ALPHONSUS DE LIGUORI
SAINT OF BOURBON NAPLES AND
FOUNDER OF THE REDEMPTORISTS
1696-1787

St Alphonsus de Liguori, 1696–1787, in the early years of his episcopate. This is one of the five authentic portraits still extant. When preaching he removed his glasses.

ALPHONSUS DE LIGUORI

SAINT
of Bourbon Naples

1696-1787

FOUNDER
of the Redemptorists

FREDERICK M. JONES

Liguori
LIGUORI, MISSOURI

Published by Liguori Publications
Liguori, Missouri

Originally published in Ireland by Gill & Macmillan Ltd, Goldenbridge, Dublin 8 (1992) with associated companies throughout the world.

Library of Congress Cataloging-in-Publication

Jones, Frederick M.
   Alphonsus de Liguori : the saint of Bourbon Naples, 1696–1787, and founder of the Redemptorists / Frederick M. Jones — 1st U.S. ed.
   Originally published: Dublin : Gill and Macmillan, c1992.
   Includes bibliographical references and index.
   ISBN 0-7648-0376-X
   1. Liguori, Alfonso Maria de', Saint, 1696–1787. 2. Christian saints—Italy—Biography. I. Title.
[BX4700.L6J66 1999]
271'.6402—dc21
[B]   98-39647

All rights reserved. No part of this publication may be reproduced, stored in a retrieval system, or transmitted in any form or by any means—electronic, mechanical, photocopy, recording, or any other—except for brief quotations in printed reviews, without the prior permission of the publisher.

Copyright 1992 by Frederick M. Jones
Printed in the United States of America
03 02 01 00 99   5 4 3 2 1
First U.S. Paperback Edition 1999

To the Memory of

*Fathers William Gaudreau, Robert Culhane and
Thomas Madigan, Redemptorists*

*whose appreciation of Alphonsus de Liguori was always an
inspiration*

'Ognuno tiene i suoi difetti. Io ne ho piu degli altri.'
(Everybody has defects of character. I have more than others.)
Alphonsus de Liguori, Letter of 3 August 1755

'If the biographers of the saints would write of their defects as well as of their virtues, their biographies would be more voluminous.'
Comment of Alphonsus de Liguori to one of his Novices

'No one is so much himself as the saint, who disposes himself to God's plan, for which he is prepared to surrender his whole being, body, soul and spirit.'
Hans Urs van Balthasar

Contents

Acknowledgments	ix
Genealogies, Maps and Illustrations	xi
Introduction	1

Part One 1696–1743

Lord show me your ways

1. Sic Itur ad Astra	7
2. From the Law Courts to the Sanctuary	23
3. The Apprentice Years	41
4. Scala	66
5. The Instrument of His Glory	90
6. From Out the Ruins	111
7. The Bourbons of Naples	136
8. The Lord Gives the Increase	169

Part Two 1743–1762

The Paths of the Lord

9. The Theologian From Out the Woods	203
10. Building the Edifice	228
11. The Theological Wars	262
12. Among the Brethren	296
13. Zeal for the Lord's House	330

Part Three 1762–1787

Reaping the Harvest in Life and Death

14. A Mitre in the Caudine Forks	357
15. The Care of All the Churches	396

16. The Return to Pagani	423
17. The Regolamento	441
18. Waiting on the Lord	474
Epilogue	488
Appendix: Chronological List of Alphonsus' Writings	491
Notes	495
Bibliography	526
Index	529

Acknowledgments

There is a long list of confreres and helpers without whose assistance this biography would never have been completed. Many years ago I was invited to undertake the task of writing an original life of Alphonsus de Liguori by Father Michael Curran, Provincial of the Irish Redemptorists, who had responded to a suggestion from Father John B. Whyte, C.SS.R. Of the many kind confreres who assisted me in my researches over the years, mention must be made of Fathers R. Telleria, Orestes Gregorio and Domenico Capone, the first two of whom have now joined Alphonsus in the glory of heaven. Without the unfailing courtesy and expertise of Father Andrea Sampers my work in the General Archives in Rome could not have been accomplished. Father Francis Hawkins, the English Assistant General at the time, was a charming host as superior of Sant' Alfonso, the General House. In Naples, and in the various Redemptorist Houses there, I met with nothing but generous hospitality and willing co-operation. A special word of appreciation is due to the late bishop of Sant' Agata dei Goti, the successor of St Alphonsus, Ilario Roatta, with whom I stayed and who facilitated my work in the diocese in every way. I remember particularly his invitation to address his clerical students in the seminary which was so dear to Alphonsus. Rationalisation of diocesan administration throughout Italy has meant that St Agatha of the Goths no longer exists as a separate diocese; it was absorbed into the neighbouring diocese of Telese.

Work on this biography, suspended for some years due to various other commitments, was resumed at the invitation of another Provincial of the Irish Province, Father Raphael Gallagher, who has facilitated and encouraged the work in every way, even reading some of the chapters at different stages. But the one who suffered most during its preparation was Father K. H. Donlon, who courageously read the various drafts of the manuscript and equally courageously indicated the emendations and corrections which should be made. To him a special word of thanks and appreciation is due. But he must not be held responsible for the inadequacies and imperfections, whether literary or hagiographical, which remain. For them the author shoulders full responsibility, remembering the comment of Alphonsus de Liguori himself — who suffered more than his share from his publications — that anyone who ventures to publish must prepare himself to be torn asunder. The only perfect authors, he knew, were those who never published a line themselves.

And what would authors who cannot master the complexities of an electronic typewriter, not to mention a Word Processor, do without a cheerful and efficient secretary with inexhaustible patience? Mrs Anne Hughes is one of these invaluable persons and to her I express my sincerest thanks for the hours she spent on this manuscript. So if the name of the author is the only one that appears on the title page of this biography, all those I have gladly mentioned deserve their spot as well.

I wish to express my thanks to my colleague David McNamara for his assistance in preparing the Maps which should facilitate the reader in locating the towns and areas mentioned in the text.

I am indebted to Jim Fitzpatrick of Belfast and to the Provincial and Vice-Provincial Superiors of the Redemptorists throughout the world who have supported the publication of this biography of Alphonsus de Liguori. A specific mention is the only way I can express my thanks to the superiors of the Redemptorists of Vienna, North Belgium, Zaire, Baltimore, Richmond, Munich, Amsterdam, Cologne, London, Pretoria, St Louis, Dublin, Cebu, Bangalore, Fortaleza, Tokyo, Canberra, Manila, Ipoh, Oakland, Edmonton, Yorkton, San Juan and the General House in Rome.

I should also like to express my appreciation of the assistance given to me by my editor, Bridget Lunn.

Frederick M. Jones, C.SS.R.
Marianella, Dublin 6
September 1992

Genealogies, Maps and Illustrations

Genealogies   *page*
1. The Liguori Family   *12*
2. The Bourbons of Naples 1734–1861   *138*
3. The Family of Don Hercules de Liguori, brother of Alphonsus   *478*

Maps
1. The Bourbon Kingdom of the Two Sicilies   opposite page 52
2. Naples and Scala   opposite page 180
3. Foundations and Missions 1732–1756   opposite page 308
4. The Diocese of St Agatha of the Goths 1762–1775   opposite page 436

Illustrations

Frontispiece: Alphonsus in his episcopal robes

- *Between pages 52–53*
1. Naples: the *Incurabili* and the Law Courts
2. Father Matthew Ripa; Scala
3. Alphonsus as a young missionary priest
4. Scala: the *Casa Anastasio* and the *Grotto*
5. Brother Vito Curzio's graffito at Scala
6. The monstrance of the 'Apparitions in the Host'; the confessional grille at Scala
7. Title page of an early draft of the *Rules* of the missioners of the Most Holy Saviour

- *Between pages 180–181*
8. Tramonti and Campinola: scene of the first missions

9. A village church near Pagani where Alphonsus preached
10. A typical 18th-century pulpit of Bourbon Naples
11. Façade of the cathedral of Amalfi, scene of the 1756 mission
12. The people of the countryside for whom Alphonsus worked
13. Typical inhabitants of the Abruzzi and the Basilicata
14. Frontispiece of the *Medulla Theologiae Moralis* of Busenbaum; title page of the first edition of Alphonsus' *Moral Theology*

- *Between pages 308–309*
15. Title page of the sixth edition of Alphonsus' *Moral Theology*
16. A page of the *Glories of Mary* in Alphonsus' handwriting
17. The church and monastery of Ciorani
18. Pagani: the Basilica and the room where Alphonsus died
19. Deliceto from the Redemptorist monastery
20. Deliceto: the monastery as it is today with the entrance to the church
21. Sant' Agatha of the Goths: two views of the episcopal city

- *Between pages 436–437*
22. Statute of St Alphonsus in the piazza of Sant' Agatha
23. The plaque commemorating Alphonsus' years in Arienzo
24. Charles of Bourbon and his queen Maria Amalia
25. Goya's portrait of Charles III
26. Ferdinand IV of Naples and his queen Maria Carolina of Austria
27. A contemporary caricature of the Marchese Bernardo Tanucci
28. The opening pages of the *Regolamento*

INTRODUCTION

Alphonsus de Liguori is easily accessible historically. His life spanned virtually the whole of the eighteenth century; born in 1696, he died in 1787, two years before the fall of the Bastille. While the majority of saints have to wait until after their deaths before their life stories are written, he belongs to that small category of saints who found biographers while still alive. Ignatius of Loyola, Francis de Sales, Vincent de Paul all attracted contemporary biographers. Alphonsus had two members of his Congregation, Anthony Mary Tannoia and Joseph Landi, who independently of each other set themselves the task of recording the details of his life.

Father Landi's work, *Istoria della Congregazione del SS. Redentore*, eventually found its way to a lumber room in the monastery of Materdomini; there it attracted the attention of the local cobbler, totally unlettered, who began to use the unwritten pages of the manuscript to measure shoes for his last! Rescued from impending destruction by a young Redemptorist, Father Lammanis, who recognised its value for posterity, the manuscript was placed in safe keeping until it found its way to the General Archives in Rome about 1870 where it is now available, still in manuscript.

Tannoia was more fortunate though he, too, had a narrow escape when Alphonsus on one occasion discovered part of his notes. The completed work was published in Naples in three volumes from 1798 to 1802 and has remained an essential source for all subsequent biographers. Fortunately its shortcomings and inevitable inaccuracies can now be rectified as a result of later research.

Father Tannoia (1727–1802) could have heard of Alphonsus de Liguori and his missioners as he grew up in Corato near Bari in southern Italy; the missioners of the Holy Saviour, as they were then called, had already extended their activity from Scala overlooking Amalfi, across the Appennines to Apulia and the Terra di Bari. In 1744 Alphonsus had established a mission house in Deliceto within easy reach of Lacedonia, where Anthony's family had moved after his father's death. Two years later, in 1746, Tannoia, then nineteen, entered the novitiate at Deliceto where he found five or six other novices to welcome him, among them Joseph Landi. Tannoia's first meeting with Alphonsus took place in October 1746 as he recalled, exactly fifty years later, when he gave evidence under oath at the process of canonisation. Alphonsus was then fifty years old, at the height of his missionary and theological activity, well established as Rector Major of his Congregation and out of the shadow of the domination of Bishop Falcoia. The young Tannoia was immediately impressed; the memory of that first meeting never left him. A few weeks later, in November, Alphonsus probably clothed him in the habit of the Redemptorists and left him to begin his training as a novice under Father Paul Cafaro.

While still a student Tannoia conceived the idea of preparing to write the life of his founder. He was a young theological student when he interviewed Alphonsus' mother to gather details of the early years of her son's life. Anyone with a feeling for how things were in those days would appreciate that this interview must have taken place with the permission of Tannoia's immediate superiors but certainly unknown to Alphonsus himself. From that time onwards Tannoia kept a record of Alphonsus' activities, his missions, his conferences to the communities, his letters, his *obiter dicta*. Little of importance escaped him; when not in the community with Alphonsus he commissioned other members to take notes for him. The biographical task suited him perfectly. He possessed a genuine literary flair and produced lives of many of his Redemptorist colleagues as well as lives of local saints and a history of Our Lady of Consolation at Deliceto where he spent the greater part of his life. His delicate health unfitted him for the rigours of the missionary life in those early days. Highly esteemed by Alphonsus, he was entrusted with various offices in the Congregation such as novice master, local superior, consultor, procurator, which fitted in well with the fact that he was unable to spend months away from home on missionary campaigns in the Abruzzi or Calabria like his more robust colleagues. Everything conspired to facilitate his literary activity, and his other great interest — indeed, passion — bees. They were his life-long hobby. Two years after the publication of his life of Alphonsus he published his *magnum opus* on *Bees, Their Usefulness and Correct Manner of Cultivation*, which earned him a lot wider fame than his biographies, as well as honorary membership of scientific academies in Florence and Bologna.

Tannoia was at Alphonsus' bedside when he died in Pagani, 1 August 1787. For the next ten years he intensified his collecting of material for the 'life'. He travelled to the various places where Alphonsus had preached; he interviewed those who had recollections of him either as a missioner, a bishop, a counsellor or a colleague. The notes he made of these interviews are still preserved in the Redemptorist General Archives as a monument to his indefatigable commitment to his task. Finally the first volume of his work appeared in print in Naples in 1798, *Della Vita Ed Istituto Del Venerabile Servo Di Dio, Alfonso Maria Liguori, Vescovo Di S. Agatha De' Goti E Fondatore Della Congregazione De' Preti Missionarii Del SS. Redentore*. Two further volumes appeared at two yearly intervals to bring the task he had begun fifty years previously to completion in 1802. With a sense of personal martyrdom shared by other historical and literary greats he complained of his age and failing health (which was still equal to publication of his work on bees) and of the fact that he had received no assistance from his confreres in his efforts; he begged for the benign understanding of those who detected errors in his work and their prayers after his death.

Few will deny that Tannoia's work is a masterpiece of its genre, worthy to take its place beside similar efforts of Abelly, Polanco and Ribandeneira. Praised by Italian literary critics and by bishops and priests throughout Europe in the last century it has been translated into a number of languages. More than that, it has been the main source for the series of biographies of Alphonsus which followed his canonisation in 1839 and his proclamation as Doctor of the Church some thirty years later. Cardinal Villecourt's *Vie et Institut de Saint Alphonse M. de Liguori*, Tournai 1863, Cardinal Capecelatro's *La Vita di Sant Alfonso de Liguori*, Roma 1893 and finally the classical two-volume French life by Father Augustine Berthe, *Saint Alphonse de Liguori*, Paris 1900, which was virtually the 'official General Curia' biography, all owe their main orientation to Tannoia, despite the addition of further archive material which was then becoming available.

Father Karl Dilgskron, an Austrian Redemptorist and, like Berthe, a consultor to the Superior General, was the first to adopt an independent approach to the life and work of Alphonsus. His carefully researched life, *Leben des Hl. Bischofs und Kirchenlehrers A.M. de Liguori*, Regensburg 1887, showed a refreshing willingness to challenge many of the accepted aspects of Alphonsus' life, and to depart, if necessary, from the line adopted by Tannoia. Tannoia's work, admirable in so many ways, still leaves a lot to be desired from both the hagiographical and the historical points of view. His work was constrained not only by the fact that the process for the canonisation of Alphonsus was in progress but also by the accepted pattern of saints' lives at the time — pious parents, pious youth, emphasis on the extraordinary and the miraculous such as visions, cures, prophecies, levitation, ecstasies, even bi-location, during the course of the saint's life and a corresponding reluctance to portray him as a human being with human frailty. The 'angelic' was emphasised to the exclusion of the 'human'. Some incidents, complicated and not always redounding to the good name of the Congregation, were glossed over or dismissed innocuously in a few lines, leaving the innocent reader unaware of the conflicts that took place and the depths of feelings aroused. One such was the famous Chapter meeting at Ciorani in 1764 which Alphonsus left prematurely in anger and disgust; another was the question of the *Regolamento* which had such tragic consequences for Alphonsus and his Congregation in Naples. In this latter case the main protagonists were still alive; feelings still ran high and a full revelation of the intrigues and deceptions, if such there were, would only have opened up old wounds and enkindled new dissension. Equally difficult was Tannoia's task when recounting Alphonsus' negotiations with the Bourbon Court in

Naples in his efforts to legalise the establishment of his Congregation. The full story of the efforts Alphonsus had to make with Charles III and Ferdinand IV (who was still alive) and their ministers, especially Bernard Tanucci, and the frustrations he suffered when the survival of his work depended on the benevolence of one or the other, could not then be described.

Historical research during the last fifty years has gone a long way towards rectifying the shortcomings of Tannoia. The re-organisation of the General Archives of the Congregation in Rome and in particular the untiring work of archivist Father Andrea Sampers have opened up opportunities to complement the picture which emerges from Tannoia's volumes. A group of Neapolitan historians, Gregorio, Fredda, Capone, Majorano and Marrazzo, have taken the lead in producing scientific monographs of the highest standard clarifying many aspects of the origins of the Redemptorists and of the life, work and writings of Alphonsus. The publication of *Spicilegium Historicum* by the members of the Historical Institute in Rome has made available a further mass of documents indispensable for a balanced historical picture. But by far the most valuable contribution to Alphonsian studies in this century has been the work of the Spanish Redemptorist, Raimundo Telleria, *San Alphonso Maria de Ligorio*, Madrid 1950/1951. For twelve years, Telleria, with amazing dedication, spent his time searching through the state and ecclesiastical archives of Rome, Naples, southern Italy and Sicily in quest of Alphonsus de Liguori; despite the difficulties occasioned by war restrictions he plodded on unremittingly, overcoming immense frustrations to produce, if not a conventional biography, certainly a mine of new information directly and indirectly connected with the Redemptorists, their founder and his family. His work is now, along with Tannoia, indispensable for all future studies.

I was privileged to be able to make my own researches for some years in the General Archives in Rome, in the episcopal archives of St Agatha of the Goths and in the Redemptorist archives of the Neapolitan Province. While it would be premature to claim that it is now possible to write the definitive biography of Alphonsus de Liguori — such a claim was made as early as the end of the last century when Berthe's *Life* appeared — we are certainly in a much better position to bring his life and work into more accurate focus. And we are no longer anxious to suppress his human frailties. Rather does his greatness shine through more clearly as we witness his struggle to overcome them. And yet his life had so many facets to it; his work, pastorally, spiritually and theologically had such an impact on the life of the Church throughout the world during the nineteenth century through the First Vatican Council and right up to Vatican II that no one presentation of his life could presume to encompass them all.

Part One

Lord Show Me Your Ways

1696–1743

CHAPTER ONE

SIC ITUR AD ASTRA

– *I* –

It was quite in keeping with the history of the kingdom of Naples that Alphonsus de Liguori should have been born under Spanish rule, should have grown up and studied under the domination of the Austrian Hapsburgs and should have worked as a priest, missioner and bishop in an independent kingdom of Naples under the newly established dynasty of the Neapolitan Bourbons. Three changes of rulers within a period of forty years may have been unusual even in Naples but it caused less surprise there than anywhere else; few kingdoms have known so many different rulers in the course of their history. Phoenicians, Greeks, Goths, Lombards, Normans, Angevins and Spaniards, all in turn were masters of the south of Italy leaving their mark in the variety and multiplicity of its dialects, in the complexity of its legal codes and in the characteristics of its inhabitants. The kingdom of Naples is a palimpsest which bears still the imprints of its successive conquerors. In the days of the *vecchia Italia* before the *Risorgimento*, Italy, it was said, ended at the Garigliano, the river which, rising in the slopes of the Abruzzian Appennines, winds its torturous course of some sixty miles through the *Terra di Lavoro* until it empties itself in the Tyrrhenian Sea a few miles south of Gaeta: there the kingdom of Naples began. For a Neapolitan, to cross the Garigliano was to go into another world — like crossing the Rhine for a Frenchman or like passing the Statue of Liberty for a European emigrant in the twentieth century. A line drawn diagonally across the peninsula from the mouth of the river Tronto on the Adriatic to the lake of Fondi on the west coast below Terracina divided the kingdom of Naples from the Papal States in the north. When the ruler of Naples had the good fortune to be ruler of the island of Sicily as well — which did not always happen — his kingdom was referred to as the Kingdom of the Two Sicilies, out of deference to the susceptibilities of those who lived beyond the Faro.

The last conquerors of the kingdom of Naples in the period preceding the birth of Alphonsus were the Spaniards. The brilliant military genius of the Great Captain, Gonsalvo de Cordoba, routed the French on the banks of the Garigliano in 1503 to deliver the heritage of Barbarossa and the Hohenstaufens into the possession of Ferdinand the Catholic. The Treaty of Barcelona between Pope Clement VII and the Emperor Charles V in 1529 confirmed the Spanish domination which was in any case a fact with Spanish garrisons securely lodged in both Naples and Sicily. For almost two hundred years Spain ruled the kingdom through Spanish viceroys; while one has to search for the evidence of other conquerors in the old city of Naples, the evidence of Spanish occupation is at every hand's turn from the imperial eagles of Charles V over the Castello Capuano to the *Toledo*, the name by which the Neapolitans still call the great central thoroughfare of their city which was laid out by the viceroy Pedro de Toledo in 1536 and which has defied all subsequent efforts to rechristen it. For two centuries Spanish and Neapolitan blood mixed as the two peoples intermarried and to the already complex characteristics of the people of the *mezzogiorno* were added the intense religious spirit of the conquistadores, a new love of pomp and ceremonial, a new and petulant sense of punctilio and *stima propria*. The Spanish language was widely used among the nobility; it was the official language in many convents and monasteries; Spanish names with only a transparent Neapolitan covering abounded, Spanish manners and customs, Spanish etiquette were in vogue, Spanish saints and devotions became popular among the people. One does not have to search far to explain Alphonsus de Liguori's devotion to Teresa of Avila or to John of the Cross.

In 1700 the King of Spain, Charles II, last of the Spanish Hapsburgs, an imbecile and an invalid all his life, died without successors, leaving his dominions to Philip of Anjou who became Philip V of Spain, the first of the Spanish Bourbons and grandson of Louis XIV of France. While Europe went to war to redress the balance of power which had been upset by this sudden acquisition of territory by the Bourbons, Naples accepted its new ruler gladly; Bourbon or Hapsburg, it was all the same to them. In 1702 the young and courageous Philip of Anjou was rapturously welcomed in the bay of Naples when he came to claim possession of his inheritance. In May he made his solemn ceremonial entry into the city through the Porta Capuana and went in procession through the *Via dei Tribunali* to the Duomo for the *Te Deum* presided over by Cardinal Cantelmo. But his possession of the kingdom was short-lived; in 1707 the Austrians, aided by a small group of the nobility, gained control and were confirmed in it by the treaty of Utrecht in 1713 which concluded the long struggle of the Spanish Succession. For twenty-seven years—the formative years in the life of Alphonsus—Naples remained under the domination of the Austrian Hapsburgs and was ruled from Vienna through a viceroy in Naples. The net result of the war for the Neapolitans amounted to an Austrian viceroy instead of a Spanish one.

– II –

On Thursday 27 September 1696 Alphonsus de Liguori was born at his parents' home at Marianella on the outskirts of Naples; it was thirteen hours after the *Ave Maria* according to the Neapolitan method of reckoning the time, or about eight o'clock in the morning. Two days later he was taken to the capital to the parish church of *Santa Maria dei Vergini* where he was baptised and provided, *more nobilium*, with an adequate array of heavenly protectors, Alphonsus Mary Anthony John Francis Cosmas Damian Michael Gaspar. The choice of names is easily explained; Alphonsus was traditional among the Liguoris as a glance at the family genealogical tree will show, while Cosmas, Damian and the Archangel Michael were the liturgical patrons of the days of his birth and baptism; Mary he owed to the quite remarkable love of his mother for the Blessed Virgin, Anthony and Francis to her devotion to these saints which she learnt from the Franciscan nuns with whom she was educated. The baptismal register of the parish of *Santa Maria dei Vergini* with the record of that day is still preserved, almost miraculously, since the church was destroyed by bombing in the last war; other hands than those of Don Giuseppi del Mastro, the parish priest of 1696, have completed the history of the child who was then regenerated to new life in Christ by adding in the margin, 'Beatified, September 1816. Canonized 26 May 1839. Declared a Doctor of the Church, 23 March 1871.'

Society in the kingdom of Naples at the time of Alphonsus was divided simply into two classes, the nobility and those who were not. Titles of nobility abounded, prince, duke, marquis, count; all were jealously prized and often accumulated in the same family through arranged marriages. Naples alone boasted a thousand titled families. The family to which Alphonsus belonged was ranked among the lesser nobility; though authentically 'patrician' in the Neapolitan sense their status had been acquired not through land but through royal grant for service in some area of administration. Spanish usage entitled them to use the prefix 'Don'. The Liguori[1] had figured prominently in the life of Naples for over five hundred years at the time of Alphonsus' birth; in the sixteenth century in the heyday of the Spanish domination one of the family genealogists, following the current vogue, boasted of their Castillian origins. For centuries different members of the family appear in influential positions at court, in the royal service and in the government of the city of Naples. At a time when rank counted for so much the family was firmly established among the recognised nobility of the kingdom; their coat-of-arms of blue and gold with a lion rampant displayed the device, *Sic Itur ad Astra*.

Don Joseph Felix de Liguori (Don Giuseppe), Alphonsus' father, was born in 1670 in the village of San Paolo in the diocese of Nola, sufficiently near to the capital to be legally a citizen of Naples; while still young he came with his parents to live in the city just outside the walls at the *Porta San Gennaro*. At the age of fifteen Joseph entered the Spanish naval service and by the time of his marriage in May 1695 to Donna Anna Caterina Cavalieri had risen to the modest position of an ensign in the Royal Galleys. Life in the galleys was rough even for an officer. In 1764, some twenty years after the death of Alphonsus' father, the English novelist, Tobias Smollet, visited the galleys of the king of Sardinia in the harbour of Ville Franche. In his *Travels through France and Italy* he expressed himself disgusted at the sight of 'about two hundred miserable wretches, chained to the banks on which they sit and row when the galley is at sea', even though he admitted that their lot was a just retribution for their crimes against society. 'The accommodation on board for the officers is wretched. There is a paltry cabin in the poop for the commander; but all the other officers lie below the slaves, in a dungeon, where they have neither light, air, nor any degree of quiet; half suffocated by the heat of the place, tormented by fleas, bugs and lice, and disturbed by the incessant noise overhead.'. The harsh discipline too shocked him, though he realised that only in this way could so many men of such mixed race and dubious character be kept under control. 'The slaves seem nevertheless quite insensible of their misery, like so many convicts in Newgate: they laugh and sing and swear and get drunk when they can.'[2] Don Joseph proved himself a successful officer; before his retirement he had risen to the position of Capitano Comandante della Galera Capitana — Commanding Officer of the Flagship of the Royal Squadron. But his long years in the galleys left their mark upon his character, making him harsh in manner, intolerant, a martinet at home and altogether unaccustomed to the experience of having his decisions questioned, as Alphonsus was to learn to his cost.

Don Joseph was twenty-five when he had the good fortune of marrying Donna Anna Caterina Cavalieri, one of those mothers whose lives of self-sacrifice and prayer seem in themselves to be a sufficient explanation of the holiness of their children. Even more so than the Liguori family the Cavalieri could boast of their ancient lineage and nobility. Certainly whatever difference in social rank there was between the two families was in favour of the Cavalieri. Donna Anna was the youngest daughter of Don Federico Cavalieri and Donna Elena d'Avenia, both of whom could trace their ancestry to Spain. Their first child, Emilio, joined the missionary society of the Pii Operai, became bishop of Troia and died in the odour of sanctity;[3] two of their daughters became Franciscan nuns in the 'cappuccinelle' of Pontecorvo, in Naples, while yet another son became a judge. Altogether they were a remarkable and distinguished family. Anna Caterina, the youngest, was orphaned of her mother while still only a child with the result that she was reared in the convent where her sisters were nuns and where she remained for fourteen years as an *educanda* until she returned home to attend to her father, a minister of state of the Royal Council of Santa Clara, renowned both for his integrity and his deep christian piety. Her marriage to Don Joseph de Liguori, which would have been arranged for her, was celebrated in the chapel of Santa Restituta in the cathedral of Naples with all the magnificence which was customary among the nobility at that time. In this same chapel, their eldest son, Alphonsus, was later to preach on several occasions both as priest and as bishop.

Don Joseph brought his bride to live at the country casino of Marianella which had been given to him by his father and it was here that Alphonsus was born the following year. Seven other children followed; Antonio, born in 1698 became a Benedictine of the Cassinese congregation and died in the abbey of San Severino in Naples with a reputation for holiness. He had been Novice Master and according to Tannoia his life was shortened by his practice of penance. Twin girls, Maddalena and Barbara, followed in 1700, of whom the first died as an infant; a third boy, Cajetan, was born in September 1701 and became a priest in the diocese of Naples. He lived at home, a virtual recluse, his ministry centred on the chapel of San Gennaro in the cathedral. Two girls, Anna and Teresa, followed. Anna and her elder sister Barbara entered the convent of St Jerome and only appear once again in the family history when they took legal action against their father to secure their dowries; Teresa, who was Alphonsus' favourite sister, was married at the age of sixteen to the Duke of Praesenzano, and her unfortunate married life with a widower much older than herself certainly influenced him when he wrote of the unhappy lives of so many married people whom he knew. Finally there was Hercules, the benjamin of the family, born in 1706, twice married and who handed on the family name about which Don Joseph was so anxious. Don Joseph's consuming passion in life was the advancement of his family in every possible way. The branch of the Liguoris to which he belonged was not rich and with only his naval salary he probably had to rely mainly on his wife's very adequate dowry in the early years of married life. But he set himself to increase the family fortune and in this he succeeded for by 1725 when Alphonsus legally renounced his right of primogeniture the family was moderately opulent, owning two properties in Naples besides the country villa at Marianella. Legally their possessions were assessed at some 40,000 ducats, which would provide an adequate inheritance for each member of the family to maintain their social status.[4] Hercules inherited all his father's financial ambitions and amassed an even greater fortune for himself by astute transactions coupled with a considerable degree of parsimony. But the social and political upheavals of the closing years of the century with the flight of the Bourbons, the arrival of the French and the waywardness of his heirs dissipated most of what he had acquired.

Duties in the galleys necessitated Don Joseph's absence from home for long periods; besides guarding the Naples coast the galleys swept the Mediterranean as far as Spain, Morocco and Algiers in the west, Palestine and Greece in the east, in search of corsairs and pirates who preyed on shipping and unprotected coastal villages. As a result the dominant formative influence in the Liguori household was Donna Anna, the direct opposite of her husband in almost everything, gentle, cultured, refined, devout with a cloistral piety. She never went to the theatre or to other public amusements; she spent long hours in prayer, recited the monastic breviary, fasted

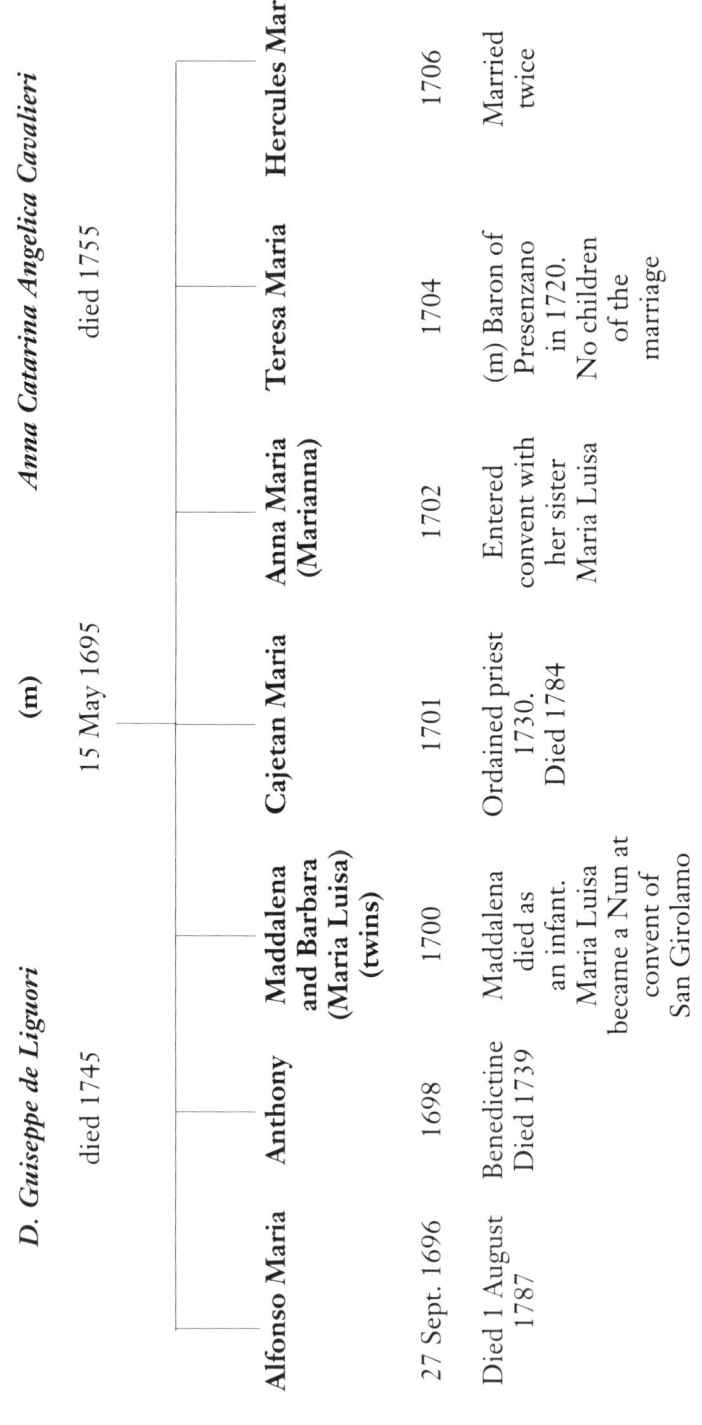

rigorously and practised severe corporal austerities like any contemplative nun of those days. It is hard to resist the thought that were it not for the family circumstances which demanded her presence at home with her ageing father, Donna Anna would have found her way into a convent. She was inclined to be of an over-anxious disposition and suffered much from scruples; only some time before her death did she gain complete peace of mind. She took her responsibilities as a mother very seriously, inculcating in her children a love of prayer and self-denial of which she gave such a remarkable example in her own life. As an old man eighty years later in Pagani, Alphonsus still had the note-book with the prayers he had learnt from her. Cajetan recalled how his mother gathered them together for prayers each morning, how she taught them their catechism each evening and recited the rosary with them before they retired for the night. Each week she saw to it that they went to confession to the Fathers of the Oratory. It was from her that Alphonsus learnt his love for the Mother of God and the practice of special devotions in her honour to which he was faithful as long as he lived; he was not exaggerating when he said that whatever good there was in him as a young man he owed to the care of his mother.[5]

In order to facilitate the education of his growing family Don Joseph moved from Marianella to the centre of Naples when Alphonsus was about six years of age. While there were *convitti* for the education of the sons of nobility Don Joseph opted for the private education of his sons at home, and competent tutors for this purpose were more easily available in the city.[6] The principal tutor was a Calabrian priest, Don Domenico Bonaccia who taught Alphonsus Latin, Greek, French, Spanish and Italian as well as history, mathematics and the rudiments of physics which under the influence of Descartes was all the rage; later another priest, Don Carminiello Rocco initiated him into the mysteries of philosophy consisting mainly of cosmology and psychology. But the intellectual graces were only a minor part of the cultural equipment of the complete Neapolitan *cavaliere* which Don Joseph wished his son to be and other tutors were engaged to instruct him in the elements of sketching, painting and architecture for which he showed considerable talent. Later in life he outlined the designs of his monasteries, while his oil paintings and sketches of religious themes such as the Crucifixion and Our Lady were to be found in the oratories and refectories and used by him as visual aids on missions. Tannoia argues rather unconvincingly that his parents refused to allow Alphonsus to be initiated into the arts of dancing and fencing both of which were part of the normal training of the nobility. Whatever about dancing, Alphonsus certainly wore his dress sword which was *de rigueur* for a Neapolitan nobleman.

But there is no argument about the part that music played in his education. Surprisingly enough Alphonsus' father possessed a remarkable talent and love for music which his son inherited. Don Joseph's excellent judgment in matters musical is evidenced in the choice he made of Gaetano Greco as music tutor for his son. Greco, a pupil of Alessandro Scarlatti whom he later succeeded in the chair of music at the famous Conservatorio dei Poveri di Christo in Naples, has several operas to his credit though his greatest claim to fame is the fact that he was the teacher of both Durante and Pergolesi.[7] Under the guidance of Greco, Alphonsus devoted himself assiduously to both theory and practice and acquired considerable proficiency on the harpsicord and also as a composer.[8] His father insisted on three hours' practice a day and on one occasion adopted the drastic expedient of locking both pupil and teacher together in the music room lest they should shorten the time of their studies. As a priest and missioner Alphonsus found an opportunity of satisfying his love of music by composing hymns for the people which he taught them himself and sang with them from the pulpit. This love never left him. At recreation in his communities he played the harpsicord and even as an old man of over eighty the scholastics got him to play for them in the house of studies at Pagani; on his day of recollection each month as a religious he left aside all distracting tasks such as letter-writing, study of theology and preparation of sermons but had no scruple in spending some time at the harpsicord.

Alphonsus' education was thus broadly based and calculated to make him a cultured and learned Neapolitan nobleman in a society where the arts and cultural activities were experiencing a remarkable renaissance; in many ways Bourbon Naples in the eighteenth century became one of the great social and cultural centres of Europe. At the same time his parents were equally attentive to his religious formation. Fonso, as he was called at home, was seven when his mother placed him under the care of her own spiritual director, Father Thomas Pagano. Pagano, who was to remain Alphonsus' director of conscience for nearly thirty years and who was to guide him wisely through many spiritual difficulties, was a true son of St Philip Neri, gentle, cultured, placid, a christian gentleman in everything. His direction of souls was characterised by great kindness, firmness when necessary and emphasis on the love of God. He prepared Alphonsus for his first communion which took place in the rich baroque church of the Oratorians or Girolamini as they were popularly styled in Naples. Attached to this church were at least five different sodalities catering for the spiritual needs of the various sections of the faithful to whom the Fathers of the Oratory ministered. Since the remarkable transformation worked by the Oratory of Divine Love in Italy in the early sixteenth century, these 'oratories' serving a spiritual elite had multiplied. With a restricted number of members, a special chaplain, a strict rule of conduct for members and an extended period of probation before admission, they achieved much for the sanctification of the laity. Shortly after his first communion at the age of nine, Alphonsus became a member of the Sodality of Young Noblemen under the patronage of St Joseph. He remained a member until August 1715 when, after graduation from the university, he progressed to the Sodality of Doctors. Under the rules of the sodality the boys came together regularly for lectures, spiritual reading, Mass and the reception of the sacraments. To these spiritual activities were added concerts, plays, operas and excursions to the countryside accompanied by the Fathers, all of which was in the pure Oratorian tradition of Philip Neri who used to take his Roman protégés to the Janiculum or the Coelian Hill to recreate themselves.

It was on one of these excursions that there took place an incident which has been much embellished by the saint's biographers. The Oratorians had taken their young sodalists to their wooded villa on the hill of Capodimonte overlooking the city from which there is one of the most magnificent views in all Naples. At the foot of the hill lies the semicircle of the city outlined by the broad sweep of the bay; the islands of Ischia and Procida are clearly visible, with Capri and the mountains of the Sorrento peninsula closing the horizon to the south; to the east rises Vesuvius. A group of boys improvised a game of bowls, *il giuoco delle bocce*, played, it would seem, with oranges. Alphonsus, invited to join, declined on the plea that he had not played before and consequently would be more of a handicap than an asset to his side. Eventually, however, he was persuaded. It may have been 'beginners luck' or perhaps a natural talent for games but whatever the reason Alphonsus performed most unlike an amateur, and brought victory to his side; it looked as if his refusal to play in the beginning had been a deliberate deception. When the stakes were being paid over, the leader of the opposing side vented his anger on the young Liguori — he was then twelve — in no uncertain terms. The rough phrase that he used — '*parolaccia impura*' says the account — offended Alphonsus who considered it a sin. 'So you are prepared to offend God for a few carlins,' he replied and, returning the money, left the group. When the time for return to Naples arrived Alphonsus was not in the company. After some search they located him in a grove on his knees before a small picture of the Madonna which he had fixed to a tree; the unseemly language of his companion demanded some reparation from him.

Don Domenico Villani, a school companion of Alphonsus who was present at the incident, recounted the story in the Redemptorist house at Ciorani many years later as evidence that in his opinion Alphonsus was a 'saint from his youth'. The only other incident which is recounted of his youth shows him in a more normal light and gets less prominence — a raid on the neighbouring Caravita lemon orchard. When he looked back on his boyhood in later life, he regretted that on that occasion he had taken some lemons from the garden.

– III –

When Alphonsus, under the guidance of Don Bonaccia, completed his humanities, his father decided that he should read law at the university of Naples with a view to a legal career. Alphonsus most probably was not consulted since in the patriarchal society in which he lived, marriages and the careers of children were arranged for them by their parents — especially by parents of the type of Don Joseph. Don Joseph's decision was a wise one, dictated by the fact that in Naples the law, besides being lucrative, was the gateway to a possible public career. Lawyers and bankers climbed steadily to political power. *Dat justinianus honores* was true, then, as now. The Neapolitans had a passion for litigation. It was said that when a Neapolitan noble had nothing to do — which was a frequent occurrence — he locked himself in his study to see if he could initiate legal proceedings against anyone on any pretext whatsoever. Don Joseph's two daughters, as nuns threatened legal action against him in connection with their dowries; Hercules fought several legal battles to increase his property, one of them against his own sister, Teresa. As a consequence of this general interest in law and the volume of legal practice available, legal studies attracted a following only less numerous than candidates for holy orders.

The university of Naples, founded by Frederick II in 1224, had greatly declined by the year 1700; the number of students which a century earlier was as high as 6,000 was now reduced to less than one sixth of that number and many of these, if not the majority of them did not attend lectures. After matriculation they pursued their studies in private academies, directed very often by university professors unable to subsist on their salaries. The students then presented themselves at the university only for registration and examination purposes. So few were the number of students actually following lectures that the faculties were all housed in a few halls in the Dominican monastery of San Domenico Maggiore. Contemporaries make frequent references to the more than ordinary lawlessness and immorality of the students who were only kept in check by the presence of a detachment of soldiers assigned for this purpose. Reforms had been initiated however, which, under Charles III, improved matters generally; with the coming of the Bourbons the university regained its reputation for learning and acceptable standards. The faculty of law was the one faculty which had anticipated later reforms and already by the opening of the century had reorganised itself and was flourishing, many of its professors enjoying an international reputation. In the first weeks of October 1708, Alphonsus, then in his thirteenth year, presented himself to the professor of rhetoric, Giovanni Battista Vico for the entrance examination; a few weeks later he was present as a matriculated student at Vico's remarkable inaugural lecture, *Il Metodo degli Studi del Tempo Nostro*, delivered in solemn session in the presence of the Austrian Viceroy, Cardinal Grimani.[9]

Vico, philosopher, historian and jurisprudent, was one of the most original thinkers of his day and was the first of a series of remarkable professors with whom Alphonsus came in contact. He was the high priest of the *scienza nuova*, the new learning, a genius who has influenced the evolution of European thought right down to the present day. Vico and Alphonsus would have met each other regularly in the course of the following years in university circles and particularly in the legal *salotto* held in the Caravita palace; Canon Giulio Torni, in whose house Alphonsus studied theology, was on intimate terms with Vico, yet despite all this and the fact that their outlook on life and religion were so different, Alphonsus never once refers to him in any of his writings or letters, which is all the stranger considering the frequent critical references he made to so many other less distinguished of his contemporaries.

By the end of October 1708 Alphonsus was registered as an *istitutista*, the name given to the first-year law student in Naples since their main study was the *Institutiones* of Justinian. There was nothing exceptional about the age at which Alphonsus matriculated; he may have been a year or so in advance of many of his contemporaries though others may have been a month or so younger. Recent researches have also shown that his inscription in the university was not a formality but that he did in fact attend lectures, even though, as was normal, private tuition would have continued at home. The course, extending over five years, was a complicated one involving the study of Roman law and of the other various legal systems, Norman, Suevian, Angevin and Aragonese which went to the making of Neapolitan jurisprudence. The faculty had twelve chairs, seven in civil law and five in canon law. The general atmosphere was strongly anti-Roman in spirit; the professors by their writings and mode of thought were laying the legal foundations for that state control of the Church which characterised the Bourbons of Naples as it did the rest of the European governments at that period. The whole system of Church-State relations in Bourbon Naples which went under the name of regalism and which is associated with the name of Bernard Tanucci, was built on the legal foundations laid during these years in the faculty of law.

The most illustrious professor in the faculty of civil law was Domenico Aulisio whose rare competence in every branch of learning, but especially in law, was reflected in the large attendance at his lectures; when these were later published by his equally famous pupil, Pietro Giannone, they gained European fame. Aulisio was the real initiator of the anti-papal movement in the university which found a genial exponent in Giannone whose *Istoria Civile del Regno di Napoli* became the bible of the anti-curialists. Published in 1718 when Alphonsus was beginning his career as a lawyer, it was translated within a short while into English, French, German, and became one of the main formative influences of eighteenth-century European thought. Montesquieu wished for something similar to be written by a Frenchman; Gibbon in his Memoirs professed to have been much influenced by reading it.[10] Next in importance in the legal faculty was the professor of feudal law, Nicola Caravita, who was even more aggressively anti-Roman and whose writings were put on the Roman index; his *Nullum Ius Pontificis Maximi in Regno Neapolitano* was published the year before Alphonsus matriculated. Caravita was the foremost lawyer of his time in Naples with a reputation which he yielded ultimately only to the brilliance of his son Domenico. Alphonsus was on very intimate terms with both father and son who invited him as a student to form part of the legal group which gathered for discussion in their palazzo; here he became personally acquainted with the leading figures in the legal world of the capital and learnt at first hand the theory of regalism and the aspirations of those who professed it and which as a bishop and founder of a religious order he had to struggle against all his life. Two priests, both strongly anti-Roman in outlook, Canon Gennaro Cusano and Nicola Capasso were the leading professors in the faculty of canon law. Capasso was also a poet, a scathing critic and lampoonist who later was vividly impressed by Alphonsus' simple unadorned style of preaching and came to listen to him on several occasions. Finally, best known of all in the faculty of law, at least to the students, was Domenico Campanile whose lectures were so uninspiring that he delivered them faithfully at the first hour each morning to empty benches!

Alphonsus' legal and philosophical studies at university level took place, then, in a hotbed of regalism and anti-Romanism on the one hand and in a philosophical climate which aroused the anger of the Holy Office on the other; it was felt that Vico's teaching spawned a generation of atheists. Exposed as he was to both these currents of thought Alphonsus later became their great opponent, the ardent upholder of papal rights and the preacher of belief in God and the love of Jesus Christ. But one must be careful not to exaggerate. The general atmosphere was not officially irreligious; corporately the staff and students professed their religious beliefs at the opening of each academic year and at the conferring of degrees. During the sitting of the Royal Commission before the Bourbon reform one of the professors' strongest complaints concerned the lack of a special university chapel for the use of students and staff — a lack which they were able to make good, however, by using the adjacent church of St Dominic. The conferring of degrees was an occasion for expressing belief in the doctrine of the Immaculate Conception which had not then been defined. All during Alphonsus' lifetime one comes across the contradiction of impiety and simple faith existing side by side in individuals such as those of the royal family and Tanucci, and indeed in society at large. Charles III and his son Ferdinand were staunch believers in the divine right of kings, opponents of the power of the papacy and everything Roman and at the same time intensely devout in their private lives with a simple childlike piety which delighted in the making of Christmas cribs; Tanucci hated the Roman Curia, the Jesuits, the Jansenists and the French, especially Voltaire, with an equal hatred; when he had to accompany the king on hunting expeditions he complained about missing his daily Mass.

During his university years Alphonsus continued, as the records show, to be a faithful member of the sodality at the Oratory, occupying various offices like sacristan and novice master or director of aspirants. As he grew older he was initiated into the full circle of Oratorian piety and allowed to practise, in common with the other senior members, certain corporal austerities such as the use of the discipline, a normal feature of the piety of the time. Don Joseph continued to rule his home as if he were ruling his galleys; he was the master and his word was law. He was determined that his eldest son should devote himself assiduously to his studies. Alphonsus enjoyed a game of cards with a group of fellow students in the nearby palazzo of the marchese Cito, whose son Baldassare was also reading law.

Don Joseph regulated rigorously the amount of time to be spent in this pastime, about an hour each evening. On one occasion when Alphonsus overstayed the allotted time, he found that his father had spread out a pack of cards on his study table in place of the law books and greeted him with the remark that he seemed to be more interested in card playing than legal studies.

The political constitution of Naples was a complicated one; while all effective power was at this time in the hands of the viceroys and after 1735 in the hands of the king and his ministers, the nobles had their own local parliaments or assemblies known as *sedili* whose origins went back to the time when Naples was a self-governing republic under the Byzantine empire, somewhat like our own city councils or corporations. Of the original twenty-nine only six of these assemblies survived the course of history, two for the provincial feudal nobility, three for the urban nobility and one for the people or commons.[11] They had become in fact little more than ceremonial hereditary corporations with few executive responsibilities. But membership was still valued as a badge of nobility and ancient lineage. The Liguori family belonged to the *sedile* of Portanova which held its sessions in the council rooms beside the church of Santa Maria in Cosmedin, now known as Santa Maria di Portanova. There can still be seen in the small church the heraldic arms of the different families who composed the *sedile* and who came to Santa Maria for their religious functions. Don Joseph took his membership seriously and introduced Alphonsus in September 1710 when he reached the required age of fourteen; later at eighteen he was fully and officially aggregated.

The registers show that he attended the sessions regularly from 1710 until he became a cleric in 1723 when his attendance became sporadic. The last occasion on which he went to the deliberations of the council was as a missioner in 1742 when his main reason was to claim the modest remuneration to help in the building of his new monastery at Ciorani. Official dress was *de rigueur* for a non-cleric, the ceremonial sword, the wig, the ermine-edged short coat. As a young boy his functions in the assembly were ceremonial, such as Cross Bearer for the liturgical ceremonies of Holy Week. His only important official act was in 1722 when he was elected by the members of the different *seggi* to present a memorial of welcome on their behalf to the new Austrian viceroy, Cardinal Frederick Althann.

In January 1713 Alphonsus in his seventeenth year, having completed his legal studies was ready to present himself for the doctorate examination. A decree of 1619 laid down that the candidate should have reached his twenty-first birthday before his degree but this enactment had long been a dead letter and the university authorities were content if the candidate had begun his seventeenth year. Alphonsus, consequently, had no difficulty in securing a dispensation of three years and eight months as regards his age and of one semester as regards attendance — another ordinary practice which was later regularised in the reform decrees under Charles III. Alphonsus was about a year younger than the average age of those who took their degree; of his own classmates, three, among them his cousin, Francis Cavalieri and his card friend, Baldassare Cito, were not yet eighteen and received similar dispensation as regards age and attendance. The necessary dispensations for Alphonsus were signed on 10 January and the following week he presented himself for the preliminary examinations. The examiners asked him to treat *De clericis conjugatis* from the Decretals and *De Secundis nuptiis* from the Code of Justinian; satisfied with his handling of the material prescribed, they fixed Saturday 21 January for the doctorate. The final examination was mainly ceremonial; in the hall of the chancellor the relatives of the candidate were assembled; the candidate read his paper, two or three points were brought up by way of objection and finally the examiners cast their votes. The conferring followed immediately. The student was invested with a doctor's cap and gown, a doctor's ring was placed on his finger. Alphonsus often recalled with amusement how the gown was much too large for him and how it fell in ample folds around his legs. He was then handed his diploma and presented with a *corpus* of both civil and canon law. Finally on his knees before the assembled members of the faculty he swore to defend the doctrine of Our Lady's Immaculate Conception in a ceremony imposed by the Spanish viceroy, the duke of Osuna, a hundred years previously, in face of severe opposition from many theologians:

> I, Alphonsus Mary de Liguori, humble servant of the ever Blessed Virgin Mary, Mother of God, prostrate at the feet of the Divine Majesty and out of respect for the Ineffable Trinity of One God and Three Persons, Father, Son and Holy Ghost; and invoking the testimony of the inhabitants of the Heavenly Jerusalem, believe with my mind, and embrace with my heart and proclaim with my lips that thou, the ever Virgin Mother of God, wast preserved by a singular privilege of the same omnipotent God from all stain of original sin in the first instant of your conception or of the union of your soul and body. I will proclaim this, my belief, in public and in private until my last breath and with the help of God I will defend it and get others to defend it.
>
> So I profess, so I promise and so I swear. May God help me and these His holy Gospels.

The young Liguori was now a member of a powerful but overcrowded profession, almost as overcrowded as the priesthood for which he was to leave the law courts. When Tanucci, a few years later, set himself to restrict the numbers in the legal profession, nearly 50,000 people in Naples depended for their livelihood on the courts of justice; judges, lawyers, counsel and notaries alone numbered 15,000. The courts were divided into four sections according to the nature of the matter in question, the Concilio Collaterale, the Concilio di Santa Clara, the Camera Reale della Sommaria and the Corte Grande della Vicaria. Most of Alphonsus' dealings were with the Vicaria which had both civil and criminal jurisdiction; his last case, which brought his legal career to an end, was before the Sommaria. Court sessions were held in the Castel Capuano just inside the Porta Capuana, in what was once a royal palace but was converted into the Palace of Justice by Don

Pedro de Toledo in the time of the emperor Charles V. The main entrance to the vast rectangular cortile was through a doorway surmounted by the imperial eagles and the device of the emperor, *Plus Ultra*; at the entrance lawyers entitled to wear sword and dagger deposited them in the guardroom and in their chambers donned the legal dress of ruff and straw hat or *paglia* which gave them their dialect name of *paglietti*. The vast building still stands, much as it was in the time of Alphonsus, with the exception of the exterior which has been completely renovated; the halls are still there which once echoed with all the excitement of a Neapolitan court and which seemed so strange to Montesquieu when he attended the court sessions in 1729, six years after Alphonsus' last appearance. The day's hearings began with Mass in the Capella della Sommaria, attended by judges and lawyers.

Alphonsus' degree did not mean that he immediately took his place in the courts; a further period of practical training was necessary before that. He was apprenticed by his father first to Don Luigi Perrone and, after his death, to Don Andrea Giovene, two well-known lawyers with whom he worked for some years as an assistant, familiarising himself with court routine. Only at the end of this period was he entitled to wear his lawyer's toga and appear in court. Side by side with this practical initiation into the legal world Alphonsus continued his studies at the Caravita salon which did not confine itself to legal disciplines but included literary, historical and philosophical studies as well. At the meetings with the young lawyers, Don Domenico Caravita proposed some point from the Pandects or from the Code of Justinian for discussion; in simulated sessions of one of the courts he sat as judge himself and appointed the students in turn to plead before him.

Alphonsus was nineteen or twenty when he began his career at the Neapolitan bar as a junior advocate; unfortunately we know almost nothing about the details of his career. The faint hope that research in the civil archives of Naples, now scattered throughout Italy, might shed some light on the work he undertook has not been fulfiled. The primary source of information, the Catalago delle Sentenze for the years 1715–23, which listed all the cases and the advocates involved, perished in the political upheavals in Naples in the last century. If we can believe Father Pier Luigi Rispoli, one of the saint's early biographers, who claimed to have studied this source, Alphonsus was successful in all the cases entrusted to him.[12] We have abundant evidence, however, for the fact that he did not lack clients sent to him either by his influential friends or his own highly placed relatives. He became the family lawyer of the important Ruffi family while the fact that two of his uncles were judges of the Vicaria and regents of the Collaterale would have helped to attract a clientele.

Not merely were the members of the legal profession in Naples powerful, they were also considerably corrupt. Forming virtually a state within a state their power led to the accumulation of privileges and exemptions inevitably spawning corruption both among themselves and the judiciary, which was recruited totally from among their ranks. The administration of justice was consequently considerably flawed, leading to a blatant perversion of justice in favour of the rich and the nobility. Baldassare Cito, one of the incorruptible members of the bench and a friend of Alphonsus, was banished from the capital when a local potentate disagreed with his impartial verdict. When the Bourbon regime took over in Naples a few years later they were inundated with petitions for the reform of the *magistratura*; their popularity owed much to the fact that they immediately addressed the task, entrusting it to Tanucci, himself a lawyer, who set to work with his usual energy and persistence. Despite intense opposition he succeeded in transforming the whole legal profession within a decade. But these reforms were still in the future when Alphonsus drew up for himself a code of conduct in the exercise of his profession; it is against the background of the prevailing corrupt climate that they must be judged. He set for himself a high standard of personal integrity and moral uprightness:

1. Not to accept unjust cases since they can compromise one's conscience and one's integrity.
2. Not to employ unjust means in the defence of a case.
3. Not to cause one's clients unnecessary expense.
4. To defend one's client with the same energy as if his case were one's own.
5. To study the case conscientiously so as to be fully conversant with it; remissness could seriously compromise the result. The lawyer who loses a case through his own negligence is under an obligation to compensate the client for any losses he suffers.
6. A lawyer should not undertake any case which is beyond his capabilities or to which he has not the time to devote himself thoroughly.
7. A lawyer should have a great reverence for justice and integrity. He should be truthful and sincere, diligent and assiduous.
8. A lawyer should not neglect to call on God's help during the case since God is the source of all true justice.

CHAPTER TWO

FROM THE LAW COURTS TO THE SANCTUARY 1713–1723

– I –

The ten years between Alphonsus' graduation as a lawyer and his decision to become a priest in 1723 are now much better documented and as a result we are able to paint a more complete and balanced picture of his adolescence and early manhood than emerges from the pages of Tannoia. In many ways it was a troubled period in which his scrupulosity and anxiety complex clearly manifested themselves even though there is also evidence that he was still able to enjoy many of the normal aspects of adolescent social life in Naples at the time. The Roman authorities were not at all impressed at the process of canonisation by the efforts to minimise these aspects of his life; his life, they felt, was quite normal for a young Neapolitan, with its 'social evenings, musical soirées, parties, theatres and various other amusements'.[1]

It is equally clear that during these years Don Joseph occupied centre stage in all family matters; if Donna Anna was the centre during the children's early years, Don Joseph now had firm control of all family arrangements; one feels he organised them as he did the Fleet. To accustom them to the rigours of life as he experienced it in the navy, he insisted that the boys sleep on the floor once a week; he began to plan their future careers just as he had done for Alphonsus; he drew up marriage plans, seeking out suitable partners, always with an eye to wealth and social status.[2] He would not tolerate any deviation from his decisions. The two surviving eldest girls Maria Louisa and Anna Maria were despatched, as was the accepted custom, to a nearby convent for their education, Maria Louisa when she was nine, Anna Maria, with a papal dispensation, when she was five. Dressed in religious habits and sharing as far as possible the life of the nuns, even to the matter of enclosure and visits from family, such young girls were often referred to as *vergini in capillis* since if they later wished to become novices in the convent their hair was symbolically cut at their reception ceremony. Both Alphonsus' sisters did in fact enter the convent of San Girolamo where they had been educated; when the time came for them to enter they returned home for a few months of preparation and final decision before their formal Clothing Ceremony as novices.

Maria Luisa was professed in 1716, Anna Maria two years later. It is worth noting that Alphonsus never lived with these two sisters during their or his adolescent years; at most he would have known them as young children and during their few weeks at home before returning finally to the convent. Nor is it without interest that Anna Maria soon fell into bad health, both physical and mental. Her neurotic scrupulosity became so well known throughout the Neapolitan clerical world that in the life of Father Giambattista Cacciottoli, S.J., published in Naples in 1751, her sad condition as a victim of scruples was referred to publicly.[3]

Antonio, the second son, apparently posed no problems for Don Joseph in his domestic arrangements; he slipped off quietly to the Cassinese Congregation of the Benedictines around his fifteenth birthday; three years later in 1716 he was professed as Benedict Mary. Cajetan, the next boy, was not so easily settled. Don Joseph decided that he too should join the clerical ranks but realised that a rich benefice with adequate financial returns was necessary for his support as one of the Neapolitan home-based clergy. In 1715 he presented Cajetan, just fourteen, to the duke of Gravina-Orsini as a candidate for the benefice of the Abbey of San Matteo de Ferrilli which was at the disposition of that powerful family. Nothing came of it, with the result that Cajetan was once more on Don Joseph's hands. Some twelve years later in 1728 Cajetan resumed his progress towards the priesthood with greater maturity and purpose; Alphonsus was by then two years a priest. Ordained in 1730, Cajetan secured a modest benefice for his support, in the church of S. Anna dei Lombardi, in 1734; two years later he improved his economic situation considerably by becoming Chaplain of the Treasury of St Januarius in the Cathedral, a lucrative position he retained until his death in 1784. He lived his life as a typical Neapolitan clerical gentleman with his liveried servants; cultured, kind and gentle but, unlike his elder brother, caused scarcely a ripple on the pastoral scene in Naples.

Don Joseph was now able to focus his full attention on Alphonsus; besides him there only remained Teresa and Hercules, the benjamin of the family. Their future would be arranged in due course. Alphonsus was the centre of all Don Joseph's hopes. His successful university studies augured well for a brilliant legal career; a marriage to a richly endowed member of the nobility would be the crowning achievement. The central position of Don Joseph in the Liguori household is the key to the difficult decade that was now beginning in Alphonsus' life; his activities and development were to be closely monitored by his domineering parent.

By 1715 Alphonsus had outgrown the Sodality of Young Noblemen in the church of the Oratorians where under the guidance of Father Pagano we

have seen him develop spiritually. He now progressed to the Sodality of
Our Lady of the Visitation, or *Congregazione dei Dottori* for university
graduates, still under the guidance of the Oratorians. Besides their religious
and cultural exercises the *dottori* devoted themselves to very practical works
of charity among the poor of the city. Not far from the church of the
Oratorians was the hospital of Santa Maria del Popolo, the refuge of the
needy and the outcast, referred to usually as the *Incurabili*, a name given to
similar hospitals in nearly every Italian city in those days.[4] The *Incurabili* of
Naples had been founded in the early decades of the sixteenth century by
the Venerable Maria Longo, a Catalan widow, and was one of the largest
and best organised hospitals of Europe at the time, catering for about eleven
hundred patients, both male and female. Here young men and women of
Neapolitan society took their turn ministering to the sick and aged in what
was then the most practical form of the lay apostolate. The Fathers of the
Oratory paid for the upkeep of forty-eight beds while their sodalists on
certain days of each week attended to the needs of three hundred and ten
patients assigned to them by the hospital authorities, making beds, changing
linen, washing the sick, feeding the more helpless and performing the other
services demanded by geriatric patients. Modern hygienic methods and the
advance of medical science have reduced the unpleasantness and danger of
such tasks but in those days voluntary service in the *casa degli incurabili*
demanded real courage and often heroic charity like that of St Camillus in
Rome or St Francis Xavier in Venice.

Alphonsus was faithful to his work among the poor of the *Incurabili* until
he became a cleric in 1723, a period of some eight years; it was here that he
first experienced the real happiness to be found in God's service and appropriately enough it was here too that God finally and unmistakably called
him to the priesthood. Not satisfied with membership of one lay charitable
organisation Alphonsus followed his father into another. Don Joseph had
been a member of the *Congregazione dei Nobili di Santa Maria della Misericordia*
for many years when he insisted on Alphonsus joining him. The *Misericordiella*,
as the society was conveniently known, had been established by St Cajetan,
the founder of the Theatines, as an association for the lay apostolate of the
Neapolitan aristocracy. It attended to the spiritual and material needs of
clerics in the two ecclesiastical prisons of Naples (one of the archbishop,
the other of the papal nuncio), and maintained a hostel for pilgrims as well
as a small hospital, while in 1700 it took upon itself the further charitable
activity of burying the poor. The association flourished, had its own private
chapel and a special chaplain with his specific duties clearly detailed. The
members followed a prescribed programme of religious duties and devotions
with regular meetings to which was added the humiliating task of questing
weekly in turn for support for their charitable activities. With whatever
funds were available the associates then maintained their hospital, brought
food and clothing to the ecclesiastical prisons and arranged decent obsequies
for the indigent. Dressed in a long white cloak with a scarlet mozzetta or
cape to which was attached a capuche or hood, they were a striking and

familiar sight in the streets of Naples as they sought alms for their charities or accompanied the funerals of the poor with chanting to the local *terrasanta*.[5]

Alphonsus' father was a totally dedicated and exemplary member of the *Misericordiella*. For all his rugged ways he was at heart a man of simple piety and fundamental goodness; in his cabin he kept four miniature statues representing Our Lord at different stages of His Passion which helped to bring his mind to spiritual things while away at sea. On his retirement from active service he made the *Misericordiella* the centre of his spiritual life; when he died some fifteen years later he was accorded the privilege of burial in its private *terrasanta*. After his year of probation, Alphonsus took part with his father in all the activities of the sodality from about 1716 onwards; it was only when he became a deacon in 1726 that he formally resigned his membership in favour of his brother Hercules. To the *Misericordiella* Alphonsus owed his acquaintance with the five psalms of the Holy Name of Mary, attributed to St Bonaventure, which the sodalists recited in choir at their meetings. These psalms became one of his favourite devotions in honour of the Mother of God and he later bound himself by vow to recite them daily; at the end of his life he knew them by heart and would recite them from memory.

The picture of religious practice in the Liguori family would not be complete without reference to the enclosed retreats which Don Joseph made each year with either the Jesuits or the Vincentians, usually during Holy Week. Alphonsus was about seventeen when he accompanied his father on one of these retreats for the first time, probably the year he graduated from the university. Later, if his father was detained on duty in the galleys, he went alone. We have it from his own lips in later years how much these days of meditation and prayer meant to him; the retreat of 1722, as we shall see, stood out particularly in his memory as the really decisive one, the beginning of his conversion, as he engagingly called it, in the language of the saints.

The accumulation of religious practices in the rather narrow and oppressive Liguori household should not be allowed to obscure the more normal aspects of Alphonsus' adolescence nor to imply that he did not behave as naturally as many other young Neapolitan noblemen blessed with similarly devout parents, the advantages of status, education and modest wealth. Just to concentrate on the religious activities is to get the whole picture out of focus. His life was edifying undoubtedly but probably no more so than that of many others in that enigmatic society; he himself compared his own conduct unfavourably with that of his closest friend from one of the most distinguished families of Naples, Francis Capecelatro, duke of Casabona, whose christian conduct was a source of inspiration to him. Alphonsus played cards a lot; contemporaries remembered him as sharing to the full the great passion of eighteenth-century society for *terzilgio*, *ombre* and *pichetto*; today he would be a committed Bridge fan.[6] Hunting and fowling, later to be the passion of the Neapolitan Bourbons, he also found congenial and devoted considerable time to them but his defective vision and the fact that he had to wear glasses soon made this sport impossible for him. His greatest interest, however, was in theatre and music.

He frequented the San Bartolomeo, the finest theatre in Naples until it was demolished in 1737 to make way for the San Carlo Opera House of Charles III, and the Teatro dei Fiorentini, the home of Neapolitan *opera buffa*. At the San Bartolomeo he would have attended *Aci e Galatea* by Handel, the *Tigrane* and *Carlo, re d'Alemagna* of Scarlatti, as well as operas now forgotten by composers such as Mancini and Popora. His interest was centred on the music, not on the plot or the acting. He recalled later how he used to lose himself as he listened to it and how he was able to copy out the more tuneful arias when he returned home and play them on his harpischord.[7]

The Liguori family flourished under the Austrian regime; Don Joseph in particular improved his status considerably. Whatever loyalties he possessed were towards the Austrian Hapsburgs, with the result that promotion and high commendations for his faithful service came to him from Vienna. By the summer of 1731 he was Captain Commander of the Flagship of the Fleet. The financial position of the family had also been consolidated, reflected in the fact that their home was well supplied with Muslim slaves captured by the royal galleys. Most of the noble families of Rome and Naples at that time kept these servants who were hired out from the galleys but could be recalled to service when required. Alphonsus had his own personal liveried footman who accompanied him wherever he went, to the courts in the morning, to the Caravita palace and the social rounds or theatre in the evening. One of these footmen, a native of Rhodes, named Abdala, has escaped from anonymity into the pages of history. Abdala was much impressed by the kindness of his young master and more so by the example of his life with the result that he asked to become a Christian. Alphonsus took him to his kinsman, Father Mastrillo, at the Oratory, who questioned the young slave as to whether his desire for baptism was not merely a device to secure his release. Convinced of his upright dispositions, Mastrillo had him ransomed from the galleys and began his instruction in the faith in May 1715. Some weeks later Abdalla fell ill and was taken to the *Ospidale della Pace*, under the charge of the Fatebenefratelli, the Brothers of St John of God. On the night of 21 June his condition became critical and he asked to be baptised. Word was sent to Father Mastrillo who saw to it that the young man was baptised at once; a few hours later the former Mohammedan slave, now the neophyte Joseph Mary Philip Felix Marcell, died — the first fruits of the missionary labours of Alphonsus de Liguori.

Another incident concerning a Mohammedan slave in the Liguori household was a less happy one but more indicative of the family climate. At the conclusion of a reception in the Liguori palace one of the servants was slow in bringing a torch to light the guests to their carriages. Don Joseph, highly sensitive to anything which might tarnish the family reputation, was furious at the lapse. When the guests were gone he vented his rage on the unfortunate slave. Alphonsus took the part of the servant and losing his own temper — which erupted as easily as his father's — told the latter in so many words to have some consideration for others. 'When you start, there is no end to it,' he said. Enraged, Don Joseph struck him, whereupon Alphonsus turned, retired to his room and refused to appear for supper. It took all the gentleness of his mother to restore peace to the family; at her request Alphonsus came to table and begged his father's pardon for the incident.

Having determined his son's profession, regulated his studies and to a large extent the practice of his religion, Don Joseph finally directed his attention to the important question of marriage. His efforts to get Alphonsus married were spread over a decade and were the real source of friction between father and son and a cause of pain to both. Two attempts are well documented though there were certainly others; the idea was never far from Don Joseph's mind.[8] Some time about the beginning of 1710 he planned a marriage between his eldest son and Teresa, daughter of his kinsman Don Francis de Liguori, prince of Presicce. The choice had much to recommend it according to the ideas of the time; her father's wealth guaranteed the girl a rich dowry, the noble blood of the Liguori would be preserved by uniting two branches of the family. The decision, of course, did not lie with the proposed partners, Alphonsus being about thirteen, Teresa not yet seven. The proposal, for a variety of reasons, came to nothing but it had an intriguing conclusion. As a child Teresa was sent to the Carmelite Convent of the Most Blessed Sacrament to be educated; there she determined to remain and despite efforts to make her return 'to the world' she persisted and consecrated herself to the Lord at the age of sixteen as a Carmelite nun. Four years later she died after much suffering and with a considerable reputation for holiness. In 1761 on the eve of his appointment as a bishop, Alphonsus acceded to the request of the Mother Prioress to write the life of the girl whom his father, at least, once thought of as his bride. *The Life and Death of the Servant of God, Teresa Mary de Liguori*, is an unsophisticated account, wholly in the style of the time, of one whose only ambition was to belong to God and who proved her fidelity in the midst of great anguish of spirit.[9]

There can be little doubt that Alphonsus at some time became aware of his father's plans for him in regard to Teresa and presumably so did she. As he dictated his biography of her to his amanuensis, Father Criscuoli, he recounted the full story. 'I know this for a fact because the servant of God told me while he was dictating Sister Teresa's life to me', Father Criscuoli declared under oath at the process of canonisation in the diocese of Nocera. And yet there is no mention of marriage proposals in Alphonsus' account of her life; not even the slightest hint that Teresa herself or the author had any idea of what plans their parents had for them. Behind the simple straightforward words of Alphonsus' biography we can now see the hidden story:

> Sister Teresa, then known as Donna Teresa, was only sixteen, possessed of a considerable private fortune, and endowed with remarkable gifts

and qualities which made her attractive to everybody, when she consecrated herself to the love of her divine spouse and became a religious. At home in her father's house, despite pressing invitations, she constantly refused to frequent the theatre or to attend social soirées or other forms of entertainment.

Despite this set-back Don Joseph continued to plan for the marriage of his eldest son as indeed he did for the other marriageable children on his hands, Hercules and Teresa. There is an amusing side to much of his activity. The negotiations for the formal *fidanzamento* or betrothal between Hercules and one Donna Maria Vincenza Sersale were on the point of being concluded; clothes had been made, the appropriate jewellery ready to be exchanged, when the young lady, an *educanda* in the convent of San Girolamo, suddenly changed her mind and announced her intention of becoming a nun. Don Joseph, away at the time on active service, knew nothing of the cancellation of his plans. On his return in time for the celebrations, as he thought, he drew up the fleet in the Bay in view of the Sersale palace and fired a salvo of guns by way of salute to his future daughter-in-law. His embarrassment was total when he learnt of the collapse of the proposals and more so when there emerged a suspicion that Alphonsus — by then a priest — was instrumental in getting the girl to change her mind.[10]

In 1720 Don Joseph successfully concluded negotiations for the marriage of Teresa to Don Domenico de Balzo, duke of Presenzano; she was sixteen, he a widower of twenty-seven. He then proposed the marriage of Alphonsus to another member of the duke's family; it would have been a tidy arrangement. As it turned out it proved to be Don Joseph's last attempt before admitting to failure in bitter rage and frustration; it took him years to come to terms with his disappointment. Alphonsus was twenty-four at the time, nervous, scrupulous in sexual matters, confused as to his future, torn between his duty of obedience to his father and loyalty to his family according to the theology of the time, and a persistent desire for the priesthood which had begun to haunt him. When this idea came to him first we do not know with precision — most likely about the age of sixteen. He may well have confided in his mother who would have urged him to consult Father Pagano at the Oratory. Then during one of the enclosed retreats made with the Jesuits he made a definite promise, perhaps even a private vow, to join the Theatines whom he knew from their two churches and monasteries in Naples and particularly from that of San Paolo Maggiore where his family connection, Father Dominic Liguori, was superior.[11] But he was refused — or was dissuaded — whichever way one wishes to interpret the position, and the recollection of this unfulfilled vow returned to torment him in his recurring bouts of scruples later on. With this background we can imagine in what frame of mind he took part in the social round of Neapolitan society in obedience to his father's wishes, the entertainment, the visits and musical evenings at which he was called upon to play the harpsichord and to display himself as an eligible batchelor in the presence of hopeful *zitelle* eager to attract his attention.

From his mother and from the whole nature of his upbringing he had developed all the symptoms of a deeply rooted scrupulosity of neurotic proportions, which was to be with him throughout his life. He was particularly sensitive in the matter of chastity, an attitude which manifested itself in his adolescent years in the course of normal sexual development. The fear of committing sin at night filled him with anxiety; scruples about whether he had consented to sexual pleasure tormented him. We have it on the explicit testimony of his brother, Cajetan, that Alphonsus adopted the expedient of tying his hands together in a canvas bag before retiring to rest, lest he should touch himself immodestly, as he feared, during the night. Stemming from this inability to integrate the fact of his sexuality was his uncomfortableness in the presence of women, due perhaps in part to the natural awkwardness of adolescence but more so as time went on to an ever present fear of sinning. In the presence of women he felt he should keep his eyes cast down; in the theatre he removed his glasses so as not to see the females on stage. Apparently the very sight of women — even his own in-laws — disturbed him sexually and troubled his scrupulous conscience. It took him years of what must have been agony to come to terms with himself in this matter; he poured out his worries to his confessors and directors, recorded their instructions in a personal note-book which he consulted from time to time, vowing blind obedience to their directions, as we shall see later. One sentence recorded in his note-book reveals everything: 'Speaking with women is not an occasion of sin *per se* even though it causes some sexual arousal.'[12]

Communication between father and son must have been virtually non-existent during these years, otherwise it is difficult to understand how Don Joseph could have persisted so insensitively in the task of securing Alphonsus' co-operation in his marriage plans. Did he ever suspect for a moment what his son was going through as he struggled with himself in the matter of his priestly vocation? Why was Alphonsus so terrified of intimating to his father the real reason for his reluctance to commit himself to marriage? The nearest he came to giving his father a reason for his refusal of all offers was to plead indifferent health, recurring asthma and a definite bronchial weakness. A well-documented incident in the home of the duke of Presenzano should have taught Don Joseph the futility of his efforts. On the occasion of a visit to the castle of Presenzano hopefully arranged by Don Joseph, Alphonsus was induced to play the harpsichord while a possible fiancée attempted to sing. When she came to his side and looked lovingly into his face, as was customary on such occasions, Alphonsus turned away; nothing daunted the young lady went around to face him again only to find that Alphonsus had turned away once more. With an untranslateable comment in Neapolitan dialect on her lawyer partner the young lady ended the whole affair.[13]

The picture that contemporaries drew of Alphonsus at this time clearly indicates that he must have been a very attractive young man from the physical point of view. He has suffered more than most saints from the so-called portraits that found their way into nineteenth-century editions of his work all over the world; the black and white line drawings of him in his old age, virtually hunch-backed, unshaven, unkempt, verge on the repulsive. Yet by these caricatures is he most commonly recognised. Certainly the weight of years and a variety of illnesses, especially an arthritic curvature of the spine, deformed him considerably as well as causing him great pain. But in his early manhood as well as being successful in his profession, highly esteemed for his forensic talent and his irreproachable personal conduct, he was also physically attractive. He was of medium height, of slender build, with a broad forehead, black receding hair which enlarged the area of his brow, and with a markedly aquiline nose. His eyes were light blue, his mouth small with a gentle expression as if he were continually smiling; his voice clear and penetrating while his carriage was upright and distinctive. The one physical defect from which he suffered was shortsightedness; he was mildly myopic necessitating glasses even as a youth. These were not, however, anything of a social handicap; in Naples at the time they were quite fashionable. Alphonsus had a fine sense of dress; one of the canons of Naples Cathedral recalled him as always elegantly dressed and accompanied by his footman — in marked contrast to the poverty of his clothes in later years as a missioner and as a bishop.

Underneath the external composure was a very ardent nature with an explosive temper inherited from his father but which subsided again as easily, leaving him distressed and repentant. This exterior gentleness of manner concealed a strength of will which his father knew all too well and which he called stubbornness and yet with it there went a habit of obedience and submission such that in after-life he could only recall one deliberate refusal to carry out his father's explicit command — that was when Don Joseph asked him to take part in a private opera with other young men and women in the house of a family friend. Here, what we can readily surmise was a clash between his sensitivity in the matter of sexuality and the obedience due to his father, was resolved anxiously in favour of safety in the matter of chastity. These characteristics which marked his adolescence and early manhood can be clearly traced in his conduct at a different level in succeeding years.

His sense of obedience and readiness to submit himself to his father's wishes later emerged as total obedience to his various directors of conscience, and complete abandonment to the designs of God in his regard; the stubbornness of which both his parents at times lamented became the strength of purpose which characterises all the saints in the difficulties of their ascent to God and the execution of what they see as His wishes. While the Promoter of the Faith in the process of canonisation had numerous objections to raise about his life he could only express astonishment at Alphonsus' heroic steadfastness in overcoming the difficulties connected with the foundation of his missionary society.

– II –

The enclosed retreat of 1722 made with the Vincentian Fathers during Holy Week marked the turning point in Alphonsus' life and spiritual development.

Forty men, among them the social elite of Naples such as the Carafa, the Capecelatro, the Filomarino and Spinelli families began the spiritual exercises under the direction of Father Vincent Cutica, superior of the house for twenty years and a well known missioner in the kingdom. There was a striking contrast between his approach and that of the gentle Pagano to whom Alphonsus was accustomed. Perhaps Cutica decided that fear, aroused by the thought of hell and damnation, was necessary to elicit some religious response from the majority of his audience; be that as it may, he left no dramatic stratagem untried to instil terror into them. During a conference on hell the Vincentian had the lights extinguished and then related the following incident:

> Eleven years ago in the city of Florence a young nobleman was living in sin with a married woman. Neither prayers nor threats were able to get him to change his life. After some time his sinful companion died suddenly and the young man, almost distraught with grief, came to our house of St James to make a retreat. On the evening of the first day it was noticed that his place at supper was vacant; thinking that he had mistaken the time the father in charge sent up to his room for him. They knocked on his door, then opened it only to be driven back by a cloud of smoke. They immediately thought fire had broken out and that the young man was in danger. They found him lying on the floor unconscious with the priedieu burnt in the place where he had knelt; on the picture of the Crucifixion before which he had been praying were the imprint of two hands burnt into the canvas. When the young man regained consciousness he declared that his sinful companion had appeared to him as he knelt in prayer and said, 'Through your fault I am now in hell. Do not trouble to pray for me but think of yourself and of your own salvation. God has allowed me to appear to you. And in order to remove any hesitation from your mind I will leave the imprint of my hands on the picture of the Crucifixion.

Calling for lights again and fixing his eyes on the forty men in front of him Father Cutica then produced the picture to which he had referred. In the silence that followed there was ample evidence of the effect of his illustration. 'Look at this picture and draw your own conclusions' was all he added as he made a dramatic exit.[14]

This fear-of-God approach together with the terror aroused by the thought of hell and damnation did considerable psychological damage to Alphonsus with his scruples and his sensitivity; the concept of God which underlay that approach can have done nothing to alleviate either one or the other. Rather it deepened what was in danger of becoming a serious and deep-seated neurosis. From his own personal notes over the next fifteen years we shall see the repeated efforts he had to make under the guidance of his spiritual directors to rid himself of the notion of God as a punishing tyrant and replace it with a sense of the love of God as the kindest of Fathers. The notion of the fear of God left him psychologically scarred.

Nevertheless this retreat of 1722 was his 'conversion' retreat; the previous two or three years during which he had participated in the normal round of Neapolitan society were considered as marking a loss of fervour on his part. There would now, however, be an end to theatres, operas, soirées and card playing with his friends. Decisions taken during these days of Holy Week in 1722 determined his whole future. In September following the retreat he was confirmed, being then twenty-six. When this apparent negligence on his part was objected to at his canonisation it was explained in reply that it was the accepted practice in Naples to defer the reception of this sacrament until comparatively late in life; in convents it was the usual prelude to religious profession. The tempo of Alphonsus' spiritual life increased; he now communicated several times a week following his weekly confession. His favourite devotion was the Forty Hours Adoration of the Blessed Sacrament, which was organised throughout the year in the different churches of the city. He spent long hours on his knees hidden away in a quiet corner enjoying all the spiritual consolations with which the Lord usually regales the beginner in the early stages of the spiritual journey. This was, in fact, to be one of the happiest periods of his whole life; the anxieties of conscience and the darkness of spirit which marked the first years of his priesthood were still to come. In 1745 in the monastery which he founded at Ciorani he referred to these days in the introduction to his book of Visits to Jesus in the Blessed Sacrament in words which are clearly autobiographical:

> Where have souls who love God found courage to make important resolutions if not before the Blessed Sacrament exposed? Who knows but you too will one day resolve before the Sacred Monstrance to give yourself completely to the Lord. I feel an obligation to declare publicly in this little book — at least out of gratitude to Jesus in the Blessed Sacrament — that I owe my vocation to the visits I made to the Blessed Sacrament, however tepid and remiss I may have been. It was my misfortune to have lived in the world for twenty-six years. You will be fortunate if you are able to dedicate your life at an earlier stage than me to the Lord who gave himself completely to you.
>
> You are fortunate, I say, not only in the next life but also in this. Believe me, parties, banquets, theatres, social soirées and amusements are nothing but futility; they are the main attractions the world has to offer but attractions full of bitterness and thorns. Believe me who has experienced it all and is now regretting it.[15]

Alphonsus' attendance at the Forty Hours Devotions throughout the city did not go unobserved nor were they without effect on the lives of others. One of his first companions some ten years later in the foundation of his new missionary society was the great priestly gentleman, Father Giovanni Mazzini. Though well over ninety years of age he testified at the process of beatification of Alphonsus that he had often observed him lost in prayer in some city church when he himself was a young cleric:

> I was with two fellow priests when I saw Alphonsus for the first time in the church of the Oratorians. The appearance of this young man, richly dressed, attractive and composed, modest and friendly, obviously of noble lineage, who prayed with such fervour on his knees was a source of great edification for us, which was increased when we found him in every church where the Forty Hours Devotion was in progress. When we had concluded our own short visits we left the young man behind us and we commented among ourselves on his exemplary conduct. I thought to myself what a shame it was for me, a cleric, to be outdone in piety by a man of the world. We were anxious to know who he was and to speak to him but neither of these did we succeed in doing. A considerable time afterwards we found the young man again in the same prayerful posture before the Blessed Sacrament but now dressed as a cleric. As he left the church we spoke to him and he told us his name was Alphonsus de Liguori.

The retreat of 1722 also marked a crucial stage in the clarification of Alphonsus' vocation to the priesthood. The last work he wrote as a bishop was a translation of the psalms which he dedicated to the reigning pontiff, Clement XIV. As was his custom he sent many complimentary copies to different people; one was to the superior of the Vincentians in Naples, Father Lemêtre. In an accompanying letter Alphonsus informed him that it was in the Vincentian house in Naples that he finally determined to 'leave the world' — as the quaint phrase in use at the time described becoming a priest or religious. It took Alphonsus years to make a definite decision to become a priest; it was virtually wrung from him after years of agonising introspection. Unfortunately, he was later always very reticent about the details of the various stages of that long journey of hesitation and doubt. At any rate his determination did not come to him overnight, he was not struck down on any road to Damascus. The forensic debacle which was his last painful experience in the Naples courts was not the origin of the idea; it merely hastened a decision which was long maturing. Undoubtedly he was psychologically hesitant at this stage of his life. But on the other hand, it must be said in his favour, that he was the eldest son and the eldest son, moreover, of a father for whom family status and advancement which had all the force of religion, was centred on his success in secular life and subsequent marriage. His obligation to remain a practising lawyer seemed clear. In the atmosphere of the time it was a matter of conscience for children to obey their parents and especially their fathers, in the matter of choosing both a state of life and their marriage partner. Alphonsus himself included a question on this in an examination of conscience he drew up in 1755. Moral theologians in Naples took a long while to come to the conclusion that children could become priests and religious despite the opposition of their parents and that parents were not to impede their children's entrance into religion.[16]

Furthermore, there was the added complication that in Naples, both legally and from the point of view of the ecclesiastical authorities, the entrance of a family heir into the clerical state entailed several difficulties which necessitated special dispensations. An ecclesiastical decision in Naples in the year 1700 laid down that an only son, a first-born son, or those who had brothers already in the clerical state, were not to be accepted.[17] It may well have been considerations such as these, together with a personal knowledge of Don Joseph's reactions, which influenced the Oratorians and Theatines in turn to reject Alphonsus' request to become one of them. And yet, Alphonsus' decision on Easter Sunday 1722 at the end of his retreat with the Vincentians seems to have still been tentative, something rather in the nature of remaining celibate and awaiting clearer indications concerning any further step; one thing was at last clear to him and that was that he should not marry.

– III –

The climax of Alphonsus' career as a lawyer and the turning point of his whole life came in the year following his 'conversion', when he was retained by Don Filippo Orsini, duke of Gravina, to prosecute his claim for some 600,000 ducats against the estates which the Grand Duke of Tuscany, Cosimo de Medici, held in the area of Amatrice in the Abruzzo.[18] The Amatrice fief had a long and involved history going back two hundred years to 1538 when the Emperor Charles V rewarded his loyal soldier Alessandro Vitelli with a vast grant of land at Amatrice. In less than a hundred years the estates had passed through marriage out of the Vitelli family to a branch of the Orsini family, the last member of which, Alessandro, besides murdering his wife, mortgaged the estates to his kinsman, the duke of Gravina. On Alessandro's death — surprisingly from natural causes — without heirs in 1692, the rich spoil of the Amatrice estates was claimed through right of inheritance by the Grand Duchess of Tuscany, Vittoria de Montrefeltro della Rovere, a formidable personage in more than name, and a descendant of the original owner, Alessandro Vitelli. In 1693 the Royal Chamber of Naples, at the instance of the Treasury, sequestered the estates and regranted them to the Grand Duchess on payment of 28,000 ducats. The terms of the grant ran: *die 3 Maii 1693 fiscus cedit in beneficium Serenissimae magnae ducissae Hetruriae civitatem Amatricis in novum feudum* (the Treasury grants to her Serene Highness, the duchess of Tuscany, the city of Amatrice, *as a new fief*). The fact that the Grand Duchess now possessed these estates, first, as a result of a regrant by the Treasury, and secondly, under the clause *in novum feudum* which her astute lawyers had succeeded in having inserted into the charter, were legal points of vital importance.

A series of lawsuits concerning these estates now followed which were to drag on for forty years and were to make legal history in more ways than one. First in the field was the Hapsburg Emperor Charles VI who laid claim in 1716 against Cosimo de Medici who had inherited Amatrice on his mother's death in 1694. The political situation was, of course, entirely favourable to the Emperor's intervention. His lawyer, Giuseppe Sorge, claimed that the grant of 1693 did not establish a *new title* to the possession of the estates; legally this was equivalent to saying that the duke of Tuscany held the Amatrice fief by right of inheritance and according to the original grant of Charles V and not in virtue of the grant of 1693. Consequently the duke inherited not merely the assets of the estates but the liabilities as well. Sorge's analysis of the nature of feudal fiefs and their tenure, which he published in Naples as a result of this *cause célèbre*, immediately became a *locus classicus* of feudal law in Italy.[19] Encouraged by the favourable progress of the emperor's claim through the law courts, Don Felippe Orsini, duke of Gravina, considered it a propitious time to prosecute his own claims against the estates. He filed his suit in 1720 in the Regia Camera della Sommaria and it was finally listed for hearing in the summer of 1723. By this time the best legal brains of the capital were engaged in the case, Sorge, Ruffo, Camarota, Caravita, Orazio Rocca, Francesco Iovino, Domenico Bruno, Francesco Onofri, Antonio Maggiocchi and finally Alphonsus de Liguori.

Every lawyer in the capital was familiar with this case; its passage through the courts had given rise not merely to discussions but to legal publications of all sorts. It was centre stage on the legal scene from the very first year that Alphonsus began his legal studies; inevitably it must have figured in the student discussions in the various legal *salotti* he frequented. That he was now invited to join the array of legal talent involved in the case is sufficient indication of his standing as a lawyer, apart altogether from the fact that the de Liguori and Orsini families were on intimate terms. Alphonsus prepared his brief with great care in conjunction with Giuseppi Sorge whose opinion and approach he fully shared. The kernel of their submission was that the fiscal decree of 1693 did not alter the nature of the original feudal grant; they were not prepared to concede that the phrase *in novum feudum* made any essential difference. In this Alphonsus was following the opinion not only of Sorge but also of another recognised authority on feudal tenure, Giovanni de Rosa, whose work on this subject, published in Naples in 1713 treated explicitly of the point at issue, *nova qualitas non facit feudum simpliciter novum*. Sorge on his part was prepared to go even further in dismissing the importance of the disputed clause; he outlined the absurd legal consequences that would follow were such a clause to be interpreted as altering the nature of the original concession. Neither Alphonsus nor Sorge was ready to concede any weight to the opposing opinion, and this attitude was, in the event, to prove disastrous. The case was called towards the end of July 1723. Alphonsus, twenty-seven, was the first to speak and put his case with force and clarity. His line of argument was easy to follow. The title of the Grand Duke of Tuscany was *antiquum* and not *novum*. He traced the history of the original grant of Charles V; he showed that the Grand Duchess Vittoria possessed a legitimate title of inheritance to the estates in 1692; he discussed the confiscation of the estates and the transactions with the Treasury a year later, recalling the accepted principle, *feudum quod retinetur ratione alicuius transactionis cum Fisco dicitur antiquum non novum*. The fiscal decree of 1693 only confirmed and did not set aside the ancient title or, in the legal terminology of feudal jurisprudence, *nova qualitas non facit feudum simpliciter novum*. It followed then that the claims of his client, the duke of Gravina, against the estate had not been extinguished by the proceedings in 1693.

To Alphonsus the case seemed irrefutable; he finished his exposition certain of success. What happened next is clear from his own account thirty-five years later when he recounted the incident to his companions in the monastery at Pagani.[20] Unimpressed by the main thrust of Alphonsus' argument, the Medici lawyers concentrated on the grant of 1693, drawing the attention of the judge to the phrase *in novum feudum* which Alphonsus' line of argument dismissed as incidental. They insisted that this clause did in fact alter the whole position: for them it was decisive. To the astonishment of Alphonsus the presiding judges readily upheld the submission of the Medici counsel, and the whole Orsini case as prepared and presented by him collapsed irretrievably. The claim of his client was summarily dismissed. Alphonsus could only concede defeat and retire in humiliation and confusion.

It is now clear that there was much more to the court room encounter than the legal complexities of feudal tenure; nor is it any longer possible to accept the romantic version that Alphonsus, despite his months of study and consultation, had incredibly neglected to give due weight to a negative particle as some biographers would have us believe. Behind the scenes there was bribery and political interference at the highest level. Giovanni Battista Cecconi, the Medici agent in Naples, was quietly active on behalf of his master, as his despatches to Florence, recently studied, now clearly show. His intrigues reached as high as the Austrian Viceroy in Naples, Cardinal Michael Frederick d'Althan, who pressurised the judges in favour of the Medici with the connivance of Mauleone, President of the Camera Regia della Sommaria where the case was heard. Cecconi reported to Florence with a good deal of satisfaction that he had presented his Eminence with the gift of a pair of bears and (with an eye to detail) thoughtfully, male and female — *due piccoli orsi, maschio e femmina*.

This was probably Alphonsus' first experience at close quarters of political interference with the courts of justice. He returned home wounded in his pride, exposed as a lawyer who had incorrectly interpreted vital legal documents, disillusioned as regards the administration of justice. Psychologically he was shattered, unable to face his legal associates or even to appear in public. He locked himself in his room for three days refusing to eat or to see or talk to anybody. His father who was absent at the time of the court case returned home a day or so afterwards to learn of the debacle. His patience with Alphonsus was now exhausted; he had had enough. When his wife expressed her fear that Fonso would kill himself by his refusal to eat, Don Joseph replied irately that he did not much care whether he did or not. His mother urged Alphonsus to mix in society again and to take part in the social rounds of the city. 'Mother, I hate them with all my heart,' was his reply. Don Joseph tried to entice him to return to his legal practice; it would have been easy for him to re-establish himself in the courts since Don Joseph had court business which he wished Alphonsus to handle. But Alphonsus was determined not to return. Donna Anna still hoped that the effects of the defeat would wear off but on this occasion her husband divined the true situation more accurately. 'No,' he said, 'Alphonsus is stubborn and will not easily change his mind.'[21]

Slowly Alphonsus began to reconstruct his life again but this time almost on monastic principles. The hot summer months of August, September and October were months of more than usual tension in the Liguori household; discussions concerning the future were interminable. For his part Alphonsus spent his time mainly in prayer and spiritual reading in his room; if he went out it was to some church for the Forty Hours or to the *Incurabili* or to the Girolomini for confession and consultation with Father Pagano. The chronological sequence of events leading to the final decision is somewhat confused but the events themselves are not in doubt, vouched for, as they are, by the personal reminiscences of Alphonsus himself. During the novena in preparation for the feast of the Assumption of the Blessed Virgin he happened to enter the church of Our Lady of Ransom where a preacher unknown to him but with a German name was speaking about the Mother of God. It may have been at the end of the sermon that Alphonsus knelt before the statue of Our Lady of Mercy and ungirding his sword placed it at the feet of Our Lady like some medieval knight as a symbol of his dedication to her and as a sign of his resolve to become a priest. If the gesture seems to us theatrical we can only try to share the gracious spirit of those years when such chivalrous acts still had significance. Ever afterwards this tiny church retained a special place in Alphonsus' affections; when in Naples, even as a bishop, he never neglected to visit it and to relive those moments.[22] On the eve of his departure from Naples in 1770 on what was to be his last visit he went down alone to the church to take his farewell; on his return he informed his friend Don Salvatore Tramontano in whose house he was staying, 'This evening I said,"a rivederci in Paradiso," to the Madonna.'

Don Joseph made his final effort to bring Alphonsus back to his former way of life on Sunday 29 August, the official birthday of the empress Isabella. Elaborate festivities were arranged, a Te Deum in the viceregal chapel, salvoes of artillery from the ramparts, a state reception and a *cuccagna* — to the delight of the *lazzaroni* — in the palace grounds in the evening.[23] Don Joseph asked Alphonsus to accompany him to the palace; Alphonsus begged to be excused and no arguments on his father's part were able to change him. Exasperated, the good captain lost his temper completely and told his son that from then on he could go just where he pleased — the contemporary account mentions that he used 'pungent phrases'. Entering his carriage and avoiding the city, Don Joseph drove out to his villa at Marianella where alone with himself for three days he tried to come to terms with what was happening to his son.

For his part, Alphonsus resumed his round of church visits and his work with his companions at the *Incurabili*. It was while working there that the thought of the vanity of the world and all it could offer came home to him with startling clarity; the phrase, 'what doth it profit a man if he gain the whole world and suffer the loss of his soul' seemed to resound in his ears; he felt an insistent call from God to have done with hesitations and to leave the world without delay and consecrate his life to God's service.[24] Once more he withdrew to the quiet of his room, allowing his decision to mature. Finally he went back to Father Pagano to announce to him that he had finally made up his mind to become an Oratorian. Pagano asked for a year to consider the matter. But now Alphonsus was determined that there should be no further vacillation; he wanted to be accepted immediately.

While the decision cannot have been in the nature of a surprise to Don Joseph, he was still not prepared to acquiesce in it; the struggle between Alphonsus and himself went on for weeks. One can understand the feelings of the father as he saw his dreams dissolve, and feel for him in the bitterness of his disappointment when his plans were finally frustrated. But if God was working his purpose in the soul of Alphonsus He was at the same time beginning his work of purification in the soul of his father. By disappointment He brought Don Joseph to realise the value of the spiritual over the material, leading him ultimately before his last voyage to eternity to a deep spirit of detachment from all things earthly. But such a transformation was still in the future; at the moment his mood was explosive since nothing he could do was able to shake the determination of his son. Alphonsus explained that the idea had been in his mind for a long while but that he had hesitated to take the final decision. But now he was convinced that it was God's Will and that he would endanger his own eternal salvation if he did not answer God's call.

Unequal to the struggle Don Joseph called in some family friends to support him, the Benedictine Abbot of San Severino where Anthony was a monk, Canon Pietro Marco Gizzi from the seminary, the Vincentian Father Cutica who had preached the sermon on Hell, Father Pagano, Mons. Emilio Cavalieri and even Don Muzio de Maio, head of one of the sections of the law courts, probably with the intention of proving to Alphonsus that a legal career was still open to him.

But it was the intervention of the saintly Mons. Emilio Cavalieri, Donna Anna's brother, a member of the missionary society of the Pii Operai and bishop of Troia, that was decisive. He had himself experienced similar opposition from his father in following his vocation and had eventually renounced his right of primogeniture in order to enter the clerical state. Reluctantly Don Joseph was brought to agree to a compromise, that Alphonsus should become a priest of the diocese of Naples and not an Oratorian. Alphonsus was loath to accept the decision but agreed on the insistence of Father Pagano, Canon Gizzio and Mons. Cavalieri. In the middle of October Don Joseph presented his son to the Cardinal Archbishop of Naples, Francesco Pignatelli, who accepted him for ordination. On 23 October in a private ceremony in the Cardinal's palace Alphonsus donned the clerical soutane for the first time. Don Joseph refused to be present at the ceremony. In Naples the news caused a sensation; some attributed it to *una forte ippocondria*, to a mixture of spleen and disillusionment; in the Caravita household, the centre of the legal world where Alphonsus was so well known, the verdict was simply that he was out of his mind.[25]

CHAPTER THREE

THE APPRENTICE YEARS 1723–1729

– I –

Alphonsus' ecclesiastical training owed little to the norms of the Council of Trent which nearly 200 years earlier had instituted the seminary system; the Council's decrees on this, as in other matters, had to a large extent remained a dead letter throughout the kingdom. Most of the bishops were content to cater for such education as their priests received in their own episcopal residences or by giving them little more than a practical initiation into clerical practice in the homes of other clerics. Conditions in Naples itself were slightly more in keeping with the spirit of Trent since it did possess a central college attached to the cathedral with a professorial staff where candidates for the priesthood could follow a course in the humanities, philosophy, law and theology. The establishment of a formal seminary only came about some ten years later as the main pastoral initiative of Cardinal Spinelli who became archbishop in 1734. At the time of Alphonsus the majority of those who were studying for the priesthood in the city maintained at most external contact with the college and its professors; they lived at home with their families, wore ecclesiastical dress, were assigned to a church where they worked under the supervision of the incumbent priest, and studied theology either in private or under the guidance of self-constituted tutors. The system, for all its haphazardness, was not without its advantages for one of mature age and decision like Alphonsus. It developed a sense of responsibility and brought the aspirant into immediate contact with the milieu in which he would exercise his ministry if he had genuine pastoral aspirations.

Alphonsus now wore the black soutane of the Naples diocese with a plain black cincture and white collar which he later adopted for his own missionary society; he had to wear his hair short and the wearing of wigs was strictly forbidden. Violation of this law could entail a custodial sentence in the archiepiscopal prison. The very sight of his son in clerical attire was enough to enrage Don Joseph who turned away in disgust when he saw him. For two years he hardly addressed a word to Alphonsus; out of loyalty to him some of his friends such as Don Muzio di Maio, head of the law courts, refused to welcome Alphonsus back to their homes. The final thawing of relations between father and son did not come until Don Joseph heard Alphonsus preach to an enthralled congregation in the basilica of the Holy Spirit some five years later. The encomiums which Alphonsus received on this occasion and the glory reflected on the family as a consequence were sufficient to enkindle once again Don Joseph's pride in this eldest son and to assuage his opposition to his clerical calling.[1]

Alphonsus was assigned to the Church of Sant'Angelo à Segno — also known as San Michele — in the via dei Tribunali, to be initiated into clerical practice by one of the most exemplary priests of the city, Don Aniello Pacifico who had served the little church and its congregation since 1694. The church, if it can be called that, is no larger than a large room with accommodation for about one hundred people. It is still in existence today, mainly unchanged, with its flight of steps leading from the fish and fruit stalls of the narrow street — unchanged, that is, except for the statue of the saint in episcopal robes who began his clerical career within its walls. Besides assisting the parish priest in the liturgical ceremonies and in being responsible for teaching the children of the area catechism Alphonsus' duties made him at once sacristan, altar boy and church cleaner.

The diocesan statutes in the section *De Vita Clericorum* laid down certain rules of conduct for candidates for the priesthood. They were forbidden to attend the theatre or other social functions, to be in the company of young women in carriages or on excursions. On the positive side they were to attend in choir at a special Mass every Sunday in the Vincentian church, followed by spiritual and theological instruction. For some reason which we do not know, Alphonsus was exempted from this rule and was bound to attend only once a month. A decree of 1721 further enjoined on the candidates enrolment in one of three confraternities of priests formally recognised in the diocese; membership of one of these sodalities was obligatory and was the main source of priestly formation, a unique system which despite obvious shortcomings produced remarkable results.

The first of these 'clerical corporations', founded by Father Pavone, S.J. was attached to the Jesuit church of the Gesù Nuovo; under the patronage of Our Lady's Assumption the members were known simply as the Pavone Fathers. The second was under the direction of the priests of the Pii Operai — the Pious Workers — and attached to their church of San Giorgio Maggiore; from their titular feast of Our Lady's Purification they were often referred to as the Purità Fathers or more irreverently as the *Giorgini*. The third association attached to the cathedral itself was called the Congregation of the Apostolic Missions or simply the *Propaganda*. Established in 1646 by a Father Sansone Carnevale with the dual purpose of arousing interest among the priests of the diocese in the foreign missions — hence the name, Propaganda — and of improving their level of spirituality, culture and theological learning, the

Apostolic Missions had in fact succeeded in improving the general standard of priestly life among some at least of the Naples clergy. By 1720, however, they had virtually forgotten the overseas missionary ideal and were occupied exclusively with clerical formation and with missions to the people of the Kingdom of Naples. It was the most exclusive of the three clerical groups, and the members, known, not without a tinge of malice, as the 'Illustrissimi', regarded themselves as superior to their brethren in the other two groups. They were the spiritual and intellectual elite among the clergy, boasting from among their members three Popes, numerous cardinals and bishops; significantly the hierarchy of the kingdom was to a large extent chosen from among them.

Alphonsus, whether by choice or assignment we do not know, became a member of the Apostolic Missions; the fact that two of his relations, Canon Peter Mark Gizzio and Canon Julius Nicholas Torni, were actually influential members at the time may have had a bearing on the decision. He owed everything in the way of his priestly formation to the Apostolic Missions — his spirituality, theological initiation and practical introduction into the theory and practice of preaching, especially popular mission preaching. If it is true that he was a Neapolitan through and through then it is equally true that he was a genuine product of the Apostolic Missions. When he applied for membership after his acceptance by Cardinal Pignatelli in 1723 the association totalled one hundred and ten members. Their year, reckoned from July to June rather than January to December, began with the election of superiors and officials whose term of office was for one year only. Every Monday the members met for academies in theology, spirituality and missionary theory and practice; attendance was carefully monitored. Meditation, assiduous study, examination of conscience together with regular practice of corporal penance as practised in the spirituality of the time, were inculcated as the essential basis for priestly holiness. Twice a year a jury of twenty-four members specially chosen for the task undertook the *Refirmatio* or *Scrutinium* in which the lives and conduct of each member, including the superiors, were subjected to close examination, resulting in confirmation or suspension of membership as the case warranted. Eucharistic piety in the form of the Forty Hours devotion and visits to the Blessed Sacrament was a feature of their spirituality. Founded with Our Lady, Queen of Apostles, as their special protectress, devotion to our Lady was also characteristic. Their great spiritual mentor was St Francis de Sales whose works were read and studied and whose spirituality was their inspiration. Each year in October — *post aquas* — the members made the spiritual exercises for eight days together in the cathedral complex; the conferences, it was laid down mercifully, were not to exceed one hour and a quarter. The annual General City Mission, held in the cathedral or in the vast basilica of the Holy Spirit and always conducted by the members, immediately followed. At the end of the city mission, in which all the members were expected to take part, smaller missionary groups were detailed to preach missions to the people the length and breadth of the Kingdom until the following May.

The Apostolic Missions played a major role in the evolution of popular missionary preaching, technique and organisation; they devised and institutionalised a missionary method which Alphonsus was to perfect and which with local adaptations was to spread throughout Europe and North America in the following century. Alphonsus' introduction to missionary method was here in the school of the Apostolic Missions. A Neapolitan mission, for all its apparent simplicity, was no haphazard operation; it was both highly organised and sociologically sophisticated. Anything up to twenty members were required, posing a logistic problem from the very outset. The duties of each member of the team, from the superior and his assistant to the member known as the porter or door attendant, were clearly detailed. Services began at first light in the morning, comprising a meditation for the people, preparation and thanksgiving for communion, and a special sermon of a devotional nature which was not to conflict with the main sermon of the evening. The rest of the day was filled with a variety of exercises each with its own method and purpose, such as catechetical instructions, singing and explanation of the rosary, special services for boys and girls, the spiritual exercises for the clergy and in some cases for nuns; separate meetings for different groups such as soldiers, prisoners, and the inevitable 'devout women' disrespectfully referred to as the *bizzocche*, with appropriate instructions; devotional processions with statues, lighted candles, flowers and singing through the town or countryside, brief sermons in the streets and village squares known as the *sentimenti*, — those little discourses so characteristic of the traditional Neapolitan mission. And on certain occasions there were the acts of public penance. It all led up to the climax of the day, the *Predica Grande* or Great Sermon, an oratorical tour-de-force which could last as long as two hours, where every emotion was played upon and which was only entrusted to the most experienced missioner. The confessors with their appointed Penitentiary at their head — the priest with special faculties for the absolution of reserved sins and who set the tone for confessional practice — spent long hours throughout the day and night in the ministry of the confessional. Prayer together, study conferences and chapters of faults where remissness on the part of any member or failure in their duties were brought to light for correction, filled in whatever free time was left for the missioners. It was all highly complex and well-thought out to make maximum impact on the lives of the people.

Missionary apprenticeship, especially in the Apostolic Missions, was long and frustrating; strict seniority and obedience to the superior of the mission were to be observed. Alphonsus, despite his age and experience as a lawyer at the highest level in Naples, spent his early years as an active missioner with nothing more responsible to do than recite the rosary, lead the processions through the streets and catechise the children, especially during the Great Sermon, lest they disturb the preacher. His first major appointment was for the morning meditation; it was four years before he graduated to the *Predica Grande* and then it was only outside Naples and not in the city itself. He learnt his trade from the bottom rung upwards, working his way through all the stages until with his wonderful voice and sincerity of purpose he became for twenty years the most renowned missionary of the Kingdom. Later when he came to codify his own mission methods, the choice and plan of sermons to be preached, and above all the approach to confessional practice, he spoke from experience and a deep knowledge of the people; he was no mere theorist.[2]

– II –

The conscientiousness with which Alphonsus devoted himself to his clerical formation can be gauged from the rules of conduct which one of his earliest biographers who had access to documents now destroyed, claimed he drew up for himself.[3] He had drawn up norms for himself as a practising lawyer; it was totally in character that he would have done the same thing for himself in his preparation for the priesthood. 'The seminarian', he wrote, 'who wishes to sanctify himself as a priest should

1. associate with priests of exemplary life and endeavour to imitate their conduct.
2. He should visit the Blessed Sacrament especially in those churches where there is Exposition.
3. He should make every day at least an hour of mental prayer so that he will learn to live with fervour and recollection.
4. He should read the lives of those saints who were priests and which show him an example of priestly holiness and stimulate him to follow their example.
5. He should be particularly devoted to the Blessed Virgin, Queen and Mother of the Church.
6. He should guard his good name since the reputation of the whole clerical state is at stake.
7. He should be deferential to all yet reserved and especially guarded in his conduct with women.
8. He should be submissive to all the decisions of his superiors since such is the Will of God.
9. He should always wear the clerical soutane and tonsure; he should be modest in his comportment, shunning vanity and affectation.
10. At home he should be congenial; dedicated to his studies, exemplary in church especially during the sacred functions.
11. He should confess at least once a week and communicate more frequently.
12. He should flee every fault and endeavour to practise every virtue.'

During these years of preparation for the priesthood Alphonsus associated with a group of students who appear again and again in his life; some later associated themselves with him in his new missionary initiatives, others became prominent members of the ecclesiastical establishment throughout the Kingdom and rallied to his support in difficult times. His greatest friend was undoubtedly Giovanni Mazzini, some eight years younger than himself, who had first noticed him praying, while still a lawyer, in the various churches of Naples. Their friendship was to last a lifetime and beyond. Mazzini lived to give evidence when the process of beatification of Alphonsus was opened. With a number of others, Domenico Letizia, Vincenzo Mannarini, Luigi Lago and Michele de Alteriis, to mention but some, they formed themselves into a loose confraternity who prayed, discussed and studied together. Their usual routine was to visit the Blessed Sacrament, spend some time in prayer and after Benediction retire to where they could discuss some point of theology and spirituality; it was a good method of substituting for lack of the formal exercises of an enclosed seminary.

At first their meetings took place in the open; the Neapolitan evenings are conducive to just such gatherings. Some young men joined them from time to time and this became a regular feature until suspicions were aroused as to the real purpose of these gatherings. Some dismissed them as pious humbugs; others saw in them the beginnings of a dangerous sect along the lines of the Quietists or Molinists. Memories of the controversial gatherings organised by Miguel Molinos in Rome just a generation earlier were very much alive in the minds of the ecclesiastical authorities; the bishops of the peninsula had been circularised by the Roman authorities not to tolerate the existence of unauthorised confraternities of either sex. A local convent of nuns reported the gatherings to the episcopal vicariate; the more hysterical even suggested that the seminarians' meetings should be reported directly to the Holy Office. Instead Cardinal Pignatelli was satisfied with putting an end to those meetings which took place outside with lay participation. The clerical group continued to meet indoors in the different houses of the members and finally ended up with a more or less regular meeting place provided by Alphonsus. Recalling those days in his testimony at the process of beatification, Mazzini declared that

> we resembled a religious community. In the room we erected an altar and recited the Divine Office in choir, the litany of Our Lady and other prayers. We made mental prayer in common and afterwards took the discipline. We dined together placing a statue of the Divine Child at the head of the table to act as our superior. Before it was an empty plate on which we placed part of our food to be given later to the poor.[4]

Alphonsus' life at home was on similar lines. Assiduous in study, he devoted considerable time to prayer in his room; he was restrained in eating and began a regime of corporal penance which frightened the other members of his family. His mother feared for his health which was never regarded as robust and she even approached Father Pagano, his director, in an effort to get Alphonsus to lessen his austerities. This is the period of his life corresponding to what we call the youthful indiscretions of the saints. But we must not forget that his practice of penance followed the accepted pattern of spirituality at the time; compared to that of the Jesuit missionary, Father Paul Segneri, there was nothing out of the ordinary about his regime. Moreover, he was following the guidance of a very wise and moderate

THE APPRENTICE YEARS 1723-1729

director who must have known the graces which God was giving his spiritual son as well as the penitent's own special needs.

Alphonsus' theological studies prior to his ordination to the priesthood lasted for just three years and two months, from October 1723 to December 1726; for three months of this period he was seriously ill. The diocesan Synod of Naples in 1726 lists some eight or nine professors of the various branches of theology some of whom we can reasonably surmise helped to form the future moral theologian and doctor of the Church but we can be sure of only three, Don Alessio Mazzocchi and Don Julius Torni from the cathedral, and the Oratorian, Father Pagano, who influenced every aspect of Alphonsus' development. Mazzocchi enjoyed a European reputation as a scripture scholar while Torni — like Alphonsus, a former lawyer — was considered the great intellectual luminary of the diocese. Undoubtedly his was the main influence in Alphonsus' initial theological formation. Born in Naples of Florentine parents, Torni studied with the Dominicans in Naples where he was the star pupil of Father Gregorio Selleri, later Master of the Sacred Palace and Cardinal. From Selleri Torni developed a passion for St Thomas Aquinas and his teaching. 'I cannot conceal' he wrote, 'that it was my love for St Thomas whom I have venerated from my youth which has sustained me in the monotony of my theological labours. That love and veneration I hope to maintain until my death; the writings of St Thomas which were the mainstay of my young days will be, I trust, the intellectual nourishment of my soul until the end of my days.' Torni's main published work was his *Annotations on the Commentaries of Estius*, which he published in Naples in 1720. It was the fashion of theological writers in those days, so different from our own, to tag their theological publications on to the work of some established author until their own names became accepted, rather than launch out presumptuously themselves. Alphonsus was to follow this practice of theological modesty years later in his own first major publication in the field of moral theology.[5]

From his published work we can gather the theological opinions which Torni passed on to his pupils. He taught the doctrine of the Immaculate Conception of the Blessed Virgin and her corporal Assumption into Heaven; he encouraged the frequent reception of Holy Communion in contrast with the Jansenist teaching of Arnauld's *De La Fréquente Communion*. Only on the question of the efficacy of grace, which preoccupied theologians during the Jansenist controversies, did he hesitate to follow without question the teaching of his Dominican masters. By doing so he left the way open for Alphonsus to elaborate his own highly personal and eclectic approach to the question of the workings of God's grace. Two French theologians through their theological writings complete the picture. The saintly bishop, friend and biographer of St Vincent de Paul, Louis Abelly, provided the main source for Alphonsus' dogmatic studies; his *Medulla Theologica* had a wide circulation throughout European seminaries as the ideal manual of doctrinal initiation. Pastoral in its orientation, it avoided purely speculative questions; succinctly it gave the basics of dogmatic teaching and pastoral application — afterwards

Alphonsus recommended its use for his own students. As a result of his teaching on the doctrinal authority of the Pope, his theological positions with regard to Eucharistic and Marian devotions, Abelly became a *bête noire* of the Jansenists.

Less fortunate from one point of view was the choice of manual which Alphonsus was given for his initial studies in moral theology. François Genet's *Morale de Grenoble* was the bible of the rigorist school of moral theologians and provided the norms for rigorous pastoral practice. Genet, a brilliant theologian, born at Avignon in 1640, published his work on moral theology while still in his early thirties; soon afterwards, despite the outcry which his rigorist tendencies evoked, he was made bishop of Vaison. Thirty years later his moral theology was translated into Latin, making its way into Italy. In all probability the third Venetian edition of 1713, incorporating the decrees of the various Italian diocesan synods, including those of Naples, was the manual which provided Alphonsus with his first introduction to the study of moral theology, the delicate science of guiding consciences in their relations with God.[6]

Every indication points to the fact that Torni was Alphonsus' professor in moral theology as well — or, at least, one of them; strange that he who was so liberal in other aspects of his teaching should use such a rigorist author, even though it was by far the most widely studied manual in the seminaries at this time. However, Torni was possessed of an excellent practical judgment which would have allowed him to temper in practice the severity of the opinions which he may have upheld in theory, a point which Alphonsus soon noticed. He never made any secret of the quality of his introduction to moral theology: 'I admit quite frankly that when I commenced my course of moral theology I had a professor who followed the rigid opinion and I for my part, like so many others at that time also defended it wholeheartedly.' 'You know', he wrote in reply to an adversary who attacked him for his lenient views, 'that from the very beginning of moral theology I always had professors who taught the rigid opinions. The first volume of moral theology which was put into my hands was that of Genet, the leader of the rigorist school. And I also as a consequence was for some time myself a defender of the rigorist view.' The development of his views over the next twenty years before his first major publication in the field of moral theology is a story of assiduous study, wide pastoral experience as a missioner and confessor, a deep sympathetic understanding of the lives of the simple people to whom he ministered and long personal suffering in his own conscience as he tried to free himself from the agony of scruples which the various elements of his formation had induced.[7]

The name of Father Pagano must never be omitted from the list of Alphonsus' teachers. He was more than a confessor and counsellor; he supplemented the official teaching from his own wide learning and writings. Unfortunately to this day they remain unpublished in the archives of the Naples Oratory but they bear eloquent testimony to his wide study of St Thomas and his benign views in the area of moral practice. The private tuition which Alphonsus received from Pagano was an important corrective in his theological formation.

On 23 September 1724, almost a year after his acceptance by the Cardinal as a candidate for the priesthood, Alphonsus received the Tonsure; three months later on Saturday 23 December, Bishop Salvadore Miroballo, assistant to the Cardinal, conferred on him the four Minor Orders. Testimonials from his parish priest declared that he had taken part in all the parish functions during the previous year, including the ceremonies of Holy Week; he had been assiduous in catechising the children and had even gone out into the streets to gather them for instruction. From the cathedral Don Michele de Salone testified that he had participated in all the spiritual exercises for students without missing a single day. Father Cutica from the Vincentians vouched for his presence once a month in their house and to the fact that he had communicated on each occasion. Conspicuously absent from the Tonsure ceremony was Don Joseph; his disgust at his son's priestly vocation had not sufficiently subsided to permit him to attend in any spirit of acceptance. However, he had complied with canonical requirements some months previously when he legally arranged for a patrimony of forty ducats per year for his son. On his ordination to the priesthood Alphonsus would reciprocate by legally renouncing his right of primogeniture.

After minor Orders the tempo and the intensity of Alphonsus' preparation for the priesthood increased. The more structured regime he was now facing was due to the fact that he had begun his period of probation for formal membership of the Congregation of the Apostolic Missions in November 1724. With his relation, Canon Gizzio, as 'novice master', the period of probation was the equivalent of a religious novitiate, though not in any canonical sense. The members of the Congregation—their official title — did not take either public or private vows of religion; they continued to live at home and were bound to the society only by a promise of obedience and co-operation in the work of the missions. But the period of probation entailed regular attendance at spiritual conferences, classes in theology, academies of sermon practice, together with the visiting of the sick members of the society. Participation in an actual mission completed the programme. Alphonsus' first missionary experience was in November 1724 when he accompanied the mission group to the island of Procida where he was assigned to teaching catechism to the fisher folk.

Early in 1725, still during his period of probation, he added to his commitments by applying to become a member of the *Confraternita dei Bianchi* (church life and spirituality at the time being characterised by the multiplicity of such sodalities). The *Compagnia di Santa Maria succerre miseris* or simply the *Bianchi della Giustizia* was an association of priests and laymen whose function was to attend to the spiritual needs of the criminals of the Naples prisons, to support their widows and orphans and specifically to assist spiritually at the executions of condemned criminals and to bury them — not altogether unlike the *Misericordiella* of which Alphonsus was already a member. The *Bianchi* wore a white habit with a capuche and white cincture, hence their name. Dressed in their habits, the members of the confraternity accompanied the condemned criminals on their last journey to the gallows erected in the Piazza del Mercato, where the crowd gathered to witness the macabre spectacle of a public execution with all its gruesome routine culminating in the function of the *tirapiedi* who clung to the prisoner's feet and swung with him into space to ensure that the spinal cord was severed. It was in this piazza, still called by the same name, that public executions took place in Naples from the middle of the thirteenth century onwards; here Charles of Anjou decapitated Conrad of Suebia and it was here that public executions were carried out right up to the beginning of the nineteenth century. With a nice sense of social distinction typical of the *ancien régime*, two permanent gallows were erected, one for the execution of the nobility, and the other for the hanging of the ordinary plebian criminal; a third structure catered for the more common whipping of petty criminals. In February and March 1725, Alphonsus presented himself to the assembled members of the confraternity, making the three formal petitions to be received among them. 'The desire which I have to devote myself assiduously with the help of God's grace to all tasks which are for the glory of God and the salvation of souls, embolden me to petition your most illustrious lordships to admit me among the members of this holy brotherhood.' His application, supported by Fathers Pagano and Nicholas Sicola of the Oratory and another influential friend, the Jesuit, Father Dominic Manulio, was favourably received. In April 1725 he was admitted.

The registers of the confraternity show that Alphonsus assisted at several executions after his ordination to the priesthood; on occasions in 1727 and 1729 he was also summoned to assist at executions outside the city. The Tribunals of Justice would automatically inform the confraternity when an execution was to take place. The members then arranged to assemble in their own Oratory, which can still be seen in the via dei Bianchi, to begin a programme of prayers for the unfortunate condemned person. Certain members were then assigned to immediate participation in that particular execution. They visited the condemned man in his cell and accompanied him in procession through the streets to the Piazza del Mercato; they remained with him to the last moments of life and the final anointing.

The pastoral experience gathered in such stressful circumstances is reflected in the instructions Alphonsus later incorporated in his moral writings for those priests who would have to assist at the execution of criminals; they are to be found in the *Pratica del Confessore* and the larger work known as the *Homo Apostolicus*. Years later he published a special pamphlet on the method of assisting those condemned to death; now almost a forgotten work — no English translation apparently was ever printed — it repays reading not least for the gentle spirit and the sense of the mercy of God which pervades it. It comes clearly from the heart of a priest who has experienced what he writes about; no one could simulate such authenticity:

It is a work of great charity to assist the dying but it is much more meritorious to assist those condemned to death since they deserve greater compassion on account of the sad condition in which they find themselves. Those unfortunates now see death right in front of their eyes, which in a day or so will snatch them from this world. St. Paul exhorts us to console those 'who have all kinds of troubles' (2 Cor. 1.4) and who can ever be in greater affliction from every point of view and more worthy of our compassion than an unfortunate criminal under sentence of death for his mideeds? The unfortunate man is guarded constantly by the ministers of justice in the depths of his prison, abandoned by his relations and friends. He is afflicted by the fear of Hell which he has merited by his sins; by the thought that he is going to die by the hands of the executioner when he believed he had still many years of life left to him; by the thought that he is going to die in public as a criminal a death of opprobrium; by the sufferings of leaving his parents, relations, wife and children without support and guidance. On account of all these sufferings the priest should with all possible diligence endeavour to console him.

Above all he should be careful not to speak to the condemned man of the rigours of the Divine Justice or of similar things which inspire terror. He should place before his eyes the Divine Mercy and God's Will to save all men. From the very first moment he speaks with the condemned man let him call him cheerfully by his christian name and greet him with 'God wishes to save you; He is calling you to leave this life of misery to take you to the other world where he wishes to make you happy for all eternity. So now make a good confession; all you have to do is to be sorry for the offences you have committed against God and He is waiting with his arms open to embrace you and make you eternally happy in Paradise.'

The treatise then suggests appropriate reflections to be put to the condemned man to alleviate his various worries. There were clearly bitter memories in Alphonsus' mind when he goes on to comment that the

> greatest sorrow for priests who assist the condemned is when they say that they do not wish to pardon their enemies who were the cause of their condemnation . . . .
>
> It is more difficult still to convert a condemned man who, as a result of his crimes, has reached the stage of hating God. But we must do what we can for him. He says perhaps that God hates him and only created him to send him to Hell and for this reason sent him his present misfortune. The priest should reply, 'No, my son, God does not hate you but only your sin; repent of sin and God will no longer reject you. And realise that even though at the moment you hate God He still wishes you well and is waiting to embrace you and bring you to Paradise; you have condemned yourself to Hell by the crimes you have committed. In spite of all that, God is ready to pardon you if you

repent of having offended him. How can you say that God hates you when He died crucified out of the love He bore you. Love Him then in return, my son, do not hate Him any more because He has not deserved this from you.'

If he still continues obstinate exhort him to have recourse to the Blessed Virgin and make him say: 'Mary, Mother of God, see that I am near to damning my soul. You can help me, have mercy and compassion on me.'

All these considerations and reflections are good but when one comes across a condemned man who remains obdurate then there is more need to increase prayer than to increase words. The priest should recommend him in his own prayers to Jesus Christ and to the Blessed Virgin and get others to pray for him, especially religious communities. Let him also see to it that Masses are celebrated for the man's conversion since such a spiritual condition cannot be cured without much prayer.'

Alphonsus' membership of the *Bianchi* remained a cherished memory with them. In 1831 they placed themselves under his special patronage; on the centenary of his death in 1887 they published the documents from their archives authenticating the details of his pastoral ministry among them.[8]

In September 1725 after the obligatory retreat of ten days Alphonsus was ordained a subdeacon in the chapel of the Santa Restituta in the cathedral in the ordinations '*post Crucem*'; the following year in April he was ordained a deacon; it was the Saturday known in the liturgy as *Sabbato di Sitientes*. The hopes which his professors and superiors in the Apostolic Missions had for his future were conveyed to the Cardinal in the canonical reports demanded before ordination; impressed, he immediately granted him faculties to preach in the churches of the city. Alphonsus preached his first sermon in the small church of San Giovanni in Porta near the hospital of the *Incurabili* during the Forty Hours devotions. Providentially still in existence, this was the church frequented by the Cavalieri family, which allows one to surmise that his mother may well have been present; Don Joseph certainly was not. By some remarkable chance the original manuscript of this first sermon is still preserved, consisting of six folios with the last two pages blank. The pages were divided in two, with writing on the right half leaving the large margin on the left for alterations and corrections. At one point of the manuscript on the left side is added the word 'shorten' — excellent advice for preachers both young and old. The sermon was entitled 'Jesus, Our Shepherd and Lamb' which sounds more acceptable in Italian as *Pastore e Agnello*, the text being the words of St John the Baptist, 'Behold the Lamb of God'.

> On one occasion St. John, the precursor of Christ, while in the company of his followers was asked if he were the promised Messiah. Full of confusion and humility he immediately replied, 'I am not the Christ. I am not worthy to open the latch of his shoes.' Seeing in the distance

The entrance to the hospital of the Incurabili in Naples. While working here among the sick the full impact of the gospel sentence, 'What doth it profit a man if he gain the whole world and suffer the loss of his soul,' came home to Alphonsus.

The cortile of the old Palazzo dei Tribunali where Alphonsus lost the case concerning the feudal estates at Amatrice

The statue of Father Matthew Ripa on the roof of the Chinese College in Naples which he founded to train priests for the Chinese mission. After his ordination Alphonsus made the Chinese College the centre of his priestly ministry. He only left it to found his new missionary society in Scala.

The episcopal city of Scala, high in the folds of the Lattari mountains, where Alphonsus laid the foundations of his new missionary society of priests

Alphonsus as a young priest (authentic contemporary portrait)

The Casa Anastasio before its restoration in recent years. This was the first permanent 'monastery' of the Missionaries of the Most Holy Saviour at Scala.

Scala. Just in from the top right-hand corner can be seen the chapel built round the cave in the hillside where Alphonsus prayed for guidance in the early years of his new missionary society.

The crest of the new missionary society which Brother Vito Curzio scratched on the walls of the kitchen area of the Casa Anastasio

The monstrance of the 'Apparitions in the Host' which occurred in Scala in 1732. Alphonsus was not present at the time but he was sufficiently impressed to incorporate certain elements of the mysterious appearances in the host in the Emblem and Seal of his Congregation.

The confessional grille in the nuns' convent at Scala where Alphonsus directed Sister Maria Celeste Crostarosa and heard of her revelations about the two new religious institutes

Sketch of the title page of an early draft of the Rules and Idea of the Institute of the Congregation of the Most Holy Saviour *with the proposed Congregation logo. Probably from the pen of Alphonsus de Liguori himself*

his beloved Redeemer approaching, he exclaimed, 'Behold the Lamb of God who takes away the sins of the world.'

With this introduction Alphonsus directed his congregation's attention to the Blessed Sacrament where they would find Jesus as their Pastor and Victim.

> Now I want you to pay attention to me since I wish you to understand how in the Blessed Sacrament we have *il nostro Caro Gièsu* as Shepherd and Victim. He is there as Pastor to exercise on our behalf all the duties that a good shepherd performs for his flock. He is there as Victim to give us confidence and to obtain for us at the same time from God the pardon of our sins.

As he concluded the first section of his sermon, Alphonsus, in typical missionary style, apostrophised sinners in ringing tones—hardly relevant, one would surmise, to the devout congregation in front of him.

> O unfortunate and deceived people why do you flee from your dear Shepherd? Where are you going? From whom are you fleeing? You are heading straight into the jaws of wolves; you are going to make yourselves slaves of the devil who wishes for nothing more than to take you with him into misery for all eternity. Turn instead to your loving Shepherd; do you not hear how he calls to you from that altar to turn back to him since he wishes to pardon you?

There is nothing remarkable about the sermon. A typical first effort from a deacon, it conformed in theme and concept to the accepted pattern of devotional preaching at the time; it may certainly appear to some temperaments unacceptably *dolciastro* or mawkish. In the original, however, it had one characteristic which was in no way accidental and which is lost in translation. Alphonsus used the dialectical forms of the ordinary Neapolitan; he avoided the artificial tone and literary conceits of the fashionable society preachers. In this he was true to the teaching of his instructors in the Apostolic Missions who were in the forefront of a revolt against the florid rhetoric and artificial pronunciation of the court orators. They even laid down the acceptable pronunciation of the name of Jesus in their dialect; it was to be *Gièsu* not *Gesù*. Alphonsus' first sermon signalled his acceptance of this direction in popular preaching. The teeming unlettered population of Naples and the countryside were to hear the Word of God preached in a simple and direct manner which placed no obstacle to their understanding. It is no exaggeration to say that he even developed some sort of fixation in the matter, leading him to at least two incidents of rather intemperate anger, one when he preached a retreat to the Apostolic Missions and another as he listened to a sermon from a member of his own missionary group.[9]

The years of preparation for the priesthood had taken their toll. The combination of study, apostolic activity, the rigorous regime of corporal austerities together with growing anxieties of conscience which we shall have to examine at length at a later stage, proved too great for Alphonsus' physical and psychological resources with the result that towards the end of August 1726 he broke down in health, the first of at least three similar incidents in his life. The nature of the illness is not described for us but all indications are that it was psycho-somatic in origin, some form of nervous breakdown. So alarmed did the family become that the Last Rites were administered. Alphonsus placed the restoration of his health in the hands of the Mother of God and at his request the statue of Our Lady of Mercy at whose feet he had left his sword three years earlier was taken from the church and brought to his room. According to his brother Cajetan an amelioration of his serious condition followed and a few days later he was declared out of danger. Slowly he built himself up again physically and mentally for his ordination to the priesthood which was due in December; the parish priest of Sant'Angelo à Segno reported that he was absent from the parish and his duty of catechising the children for three and a half months 'per la sua grave indisposizione'.

A further retreat of ten days in the Vincentian House was the final preparation for the priesthood which he received on Saturday 21 December 1726 in the cathedral of Naples. He was in his thirty-first year. In all probability his first Mass was sung in the little church of Sant'Angelo, assisted by the rector, Don Aniello and his brother Cajetan, a tonsured cleric. There is no extant account of the feelings of Donna Anna and of Don Joseph who was still not reconciled to the clerical vocation of his son and who may well have been severely distracted during the ceremonies of Ordination and First Mass with the thought of a possible episcopal see to salvage something from the ruins of his hopes for family greatness which he had built on the career of his eldest son.

– III –

There was no shortage of clergy in the archdiocese of Naples when Alphonsus was added to the number; one of the great problems of the Kingdom, for Church and Government, was the excessive number of both priests and religious. For the diocese of Naples alone with a population of about 400,000 in the city and countryside, there were at least 1,500 priests not counting religious priests in one hundred monasteries. The Cathedral Chapter alone consisted of seventy canons whose pastoral activities inside the cathedral were slight and whose pastoral solicitude outside was non-existent. A group of seventy-two priests 'ministered', if that is the right word, in the small church of San Michele in the via Toledo. The number of churches was correspondingly excessive; besides the thirty-five parishes with their respective churches into which the diocese was divided there were at least one hundred rectorial churches depending on civil administrators and at least twice that number of small churches or oratories serving the 200 pious confraternities or brotherhoods. Tannoia at the end of the century announced triumhantly in his work on *Bees* that there were 514 churches in Naples requiring beeswax for their candles! In the centre of

Naples to this day, despite the ravages of 200 years, churches and oratories of confraternities in various stages of decay follow each other in bewildering profusion.

The excessive number of clergy was not a peculiarly Italian and still less a Neapolitan problem; it affected many European countries in varying degrees of acuteness. The disedifying consequences of a too numerous uneducated and pastorally uncommitted clerical proletariat had occupied the attention of the Council of Trent; its wise decrees, if they had been courageously implemented, would have gone a long way towards remedying the situation. Besides laying down norms for the education of the clergy it instructed bishops to ordain only those necessary or useful for the pastoral demands of their people. Successive popes from the time of Paul V (1605–21) had attempted to remedy the situation in Naples but with little success. In an official report to the King as late as 1779 Ferdinand de Leon gave the total number of priests and religious in the Kingdom as 75,000, an incredible figure taking into account that the Holy See and the King had agreed in the Concordat of 1742 to take steps to reduce the number.[10]

The 'enormous' number of clergy — to use the word of a royal decree — was not due to any sudden flowering of genuine vocations; it was the consequence of economic and sociological factors rooted in the position of the Church in the *ancien régime* which only the French Revolution and the Code Napoleon would succeed in altering. Central to the problem were, first of all, the Church's immunity from taxation, and secondly, the family system of inheritance known as *maiorascato* (abolished by the Code Napoleon) whereby the eldest son took all the available property, leaving the other sons — of whom there were usually a number — deprived of inheritance and under strong pressure to accept clerical tonsure as a means of escaping taxes on whatever property or income they would be able to acquire. Not merely was actual church property immune from taxation but whatever property was constituted as patrimony for clerics, together with their own private possessions, was immune as well. As a consequence, the Kingdom swarmed with fictitious grants of property to the Church, with fictitiously constituted patrimonies and tonsured clerics who had no intention of proceeding to priestly ordination; their sole purpose in wearing a clerical soutane was to escape the royal tax agent. Nor was this all. Taxes levied at town gates on wine, corn and fruit were not paid by clerics, they could also buy other state-taxed commodities free of impost. And what was true of the individual cleric was also true of ecclesiastical corporations such as religious orders, confraternities and churches. The 'dead-hand' of the Church on the state finances was the source of a multiplicity of abuses.

This whole social structure opened up a vast field for corruption. The main accusation against the clergy was that they did not scruple to descend to fraud and deceit in the matter of their immunities. By simulated titles and by claiming that property was theirs which was not in fact so, they secured a tax-free existence for their families and even for others who were willing to pay them in return for fraudulent claims. Several families in some cases lived on the flow of commodities which came to them tax-free through one of the so-called clergy. The saddest consequence of this vast web of deceit and intrigue was that the good name and credibility of the Church and the clerical state suffered enormously with inevitable loss to the spiritual welfare of the faithful. No less baneful was the effect on the self-styled clergy themselves. There came into existence a whole army of unworthy clerics whose motives for wearing the soutane were scandalous at best, their conduct far from priestly. Disregarding the often superior and malicious comments of English, French and German correspondents who painted such an appalling picture of clerical degradation in Naples, we can more readily accept the report of the Papal Nuncio to Rome in 1736 — Alphonsus was ten years a priest at the time — when he wrote: 'Now more than ever the Kingdom is full of useless and wandering clerics and priests, ordained without benefice or patrimony and without any means of livelihood. They practise the lowest and most abject trades and I do not mention the scandal they give the faithful nor the harm they cause the State by their undisciplined way of living.' In the strongest terms the Nuncio called for the elimination of such clergy who were for the most part ignorant and lawless. Cardinal Aquaviva, a member of Pope Benedict XIV's commission to conclude the Concordat with the Neapolitan court, forcefully described the amount of fraud, perjury and injustice which the Church's immunity from taxation gave rise to and the amount of odium it brought on the rest of the Church with deplorable consequences for its spiritual mission.[11]

If conditions in the city of Naples were bad the general degradation of the clergy in the rest of the Kingdom was even more appalling. While there were in every diocese priests whose education, pastoral zeal and priestly virtues were of the highest standard — many of them like Fathers Paul Cafaro and Francis Xavier Rossi joined Alphonsus as priests — the numbers who became clerics for purely economic motives and were ordained without sufficient education was inordinately high. Many were not merely ignorant but almost unlettered as Alphonsus was to experience as a missioner throughout the various dioceses and later as a bishop in his own. Benedict XIV with his own mordant humour suggested that some ecclesiastics did not know whether the Trinity was a mystery of their faith or the name of a mountain. In many towns their numbers ran to hundreds; they formed a sort of clerical proletariat, not to say rabble, undisciplined, unamenable to law, a problem for the Church and Government. The figures given for these clerics throughout the Kingdom are at times staggering; Altamura with a population of some 15,000 inhabitants had nearly eight hundred clerics or one for every twenty of the population. Capua with 8,000 inhabitants had seventy priests of whom fifty were canons. And it was not just the centres of population which had this problem; the situation was just as bad in the various *cittadine* and villages throughout the countryside or perched on the side of a mountain. And the clerical army comprised all ranks from bishops down to those in minor orders and tonsure. To these could be added the so-called *diaconi selvatici*, laymen who worked in every church and cathedral and who claimed participation in clerical privileges and immunities.

And yet, generalisations can be both misleading and unfair. The picture of clerical life in the Kingdom of Naples has to be sensitively drawn; it is too easy to concentrate on the scandalous clerical behaviour retailed for us by those visitors who were attracted in droves from northern Europe to Bourbon Naples in the eighteenth century. No outrageous detail escaped them any more than it escapes their counterparts today. It was true that Don Paolo Moccia, a priest, was one of the curiosities of Naples; he was in charge of the Royal Pages, was an excellent Latin and Greek scholar and an aquatic performer who stark naked put on a swimming display for Casanova when he too visited the Bourbon capital. It was true that at one end of the scale there were Neapolitan clerics no better than their fellow *lazzaroni* and no less frequently in jail while at the opposite end there were others like the Abate Ferdinando Galiani, ambassador to France, thoroughly cynical, agnostic, foppish, macchiavellian and the darling of the *salon* culture both in Paris and in his native city. But it is equally true that the Kingdom of Naples in the eighteenth century produced more than its quota of canonised saints and learned theologians, together with its full complement of admirably pastoral priests and bishops. When Alphonsus was canonised in 1839 two of his Neapolitan contemporaries, Father Francis Jerome, a Jesuit, and Father Giuseppe della Croce, the Alcantarine Franciscan from Ischia, were honoured with him. Nor were these isolated exceptions; if Alphonsus emerges as the dominant religious figure of the Italian *settecento* there were a host of others whose lives more than illuminated the shady side of the picture.[12]

But it cannot be denied that the unreasonable accumulation of privileges and consequent abuses among the clergy gave rise to anticlericalism in its true and original meaning — that is, to a race of men whose sole spiritual nourishment was anticlericalism, who made anticlericalism the sole item on their programme and who took the view that it alone would suffice to remodel governments, to perfect society and lead the way to happiness. If Voltaire was the high-priest of anticlericalism, then many of the king's ministers in Bourbon Naples, headed by Bernard Tanucci, were his ardent imitators both in theory and practice. In the circumstances it is difficult to blame them. And equally it is a measure of Alphonsus' achievement that in such an atmosphere he was able to establish another missionary society and earn the respect, even the admiration, of men to whom everything he stood for was repugnant.[13]

The lives of the saints and their writings must always be assessed against the background of their time and milieu; this is particularly true of the long life and prolific literary output of Alphonsus de Liguori. Only against the background of the conditions prevailing in Bourbon Naples in the *settecento* does much of what he did and wrote make sense. In every mission he insisted there should be spiritual exercises for the clerics of the area, canons, priests, deacons, subdeacons and clerics in minor orders. If possible they were to be organised into a clerical confraternity for which he on occasions drew up the rules as indeed did others of his missionary companions. When he warned in his retreat to candidates for ordination against entering the clerical state from unworthy motives we can well understand what he had in mind. When he discussed the question of fictitious patrimonies we know the extent of the problem. When he urged those already ordained to lead truly priestly lives even though they had embraced the clerical state without a genuine vocation, when he urged on them zeal for souls and the necessity of making their priesthood of some spiritual value to others, he was addressing a motley crew of clerics who may never have preached a sermon, never administered a sacrament, never acquired any theological learning beyond the bare minimum which too indulgent bishops or the Chaplain General required for their ordination. When he wrote — to the amazement of those who read it today — that priests in the congregation which he had founded would save more souls in one year than in ten outside it, he merely stated the obvious, since, living in their homes they seldom undertook the slightest pastoral initiative.

Not surprisingly Alphonsus was clearly reluctant to encourage young men to become priests of the type we have described. His instructions to confessors in this matter is inexplicable without an appreciation of the prevailing conditions. 'Young men who express a wish to become priests while still intending to live at home should not readily be encouraged to do so without a serious investigation over a long period of time of the uprightness of their motives, their education and intellectual capabilities. For someone to be a good priest at home (they are rarely found, in fact, *very rarely*) he would need to lead an exemplary life, avoid gambling, laziness, bad companions, be assiduous in prayer and the frequentation of the sacraments — *sed quis est hic et laudabimus eum?*. Otherwise they place themselves in almost certain danger of damnation especially if they become priests at the instigation of their parents for the purpose of increasing the family wealth.' [14]

– IV –

As a member of the Neapolitan clergy Alphonsus belonged to a group who were in the main better educated and behaved than those in the rest of the Kingdom. Since the year 1700 successive diocesan synods had passed legislation to check abuses and neither Cardinal Pignatelli nor his predecessor, Cardinal Cantelmo, could be faulted in their energetic promotion of the reform programme.[15] Yet the basic problems persisted. The number of clergy was excessive, their pastoral solicitude and general level of theological education left a lot to be desired. Exceedingly well-off for the most part, they lived with their families. A great number were employed as tutors, a lucrative enough profession; others became commercial stewards for the financial enterprises of the nobility — a type of business executive. After ordination few of them continued their theological studies to qualify themselves for the ministry of the confessional. The highest ambition for many was to secure a chaplaincy in one of the city confraternities where the sum total of their priestly duties was the celebration of Mass — very often as rapidly as possible — and presiding over the meeting of the brethren from time to time; their place of honour in the choir stalls of the confraternity oratories can still be seen. With such minimal demands for their ministerial activities they were able to engage in other non-clerical occupations. Within this framework they could, of course, still lead lives of personal holiness and there were some who did, but *otiositas* — a word used by Alphonsus — especially of the type generated by the Neapolitan sun, is not altogether conducive to the spiritual combat.

Alphonsus' own brother Cajetan was a typical example in many respects of the better class of Naples priest, somewhere between the clerical *lazzaroni* and the *sacerdoti di salotto*. Probably without any choice in the matter, he was destined by his father for the clerical state long before Alphonsus upset the paternal dispositions by his own decision. He received the tonsure at the age of fourteen in 1715; for twelve years afterwards he made no further progress until, after Alphonsus' ordination, he resumed his clerical career and was finally ordained in 1730. Provided with a rich income from benefices and the Cathedral Chaplaincy he lived at home as a priestly aristocrat with his own carriage and liveried servants, untroubled by any great pastoral solicitude for the souls around him.[16]

Alphonsus conformed initially to the pattern of priestly life in the diocese after his ordination to the extent that he lived at home with his parents for three years until 1729; Don Joseph insisted that he should have his own personal servant — his *lacché* to use the Neapolitan word — to accompany him wherever he went. Within a few weeks of ordination he renounced his right of primogeniture in favour of his youngest brother Hercules, in full legal form before a Notary. In the event of Don Joseph's death Hercules undertook to provide Alphonsus and his servant with board and lodging and an annual income of sixty ducats together with the income already settled on him by his father. Other dispositions catered for the possibility, soon to be realised, of Alphonsus' leaving the parental home. But the most significant insight into the whole family transaction is provided by the possible alterations to the financial arrangements in the event of Alphonsus' being promoted to such ecclesiastical benefices as a canonry in the diocese, a chaplaincy in the Treasury of the Cathedral or even *altra dignità maggiore*, in other words, a bishopric. Clearly Don Joseph was not going to relinquish his dreams too easily, while Hercules, not the most generous of men and not beyond a little manipulation, must have calculated that revenue from these likely sources would relieve him of the burden of supporting his brother.[17]

If we are to accept his own personal recollections years afterwards, Alphonsus' first inclination after ordination was to lead a virtual monastic and contemplative life at home in silence and withdrawal from outside contacts. But he soon altered direction in favour of the active apostolate. The first three years of his priesthood spent at home until he left for a chaplaincy in the Chinese College were characterised by assiduous study and intense pastoral activity. Within a year he had successfully negotiated his final theological examination and was granted the full canonical faculties of the diocese for hearing confessions, where he was at first to experience great difficulties due, among other reasons, to the rigidity of his theological training. Preaching, on the other hand, seemed to come naturally to him; he was at home in the pulpit from the very outset of his ministry. His sermon notes reveal his preparation for the homilies delivered in various churches of the city; he preached mostly at the Forty Hours Devotions where the themes were remarkably similar. Key words jotted down as aide-mémoires in his private notebook such as 'confidence, sacrament of love, desire, fire of love' allow us to recapture the spirit of what he had to say. The most remarkable aspect of the *fervorinos* was not the content but his fidelity to the simple style of preaching which had marked his first appearance in the pulpit. He was ultimately to do for preaching in the Kingdom of Naples, both by his writings and his example, what Vincent de Paul had done in France. The revival of the art of preaching *al'apostolica* — to use his own phrase — which the fashionable preachers of the time had destroyed, was to be one of his greatest achievements.

Nicholas Cafasso, a well-known cleric and one of Alphonsus' former professors in the faculty of law at the university, was seen frequently among the congregation when Alphonsus preached. He was much feared in high society in Naples as a lampoonist and satirist; his irreverent remarks spared neither clergy nor religion and least of all the affectation of the society preachers. On meeting Cafasso one day after a sermon Alphonsus jokingly asked him 'Are you preparing some *barzelletta* against me?' The reply was totally unexpected. 'No! I listen to what you have to say with great pleasure since you do not affect those purple patches and rounded periods but simply preach Jesus Christ crucified.'

Missionary activity with the members of the Apostolic Missions now began to take up more and more of his time. His first assignment as a priest was with a group of eleven others in the mission at Posillipo early in 1727; from then on his name appears regularly among the lists of missioners appointed for missions both in the city and further afield. After Posillipo he was down in Terlizzi in Apulia near Bari; in April with sixteen companions he was in the episcopal city of Campagna on the southern slopes of the Picentini mountains south of Salerno. Following the summer recess he began again in the cathedral in Naples in the annual October mission; after that he was fully occupied for the next three months in a series of missions throughout the enchanting villages and *frazioni* that dotted the slopes of Vesuvius. Despite his age and experience he was the junior member on all these expeditions serving his apprenticeship under such experienced leaders as Canon Torni, Filippo Aveta and Francisco Caraffa — all future bishops.

His participation was restricted to the recitation of the rosary, the catechesis of the children and other special groups and on occasions to some *sentimenti* in the open air. His first major assignment was the morning meditation in the Naples cathedral in October 1727; in Resina, built above the buried town of Herculaneum, he heard his first confessions as a missioner in January 1728. Not until April 1730 was he assigned to the main evening sermon, the *Predica Grande*, in the parish of Capodimonte looking down upon the city; it marked the end of his apprenticeship.

Towards the end of 1731 he was appointed superior of a mission band for the first time — significantly outside Naples. He led a group down to the heel of Italy to preach in Nardo and Polignano à Mare, south of Bari. There too he was elected for the first time Penitentiary, or head of the confessors, which was an acknowledgment of his competence in the field of moral theology and confessional practice; within a space of three years he had established his reputation as a moralist among his brethren. On the return journey to Naples he passed through Foggia where the local bishop requested him to preach a special novena in honour of Our Lady following a severe earthquake which had inflicted much damage to the city. This he gladly did only to be publicly reprimanded on his return for undertaking an assignment without permission from Naples. Despite this setback his reputation in the Society was now such that one of the richest benefices at the Society's disposal and usually reserved for their foremost preacher was assigned to him. With his patrimony income and now the revenue of this benefice he was financially without worries.

The final proof of his standing among the members of the Apostolic Missions came in October 1732 when he was appointed to preach the spiritual exercises to his brethren in the cathedral from the sixteenth to the twenty-third; his appointment brought out a record attendance, including the Cardinal. By this time, as we shall see, Alphonsus was deeply involved in assembling his own group of missioners, a project which temporarily at least was to put him at odds with the society. Nevertheless his membership of the Apostolic Missions survived misunderstanding and threatened expulsion; he remained a member all his life, taking part in their activities whenever possible and later summoning them to his diocese to conduct a series of missions. From 1779 onwards he figured each year in the Society's *kalendarium* as the doyen of the members; when he died they honoured him by a special service of remembrance at which all the members assisted and one Don Onofrio Scoppa delivered the panegyric.

– V –

Despite his commitment to the Apostolic Missions and preaching engagements in the city, Alphonsus' pastoral zeal was still not satisfied; he found a further outlet among the poor and unlettered population of Naples during the months when missionary activity ceased. He wanted to convert the whole world at one blow, commented Father Gregorio Maria Rocco, a Dominican who was on intimate terms with him and was a well-known popular missionary himself. Alphonsus' enthusiasm had ample scope among the *lazzari* or *lazzaroni* of Naples, a unique brand of urban proletariat and even then a legend throughout Europe. Children of the sun, vivacious, full of natural gentleness and goodness, they fell into the depths of depravity from the appalling social conditions in which they lived. Without education, without employment or sources of income beyond the use of their extremely sharp wits, they gained a reputation throughout Europe for every manner of deceit and roguery. Yet in the words of a contemporary they could so easily be led to the heights of goodness.

Alphonsus, though himself a member of the Neapolitan nobility who lived their lives for the most part oblivious of the misery of their fellow Neapolitans, had already as a layman experience of these unfortunates in the hospital of the *Incurabili*; from the earliest days of his clerical career he had worked for these same poor when he catechised their children in the parish of Sant Angelo à Segno. Now as a priest he consciously orientated his ministry in their direction. In this he was not alone. The names of at least ten others who like himself saw through the squalor and ignorance of the *lazzaroni* to their inherent goodness, have come down to us. Among them were some of those same seminarians and young priests who with Alphonsus had formed themselves into their own fraternity for the practice of priestly piety and study. Their work among the *lazzaroni* was the outcome of their prayers and reflections together.

The crying need was for organised religious instruction in a manner adapted to their special needs and situation since the *lazzaroni* were naturally suspicious of the clergy, at times even hostile. No one person can claim credit for the pastoral initiatives which seemed to spring up almost spontaneously throughout the city wherever the *lazzaroni* gathered, and certainly not Alphonsus though he did make a major contribution to the development of the movement. Groups of the poor and uneducated men and boys of the various districts such as the Conceria, the Mercato and the Pigna Secca were brought together for instruction in the very rudiments of religious knowledge and practice. As the movement grew, the form of the gatherings took definite shape — religious instruction of the most elementary type, a talk in their own dialect and accent, the recitation of the rosary, the singing of hymns. The meetings began at the sound of the Ave Maria, the ringing of church bells, which in those days signalled the end of the working day; the venues were the open spaces in front of churches or in the angles of the various piazze. A motley crowd of Neapolitan poor would gather — soapmakers, ragpickers, rag sellers, barbers, chestnut sellers, labourers of all types. From the open air the gatherings at times went indoors to whatever accommodation they could find. In those days before the existence of parish centres, they most frequently ended up in cellars at the back of wine shops or at the rear of a barber's premises. And all the time the formula was the same: catechism, sermon, rosary and above all, singing without which no genuine Neapolitan of whatever class would consider he had been in touch with God.

The movement spread; so numerous were the centres where the *lazzaroni* gathered that soon there were no more seminarists or priests with sufficient apostolic interest to act as chaplains; the only alternative was lay catechists. More perhaps from necessity than from theory or overall planning Alphonsus and his companions saw the need for training their lay followers sufficiently well to enable them to act in their turn as instructors or catechists. Alphonsus' right-hand man in this experiment was one Pietro Barbarese, a school teacher, probably only a little better informed than his pupils. As a young man of twenty-six he had been captivated by Alphonsus as a priest and took him as his spiritual mentor. Together they trained a group of catechists who took charge of the meetings when clerics were not available.

Historians have given this lay movement which has not yet been fully researched the name of *Capelle Serotine* — literally, the *Evening Chapels*. Around it has grown up a whole Neapolitan folklore of piety, humour and heroism which has fascinated church historians and sociologists ever since. Benedetto Croce himself fell under the spell of the stories connected with it, even venturing an unlikely explanation of why the members were sometimes referred to as the *Costatelle* while others claim they were known as the *Braciole*. Basically a religious movement to organise the *lazzaroni* into oratories or confraternities similar to those which existed for the upper social classes, it comprised various elements such as religious catechesis, prayer, education, leisure activities whether indoor or outdoor according to the season, charitable activities such as visiting the sick in the various hospitals for the poor. Each centre was a pious confraternity, a trade union movement, a recreation centre and some form of catholic action all gathered into one. In its early years the movement recalled in many aspects the simplicity and ingenuousness of the first Franciscans and their *fioretti*.[18]

Many of the lay catechists boasted of pasts spent far from the shadow of a church. Luco Nardone before his 'conversion' — all the stories insisted on a conversion experience — had been a soldier of fortune, Ignazio de Chiaia a potter, Bartolomeo a hawker of books, Antonio Peninno a buyer and seller of eggs, Leonardo Cristagno — known simply as Nardiello — sold his roasted *castagne* round the streets from the back of a mule. All learned to preach, give religious instruction and, in the words of a contemporary biographer, 'snatch souls from hell and bring them to Christ'. Nardiello became such a well-known character that on his death in 1776 a local doctor published his biography. Endless stories, all with an unmistakably Neapolitan flavour are told about the *Cappelle* and their members, especially about those who became religious and lived lives of remarkable prayer and penance. Brother Giuseppe, an Alcantarine, lived to vouch for Alphonsus' part in his conversion. Another Franciscan, Fra Angelo, who died with a reputation for authentic holiness of life, loved to recount the story of his vocation. As a young man whose sole source of income was carding wool, he went to a barber shop in the Pigna Secca one Sunday; this was an area on which Alphonsus concentrated a lot of his attention. He was surprised at the number of young men of his own age, not all of them well groomed, who passed through the room into the rear of the shop. Out of curiosity he followed them to find a room full of others like himself, in front of a statue of the Madonna. They were waiting for Alphonsus who on this occasion did not turn up. His place was taken by the barber himself who gave some religious instruction and then presided at the recitation of prayers. Impressed, Fra Angelo continued to frequent the circle, met Alphonsus, ultimately abandoned his wool carding and joined the Franciscans in Santa Lucia al Monte.

As was only to be expected, the gatherings of so many men on a regular basis gave rise to suspicion; the city police were put on their guard. One of the secret police in disguise infiltrated a meeting at which Alphonsus spoke to the members about preparation for the feast of Our Lady's Nativity on 8 September. The agent's familiarity with liturgical and devotional matters must have been minimal even by Neapolitan standards, for his report assessed the talk as highly suspicious; it was, he felt, all in some cryptic code which aroused his fears that some plot against the state was in the offing. As a result the police swooped the next day and arrested a number of the participants, among them Barbarese and Nardiello. Alphonsus contacted Cardinal Pignatelli to give a true explanation of the situation; relieved, the Cardinal was able to reassure the civil authorities and secure the release of the innocent men. Accepting in principle the apostolic value of the efforts of Alphonsus and his companions, the Cardinal gave his full support to the movement but urged great prudence lest undesirable elements might make use of the meetings for their own sinister purposes. Having survived many initial difficulties the *Cappelle Serotine* became a feature of Catholic life throughout the city; within a few years there were up to seventy-five centres catering for the religious formation and general development of the most deprived elements of Neapolitan society. The *Cappelle* survived in one form or another right down to the end of the last century; time and time again proposals were made to modernise it and adapt it to changing social conditions.

The ministry among the *lazzaroni* prompted the first of Alphonsus' devotional writings, a modest pocket-sized manual of twenty-four pages containing a set of seven simple meditations, each with three sections, on the eternal truths, one for each day of the week, to be read to the men at their meetings, and which would form the basis of simple prayerful reflections. Thousands of copies of this booklet, entitled the *Massime Eterne*, the Eternal Truths, were printed between 1728 and 1730; they were distributed free to the men and later to the people on the missions. Unfortunately, not one of these original copies has survived but the little work, reprinted literally tens of thousand of times since then, either alone or with other simple works of devotion, has become virtually synonymous with Alphonsus and his piety. And perhaps with a good deal of justification. Certainly it set the tone and motive for all his later writings. Whether of a theological or devotional nature they were always seen by him as an instrument of the apostolate, a means of saving and sanctifying souls, an apostolic medium through which the Word of God was preached as effectively as in the pulpit. In his writings no less than in the pulpit there was to be no room for self-advertisement.

Alphonsus' direct involvement with the *Cappelle* came to an end in 1732 when other commitments drew him from Naples to Scala above Amalfi on the Lattari peninsula. Just as with the Apostolic Missions, he was never to lose interest in the work where he really found himself for the first time and where he felt very much at home. The memories of his work among the *lazzaroni* and the incidents connected with the different characters were cherished by him to the end of his life; on his visits to Naples he sometimes found time to visit one of the centres. He was an old man of ninety, within a year of death, when he learnt that even the coachmen of Naples had profited by the work of the *Cappelle* and were showing signs of unwonted honesty. It was a miracle of grace almost impossible to believe since Neapolitan coachmen were apparently known in those days as the most disreputable among the dregs of society. When he was told they were taking to piety his own sense of humour came to life and he laughed as he commented, 'Holy Coachmen! And in Naples! Gloria Patri!'

CHAPTER FOUR

SCALA
1725–1731

– I –

In June 1729, Alphonsus at the instigation of his friend, Gennaro Sarnelli who like himself had abandoned the law-courts to study for the priesthood, left home to take up residence in the newly established Chinese College, known as the Holy Family. The decision was influenced at least to some extent by the approaching ordination of his brother Cajetan; two priests in the family home would only add to the problems which already surrounded the exercise of his priestly ministry. The foundation of the Chinese College was the achievement of a remarkable priest, Don Mateo Ripa. After a somewhat dissipated youth he was converted by a sermon of Father Anthony Torres of the missionary society of the Pii Operai; with Torres as his director he decided after a number of years to become a priest. At the request of Clement XI he devoted his life to the Chinese Mission where he went in 1707 by way of London and the Cape of Good Hope. In China, Ripa displayed all the genius for missionary endeavour one associates with the Jesuit missionaries a few generations before. He saw that the great need was for more and more priests; with this in mind he returned to Naples in 1724 with four Chinese aspirants and a lay professor of the Chinese language, determined to establish a college for the preparation of priests for the mission. It took him five years of negotiations in Rome, Vienna and Naples, more wearying and frustrating than his missionary labours, before he was able to open his college at Easter 1729. Montesquieu, in Naples at the time on the Grand Tour, informed 'le bon ecclesiastique, Don Mateo Ripa' that he would have been more profitably employed in establishing a lay oriental institute than an ecclesiastical seminary. Undeterred, Ripa persisted in his project and opened the College as a *convitto ecclesiastico* as well. Alphonsus joined as one of the first *convittore*.

His new surroundings suited him ideally. He had tried, on his own admission, to turn his room at home into a monastic cell, a place for prayer and penance. But the atmosphere, together with all the comings and goings of family life, was not conducive for what he had in mind. Here instead he had all the peace and solitude he required. A cell which looked into the College chapel allowed him to pray before the Blessed Sacrament without leaving his room. Here too he could perform his penances undisturbed by family curiosity. Ripa assigned him to take care of the church where he immediately found an outlet for his zeal when not absent with the Apostolic Missions. Father Fatigati, a colleague of Ripa's and superior of the College, declared that Alphonsus spent his time praying or studying, preaching or hearing confessions. Within the space of a few months he had turned the church into a permanent mission where the poor of the neighbourhood came for instruction and the sacraments; it was ideal too for members of the *cappelle* who came from all over the city.

It was in the Chinese College that his kindness and understanding as a confessor first became known; penitent after penitent was moved by his sympathic understanding. Drawn by the reputation of the confessor in the new College, Giovanni Olivieri, a government official, made his way up the hill to the College to put an end to a wayward life. He was received so kindly by Alphonsus that his confession was the beginning not only of a lasting conversion and an exemplary christian life but of a lasting friendship — perhaps the only one at this human level that existed in Alphonsus' life. He became sincerely attached to Giovanni and stayed in his home in Naples on many occasions later. Giovanni's sister Angela, who lived at home as a *bizzocca*, was no less devoted to him than her brother. It was probably one of the few places where he felt sufficiently at ease to relax. On his death-bed Giovanni sent for Alphonsus who came immediately, which, he said, he would not have done for the Cardinal.[1] Giovanni more than repaid his debt of gratitude by financing the publication of the *Visits to the Blessed Sacrament* and more importantly Alphonsus' first major work in the field of moral theology, his annotations on the *Medulla Theologiae Moralis* of Father Busenbaum. On the title page of the first edition in 1748 is stated in small print: 'published at the expense of Don Giovanni Olivieri', a line which conceals a story of over twenty years of friendship.[2]

In the college chapel Alphonsus initiated retreats for the young ladies of the city, a ministry which resulted in numerous vocations to the religious life throughout the Kingdom and which was the beginning of a lifetime's correspondence with the many sisters whose vocation he had discerned and whose conscience he continued to guide. One young lady whom he met in the Chinese College he directed to the Carmelites; later as Sister Maria Angela of Divine Love, she was the foundress and first superioress of the new convent of Carmelites in Capua where she became the confidante of the Queen, Maria Amelia of Saxony, wife of King Charles III. Despite her enclosure she was a frequent visitor to the royal palace at Caserta. At a particularly critical juncture for the survival of his new group of missionaries, Alphonsus did not hesitate, enclosure or no, to enlist her influence at Court on his behalf, but as it turned out, not with any great success.[3] One of his greatest triumphs was achieved with an unfortunate girl of the streets named Maria, whose mother brought her to him in desperation. The girl's struggle to alter her way of life went on for months. After her first conversion and her promise to amend her ways she returned to the streets. Alphonsus prayed for her and enlisted the prayers of others, particularly of convents. Alphonsus himself described the hell of bitterness, anger and unbelief which the girl went through, ending in threats to commit suicide. But grace finally triumphed. Maria's second conversion was final; after a period of training in a school for girls in Naples, she settled into life in a *conservatorio* for girls established by Bishop Falcoia in Castellamare, where she lived until her death a life of penance and prayerful union with God.[4]

The fundamental dynamic of Alphonsus' life during these years came from his sense of the dignity and obligations of the priesthood. The points of reference which he drew up for himself at this time, reflecting the priestly spirituality of the day, are to be found later in his preaching and writings for priests and seminarians:

1. I am a priest and my dignity surpasses that of the angels. I must therefore cultivate great purity and as far as possible live an angelic life.
2. Since God deigns to obey my words as a priest, I must obey the voice of God, the inspirations of his grace and my ecclesiastical superiors.
3. Since the Church surrounds me with great respect, I, in turn, must honour the Church with my whole life, my zeal and my labours.
4. Since I offer Jesus Christ to God, I must clothe myself with the virtues of Jesus Christ to prepare myself to deal with the Holy of Holies.
5. The people see in me the minister who reconciles them with God and for this reason I should be personally pleasing to God and possess his friendship.
6. Sinners look to me to free them from their sins; to them I must devote my life, through prayer, example, preaching and availability.
7. I must prepare myself by constant study to defend our religion and to stem the tide of error and unbelief.
8. The two great enemies of the priestly life are ambition and laziness which have destroyed the faith of many ministers of the altar.
9. To be pleasing to God I must endeavour to be recollected, constant in prayer, attend to the sanctification of my soul and the salvation of my neighbour even at the cost of my own life.[5]

Freed from the restrictions imposed by his home environment Alphonsus was more unrestrained in his programme of personal asceticism. Besides fasting strictly on certain days he sprinkled his food with unpalatable herbs to destroy the pleasurable taste, wore hair shirts, and scourged himself to blood. He found a prescription for a home-made ointment which he copied into his private note-book and which he made up himself and applied to the wounds which his flagellations inflicted.

– II –

By the time Alphonsus transferred residence to the Chinese College he was in the grip of scruples which had begun to manifest themselves before his ordination, and which, in one form or another, were to remain with him until his death. They affected him with varying degrees of intensity depending on circumstances; the weather was believed to be responsible for an intensification of his worries during the autumn months. His scruples were at their most distressing for a period of roughly ten years; after that the therapy of blind obedience to his directors enabled him to come to terms with himself and his doubts. He still had to struggle with his conscience in the matter of which moral principles to follow in the ministry of the confessional but to a large extent his personal sufferings and embarrassment had ended. There were periodic outbreaks of scrupulous anxiety throughout his life but he was able to cope, with the help of his directors of conscience. The agitation of the last few months preceding his death was caused more by a medical condition than by scruples.[6]

The classical manifestations of the scrupulous conscience are centred round three aspects of one's life — namely, past sins, even though confessed and absolved; sexual sins, usually of thought; and finally a morbid fear of committing sin by one's conduct at the moment. Around these three areas the scrupulous conscience gyrates restlessly. The first indication of scrupulosity is the interminable turning back to past sins, real or imaginary, which no assurance from one's confessor can relieve; once one anxiety is removed, the tortuous mind of the scrupulous person finds some aspect which seems not to have been properly understood or considered. The description of Alphonsus' scruples and mental anxieties, recorded for us by himself in his personal note-book reads like a classical clinical case-history, illustrating every possible aspect of this condition. He manifested all the symptoms — he was worried about the past, he was fearful of committing sin, anxious, never satisfied. One doubt resolved, another immediately raised its head to torment him. Satisfied for a while, the whole cycle began again — doubts, fear of having offended God, the possibility of damnation. Then once more, consultation, advice, everything clear, peace of conscience restored, but only momentarily. His directors endeavoured to give him a formula which would cover all eventualities but, of course, in vain. The scrupulous conscience of its very nature will not be reassured; the very advice itself, its meaning and interpretation, becomes a source of deeper anxiety.[7]

His scrupulosity ranged over every aspect of his life, past and present, as well as his ministry. His sensitivity in the matter of sexuality still continued to torment him, both as regards his own person and others. Pagano forbade him to confess bad thoughts, nocturnal pollution or anything of that nature. In the family home some paintings of the Rape of the Sabine Women disappeared — removed by Alphonsus, much to the annoyance of his brother Hercules, who had purchased them. Worries assailed him about his university studies and his doctorate degree, about the games of cards in the home of his friend, Baldassare Cito, about tax obligations on the family property in connection with his patrimony and the legal transactions with Hercules. The scruple about his doctorate — the exact nature of which we do not know — was resolved when he was instructed not to worry further in the matter since whatever he had done was the accepted practice and everybody else did the same thing. The thoughts of becoming a religious which he nurtured in his adolescent years and the resolutions he had made in this regard, returned to haunt him. Was he still bound by the vow he had made? Did altered circumstances remove the obligation? Was it validly commuted by Pagano or should he have recourse to Rome? Was the idea that came to him of giving his books to the Chinese College binding in conscience? Were his faculties to preach valid? If he stood where he could be clearly seen by everybody when preaching, was he pandering to his natural vanity?

Ordination to the priesthood brought with it a whole new and extensive field for his worries. The recitation of the Divine Office became a torture. He worried about distractions to the extent of believing that he had not complied with his obligations. He began to repeat the Office. Pagano intervened at once to forbid him ever to repeat what he had said. Pagano suggested that he could recite the office with another, only to find that Alphonsus was now worried that he was responsible for the shortcomings of his companion. The obligations which the virtue of charity imposes to point out to others the evil of their ways — a risky operation at the best of times — worried him, until both Pagano and Torni insisted that he was to disregard completely this aspect of the virtue; as far as he was concerned the obligation of fraternal correction simply did not exist. His scruples assailed him at the most embarrassing moments — when he was in the middle of the formula of absolution in Confession, when he was about to begin the celebration of Mass, at the Consecration, at his own Communion. Pagano made him enter in his note-book the simple instruction that once he put on the amice as he vested for the celebration of Mass, he was not to hesitate further: 'so my confessor instructs me' ran the simple entry. Before Mass he worried whether he had broken the fast by accidently swallowing water while washing; he purified the Paten after the Communion interminably in case any particles of the Sacred Host escaped his diligence. Pagano dealt with these areas by laying down categorically that Alphonsus was never to omit the celebration of Mass no matter what sexual arousals occurred during the night, nor was he to seek Confession beforehand; when purifying the Paten he was to leave most of the work to God's angels.[8]

His hesitations began to extend themselves to normal everyday commitments; Pagano consequently had to lay down a definite programme to cover every eventuality. As regards his favourite devotion, the Forty Hours, Alphonsus was to attend each day for an hour and a half of prayer, but not for any longer. In the winter season when the *tramontana*, the cold mountain wind from the snow-covered Appenines, made conditions unpleasant or when the *libeccio* blew from the Mediterranean with its quota of rain, he was not to go a long distance but to be satisfied with a visit to some nearby church.

In other climatic conditions — as a Neapolitan he reacted sensitively to wind and rain — even when the trying *scirocco* was blowing, he could go out, since, in Pagano's opinion, 'even getting out of doors was in itself a help to his "*ippocondria*"'. When he had a severe chest cold — and he suffered all his life from some form of chronic bronchitis — he was to remain in bed for two days and was not to celebrate Mass. As regards his commitments to the Apostolic Mission, he was always to say 'yes' when requested but he was then to put the request to his confessor who would give or refuse the final permission to undertake the engagement. When in doubt as to the more perfect course of action, he was to choose freely whichever course he wished, a solution which did not appeal to him and to which he objected since here precisely lay his problem.

The ministry of the confessional was an area where Alphonsus' scruples multiplied. He found it difficult to make the transition from theory to practice — what was his responsibility as regards questioning the penitent to secure a full confession, what questions were to be asked of different type of penitents from children to adults with little or no instruction in the theology of the sacrament, how was he to judge that the penitents were in the right frame of mind to receive absolution? How was he to deal with those who confessed sacrilegious confessions and Holy Communion received in sin — a common problem in the countryside? He seriously contemplated abandoning this aspect of his priestly ministry altogether until his directors insisted that he was to continue even if he made 'a hundred thousand errors'.

The theological formation which he had received had much to do with his initial hesitations in confessional practice. Genet had fixed his mind in a vice from which it took all the patient efforts of Pagano and the professor of theology, Torni, to free it. When two opinions, for and against a course of action, seemed of equal weight, Genet's advice was to suspend judgment and not to act without further consultation; if, for some reason, one had to take a decision then it had to be for the safer course, which meant in practice the imposition of a further burden on the unfortunate penitent. The result was that confessors, and among them the young Alphonsus, were faced on numerous occasion with the decision to defer or refuse absolution. It was all so logical in theory, so frustrating in practice. There was the further consideration that Alphonsus was gradually coming to the conclusion that this confessional practice was out of harmony with the spirit of Christ and the gospel. Quite simply it did not work either with the uneducated people he encountered on the missions or the penitents like the prostitute Maria who came to him at the Chinese College. He was learning from bitter experience and personal anguish of conscience that imposing obligations where there were none, deferring or refusing absolution as the virtual norm, could not be the right way of dealing with souls whom he wished to bring back to the life of grace and the sacraments. It was only at the cost of severe mental suffering that he was eventually able to lay aside the set of rigorous principles he had learnt and devise others more in keeping with the spirit of the Father in the parable of the Prodigal Son. His suffering of conscience was the price he had to pay as he evolved his own approach to dealing with sin and sinners.

Scruples of conscience may at times be beneficial to the soul, as spiritual writers do not hesitate to point out and as Alphonsus was well aware; they can purify one's conscience and make it sensitive to the inspirations of grace. Alternatively, however, if not brought under control by skilful guidance and acceptance of direction, they can impair all one's mental processes, paralyse one's judgment and in extreme cases lead to a total mental and physical breakdown. Pagano clearly foresaw this danger with Alphonsus, familiar as he was with his whole family background; a rigorous theological formation was not the only source of the problem. Pagano's handling of the situation over a period of six years was masterly; infinitely patient, sympathetic and at the same time decisive and trenchant, he was the ideal spiritual director for Alphonsus during those years.

Pagano's efforts were directed from the outset to ensuring that Alphonsus did not lose his power of coming to a decision; he was to make up his mind and come to a definite decision in the confessional in all but the most exceptional and intricate of problems. 'In doubt as to which course to take,' insisted Pagano, 'take whatever course you like, but *act*. Unless you can swear that what you are doing is clearly sinful, *act*.' He wanted to lead the young confessor away from dependence on others to the liberty of acting with serenity. Finally in exasperation he pointed out to Alphonsus that if he did not overcome his scruples he would lose his mind, render himself useless as an apostolic priest and perhaps, worse still, fall into despair and lose his soul. For all his gentleness Pagano could make a point when he wanted to and he threatened to refuse absolution if his instructions were not carried out. The warnings struck home: Alphonsus dutifully entered into his note-book the possibility that he would 'go mad' — *perdere il cervello*. And it came home to him that what he had gone through already was not far removed from that ultimate catastrophe — '*il pericolo in parte gia sperimentato di perdere la mente.*'

Pagano realised that Alphonsus would have to curb his excessive introspection; it was this tendency which was threatening to paralyse his judgment. Not merely was Alphonsus to decide things for himself without consulting others, he was not even to think of the principles on which he was basing his judgment. He was to make his mind a blank — *pensare à niente*. He would have to train himself to come to decisions, as it were automatically, drawing unconsciously on the norms of judgment which he had assimilated. He was to stop thinking of himself and of his worries; when his mind was troubled either by doubts or temptations he was to get out and talk to others. Even the instructions which he had been given and which he had written down in his note-book — Pagano had made some entries himself so that there would be no mistake — were to be read no more than once a week.

During these difficult years Alphonsus' mental equilibrium and his judgment were preserved not merely by the skill of Pagano's counselling but also by his own total obedience in faith to his spiritual directors. Reminiscing as an old man, he confided to one of his confreres that 'early in life he suffered intensely from scruples but was cured by his blind obedience to Father Pagano'. 'Scruples are good', he declared, 'when they go hand in hand with total submission to one's director.'[9] Using the same words that had been used to himself, he informed his sister Anna Maria, who was also a victim of scrupulosity in her convent, that she would go mad and would never be cured unless she learnt to obey her confessor. His own docility was not achieved without an effort on his part nor all at once. From his study of the spiritual writings of St Teresa of Avila and St Francis de Sales, he realised what was demanded of him. His spiritual note-book has a list of quotations from the writings of these saints dealing with obedience to one's director and the necessity of following his advice blindly. He applied Our Lord's words, 'who hears you, hears me', to the instructions he received from Pagano: 'the best course', he copied into his diary from Francis de Sales, 'is to walk under divine providence through the perplexities and darkness of this mortal life.' 'There is no more secure way of avoiding the snares of the devil than to do the bidding of one's director,' he copied from St Philip Neri. 'No one who obeys will ever be lost,' he read in the writings of St Teresa. Fortified by these admonitions from the saints he steeled himself to obey blindly no matter what the cost.

The therapy was life-long and at times distressing. Inevitably it left its mark on his personality and conduct. He became absolutely dependent on others both in regard to the smallest detail of his spiritual life such as his acts of self-denial, and in regard to major decisions concerning the foundation of his missionary society, his bishopric, his retirement. Fathers Pagano, Falcoia, Villani, Cafaro, Mazzini and a number of others who at one time or another were his spiritual directors, had absolute control over his conduct; whatever they said in this capacity he carried out without further hesitation. As a bishop, the Apostolic Missions invited him back for a special sermon in Naples; the request had to be referred to Father Villani who made the decisions in these matters. Anxieties and doubts on several matters did return to disturb him from time to time during his life as a missioner, superior and bishop but a word from his confessor immediately calmed his anxieties.

The final element in the therapy was to alter his concept of God. Bishop Falcoia who directed him for some eleven years from 1732 felt that Alphonsus was inclined to be too fearful of God. He was to endeavour to alter this attitude and move from fear of sin and punishment to feelings of love and hope. 'Seek the way of peace,' he was directed. 'Travel by the road of the love of God, ridding yourself of that fear which has so disturbed you.' Alphonsus in obedience copied into his note-book the relevant texts of scripture, 'I have come that they may have life'; 'Come to me all you who labour and are burdened'; 'Cast all your cares on the Lord' and a whole litany more. The love of God which casts out all fear becomes a dominant theme in his preaching and writings, culminating in his devotional master-piece, *The Practice of the Love of Jesus Christ*, which he published in 1768. It was, he felt, the most useful of all his writings even including his moral theology.

And yet, side by side with the problems of his own conscience went his mastery over the consciences and spiritual problems of others. From 1730 onwards the number of his penitents increased steadily. As the leading missioner of his day, he spent long hours in the confessional; bishops, priests, religious as well as lay people sought his advice and direction. With them, whether in the confessional or in the hundreds of letters of direction which he wrote, there was no hesitation; his judgment was clear and penetrating. In the decisions that he gave, the corrections and admonitions that he administered, he spoke with assurance. He showed special sympathy to those who like himself had experienced the agony of a scrupulous conscience; in his dealings with them he was able to draw on what he had been through himself. His treatment of the problem of scruples — which were much more widespread then than now — in his moral theology writings became normative for generations of theologians who considered that he had said the last word on the subject. His pamphlet, *Rest for Scrupulous Souls* first published in Naples in 1751 and widely diffused since then throughout the whole Catholic world has even in this century been regarded by psychiatrists as a masterpiece.[10]

Pagano was anxious to prevent Alphonsus' scrupulosity becoming known to too wide a circle; he forbade him to mention his doubts to others. It does not seem that his missionary companions or the generality of his fellow priests were aware of his problems, certainly not to the extent of lessening their esteem for him as a missioner and a confessor. On one occasion during the polemics caused by his writings concerning the use of a probable opinion, one adversary made use of the fact of his scrupulosity as an argument *ad hominem* but it was an isolated incident. As far as one can judge, his scruples were his own secret and that of his spiritual directors. As the years went by, however, the fact of his scrupulosity could not be concealed; by the closing years of his episcopate it was common knowledge.

– III –

Alphonsus' commitment to the Apostolic Missions continued unabated. Generally recognised now as one of their foremost missionaries he was constantly in demand in the city of Naples and in the missionary journeys which the members made into the rest of the Kingdom. Missionary activity in the countryside had been curtailed during the autumn of 1729 due to an outbreak of pestilence with the result that an intense programme of country missions was planned to begin in January 1730. On the fourteenth, Alphonsus with some twelve others set off for Marano. Dressed by choice in a worn and patched soutane to show his solidarity with the poorer elements of society, he deeply offended his brother Hercules' sense of clerical propriety. During the mission itself some of the people expressed their disapproval as well. 'What can you expect from a beggar like that' was one of the comments which made its way back to the Liguori household in Naples.[11] From Marano the missionary band moved on to Casoria where they preached until Holy Week. After Easter they re-grouped for the mission of Capodimonte where Alphonsus was entrusted with the *Predica Grande* for the first time in his career. Back in Naples itself after a week in Capodimonte, Alphonsus found himself assigned to the mission in the vast church of the *Annunziata*, one of the most remarkable centres of ecclesiastical activity in Naples at the time. When the mission here was concluded he returned to the Chinese College exhausted, almost on the verge of a nervous collapse. A proposal from a number of his companions to take a break on the coast of Amalfi was willingly accepted.

With four or five other companions, among them Giovanni Mazzini, recently ordained, and Vincenzo Mannarini, a member of Ripa's community at the Chinese College, Alphonsus left Naples towards the middle of May for Vietri sul Mare on the Lattari Peninsula in the gulf of Salerno. From there they set out by boat for Minori further down the coast planning to spend some time relaxing at the presbytery attached to the shrine of St Nicholas, as had been suggested to them by Don Giuseppi Pansa, a colleague of Alphonsus in the Apostolic Missions and like him an ex-lawyer who had abandoned the law courts for the priesthood. Unable to land at Minori on account of the rough seas they put ashore at Amalfi. Here they were persuaded to abandon their original intention. One of the priests of the locality suggested instead that the hermitage of Santa Maria dei Monti, perched high on the mountains overlooking the medieval city of Scala was the ideal place for what they had in mind. There would be simple accommodation and a church for Mass, and they could spend some of their leisure time ministering to the shepherds and goat herds who pastured their flocks there. May, moreover, was the month of popular pilgrimage to the shrine of Our Lady in the church, where a late sixteenth-century wooden statue of the Mother of God with the Child Jesus on one arm and the open Book of the Scriptures resting on the other was an object of devotion for the simple dwellers of the mountains.

The ascent to Santa Maria dei Monti began at the village of Atrani and continued right up the side of the mountain to Scala; the wonderful present-day tourist road which zig-zags its way up to Ravello and Scala was not then in existence. The group went by mountain path until they came to Scala clinging to the side of the mountain 1,300 feet above sea level. They went through the city which was to become so intimately associated with the name of Alphonsus in the future, through the *frazione* of Santa Catarina and ever more steeply up the side of the mountain to where, at a height of over 3,500 feet, rose the sanctuary of Santa Maria dei Monti, built on the site of an ancient pagan sanctuary. Here was an ideal place to rest for a while close to nature and its beauty; to the north through the hills lay the fertile plain presided over by Vesuvius, with the rich villages of the valley of the Sarno now filled with a thousand memories of Alphonsus and his missionaries — Angri, Scafati, Pagani, Sarno, Santa Maria la Carità; to the east lay Tramonti and the gap of Chiunsi, the first area to be evangelised by Alphonsus and his missionaries of the Most Holy Saviour, while to the south stretched the bay of Salerno with Paestum and the peninsula of Licosa on the horizon. All around the sanctuary stretched a fertile plateau rich with pastures and peopled at this time of the year with herdsmen and very often with their families. No sooner had the news of the arrival of a group of priests at our Lady's Sanctuary spread to the numerous hamlets situated on the foothills of Tramonti than the inhabitants flocked to take advantage of their presence; they had been without a chaplain for years. They were a generous people, avid for the word of God and the grace that comes through his ministers and the sacraments, but unlettered and uneducated, deeply superstitious and abysmally ignorant of the very fundamental truths of religion.[12]

The priests, who had come for a rest from their labours, were prodigal of their time; catechesis, religious instruction in the very fundamentals of the faith, confessions, Mass and preparation for the reception of Holy Communion and inevitably the recitation of the rosary and Benediction, all these turned the sanctuary into a place of mission. For Alphonsus the whole experience was a frightening revelation of the ignorance and spiritual abandonment in which souls within a few days journey of Naples were living; no group of missionaries came here to preach or instruct these people while within a few hours distance there were over fifty priests in Scala and twice that number in Amalfi. The memory of these people and their spiritual needs haunted him; here was sown the seed which later germinated into the group of missionaries who would minister by means of missions to the spiritual needs of neglected souls especially in country areas throughout the Kingdom.

Alphonsus and his companions spent some four weeks at the sanctuary. Restored in health he preached in the cathedral for the bishop of Scala, Mons. Guerriero, on devotion to the Blessed Sacrament on the Sunday after the feast of Corpus Christi. The nuns of the Visitation two hundred yards from the cathedral insisted on a special conference for themselves and Alphonsus duly obliged. He had already heard of this convent and its complicated history in Naples where it was the subject of intense clerical curiosity; the nuns and the alleged revelations that had taken place in the convent had fuelled clerical gossip enormously. First-hand experience of the community would have been of great interest to Alphonsus. He returned to Naples in time to cast his vote in the election of Father Torni as current superior of the Apostolic Missions and with an invitation from the bishop to preach the Novena of the Holy Cross in the cathedral in September and the spiritual exercises to the nuns. But first these requests would have to be submitted to Father Pagano for his judgment, and with good reason too.

– IV –

The episcopal city of Scala perched high on the mountains directly above Amalfi had been steadily declining since the later middle ages when it had ranked among the important republics of the Mediterranean coast. At one time it boasted a population of nearly 30,000 inhabitants but in 1730 only the medieval cathedral of San Lorenzo and the remains of the palaces once owned by rich merchants evoked the glories of the past. The population of the city had dwindled to about 1,500. Its days as a diocese with its own bishop were also numbered; in 1818 Pope Pius VI would suppress the united diocese of Scala-Ravello and incorporate it into the archdiocese of Amalfi of which it still forms part today. But unimporant as it may have been numerically, the name of Scala had been the centre of ecclesiastical gossip since the end of 1725; the clerical world and even the vice-regal court had been alive with stories about the happenings there, mainly focused on the convent of the Immaculate Conception. Like the city itself the local *conservatorio* dedicated to Our Lady's Immaculate Conception had been in decline in more ways than one when two missionaries of the society of the Pii Operai, Fathers Thomas Falcoia and Father Maurice Filangieri preached a mission there in 1719. At the request of the bishop they undertook the dangerous task of the spiritual renewal of the convent, a request which they might well have hesitated before accepting had they known the amount of gossip, ridicule and sufferings their efforts would entail.

Thomas Falcoia was to be one of the three central figures in the whole complicated saga; Sister Maria Celeste Crostarosa and Alphonsus himself were the other two. Falcoia was a well-known missionary in Naples at the time and had become acquainted with Alphonsus in the first place through his uncle, bishop Cavalieri, then through the Apostolic Missions. Their friendship deepened when Alphonsus took up residence in the Chinese College. Falcoia was some thirty years Alphonsus' senior. Born in Naples he had entered the missionary society of the Pii Operai where he had the Venerable Luigi Sabbatini for his master of novices. After his ordination he continued his theological studies at the 'Sapienza' in Rome. He had spent some years as a missionary in the Papal States when he was made superior of the house of Santa Balbina in Rome in 1696, the year Alphonsus was born. After filling most of the offices of authority in the society he was finally elected Superior General for the statutory term of three years, a period which he, probably correctly, considered too short and which he accordingly endeavoured to change with the result that he found himself for his pains once more a simple missionary back in Naples in the community of San Nicola alla Carità. Despite his absence from the Neapolitan scene for so long he quickly established himself as a much sought after missionary and a person of influence in the ecclesiastical world of the capital. He had been for years the close friend and spiritual director of Father Matthew Ripa and had helped him considerably in the establishment of the College where Alphonsus was to take up residence.

On the conclusion of the mission in Scala, Falcoia and Filangieri turned their attention to the convent of the Immaculate Conception which had been without vocation-intake since the early years of the century. As a result of their efforts, on 15 May 1720 eleven postulants under the guidance of the new superioress Mother Maria Giuseppa Schisano arrived in Amalfi by boat from Vietri en route to Scala; as the flotilla bringing the 'sisters' passed along the coast the military fortresses fired salvoes of welcome. On the twenty-second Mons. Guerriero solemnly established the nuns in the convent which had been materially restored through the generosity of local benefactors. The sisters adopted the Rule of the Visitation Sisters and clothed themselves in the Visitation habit. The Visitation Sisters of Naples, however, refused to recognise this new foundation or to send them a mistress of novices to initiate them into the Visitation way of life, which was just as well perhaps, since Mother Giuseppa, an ex-Carmelite of the reform of Sister Serafina of Capri, had her own ideas about it and how the sisters should live. Despite the fact that the bishop had appointed two of the local canons to attend to the affairs of the convent, Father Falcoia in fact took full charge, visiting it as frequently as he could and impressing on it his own spiritual imprint. Like his mentor, Father Sabbatini and in the tradition of his own missionary society, he directed the whole spiritual and religious life of the sisters to the close personal imitation of Jesus Christ, a significant fact in the light of later developments and disagreements. The bishop of Scala was content — at least in the early years — to allow Falcoia abundant scope for his activities; not so his superiors in the Pii Operai who only reluctantly tolerated this ministry since it withdrew him from active participation in the work of missions among the people. The convent flourished under his guidance; there was no shortage of candidates and Falcoia spent months on end instructing the novices and preparing them for religious profession. He was in his element; the sisters were devoted to him, convinced that among his other gifts was his power of working miracles — a charism which undoubtedly was of great assistance to him in his task. He had cured the superioress of an illness through a command of obedience and had followed this up by ridding the monastery of a plague of scorpions by his prayerful command to them to depart.

The beginning of 1724 saw a further influx of postulants to the convent in the persons of three Neapolitan sisters, Ursula, Julia and Giovanna Crostarosa, whose lives, and especially that of Julia, now began to occupy centre stage in the continuing Scala saga. The Crostarosa sisters belonged to a family of twelve born to a Neapolitan lawyer and doctor in *utroque jure*. Julia, born in 1696 just four weeks after Alphonsus, was a highly intelligent woman and a natural leader; her two sisters, Ursula her senior by eight years and Giovanna her junior were led by her totally, and were to follow her through all the vicissitudes of a stormy and troubled life.[13] Julia claimed mystical graces from an early age; according to her autobiography, she was little more than six when the Lord made her aware of His presence and communicated various mystical insights to her. Her spiritual life developed precociously and her autobiography alludes to succeeding periods of fervour and lukewarmness similar to those to be found in the life of Teresa of Avila. At the age of fifteen she had her own spiritual director; two years later at his direction she made a vow of chastity and began to communicate daily, which was unusual at the time. A period of spiritual darkness followed which came to an end abruptly at the singing of the *Gloria* in the Mass of the Resurrection on Holy Saturday. In May 1718 with an impetuosity which was characteristic of her, she entered the Carmelite Convent of Marigliano at the age of twenty-one, accompanied by her elder sister Ursula. Six months later when they began the formal novitiate Julia became Sister Candida del Cielo, which does not sound felicitous in translation, and Ursula took the name of Sister Columba of the Holy Spirit. Within a year Julia had made her mark; she was appointed Novice Mistress. At this time too she began her writings, partly autobiographical, partly spiritual; among her earliest efforts are to be found, significantly, outline Rules for religious communities based on the various redactions of the Carmelite Rule with which she was familiar but also giving scope to her own spiritual insights centred mainly on the imitation of Jesus Christ, and which she claimed were revealed to her in her mystical experiences.

Through one of those coincidences of which this whole story is full, the Fathers of the Pii Operai, led by no other than Father Falcoia, arrived in Marigliano to conduct a mission, in the course of which, as was the custom, they preached the spiritual exercises separately to the nuns. By this time, 1722, the youngest of the Crostarosa sisters, Giovanna, had joined her two sisters. Julia, or Sister Candida, had made up her mind merely to seek Falcoia's blessing during the course of the retreat but she believed that the Lord communicated to her in prayer His wish that she should reveal to Falcoia the state of her soul and the whole story of the Lord's dealing with her from her youth. A similar intimation, she felt sure, would be given to Falcoia independently, to prepare him for the arrival of his new penitent. The upshot was that Falcoia left Marigliano deeply impressed by Sister Candida. She, on her part, had heard from him all about the convent in Scala and the efforts being made there under his guidance to re-establish the religious life in all its fervour. It is difficult not to conclude that Falcoia was already thinking of the possibility of recruiting her for Scala and that she herself saw an opening there and was not at all averse from the suggestion. Within a few months the possibility became a reality. Unable to tolerate any further the continual interference in the affairs of the convent from the eccentric and shrewish duchess of Marigliano, Isabella Mastrilli, through whose generosity the convent had been established in the first place, the local bishop gave orders for its closure and instructed the sisters to seek other convents where they could continue their religious lives undisturbed. The three Crostarosa sisters left Marigliano in October 1723 for the family villa on the shore of the bay of Naples at Portici to assess the situation. Julia wrote to Falcoia who replied immediately that 'the Lord wished her in Scala'. Accepting his decision she further chose him as her spiritual director.

Years later in the isolation of her convent in Foggia and many years after the death of Falcoia she recalled with hindsight the painful consequences of this decision which, had she foreseen them, might have made her hesitate. 'The Lord', she wrote, 'placed me under the guidance of this priest in order to make me experience the precious fruits of the Cross which as yet I had not suffered. And yet he was a great servant of God,' she concluded.[14]

Having refused a proposal made to her through the influence of her father to establish a new convent in the region of Tramonti and having overcome the reluctance of Ursula to go to Scala where Falcoia was the only spiritual director permitted to the sisters, Julia led her two sisters there in January 1724. Clothed now in the habit of the Visitation Sisters they commenced their novitiate at the end of the month, Julia taking the new name of Sister Maria Celeste of the Holy Desert, Ursula that of Sister Maria Illuminata of the Holy Cenacle and Giovanna, the youngest, that of Sister Maria Evangelist of Jesus. In the normal course of events their profession would have followed in 1725 after a year's novitiate but due to a series of events which embroiled the whole convent and most of the ecclesiastical world as far as Naples initially and as far as Rome later on, the Crostarosa sisters were not admitted to religious profession until December 1726. Sister Maria Celeste's mystical gifts continued to flourish in the new surroundings of Scala; for the moment relations between herself and the spiritual director of the convent, Falcoia, went smoothly. Of her mystical graces there can be no doubt; the Lord led her through penance and contemplative prayer to a deep union with himself. But it was an inauspicious time to be a mystic in Naples and indeed in the Church at large; all forms of mystical prayer with the gifts that attend them had been compromised by the Quietists who had left a legacy of suspicion attaching to anything more out of the ordinary than the accepted Ignatian meditation. Celeste, moreover, had her own approach to the central question of the imitation of Christ, based on the Pauline concept of Christ living in her. She spoke of the living Presence of Christ in us through His Spirit, making us sharers, participants in His life, virtues and works. As a consequence, for her to imitate the virtues of Christ was more than a moral or ascetical practice, it was in her language, a living participation in the life-dynamic of the Saviour. This approach she brought to her understanding of the religious life and of all missionary activity as well.[15] Celeste's theological and mystical insights might not have proved disturbing either for herself or others were it not for the fact that she was addicted to writing them all down. Hand in hand with this went her facility in writing Rules for religious communities, communicated to her in her visions of the Lord and based on her approach to the imitation of Christ. From her years in the Carmel of Marigliano she may have cast herself in the role of another Teresa of Avila. Throughout the history of religious groups a mystic and visionary has nearly always been an uncomfortable guest though it is invariably herself who has to pay the heaviest price for her mystical gifts. It was to be no different with Celeste whose heroic virtues and authentic mystical gifts have only recently been fully recognised. She was still a novice when in April 1725 she began to have visions again. After Communion the Lord united her in mystical union with Himself and conveyed to her that a new Institute was to come into existence through her, based on the imitation of Christ and His virtues. The 'visions' or spiritual insights continued each day after Communion; the Lord appeared to her in the Sacred Host clothed in the red and blue habit of the new Order. Finally He instructed her to write the Rule which He would dictate. While she was to be in some way the foundation stone of the new congregation, it was not to claim for itself either a founder or foundress; for her pains Celeste would receive neither praise nor commendation. Instead, her lot would be such derision and persecution that the sufferings of Christ would be verified in her.

It is impossible to determine how much of this last message was an objective communication or just a very perceptive anticipation of the likely outcome of what she felt called to do. We can leave the discussion of her 'visions' to others. The historical facts are that with the permission of the Mistress of Novices and the ordinary confessor of the convent, Canon Pietro Romano from the diocesan Chapter, Sister Maria Celeste began to write down each day, for an hour after the reception of Communion, the new Rule which was to guide the spiritual destinies of the convent. Everything was done with the greatest secrecy; only seven or eight other sisters were privy to the revelations taking place among them and they vowed to fast for forty days for the successful outcome of what was referred to as 'the enterprise'. Even the superioress, the formidable Mother Maria Giuseppa was not brought into the circle of confidants—a tactical error of the first magnitude and one fraught with serious consequences for the future. Celeste explicitly excluded her since she considered the superioress 'very simple and ignorant of spiritual matters, especially of the gift of extraordinary prayer'. Falcoia was absent in Rome during these exciting months and could not be contacted. The first outsider to know of the events in the convent was Father Filangieri to whom the 'visions' were made known towards the end of June. His first reaction was enthusiastically favourable though he gradually altered his stance as the days went by — ending up in total opposition. After some time word reached Scala that Falcoia had returned from Rome and was in Naples. Immediately Sister Maria Angela, the novice mistress who had carried the burden of the revelations so far, sent off to him a large packet of letters detailing the events of the last two months; wisely she kept the copy of the Rule on the innocent pretext that other copies had yet to be made. Falcoia's reaction was predictable. In the strongest possible language he attacked Maria Celeste for her pride and presumption; she was 'mad'; her visions were fantasies of the devil. She was to burn the so-called Rule at once and to abstain from Communion until the feast of Our Lady's Assumption.

Falcoia's reply, dated 'the end of June' did not reach the convent in Scala until 17 August so his drastic action in regard to Celeste was not put into effect — a fact which was immediately interpreted by Maria Celeste as an intervention on her behalf by Providence and which went a long way towards confirming her belief in the authenticity of the revelations. In the meantime Sister Angela sent Falcoia a copy of the 'Rule', which calmed him somewhat and allowed him to orientate himself before visiting the convent in September.

News of the 'revelations' were now circulating in Naples. Falcoia consulted some theologians and canon lawyers in the city for their opinions which were predictably non-committal. Leaving aside altogether the question of the nature of the revelations, they found nothing worthy of censure in the Rule but its acceptance would depend among other conditions on the unanimous consent of the sisters. Having further discussed the matter with the bishop of Scala, Falcoia in September 1725, and with Filangieri at his side, addressed the assembled sisters and proposed that they should vote for acceptance or rejection of the Rule once and for all. There was a totally favourable response until the superioress, Sister Maria Giuseppa, played her trump card. As superioress she had been excluded from all consultation in connection with the affair; she had not been informed of the so-called visions or of the fact that the novice Maria Celeste was writing a new Rule for the convent. Her intervention was decisive on two points. First her opposition succeeded in rallying other sisters to her point of view; secondly with the community now totally split there was no immediate hope of having the new Rule accepted. There were two distinct camps diametrically opposed to each other, one supporting Maria Giuseppa against the new Rule, the other supporting the novice mistress, Sister Maria Angela and the visionary Maria Celeste.

After her initial victory Maria Giuseppa concentrated all her influence against Celeste and her director Falcoia. Her message was simple: the adoption of the new Rule would lead to spiritual anaemia and the death of the convent. Gradually she succeeded in turning the bishop of Scala and Father Filangieri against Falcoia; for a while there was the possibility that Maria Celeste would be expelled, in which case her sisters would have followed. But the balance shifted considerably when in June 1726 Maria Giuseppa came to the end of her term of office, to be replaced, unkindest cut of all, by Sister Maria Angela. This appointment, however, did little to restore unity among the sisters and the divisions were exacerbated when at Christmas 1726 the Crostarosa sisters were professed. Changes had also taken place among the hierarchy of the Pii Operai, and Father Filangieri was now the new superior general. Naples was buzzing with stories about the convent of Scala with Falcoia in particular becoming the object of ridicule for allowing himself to be deceived by the so-called revelations of a neurotic visionary. In an effort to put an end to the whole affair and to extricate his society from the damaging publicity, Filangieri as superior general formally forbade Falcoia to have anything whatsoever to do with the convent; on no account was he to visit it or to play any part in its affairs through his advice or direction. This drastic decision went a long way towards restoring some sort of peace, at least outwardly, to the community; the sisters accepted the decision with delight or dismay according to which side they had taken in the controversy; the bishop of Scala was relieved to have one worry less in his diocese and entrusted the direction of the convent to the gentle guidance of Canon Pietro Romano.

Falcoia acquiesced in the decision of his superior. His letter of farewell to the sisters in Scala was a masterpiece of subtlety allowing each side to interpret it as they pleased:

> My beloved daughters in the Lord,
>
> I now know for certain that you are all very dear to the Lord and that it is His purpose to make you all saints and to do great things for His glory and honour since He has providentially removed from amongst you the greatest obstacle to your perfection. Furthermore He wishes to heal all the wounds that have been opened up not through any fault of yours but due to my negligence and my fault. I wish you to understand that Father General considers me to have been deluded and inept which I admit that I am. On the other hand he loves you all dearly in the Lord and as a good spiritual father wishes to free you from all dangers and to help you positively in every way he can. And this is why he has decreed that I should have nothing further to do with your community. He will see to it that you are entrusted to the care of some Father who will be solicitous for your spiritual advancement. You can see from this how deeply indebted you should be to Father General!
>
> I, for my part, and thinking only of your good and God's glory and out of my esteem for you all, accept this decision in peace even though my pride has been hurt.
>
> Rest assured then that Divine Providence and the solicitude of our Father General will not leave you neglected but that you will have a Father Director much more capable than I have been of attending to your welfare; he will make up for my shortcomings, repair all the harm I have done, remove the blemishes caused by my weakness, inadequacy and wickedness during the time I was serving you.

His letter to Maria Celeste around the same time had a completely different ring to it:

> My dear daughter in the Lord,
>
> I trust in God that our common enemies will suffer confusion and be defeated by God's power and that they will not prevail in the terrible trouble they have caused. And so I shall be able to see you again. Pray the Lord to give grace and guidance to those who have such need of it. . . . I shall not be able to go to Scala until things take a turn for the better.[16]

For the next few years the convent in Scala ceased to make the headlines but the calm was more apparent than real. Opposition to the new Rule as well as Celeste's determination to see it accepted were stronger than ever.

She succeeded on occasions in corresponding secretly with Falcoia; likewise Filangieri, not to be outdone, kept in contact in the same way with the ex-superioress, Maria Giuseppa. And then the whole situation changed once more when early in 1728 Filangieri came to the end of his term of office to be succeeded by a personal friend and admirer of Falcoia who was himself elected to the General Council. The way was thus opened for him to resume his work for the sisters which he did tentatively at first since he had to overcome the reluctance of Mons. Guerriero and because he was conscious that the balance of peace in the convent could easily be disturbed. The following year, 1729, Falcoia, still with his heart set on seeing Maria Celeste's Rule in operation, discussed the whole affair with Alphonsus in the Chinese College where their meetings became the foundation of mutual admiration and of a lasting friendship. Alphonsus' immediate reaction was one of scepticism; at no time in his life was he easily impressed by so-called revelations and visions, particularly those which carried with them instructions for future action. The writings and acceptance of a new Rule fell into this category. When he wrote about visions and revelations some years later in his treatise on the direction of souls, he expressed severe reservations about such divine communications. At most was he prepared to concede that nothing should be done just on the word of the visionary; great caution was imperative until further confirmation could be secured. 'The safest course for the director,' he wrote, 'is not to attach any great importance to them since there are more false visions than true ones.'[17]

Providence seemed to be working in favour of Maria Celeste. Early in 1730 Father Filangieri, who had developed into an implacable opponent of the visions and the new Rule, died; if that did not tip the balance sufficiently in favour of Crostarosa, the news of Father Falcoia's appointment a few months later as bishop of Castellamare di Stabia on the bay of Naples and just over the mountains from Scala certainly did. The news brought great joy to his friends in the convent who saw victory for the new Rule in sight. This then was the situation when Alphonsus after his holiday at Santa Maria dei Monti visited the convent and gave a special conference to the sisters. We have no details of what he said or whether he talked individually to Maria Celeste or not; in view of his instructions to directors on how to deal with those who claimed to have received revelations from on high, the virtual certainty is that he did not. On his return to Naples he submitted to Pagano bishop Guerriero's request that he should preach the Novena of the Holy Cross in the cathedral and follow this with the spiritual exercises in the convent. Pagano refused permission for the retreat in the convent; his reasons are abundantly clear. He did not wish to see Alphonsus involved in a situation which was not only complicated but fraught with danger for his reputation as a priest. For five years Naples had heaped ridicule on the happenings at Scala and the involvement of bishops and priests in what was seen as the scheming of a neurotically ambitious woman. Finally, however, Pagano gave the necessary permission but only with great reluctance and when the irate reaction of the bishop of Scala became known to him. In retrospect it was this reluctant permission which was to determine Alphonsus' whole future.

– V –

Assisted by Father Giovanni Mazzini and Father Vincenzo Mannarini, his colleague in the Chinese College, Alphonsus preached the Novena of the Holy Cross in Scala in September 1730; from the cathedral he went alone to the convent to begin the spiritual exercises. Armed with full authority from Mons. Guerriero he first undertook an objective examination of the revelations and the new Rule. Despite his initial prejudice he gradually became convinced of the authenticity of Maria Celeste's experiences and that her insights and projects were from the Lord. The fervour of the community impressed him greatly. He then interviewed the sisters individually and among them Maria Celeste who made a favourable impression on him — the beginning of a deep friendship and mutual respect which was to survive the misunderstandings and rejection which were hers for the rest of her life. In obedience to his instructions she wrote a full account of her visions which she gave to him and which he carefully preserved, indicating on the back of the manuscript the source and contents of the document. In the course of his retreat which he based appropriately enough on the master idea of the new Rule, the imitation of Jesus Christ, his attitude to the revelations began to change. His scepticism gave way to acceptance and he became convinced that the establishment of a convent of sisters following Celeste's Rule was the work of God. His verdict delighted Maria Celeste and her supporters. To complete his task he addressed a special conference to those other sisters who up to that time had opposed the introduction of the new Rule, burdening their conscience with the responsibility of impeding the glory of God. Mons. Guerriero was particularly reassured at the outcome of the visit and the retreat. The way was now clear for his approval if and when the nuns decided to accept the new Rule.

The annals of the convent relate a charming incident which it was said took place on the morning of Alphonsus' return to Naples — the authenticity of which need not trouble us. The sister cook was beginning to prepare a *pizza* for Alphonsus to take with him on his return journey when she invoked the help of Our Blessed Lady in what would seem to be a rather straightforward culinary undertaking. At the mention of Our Lady's name the sister became rapt in ecstasy. When she recovered her senses the time for departure had arrived. To her surprise she found the *pizza* beautifully cooked despite the fact that in her ecstasy she had omitted to kindle the charcoal fire. With magnificent aplomb and as if nothing had happened she presented the *pizza* to the departing retreat director with the words 'Eat this, Our Lady cooked it for you'. The story possesses as distinctive a Neapolitan flavour as the *pizza* itself; the fact that it was recorded for posterity in the annals of the convent tells us more about the sisters than all the formal investigations.

Falcoia was delighted beyond measure at the outcome of the retreat. The nuns had lost no time in writing a full account to him in Rome where he was for his episcopal ordination. They were enthusiastic about the retreat conductor and were already looking forward to the acceptance of the Rule of Maria Celeste and the wearing of the habit of the new religious order the following year. At the same time Falcoia insisted that no steps should be taken until he had returned to his diocese; he was anxious that direction of the affair should not slip in any way from his grasp.

For this reason Alphonsus was not to speak of the new institute to anyone until they had met and discussed the matter together. Back in Naples Alphonsus communicated his experiences to Pagano and Torni who were both immediately apprehensive; they realised that Alphonsus could easily allow himself to be carried away and become entangled in the whole affair which they still regarded with considerable scepticism. They urged him not to involve himself further. Torni for his part would see to it that Alphonsus was fully occupied in missionary work.

On 15 October, the feast of St Teresa, Alphonsus received a package of letters in Naples from the convent in Scala; his obvious delight at the very sight of the envelope did not escape the notice of the courier who delivered the letters. Virtually every one of the nuns had written to him individually, among them Maria Celeste who made no effort to hide her feelings towards him. She assured Alphonsus that he was always in her prayers; united with him, she made her Communion. And she prayed that their friendship would be blessed by the Lord for His honour and glory. A warning on the margin of the letter requested Alphonsus not to mention to Falcoia that she had written to him.[18] At the end of the month Alphonsus replied at great length in a letter addressed to the superioress Maria Angela; it is one of the earliest of his letters extant — effusive, enthusiastic, brimming over with piety, at times calm and matter-of-fact, at times bordering on the hysterical. He assured the sisters that the memory of Scala was still with him, a memory which far from being a source of distraction brought him nearer to the Lord. He would never forget them, they would for ever have a large share in his prayers. 'Let us give our hearts to Him who calls and cast out of them everything that is not God. And in order to give ourselves entirely to Him let us empty our hearts even of ourselves so that God will find no obstacle there to prevent Him filling them completely Himself.'

Ingenuously he poured out his woes to them, revealing the darkness of soul he was experiencing, the fears that were assailing him:

> I should like you to know that, as I have said, I have paid dearly for Scala and am still paying for it. Here I am in the middle of a tempest; sometimes I can see neither heaven or earth. I find myself, as it were, in a dark cavern where there is no order but a terrible experience of horror — *ubi nullus ordo, sed terribilis horror inhabitat*. But may the Will of the Supreme God always be done! And if that is that I should be damned,

then if it is for His greater glory, so be it! Pray for me that I do not offend Him since it is not for His glory that I should do so. And for the rest, Lord, here I am: Hell is too little for me.[19]

He concluded by sending them a poem he had written in honour of Our Lady. In the course of the letter he mentioned thirteen sisters by name with a personal message for each to be read to them privately. Significantly there was no message for Maria Celeste even though there was one for her younger sister, Maria Evangelista. The omission may well have been intentional, motivated by a desire to humiliate Maria Celeste before the assembled community — an accepted spiritual therapy, according to Alphonsus' own principles, in dealing with visionaries and recipients of revelations.

After a busy autumn of preaching engagements far from Scala and cut off from communication with the convent, Alphonsus found himself in February of the following year 1731 preaching a retreat to nuns in Amalfi. There is no indication that from here he was in touch with Scala. While in Amalfi he fell ill; Falcoia, now established in his diocese, was alarmed, not altogether altruistically:

> I was sorry to learn that you were ill in Amalfi and was within an inch of going to visit you. Now I hear to my great delight that you are well again and restored to strength to continue your work for the glory of God. . . .
>
> You must continue to humour the bishop of Scala for me concerning the affairs of *our monastery*. I am given to understand that thanks to you he is prepared to allow our nuns to change their Rule but I suspect that he wants to arrange things according to his own ideas. I ask you to use your usual diplomacy to see that he leaves to me the question of adjusting the Rule and of launching this new Bark. I am fully qualified to look after the affairs of the convent and of the nuns since I have directed this work for many years. And I have already foreseen, taken into account and dealt with, all the difficulties that the bishop thinks might arise in the matter. In good time I shall let him see the Rules and Constitutions as I have adjusted them.[20]

Falcoia was totally committed to having the Rule of Crostarosa accepted in the convent. Despite his initial unfavourable and aggressive reaction he soon became convinced of the authenticity of the revelations and supremely confident of his own competence in dealing with the matter. There was always in him something of the suppressed religious founder. Thoughts of establishing a new religious group of missionaries had been with him since his days in Rome; he found an outlet for this talent in organising a group of priests in Taranto in the very south of Italy into a local congregation or sodality under the title of St Michael and providing for them a rule of life — an undertaking which, as we have seen, was the usual way of organising the surplus clergy throughout the kingdom of Naples at the time. But Scala and Maria Celeste provided a more exciting challenge, with the background of visions and revelations and an outline Rule which still had to be fleshed out in detail. Here Falcoia felt particularly assured because of his own experience of community life in the Pii Operai and his wide experience in Rome and throughout the kingdom. While he consulted widely and loudly protested his willingness to listen to suggestions — *ch'io non sara duro nel mantenere le mie proposizioni* — he was in point of fact rigid and unbending in wishing to have his own point of view and decisions not only accepted, but, at times, accepted without question.

Pagano and Torni succeeded in keeping Alphonsus from playing any further active role in Scala for the moment, much to the disappointment of Maria Celeste who longed for his presence. She expressed her displeasure at the attitude of both of them and promised to take up their prohibition with Falcoia. 'I cannot convince myself', she wrote 'that your visit here and your getting to know us was not the work of God.' His illness upset her and she felt ill herself — 'since we are good friends, we have also been ill together'. Alphonsus sent her a statuette of St Teresa as well as some medicine for her to take which she did and for which she was very grateful.[21] Due to the influence of Alphonsus, Mons. Guerriero overcame his suspicions of his fellow bishop and allowed him to resume his work for the convent. In May 1731 Falcoia presided at the nuns' chapter in which they voted finally to accept the new Rule, a decision which was in point of fact a vote for the establishment of a new religious Institute. Days of prayer in preparation for Pentecost followed. Finally on the feast, 13 May, Falcoia gave a conference to the assembled sisters on the text of St Paul, 'Whoever are baptised in Christ have put on Christ,' (Gal.3.37) and the new religious order of the Sisters of the Most Holy Saviour was formally established with the approval of the bishop of Scala. Alphonsus was in Naples, prevented from participating personally in the celebrations, by direction of Pagano.

Thrilled at the outcome of his efforts after six years of set-backs and great personal suffering, Falcoia wrote to Alphonsus from Castellamare that all was well; peace and harmony had characterised the establishment of the new Institute. He then drew up an Apologia which he had distributed to the clergy in Naples in an effort to counteract the unfavourable gossip. In some clerical conferences the document was read in public and was well received. The improved atmosphere allowed Pagano to relent somewhat in his attitude with the result that Alphonsus was present in Scala some three months later when on 6 August the feast of the Transfiguration of Our Lord, the nuns donned for the first time the new habit of red and blue in memory of Our Saviour. The transformation of the convent from being an unrecognised community of the Visitation Sisters was almost complete. There was still a considerable amount of work to be done, however, before the details of their religious life could be finalised. The Rule of Crostarosa, in the form of utterances from God the Father and His Son, Jesus Christ, had to be supplemented to deal with the practicalities of everyday life. Falcoia was now only too eager to share this task with Alphonsus whose intervention had proved decisive. Without him and his influence with the bishop of Scala together with his favourable judgment on the nature of the revelations and the Rule itself, the new Institute would never have come into existence, a fact which Falcoia readily conceded.[22]

Besides his work on the Rule Alphonsus interested himself in details such as how the sisters should read at table. They were to pause at the end of sentences and be careful to read slowly and in a strong voice so that all could hear. Everything appeared to be going smoothly; the nuns had settled in to the new Rule, the bishop was flattered that a new group of contemplative religious had come into existence in his episcopal city; Falcoia was delighted at the progress of 'his dear daughters in the Lord'; clerical gossip in Naples was silenced. But the calm was deceptive. Within a few months the whole cycle of events would start again, visions, revelations, another new Rule and another congregation — this time a missionary congregation of men. Tongues would wag again and Alphonsus would be the principal victim of their ridicule.

CHAPTER FIVE

THE INSTRUMENT OF HIS GLORY
1731–1732

- I -

The founders of religious orders bear little resemblance in reality to the romantic portraits we paint of them. We often imagine that the idea of founding a new religious family strikes them in prayer as a result of a special revelation, whereupon with total dedication they set out with absolute assurance, like Crusaders, knowing where they are going and what they are destined to achieve. The reality can be very different. Few religious founders have cast themselves in that role either consciously or willingly. Many found themselves at the head of a group of followers almost without realising it or without any definite vision for the future; others found themselves in new apostolic ventures reluctantly.[1] Alphonsus de Liguori was far from casting himself in the heroic role of a religious founder; the initiative in what he undertook came mainly from others. He was in the depths of spiritual darkness, tortured with scruples, unsure of his future, hesitant and indecisive when he found himself playing a key role in the establishment of a new missionary society. He was the most unlikely of founders; if any man was ever led unwillingly to the task it was he.

As late as 1731, five years after his ordination and with considerable missionary activity already behind him Alphonsus was still not sure of what the future held for him or where he should exercise his priestly ministry. He had already considered joining the Oratorians and the Theatines; in the Chinese College he was attracted to the work of the Chinese Mission and Ripa felt quietly confident that soon he would have him as a valuable member of his young society. When Ripa spoke of the missionary needs of the various areas he had visited on his journeys to China, such as the southern tip of Africa, which he referred to as the Cape of Good Hope, and India, Alphonsus grew more confused than ever. Was the Lord calling him to some such place? His recent pastoral experience of the abandoned souls on the mountains above Scala brought home to him that there was a China nearer at hand waiting to be evangelised. His mood of uncertainty was all pervasive but for the moment he had to be satisfied with the Chinese College and the Apostolic Missions. There was, he felt, something that God wanted him to do if only he could be certain. Every reputable spiritual counsellor in Naples must have known about his search since he discussed the whole matter not merely with Pagano, Torni, Gizzio, Ripa but also with the Dominicans, Jesuits, Franciscans, Vincentians as well as bishops and his own priest friends.

Maria Celeste continued to write at length from Scala, worried about his health, anxious that he should not overburden himself with apostolic labour. Her 'visions' and her mystical insights continued unabated; she 'saw' Christ present with them in choir at the recitation of the Office; He appeared to her at other times as a pilgrim with specific instructions as to her conduct; most of the instructions seemed to coincide nicely with her own wishes. In her letters she did not conceal her dissatisfaction with Falcoia as her spiritual director, referring to him with less than the customary reverence simply as 'Falcoia'. He had her totally confused, *sotto sopra*. The Lord even revealed to her for her consolation that her disagreements with Falcoia were not *her* fault but were part of *His plan*. Her purpose clearly was to induce Alphonsus himself to become her spiritual director. Our Lady spoke to her about this: 'Daughter, I have sent you my son [Alphonsus] for your consolation and support. Open your heart to him and obey his instructions since you have need of assistance.' Our Lord, too, spoke to her about Alphonsus at length:

> While I was asking the Lord in prayer never to allow us to separate ourselves from his love He showed me the throne of glory which he has prepared from all eternity for you as a reward for the love which you profess for Him and for the labour you undertake on his behalf. He assured me that in this life we would never be separated from His love.
>
> One morning after Communion I received clear illumination concerning the gifts and graces of souls which the Lord has conferred on you. He said to me: 'you shall receive great graces from me by means of this soul and he in turn shall receive great graces from my mercy through you.
>
> Tell him that his labours to bring sinners to repentance are very dear to me and in particular his efforts to advance in the way of intimate union with God those souls who are in His grace; in these I am glorified and through them I shed on the world my divine Mercy.'[2]

Celeste's 'revelations' were always opportune, neatly tailored to the existing situation and to fit her own purposes; at times they appeared manipulative. Despite his initial scepticism about what Celeste had to say as a result of her mystical insights, Alphonsus summarised the references to himself and wrote them in his 'diary'; they were some consolation to him in the spiritual darkness of those years. 'Jesus loves me . . . Mary regards me as one of her dearest sons. I am under her special protection and she is with me in my efforts for the conversion of souls. The devil hates the hour when I gave myself to God and detests all I have done for the monastery of Scala but Our Lord blesses it. Celeste saw my name written in the heart of Jesus and I shall be saved [*predestinato*]. Jesus is pleased at my devotion to Our Lady and accepts me among her sons.'[3]

The climax to Maria Celeste's revelations came around the feast of St Francis of Assisi, 1731, first in the refectory at the evening meal on the eve and then after Communion next day on the feast itself. Our Lord appeared to her in glory with St Francis on one side and Alphonsus on the other. A new order of men was to be established, the male counterpart of the order of nuns but dedicated to the preaching of the Gospel. Their basic spirituality, based on the imitation of Jesus Christ, corresponded to that of the Rule of the sisters. The members were to imitate the poverty of the saint of Assisi, situate themselves near the areas to be evangelised, set out like the Apostles two by two, 'teaching all nations for the kingdom of God is at hand'.[4] They were to wear a habit of red and blue — a proposal mercifully rejected by Alphonsus from the very outset. Among their members would be those called to the contemplative life whose special vocation would not be preaching the Gospel in the physical sense but who would exercise the same ministry by their prayers. Alphonsus was pointed out as the head of the new institute.

The revelations about a new missionary group were not altogether original or unpredictable. There had in fact been much discussion about doing something for the neglected souls such as Alphonsus and his companions had encountered on the mountains nearly two years previously; the establishment of some form of missionary group had been mooted as a possibility. Celeste was treading a well-worn path: she lost no time in communicating her latest revelations directly to Falcoia whose immediate 'official' reaction was similar to his reaction in 1725 on the occasion of the original revelations concerning the new Rule for the nuns.

A curt note took her to task for her presumption in believing she was in direct communication with Our Lord. 'I do not give the slightest credence to your visions and revelations and neither should you. I have other principles to guide me besides your ramblings.'[5] Secretly he was thrilled; the revelations corresponded so completely with his own aspirations that he was ready to accept them at once. Since Alphonsus, for whom he had the highest regard, had been pointed out as the providentially chosen instrument for the implementation of the work, his enthusiasm for the establishment of a new missionary institute was unbounded. Towards the end of October he set off across the mountains to Scala from his episcopal see to investigate what had happened. Despite the strict secrecy and total silence in the matter which he imposed on the convent on his arrival, the superioress found it all too much for her and hinted darkly in a letter to Alphonsus that there was something great in the offing. 'Our Father Falcoia is here with us at the moment . . . pray the Lord that everything will work out for His greater glory. Sister Maria Celeste and Sister Columba have something to communicate to you about the matter which you know of, but so far they have not received permission to write to you. When you are informed of the matter from them do not pretend that you have got even this inkling of the matter from me.'[6]

Convinced of the authenticity of these latest communications from Celeste, Falcoia wrote to Alphonsus in almost as cryptic terms as the superioress. 'When I come to Naples I have to consult you on a matter of the utmost importance which in a certain sense concerns yourself.'[7] On the conclusion of the annual mission in Naples Alphonsus, accompanied by Fathers Giovanni Mazzini and Vincenzo Mannarini, went first to see Falcoia in Castellamare and from there on to Scala to investigate for himself. At the right-hand side of the altar as one entered the public chapel of the sisters in Scala was the confessional where the confessor heard the confessions of the sisters. There Alphonsus, with the permission of the bishop, interviewed Celeste who recounted the divine communications she had received and in the name of God demanded prompt acceptance on his part of the task the Lord was calling him to undertake. His objections were innumerable but were all waved aside; the discussion became animated and the sound of voices raised in argument carried out to the body of the church where Mazzini was praying and waiting for his companion. When they were alone Alphonsus recounted to Mazzini and Mannarini the burden of the interview. Over sixty years later Mazzini recalled the conversation at the process of beatification, and the fact that both he and Mannarini there and then offered themselves to Alphonsus as his companions in the undertaking.[8]

Alphonsus' reactions to the revelations of Celeste and to the proposals of Falcoia which apparently suggested immediate action were totally predictable; he would have to submit the whole matter to the decision of his spiritual director, Father Pagano. His initial reluctance to commit himself disappointed Falcoia even though it should not have surprised him. But he kept up pressure for a favourable reply by a letter addressed to Alphonsus at the end of November but meant more for Pagano and Ripa:

My dear Son in the Lord,

The Lord wants you, yes, He has chosen you as the foundation stone of this new edifice. I cannot imagine what reason you can have for doubting this. Doesn't your own instinct tell you? Doesn't your own inclination to embrace with courage all that is most repugnant to flesh and blood and to follow the Master who leads you on, convince you? Can these inspirations have any other source than the Holy Spirit since they are so opposed to the appetites of the Old Adam and so much in conformity with the spirit of the New, who, by way of example has Himself done so much and suffered so much for us? Enough! . . .

Salute dear Don Matteo (Ripa) warmly for me. Ask him to regard as confidential what he knows about this matter but tell him with complete confidence whatever he wishes to know since we are one, as it were, in heart and soul, wishing nothing more than the greater glory of God and the fulfilment of His divine Will. At the same time secrecy is essential lest we open a way for the devil. . . . [9]

Pagano's reaction to the whole scheme was cool, to say the least. He was sceptical about the revelations, dismissive about establishing another missionary organisation to add to the plethora already in existence. Like many more in Naples he had hoped that he had heard the last from the 'visionary' or maybe even the *impostrice* from Scala. His verdict was for Alphonsus to forget about Scala and return to his mission work, a reaction matched by that of Canon Torni.

– II –

The missionary situation proved providential. In March 1731 a severe earthquake devasted the south eastern coast of the kingdom of Naples; the culmination of a week of terror was the virtual destruction of the city of Foggia where according to contemporary accounts more than three thousand people lost their lives. In the autumn, when conditions became somewhat more normal, the bishops of the region decided to profit by what they considered a chastisement from God, to bring their flock back to repentance. For this purpose they petitioned the Apostolic Missions to send them groups of missionaries. Profiting by the situation to get Alphonsus as far away as possible from Scala, Torni assigned him to open the campaign in the city of Nardo in the province of Lecce at the furthermost southern tip of Italy. The bishop was Mons. Antonio Sanfelice, a former member of the Apostolic Missions whom Alphonsus later held up to the bishops of the Kingdom as a model for their imitation.[10]

Besides the series of sermons to the people of Nardo and the surrounding area as far as Copertino, Alphonsus gave the spiritual exercises to the various religious communities, the Poor Clares and the Carmelites being the special objects of his attention. On one occasion he travelled some twenty miles from Copertino to Nardo to console a nun suffering with spiritual difficulties. From Nardo he went on to Polignano à Mare on the Adriatic coast some miles south of Bari; having concluded the mission there he continued on up the coast to Foggia, then in the process of reconstruction. His visit was something in the nature of a homecoming since his uncle, Mons. Emilio Cavalieri had been bishop of the diocese. The actual incumbent, Mons. Faccolli received him with great respect and asked him to preach a novena in honour of the Mother of God under the title of Our Lady of the Seven Veils. This miraculous Icon of Byzantine origin had been saved from the ruins of the cathedral during the earthquake. It was the most treasured possession of the people who had venerated it for centuries and had risked their lives to save it from the fury of the Iconoclasts. Painted on wood, the picture had suffered so much from the ravages of time that it was encased in silver, leaving only the face of the Madonna still visible, and this was covered by seven veils to protect it; thus the Icon came to be called the Madonna of the Seven Veils. After the destruction of the cathedral during the earthquake, the miraculous picture was taken to a temporary church on the outskirts of the city where it was the scene of fervent manifestations of piety on the part of the shocked citizens.

In the midst of the crowds it was noticed that the face of the Madonna, though completely covered by the veils, began to appear to many who prayed before the picture. This was taken as a sign of Our Lady's favour and an indication that the chastisements of God were at an end and that the Mother of God still protected her children. Crowds flocked in pilgrimage to venerate the Icon, a fact which encouraged the bishop to take advantage of the occasion to preach a Novena by way of mission.

The miraculous picture was brought from its temporary sanctuary to the church of San Giovanni, the least damaged by the earthquake and there Alphonsus began his course of sermons. He preached with great vigour against the licentiousness of the city which had drawn down the chastisement of God on his people. One night towards the end of his sermon the congregation noticed that he appeared to fall into some form of trance or ecstasy with rays of light from the oval of the picture shining on his countenance. The effect upon the people of the city can be imagined, with the result that they flocked to the confessionals. The bishop set up a tribunal to enquire into the event and the following year sent his report to Rome to the Congregation of the Council:

> After mature examination of the facts and out of respect for the truth and having taken the advice of learned men I have come to the conclusion that the Mother of God really appeared for the consolation of her children and to protect her people. Accordingly at the request of the Chapter of the Cathedral, of the clergy and of the faithful of this city I have declared the 23rd March a holyday of obligation in the city in memory of this remarkable appearance of the Mother of God.[11]

Alphonsus was asked for his testimony forty-five years later in 1777 when the cathedral Chapter wished to have the Icon solemnly crowned:

> Alphonsus Maria de Liguori, bishop of St Agatha of the Goths and Superior General of the Congregation of the Most Holy Redeemer certifies under oath that in the year 1732 while preaching in the church of San Giovanni on several occasions and on different days the countenance of the Blessed Virgin appeared in the oval of the picture even though it was covered by a black veil.
>
> Her countenance seemed to be that of a young girl of some thirteen or fourteen years and covered with a white head scarf. She moved her face from side to side. And I add with deep devotion, consolation of spirit and with tears of tenderness, I noticed that the face appeared to be sculptured and in relief and not painted. At the same time that I saw this all the congregation who were present for the sermon saw it

too and recommended themselves to the Mother of God with ardent prayer and floods of tears.[12]

From Foggia Alphonsus went on pilgrimage to Monte Sant' Angelo, the shrine in honour of the archangel Michael on Monte Gargano, about forty kilometres from the city. He refused an invitation from the bishop of Manfredonia and the canons of the sanctuary to preach both in Manfredonia and in the sanctuary itself. In the black cave set aside as a place of devotion to the Archangel since the end of the fifth century he celebrated Mass, perhaps praying not merely for light and guidance but for courage and strength in the execution of the project which was beginning to take shape in his mind. St Michael became one of the principal protectors of his new missionary congregation. When he later secured what was to become the central house at Pagani he placed it under the protection of St Michael.

His reception in Naples on his return from Foggia was distinctly cool; this was the occasion of the public reprimand. The Apostolic Missions latched on to the fact that he had undertaken the preaching engagement in Foggia without authorisation from Naples — a totally unreasonable attitude since communication between the capital and Foggia was not possible within the time available. Nor would the reports of more apparitions and visions, this time in Foggia, have helped. But the real reason at the back of Torni's ill-humour was the fact that rumours of the new missionary society were now circulating freely throughout the city. In the three months since Alphonsus' departure for Nardo, Falcoia's efforts to keep the matter secret had failed and while there was no formal announcement concerning what was contemplated, there was no mistaking the fact that plans to establish a new religious group were in hand.

The five months from October 1731 to March 1732 had in a remarkable way been decisive in the evolution of Alphonsus' attitude to the call from Scala. On his own, away from the influence of Falcoia and out of the shadow of Pagano, he had decided — or, at least, allowed himself to be convinced — that his future lay with some new missionary initiative for the purpose of preaching the Gospel in the spiritually neglected areas of the Kingdom of Naples. It was all still very nebulous; no House, no Rule, no formalised missionary orientation, no confirmed companions. All he had to go on were the account of the so-called revelations of 1725, the incomplete draft of a Rule for Sisters, and finally an outline concerning the new congregation of men drawn up by Celeste after her mystical experiences in October. But he was sufficiently certain of what the future held for him to discuss with Mons. Constantino Vigilante, bishop of Caiazzo in April 1732 the possibility of making a foundation in his diocese when the time came. The bishop promised his full support even to the extent of indicating a suitable church and building for the missionary foundation.

There had been a change too in the attitude of Father Pagano, as welcome as it was unexpected. He too now believed that the work was 'destined to give great glory to God and to be of great benefit to souls'.[13] With his permission Alphonsus widened his consultation. His first contact was with Father Cutica at the Vincentians; he approved without hesitation. Father Manulio, the Jesuit Provincial-elect, and Father — now saint — Giovanni Giuseppe della Croce, the Franciscan, both declared the work to be from God. The main opposition was centred in the Apostolic Missions where Canon Torni and the President of the seminary, Alphonsus' own relation, Canon Pietro Gizzio, united their considerable influence against the undertaking. The root of the problem lay in the mutual jealousy existing for years between the members of the Apostolic Missions and the Society of the Pii Operai to which Falcoia belonged, rather than in any personal animosity towards Alphonsus. A new missionary society, taking its direction from Falcoia of the Pii Operai, with its implied criticism of the inadequacy of the Apostolic Missions, together with 'poaching' one of its leading members, seemed to be gratuitously insulting. The opposition concentrated its attack on three points, the absurdity of establishing yet another missionary society, the outrageous new habit of red and blue and above all the fact that it was all due to the hallucinations of a neurotic nun — revelations at any time, but particularly when they come from a nun, seem to have a decidedly infuriating effect on the established clerical world. Alphonsus was laughed at, branded as proud and self-willed. The Neapolitans had a colourful variety of invective to draw on, all of which figured in their condemnations; he was 'mad, crazy, obstinate, fanatical, obsessed, deluded, vainglorious, wanting to make a name for himself, arrogant, conceited, full of himself, mentally unbalanced, got it into his head to play the founder, out of his senses, under the influence of a deluded nun'.[14]

While internally Alphonsus continued to suffer agonies of doubt and indecision, externally he adopted a simple line of defence which he maintained persistently in the face of every insult and calumny about his involvement in the new missionary society being mooted for Scala. He was definitely not going there in response to the revelations of a nun; he was not going there out of any personal vanity or ambition to play the founder. He was not even going there out of personal choice but only after advice from every spiritual guide whose power of discernment he was able to enlist in finding out what was the will of God in the matter. To counteract this claim, Canon Gizzio, who had emerged as the main stumbling block, challenged Alphonsus to submit the whole matter to the consideration of his own confessor, Father Luigi Fiorillo, a Dominican attached to the community of San Domenico Maggiore. With the consent of Pagano, Alphonsus agreed to submit the matter to yet another judge. Fiorillo's first reaction was to confirm Alphonsus' own intuition that the Lord was asking more of him than just spending his life in the Chinese College. With a combined sense of history and Dominican loyalty he urged Alphonsus to pray to St Vincent Ferrer, O.P., the greatest missionary after the Apostles, but reminded him at the same time that his other fellow Dominican, St Luigi Bertrand, had asked St Teresa of Avila for six months to consider his verdict on her proposed reform of Carmel, and he requested the same himself. Alphonsus was prepared to give him as long as he wished.

Within a few weeks Fiorillo returned with his verdict. 'The work you have in mind is a work of God. Just as a stone falling down a mountain descends into a valley so place your plans in the hands of God. You will experience persecutions but do not let that frighten you. Persevere until you complete the work; God will be your support.' Alphonsus insisted on the verdict in writing, which he got, but Fiorillo stipulated that since the clerical climate was so paranoid about the new institute, his verdict was not to be quoted in public or attributed to him lest he too should experience some of the opprobrium the whole affair evoked. Alphonsus would have to be content with communicating it in confidence to Pagano and Falcoia. But Fiorillo's opinion was now such a vital link in the whole chain of decision that Pagano felt the obligation of secrecy imposed by Fiorillo unreasonable and that it should yield to other considerations. So too did other theologians he consulted, with the result that he allowed Alphonsus to confront both Gizzio and Torni with the judgment of their own chosen expert. True to his word Torni ceased his opposition and defended his colleague's action with the other members of the society and above all with the Cardinal. Gizzio was still sceptical.[15]

Alphonsus had also to face the opposition of Matteo Ripa in the Chinese College. Ripa had been in Rome for most of 1732 negotiating final pontifical approval for his Chinese Mission and was mainly uninformed about events in Naples. At the end of July he returned to find the clerical world alive with gossip; Cajetan, Alphonsus' brother, was the first to intimate to him what was being contemplated. He felt totally aggrieved that he had been kept in the dark about the whole matter and not a little sore that those on whom he had counted for support were being snatched away from under his very eyes, 'taken in by the alluring novelty of so-called visions', as he put it. While he was canvassing the Curia in Rome for support, his friends in Naples were sabotaging his work at its source. He confronted Alphonsus:

> I attempted to dissuade Don Alphonsus from this undertaking by pointing out that he should not abandon the certain good he was doing in our House and Church — a work approved by the Pope — for the doubtful good he hoped to achieve in a new institute.
>
> I further asked him to consider the positive harm be was inflicting on the College by leaving it and taking with him Don Vincenzo Mannarini. If Mons. Falcoia wished to establish a new society let him do so without disturbing our peace and quiet. And finally I pointed out that since the purpose of the new institute was preaching and teaching in schools he could find all that and more in our society. Since our aim was to spread the Faith to the ultimate ends of the earth and set up schools for pagans it did not seem at all a reasonable course of action to leave us with two others and take his chance with Mons. Falcoia.
>
> However despite all my arguments he remained fixed in his purpose insisting that he was certain this was his vocation.[16]

But he kept his strongest protests for Falcoia who for years had been his spiritual director and friend. He blamed everything on him. The bonds of friendship between them were broken never to be re-established. His letter to the bishop who at the time was on vacation in Ischia 'taking the waters', was angry and bitter. Falcoia replied at great length pointing out that it was not the spiritual director who gave each his vocation. That is the prerogative of Divine Providence. The spiritual director's function is only to approve or reject as the case may be. Angrily he rejected any insinuation that he was undermining Ripa's work. Rather ingenuously he disclaimed all responsibility for Alphonsus' decision — who was, in fact, merely following the path of obedience to his spiritual director, Pagano.

The protests, recriminations and torrents of abuse had reached a climax during mid-summer; towards the end of August the tempest abated and word went round that Alphonsus had altered his decision. The news was a great relief to Falcoia who suggested to Alphonsus that he should do nothing to contradict the rumour. If asked he was to pretend that he was not informed of what was happening since Falcoia had full charge and kept everything to himself. The stratagem of deception could be justified by Our Lord's own action when he pretended to the companions on the road to Emmaus 'that he was going on further' — *Jesus finxit longius ire*. The artificial calm would allow final preparations for the establishing of the group in Scala to proceed undisturbed.

– III –

During the interminable discussions of the last year, since Maria Celeste's revelations in October 1731, Pagano had come to realise that an impossible situation was developing in the matter of his relationship with Alphonsus, who was coming more and more under the influence of Falcoia. Every proposal emanating from Falcoia in connection with the new missionary project was submitted to Pagano for confirmation; without his *placet* Alphonsus refused to act. The position was becoming intolerable, so Pagano now proposed that Alphonsus should put an end to this anomalous situation by taking Falcoia as his spiritual director. The proposal was first discussed with and then approved by Father Fiorillo who was becoming more and more the final court of appeal. Alphonsus was assured this was a prudent step to take. The change took place in August 1732 when Alphonsus formally placed himself under obedience to the bishop, binding himself at first to follow his directions in everything, though later on he was to make certain significant exclusions; for the moment Falcoia was his father and director in every aspect of his life and conduct. The final decision was made at a personal meeting in Ischia from where Falcoia wrote: 'I have received you as my spiritual son and I formally confirm the contract. And I will continue to confirm it with every breath I take.' For the first time he concluded his letter familiarly, 'I remain, your most cordial Father, Thomas, Bishop.' On the margin of the letter Alphonsus wrote, 'accepted as son. Depend in everything on Falcoia who has accepted you as his son.'[17]

Alphonsus was now to look to Falcoia for guidance not alone in the matter of establishing the new missionary institute and everything concerned with it, foundations, recruitment, acceptance of mission engagements, but also in the direction of his conscience which had been under the guidance of Pagano for nearly thirty years. The change proved traumatic, opening up another area of scruples. Was Falcoia *really* his spiritual director? What about the directions already received from Pagano? The whole process of alleviating his fears and establishing norms of conduct had to be repeated. First of all Pagano made it clear that all his past directions remained in force and *for ever*, to avoid any doubt. Nothing in the change-over cancelled the norms already imposed. Obedience to Falcoia was restricted to the future and his new vocation, but did not cover the past. Falcoia too confirmed once and for all everything that Pagano had laid down, no matter whether or not he was aware what these directions were. Both his directors united in laying it down that he was never again to call into question the fact that the bishop was now his spiritual director though there is no indication what the source of the doubt was. Repeated entries in Alphonsus' personal notebook indicate how deeply the change had disturbed his conscience. A new name appears for the first time among the list of those he consulted, one Don Biase Bovis; fortunately he too had the good sense to endorse all the decisions taken. An entry tells its own story and needs no commentary: 'Today 30 August 1732. The decision confirmed with the advice of Don Biase Bovis, "to depend in everything on Falcoia who has already accepted you as his son . . . *obedience not to think any more about it or to doubt that Falcoia is my director* . . . Right! . . . Obedience not to doubt any more."'[18] But of course, the doubts did recur and demanded repeated reassurances. Wisely, however, the change did not imply the total exclusion of the gentle Father Pagano. Alphonsus continued to meet him, discuss doubts and problems with him, the main difference being that the final decision now lay with Falcoia.

– IV –

Restored to health after his annual summer cure in Ischia, Falcoia returned to Scala determined to get the new missionary group under way without further delay; there had been enough consultation. Alphonsus, he decided, should remain in Naples and continue to take part in the activities of the Apostolic Missions until the very last moment. He had been appointed the previous year to conduct the annual clergy retreat in October, a major assignment, and he had to be present for the city mission which followed immediately. So the date for Alphonsus' arrival in Scala was fixed for the first few days of November; Mannarini and Giovanni de Donato, candidates for the new congregation, would take his place in preaching the novena in Scala for the feast of the Holy Cross. In the meantime Falcoia busied himself about a site for the new foundation in or around Scala. Santa Maria della Neve did not appeal to him, Pontone with its small church attached had a lot to recommend it but lacked adequate accommodation, while both locations would involve considerable financial outlay. The other possibility was a house on the street in Scala itself, bought by the nuns as accommodation for priests who came to preach their retreats; an adjacent house would allow for expansion. Alphonsus was instructed to discuss the merits of the sites with companions and make a rough calculation regarding what capital would be available. Though Falcoia was in favour of Pontone, the outcome was the decision to avail of the sisters' house, via Torricella, 21, as a temporary expedient. The entrance led to five rooms at street level, three of them quite small; a stairs led down to the basement where there was a kitchen and two further rooms. With the house went a small garden consisting of three tiered squares of land, planted with figs and other fruit trees. A path along the side of the hill led down some steps to large fissures or caves in the rocks, one of which was used by Alphonsus as a hermitage where he prayed and performed his penances. Such was the unimposing start to Alphonsus' new missionary initiative, at least as far as accommodation was concerned. One thing the house did possess was an enchanting view of Ravello across the valley and a breathtakingly beautiful panorama through the Dragone Gorge right down to the sea at Amalfi.

The calibre of his first four associates, Mannarini, de Donato, Romano and Tosques equally left a lot to be desired. While Mannarini and Romano both lacked that total commitment the undertaking required, the other two were more dangerously flawed. De Donato was a restless priest typical of the Neapolitan clerical world at the time, while Tosques was a spiritual conman with an unlimited capacity for disrupting any undertaking into which he talked his way. Mannarini was aware of the content of the revelations in Scala in October 1731; early the following year Alphonsus had confided to him in the Chinese College his intention of undertaking a new missionary initiative inspired by their experiences with the goatherds of Santa Maria dei Monti. He was thirty-two years of age at the time, having been born in the diocese of Rossano in Calabria; cultured and devout, he became an admirer and follower of Ripa whose society he joined. When Ripa was absent from the college, Mannarini was left in charge. Ripa was outraged when his protégé informed him of his intention of leaving the Chinese College and joining Alphonsus in his missionary work. He rebuked Mannarini in no uncertain terms, insisted he make the spiritual exercises to discern fully the depths of his infidelity, and when Mannarini, with the advice of his spiritual director, persisted in his decision Ripa had him formally expelled from his society.

Pietro Romano was a native of Scala; ordained a priest he became soon afterwards a canon of the cathedral chapter. He acquired a reputation as a sound theologian or at least sufficiently proficient to exercise the ministry of the confessional. He was a spiritual son of Bishop Falcoia whom he had chosen as his director of conscience when Falcoia preached his first mission in the cathedral. As ordinary confessor of the sisters in the convent he was acquainted with the whole development first of the convent itself and then of the new missionary society for men. He more or less considered himself a member of the new body even before it came into existence and was accepted as such even though he did not leave his home in the village where he lived with his married brother, nephews and nieces. He preached several missions with Alphonsus but the new missionary society was never his first priority; when the group finally left Scala in 1738 he remained behind and took no further part in the growth of the congregation.

Father Giovanni de Donato was the oldest of the four, being in his early fifties; he suddenly appeared among the group as if from nowhere. Like Mannarini, he too was from Calabria and his arrival in Naples should have aroused suspicions at least in ecclesiastical circles where unattached clerics from the provinces had an unenviable reputation. He was already a member of a clerical missionary group in his native town of Rende not far from Cosenza in Calabria, known as the Missionaries of the Most Blessed Sacrament. In 1724, guided by their director, the Jesuit, Father Nicholas Fragiorgi, the society opened a house in Teano, north of Capua and well within striking distance of Naples. The death of Father Fragiorgi in 1731 left the society in some disarray and when the news of a new missionary group with Alphonsus at its head reached Donato — though the whole project was still meant to be a great secret — he disbanded his companions sending them back to Calabria, and arrived in Naples determined to join. His motives would appear to have been a mixture of missionary adventure and a search for further experiences since, at the same time that he left Teano for Naples and ultimately Scala, he wrote to the colleagues he had dispersed assuring them of his return to take up the work again. Falcoia, be it said to his credit, was immediately suspicious. Why should Donato wish to leave his own society which was apparently doing good work? Why make the change? 'I have my suspicions,' wrote Falcoia, 'that there is something more behind all this.' Nor was he convinced when Donato sent him a copy of his society's Rules. Finally he asked Alphonsus to interview the new candidate himself in Naples, warning him to spare no effort to get to the full truth in the matter. We have no record of the interview but the upshot was that Alphonsus accepted the new candidate and sent him on to Scala with Mannarini to preach the novena of the Holy Cross while he was himself detained in the capital. The first two priest members of the new society to arrive in Scala were, as a result, Mannarini and Donato, neither of whom remained beyond a few months. As it turned out it is impossible to determine whether they were not in fact endeavouring to recruit Alphonsus for their plans rather than he recruiting them for his.

If Alphonsus' powers of discernment failed him with regard to Donato, they abandoned him completely in his judgment of Silvestro Tosques, a plausible but dangerous adventurer in the classical mould. Tosques or Tosquez, and sometimes even Tozquez, was from Troia about twenty kilometres from Foggia in the direction of Bovino. The family, he claimed — and one must always suspect anything Don Silvestro claimed in this connection — had been ennobled by Charles V when the Emperor ruled the Kingdom of Naples. Francis Tosques, his brother, after his education in Rome, went to the imperial court in Vienna where he occupied several influential posts in the service of the Austro-Hispano government. In due course, as was only to be expected, he summoned his brother to join him. Silvestro in the meantime had developed a remarkable talent for talking spirituality; to crown it all he claimed to possess mystical gifts. In Vienna while recovering from an illness he was inspired to found a new religious order to imitate as closely as possible the life of Our Lord and his Apostles — that was one of the least of his outrageous claims. The inspiration, however, did not prevent him from accepting an appointment to Naples as Chief Superintendent of Imperial Customs, as a result of his brother's influence at Court. It was a lucrative post in itself but more attractively, held untold possibilities for personal aggrandisement. He did, in fact, whether by fair means or foul we can only surmise, become a man of considerable wealth which stood him in good stead in his ecclesiastical adventures which were now to begin in earnest. In Naples his mystical charisms blossomed rapidly. Even among the Neapolitans, no mean practitioners themselves, his glibness of tongue and his faculty for fantasising were a constant source of amazement. He was, as an observer summed it up, *dotato di una meravigliosa natural facondia*.[19] He cultivated in a special way the Carmelite Fathers near whom he lived and then gradually insinuated himself into the ecclesiastical world of the city. His greatest conquest was the gentle but entirely gullible Mannarini.

During his retreat in preparation for the feast of Pentecost which fell that year on 31 May, Mannarini felt the silence and prayer so oppressive that he slipped out from the College to go for a short walk. It proved a costly error, for near the Carmelite church he encountered Tosques who was at his most voluble and ingratiating. Mannarini was impressed by Tosques in the first place as somebody of importance, *una persona di qualità*. Tosques enthralled him with his story, how in Vienna in the imperial service he had felt that call to leave all and 'give himself to God', how he had felt inspired to establish a new religious order based on the imitation of the Most Holy Saviour and the Apostles, corresponding virtually in every detail to what was envisaged by Celeste at Scala; even the habit, seen by Tosques in his 'vision' was similar. Instead of being suspicious Mannarini was deeply affected; his own determination, wavering before the onslaught of Ripa, was now confirmed. Following on this encounter Mannarini introduced Tosques to Alphonsus and another friend who was also considering joining, one Don Cesare Sportelli. The upshot was that Tosques betook himself hot-foot to Castellamare where his story enraptured Falcoia. The account of his life, the aspirations of his youth for a religious order, so impressed the bishop that he gave his permission to visit Scala to interview the sisters who had been the recipients of the special revelations concerning the new order. It was the crowning indiscretion, as we shall see. Afterwards as he rued the havoc wrought by Don Silvestro (Tosques), Falcoia declared that his intention in thus introducing Tosques to the sisters had been to allow him to experience authentic holiness of life at close quarters. If he imagined that Don Silvestro would be satisfied with merely being on the receiving end of edification, the bishop was sadly mistaken; Tosques planned a much more active role for himself in the affairs of the convent and in particular in relation to Maria Celeste.

Tosques continued his all-conquering way with the new bishop of Scala. Mons. Guerriero had died in April 1732 to be succeeded in June of the same year by Mons. Antonio Santoro, auxiliary to Cardinal Albani in the diocese of Santa Sabina. Alphonsus, on instructions from Falcoia, paid his respects to the bishop as he passed through Naples en route to Scala; much would depend on his attitude both to the convent and to Falcoia's proposals for a new missionary society. Despite the unfavourable publicity surrounding the combined enterprise, Santoro, who was himself a religious, was content to continue the benign attitude of his predecessor and at this stage made no difficulty about his brother bishop from the neighbouring diocese of Castellamare operating in his jurisdiction. Despite his experience on the Roman scene he too fell under the spell of Tosques. He may well have been impressed by Tosques's fantasies concerning his influence with the Austrian Viceroy in Naples and his connections with the Imperial Court in Vienna, all of which Don Silvestro would have adduced to advance his standing.

Tosques remained for a whole month in Scala during which time he put on a star performance. Far from restricting his visit to a search for edification as Falcoia had fondly imagined, he began to interfere in every detail of the sisters' lives, sweeping them off their feet with torrents of spirituality. He made sure to be seen in the public chapel of the convent motionless in prayer, hands joined, his eyes closed; at appropriate times he was observed to burst into tears. With the nuns at the enclosure grille he discoursed at length on the various stages of prayer, regaling his hearers at times with the details of his own communications with the Lord. Theatrical to the last he publicly professed himself a great sinner worthy of the Lord's anger. Falcoia came to preach a retreat to the sisters while he was there. Called away unexpectedly he incredibly commissioned Tosques to replace him which despite his protestations he did, preaching dramatically one day on Death, the other on the virtue of Charity. The nuns were in a state of near exaltation and Tosques crowned the whole performance by eliciting from the bishop a promise to grant a formal diocesan approval to Crostarosa's Rule. He was the next thing to a heaven-sent Messiah.

Back in Naples in his Customs Office, he announced to all and sundry his intention of offering himself as a candidate for the new missionary congregation—a complication it could well have done without. Ripa in the Chinese College could not contain his anger when he heard the news since for some reason or other he too had been led to believe that Tosques would join him. In a few months he would realise what a narrow escape he had.

– V –

Alphonsus did not return to Scala again after November 1731 when Celeste had communicated her revelations to him until he left Naples finally a year later; he was, as we have seen, totally occupied in the meantime with missions on the one hand and consultations about his future on the other. Maria Celeste, however, kept up a regular correspondence to which he faithfully replied. She was well informed about his missionary engagements, timing her letters to reach him each time on his return to Naples. She was worried that he was overdoing things: 'Father, for goodness sake why are you testing your strength with such an amount of work. Please, not so much or the donkey will collapse under the burden. Take things a little easier since the Lord does not demand so much of you.' She wished with all her heart to see him and to have his advice in her spiritual problems which she could not commit to writing. She was praying for him day and night since even in her dreams she recommended him to the Lord. Moreover, she sent him the promised outline of her revelations concerning the new congregation, no copy of which has survived. What would the biographer of Alphonsus not give for a glance at this document in Celeste's handwriting and in her phonetic and dialect spelling which Alphonsus must have had with him during 1732 as he agonised over his future. She wrote to him even while confined to bed under doctor's care, dejected that he had not been able to respond to her requests to come to visit. One recurring theme was her increasing disillusionment with bishop Falcoia as her director; the signs of an imminent rupture between them and the implied invitation to Alphonsus to replace him were obvious.[20]

In the spring of 1732, the vicar of the convent, Sister Columba whose mystical gifts and insights about the new institute ran parallel with Celeste's, wrote to him on his return to Naples from Foggia of her longing to see him assume command of the fresh onslaught on the powers of evil which the new institute would spearhead. She had heard that he was suffering considerably as he struggled to make up his mind. She, however had no doubts:

> No more hesitation; the Lord is with you. He has chosen you for this work for His greater glory. He will be your master and guide. Do not fear. Our dear Lady and Mother, Mary, has you in her thoughts and under her care. She loves you. Why then are you afraid? Courage! Courage! dear Father. You will do great things for the glory of God. The Lord Himself will give you good companions. He Himself has assured me that He wishes to make you all living images of His holy life. No more hesitations. Fill your hearts with confidence. The greater your confidence the more you will do for the glory of God. Love Himself has marked you and your companions with a special seal.[21]

Easter came and with it the appropriate greetings from Celeste, full of mystical references: 'During these days [of Holy Week] let us sit together in the shade of my Jesus in Whom you are to be seen.' She asked him to pray earnestly to her Divine Spouse that she would obtain the grace of true humility — the irony of which will be obvious in the light of what followed between herself and Alphonsus. And she concluded her letter by signing herself his unworthy daughter in the Lord.[22] And then the whole picture changes. Don Silvestro, the Superintendent of Imperial Customs, arrives, in search of edification. Maria Celeste was completely taken in. The tone of her letters to Alphonsus altered perceptibly. She boasted that she had not been mistaken in her initial assessment of Don Silvestro, as — according to her — Alphonsus had been. It was now abundantly clear to her who would take over from Falcoia concerning the affairs of the convent; there was no need for further discernment since the Lord Himself had seen to it by sending Tosques along. And he could also act as adviser to Alphonsus in drawing up the new Constitutions and even as his spiritual guide in matters of conscience. In a mood of exaltation she asked theorically why would God have heaped such an accumulation of charisms on just one person, only a portion of which were required for his own sanctification, were it not that he was destined to employ them for the benefit of others. Her tone was domineering, peremptory, even arrogant. She had lost her balance of judgment completely. She concluded with a flourish, omitting for the first time her customary professions of humility and the protocol of requesting a blessing, signing herself 'in haste, in the heart of Jesus, Celeste'. Sister Columba showed herself to be altogether wiser and more mature in her assessment of the situation following on Tosques's arrival. Despite her efforts not to be uncharitable, her message was clear:

> I really do think that Don Silvestro must be very dear to Our Divine Lord. At the same time he is somewhat attached to his own opinion, but this defect, will, I hope, be overcome. Nobody, however perfect, is free from faults. And Our Lord does not always make known to His servants directly their shortcomings but allows them in his wisdom to be pointed out to them by others so that they may remain humble and with a low opinion of themselves and realise that they need correction.[23]

Alphonsus was deeply offended by the tone of Celeste's letters during these summer months after the visit of Tosques to the convent. He was shocked at her arrogance and resented the insinuations her letters contained. He wrote at once to the superior and then a long letter to Celeste in which he took her severely to task. Only a Neapolitan could have written it; only a Neapolitan would have accepted it:

My dear Celeste,

> A veritable dagger has entered my heart. It has deprived me of sleep, and it is all on account of you. During all these months in which there have been differences between us, you have not written one word to me in a spirit of genuine humility. In your last letter in particular I noticed how you addressed me, how you signed yourself and the clear indications you gave that you did not care one way or the other whether I believed you or not. You did not even say that you would pray for me — as if I were a reprobate! And then you concluded with 'I remain in the Heart of Jesus'. Celeste, is there any way less humble than that for even the most imperfect soul to write to me?

> I do not believe that you harbour a grudge against me, but from the manner in which you wrote, so different from your past letters, I am beginning to think that you do. I am not saying that I deserve that you should humble yourself before me; I confess that I am unworthy to kneel at your feet because I know what my life is like and what yours is. However, for all this, I have not given up hope of loving Jesus as you do, through His Infinite Mercy to me. But I do say that I expected to see and experience a greater depth of humility in a soul so united with God and so favoured by Him as you are.

And so the letter rambles on at length with torrents of reproaches on one hand mixed with sentiments of deeply felt disappointment on the other. Reprimands are softened by praise of the graces she has received from God. His insistence on her lack of humility is balanced by asking her pardon if he has overstepped the mark in what he has written. With Falcoia's permission he would even be willing to beg her pardon on his knees. Only on one thing was he adamant; he denied that he had ever said that Tosques was deluded — and he would have been correct if he had. He promised to pray for Celeste each morning at Mass that the Lord would grant her genuine humility. And he concluded dramatically by saying: 'I am not calling you daughter so that you cannot accuse me of laying claim to that which I have no right to. Viva Gesù, Maria, Joseph and Teresa.'[24]

This certainly was not a 'normal' letter in the accepted sense of the word; clearly Alphonsus was in a highly nervous and emotional state when he wrote it, even allowing for all the natural effusiveness of the Neapolitan temperament. In point of fact he was within a few weeks of leaving Naples for Scala, back in the family home and subject to enormous pressures from all sides to which were now added the final efforts of his father, Don Joseph to get him to change his mind. He was fortunate to preserve his mental balance in the midst of it all.

– VI –

Bishop Falcoia took up residence in Scala towards the end of August 1732 to make arrangements for the inauguration of the new missionary institute. His first problem was to re-establish his authority among the sisters after the disturbance caused by Tosques's visit. Then the first members of the new congregation began to arrive, Mannarini, de Donato and inevitably Tosques; they had to be settled into their new quarters in the hospice of the sisters and organised into some sort of community and provided with pastoral work to keep them occupied. On 12 September he wrote to Alphonsus in Naples giving his assessment of the situation. All was now peaceful in the convent; he had Maria Celeste under control — '*ho Suor Maria Celeste all'mano*'. If only he had known! Donato, as the senior, was regarded as superior in some indeterminate manner and was doing good work pastorally. Some rough corners on Don Silvestro were yielding to the 'oil of charity and patience' and at the moment he was behaving himself. But Falcoia sensed already the potential for disagreement and he begged Alphonsus to make a special effort on his arrival to see eye to eye with Tosques. More importantly he had to report remarkable happenings in the nuns' chapel. On Thursday 11 September during the period of weekly exposition of the Blessed Sacrament, the outline of a hill, surmounted by a cross, appeared on the Sacred Host. The cross, dark in colour at first, turned to red and the instruments of the Passion appeared. There were other signs in the Host as well, which were witnessed by the assembled sisters and their chaplain, Canon Romano. While they all reported seeing more or less the same general picture they differed somewhat on specific details of the apparitions. Terrified initially, the sisters subsequently experienced great consolation and were unanimous in interpreting what they had seen to Falcoia and Santoro as heavenly confirmation of the work of the double institute of sisters and missionaries. Prudently Falcoia warned Alphonsus that this latest occurrence in the convent should be kept secret; reports of further revelations and supernatural signs were the last thing the new institute would have wanted to reach the ears of the Naples clergy. The news, however, Falcoia hoped, would sustain Alphonsus as he struggled alone in Naples with his doubts in the matter of his vocation.[25]

As the date for his departure for Scala approached, Alphonsus left the Chinese College to return home; Ripa's anger at what was happening would certainly have been a factor in the decision. Home was certainly not entirely undisturbed either, since he had to face the opposition of his family and in particular of his father. Even though Scala was less than one hundred miles from Naples, such a separation made severe demands on family affection. But beneath the objections from that source there were other motives for Don Joseph's attitude. He had never really accepted the fact that Alphonsus was to remain a simple priest all his life; from the very outset he had set his sights firmly on a bishopric for him. He made influential contacts and discussed the matter several times with Alphonsus himself — only in later years did he desist when Alphonsus finally took him severely to task. The reports of his son's success as a missioner would not in any way have prejudiced his prospects. Quite the contrary, since success in the Apostolic Missions was the normal avenue to episcopal promotion. But to abandon Naples and take himself off to as remote a village as Scala on a hare-brained expedition as a result of a neurotic nun's revelations was the height of folly. All these emotions were mingled in Don Joseph as he attempted to dissuade Alphonsus from his decision. He first approached the Cardinal but found he had no canonical authority to intervene since Alphonsus was not one of his beneficed clergy. He then faced his son directly; he played on every possible human feeling in a hysterical scene which lasted for three hours. According to one account Alphonsus was confined to bed at the time and his father threw himself down beside him, embracing him and weeping uncontrollably. Even though he was thirty-six at the time the experience was one of the most traumatic Alphonsus ever had to endure. The memory of it remained with him all his life; it was an incident about which he was totally reticent when he shared at times the story of his life with his confreres. When he recounted it near the end of his life to his trusted friend Father Villani, his embarrassment was so acute as the memories flooded back that he bound him to absolute secrecy. Only after his death did Villani reveal what he had learnt.[26]

Alphonsus began the retreat to the priests of the Apostolic Missions on 16 October. The attendance was exceptional. The clerical students were present each day; two bishops also made the retreat while Cardinal Pignatelli was present on three occasions. His presence, which was out of the normal run of things, was mainly symbolical; he wished to signal that he was distancing himself from those among the clergy who had publicly ridiculed Alphonsus and his missionary project. The retreat was a particular ordeal for Alphonsus since he could not rely on the sympathy of his audience. On the second last day of the retreat he wrote to Falcoia begging for the command to set out for Scala and begging to be relieved of the obligation of remaining on longer in Naples. Somehow he survived the eight days of the retreat and then took part in the usual city mission which opened in the basilica of the Holy Spirit on the twenty-fifth. He preached on the morning of the twenty-ninth, on the thirtieth he gave the *sentimenti* through the streets, and his presence was also registered in the basilica on the morning of 2 November. The following day, without taking formal leave of the Cardinal, he left almost furtively for Scala.[27]

There is good reason to believe that he was not alone. His friend Father Giovanni Mazzini may have accompanied him; a new figure in his life, Don Cesare Sportelli, certainly did. But their presence was more an earnest for the future than anything else. Mazzini had hoped to be one of Alphonsus' first companions but his director resolutely opposed his joining the new group. But by his presence he wished to assure Alphonsus that he could at least rely on him when his director relented, which he did only after some years. Even more symbolic was the presence of Sportelli, a layman, but a totally different proposition, fortunately, from the one and only Don Silvestro Tosques. The son of a doctor in Mola near Bari in Apulia, Sportelli had qualified as a lawyer in Naples where he had built up for himself a considerable practice. Now aged thirty-one he was as devout a Christian as he was a brilliant lawyer. A protégé of Falcoia whom he had met at the church of San Nicola alla Carità, he followed the same path of lay involvement in the corporal works of charity as had Alphonsus. Falcoia directed his attention in due course to the proposals to found a new missionary group; he was sufficiently confident of Sportelli's intentions to assure Alphonsus that one day he would number him among his missioners, despite the fact that Sportelli was not even a cleric at the time. Several locally insoluble canonical difficulties arose about his ordination which Falcoia had ultimately to refer to the Roman authorities. However, Sportelli's vocation was an authentic one and his perseverance sufficient to overcome all obstacles. Five years later he was ordained and ready to play his part with Alphonsus in the new missionary endeavour. But for the moment he was just an interested observer.

Falcoia was waiting for Alphonsus on his arrival at Scala. His immediate task was to calm his scruples by confirming once more everything that

Pagano had laid down. There was a note too from Fiorillo telling Alphonsus to be of good heart and assuring him that he had not lost his interest in the missionary project. In point of fact he had it more at heart than ever before. He had come across nobody whom he could recommend to join but if they came his way he certainly would not hesitate to direct them to Scala. Alphonsus was not to be put out by the fewness of subjects — 'it was better to have few good ones than many'.[28] Mazzini and Sportelli returned to Naples leaving Alphonsus with as unprepossessing and heterogenous a quartet as could be imagined, none of whom were to remain with him more than a few months.

A triduum of prayer with Exposition of the Blessed Sacrament was organised in the chapel of the sisters by way of preparation for the inauguration of the work. In the presence of the two bishops, Santoro and Falcoia, some priests from the town and the community of sisters, the prodigies in the Sacred Host were repeated — three Hills, surmounted by a Cross with the various instruments of Our Lord's Passion were clearly visible for all to see. The remarkable happenings were repeated several times later on in the month. The two bishops regarded the matter as sufficiently important to bring it officially to the attention of the Papal Nuncio in Naples who would have heard about the occurrences anyway from other less reliable sources. As a result the Cardinal Secretary of State to Pope Clement XII ordered an immediate enquiry which took place within three months. There is a humourous side to the testimonies of the two bishops, as if they were somehow embarrassed about it all. Santoro said he was sitting just inside the door of the chapel so as not to confer any solemnity on the occasion while Falcoia mentioned that he was in Scala for a change of air, neither of them referring in any way to the triduum of prayer for the beginning of a new institute. No verdict was ever forthcoming from the investigation but Alphonsus later kept alive the memory of the incident when he sketched a Cross raised above three hills flanked by the instruments of the Passion as the Emblem and Seal of his Congregation.[29]

Sunday 9 November 1732 marked the inauguration of the new missionary society; to describe it as 'solemn' as is usual about such occasions is to misuse the term. In the narrow confines of the temporary chapel prepared in the largest room of the hospice of the sisters, bishop Falcoia sang the Mass of the Holy Spirit. It was the feast of the Dedication of the Lateran Basilica in Rome. A Te Deum for the graces received up to that moment concluded the liturgy. The Congregation of the Most Holy Saviour, amorphous and undefined, had begun its precarious existence.[30]

CHAPTER SIX

FROM OUT THE RUINS OCTOBER 1732– JUNE 1734

– I –

Falcoia remained with the group in Scala for six days after the inauguration ceremony. He could not have been encouraged by what he experienced; the differences of opinions and the positive dissensions among the group augured badly for the future. Even before the arrival of Alphonsus, Falcoia had found himself in disagreement with both Donato and Mannarini. His naive expectation had been that the group would sit down with him and as a result of their shared views come to agreement about every aspect of the new missionary undertaking. Their purpose was ill-defined — the establishing of a new missionary group — and it soon emerged that not even that was shared by Donato, or, consequently, by Mannarini who was always ready to row in behind his fellow Calabrian. Even supposing the existence of a common purpose among them, they had very little tangible to go on beyond the rules of Celeste for the nuns, dating back to 1725, and the brief outline she had drawn up in 1731 for the missionary order. Otherwise they were beginning *ab ovo*. What precisely was to be the purpose of the new missionary group? What would they do which the long established missionary orders and the multiplicity of diocesan missionary societies, including the Apostolic Missions and the Pii Operai, were not already doing? Was the new group to possess a characteristic spirituality and a form of life which had new dimensions? Were its missionary methods and techniques to break new ground?

True, Falcoia possessed a vision of what he wanted, which he had shared with Alphonsus and which they had discussed together and with others in Naples for over a year. But it had still to be fleshed out and codified. The reality of their ideal, however, had not sufficiently impressed itself upon the three others to allow their discussions to issue in acceptable proposals. Donato had the rule of his own congregation in his pocket, ready to hand as the model to be adopted; his reluctance to consider any other was soon apparent. Tosques was all in favour of the rule just as it was revealed to Maria Celeste provided that nothing clashed with any of his own favourite ideas. Mannarini soon began to get on Alphonsus' nerves and the antipathy he developed for his former colleague from the Chinese College became a source of new scruples for him. Romano with admirable insouciance did not allow himself to become too intensely involved one way or the other and was able to escape to his family home at the end of the day. Falcoia's presence would not have helped the group. Authoritarian in the extreme, despite his protestations that he was open to every point of view, he was not prepared to compromise with any proposals which conflicted with his own ideas. It was this great strength which secured the ultimate survival of the missionary undertaking but which at the very outset nearly saw its total destruction. In the last analysis, had it not been for the heroic constancy of Alphonsus, the new missionary undertaking would not have survived beyond 15 November 1732; within a few days of the opening of discussions the whole project seemed to be on the point of falling asunder. And the disagreement among the men in the hospice was reflected among the sisters in the convent who were kept duly informed of everything that was going on by Tosques whose disruptive charisms were now fully operative.

Falcoia returned to his diocese on 15 November; before he left Alphonsus took out his personal note-book to record the bishop's final directions. They consisted of a formal obedience to remain unshakeable in his commitment to the establishment of the new missionary group; no matter what the others did or said he was not to be moved from his determination — *even if he were to remain alone*. God would assist him; he was not to falter. Thus within a few weeks of coming together in Scala it was evident to both Alphonsus and Falcoia that the others would not remain. The sense of isolation after Falcoia's departure was intense — his one support was withdrawn. There was some consolation in the fact that Tosques, too, had departed temporarily for his Customs Office in Naples and that on the eighteenth a new recruit had arrived in the person of Vito Curzio, another layman, but of a totally different calibre. He was to be the first Brother in the new congregation, a legend even in his lifetime.

Vito was born in Bari in Apulia in 1702; his early years are fortunately shrouded in mystery. One account claims that he left his native place on account of running foul of the law, a refugee from justice. Having found anonymity in Naples he became the administrator of the estates of the marquis of Vasto on the island of Procida, which apparently suited his naturally violent and quarrelsome temperament admirably. Cesar Sportelli, whose family befriended him, summed up his life story to this point rather colourfully when he wrote that Vito's spiritual reading before he joined was pistols and swords. In a dream Vito saw himself being assisted by a priest whose face was clearly etched in his memory. Visiting the Chinese College in the company of Sportelli, he was introduced to Alphonsus, and to his amazement, recognised him immediately as the priest of his dream; it was an easy transition to recognise him further as his heavenly appointed spiritual guide. In due course he offered himself to the new missionary society. True to his word he arrived in Scala on 18 November, full of piety and determination but with a very difficult personality which it would take him years to bring under some form of control. His arrival was a great relief to Alphonsus in many ways but from the culinary point of view, a disaster, since he took charge of the kitchen with much more good will than skill.

Alphonsus was scheduled to return to Naples at the end of November to fulfil commitments to the Apostolic Missions. The few intervening days gave him an opportunity to assess his position, first of all with regard to the opposition he was certain to encounter there, and secondly, with regard to his future relations with Falcoia. His personal note-book records the outcome of his reflections. He determined to answer all criticisms in Naples simply by stating that he was engaged in his work in Scala out of obedience to Fiorillo and bishop Falcoia; it was not a capricious decision on his part, still less a response to the revelations of a nun. The proposed enterprise itself was a good one and had the approval of many bishops and priests. As regards Falcoia, he was able to clarify his position in three quite distinct areas. He had vowed to accept Falcoia as his spiritual director and to obey him in matters of conscience; there was no problem there. He now vowed never to abandon the new institute unless formally directed to do so by Falcoia or whoever succeeded him as director. But in a remarkable manifestation of independence, which one might have thought altogether out of character, he formally exempted himself from obedience to Falcoia concerning details of the new rule for the missionary institute. He determined that the final decision in the matter of the rules he and his missionaries would have to follow should be his — *à mio arbitrio*. Further, he reserved to himself the right to accept or change or interpret the new rules according to his own judgment, and he retained the right to add further restrictions to his obedience to Falcoia if he so wished. It was all remarkably clinical.[1]

These entries in his personal note-book are clear manifestations of the evolution of Alphonsus' conscience and of his gradual assumption of responsibility for the direction of the new missionary institute. While he resolutely rejected for himself the role of founder and insisted that he was led to the undertaking by obedience, he gradually came to assume leadership of the enterprise over the course of years. Full control would not be his until after Falcoia's death some eleven years later in 1743. As the years went by, however, he more and more stamped his own ideas and personality upon the work. There are two periods during which this evolution in his attitude is clearly documented; the first, we have seen, was when he was on his own in the south of Italy on mission from November 1731 to March 1732. He returned to Naples determined to take up the challenge. The second was after the departure of Falcoia from Scala when he was alone with his own reflections. One can only surmise that his experience of the few days' discussions together with Falcoia and the four others brought him to the realisation that he must play a more active role in what was happening. And then he added the final vow never to call in to question again the authenticity of his vocation to the new institute. Every aspect of the situation was now catered for according to his legal mind.

These entries of November 1732 in his note-book highlight another aspect of his personality and to some extent of his spirituality which flowed directly from his scruples and which was to characterise him all his life. Indeed, the Defensor Fidei commented on it during the process of canonisation and urged it against him. He began to multiply private vows and oaths to carry out his different resolutions — even his ordinary acts of piety and penance. Vows were reserved for major decisions, oaths sufficed for the more ordinary decisions which would now be covered by the word 'resolutions'. Whatever may have been the theological teaching prevalent at the time, on the value of acts done under vows and oaths, they apparently fulfilled a psychological need for him.[2]

– II –

Alphonsus needed all the courage he could muster to return to Naples at the end of November to take part in a mission on behalf of the Apostolic Missions in the church of the Annunciation for the beginning of Advent. His reception was anything but cordial. Soon after his arrival the members met in the chapel of the seminary to discuss the damage inflicted on their congregation by the proposed breakaway, spearheaded by him. The atmosphere was charged. Canon Gizzio took Alphonsus' departure as a personal insult; Torni, more calculating, was still very angry, if not with Alphonsus, certainly with the Pii Operai and Falcoia. There was a proposal to expel him from the society and consequently to deprive him of his chaplaincy; one would be a public humiliation; the other, a severe economic deprivation. Alphonsus sought and obtained an audience of the Cardinal who upbraided him for leaving Naples without consulting him. Alphonsus pleaded by way of excuse that he thought the Cardinal was too busy. 'You know I am willing to listen to anyone who comes to me and you say that you did not wish to inconvenience me,' replied Pignatelli, whose reception was sympathetic in the main and showed a considerable understanding of what was contemplated at Scala. The interview helped to clear the air and went a long way towards securing Pignatelli's support some months later. The immediate upshot was that the Cardinal gave directions that nothing should be done as regards Alphonsus' membership of the Apostolic Missions and the income from the chaplaincy, without his express confirmation.

Bishop Fortunato of Cassano, who seemed to spend most of his time in Naples, and who had already been consulted by Alphonsus, encouraged him to persevere in his work and suggested that he might consider resigning from the Apostolic Missions to forestall his expulsion. Fiorillo had begun to regret the haste with which he had declared the work to be from God and had given the go-ahead; on second thoughts, he wondered if it would not have been more advisable to join up with Donato and his missionaries. Since certain steps had already been taken to establish the work, however, he reluctantly agreed that it would be better to see it through. Father Mazzini alone, still frustrated by the refusal of his spiritual director to allow him to go to Scala, encouraged him not to doubt for one moment the divine origin of his vocation.

Having weathered the storm in Naples but with the threat of expulsion still hanging over him Alphonsus returned to Scala by way of Castellamare to bring Falcoia up to date with the latest developments. The immediate requirement was for some sort of written guidelines to cover all aspects of their lives from community living at home to the preaching of missions. Falcoia, who had jealously reserved this task for himself in relation to the sisters and had been occupied at it for the previous six years, now undertook to perform a similar service for the missionaries but with the difference that his decisions were subject to Alphonsus' approval. This work of drawing up a comprehensive rule for the men would drag on for years with Falcoia offering one excuse after another for the delay in producing an acceptable draft; sometimes he pleaded the pressure of his work as a bishop, at other times, his health. At any rate, nothing was finalised by the time of his death some eleven years later and it is difficult to resist the conclusion that as the years went by Alphonsus was less and less anxious to see it completed while Falcoia was still alive to insist on some of his own ideas. It was to take five more years after the bishop's death before the final draft was completed and made its way to Rome for approval.

Reunited in Scala in December with Romano, Donato, Mannarini and Vito, Alphonsus organised the first united apostolic endeavour of the new missionary society of the Most Holy Saviour. Together they preached a mission in the cathedral in preparation for Christmas. Besides the usual course of evening sermons, they gathered the people each morning for a meditation which Alphonsus directed from the pulpit. They established various 'sodalities' for the different sections of the population, men, married women, young men and girls. Alphonsus personally introduced the practice of a visit to the Blessed Sacrament each evening with Benediction and prayers. Special devotions were arranged for Saturdays in honour of the Mother of God, all of which were later to become a feature of his missionary method under the name of the 'Devout Life'.

The festive season with its prayers, liturgy and celebrations, centred, at that time, round the feast of the Epiphany rather than Christmas Day itself, was spent together in the hospice. Falcoia sent them a present of two turkeys. From Naples came a typically unctuous letter from Tosques:

> How fortunate you are to suffer cold and hunger for Jesus Christ, just as He did, especially at this time. I am not worthy, dear Don Alfonso, of this great honour. The Lord does not want me to participate in his

work as I had wished or to put on the livery of His Church; instead he wishes to purify me of my unruly inclinations. And I can only acquiesce in his Most Holy Will. You by your prayers will gain for me the necessary help in my weakness so that I may become both capable and worthy of accompanying you in following the footsteps of Jesus Christ for the good of souls.

More worthy of credence and more reassuring was the letter which arrived at the same time from Torni. He was fully aware of everything that Alphonsus had been through. He promised to continue his prayers that he would have the courage to bear all the tribulations that were facing him, so that eventually God's purpose would be realised. He assured him that he harboured no sentiment of either bitterness or dislike for him; on the contrary, he had always held him in the highest esteem and regarded him with great affection. Far from having changed his attitude he could now honestly say that he regarded him more highly than ever. Reassuringly he continued:

> Our Congregation regards you as one of its most esteemed members, as much now as ever. Nothing has been done in the matter of your chaplaincy and nothing will be done without the express approval of his Eminence. So continue to celebrate Mass in accordance with the norms of the chaplaincy until you hear to the contrary. Rest assured that as long as I am superior and the matter is in my hands, there will be no change.
>
> As regards your new institute I trust everything will be done according to the canonical norms I suggested to you and that finally you will receive the approval of the Holy See. In that way your work, founded *super firmam petram* will endure. . . .
>
> Finally I have never entertained those malicious sentiments towards you which you supposed. Quite simply I know you have been motivated by the highest ideals in all you have undertaken.[3]

Torni's letter meant a great deal to Alphonsus; Falcoia too was pleased when he learnt of its contents but he was always on his guard with Torni and resentful of his influence. He did not take easily to advice from that quarter, a fact which did not escape Torni's notice either; there was no love lost between them. Furthermore, the ambivalence of Torni's attitude to the new missionary initiative was clearly emerging. He would have been pleased to have been involved in it from the beginning provided he could have had the direction of it; he certainly wanted it in Naples rather than in Scala and he would have enjoyed whatever reflected glory its success might have occasioned. Not for nothing was he referred to somewhat unkindly as 'the cutest fox that ever walked through Naples'.

Despite Torni's optimistic prediction, time did not heal the bitterness felt by some members of the Apostolic Missions at Alphonsus' departure; the question of his membership came to a head finally a few weeks later. At the usual Monday meeting on 23 February 1733, the proposal that Alphonsus be excluded from the society and deprived of his chaplaincy was put to the assembled members. Torni, as superior, spoke strongly in Alphonsus' favour; Canon Gizzio was excused from participating. The voting went overwhelmingly in favour of the motion. But the decision required confirmation by the Cardinal which he at once refused to grant. 'Not content with destroying his reputation, they now wish to ruin him economically as well,' was his comment on the whole proceedings.

The Cardinal's intervention was decisive; no further disciplinary action was taken. The crisis in his relationship with the Apostolic Missions was over and would never again arise. Even though most of his time was now to be taken up with his own missionary society he continued to take part in the weekly academies of the Apostolic Missions whenever he was in Naples; occasionally, too, he would also join them on missions. His debt of gratitude to Cardinal Pignatelli was great. Six weeks later he travelled back to Naples from Scala to express his thanks and to receive his advice and encouragement once again in the face of what appeared to be the total collapse of the whole missionary project in Scala.[4]

– III –

The mission season opened immediately after Epiphany. Alphonsus had no intention of remaining in Scala engaged in interminable discussions with his companions about rules for the new congregation; discussions were secondary to missionary activity. He saw the evangelisation of those rural areas where missionaries rarely or ever penetrated as the main purpose of his society and he was anxious to be up and doing in the vineyard of the Lord; it was for this he had left Naples. While there was much to be admired and imitated in the missionary systems of the existing societies he was acutely aware of their shortcomings and anxious to avoid them in his own. From the very outset Falcoia rightly insisted that there should ultimately be a section in the rules dealing with the method of giving missions. The Constitutions dealing with missions in the rule finally approved by Rome did, in point of fact, come from the pen of Alphonsus, and he was later to publish a full treatise on the method of giving missions, incorporating his experience of thirty-four years. But for the moment it was a question of trial and error. At Scala he now began to prepare with his companions for their first venture together away from home. It involved the writing of sermons and instructions, an acceptance of a common approach to moral problems in the administration of the sacrament of penance. The importance of the proper administration of this sacrament was high on the list of Alphonsus' priorities; he was insistent that the missionaries should remain in an area long enough to hear the confessions of all the inhabitants. He was equally anxious to ensure, without offence, that the local clergy should *not* hear confessions during the mission. It was also important to cater for the different social classes to be found in the area and devise a method of dealing with those who did not co-operate, whether clerics or the local 'nobility'. Mannarini surprisingly threw himself wholeheartedly into the preparation — he was working 'like a dog', reported Alphonsus to Falcoia in December.

The area chosen for the first external mission was Tramonti, a region high up in the Lattari mountains between Amalfi and Salerno. Inaccessible except through the mountain passes from the coast town of Maiori or through the Gap of Chiunzi from the north, Tramonti, populated by sturdy peasants and shepherds, comprised some twelve small towns and a slightly larger number of parishes, belonging to the archdiocese of Amalfi. From the pastoral point of view it was an ideal location for missionary work with its large population, mainly unlettered, badly instructed in the rudiments of the faith, and its clergy scarcely more literate. All the pastoral problems which Alphonsus later described as endemic to the country areas of the Kingdom were present: ignorance, popular religion at its most superstitious, sacrilegious reception of the sacraments due to familiarity with the clergy who were born, reared and educated in the area, and then ministered there while still living with their families. Cut off geographically from easy contact with the outside world it was an area largely neglected pastorally. In the second half of January 1733, the first mission band of the new congregation, Alphonsus, Romano, Donato and Mannarini set off from Scala by way of Ravello and Maiori on horseback. The archbishop of Amalfi gave Alphonsus every jurisdictional faculty he could delegate. Rather than detail them he said, 'I make you archbishop of Amalfi for as often as you wish.'

Their first engagement was in Campinola; from there they went on to Pietre where they had the largest congregation, and from there to Gete. Another person joined them after Campinola and remained to the end; the indications are that it was the inevitable Tosques, never missing an opportunity of disrupting whatever fragile unity might have been achieved among the others. Before returning to Scala, Alphonsus preached a retreat to the nuns in the convent at Pocara where he made an effort to re-establish some form of regular religious life.[5]

The enthusiasm of the people of Tramonti for the missioners was unbounded. The fact that they would not accept any remuneration for their efforts and, more important still, that they insisted on sharing the simple fare and living conditions of the people, had made a deep impression. The local authorities invited them to establish a mission house in the area — an invitation which was seriously considered by Alphonsus and Falcoia but which was taken up instead by Tosques and companions a few months later, trading deceitfully on the goodwill of the people towards Alphonsus. Falcoia was thrilled at the successful outcome of the first missionary endeavour under the banner of the Most Holy Saviour; all his old enthusiasm for missionary work was reawakened as he recalled his own days as an active member of the Pii Operai. He longed to be able to leave his diocese and take his place in the work once more, even if it were only, as he said, 'to clean their shoes and wash their linen'.[6] As a consequence of the success of the efforts in Tramonti and with the good-will of the archbishop of Amalfi assured, other centres of population along the whole coast and in the neighbouring dioceses were now open to the missionaries of the Most Holy Saviour. There was no shortage of missionary opportunities, only a shortage of missionaries.

– IV –

The success of the missionary campaign in Tramonti did nothing to heal the serious divisions developing among the group; if anything their weeks together only served to highlight the areas of dissension. There was no unity of outlook, no agreement on what they wanted to achieve, still less on how it should be done. Falcoia made frequent exhortations to bring the group together; 'there is need now in the beginning of this great work for complete unanimity, as well as harmony of will, intellect and spirit, since a minor divergence at the outset becomes large at the end'. There existed a wide divergence of views on a whole range of vital issues among the group. The original rule of Celeste, which was to be the basis of the rule for the missionaries, consisted simply of an outline of nine virtues with a spiritual treatise on each one. To these outlines had to be added an exact formulation of the purpose of the new institute, a form of government, a method of preaching missions, an order of the day — everything, in fact, down to the habit, if any, of the members. Thus the opportunities for disagreement were unlimited. Donato, inspired by the work of his mentors, the Jesuits, advocated schools in villages and towns as well as the preaching apostolate. Alphonsus was opposed to schools, but was prepared to tolerate them as an initial and temporary expedient to gain the good-will of the local authorities and the people. Some favoured the recitation of the Divine Office in choir; others, after the example of the Jesuits, were opposed.

Falcoia was prepared to clothe the missionaries in a habit of blue and red. Their footwear, sandals or shoes, was another major problem. Falcoia favoured shoes of dark blue, 'to signify that all your steps are heavenwards', which was certainly pushing symbolism to its utmost limits. The nature of the vow of poverty was a source of very fundamental disagreement and continued to be so for nearly 200 years. Falcoia rejected the model of the Theatines. Tosques suggested that the members should sell all their possessions and leave them at the feet of the superior, following the example recounted in the Acts of the Apostles. Alphonsus, more realistic and knowing his fellow countrymen, was appalled at the possibilities of deceit such a practice would open up. There would not be sufficient members left to carry out the dead Ananiases, he commented wryly.[7]

Alphonsus had a simple solution to the disagreements — leave the final decision in all disputed matters to Falcoia. While this attitude reflected to some extent a psychological need in his make-up — though this was now less in evidence — it reflected at the same time a well thought-out spiritual approach. He outlined his position clearly:

> The only way to establish everything successfully is for all of us to have recourse to just one person, to whom we will all submit blindly once

we have made known our views. This one person should have experience of community life and of preaching the spiritual exercises. He should be endowed with all the learning necessary for a worker in the Lord's vineyard, be spiritual and guided by the Holy Spirit. He should have the final decision in all doubts and differences among us. And what he determines should be accepted without further opposition. Only in this way will we be able to maintain charity and union among ourselves which is vital for launching this Bark, as you yourself agree and as I have preached until I have foamed at the mouth — '*ho fatto la schiuma in bocca*'.[8]

His researches into the history of religious orders convinced him that this was, in fact, the way religious orders and their rules had come into existence. A study of the reform of Carmel operated by Teresa of Avila demonstrated how nearly the whole movement foundered for lack of central direction until Father Gratian took control. For Alphonsus the central role of Falcoia was not to be called into question. Mannarini proposed that they should elect another director but Alphonsus was adamant; it would be Falcoia or no one. The whole affair, then, finally resolved itself into a matter of accepting Falcoia as director of the whole enterprise. In favour, on one side, were Alphonsus and Romano; totally opposed on the other were Donato, Mannarini and Tosques. Tosques was undoubtedly the villain of the piece. He directed all his intrigues against Falcoia and one by one succeeded in turning Donato, Mons. Santoro of Scala and Maria Celeste against him. He insisted to Donato that Falcoia was planning to expel him from the group; he insinuated to Santoro that Falcoia wanted to be bishop of Scala as well as of Castellamare; the unfortunate Celeste fell completely under his influence.

The situation was irretrievably compromised by the time Alphonsus got back to Scala from Tramonti at the end of February 1733, to open the Lenten course of sermons in the cathedral and to plan for further missions in the Amalfi region. Tosques had withdrawn to Naples where he continued his campaign of vilification against Falcoia and, in so doing, brought the whole Scala enterprise into greater public ridicule and disrepute than ever. Alarmed at the damage being inflicted on the undertaking, Falcoia hastened to Naples to confront him but Tosques refused to discuss the matter. In the meantime, Mons. Santoro decided to take action. Disturbed in the first place by rumours concerning the nature of the relationship between Celeste and Tosques, he made a personal visitation of the convent early in March, interviewing each sister in the process. Only then did the extent of Tosques' indiscretions become apparent. He had undertaken the direction of a number of the sisters, who were unaware of his lack of theological competence. To prevent any wider consultation he had forbidden them to have any contact with Bishop Falcoia. Next, he had informed a number of the sisters that the Lord had revealed to him in prayer the names of two or three sisters who 'were especially dear to Him and were the recipient of

His special favours'. At first he had refused to reveal the identity of these 'saints', an infallible technique for arousing the curiosity and possibly even the jealousy of other members of the community. Sister Maria Raffaella however, succeeded in eliciting them from him under promise of total confidentiality only to divulge them herself under similar conditions to others, and among them to Celeste, who now knew that her name was among the 'chosen few'.[9]

In the course of his investigations, the Bishop enlisted the assistance of Alphonsus, who lectured the community at length on every aspect of the situation from the nature of revelations to the role of spiritual directors in general and Falcoia in particular. To his great surprise Maria Celeste refused his invitation to come down to the parlour to discuss matters with him afterwards. The upshot was that the bishop of Scala formally forbade Tosques to visit the convent or to have anything to do with the sisters. The decision was the correct one and long overdue. Nevertheless, it left Falcoia dismayed at the error of judgment he had been guilty of in respect of Tosques, nor was it any great consolation for him to reflect that the bishop of Scala had been equally deceived. He almost lost faith in the entire human race as a consequence. 'Praised be Jesus Christ. This has taught me a lesson before I die that the machinations of men can reach such depths. And so before I die I leave this warning to those who come after me, always to be on their guard in dealing with the laity about the things of God.'[10]

Santoro's action precipitated the inevitable break-up of the group. Donato and Mannarini followed Tosques back to Naples where they enlisted the support of Father Fiorillo in their efforts to establish their own missionary group. The formal intimation of the break-up of the group arrived from Tosques, who wrote from Naples on 20 March, refuting Alphonsus' accusation that he had disrupted the unity of the group. He adopted his usual mealy-mouthed technique of protesting his sinfulness and his willingness to suffer in silence, united with the Cross of his sweet Jesus — a line of defence which puts one's accusers at a distinct disadvantage. Within a few days, a letter followed from Mannarini, with the definite word that they were not returning to Scala but were waiting for a decision as to the next step they should take. In evident sincerity they invited Alphonsus to join them; they would receive him warmly. Mannarini's letter was dated 1st April which was Wednesday of Holy Week; it would have reached Alphonsus on Good Friday. What he dreaded had happened—he was alone with Vito Curzio on the rocks of Scala. The words he had entered into his note-book the previous November had proved prophetic — 'even if I am to remain alone, God would help me — *se restassi anche sol, m'aiuta Dio.*' At the process of canonisation it is seldom that the so-called Devil's Advocate allows his admiration of the candidate to break through. In the case of Alphonsus this is precisely what happened; the Promotor Fidei could not honestly withhold his admiration of the heroic constancy and trust in God which Alphonsus manifested at this juncture.[11]

Falcoia's reaction to the departure of the three from Scala showed him at his very best. Autocratic he may have been, and unreasonable in the quality of obedience he demanded from those he directed, but there was no doubting his deep faith and the strength of his determination to bring the new missionary institute into existence. He had never really hoped for much from either Mannarini or Donato and still less from Tosques. Their departure was a blessing, not a disaster. He struck just the right note in his letter to Alphonsus:

> You should consider the fact that these gentlemen have left you as a double blessing; we are now free of the obstacles which they placed to the work. If they did not go themselves we should have had to rid ourselves of them. And now we have the good fortune, which they do not realise, that it is more advantageous for us to suffer their departure then to have to bring it about.
>
> Let us trust in God and leave ourselves completely in his hands and we shall find that the evil will leave us. I will never leave you and God will never abandon either you or me. For the moment, three or four will be enough for the work and in his own time God will send others.[12]

The collapse of the enterprise at Scala aroused intense excitement in clerical circles in Naples once again; the gossip which had abated some months before was now more unrestrained than ever. Unfortunately, the three deserters were the first in with their account of what had taken place. Tosques was the most vicious but Donato and Mannarini were equally damaging as they coloured everything in their own favour in their efforts at self-justification. Alphonsus' name was mentioned explicitly from the pulpit as an example of what chastisements from God pride can deserve. Those Alphonus reckoned he could rely on from the Apostolic Missions, Tommaso Carace and Guiseppe Porpora, were amongst his fiercest critics. Others, more zealous still for the glory of Holy Mother Church, sent reports to the Holy Father in Rome so that he could put an end to the scandal by his direct intervention. And yet, there were some in the capital whose perception was more attuned to the mystery of God's dealings with his chosen ones. The very fury which the undertaking aroused was for them the surest indication of its supernatural origins.

This was the atmosphere when, in Easter Week, Alphonsus ventured back to the capital for consultation with the Cardinal and with his friends. Torni received him sympathetically but advocated abandoning the project and returning to Naples to resume his work with the Apostolic Missions, without ruling out the possibility of undertaking the missionary initiative from there — something he had always suggested. The reception Alphonsus received from the Cardinal was more remarkable still. He was scandalised at the bitterness which had been drummed up against Alphonsus and his missionary undertaking; he regarded Tosques with something approaching loathing. Making his own the words of the Acts of the Apostles the Cardinal declared that if the work were merely human in origin it would fail; if it were from God, no power on earth could destroy it. He approved of Alphonsus' determination to return to Scala and left him with the advice to trust more in God and less than ever in men so that God could bring success from the ruins of his first efforts.

And there were other aspects of the situation which were encouraging. Cesar Sportelli, Mazzini and a new candidate, Gennaro Sarnelli were more determined than ever to join him so that the work should start anew. A third priest, Father Francis Xavier Rossi from the diocese of Caiazzo, was not merely anxious to join but was already negotiating with his bishop for a suitable site for a house and church for the new congregation.

– V –

The dissensions among the missionaries leading to the total collapse of the work at Easter 1733 were paralleled in the convent among the sisters. The root of the trouble was precisely the same — Falcoia and the efforts he was making to complete the rule for the convent. Here again, Tosques led the opposition. The sisters split into two fiercely opposing factions, one prepared to accept Falcoia and his decisions on all matters, the other, master-minded by Tosques and supported by Maria Celeste, opposed to the bishop and his modifications of the 'revealed rule'. Over the last year Celeste had gradually withdrawn herself from Falcoia's direction; Alphonsus had not responded to the implicit invitation to replace him. Her decision to make a definite break with the bishop came in December 1732, inevitably after divine illumination in prayer. She was able to detail at least ten reasons why she should abandon the spiritual director who had guided her since her early days in the Carmel at Marigliano; to these were now added her final justification for the step she was taking: Falcoia did not pray sufficiently before directing her with the result that his directions were not replete with the Holy Spirit. Even though she later disclaimed that Tosques had influenced her in any way in her decision, his attitude to Falcoia certainly would not have helped. In 1733 when relations between Tosques and Falcoia deteriorated beyond repair Celeste came more and more to depend on Tosques. Suspicions grew about the nature of their relationship, compounded by the fact that Celeste refused to agree not to see Tosques. How could all this square with her visions and revelations, wondered Falcoia?

The bishop of Scala took action, as we have seen, in March 1733. Alphonsus had been only peripherally involved in the whole affair; his sole intervention had been the conference to the sisters. When to his surprise Celeste refused to come to the parlour to discuss matters with him afterwards, he wrote to her at great length, a virtual treatise on spiritual direction and obedience to one's spiritual father, running to over four thousand words, which he cleared with Falcoia before dispatching it. Falcoia pronounced it most appropriate, *giudiziosissima*. Alphonsus was well aware of all that was happening in the convent — aware too, of the unsavoury rumours. While he regarded Celeste highly and considered her greatly favoured by God through the gift of mystical graces, he was not blind to her defects which the last few months had brought into relief. There is a calm balance and objectivity in what he wrote, a lawyer's assessment of every aspect of the situation, a summing up for the jury. He was secure in his theological principles, penetrating in his psychological insights. Knowing how easily she could be disturbed he asked her to read the letter with all the calmness of which she was capable:[13]

> Celeste, my dearest sister in Jesus and Mary,
>
> I asked you in my last letter not to reply but since you have honoured me with one, I now ask you to read this letter and then do what God inspires you. But read it with resignation, without endeavouring all the time you are reading, to think out suitable replies. If you read with the purpose of contradicting, there will be no lack of arguments for you to employ, but you will never come to the truth; even the heretics can find arguments in the scriptures against the Church. I ask you to read this letter first and when you have done so, pray for three days in a spirit of resignation and perfect indifference, without writing to me or making notes for a possible rebuttal. Then, after that, you can do what seems best to you.

There were two important aspects which Alphonsus wished to keep quite distinct, one was her spiritual life, the other, her revelations concerning the new congregations. As a spiritual director himself, he was certainly upset that she had withdrawn herself from Falcoia's direction — according to herself, as a result of one of her revelations. For Alphonsus this very fact cast doubt on the authenticity of all her other revelations. Was it because Falcoia had humbled her and was apparently dismissive of her? 'But this, Sister dear, was necessary in order to subjugate your proud spirit and to free you from your attachment to your own opinion' — defects which others had drawn her attention to. Was it perhaps that she was led on by Don Silvestro Tosques who 'regards you as greater than St Teresa of Avila and goes about publishing your praises as far off as Vienna; so much so that he approves everything about you — something a spiritual director would be on his guard against if he wished to direct a soul prudently and to maintain her humility'.

Don Silvestro, Alphonsus went on, had seemingly taught her some strange doctrine concerning obedience to superiors, which she had been foolish enough to follow. He had no hesitation in informing Celeste that in matters of doctrine Silvestro was as wide of the mark as he could be, not merely *storto* but *stortissimo*! Alphonsus had heard him making outrageous assertions, culminating in the enormity that all those who followed Falcoia's directions were already damned, a point of view which would not have endeared him to Alphonsus. Alphonsus then compared her way of acting with that of Teresa of Avila, who followed the advice of her spiritual director even when it was diametrically opposed to what she claimed had been revealed to her in prayer. He concluded this section of his letter dealing with the problems of her soul with a personal appeal:

> Celeste, give this great pleasure to God and leave Don Silvestro. I realise that you will have to do great violence to yourself but the greater the

violence the greater will be your advance on the road to holiness. Tell me, if God wishes you to leave him, what do you wish to do? But God does not want it, you say. Ah, my dear Celeste in Jesus Christ, do you not see clearly that you are being deceived and what is worse, apparently willingly?

When he came to the question of the two new religious families, Alphonsus was equally clear on Falcoia's role in completing the rules, one for the Sisters and the other for the missionaries. He reminded her that when they had discussed all this together originally, their opinions were identical. Once again the malign influence of Don Silvestro was to be detected. If they did not leave everything in Falcoia's hands then

> Don Silvestro would certainly constitute himself director of the whole undertaking and would appoint himself infallible interpreter of all your revelations, both past and any possible future ones too! His practice up to the present has always been to cast himself in the role of director, never in that of disciple. And God help anyone who attempts to oppose him in this, as I have learnt from experience. His opinion must prevail in everything. he was barely inside the door of your monastery when he took upon himself, even though he was still a layman, the task of directing some poor sisters, who now that they have escaped from his direction, consider themselves as liberated from a dark pit. That, in itself, should be sufficient for you, Celeste, to make you reconsider your position. Hardly was he in, I repeat, than he tried to stipulate that no sister should write to Falcoia, the appointed spiritual director of the convent, without his permission. What would have happened if we had all abandoned Falcoia? And I have the impression, my dear Celeste, that it was precisely your intention that even we, the missionaries, should abandon Falcoia and depend totally on the great Oracle, Don Silvestro!
>
> If God willed that I would do it, but just at the moment, I do not feel any such inspiration.

The pattern of his own blind obedience to his spiritual directors, first Pagano, now Falcoia, was the criterion by which Alphonsus assessed Celeste's conduct.

> I hope to live and die under obedience. If you wish to follow another way, then, *à rivederci*, wherever you are going to end up. I tell you that I will never leave Falcoia even if all the others — which is impossible — were to place themselves under my direction. . . .
>
> And I wish you to know in this context, when the thought enters my mind (as a result of what I now know about you) that all your revelations from the very beginning have been nothing more than illusions — and it is certain that your present visions and intuitions which confirm you in your obstinacy, are, in point of fact, illusions, as Falcoia has written to you and as everybody recognises — one thing gives me courage and determination to persevere, namely that in

> everything I have done, I have followed the path of obedience to my spiritual director and not your revelations. So even if all your visions were illusions, I, as a result of my obedience, am secure and cannot be mistaken in my vocation.

The long letter concluded with some very direct talking. Alphonsus accused Celeste of endeavouring to exclude him from the new missionary family and he laid the blame for the break-up of their efforts to date, fairly and squarely on her shoulders. But his main concern was for her salvation. She was, he felt, on the edge of a great precipice and he feared for her unless she reflected on the error of her ways. He warned her of the danger of losing her soul — she was certainly on the way to doing so. Above all, he begged her not to reply, but to reflect on what he had written to her. 'That head of yours is quite capable of composing a reply but I wonder if it would carry much weight before the Tribunal of Jesus Christ.' His final paragraph made explicit the root of the problem:

> My dear Celeste, do you not realise the attachment you have for Don Silvestro and the attachment he has for you? It is from God, you reply, because I wish only for God. I do not believe that you have committed sin in all this but in truth, is there not much of earth in it all? In Don Silvestro you are not seeking God alone but something that is not God. Realise that you are in an earthenware vessel; realise that following Don Silvestro you are placing yourself in great danger of losing God.

Celeste did not reply for about six weeks; her *Apologia*, in reply, was dated 20 April, and was addressed not to Alphonsus but to the ordinary confessor, Canon Pietro Romano, the significance of which cannot have been lost on him. Life in the convent, in the meantime, was becoming increasingly difficult for her. She was cut off from communication with the other members of the community, even her sisters were forbidden to speak to her. She was confined to the convent 'prison' — a remote cell, isolated from the rest of the sisters. She was spied upon and her letters intercepted. Under the strain of it all her health deteriorated causing considerable anxiety for a while. Both Falcoia and Santoro began to have considerable misgivings about the whole situation. Tosques was in Vienna and Falcoia feared he could well have been intriguing there against him. Celeste had appealed to Canon Torni in Naples as the Vicar in charge of religious women and the uncomfortable possibility of an ecclesiastical enquiry into the whole affair could not be ruled out. Celeste's father, unable to travel himself, arranged for his son, a Jesuit, Father Giorgio, to remain in Scala, to ensure that his daughters were not mistreated in any way.

The situation clearly demanded immediate action. Falcoia came to Scala in May and, after consultation with Santoro, determined to settle the affairs of the convent once and for all. An ultimatum was given to Celeste to accept three conditions for remaining in the convent or else face expulsion.

She was to accept the rules of the convent as expanded by Falcoia, she was to have no communication whatsoever with Don Silvestro Tosques and she was to bind herself by vow to accept Mons. Falcoia as spiritual director of the convent and consequently, hers as well. Advised by her brother the Jesuit, Celeste willingly accepted the first two conditions but absolutely refused to bind herself to accept Falcoia as her spiritual director. There are few, if any, who would now question her liberty in this matter. But the result was that the sisters of the convent were assembled in Chapter and Celeste was formally expelled.

On the morning of 25 May, Pentecost Monday, she and her two sisters, clothed in habits borrowed from a local Benedictine community, left their convent in Scala, never to return. Her virtue was never more clearly demonstrated than in the humble dispositions with which she begged pardon of the community before taking her leave, more or less in the guise of a condemned religious criminal. God was weaving for her a mysterious pattern of life which led her through great suffering and trials to heights of heroic virtue.

Celeste had accomplished her providential mission; her revelations were the basis for two new religious families which were destined to flourish and her 'Rule' became the inspirational matrix of two rules which were later approved by the Church. There are stranger stories than hers in the history of religious foundresses but few which equal hers in suffering and misunderstanding. In all she did, Alphonsus stated explicitly that he never questioned her good will, only her judgment. And even saints can err in their assessment of others. Alphonsus himself may have erred in allowing himself to become too readily the mouth-piece of Falcoia. Her *Apologia*, which for almost 120 years remained hidden in the archives, has at last reinstated her reputation and revealed the extent to which she was calumniated. From the convent of Scala her religious pilgrimage brought her finally, after many adventures, to Foggia where she was able to establish another convent under her cherished rule of the Most Holy Saviour. Following her departure, Falcoia pursued her inexorably and forbade Alphonsus to visit her as he travelled around on his missionary journeys. But after the bishop's death, Alphonsus felt himself free to renew his acquaintance with her which he did during a mission in Foggia some years later. There she lived in great holiness of life until her death in 1755, still cherishing the respect and friendship of Alphonsus.[14]

A month after her departure from Scala, the nuns there finally accepted the rule of Celeste as completed in detail by Falcoia. In the presence of Bishop Santoro the thirty religious took their public vows according to that rule; Celeste's work had come to a successful conclusion but there must surely have been less painful ways of achieving it.

– VI –

Alphonsus was not present in Scala for the final dramatic events connected with the departure of the Crostarosa sisters; he had been away in Naples since April and on mission since early May. On his return in June he found the bishop of Scala less than well disposed to him; for some reason he forbade him to have anything to do with the sisters. He was not even to talk to the superioress. The archbishop of Amalfi had adopted a similar attitude — all due to the Crostarosa debacle and to the fact that both the bishop of Scala and his metropolitan, the archbishop of Amalfi, now felt that Falcoia should confine his activity to his own diocese. Remarkably, Alphonsus was at peace, more so than he had been for months; the departure of his three companions, and especially Tosques, proved more of a relief than anything else. He grew more convinced than ever that the work was from God, arguing that the opposition it aroused and the near collapse of his efforts were the surest indications of heaven's favour. He was unperturbed by the failure, rooted in a strange confidence and determination, sensing with supernatural intuition that the work would succeed since God willed it. He loved every stone of Scala, he said, and would not entertain any thought of transferring his missionary foundation either to Naples as Torni wished, or to Castellamare, as Falcoia always had at the back of his mind.

Left to his own inclinations, Alphonsus had undertaken a frightening regime of corporal penances which Falcoia was forced to mitigate considerably, refusing permission for certain practices and instruments of corporal austerities which he rightly considered altogether excessive. Instead, he advised him to take walks among the hills and woods and to allow himself to enjoy the beauties of nature. From the cramped quarters of the hospice a path led down to a natural cave or grotto in the face of the mountain where Alphonsus betook himself for his private prayers and penances, particularly during the summer heats. Before he died he admitted that in the Grotto of Scala — as it came to be referred to in later years — he had treated with the Mother of God and sought her counsel concerning the missionary group he was establishing. 'And what did she say to you?' asked his companion, Father Constanzo. All Alphonsus did was to repeat, 'There in the Grotto she told me many beautiful things.' In the peace of his reflections in Scala, his legal mind discovered a loop-hole in the vows he had made to regulate his relations with Falcoia as his director. On the one hand, he had made a vow never to abandon the work of establishing the new institute unless commanded to do so by his director; on the other hand, he had reserved his right of veto on acceptance of whatever rules Falcoia would suggest. Supposing Falcoia — which was not beyond the limits of possibility — dictatorially insisted on some rule with which he personally totally disagreed? What would happen in this eventuality? With Falcoia's permission he closed this avenue of escape by vowing not to leave the work even if they were to reach such an impasse in their relations.

The two new members, Cesar Sportelli and Gennaro Sarnelli, had taken up residence in Scala early in June. Sarnelli proved to be the key figure, the real saviour of the whole situation. He was six years younger than Alphonsus, and, like him, had studied and practised law successfully in Naples. He too had abandoned the law courts and by a route similar to that of Alphonsus was ordained in 1732 as a member of the Apostolic Missions. Alphonsus was friendly with him from his time in the Chinese College where they were both *convittori*. They had even given missions together and, apparently, discussed the formation of a new missionary group which Sarnelli expressed a wish to join. But his director, the Jesuit, Father Manulio, refused permission; it was an accepted hazard in those days that one's decisions had to be submitted to a director whose word was law. Manulio, who had already blocked Mazzini, now blocked Sarnelli as well.

Taking advantage of his brother's ordination to the priesthood by Falcoia in Castellamare in early June 1733, Gennaro Sarnelli continued his journey over the mountains to Scala to see things for himself. He joined Alphonsus on the mission in Ravello, taking the opportunity of judging its pastoral impact for himself, even though Ravello would not have been a typically abandoned rural area like Tramonti. Nevertheless, the mission experience confirmed his intention of offering his services to the new missionary group, though the thought of having to teach in a junior school horrified him. With a guarantee that teaching would not be his lot, he returned to Naples after a few weeks and immediately threw himself into the task of refuting the calumnious propaganda which was still circulating there concerning Alphonsus and the entire enterprise. He wrote a formal refutation of the misleading reports current among the clergy, tracing their source and confronting the gossips with the real facts. In a series of letters to Scala he detailed all he was doing. He sought a verified copy of Fiorillo's original permission to allow Alphonsus to follow his vocation. Alphonsus had come across a quotation from Teresa of Avila in the matter of obedience as the only reliable source of God's revelations, and that would be useful too. He requested an authenticated account of everything that had happened to Maria Celeste, since the news of her departure had fuelled the gossip enormously. The allegations of cruelty perpetrated against her had been particularly damaging. And since the ridicule about the new institute was still centred on the three original objections, the revelations of a neurotic nun, the ridiculous habit of red and blue, and the establishing of a new religious order, Sarnelli concentrated his defence on these points. Even more than Alphonsus, he was unimpressed by anything in the nature of alleged revelations; he totally discounted them as the source of the new missionary group. As regards a new religious order he was quite definite: 'We are a group of pastorally active priests who go from place to place helping souls in the most abandoned rural areas of the kingdom, making God known to those who do not know Him.' 'That', he said, forcefully if not elegantly, 'shut their mouths and left them without a come-back.'[15]

Sarnelli's intervention was decisive. Gradually he stemmed the tide of gossip and brought the clerical world of Naples to behave with a modicum of sensitivity and tolerance. His own departure for Scala, later in the summer, proved to be the breakthrough the work needed. He was the first priest possessed of a genuine missionary ideal matching that of Alphonsus to join the group. He was strong-willed and independent with little time for Falcoia, a sentiment which was reciprocated fully by the bishop. But his presence was invaluable for a variety of reasons, not least among them being the fact that he provided the little group of missionaries with a hard core of steel which it may have lacked up until then. Even though Falcoia did not see eye to eye with him and never really considered him a genuine member of the missionary group, Alphonsus thought otherwise and Sarnelli may well merit the title of the second founder.

– *VII* –

The increase in numbers, but above all the harmony of outlook existing among the group for the very first time, enabled them to experiment with a pattern of religious observance. The day began at a quarter past four in the morning after the regulation period of six and a half hours' sleep. Meditation together was followed by the recitation of the Hours of the Breviary, Prime, Terce and Sext. The Neapolitan breakfast was at a quarter to six, leaving five and a half hours for study and pastoral work until a quarter past eleven, when they gathered in chapel for the recitation of the Hour of None. Examination of conscience, lunch and recreation followed. There was reading at table except on what were styled recreation or free days, and Sundays. In chapel again after the meal, litanies were recited for all living friends and benefactors while the psalm *De Profundis* was recited for the dead. After the midday meal, Brother Vito distributed food to the poor. Fortunately for the community, Falcoia had intervened to remove responsibility for the kitchen from Vito and entrusted it to Canon Romano who was unlikely to allow ascetical principles to run riot.

Life began again after the midday siesta with an hour's prayer, divided between spiritual reading and private meditation, leading directly to the Office of Vespers in the chapel. There was then time for further study or pastoral work, or at certain times, for instructions in the junior school. Compline was recited at six thirty, then there was another half hour of meditation, this time together, followed immediately by the common recitation of Matins and Lauds — about which there was much discussion, and later the time for this Office was altered. The evening meal at seven forty-five was followed by an hour of relaxation which began when the bells of the cathedrals in Scala and Ravello rang out the *Ave Maria* to announce the end of the day. Night prayer at nine fifteen ushered in the period of absolute silence when all were free to retire to rest.

Alphonsus spent Thursdays in private retreat, though he did take part in the common recreation since their numbers were few. Monday, after the midday meal, was set aside for an academy of spiritual theology, without undue formality, since apparently a few jokes were not ruled out, if one is to interpret Falcoia's directions correctly — '*no si refiuta qualche parola d'ilarità*'. A more formal academy of theology was also held during the week, to which the local clergy were invited, to discuss matters of pastoral interest, sometimes in the hospice itself, sometimes, for lack of space, in the cathedral. Silence was to be observed in the house to facilitate both prayer and study. Experience was to alter certain aspects of this primitive timetable as the years went by, but the general outline survived for nearly two centuries, despite differences of climate, social habits and pastoral needs. Since the computation of the hour of the day began from the evening *Ave Maria* rather than from midnight as it does now universally, and since the hour of the *Ave Maria* varied from month to month, Alphonsus had to spend considerable time and energy drawing up an horarium for the whole year, which was finally copied out by Sportelli. Signed by both Alphonsus and Falcoia, the original has survived to this day.

Finally, there was an air of confidence about the group which had been lacking up to then. Mannarini paid a brief visit to Scala during the summer — but not apparently to Alphonsus — and floated the idea of uniting with the group once more. Alphonsus intervened immediately to reject the proposal out-of-hand; one experience was sufficient. The Scala municipality was anxious to secure the establishment of a junior school. Alphonsus agreed, both to cater for the catechetical needs of the children, as well as to foster goodwill, while the modest monetary subsidy of forty ducats would help to maintain the community. A few rooms adjacent to the hospice were secured where Sportelli, and for a short while both Sarnelli and Alphonsus himself, instructed the children. The nuns' hospice was now clearly unsuitable taking into account the increased numbers and the opening of the school; there was the added consideration that relations with the sisters were still strained. A much larger and altogether more suitable building was secured higher up the mountain overlooking the convent and the cathedral. It became known as the Hospice of the Most Holy Saviour to distinguish it from the hospice of the sisters; later it was referred to as the *Casa Anastasio* and is still cherished as the first permanent home of the missionaries of the Most Holy Saviour.

The new 'monastery' was a typical two-storey Neapolitan farmhouse, similar to many others still scattered on the hillside — slightly more spacious but offering no more concessions to luxury than the restricted dwelling they had vacated. It had the usual staircases connecting the ground and upper floors — one internal, the other external. It was sufficiently spacious for them to be able to designate a room on the ground floor as a public chapel and to set aside two others upstairs, one as a private domestic oratory, the other as a class room. When the bishop granted permission to reserve the Blessed Sacrament they had no tabernacle equipped with a key, so they took turns to spend the night in adoration until the liturgical requirements could be complied with.

The five rooms on the upper storey opened out on a *loggia* about three yards wide and some thirty long which was the most delectable feature of the property, since it allowed the members of the community to enjoy both the sun and the enchanting scenery. Brother Vito had regained control of the kitchen, where a large open furnace, resembling nothing more sophisticated than those found in the ruins of Pompei, provided him with his cooking oven. In the account of Brother Vito's life which he wrote, Alphonsus recalled that, on one occasion, Vito neglected to include some yeast in the bread he was baking, with the result that it turned out as hard as a rock. By way of retribution he allotted the concoction to himself and ate nothing else until he had finished it. Not all cooks are so considerate.

A remarkable feature of their lives together from the outset was the insistence on study, especially the study of theology in all its branches; if there was a particular emphasis it was on moral theology with special reference to the ministry of the confessional or what we would call pastoral theology. Despite their poverty and very meagre resources, there was already the beginnings of a sound theological library. Alphonsus had *folio* copies of some of the classical moral theologians in his possession. Sarnelli announced from Naples, with a sense of triumph, that he had secured a copy of *il Calepino Grande*, the classical Latin dictionary published by Ambrogio di Calepio in 1502, and would bring it with him on his return to Scala in September. Alphonsus, besides collecting material on Our Lady, which many years later saw the light of day as *The Glories of Mary*, was already concentrating his attention on problems of moral theology.

– VIII –

With the arrangements for their new residence confirmed, Alphonsus and Sarnelli embarked on a whole series of missions in the autumn of 1733. They enlisted help from other secular priests; other religious, and the Neapolitan Dominicans explicitly, were excluded, under instructions from Falcoia — the Dominicans because of their reputed rigorism in the confessional; other religious, because Alphonsus wished to evolve a mission system of his own. For the moment they concentrated their efforts at the Cava and Salerno end of the Amalfi peninsula, thus opening up a whole new area for their efforts. They were now working in a completely changed atmosphere and with a new assurance. In Naples the critical gossip had ceased; they were singing a different tune there now, wrote Alphonsus triumphantly. No one would now dare to criticise the missionary undertaking established at Scala. The missions were visibly blessed and requests came pouring in especially from the most backward areas like the Cilento, south of Salerno. Bishops, too, were requesting foundations in their dioceses, the archbishop of Salerno and the bishop of Cava being particularly insistent. The decision, however, was to make a second foundation in the diocese of Caiazzo about a hundred kilometres from Naples north of the Volturno.

Mons. Vigilante of Caiazzo was the first bishop with whom Alphonsus had discussed in great secrecy the proposal to establish a new missionary congregation as far back as the spring of 1732. Vigilante was enthusiastic then and invited Alphonsus to begin the work in his diocese. When the choice of Scala was made, mainly to be near Falcoia and Crostarosa in the convent, Alphonsus was careful to keep open the lines of communication with Caiazzo. He kept in constant touch by letter and made sure that Falcoia did the same. When his first companions deserted him, he went directly from his visit to the Cardinal in Naples in April 1733 up to Vigilante to re-open the question of a house of missions there. The bishop suggested that the foundation be made in *Villa degli Schiavi* or the 'town of the slaves', changed since then into the less insulting name of *Villa Liberi*, once the home of St Anselm of Canterbury. Situated in the northern tip of the diocese, Villa was particularly attractive from the pastoral point of view — it was the ideal centre for access to the dioceses of Capua, Piedmonte and Caiazzo itself, besides possessing a numerous population much in need of spiritual ministrations. Despite the fact that the diocesan capital of Caiazzo with a population of less than 2500 inhabitants had thirty-five priests, twenty-five of them canons, and three religious communities of priests, the simple folk scattered on the mountains and hills round Villa just fifteen kilometres distant, were spiritually abandoned. Mons. Vigilante offered Alphonsus the small church of the Annunciation or the *Ave Gratia Plena* on the outskirts of the town as the centre for his missioners. Father Francis Xavier Rossi, a local priest, offered his assistance in making the foundation.

Rossi, thirty-two years of age, was in the full fervour of his priesthood when he offered himself to Alphonsus; he had a brother a priest in the village, whose unedifying life was typical of many of the local clergy. Francis Xavier was hewn from the locality, rough and rugged but genuine and honest; a little bit of a Jansenist and very much a Gallican, he possessed a fiery nature, ever on the verge of eruption. He knew himself well enough to say that if he had remained as a layman in the world and had not joined Alphonsus, he would have met a violent death.[16] As it was, he was fortunate to escape a similar fate in the monastery. Later in life he was to become the confessor and confidant of Don Joseph, Alphonsus' father; they were well matched. But men of such tough fibre were needed for the missionary life as envisaged in the new congregation and Rossi was the ideal candidate to establish the foundation in Caiazzo. Alphonsus sent Rossi to Castellamare for Falcoia's inspection; the bishop approved of him with the hope that 'by the autumn he will be more mature and more stable and that he will become one of the foundation stones of the edifice'. And this is precisely what happened. Rossi was accepted and regarded himself as a missionary of the Most Holy Saviour right away. Falcoia determined that he begin immediately 'an anticipated novitiate', whatever that was.

Rossi duly returned to Villa to take charge of the preliminary negotiations in connection with the new foundation, which dragged on during the summer and autumn. At the end of January of the following year 1734, Alphonsus and Sarnelli, restored after the fatigue of their missionary activity in the autumn, arrived with two secular priests to open the mission in the episcopal city of Caiazzo. From there, the group, strengthened with reinforcements, among them Rossi himself, moved on to the neighbouring villages. In March, in an atmosphere of enthusiasm generated by the success of the missions, the commune of Villa handed over to Alphonsus possession of the small church with a dwelling house of seven rooms beside it. Sarnelli returned to Scala to rejoin Sportelli and Vito under the gentle care of Canon Romano; Alphonsus established himself at Villa with Rossi, to consolidate the new foundation as well as to initiate him into the spirit of the new institute and instruct him in the method of giving missions. Together they preached the first mission the people of Villa had ever experienced. Then they set about making the church a centre of pastoral activity, a continuing mission, which was always part of Alphonsus' vision for his congregation's activities. On Thursdays there was exposition of the Blessed Sacrament followed by a sermon; the other days of the week, the church bell tolled in the evening to bring the people together for the visit to the Blessed Sacrament. Saturdays were days of special devotion to the Mother of God. In the church was an altar of Our Lady of the Rosary with a painting of the Our Lady and St Dominic, a reminder that a confraternity of our Lady of the Rosary had once been established there. Alphonsus decided to revive it. He wrote to Father Fiorillo asking him to renew its incorporation into the Dominican arch-confraternity. Fiorillo replied encouragingly, 'You will have the Brief for the Indulgences and the establishment of the confraternity for the feast of Our Lady of the Rosary. Believe me I maintain all my interest in, and sympathy for your congregation. . . . Keep up your courage and may the Lord console you by sending you good subjects. Place yourself under the protection of St Vincent Ferrer who was the greatest missioner since the time of the apostles,' — he never omitted this refrain.

Alphonsus now began to plan for the total pastoral utilisation of his new foundation; missions were only part of the ministry he envisaged. He planned a building which would serve for retreats for priests and laity, for seminarians and those for ordination. He also had in mind some form of novitiate, and perhaps even a minor seminary, for the education of prospective candidates. Falcoia approved the project with something less than enthusiasm and, with the natural caution of old age, warned against going forward too quickly. In point of fact, Alphonsus had already anticipated the decision and had purchased building materials to commence the work right away; since there were no missions during Lent or high summer this was the ideal time to commence operations. Moreover, he had skilfully exemplified the well-known technique of having everything ready to begin before getting the formal permission. He donned working clothes and was mason, carpenter, labourer and architect all at the same time. Men and women from the village came to offer their assistance. With the bishop's permission, Father Rossi took upon himself the task of collecting funds for the building. Within a few months a chapel and some forty small rooms were ready for use; to spare expense, oiled paper was substituted for glass. It was all very primitive but it served its function.

The spiritual fruits of the new house were not long in making themselves evident, not alone in the locality but throughout the whole diocese. The preaching of Alphonsus, his ceaseless ministry in the confessional, the regular functioning of the sodalities he had established or revitalised, brought about a reformation in the moral standards and devotional practices of the whole area, which was the subject of comment by both priests and bishop in the diocese. Perhaps the priest of Caiazzo was exaggerating, somewhat, when at the process of canonisation, he declared that under the influence of the ministry of Alphonsus and his companions, Villa and the neighbouring countryside became a terrestrial paradise, but he was, at least, bearing testimony to a decided improvement in the religious practice of the area. Alphonsus preached to the clergy and the seminarians of the diocese; with whatever help he could muster, he evangelised sections of the diocese which had not experienced missionary preaching of the Word of God during the life-time of the majority of the faithful. Dragoni, Formicola, Fondola, Treglia, Profeti were all evangelised with Alphonsus insisting that he and his missionaries should remain in each place as long as was necessary for them to hear the confessions of all the inhabitants. The candidates for ordination from the neighbouring diocese of Capua were sent to Villa to make their retreats for ordination. The ideal of priestly holiness and above all, of priestly zeal for souls which was placed before them can easily be gauged from Alphonsus' later publications; what he wrote he had already preached.

At the end of the following year, 1735, the bishop of Caiazzo had to report to Rome on the state of his diocese. In his official *relatio* to the Congregation of the Council, he wrote:

> I have not omitted to preach the Word of God in the course of my pastoral visitations and in the cathedral, even though I am not gifted naturally for this ministry. On account of my inadequacy, I asked the Lord to send labourers into his vineyard for this purpose and He, who is never slow to answer favourably petitions which are acceptable to Him, consoled me by providing for this diocese missioners with a genuine apostolic spirit from Naples who have settled in Villa degli Schiavi, so that living there permanently in community, they may with greater profit scatter the seed of the Divine Word throughout these regions which are almost destitute of evangelical labourers. And to assure you that I am not merely using words to exaggerate what is being done for the glory of God and the good of souls, the general opinion of everybody is that these people, so unlettered, and so often led astray into the ways of sin, now walk in the true way of salvation, thanks to the sweat of these missionaries and the grace of God.

This was the first official report of the pastoral activity of the new missionary congregation to find its way to the relevant Vatican department.[17]

CHAPTER SEVEN

THE BOURBONS OF NAPLES

– I –

Naples was a fief of Spain ruled by Spanish viceroys when Alphonsus was born; he was eleven and beginning his legal studies when Austria took control and ruled the Kingdom from Vienna. He was thirty-eight and settling down to priestly life as a missionary of the Most Holy Saviour when the Bourbons arrived. His life for the next fifty years as superior of a missionary congregation, a writer of popular spirituality, moral theology and apologetics and his pastoral activity as a bishop have to be seen against the background of the changes brought about by the arrival of the new dynasty.

Alphonsus was at Villa in April 1734 when eighteen-year-old Charles of Bourbon, son of Philip V of Spain and his second wife, Elizabeth Farnese, set out from Florence at the head of a small but efficient Spanish army to claim the Kingdom of the Two Sicilies which had fallen to him as a result of the dynastic arrangements resulting from the war of the Polish Succession. Very few Neapolitans rallied to the Austrians as the Spanish troops came down the valley of the Volturno and headed for the capital; even the municipality of Villa hoisted the Bourbon flag in welcome. At Maddaloni, young Charles, wearing the jewelled sword of his great grandfather, Louis XIV, and with a retinue of two hundred followers, received the keys of the Kingdom from the nobles of the *Seggi* of Naples. Alphonsus, though he did not do so, would have been entitled to take part in the ceremony as a member of the *Seggi* of Portanuova. One of his most genuine friends, whose spiritual director he was and whose influence was later vital for him and his missionary work, Gaetano Maria Brancone, acted as their secretary. A few weeks later, on the evening of 10 May Charles made his state entry into Naples where he was received enthusiastically by the people. Cardinal Pignatelli received him formally on behalf of the nation and conducted him to the cathedral to venerate the blood of St Januarius. During the following days the hierarchy, among them Falcoia from Castellamare, rendered homage to their new sovereign in the church of San Giacomo degli Spagnuoli.

Naples took the boy king to its heart immediately; as the years went by they grew to love him and regard him as their own. When he later left to succeed to the throne of Spain in succession to his half-brother there was general regret. Young and with Italian blood in his veins he was the nearest thing the Neapolitans could hope for in the way of an independent Neapolitan dynasty. His military campaign had been conducted in a most gentlemanly fashion with few casualties on either side. The Kingdom — with the exception of some of the feudal barons — was tired of the Austrians and the Austrians were unable and unwilling to defend it; it fell readily into his hands. Fortunately, too, the King's advisers were excellent. At once he identified himself with Naples and its population. He made himself one of them and they reciprocated in a way they had never done with the Hapsburgs. In July he was crowned King of the Two Sicilies in Palermo by the primate, archbishop Basile.

The arrival of the Bourbons ushered in a whole new era in Neapolitan history not merely from the dynastic point of view but also from the social, religious, economic and cultural aspects of life as well. Naples entered upon a period of expansion and prosperity which made it one of the great capitals of Europe and one of the most characteristic kingdoms of the *ancien régime*. The splendour of its new palaces at Portici, Capodimonte and Casserta, the glories of its operas and of the San Carlo, the protocol of its Court, the flowering of its intellectual and cultural genius, the excavations of Pompei and Herculaneum made it the envy of Europe. There was peace; the population increased; there was order in government and above all order in the public finances. The new King was devout with morals above reproach, high-minded and full of the best intentions for the advancement of his people according to the principles of the Enlightened Monarchs. With his Jesuit education and confessor he commenced his reign with no animosity towards the Papacy but unfortunately his relations with the reigning pontiff began inauspiciously. Clement XII was a loyal supporter of Austria and made known at once to Cardinal Pignatelli his displeasure at the ecclesiastical reception accorded to the new king. Since the thirteenth century when Pope Urban IV invested the Angevins with the crown of Naples, it was customary for the reigning monarch to present the Pope with a white horse and an offering of 7,000 ducats on the feast of St Peter in the Vatican basilica — the colourful ceremony of the *chinea* so often described and ridiculed by Roman visitors of the period.[1] In 1735, the year following Charles' acquisition of his kingdom, both his representatives and those of the Austrian court vied in presenting the tribute to the Pope. The Austrian tribute was accepted, that of Charles rejected. The insult rankled; fanned by the advice of his minister Tanucci, the King developed a strong anti-Roman and anti-curial complex. Worse was to follow. Clement XII refused to confer the nominal papal investiture of his Kingdom on Charles for another three years, thereby considerably inflaming his anti-Roman feeling.

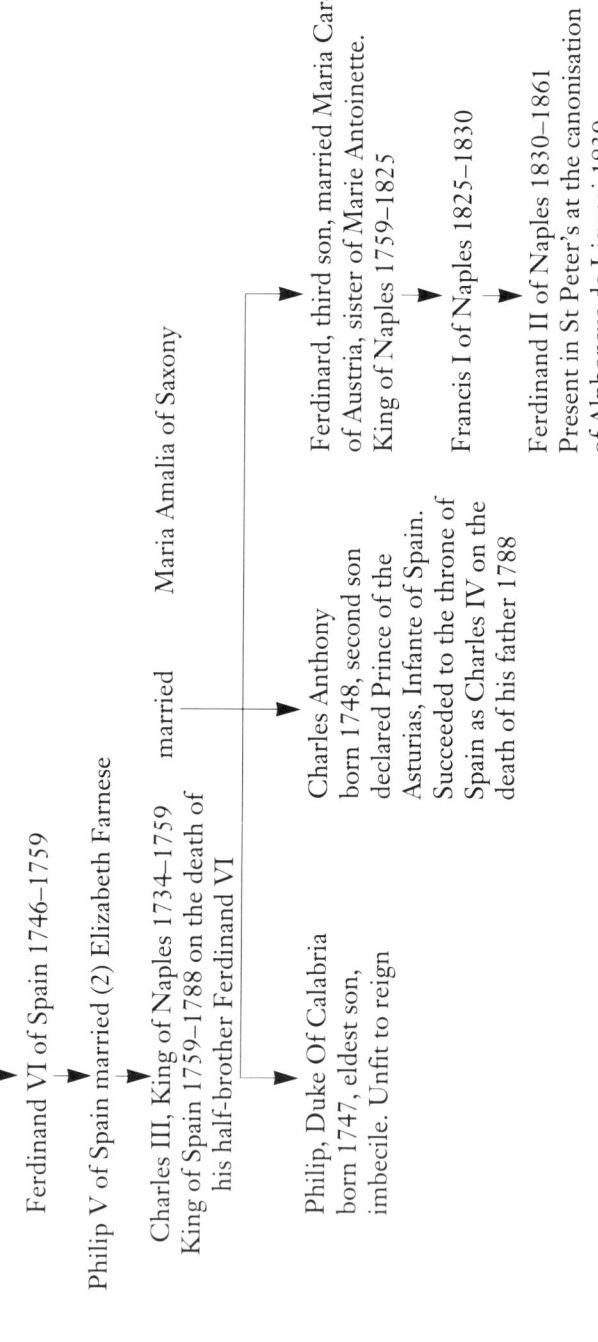

Charles set about reorganising the whole government system bequeathed to him by the Austrians. He appointed his Spanish guardian and mentor, Don Manuel de Benavides, conde de San Estaban, his principal minister and under him four Secretaries of State, three of whom figure prominently in Alphonsus' life. Brancone became Secretary for Ecclesiastical Affairs, Gioacchino de Montealegre, Secretary for Diplomatic Affairs; and Bernardo Tanucci, Secretary for Justice, who, in due course, as virtual prime minister, took over the reins of government for nearly forty years.

When Charles assembled his retinue in February 1734 prior to setting out for Naples, he included in it the young lawyer Tanucci whose loyal services during his stay in Parma and Florence had taught him what an essential member of his court he would be. Tanucci, eighteen months younger than Alphonsus, was born in the small *borgata* of Stia in the mountains of the Casentino. A severe attack of smallpox at the age of eleven disfigured him physically for life. He was educated at the seminary at Perugia and then by the Scolopi Fathers in Florence where he began to develop his anti-Jesuit prejudice. He studied law in Pisa, practised in the courts and then took up teaching in the university. He married the daughter of a count and no breath of scandal ever tarnished their married life or their devotion to their only child, Mariana. The arrival of the young Charles of Bourbon from Spain as heir presumptive to the last of the Medici brought him entry into government life, and without hesitation he followed the rising star of the Bourbons to Naples. His loyalty as well as his undoubted talents were rewarded by his appointment to the *Segretaria della Grazia e Giustizia*. It would have been difficult for the new King to have made a more inspired choice. During his ten years at the justice office he initiated a complete reform of the judicial system, unifying the various criminal and civic codes which were a troublesome heritage from medieval times and of which Alphonsus himself had bitter experience in the Gravina law suit. He restored law and order to the city and was determined to do the same for the rest of the Kingdom. His first attack was on the 'nobility' to make them amenable to the law and its penalties; there was to be the same equal justice for all. His next undertaking was to demolish the Church's position of privilege, with its immunity from taxation for itself and the clergy. The right of sanctuary enjoyed by churches, church buildings and in some cases even by ecclesiastical persons was the next area for his attention, bringing him into conflict before long with Falcoia in Castellamare. The proud inscription on his tomb in Naples announced that while in control of the State's finances for over forty years he never once imposed new taxes.

Tanucci, moreover, was that strange phenomenon in Neapolitan life, incorruptible. In a society where most of the officials were venal he was above suspicion. His sense of justice was such that he was scrupulous in not seeking his own aggrandisement as a result of his office; he died a poor man and more to the point, lived as one. He cultivated a deep personal piety which he never abandoned. He went regularly to Confession and Communion and to Mass every day. In his last Will he recommended his soul 'as a faithful christian to God, to the Divine Redeemer, to the Queen of Heaven, to his Patron Saint and to his Angel Guardian'. He requested twelve Masses to be celebrated for the repose of his soul and ordered his interment to be carried out with the Last Absolution but without 'any other function of music or other vanity' — he obviously had not accustomed himself to Neapolitan ways even in liturgical matters. All he wanted at his death was prayer and then to leave his remains in that deep silence which would not interrupt his last colloquy with God.[2]

From the beginning Rome intrigued against him; the Curia tried everything in its power to have him removed from office even before he became the dominant figure in the government. Despite the fact that he abhorred Voltaire and his hatred of the Church, he was himself consumed with a phobia against the Roman Curia, the Society of Jesus and the slightest manifestation of clerical privilege. The excessive number of clergy, the amount of property they controlled, their fiscal immunity, all these enraged him. He planned to claim the revenues of vacant benefices, to separate religious from their Roman superiors — in this he was supported by some of the bishops — to place their property under government control and supervision, to forbid legacies to the Church, to annul Wills providing for the celebration of Masses, even though he requested them for himself. Every Roman appointment had to be approved by the Royal Secretariate for Religious Affairs, a ministry of religion in modern terms; every Roman document had to pass through that office and possessed no authority in the Kingdom without the royal *Exequatur*. Every single religious sodality or confraternity, not to speak of a new missionary congregation, had to have its approval. This was the climate in which Alphonsus, first as a missionary and superior of a new congregation and then as a bishop, had to exercise his ministry, publish his books, communicate with Rome. Time and time again he had to approach Tanucci either personally or through some influential friend in order to stave off the disaster he feared for his missionary society. And yet in 1772, when he published his work on the history of heresies entitled *The Triumph of the Church*, he dedicated it to Tanucci and addressed him in the most laudatory terms, 'for your vast legal erudition and your capable administration of affairs of State. . . . Above all you will be remembered for the admirable zeal with which you have always striven to preserve untarnished our holy religion throughout the Kingdom. . . . These reasons together with the veneration I personally have for you, have induced me to dedicate this work to you.' Perhaps it was all diplomacy and tongue-in-cheek but a century later Peter Minetti, the *Promotor Fidei*, objected strongly to what Alphonsus had written when the question of declaring him a Doctor of the Church was under consideration.[3]

In 1738 the King married by proxy in Dresden the daughter of the King of Saxony, Maria Amalia; he was twenty-two, she fourteen. He met her for the first time in June of that year at Portella on the frontiers of the Kingdom of which she was now to be Queen. They loved each other at their first meeting and were utterly faithful in their marriage until her death at the age of thirty-six after some sixteen pregnancies and the birth of eleven children. Stricken with grief at his loss the King maintained his faith with her beyond the grave, resolutely refusing to marry again even when he succeeded to the throne of Spain. A member of the court circle, with the malice typical of that society, described them as the ugliest couple in the world, she with a bullet nose, crayfish features and magpie voice; he small and round-shouldered, with bad teeth, a complexion marred by smallpox and a protruding nose which is the most prominent feature of the royal portraits. The King's great passion was sport; he loved to have his portrait painted in his hunting clothes with a fowling piece in his hands. Intellectual exercises of any sort were beyond him; matters of state bored him. Hunting, fowling, fishing, anything, provided it was outdoor exercise, were his only real interests. Often at Court ceremonies and cabinet meetings he wore his hunting apparel under his royal regalia so that he could escape at the first opportunity to his beloved fields. It all stemmed from a belief which later became an obsession, that an outdoor life was essential if he was to avoid the depressive insanity which brought his father to the grave. Despite his genuine esteem for Alphonsus personally he was never prepared to accept the existence of the Missionaries of the Most Holy Saviour, and on several occasions was within an inch of decreeing their suppression. Innumerable were the occasions when Alphonsus arrived at one of the Royal Palaces and waited interminably in the ante-chambers to plead for understanding of what he was doing, fearing at the same time the destruction of his life's work.

– II –

Alphonsus was fully occupied during these exciting months of dynastic changes with his work in Villa, the preaching of missions and the search for new members for his Congregation. The arrival of the Bourbons, however, did have an immediate effect on the career of his father and also on that of Don Silvestro Tosques. Whatever his true political allegiance may have been and there is every indication that he was devoted to the Hapsburgs, Don Giuseppe was not initially *persona grata* to the new officials in the Ministry of War; his navy career was at an end. Removed from his command and deprived of his pension rights, he retired to the family home at Marianella where he devoted a considerable amount of his leisure time to painting. A few years later he would spend much of his time with Father Rossi in the new foundation at Ciorani.[4]

Just when the work he had undertaken seemed to be gathering momentum a new phase of doubt assailed Alphonsus about his whole vocation. Under Falcoia's guidance he had gained some control over his personal anxieties and he had vowed *never* to allow the authenticity of his vocation to be called into doubt. Now a fresh scruple concerning a greater good began to trouble him. It was not that he was tempted to abandon the work for some selfish reason — he could easily cope with that temptation — but he was tempted to abandon it under the specious pretext of devoting himself to the more urgent work of the salvation of souls on the foreign missions, specifically in the Cape of Good Hope which, according to Ripa in the Chinese College, was totally deprived of priests. He felt under an obligation of charity to preach the Gospel to these neglected souls. In the summer of 1734 he drew up a theological *exposé* of the whole question, centring his problem in the obligation that theologians of the time commonly imposed, of coming to the assistance of those in grave spiritual and temporal need. He sent his first draft to Pagano for his opinion; something similar he sent to Falcoia but with a stronger though implicit suggestion that he felt bound to abandon his present work in favour of the foreign missions.[5] Falcoia's reply was a stroke of genius. Instead of refuting Alphonsus' main argument concerning the obligation of charity which he was under, he affirmed it but demonstrated at the same time that the work he was engaged in was more effective for the salvation of souls than if he were to travel to Africa or anywhere else:

> Certainly your inspiration to come to the assistance of the abandoned souls in the Cape is from God and consequently is good. But I sincerely wish that your horizons could be broader still. My son, why do you wish to assist those neglected souls and not so many others who are in similar necessity throughout the rest of Africa, Asia, America and the still unknown lands, and indeed in Europe itself? Are they not souls too? Are they not like your own? Are they not in the image of God? Did they not cost Jesus Christ his Blood? Are they not capable of eternal beatitude? Are they not near to eternal damnation? Why do you not feel disturbed for them as well and why do you not wish to come to their assistance?
>
> This is precisely the purpose of our Institute — here we must concentrate all our desires. In all this we must be co-operators with Jesus Christ, we must expand our hearts with charity for all. And do you think that you, by yourself, can do all this? Our Lord himself wished the co-operation and help of his apostles and now even *our* help, though, of course, He could have done it all himself. What can you do single-handed?[6]

Falcoia concluded with the strongest possible statement about Alphonsus' vocation. 'Remain at peace and press ahead with the work of the Lord . . . never again look further than this statement and pay no attention to anything else concerning either yourself or the work you have undertaken. You have been chosen by God as the main instrument of this building and it is for you to carry His Name to every Tribe and People and Nation.'

With his mind at rest, at least temporarily, Alphonsus was able to continue his work in Villa for the recruitment and formation of new members. Falcoia had his own very sound ideas about enticing candidates to join. He discouraged 'propaganda' since 'vocations come from God'. The first move must come from the candidate himself and then it would be up to the congregation either to accept or reject the application after prayerful discernment.

It was only as a result of the members' prayers and their own fidelity to God that the Lord of the Harvest would *send* the workers. Falcoia was equally determined not to accept all those who offered themselves; quality was more important than numbers. Two clerics from Positano who presented themselves did not impress him; 'they would do nothing for us' was his verdict and he advised them to return home. His attitude is quite understandable in the light of the situation at the time. There was an abundance of clerics on all sides but few who were genuinely interested in pastoral work or in facing the hardships of the missionary life in general, and fewer still, the missionary life as Alphonsus envisaged and practised it.[7]

At the very outset of his efforts to build up his missionary society Alphonsus encountered his fellow Neapolitans' almost pathological reluctance to leave home and family and the equally strong reluctance of their families to allow them to leave, sometimes indeed on account of deep family affection but, as often as not, for less worthy motives. Don Giuseppe Chierchia from Castellamare, an exemplary priest residing at home with his mother, was an example typical of many. Despite the attraction he felt for the missionary life, his talents for it and the belief that God wanted him to engage in a more active apostolate for souls, the attraction of home and family proved too strong. 'The spirit', he quoted, 'is willing but the flesh is weak.' For months Alphonsus pleaded with him; six or seven times he wrote at length to him using every possible argument to entice him to come. 'For heaven's sake, come at once. What about your home, your mother, your brothers and sisters? Whoever does not leave all for God will never find God completely. Come at once. We are preparing for a number of missions, but as well as that we wish to have you always with us.' But the attraction of home, the affection for family proved too strong. To all the appeals, to the urgings that God needed him and was calling him, Don Chierchia remained unmoved. 'When one cannot, one cannot', he concluded. Exasperated Alphonsus retorted, 'And I say to you when one won't, one won't. However this is the end. I do not wish to annoy you further nor do we wish to have you among us any more if you do not come with all your heart. We do not take persons by force.' The upshot was that Don Chierchia agreed to join Alphonsus and his companions on missions from time to time provided that he was not obliged to pass through Scala lest his love for all it stood for should reawaken his desire to commit himself fully.[8]

Others, however, hesitated to join the new congregation, weighing its prospects in a calculating way. Don Francesco de Viva from near Villa would have been an acceptable candidate. An exemplary priest and excellent preacher he had accompanied Alphonsus on many missions but hesitated to become fully committed for the simple reason that he thought the new society had no future. What resources have you? he asked Alphonsus. From the human point of view he considered Mannarini and his companions, who were boasting of their success, a better investment. Alphonsus' reply was on an altogether different plane:

What resources have we? We have God. And what work of God was ever based on human support? Tell me what human support had the work of St Francis, of St John of the Cross, of St Teresa?

You tell me that Mannarini has more human support than we have. Then we must have more trust in God than he has. In proportion as a work is great, so much the more does Jesus Christ make it begin from nothing and surround it with contradictions so as to make it admired by all as a work of God and not a work of human ingenuity. What work was ever more destitute of human resources than the preaching of the Gospels? Don Ciccio mio, the more you talk like this the clearer it becomes that you are not called to this work since for our humble institute Jesus Christ wants men who have placed all their trust in God and not in human means.

The only thing that can ruin this institute is lack of confidence in God and placing one's trust in human means which I well know from experience since I placed all my hope in human considerations which nearly led to the destruction of the whole work. Don Ciccio, who has done what has been achieved up to now? Me or God? And that same God who has begun the work can complete it.[9]

By 1735 there were eleven 'novices' in Villa under Alphonsus' guidance, seven priests and four brothers, Sportelli, Rossi, Mazzini, Camardelli, Marocco, Don Innocencio, Michele de Alteriis and Brothers Rendina, Angelillo, Pietro and Xaverio. Mazzini had eventually succeeded in extracting permission from his reluctant spiritual director; de Alteriis was one of Alphonsus' companions from the days of the *capelle serotine* in Naples. The whole position was canonically anomalous. There was no question of a formal canonical novitiate, there were no vows not even an oath of commitment to the institute. The group was nothing more than a number of priests living together for the purpose of giving missions; they did not even possess an accepted and completed Rule. And yet both Falcoia and Alphonsus recognised that the task of building the spiritual edifice of the new society was of greater importance than the building of the material monastery of Villa.

Alphonsus could claim no expertise in the task of training the candidates. He had to rely completely on instructions from Falcoia who had been for many years Master of Novices in his own society and displayed no diffidence about his competence. 'I know well from experience what skill and prudence is needed in the task of training novices.' The correspondence between them grew more frequent and voluminous during the months Alphonsus was in charge. Falcoia's directions extended to every phase of the religious life since Alphonsus made clear his need of detailed suggestions from one with the bishop's lived experience. His instructions amounted to a virtual manual of novitiate practice, taken directly from the practice of the Pii Operai and later codified as a special Novices' Rule surviving right down to the Second Vatican Council and detailing such minutiae as the topics of conversation unbecoming to the novitiate community room. Falcoia left his mark on two centuries of unfortunate novices throughout the world.

The fundamental spirituality of the novitiate was based on the master idea of the imitation of Jesus Christ. This had been the principal insight of Maria Celeste's revelations and she had interpreted this basic idea as a living participation in the life dynamic of the Saviour. Falcoia's approach lacked the theological sophistication to be found in Crostarosa; for him it was an imitation which did not go beyond an ascetical method concentrating on the life of Jesus Christ — a greatly impoverished concept in comparison with that of Crostarosa. A special virtue was proposed for each month of the year and round this virtue the meditations, lectures and examinations of conscience were centred. An outline plan appears in Alphonsus' own private note-book. Beginning in January with the virtue of faith — the three theological virtues had been added to the nine proposed by Crostarosa to make up twelve — the novices were led each month through the theology and practice of a specific virtue, though not, of course, to the exclusion of others. It was a methodical spirituality in vogue at the time and in no way unique. Twice a week Alphonsus lectured his novices on these and other subjects while the best exemplification of the virtues he was inculcating was to be found in his own conduct. His hours of prayer, his penances which it was not possible for him to conceal in the small community despite his best efforts, the meals he took on his knees in the refectory seasoned with bitter herbs to make them less palatable than they already were, were the most effective catechesis he could provide. Yet he was well aware that he was training men for the apostolic life on missions and he wished them to be in contact with it from the beginning. On Sundays and feast days the novices were sent out to teach catechism and those who were priests — the majority in the early years — to preach a closely monitored sermon in a nearby church or even in the market-place. This was coupled with instructions on how they were to behave on missions with regard to life-style, food and accommodation, all of which were to be in marked contrast with the practice of the Apostolic Missions.

The candidate's first introduction to life in the congregation was an uncompromising examination of his motives. Brother Gennaro Rendina was greeted with the remark, 'If you have come to sanctify yourself, come in; if not please return to Naples.' In his case there was no doubt about his intentions as his fifty years faithful service was to demonstrate; others, however, were not so upright. Life for the novice began with a spiritual retreat which was to mark the definite break with the work and life he had left and his earnest commitment to the new world he had entered. Falcoia was aware, as was Alphonsus, of the Neapolitan's affection for home and his sense of being in exile if anything so much as a mountain range separated him from his native place. In this context Falcoia warned Alphonsus against allowing the novice to return home on the pretext of being ill:

> Do not permit the novices to return home to be attended to when they are ill; if this once began it would be the end of everything. At the same

time show every kindness and attention to those who are ill so that they will not have any wish to return home. Only very special illnesses such as tuberculosis would necessitate one's native air. But the ordinary illnesses, even if mortal, cannot be regarded as an excuse.

When you hear that relations are ill, you can allow them to go see them to console them, especially if they are priests and the parents request their assistance at this time. The general rule is that they do not go home and according to the Gospel that they 'allow the dead to bury the dead', but there are a variety of grave emergencies such as the salvation of souls, the particular character of a novice, which would be a reason for dispensing this general norm.

These reasonable instructions were interpreted by Alphonsus in an equally reasonable way. What he wrote later in some of his treatises on the priesthood and the religious life about detachment from one's home, parents and relatives must always be considered in the light of his own practice and against the background of social conditions in Naples at the time. False interpretations by later generations of his non-Neapolitan successors have done his reputation considerably less than justice.

Falcoia warned Alphonsus not to be over impressed by initial fervour:

I am delighted that the novices are behaving well and I hope to God that they will continue to sanctify themselves and later be instruments for the salvation of many souls. But it is good not to be over impressed by these beginnings but to use their present fervour to lead them with all possible prudence to lay a solid foundation. It is important to accustom them to the practice of solid internal virtue, such for example, as self-knowledge, uprightness of intention, charity and recollection.

According to the ideas of the times Falcoia considered games unsuitable for novices and apparently for no other reason than that they occasioned novices undue fatigue which might be detrimental to their general health: 'As regards games, even *Palla* (a not too vigorous form of bowls) I do not think them suitable except a few times a year on occasion of some extraordinary recreation and then in moderation. Do not tire out the novices since fatigue is more prejudicial then you might think. For relaxation and distraction take them out for a walk when you can.'

Again and again Falcoia returned to the question of mortification and corporal austerities which were so much part of the spiritual scene at the time. He was fearful lest the fervour of beginners and Alphonsus' inclinations in that direction might lead them to overstep the bounds of prudence, which in point of fact, in certain cases, did happen:

As regards mortification, be cautious. Study the strength and needs of each one so that even for the less robust the regime does not become too rigorous. Try to achieve that they themselves wish to be mortified and that it comes from them spontaneously. Do not give them permission for outlandish practices; external mortifications are good but after the manner of salt. Make sure that there is a spirit of family happiness among them.

Falcoia's fear that Alphonsus might in those early years be less than prudent in recommending external mortifications to the novices was matched by a fear that he could also be excessive in his manifestations of kindness. There was an incident at Scala, the precise nature of which we do not know, when the four non-clerical candidates were there, which elicited a warning from the bishop. 'Guard your heart from certain manifestations of kindness — *certe tenerezze* — which betray a suspicion of inordinate attachment, even though thoroughly spiritual. Perhaps it was the jealous love of God for you which allowed this incident to take place; I am certain it came from God.' A few weeks later Falcoia used the same word again when he explained to Alphonsus that he must lead the novices away from attachment to the world but 'by degrees and with supreme gentleness but with seriousness and without your usual manifestations of kindness, *senza le sue tenerezze*, and at the same time with all charity.'[10]

Inevitably there were disappointments; at least four of those who gave such promise of being edifying members left, some like Brother Angelillo, to spread stories of the frightening regime and severe austerities to which they had been subjected. Alphonsus' most traumatic experience was occasioned by the confrontation he had with the De Alteriis family whose son, Michele, had presented himself at Villa. He was thirty-two years old, many years a priest and should have been well able to make his own decisions in life for himself. But his father had other ideas. When his son left home to enter the novitiate he decided to abduct him by force. Leading an armed band he arrived at Villa like some crusader braving death to rescue a valuable captive. Warned beforehand, Alphonsus moved Michele to Caiazzo and then, keeping ahead of the search party, into hiding in Naples where the father, hot on the scent, caught up with him. The matter was put to the Cardinal for his mediation; his decision was that Don Michele should spend some time alone with the Vincentian Fathers to make up his own mind about his future ministry as a priest. Towards the end of February 1736 Alphonsus visited him there in the very house where he himself had finally determined to become a priest. Michele, however, decided to cede to the wishes of his parents, and perhaps even of the Cardinal, and return home. Alphonsus' remark that the parents' action would cost them dearly was recalled when a few months later, death claimed their eldest son, Nicholas. 'God who was denied one, has claimed the other,' was the father's comment.

– III –

Though Alphonsus protested his love for the rocks of Scala he was well aware that the declining episcopal city perched high on the Lattari mountains was not an ideal mission centre. The original hospice of the nuns had been too small, the new Casa Anastasio was only a slight improvement. The main draw-back was its inaccessibility and the difficulty of travelling to fulfil their missionary engagements which were no longer confined to the Amalfi coastline. Villa was eminently more suitable. There had been several requests from other areas for foundations due to the favourable reports beginning to circulate about the work being done by the missioners of Villa. Both Falcoia and Alphonsus had set their hearts on a foundation in the more populous area of Salerno where scope for their type of mission work was unlimited. The arrival of Father Gennaro Sarnelli as a member of the congregation opened the way for another foundation which was to become — at least in the judgment of many contemporaries — the mother-house of the congregation.[11]

The wealthy Sarnelli family had their seat in the enchanting *borgata* of Ciorani lost in the folds of the Salerno mountains; most of the 500 inhabitants lived as feudal serfs on the family estate where Baron Angelo Sarnelli, head of the family, held sway. During the usual mission season at the beginning of 1734 Alphonsus and Gennaro — despite the fact that his father was the local lord — preached a mission in Ciorani and the neighbouring villages. The response was, as usual, enthusiastic. Immediately the possibility of establishing a mission house was broached. Falcoia went to Ciorani himself to ascertain whether the area was suitable.

Negotiations with both the civil authorities for the transfer of the property and with the archbishop of Salerno, Mons. Fabricio de Capua, dragged on for a considerable time. The archbishop was the first to sign, giving permission for the foundation on two conditions, that good missioners be appointed to the house and an annual tax of a pound of wax be paid to the episcopal treasury as a sign of the dependence of the house on the bishop. A few weeks later Alphonsus signed the civil accord in the office of the Public Notary at Bracigliano. The Sarnelli estate agreed to pay the missioners two hundred ducats annually from the revenue of the vineyards. Alphonsus in turn undertook to establish a centre for missioners and to give each year in Ciorani itself 'the exercises of the glorious St Ignatius'—it is easy to deduce that the Baron had a son a Jesuit—and to preach in the village every three years a formal mission, this time presumably according to the method of the missionaries of the Most Holy Saviour. The exercises of the Devout Life in the parish were to include special celebrations each Saturday in honour of the Mother of God.

Leaving Mazzini in charge of the novices, Alphonsus accompanied by Father Rossi and Brother Rendina set out from Villa for Ciorani in March 1736. The journey took two or three days; the night of Saturday 3 March was passed at Nocera dei Pagani and the following morning, following the plan drawn up by the Sarnelli family, the missioners set off on horseback to travel the few miles to Ciorani. At the approaches to the village they were met by a cavalcade of horsemen and the usual salvo of guns greeted their arrival at the estate. Without delaying over the formalities Alphonsus gathered the people into the village church of St Nicholas, thanked them for their welcome and from the pulpit announced the mission which was to begin the next day. From all the surrounding villages, Bracigliano, Carife, Casale and from as far distant as Mercato San Severino the people flocked until the church was unable to contain the crowds. The missioners were lodged temporarily by the Baron in some rooms at the southern end of his palace, right above the local wine shop and next door to what served as the baronial prison. The noise from both establishments was reported to have disturbed the recollection and prayer of the missioners.

Alphonsus who was the superior, transferred his temporary ministry from the parish church to the church of Santa Sofia attached to the baronial residence and began to work at once on the building of a monastery, a church and a large wing for retreatants. The Baron proved cantankerous to deal with, jealous of his dignity and insisting that his noble status should be exteriorly acknowledged by Alphonsus and his companions just as it was by his feudal serfs on the estate. At the same time he was generous in providing the missioners with timber and stones from the estate. By the summer of 1736 the work had commenced and the same pattern of enthusiasm which characterised the people of Villa was repeated here. From the neighbouring villages men and women came in turns to help the work, especially on Sundays and Church holidays; under the usual licensing system all were able to lend a hand. The work was under the direction of Father Rossi whose genius lay in that direction. One whole section of the building was completed by the summer of 1738 when the new monastery was inaugurated in the presence of the Baron and the clergy of the diocese. While there still remained a considerable amount of the planned building to be completed there was now a sizeable church for the public, an oratory on the first floor for the community as well as a considerable number of small rooms. The work of retreats for clerics, priests and those for ordination as well as for the laity began at once with such numbers that on many occasions the overflow had to be housed in a section of the Baron's residence, with one of the halls being used as a chapel. Members of the community slept where they could; Alphonsus frequently took his rest under the stairs.[12]

The house at Ciorani was barely habitable when it had to accommodate the two existing communities of both Scala and Villa. A pattern was emerging which was to be repeated in every single foundation the missionaries of the Most Holy Saviour made in those early years. After the initial enthusiasm which greeted the arrival of Alphonsus and his companions the community settled down to its permanent ministry both at home in the church and on missions. Then from one source or another opposition arose, sometimes from jealousy, sometimes from economic motives. Law suits were threatened, there were appeals to the King and his ministers in Naples, at times even violence took place until eventually the missioners were either victorious and allowed to continue in peace or were forced to abandon the foundation. The community at Villa had appeared to be well established, in the monastery the work of retreats to the clergy and laity was flourishing, missions throughout the area were in great demand. Under Father Mazzini's direction the novitiate was stabilised. Then the storm broke. The main source of opposition was a section of the local clergy. They began a campaign of calumny against the missioners and against Alphonsus himself which reached even to court circles in Naples. The Prince of Colubrano, feudal lord of Villa degli Schiavi, on whose estate the missioners' residence was built, lent a ready ear.

The unpleasant atmosphere was only the prelude to an explosion of hatred. One of the local priests was living in open concubinage; the Fathers denounced the scandal publicly. With his mistress the priest planned revenge. A bribe to the Prince of Colubrano left them full liberty of action. On the morning of 2 June 1737 when the Brother opened the church door after ringing the morning Angelus he was met by a band of armed men together with the Mayor of the town. They demanded the keys of the property and the immediate departure of the community.

Father Mazzini appealed to the bishop for his assistance. He, however, was powerless to lift the blockade of the monastery but offered to place at their disposal another small monastery and church at Vignanello. Alphonsus' efforts with the Prince were to no avail; frustrated he met Mazzini in Naples to discuss the crisis; from there they went to Castellamare to consult with Falcoia. The decision was to abandon Villa at once in the interests of peace and in the spirit of the Lord who instructed his Apostles to leave the place where they were persecuted and go to another. The bishop of Caiazzo, a long-time friend, felt deeply let down by the decision, even threatening to institute proceedings in Naples with the King's ministers to secure their recall. This was the last thing Falcoia wanted since in the prevailing climate it might well have brought on greater trouble still. Alphonsus was able to see a good side to the debacle since he felt their meagre numbers were already dispersed too widely. He let Falcoia know his thoughts on 12 July 1737:

> Father, permit me to let you know my opinion on two points. First, from now on we must think well before accepting unpromising foundations, since although it is true that we can abandon them whenever we wish, there results great harm and discredit to the whole institute. It is then reported, as it has been in the case of the diocese of Caiazzo, that we were expelled.
>
> Secondly, I ask you now since we are so few to allow us all to live together. I am consoled to think that it is for this purpose Our Lord has arranged for us to leave Villa. Where the subjects are too few — your Excellency knows this well, but I have now learned it from experience — observance languishes, so does fervour and consequently one's perseverance is endangered. In a word everything declines. Our days of recollection, our spiritual exercises, fall into neglect. For myself from the time I have been so much on my own I cannot recall having made the spiritual exercises in complete retirement. We were so few I had to occupy myself with some work or other.

Alphonsus concluded with an amusing aside. He informed Falcoia in the strictest confidence that poor Father Rossi was not what he should be from the spiritual point of view though he did take some of the harm out of it by asserting that he himself would be the worst of all if he had continued to live in a small community.[13]

The shock of having to abandon Villa was followed within a few months by departure from Scala. Once again the enthusiasm of the local clergy for the presence of the missioners had diminished considerably since their ascetical life-style and pastoral activity threw into sombre relief their own lack of both. Inevitably too the population was driven to unfortunate comparisons. There was the further complication that the troubles of the convent, which had apparently disappeared with the departure of the Crostarosa sisters, surfaced once more. The old factions revived. Some of the sisters longed for the easier days when they were freer under the old Visitation Rule; the standards set by Alphonsus in his discourses to the nuns were too demanding. Neither was the bishop as well disposed towards the missionaries as before and he came to resent Falcoia's activities in his diocese more and more. The atmosphere was such that Falcoia took the final decision to abandon Scala on August 25 1738, instructing Mazzini to lead his small community to Ciorani where they would find some form of accommodation. Two days later Mazzini with Fathers Villani and Marocco and Brothers Vito and Gaudiello left for Ciorani but not before Vito scratched on the stucco around the open fire the Arms of the Congregation and the date A.D. 1738, a *graffito* which has survived to this day, a silent witness to the heroic beginnings at Scala. It was almost six years since the first candidates in search of a new missionary congregation had arrived on the mountain. Good Canon Pietro Romano remained behind and does not figure again in the history of Alphonsus and his companions.

– IV –

The Ciorani foundation provided Alphonsus for the first time with a suitable centre where he could establish a degree of stability and observance for the institute. There was an atmosphere of peace and quiet totally conducive to prayer and also to study which was becoming a feature of life at home and for the missioners on their return from their missions. Already there was the nucleus of a sound theological library; Alphonsus snatched every moment of freedom from his activities and prayer to begin his writing ministry — but more of this later.

From Ciorani easy access to the neighbouring diocese facilitated the work of the missions for which there was constant demand. The ministry of the enclosed retreats was so successful that the house had to be enlarged, much to the horror of Father Rossi, who declared with great worldly wisdom that the coffers were empty. There was a face-to-face confrontation with Alphonsus. 'Don Saverio,' he is recorded as saying, 'you build as if you were a person of the world. They collect money first of all and when they have sufficient they begin to build. We, on the other hand, who have our trust in God, operate in a completely different way. We begin the building first and then look for the money. They build from what they collect; we build with the assistance of Providence.' The economic practices of the saints cannot always be recommended for imitation but in this case the Lord responded and the money for the building was forthcoming from one source or another. The Archbishop of Salerno regarded the new monastery with its retreat facilities as sufficiently important for the spiritual welfare of his diocese to tax the various parishes to assist in meeting expenses. Alphonsus devoted all his personal income to the project. On the installation of a new member of the *seggio* of Portanova a small gratuity was paid to all who attended. In order to secure this money for the congregation he made sure to attend these special meetings, arriving in his missioner's soutane to the disgust of his brother, Hercules, resplendent in formal dress for the occasion. On one such occasion when he returned to Ciorani with the modest pittance for his attendance, he announced with undisguised glee, 'I did not refuse my vote to the new member, even though he was not a noblemen but a simple baker.'[14]

But there were other worries besides the building and the lack of funds. Just when everything seemed to be falling into place, two of his most promising workers, Fathers Carlo Maiorino and Giulio Marocco fell victim to the Neapolitan nostalgia for home. Maiorino's case was aggravated by the naive illusion which he harboured that he was indispensable to his native parish of Saragnano near Mercato San Severino. Unable to cope with these two emotions he left Ciorani secretly, taking leave of no one. No sooner was he at home than he was smitten with remorse. He wrote to Alphonsus in extravagant terms which were perhaps a manifestation of his fundamental immaturity:

> Prostrate, I beg pardon of God and of you for having failed you. But I assure you that I never had the slightest intention of causing you the least displeasure since I have always sung the praises of your virtues and the wonderful example of your life. And I do so now and I will continue to do so for the future.
>
> How happy you all are. I deplore my misfortune. In all truth he who does not envy you shows that he does not know God or else has little judgment. Even though I do not deserve to ask anything, I ask you in the name of Jesus and Mary that you have compassion on Saragnano where the flame of its former religious fervour has dwindled. Only you and your fellow missioners would be able to rekindle it by coming one day to preach a mission and thus rekindle the flame.[15]

The defection of Maiorino began to cause Alphonsus severe misgivings about Father Marocco, a native of Caiazzo who had been another of his novices at Villa. He had permitted him to return home to partake of the infallible Neapolitan nostrum for all illnesses, his 'native air'. Marocco was a member of an aristocratic family who possessed the right of patronage to the post of *Primicerio*, one of the most important and lucrative positions in the Cathedral Chapter. From the length of time he was away it began to dawn on Alphonsus that the family fortune and the cathedral dignity and not his health might be the real reason for his reluctance to return. A first letter of recall in July 1740 brought no reply; a final letter of appeal the following month, tells its own story:

> My dear Don Giulio,
>
> I am afraid that my letters are annoying you at the moment. But what else can be done? The affection which I have for you, one of the first members of our little congregation, impels me to write to you.
>
> You were previously so detached from your relatives. Why do you now allow yourself to be overcome by the devil of human attachments? Do you wish to be like De Alteriis whom you once condemned so roundly? At least he could allege that the Cardinal was forcing him to remain at home. Do you think perhaps that we will not receive you now with the same affection as before? Here you will find more than brothers and more than a mother. Here everyone is longing to see you again, even though you may have almost rejected us as your brothers.
>
> For goodness' sake delay no further lest the devil gains victory over you. What further excuse have you for remaining at home? You say you wish to go to Naples to take advice! Take advice from the Lord and you will return at once, wherever you are, to Ciorani.
>
> I pray you to return the minute you receive this letter, at least out of love for the Madonna. Maybe it will turn out that your pains will disappear when you leave Caiazzo. We are aware that you will come back to us 'good for nothing', but among us you will find exquisite charity. And we will receive you even though you are not able to do anything. We wish to have you, not because you are useless but because you are our brother and we do not wish to see you separated from us.
>
> I can't say anything more. When you read this, take advice from the Crucifix and make your resolve there, right away. . . . [16]

But on this occasion as on so many others, Alphonsus' appeals fell on deaf ears. When family fever struck a Neapolitan the disease proved virtually incurable. The departure of Giulio Marocco was a particularly sad disappointment for Alphonsus; he had been one of the first to join in Scala in 1734 after the initial debacle when Alphonsus had to start all over again. With Rossi, Mazzini, Sportelli and Sarnelli he had come to be regarded as one of the pillars of the institute, a founding father, as it were. Of the six companions of Alphonsus whom history places in that category there are two we still have to meet, Fathers Andrea Villani and Paul Cafaro. They were born within a few months of each other and not very far from each other in the Salerno archdiocese. They had both been ordained when they met Alphonsus in the course of his missionary activity in the years 1736 and 1737 but while Villani was able to join up at once and was among the group at Villa, Cafaro found his bishop reluctant to permit him to leave his ministry as parish priest. It took him nearly five years before he was finally released with considerable bad will to join Alphonsus in 1742. Villani, on the other hand, was by that time well established as one whom Alphonsus consulted frequently and on whose judgment he relied considerably. He was to be his official consultor in the canonical sense for nearly forty years and on Alphonsus' appointment as bishop, was to be his Vicar, finally succeeding him by right of succession on his death. Villani survived all the intrigues and upheavals of the last years of Alphonsus' life which would have submerged a less adroit manipulator.

The defection of Maiorino and the inevitable departure of Marocco brought home to Alphonsus the need for some bond of stability in the congregation which would offset the instability of some of his companions. Some in point of fact had already taken a private vow of obedience to Falcoia which they renewed each year; some, too, like Alphonsus had placed themselves under his spiritual direction as well. Others, like Villani, rejected both these expedients. Beyond these private vows which were at the discretion of each member there was nothing more binding them to the group and the work of the missions than their zeal and enthusiasm while it lasted. There was no definite commitment to the congregation seen as a response to a vocation chosen out of love for God. The matter must have been discussed with Falcoia though there is no record of this. Finally it was decided to take a vow of perseverance in the institute very similar to that of the Pii Operai. The mission season was at an end and all the members, with the exception of Sarnelli who was in Naples on his anti-prostitution campaign, were gathered in Ciorani when they took the first steps to establish a formal juridic bond in the congregation.

It was the eve of the feast of St Mary Magdalen in June 1740. The first Vespers of her liturgy were recited. This was followed by a discourse from Alphonsus. Each one then in turn recited the formula of a vow of stability drawn up by Alphonsus and transcribed in the distinctive handwriting of Sportelli:

> Eternal, Omnipotent and Most Loving Lord, I, . . . numbering myself without any merits of my own among the members of this Congregation of the Most Holy Saviour, in order to serve you with all my strength by imitating as far as possible the adorable life of your Divine Son and my Saviour Jesus Christ; confiding at the same time in your infinite goodness and motivated by the desire of dedicating myself entirely to your love and to serving you with all my strength by the imitation of the life and virtues of Jesus Christ, which is the only way of pleasing you and is the principal end of this holy institute.
>
> After many days of prayer and reflection, prostrate in your presence and in the presence of my dear mother Mary, St Michael, St Joseph, the Holy Apostles, St Mary Magdalen, St Teresa of Avila and of my Angel Guardian and of the Guardian Angel of this Congregation, and finally in the presence of the whole court of heaven I bind myself and vow before Mons. Falcoia, bishop of Castellamare and Director of this

> Congregation to persevere in it until death with the help of the Divine Grace and Blood of Jesus Christ.
>
> This vow I intend to take with the understanding and condition that it can be dispensed only by the Superior General for the time being and by the Supreme Pontiff and by no one else . . . [17]

One by one the nine members of the group signed the formula, beginning with Alphonsus followed by Mazzini, Sportelli, Rossi, Villani and Brothers Rendina, Francis Tartaglione, Gaudiello and last of all, Vito Curzio. Vito, as senior of the Brothers, should have signed first among them but never losing an opportunity for the theatrical insisted on placing himself in the last place. The parchment was then sent to Falcoia who wrote on the left hand side of the last page, 'I accept and confirm the offering which you have made freely to God. And whoever in future wishes to be considered a member of this holy Congregation must do likewise at the end of two years of probation.' The document was then returned to Ciorani where it was carefully preserved; the names of those who entered for some years afterwards were in turn added to it, making it the first official register of the Missionaries of the Most Holy Saviour.

The introduction of a vow of perseverance gave the missionary society a new juridical status; it is for canon lawyers to describe how this fitted into the accepted canonical patterns at the time. Up to this the members were neither diocesan priests nor religious priests, even if they performed certain religious duties in common. Now, however, membership became a more serious commitment and, more significantly, a way of life, a life-long dedication. Since there were numerous missionary societies throughout the Kingdom in which local priests worked for a while, gave a few missions as zeal or curiosity prompted them and then resumed the untroubled tenor of their lives *en famille* there was always the danger that Alphonsus' companions would see in the Congregation of the Most Holy Saviour something similar. But in the minds of Falcoia and Alphonsus it was to be something more — what precisely would only evolve with time. But already it was quite distinct from the Apostolic Missions in Naples, and from what was evolving in the novitiate it would also possess a distinct spiritual physiognomy based on the imitation of the life and virtues of Jesus Christ. Remarkably there was no explicit mention in the vow formula of the nature of the apostolate to which the members would dedicate their lives; it was all contained implicitly in the imitation of the Saviour. Beyond this vow of stability there were no other vow commitments; the traditional vows of religion, poverty, chastity and obedience would emerge three years later after the death of Falcoia.

With his followers now concentrated in Ciorani which became the centre of the work, the missionaries soon came to be known popularly as the *Cioranisti*, a name to which Alphonsus took exception. Nearly twenty years later, preaching in Pagani he told his congregation that he was pained they were still calling the missioners *Cioranisti* and not what the Holy Father wished them to be called, the Fathers of the Most Holy Redeemer.[18]

– V –

If we are to judge by the frequency of the correspondence between them relations between Alphonsus and Falcoia cooled somewhat after 1737; there was no formal rupture but Alphonsus began to act more on his own initiative — one hesitates to say, independently. It may also have had something to do with the fact that Falcoia came more and more to rely on Sportelli. In that same year the bishop had succeeded in overcoming whatever canonical difficulties lay in the way of Sportelli's ordination to the priesthood. Together they had travelled to Rome to argue their case face to face with the Roman authorities. The outcome was that Sportelli was ordained by Falcoia in his cathedral in May 1737. He now spent considerably more time with the bishop in his residence at Castellamare, acting as his secretary, valet and confidant. It was something of a family affair since his widowed mother who had taken religious vows was also in Castellamare where Falcoia had appointed her superioress of the *Conservatorio* for the education of orphan girls.

Falcoia's autocratic manner of directing the whole undertaking was beginning to irk Alphonsus. The decision to abandon Scala and to send the community from there to Ciorani was taken by Falcoia without reference to him, perhaps bringing back memories of the fact that he was also absent from Scala when Maria Celeste was expelled; that decision too had been taken without consultation with him. Furthermore when all were assembled in Ciorani Falcoia took it upon himself to assign the various community offices among the members. His decisions were addressed to Sportelli in the absence of Alphonsus with instructions not to pay any attention to what other members of the community were saying; there were clearly murmurs of discontent among them. Under Alphonsus' guidance the community at Ciorani set aside the summer months of 1739 for a period of prayer, study and retreat. One of the subjects chosen for study was the theology of obedience which was of immediate relevance. Different opinions emerged concerning the concept of 'blind obedience' and whether it was less perfect to outline to superiors difficulties in the execution of their commands which they might not be aware of. The whole discussion centred around the teaching of the Jesuit spiritual master, Alphonsus Rodriguez, whose treatise *Esercitio di perfettione e di virtù christiane* had become, even then, the bible of novitiates. Alphonsus shared the view held by Rodriguez that it was in no way against the highest perfection to point out to superiors difficulties of which they might have been unaware, provided this was done in a spirit of indifference and a willingness to carry out whatever was finally decided. Falcoia would have none of it. He believed that every superior possessed in himself a ray of divinity. Not merely that, which was incredible enough; he held that God went guarantor for every command of a superior even if he were not a bishop. 'Who hears you, hears me' was as valid for the superior of Ciorani as for the Apostles. In a real sense for Falcoia, a legitimate superior took the place of God; he was God's Vicar. Falcoia's arguments which,

[156]

significantly, were shared by Sportelli, did not succeed in convincing Alphonsus who was not prepared to accept that superiors possessed the Holy Spirit and the gift of infallibility to the extent that they could not be mistaken in what they commanded. Little wonder then that Alphonsus at the end of his retreat with the community made the resolution that 'he would always speak well of Mons. Falcoia and would not complain about him'.[19]

Apart from differing theologies and the fact that Falcoia wanted to have a finger in every detail, there were two main areas of disagreement between himself and Alphonsus. The first was that the bishop felt that Alphonsus was too frequently absent from Ciorani and the second was his continuing involvement with the Apostolic Missions in Naples. The demand for the services of the *Cioranisti* for missions and preaching engagements continued to increase; Alphonsus was absent from Ciorani for weeks on end in the course of the mission season. Falcoia expressed anxiety about this excessive activity, first of all from the point of view of his health, then from the point of view of his spiritual life and finally because he was needed at home for the spiritual guidance of the community. 'You should know that it is important to attend to one's own soul and one's own body and to build up the members of the community as well as the people of the villages. My son, do not allow yourself to be persuaded otherwise; it is a greater service to the Lord to form good missioners than to give missions, especially in the beginning of the work. In the beginning of the growth of the tree it is more important to make sure that it strikes root well rather than endeavour to pluck some meagre fruits out of season.'

But the main cause of the growing tension between them was the fact that the Apostolic Missions continued their claims on Alphonsus' services, insisting that as a member beneficed with one of their most lucrative chaplaincies he should work for them when called upon to do so. The income of the chaplaincy was so badly needed that Alphonsus chose to leave himself at the disposal of the Apostolic Missions when they required him which they very often did.

They had to write to Falcoia, however, each time they called upon Alphonsus' services. Falcoia grew exasperated at the repeated requests and he made known his displeasure in no uncertain terms:

My Son,

Regarding what you write to me about the Fathers of the Congregation to which you formerly belonged, all I can say is that this blessed Congregation may prove to be a very great temptation for you — I do not mean in a bad sense. On no account must you fall between two stools; he who wishes to serve two masters, ends up serving neither. The many demands which they make on you does not please me at all; eventually under various pretexts they will detach you from your present work.

And the worst aspect of it in my opinion is that the root of the problem is human respect and the financial aspect of your chaplaincy.

> This cannot be pleasing to God since your reliance on Providence is thus weakened. And I feel that trust in Providence is all important.
>
> My Son, you have been entrusted with a sublime task — a work from God, a work which will bring great fruit to the Church of God. *Age quod agis* and do not allow your interests to be divided. Remember the saying from Osee, 'their heart is divided and so they shall perish' (10.2). I am not telling you to be rude or to inconvenience them. But by degrees you must intimate to them that your first interest above all others is the work that the Divine Majesty has entrusted to you; that the harvest is great, that the field you have been given to cultivate is immense, that you have not time to be always at their disposition since you have already too much to do both within your own Congregation and outside it. And finally that the number of members you have is so very small.
>
> And then if they wish to deprive you of the chaplaincy, Divine Providence is not thereby exhausted. Since your work is from God, God has to look after it. Perhaps he will suffer you to feel the pinch just to test your confidence or even as a punishment for the greater confidence you have placed in human assistance rather than in him. At least this is my opinion.[20]

Despite the strength of Falcoia's feelings so clearly expressed, Alphonsus did not surrender his chaplaincy and the Apostolic Missions continued to call on his services. A few months later they requested him to preach the clergy retreat in Naples despite the fact that he had already preached to them seven years before. The superior, Don Francesco de Rosa made his approach through Falcoia; the tone of his letter was peremptory which cannot have been too pleasing to the the bishop:

> As Superior of this Congregation of the Apostolic Missions here in this cathedral I require (*mi necessita*) the services of Don Alfonso de Liguori, one of our most esteemed members, to give the spiritual exercises to the clergy in the coming month of October. But since I know that Don Alfonso depends in everything on the wise and prudent counsels of your Lordship, I have recourse to your kindness requesting that you would favour me by giving him an obedience to accept this work.
>
> And at the same time you could tell him that on account of the weakness of his health as a result of his incessant missionary labours he is not to think of composing new sermons. He can use those same meditations which he gave to the clergy here seven years ago. And I can assure him that the clergy and myself wish to hear him again since he preaches with a fervour of spirit and great efficacy because the Word of God in his mouth is strengthened by the exemplariness of his own life. . . . I trust that your Lordship will have the goodness not to deny us this favour and to help us in this matter.[21]

Falcoia's initial reaction was to refuse permission but under pressure from Naples he reluctantly consented. In his letter to Alphonsus he suggested that he should include at least one new conference on the imitation of Jesus Christ which apart altogether from being appropriate for priests should present no great difficulty for him since it was by now so much part of the spirituality of his own congregation.

Then in November of the following year, 1740, Cardinal Spinelli of Naples decided to embark on a spiritual renewal of his diocese in response to a call from the new Pope, Benedict XIV. Benedict, who was anxious for a *rapprochement* with the Bourbons, took immediate steps to arrive at an agreement with the young King Charles and his ministers in the matter of Church privileges and the excessive number of clergy throughout the Kingdom. At the same time he was anxious to promote a deepening of christian life and practice among the people. In response, Spinelli decided to initiate a whole series of missions throughout his diocese and to establish the practice of mental prayer in common among the people, a decision which appealed to the piety of the King. It also commended itself to his ministers anxious for any initiative which could provide a moral uplift for the people. The Cardinal's decision was greatly influenced by Father Sarnelli who spent most of his time in Naples engaged on just such a campaign and who had ready access to him. Prompted by Sarnelli and impressed by the accounts of the work being done in the Salerno area by Alphonsus and his colleagues, Spinelli proposed that they should open a house in the archdiocese, if not in Naples itself, certainly somewhere among the surrounding villages. Alphonsus was in a dilemma; he was reluctant to dissipate his forces any further and was particularly anxious not to offend the susceptibilities of the Apostolic Missions by entering into competition with them in Naples itself. At the same time he had no wish to offend the Cardinal in any way since he was well aware that he would need all his good will and support in the future.

Spinelli's request to Falcoia spoke of his great esteem for the work being done in the new congregation:

> I have learnt with great satisfaction of the work that Alphonsus de Liguori and his companions are doing for the spiritual welfare of the people in the neglected villages of the countryside and for the rural clergy. I have resolved to avail myself of his zeal to console my heart which is really tormented by the thought of the multiplicity of spiritual disorders prevalent in the villages of my diocese both among the people and the clergy.
>
> I fully appreciate that his companions are not numerous but I will be satisfied if he takes part himself with just one other companion. I therefore ask your Excellency as Director of this Congregation to support my request which is so much in harmony with the vocation which Don Alfonso and his companions follow and that you will send them to me out of obedience.

The letter was certainly from the Cardinal but the inspiration behind it was clearly Sarnelli who had primed the Cardinal on what to write and what approach to adopt. Alphonsus himself was privy to what was happening; Sarnelli kept him fully informed. He knew that there was question of establishing a house for himself and his missioners; Sarnelli informed him that he would join the community. The gentle deceit was not lost on Falcoia; he saw through the whole conspiracy at once.[22]

Falcoia replied to the Cardinal without delay, indicating all the reasons why he could not accede to the request, the small number of priests, their weak health due to excessive work, the danger of destroying all that had been achieved up to that by further dissipating their efforts. More to the point he reminded the Cardinal of the 'great number of priests and clerics, missionary congregations and religious orders' in Naples. Most amusing, however, were his protestations that he did not possess all the authority over the new Congregation which the Cardinal attributed to him. 'As regards myself, I do not possess all the authority you think I have to insist on transplanting and nourishing this frail plant. In fact, I am no more than a frail support and it is only the humility of these servants of God which makes them rely on me to some extent.' It was well that this declaration came from himself and not from Alphonsus. And at the same time it may have been an indication that Falcoia realised that the new Congregation was beginning to have an independent existence of its own.

The Cardinal was not to be gainsaid; he knew how to interpret even the most impassioned letters of his fellow countrymen, including those from bishops. He pointed out to Alphonsus ultimately that he was still his superior by virtue of his continuing membership of the Apostolic Missions and as a consequence was entitled to command him to undertake the work. Against the wishes of the Apostolic Missions, Spinelli named Alphonsus superior of the whole general mission, giving him authority to summon any member he wished from the three congregations of missioners in the capital. The upshot then was that to the displeasure of Falcoia and the delight of Sarnelli, Alphonsus found himself at the head of a missionary band of some twenty priests, many of them young and zealous, eager to campaign under the direction of one whose reputation as the foremost missioner of the diocese could not be questioned. Among the group were at least ten who within a few years were appointed bishops throughout the Kingdom, thus opening up their dioceses to the new missionary Congregation. Among them too figured Don Michele de Alteriis, the same who was kidnapped by his parents from Villa.

After a solemn inauguration by the Cardinal, the general mission opened in Afragola in May 1741; it continued with the usual interruption for the summer heats until August of the following year 1742. It took the missioners to between forty and fifty rural parishes with their large population and over six hundred clergy. As well as Sarnelli, Alphonsus at different times during the eighteen months summoned Fathers Villani and Cafaro and Brother Francis Tartaglione to accompany him. The Cardinal put a house and church in Sant Agnello near Barra on the slopes of Vesuvius at their disposal with the secret hope that it would be a permanent centre for the missionaries of the Most Holy Saviour. Alphonsus passed the summer months there and used it as the assembly point of the whole missionary operation. The list of villages evangelised reads like a tourist guide to the beauties of the slopes of Vesuvius, Bosco Tre Case, San Giorgio à Cremano, San Giovanni à Teduccio, Ponticelli. The Vesuvian countryside, which was such a worry to Sarnelli from the pastoral point of view, was a typical cross-section of the whole Kingdom with all the inveterate abuses which years of pastoral remissness had allowed to take root and flourish — blasphemy, the cursing of the dead, concubinage, clerical as well as lay, the practice of engaged couples living openly together, the licentiousness connected with the harvesting of the grape crop in September and October and the wine festival in November. As well as the appalling ignorance of the fundamental doctrines of the faith and the spiritual and intellectual inadequacy of the clergy there was the all-pervading atmosphere of intense popular superstition to be overcome and the family feuds and hatreds of tightly knit communities.[23]

Alphonsus was the inspiration of the whole operation. He reserved to himself the preaching of the night sermon for the greater part of the mission; on occasions he preached two or even three times in the day. Learning by experience he was ready to experiment with new approaches such as separating the men from the women for a part of the mission and then bringing the whole population together for the final days. No mission was declared closed unless all the confessions had been heard by the visiting priests; in places where the population was particularly numerous the missioners remained on after the preaching to complete their ministry in the confessional. Abandoning the emphasis on the motive of fear, Alphonsus came more and more to insist on means of perseverance such as the establishment of sodalities, the practice of prayer and meditation on the Word of God together in church, the establishment of schools for the education of the young, and catechetical instruction for all on Sundays. His own conduct set a high standard for his companions. He ate frugally, insisting on the ordinary food of the people and even that he seasoned with bitter herbs. He laid down strict dietary norms for all the missioners— much to their displeasure. He allowed them meat balls of magpie on Christmas Day by way of exception but not the *pizza* they were hoping for — even the Cardinal could not refrain from laughing at this decision when the missioners recounted it to him. Alphonsus continued his regime of penances just as if he were at home in the monastery. The poverty of his clothes caused him at times to be mistaken for a beggar; as he arrived on horseback in one village he was pointed out as probably the cook of the group. While he reluctantly permitted the Neapolitan missioners to travel in coaches he insisted that he himself and his own missioners should travel by mule. He reserved for himself the worst accommodation, insisting that his companions take the best rooms in the allocation of sleeping quarters. He was particularly assiduous in the ministry of the confessional insisting that his companions should be equally so — at times to their disgust. On one occasion when he came late to a meal from the confessional the local priest remonstrated with him. 'I have come to save souls, not to eat,' was the reply.

Spinelli, remembering that Falcoia had been unwilling to allow the Missionaries of the Most Holy Saviour to preach in his diocese, pointedly asked Alphonsus on his return to Naples after the first round of missions if he did not now believe that his diocese needed missioners as much as any other.[24]

During the months of Alphonsus' missionary work in Naples, Falcoia grew more and more annoyed at what was happening. He considered Alphonsus' presence in Naples at the head of the Cardinal's band of missioners as a dereliction of his commitment to his true vocation of establishing a new missionary congregation. Further, he felt that the missions in the Naples area should not have received the priority Alphonsus was giving them — there was more to be done for the authentic work of the Congregation from Ciorani. He saw the Congregation which he had nourished departing from its true purpose — the imitation of Jesus Christ through evangelising the poor in the most needy dioceses and not in Naples where Spinelli had abundant resources and priests. In his anger Falcoia felt that nothing was right. In Ciorani the work was collapsing, the members of the community were overworked and ill, observance was in decline, the novices were deprived of proper formation at all levels but especially from the spiritual point of view. And he was totally opposed to any mention of a foundation near Naples such as the one proposed at Barra which could only draw the members of the Congregation into the ecclesiastical world of Naples with ruinous effect. Falcoia sent Alphonsus an ultimatum to return with an explicit threat that if he agreed to such a foundation there would be a division in the congregation between those who would wish to go with him and those who would remain in Ciorani under Falcoia — it would be the Mannarini situation all over again, with Alphonsus on this occasion cast in the disruptive role. Falcoia even contemplated replacing Alphonsus with Sportelli as superior of the Congregation.[25]

As far as Falcoia was concerned the root of the problem was Father Sarnelli. They had never seen eye to eye from the beginning and Sarnelli had pointedly excluded himself from the list of those who submitted to the spiritual direction of the bishop. They had clashed too in their differing attitudes to the convent at Scala. In Naples Sarnelli insisted that he was a member of the Congregation of the Most Holy Saviour as he threw himself unreservedly into his two-pronged apostolate of ridding Naples of prostitutes and establishing the practice of mental prayer throughout the various parishes. Alphonsus had no difficulty in allowing one of the Brothers of the Congregation to remain in Naples with him, something which Falcoia strongly objected to. Sportelli was not helping the situation either. From Ciorani he kept Falcoia fully informed of every detail which took place in the house from the slightest indisposition of a member of the community to their smallest human foibles. When he was able to find a few free days he went to Castellamare to be with the bishop and to be nurse, butler and secretary all rolled into one.

To add to his failing physical and mental condition, political troubles were piling up for the bishop who was approaching eighty years of age. Towards the end of 1741 one Gennaro de Maio took refuge from his creditors in the church of San Mateo in Castellamare from where he was dragged out violently to face charges. Falcoia chose this insignificant incident to assert the Church's right of sanctuary; he excommunicated those who had laid hands on the debtor and affixed the decree of excommunication in public. It was an error of judgment which brought considerable sadness to the final months of his episcopacy. This was just the opportunity the Bourbon Court in Naples was waiting for; at once the King's Ministers seized upon the incident as a trial of strength between the Government and the Church. Falcoia was summoned to Naples *ad audiendum verbum*, threatened with the confiscation of his property and the property of his diocese and ordered to remain in Naples under virtual house arrest or face exile in Terracina. From the villages of the slopes of Vesuvius Alphonsus followed the trials of his director with sympathy. From Rome and Naples came the intervention of the Nuncio and the Pope, Benedict XIV, resulting in a compromise which resolved the matter early in 1742.

These events explain to some extent Falcoia's rather hysterical reaction to Alphonsus' missionary activity for the Cardinal. Quite simply he was no longer able to cope either with the affairs of his diocese or the direction of the new congregation which had taken on a dynamic of its own. For his part Alphonsus found himself torn between his desire not to offend the Cardinal and at the same time his duty to attend to the building up of his own Congregation. He spent hours with Spinelli endeavouring to overcome his unwillingness to allow him to depart; he took his place again and again in the episcopal ante-rooms waiting for audience. From Castellamare Falcoia in a fit of pique forbade him to plead his vow of obedience to himself as an argument to be used to obtain his release — this, he claimed, would be a sinful manifestation of alleged virtue. Finally on condition that Alphonsus continued the series of missions right into August, the Cardinal agreed that he could return to Ciorani and hand over the direction of the missionary campaign in the diocese to Sarnelli. Falcoia was relieved at the solution but aghast at the idea of Alphonsus or anyone else for that matter continuing to preach during the heats of the dog-days, the Solleone.[26]

The eighteen months with Sarnelli and the other Neapolitan missioners in the Naples area was an important experience for the development of Alphonsus' concept of mission techniques. Besides experimenting with various expedients such as separate days for men and women, the main development was in the area of what was called the exercises of the Devout Life and the cultivation of exercises of 'popular devotion' which was becoming a feature of the Alphonsian mission. He established the practice of prayer together in church, morning and evening, and a daily visit to the Blessed Sacrament and Our Lady. Once a month there was the Preparation for Death with exposition of the Most Blessed Sacrament. In each parish he erected a Calvary to increase devotion to Our Lord's Passion, especially on Fridays.

More important still, Alphonsus' eyes were opened to the danger of being too dogmatic and rigid in interpreting the purpose of his new institute. There were abandoned souls within a stone's throw of Naples as well as among the mountains of Tramonti and the Cilento. His own understanding of the work to be done was evolving more rapidly than was Falcoia's. The very success of the missions he had organised proved embarrassing from other points of view as well. Spinelli suggested that his own missioners from the Apostolic Missions should follow the method of the Cioranisti and even undergo in-service training with them. Success too brought talk of a mitre for Alphonsus — the inevitable criterion of success in Neapolitan ecclesiastical circles.[27]

– VI –

During the period of Alphonsus' absence from Ciorani, candidates continued to come forward to join the Congregation — some of them receiving their formation in Ciorani, others being introduced directly to the missions, making them part of their training. Among the latter was Father Paul Cafaro, the last of the 'founding fathers'. Born in 1707 in Cava dei Tyrreni, a fruitful area for genuine priestly vocations, he entered the diocesan seminary at the age of thirteen and was ordained eleven years later. In 1735 he was appointed priest in charge of a parish. The following year Alphonsus gave a mission in Cava and preached the spiritual exercises in the local convent. Deeply impressed, Father Cafaro requested permission of his bishop to leave the diocese and join Alphonsus; only after five years insistence did he receive a very grudging permission to go. He joined Alphonsus and Sarnelli on the Naples missions which was considered adequate novitiate training. He came back to Ciorani to spend some months under the guidance of Father Mazzini before taking his vow of perseverance on 9 November 1742, the tenth anniversary of the foundation of the missionary group in Scala. Cafaro's arrival completed the list of the Founding Fathers, Mazzini, Sportelli, Sarnelli, Villani and Cafaro. He was a great ascetic embracing a regime of fasting and corporal austerities which must have stretched human endurance to the limits. When Falcoia died Alphonsus chose him as his spiritual director.

Alphonsus was back in Ciorani by the end of August 1742, tired and with nothing more to show for his absence than a long beard and very few ducats in his pockets. Spinelli had given him 500 ducats which was barely adequate for the support of himself and his companions and the upkeep of the house and church in Barra for the whole eighteen months. He now found himself fully occupied with a host of problems. Besides the spiritual formation of the community, including the novices, which Falcoia declared had been neglected in his absence, and the increasing demand for missions which he had to deal with, there was the annoyance caused by Baron Sarnelli who continued to demand further signs of deference to his position as the local feudal lord. Besides the special reserved area in the church, he now insisted on special carpets as well. The congregation was to stand at his entry and bow respectfully as he proceeded up the church to his place. He was to be addressed as *Illustrissimo*. Father Rossi found it all too much for his explosive temper and was forbidden to get involved in any way — a necessary precaution for the Baron's personal safety. Falcoia had grown so accustomed to interfering during Alphonsus' absence in Naples that every little detail of administration had to be referred to him for decision, including the question of the Baron.

There was also the important affair of the new foundation at Pagani. The question of a foundation there followed the familiar pattern — a successful mission, local enthusiasm, a request for a foundation which once set in train was inevitably followed by increasing difficulties. Alphonsus and his companions had preached a successful novena for the feast of Our Lady of the Rosary there in 1738 and he had made several subsequent visits for other preaching engagements. Pagani, with a population at the time of about 8,000 inhabitants was situated on the edge of the fertile plain stretching from the Amalfi peninsula northwards to the city of Nola. The site offered several obvious advantages as a missionary centre. While Ciorani opened up the approaches to the south past Salerno and into Irpinia to the east, Pagani afforded easy access to the heavily populated missionary area south of Vesuvius as well as to the Amalfi peninsula through the Gap of Chiunzi. The local bishop was enthusiastic for the foundation, while the retired parish priest of San Felice, Don Francisco Cataldi, who was already negotiating with the Vincentians in Naples for the establishment of a missionary foundation, now decided to offer the same facilities to Alphonsus and his new missionary society instead. Late in 1741 three Fathers and Vito Curzio took up temporary residence in a section of the considerable *palazzo* occupied by Don Francesco, using a ground floor as a public oratory and going down to the chapel of San Domenico at the edge of the town when there was a liturgical function to be performed. From Pagani the missionaries set out on their preaching campaigns and then returned home to continue their missionary work among the people.

It was to prove a very precarious existence for many years. In July 1740 Brancone, as Secretary of State for ecclesiastical affairs, communicated secretly to all local authorities a royal decree forbidding the construction of new churches or the establishment of new religious institutes without previous royal permission. Sensitive to any false move which could provoke the wrath of the Bourbon authorities and the destruction of his whole work, Alphonsus contacted Brancone, the first of a long series of visits he would have to make to the Bourbon seat of administration in the course of his life. With less than ingenuousness he pleaded that the house in Pagani was not in fact a 'new' foundation but rather a replacement for Scala which they had given up due to its insalubrious climate and difficulty of access — not mentioning that this had taken place four years before and owed more to local and episcopal opposition than to climate and access problems. Brancone signed a provisional *placet* for Alphonsus and his companions to live in Cataldi's private residence and to open a private oratory. With this slender thread of legitimacy Sportelli, Mazzini and Giordano attempted to establish themselves. All went well for a while but inevitably the climate changed, and opposition to the foundation began to gather momentum, orchestrated by one Don Domenico di Maio, successor of Don Francesco as priest in charge of San Felice. Influenced by the fact that they were living on sufferance without church or residence of their own, Sportelli contemplated abandoning the whole undertaking. But Falcoia, within a few months of his death, forbade them to leave: 'This is the work of the devil. Pay no attention and do not fear. Just go ahead and the Lord and St Michael will protect you. Dedicate your new church to St Michael.'

This was virtually Falcoia's last dealings with Alphonsus and the Missionaries of the Most Holy Saviour. The confrontation with the Bourbon authorities had proved a shock to his system from which he never recovered; more and more he found himself unable to cope with the burden of administration in his diocese and of directing the missionary congregation. During the early months of 1743 his health deteriorated. Alphonsus, absent on mission, assigned Sportelli and Brother Francis to go to Castellamare to assist in every possible way. From Ciorani all the members of the Congregation signed a common letter which Sportelli read for him; from the mission Alphonsus continued to send him assurances of prayers and requested that when the bishop saw the Madonna he would recommend them all to her. On Easter Saturday, 20 April 1743, just a month after his eightieth birthday, Falcoia died. None of his colleagues from the Pii Operai were with him at his deathbed — only his own diocesan clergy and members of the Missionaries of the Most Holy Saviour. It was on account of them and of his work on behalf of the convent of Scala that he became marginalised from his own society and virtually forgotten by them. In his Will, drawn up in March, he left his body to the Nuns at Scala, his heart to the cathedral in Castellamare, and to the Congregation of the Most Holy Saviour, the treasured possession of his favourite picture of the Madonna. But news that his body was to go to Scala met with total opposition from the people of Castellamare; they placed a guard on his remains, refusing to allow those who had come from Scala to arrange the transfer to carry out the bishop's wishes. So the remains of Falcoia remained in his episcopal city and were interred peacefully in his cathedral.[28]

The death of Falcoia left a void in the life of Alphonsus which would never be filled. It also marked the end of the first phase of the history of the Missionaries of the Most Holy Saviour. To the establishment of this new institute Falcoia had brought an unshakeable confidence that the work was from God and must succeed; at no time did the slightest doubt concerning the ultimate success of an enterprise which humanly speaking had little to justify it and seemed doomed to failure so very often, even seem to cross his mind. In the presence of his metropolitan, the archbishop of Salerno, he declared as he received the Last Rites that the institute was the work of God and that it would spread like the grass of the fields.

He was a man of great contrasts and at times of contradictions. Autocratic and jealous of his authority, he could not tolerate that his decisions were not carried out unquestioningly. At the same time he generously saw in Alphonsus the chosen instrument for the establishment of a work which he had failed to set up himself. And if towards the end he seemed to rely on Sportelli more than Alphonsus he never in fact retracted his belief that Alphonsus was the chosen instrument of God. He was able to see the calibre of the man behind the scruples and hesitations. In the very last letter that he addressed to him in the summer of 1742 when they were at odds with each other about the Spinelli missions, he reassured Alphonsus that 'he esteemed him as the apple of his eye. And I trust that the good Lord will enable you to do great things for his Divine honour and glory.'

Falcoia's ideas of spiritual direction were not untypical of the time though undoubtedly reinforced in practice by his autocratic temperament. For him the Holy Spirit did not speak to the penitent directly; all divine communications were through the director who became, as it were, the mouthpiece of the Spirit of God for the penitent. Maria Celeste suffered under this attitude and was crushed by it. Alphonsus was more fortunate in that Falcoia's autocratic methods matched his psychological and spiritual needs at the time better than did the gentler guidance of Pagano and consequently he was able to handle the difficulties of Falcoia's guidance successfully even though at times he could not have found it easy to do so. He learnt to depend totally on Falcoia in two areas: one, the establishment of the new missionary congregation; the other, his personal spiritual difficulties and scruples. In both these areas he sought no assurance other than the word of his director. Since the distance between them at times made consultation difficult, Falcoia wisely allowed him to consult his 'local' confessor on the spot and to follow his immediate guidance in the practical doubts and anxieties of every day. In this way the list of Alphonsus' 'confessors' grew; Father Fiorillo helped him in Naples, Don Silvestro Sangiorgi, rector of the seminary at Caiazzo came to his assistance in Villa, and Fathers Mazzini, Sportelli, Sarnelli and Rossi at one time or another when he grew disturbed at home. But their advice was always subordinate to the final decision of the bishop.

And yet for all his apparent severity Falcoia was at heart a tender father with a deep sense of the vital importance of the simple love of God in one's life. He diagnosed, early on, the need for Alphonsus to alter his concept of God away from fear to one of love and trust. The most touching parts of his direction of Alphonsus are to be found in those letters where he explains in simple terms the significance of the gospel injunction, 'You shall love the Lord your God with all your heart.' 'It implies two things,' he wrote, 'one that you remove all obstacles, which is the same as saying that you have freed your heart from all that is not God and have freed it totally. Anything that is loved, that is not God, divides the heart at very least. So you cannot say with truth that you love God with all your heart when it is shared with creatures, and among these the worst is oneself. And the second is to unite oneself with the Divine Majesty. One rests in the Lord with Him as centre; one unites one's will with His, one wishes nothing other than what He wishes, one directs all one's efforts to carry out God's will in everything, even the smallest.' To love God with one's whole heart, that was the secret. What did it really mean in practice? Falcoia explained it all so simply that Alphonsus copied into his personal note-book, first his resolution 'to avoid the slightest deliberate fault' and then secondly how to sanctify everything he did. 'At the beginning of every action to say, Jesus and Mary, help me, to unite what I do with the intentions of Jesus and Mary and lastly to offer all my actions in this way to God.'

Chapter Eight

The Lord Gives the Increase 1743–1750

– I –

Falcoia had expressed contradictory views about the survival of the missionary congregation after his death; in a letter to Spinelli he expressed his fear that after his departure the congregation would disintegrate due to conflicting ideas among the members. At the same time he is reported to have said on his death-bed that the new missionary society would continue to flourish. He was right on both scores. Conflicting attitudes did emerge among the members which were a constant source of worry to Alphonsus and at the same time the society grew in numbers and repute and foundations multiplied.

The immediate problem on the death of Falcoia was the appointment of a superior. Although the outlines of the Rule for the new congregation, which had been in the making since 1732, provided for an overall superior with the title of Rector Major to distinguish him from the local superiors, there had been no attempt to establish the position or appoint anyone to it while the bishop lived. No attempt had been made to codify the relations between Alphonsus and the bishop or to delineate their particular spheres of authority; instead a *modus vivendi* had evolved which, whatever the strains upon it, worked tolerably well for eleven years. Now there was need to regularise the governmental structure. Alphonsus, absent on mission when Falcoia died, was not present at his obsequies. He summoned all the clerical members of the congregation to meet in Ciorani on 6 May 1743, not three weeks after the bishop's death. The Brothers who were nearly as numerous as the priests, did not have a vote in any of the electoral procedures. On the first Monday in May, Alphonsus, Sportelli, Rossi, Mazzini, Villani, Giordano and

Cafaro assembled in Ciorani for the first General Assembly of their missionary congregation. Sarnelli was still in Naples with the Cardinal. Whether he was summoned to attend or not, he did not, in point of fact, participate in any way in the deliberations and decisions of the assembly. The first three days were spent in retreat and prayer for the repose of the soul of Falcoia. Mass was celebrated for him each day and Alphonsus delivered the panegyric. On Thursday 8 May the real work of the assembly began. There was a Votive Mass of the Holy Spirit preceding the first meeting of the seven members at which Sportelli was elected President of the Assembly and Mazzini its secretary.[1] In the rough draft of the proposed Rule for the congregation it had been generally accepted that a two-thirds majority of the votes was required for the election of the Rector Major. This was confirmed by the group and consequently five votes were required for a candidate to be elected to the office of Rector Major. Sportelli as President addressed the members, pointing out to them that in casting their votes they were to consider solely the glory of God and the good of the congregation. Even if they were all gifted by God with special graces and valuable talents, he pointed out, there still existed degrees in the distribution of God's gifts just as star differed from star in brilliance. Alphonsus gave no indication that he expected the position to go to him as of right. At any rate, the first three scrutinies did not provide the required majority. Unfortunately we have no record of how the votes were distributed beyond the simple fact that Alphonsus, even if he did get the majority of votes — and we cannot be certain of that — still did not receive the necessary five. Taking it for granted that he did not vote for himself this means that at least two, and maybe more, of his six companions did not immediately vote for him as Rector Major.

After the third ineffectual scrutiny, Sportelli suspended the session. On his direction the members took themselves off to the chapel or their rooms for private prayer and reflection. When they were reassembled, Alphonsus was elected Rector Major on the first scrutiny unanimously — in other words, he received all the votes except his own. He saw the election as the manifestation of the Will of God for him and it was in that spirit that he assumed the direction of the congregation. This he was to declare explicitly when, within a few years, his position as superior was under attack.

Various theories have been advanced as to why Alphonsus' election as Rector Major on the death of Falcoia was not a mere formality and why some of his companions hesitated to elect him. Who were the other candidates who received votes and whom did he himself vote for? None of these questions can now be answered definitively since the results of the scrutinies are not contained in the account of the assembly's proceedings drawn up by Mazzini as secretary. But the other most likely candidate was Sportelli, and his supporters may well have felt that he would adhere more rigidly to the line laid down by the bishop. Alphonsus had already shown his readiness to take an independent approach which was well demonstrated in his initial willingness to accept the Cardinal's offer of a foundation at Barra. They may also have felt that he was likely to be absent for long periods on preaching engagements. But all this is surmise and the only historical conclusion that is valid is that he was not the undisputed choice as the first superior of the Missionaries of the Most Holy Saviour.[2] While the nature of the office to which he was finally elected had still to be worked out in detail, there were two aspects of it which caused dissension from the very outset and were to have serious consequences in the future. The office of Rector Major was for life and was to be exercised with no such restrictions as the necessity of securing the consent of his advisers which is laid down in modern Canon Law for similar offices. Falcoia insisted that the government of the missionary congregation should be in the hands of one person, modelled to some extent on the papacy — *il governo per un capo solo, a forma della chiesa* — and Alphonsus was determined from the very outset to maintain it as such, whether out of veneration for the wishes of Falcoia or from personal conviction, we do not know.

On the day following his election, Alphonsus assembled all the Fathers and Brothers in the domestic chapel of the monastery where they pronounced the traditional vows of poverty, chastity and obedience as well as a vow of perseverance in the congregation until death, before Alphonsus as the first Rector Major; he himself took the same vows before the assembled capitulars. With the vow of poverty went a vow renouncing ecclesiastical dignities, benefices and offices outside the congregation, while to the vow of obedience was added a vow to go on missions overseas to the 'infidels' if commanded to do so by the Pope or the Rector Major. The formal profession of the three vows of religion represented the acceptance of Alphonsus' line of thinking about the congregation rather than that of Falcoia who may well have envisaged for the new missionary society just something similar to the oath of perseverance on the model of his own society. The members of the Chapter at Ciorani were fully aware that the profession of vows commonly associated with religious orders might arouse the suspicions of the Bourbon Court in Naples for whom the least mention of anything in the nature of a new religious order was abhorrent. Accordingly they passed a decree declaring that they were not a religious order 'but a congregation of priests similar to the Fathers of the Mission (Vincentians) and the Pious Worker Fathers but with this difference that the Fathers of our least congregation must attend in a more particular way to helping country people and that therefore they must always live outside the cities and in the centre of the dioceses.' In point of fact the profession of vows, for all the cautionary declarations of the Chapter, did differentiate the missionaries of the Most Holy Saviour from both the Pii Operai and the Vincentians as far as canonical identity was concerned. But that is altogether another story.[3]

Besides electing their own first superior the Fathers at the May meeting made certain decisions about the practice of the vows, about the government of the congregation, the method of giving missions and the formation of candidates. It was a totally new experience for them to be discussing and deciding matters which up to this had been solely within the competence of Falcoia and to some extent Alphonsus himself. The group, however, was anxious to get back to the actual work they already had in hand; Sportelli, Mazzini and Giordano had urgent matters to attend to in Pagani, Alphonsus and the others had missionary commitments that could not be deferred. Missioners, by nature, are notoriously impatient of chapter meetings. So the decrees show all the signs of being devised in haste and assembled without any order or precision. The need for a definite set of Rules and Constitutions was obvious; despite the various drafts which had been drawn up by Falcoia and Alphonsus there was still an enormous amount of work to be done collating the various texts and producing a final text. For the moment, with veneration for Falcoia at its height, the Fathers passed a resolution that 'what has been established by our deceased Father and Director, Mons. Falcoia must always be totally adopted and observed.' And the final decision was 'that a Father should be appointed to collate the Rules and Constitutions left dispersed by our Founder.' Falcoia had written some years before that these documents could be found conveniently in the drawer of his desk. Within a few months this work of drawing up a definitive text would run into serious difficulties and incur the displeasure of Alphonsus.

– *II* –

Besides the need for the definitive formulation of the Rules for the congregation and the ultimate approval of Rome, there were more immediate problems facing Alphonsus on his election as Rector Major; he now came face to face with all the difficulties which Bourbon regalism was to create for the continuance of his missionary society. Despite the conciliatory efforts of Pope Benedict XIV to come to terms with the reasonable grievances of the Neapolitan government and the Concordat which was signed in 1741 between them, Charles III and his ministers continued to restrict the freedom of action of the Church in their dominions. The decree of 1740 forbidding new foundations, which had sent such a shock of horror through Alphonsus and his companions, was just the first instalment of anti-Church and anti-Roman edicts. Further decisions would make it necessary for all decrees and rescripts from Rome to receive the royal *Exequatur* before they could legitimately be put into execution in the Kingdom. The concession of this approval was in the hands of the Cappellano Maggiore, who, though always a cleric, was as often as not as regalistic and anti-Roman as the King's ministers themselves. Restrictions on religious liberty continued to multiply; royal approval for the publication of books even of a theological nature was now required. In the light of the sufferings and misunderstandings which darkened Alphonsus' last years it must be remembered that whole generations of educated and well-meaning people, including many clerics, grew up for whom no church law was binding in the Kingdom unless it was approved by the King or his ministers. There were even some members of his own congregation prepared to refuse obedience on the pretext that the Roman approval of the Rules and Constitutions had not received the royal *Exequatur*.

The first major concern was the foundation at Pagani. Armed with the royal approval obtained through the good offices of Brancone and with some money from the retired priest, Don Francesco, and the rest borrowed from the rich convent of Santa Clara at Naples, Alphonsus purchased a site for his church and 'house' on the outskirts of Pagani, known as the 'Cantilena'. The plans for the buildings were drawn up by the Neapolitan architect, Pietro Cimafonte, the same who had worked on the house at Ciorani. In July 1743 two months after Alphonsus' election as Rector Major, the Vicar General of the diocese laid the foundation stone amid general rejoicing. And then the opposition really manifested itself. The diocese had over 300 priests, not including ten monasteries of religious who saw in the arrival of the new missionaries a threat to themselves and perhaps a reproach to their own pastoral negligence. The relatives of Don Francesco, who were anxious to have his money for themselves, and a number of disgruntled clergy made common cause. They first instituted legal proceedings against the Fathers of the Most Holy Saviour in the bishop's court with unfortunate results for themselves. Undaunted, they decided to take their case to Naples where they were assured of a hearing because of the anti-clerical temper of the courts. For good measure they entered a similar petition in Rome with the Congregation of Bishops and Regulars. Every possible accusation was brought against the missionaries; they were in Pagani illegally — despite the fact that they had a royal decree; they were building a 'monastery' and not just an ordinary 'secular' house. In Rome their adversaries had the effrontery to complain that they had formed themselves into a missionary congregation without papal approval, they were trading in religious objects and taking money from the people. Most intriguing of all was the accusation that they were introducing dangerous novelties in their missions throughout the various dioceses.

Alphonsus had to exercise extreme vigilance to counteract every move of the opposition. He drew up a legal document proving that the foundation in Pagani was both 'lawful and legitimate', *lecito e legitimo* — an eight-page folio defence which delighted Sportelli for its clarity.[4] To Brancone he addressed a memorial proving that the design of the house does not constitute a 'monastery' — it lacked cloisters. He used all his influence in Naples, even sending one of his novices, the well-connected Sanseverino, to make the necessary contacts. He organised his various friends among the hierarchy, from Spinelli in Naples to Vigilante in Caiazzo, to testify their approval of himself and his missioners. He pleaded, then threatened, feeling that 'a call to arms', as he styled it, might achieve results; the best method of defence is attack. Even so, for a while in 1745 he seriously considered abandoning the foundation in frustration.

There were incredible incidents during the long drawn-out struggle. The original decree granting royal approval specified a house and public church, *casa con capella publica*. By bribing the registrar of the royal decrees the brief was made to read *senza capella*, 'without a church'. When Alphonsus discovered the deception he sent Sanseverino post-haste to Brancone to make it known. The marquis immediately altered the document with a stroke of his pen, restoring it to its original meaning. The next encounter was more thrilling still. The following summer of 1744 when work on the church and house was approaching completion, the opposition succeeded in obtaining a court decree of *nihil innovet* from the marquis of Fraggiani. It was a type of injunction which had the effect of suspending work on the building and maintaining it in the state in which it was, namely an uncompleted shell. Warned secretly of the contents of the decree, which arrived in Pagani on Friday 17 July, Sportelli contacted Alphonsus in Ciorani; together they devised a stratagem in reply. The local magistrate, who was a friend of the Fathers, refused to take action on the grounds of a legal quibble pointed out by Sportelli, himself a lawyer, namely that the decree was addressed to the superintendent in Salerno. This allowed for a breathing space. All day and night Sportelli and Brother Rendina laboured with what help they could secure, to make the house habitable and the church operational. When the official arrived from Salerno on Sunday he was faced with a *fait accompli*, the church was in use, Mass was being celebrated, Sportelli had preached and confessions were being heard. The temporary nature of the arrangements were obvious to him, the rough clay floor covered with straw, the walls unplastered, the altar without a tabernacle, the windows without glass. A picture of St Michael the archangel, the church patron, graced a hole in the wall. Innocently Sportelli expressed his willingness to abide by the decree *nihil innovet* — celebrating Mass, preaching, hearing confessions. The official realised that he had been completely out-foxed legally for he reported back to Naples:

> I presented myself this morning at Pagani and demanded of Father Cesare Sportelli that he show me the authentic document of the Royal permission and that in the meantime he desist from all further work on the building. He replied that he and his companions were established in Pagani by gracious grant of the King, whom God preserve, and that they were more than anxious to comply with the dispositions of his Majesty and that in obedience to this they would show the Royal Decree in the royal Chambers on request and that they would at once put an end to the work, which they did in my presence, by dismissing the workers.

Fraggiani could only admit defeat and swallow it with the best grace possible. It was all so typically Neapolitan.

The legal battle for Pagani dragged on for years. The litigation connected with it became famous in the Naples court, since the opposition to the Fathers in Pagani was led by one of the most anti-clerical of lawyers, Don Francesco Cailo, another contemporary of Alphonsus at the bar. The struggle developed into a legal duel between them, a spectator sport for court watchers. In Pagani itself there was a period when the members of the community were publicly insulted in the streets; an attempt was even made to blow up the whole building. More imaginatively some of the opponents of the foundation gathered under the windows at night time to mimic their sermons and their manner of preaching. Alphonsus himself suffered on his visits as well. He was publicly called an 'ignoramus', while one cleric in the company told him that if he wished to rob the people it would have been more manly to assault them on the highways rather than under the pretext of religion. His reply has been recorded. *'Dio sia benedetto*, have I renounced my home and my inheritance to be treated as a robber in Pagani.' But ultimately all resistance came to an end, due in the main to a number of conciliatory compromises agreed to by Alphonsus. In September 1747 the novices, led by their novice-master, Villani, walked from Ciorani singing hymns along the way, to take up residence. Mazzini, the new rector, greeted them with an improvised para-liturgical service of washing their feet. It had taken nine troublesome years to establish the house and church at Pagani where the body of St Alphonsus, Doctor of the Church, is now venerated.[6]

The opposition to the Pagani foundation had one quite unintended result for Alphonsus and his missionaries. The objections raised in Rome were referred to the various episcopal authorities in the Kingdom of Naples as was the usual Roman curial practice. The outcome was that the bishops sent glowing encomiums of the new missionary group to the Roman authorities, their edifying lives, the effect of their missions on the religious practice of the people. Bishop De Dominico of Nocera went straight to the point. 'Before admitting them to my diocese I assured myself of the value of their activity because I summoned them to my diocese to give a mission. When I saw with my own two eyes the indescribable good — which still remains — done by them I determined to bring them to my diocese.' Bishop Vigilante of Caiazzo generously confirmed the excellent work they had done in his diocese and did not conceal his disappointment at their departure. All of this was of immense benefit to Alphonsus a few months later when, greatly daring, he had the courage to seek Roman approval for his Congregation.[7]

– III –

The problems connected with the foundation at Pagani did not deter Alphonsus from planning another foundation on the other side of the Appenines which would cater for missions in the area of the Abruzzi, Apulia and the Basilicata.

With the number of vocations increasing steadily if not dramatically he was ready to consider seriously a proposal to establish a missionary centre in the almost derelict Sanctuary of Our Lady on the edge of the mountain town of Deliceto. The proposal originated with a former governor of the town who recommended the missioners to the patron of the sanctuary, Canon Casati:

> There is here in the diocese of Salerno a new congregation of missioners, quite unlike the ordinary run of priests. They are not seekers after money; they have sacrificed their own comfort and are ready for all

hardships and fatigue to come to the assistance of the most abandoned souls. Among them are members of noble families and of social status like Don Alfonso de Liguori, a Neapolitan nobleman of the *seggio* of Portanova. He is well known, I think, to the prince of Castelleneta, Lord of Deliceto, and a member of the same *seggio*. In a word they are men of worth and live a life of exemplary strictness. The Fathers are going towards the end of the year to give missions in Bari. I thought you would be glad to take the occasion of their journey to invite them to preach a mission at Deliceto either on their way there or on their return.

With this introduction Alphonsus set out from Ciorani in early December 1744 with Fathers Cafaro, Genovese, the student Francesco Sanseverino and a novice. The journey through the snow-covered Appenines took the best part of a week. Near Bovino they left the road that led on to Foggia and turning to the right went up into the mountains until they reached Deliceto perched 1,600 feet above sea level. It was a typical medieval town built under the shadow of a Norman castle which still dominates the whole area; even today it has changed little from the time when Alphonsus and his companions rode in for their first mission. In its inaccessibility time has left it untouched; it stands like a sentinel guarding the fertile plain stretching south to its sister town of Sant' Agata di Puglia and northwards across the Apulian plateau to the confines of the Molisse and the Abruzzi. Besides its missionary significance for Alphonsus, its greatest claim to fame was the fact that it was the favourite hunting place of Charles III and the place that most bored Tanucci when he was forced to be a member of the royal retinue.[8]

The mission in Deliceto was a revelation. The bishop of the diocese of Bovino in which the town was situated, and even the priests, numerous as usual, were filled with enthusiasm. Particularly impressed, at least at the outset, were the Maffei, the ruling family of the town and agents of the feudal overlord. Later they were to come within an inch of destroying the whole congregation. Alphonsus was elated at the reception they had received: 'They have accepted us as angels from heaven,' he wrote.

> The people here are most affectionate and docile and there is very little litigation. They are all mostly country folk, inclined to piety and not given to any vices.
>
> The countryside is fertile and there is an abundance of everything, wood, grain, vegetables, good wine, excellent cheese and plenty of good fruit. There are cows, sheep and goats and there is a certain type of *ricotta* the like of which I have never tasted before.

There was no prospect of a foundation within the walls of the town on account of the already excessive number of priests but just six kilometres outside the town and separated from it by a steep ravine was a sanctuary of Our Lady of Consolation. Although its origins stretched back to early times the modern history of the building dated from the fifteenth century when Blessed Felix of Corsano, an Augustinian hermit, built a shrine of Our Lady and a small hermitage where he began the reform of the Neapolitan province of his order. By the middle of the seventeenth century the order had again declined and the Augustinian house was closed by papal decree leaving the sanctuary to caretakers. Two attempts to establish new organisations there failed and when the sanctuary was offered to Alphonsus as a missionary centre it was largely in ruins; the chapel could accommodate only about thirty people. But geographically the site was very attractive. From Deliceto the way was open for missionising the whole eastern section of the Kingdom. At the very doorstep on the fertile plains of Apulia were thousands of shepherds, who came down from the mountain fastnesses of the Appenines during the winter months to pasture their flocks. Immediately Alphonsus set his sights on these pastorally neglected souls as the principal object of his missionary efforts; within a few weeks of the Deliceto mission he was in contact with the civil authorities in Foggia to see what arrangements could be made. He was hopeful that since the sanctuary was a few miles away from the town there would be little likelihood of objections from the local clergy; he was once again to be proved totally wrong. The local bishop, however, was more than favourable. Mons. Antonio Lucci, a Franciscan, after a distinguished career in Naples and later in Rome at the church of the Dodici Apostoli, was sent as bishop to Bovino in 1729. Before allowing the new missionaries into his diocese he consulted his sources in Naples; their reply removed any doubts he may have had:

> These fathers have as their object the preaching of missions. In the dioceses where they have worked they have instructed the people admirably in the doctrines of the faith, sanctified them by the administration of the sacraments through their preaching and with the practice of prayer and meditation in common. They are excellent theologians, particularly in moral theology; they preach very well and what is of more importance they are contented with what they get and do not meddle with other affairs.[9]

Before Christmas 1744 all legal arrangements were made for the transfer of the sanctuary of Our Lady of Consolation to the care of the missionaries of the Most Holy Saviour. The revenues guaranteed to the Fathers were meagre, a total of 76 ducats per year. Alphonsus planned to bring a Brother from Ciorani to attend to the cultivation of the two fields which went with the property. A few weeks later on 9 January 1745 the royal permission was granted to Alphonsus and his companions to reside in Deliceto with the usual *caveat* that they were not to build a 'convent' but simply a secular dwelling for their accommodation and that they were to remain subject to the local bishop like secular priests living at home. 'His Majesty', wrote Brancone to Alphonsus, 'has learnt with great personal satisfaction of the spiritual good which has resulted to the faithful from the missions and labours of your Reverence. His Majesty prays that you may always maintain and even increase this spirit in favour of souls who are so numerous and who are almost abandoned.'

A copy of the Rules and Constitutions of the new congregation was sent to the bishop of Bovino for his approval which followed in due course. In the presence of the vicar General of the diocese, Alphonsus took possession of the sanctuary at the end of March 1745 and installed himself and his companions among the ruins of what was once a Marian shrine. He set himself to work to make the place habitable. It was necessary to start building at once so he took upon himself the function of architect, drawing up a simple plan which still exists, with sufficient rooms for retreatants as well as for novices and missioners. While the building was still in progress Alphonsus installed a community of six Fathers, three Brothers and the novices under the direction of Father Paul Cafaro, who found the place well suited to his ascetic and contemplative temperament.[10]

The hardships suffered by the community at Deliceto in those early days became legendary. The foundation revenues were hopelessly inadequate. There were no pilgrims to the shrine to help the upkeep of the community; the missions, though flourishing, were given without stipend and few bishops and fewer priests offered anything to the missioners for their labours. One of the first novices in Deliceto, in 1745, Father Celestine de Robertis, recalled the hardships of the community and, even allowing for a little over-emphasis, he conveyed a grim picture:

> Hunger, cold and want were the norm. Our ordinary fare was a *minestra* of vegetables, usually badly cooked since the cooking stove was not adequate for all the demands on it. From time to time we had the good fortune to get some scraps of boiled meat. The bread, made from bran, was as black as our soutanes and hardly more appetising. For *dolci* we had either boiled beans or roasted chestnuts. Linen was also in short supply; we had only one blanket each and at night we had to use our cloaks as bedclothes. Cold draughts blew in through the cracks in the windows at night time. In the winter we were snow-bound and on occasions as a result, without flour or bread. At times during the winter it was torture to celebrate Mass since with the cold, one's hands were frozen and one's fingers numb so that it was almost impossible to handle the Chalice or make the sign of the Cross with the Sacred Host. Very often in our domestic meetings in view of these hardships, our Rector Major (Alphonsus) would encourage us to bear them cheerfully, saying, 'Fathers and Brothers, have we by any chance come here to the mountains of Deliceso to enjoy ourselves and not to suffer for the love of Jesus Christ?[11]

The protracted negotiations in connection with the two foundations at Pagani and Deliceto did not interrupt Alphonsus' missionary labours. Since his arrival east of the Appenines towards the end of 1744 he and his companions were in constant demand. Benedict XIV, whose first pontifical act had been to issue a papal letter encouraging missions in Naples, followed this up in September 1746 with a fuller encyclical *Gravissimum Supremi Apostolatus* addressed to all the bishops of the kingdom of Naples urging them to renew the spiritual life of their dioceses by a series of missions in every parish. The Pope himself had experienced the value of missions while he was bishop in Ancona and Bologna and he was anxious to set on foot a spiritual renewal in Naples with whose monarchs, Charles and Maria Amalia, he was now on the warmest terms following their official visit to Rome in 1744. His proposals met with the fullest approval of the King and his ministers not from purely supernatural motives but because they believed the missioners contributed considerably to the task of eradicating civil as well as religious abuses, and more effectively and at less cost than their own militia and law courts. Accordingly they were prepared in certain circumstances to support the work financially. Cardinal Spinelli was named as Papal Delegate for the implementation of the papal decree and in apportioning of areas to be evangelised he entrusted Alphonsus and his missioners with the task of missionising the dioceses of Bovino, Troia and Foggia.

As a result of the Pope's intervention the year 1745 ushered in a period of exceptional missionary activity for Alphonsus and his companions which was to continue right up to the time Alphonsus preached his last mission in Nola in 1759. Gathering together all the Fathers he could spare from Ciorani and Pagani he deployed them over the three dioceses. This was the most extensive campaign he had yet undertaken with his own priests. From September 1745 the groups of missioners went from town to town and village to village on horseback, staying as long as was necessary for preaching and the hearing of confessions, living together as far as possible with all the spiritual exercises in common as if they were at home. The response of the people was most encouraging. They were in the main simple, unlettered, badly instructed, given to violence and blasphemy—the area was a centre of brigandage. At the same time they were full of all the popular religious superstitions, given to externalisation and even theatricality in the practice of religion. This was an aspect on which the missioners, professionals in their techniques, learnt to capitalise. During the act of contrition one night at the end of a sermon in the course of the mission in Arcadia, the rosary beads placed on the statue of the Madonna in the sanctuary fell noisily to the ground. Silence fell on the congregation. Not one to miss such an opportunity, Sportelli, who was preaching, stopped his sermon; taking the rosary in his hands, he held them high as a sign of the Madonna's displeasure. The effect on the people was dramatic.

The episcopal city of Troia, which was next to be evangelised, had acquired an unenviable reputation as a difficult place in which to preach; it had been the graveyard of many an orator's reputation, resembling somewhat those local opera houses where fans hooted to tears the visiting *prima donnas* they disliked. The renowned missioners of the Kingdom faced the prospect with trepidation. One Father Santorelli left after his third sermon; the great Carace from the Apostolic Missions failed to measure up to their standards and one particularly unfortunate missioner, Don Filippo Avveta, was brought down from the pulpit in the middle of his sermon. Alphonsus assigned to himself the *Predica Grande*. The fact that his uncle had been a venerated figure as bishop of the diocese was a helpful introduction. Then one night as he was going out to preach, news of his father's death arrived from Naples. Having prayed first in the sacristy for the repose of his soul he entered the pulpit and made the public announcement and asked the congregation to join him in prayer for the repose of Don Giuseppe's soul. Soon the people of Troia were open to the grace of the mission.

Having concluded the missions in the dioceses of Bovina and Troia Alphonsus gathered his forces, twelve Fathers in all, for a six-week mission in Foggia some twenty kilometres distant. It was exactly thirteen years since he had been there, paying for his enthusiasm in preaching after the earthquake with the public reprimand from Torni at a meeting of the Apostolic Missions on his return. The city had been completely restored in the meantime, achieving a stable population of over 15,000 which was swollen even more by the influx of winter dwellers from the Abruzzi with all the problems that this migration entailed. The mission presented the greatest challenge yet to the Missionaries of the Most Holy Saviour. Apart from having the greatest concentration of missionaries he had yet assembled for any one place, Alphonsus realised that Foggia presented special pastoral problems not generally associated with the rural areas of the Kingdom where his work had been mainly centred up to the present. Its moral standards were notoriously low despite the memory of the destruction of the city in the earthquake. It was the centre of a flourishing trade in banned books which made their way to the city from Venice and from there throughout the rest of the Kingdom. Sportelli reckoned it had over a thousand prostitutes. The task demanded a degree of organisation and planning greater than what was called for in rural communities. Dividing his forces among the three parishes of the city, Alphonsus reserved for himself the preaching of the mission in the collegiate church as well as the preaching of the spiritual exercises in the convent of the Clarissae. Much depended on the success of this mission both for the reputation of his missioners and their method of conducting missions; success from the human point of view was vital for the ultimate acceptance of the new missionary society in the ecclesiastical world of Naples.

Alphonsus' opening sermon, *la predica della Chiamata* has come down to us almost verbatim as it was preached.[12] It was simple in language, with considerable scriptural references, especially from the Old Testament, and highly dramatic. Alphonsus began:

> On this the first day of the mission, before I address you, my dear people, allow me first to speak to God who has sent me here to preach to you. I ask Him to let me know what He wishes me to say to you.
>
> My Lord and my God, you have sent me here to preach in Foggia. Here I am in this pulpit. What do you wish me to say to this ungrateful city and to these, your unfaithful servants, who have come to listen. You are disgusted with them and rightly so. You have done everything possible to secure their conversion; you have heaped favours on them

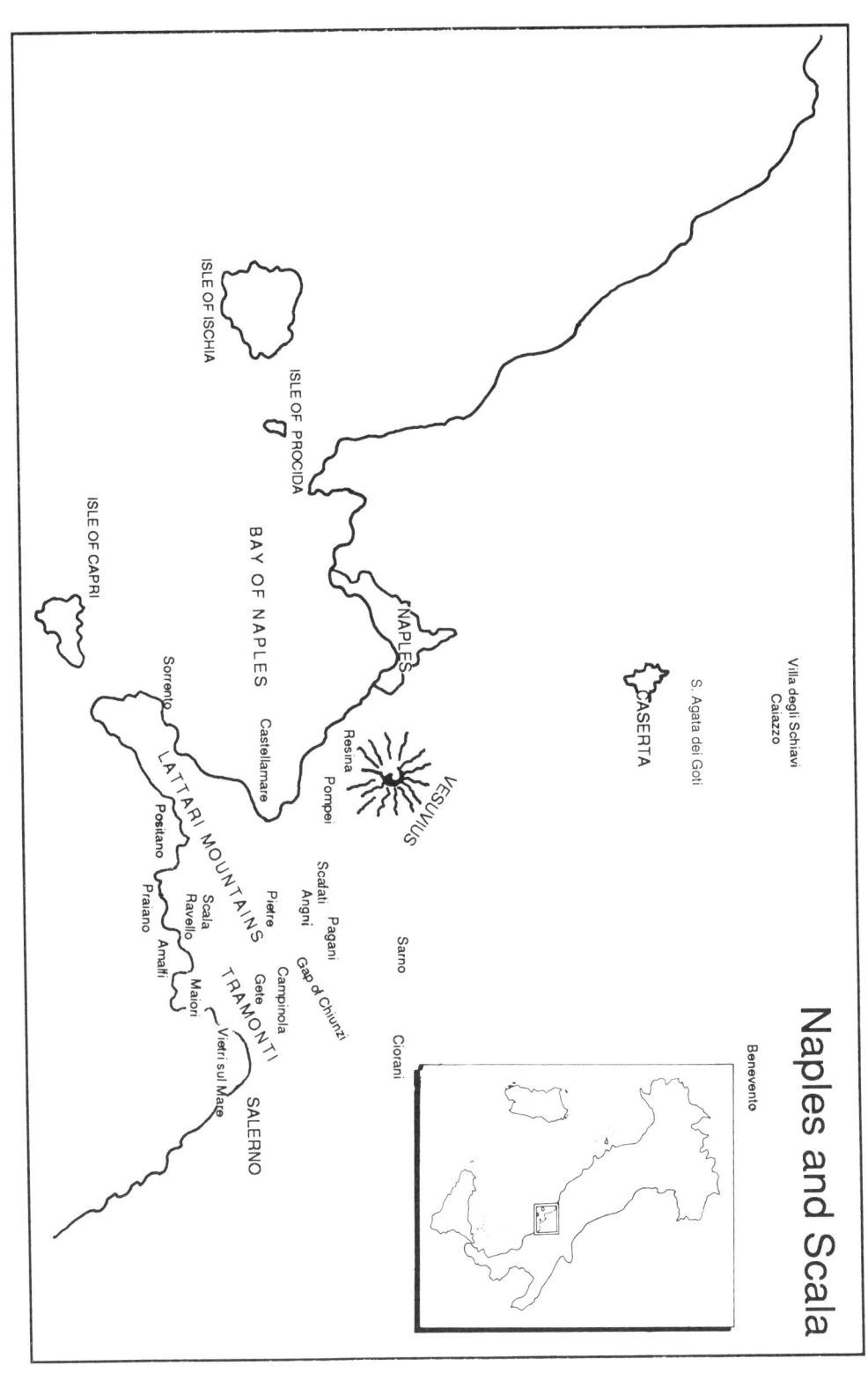

Tramonti and Campinola. The first missions of the new missionary society of the Most Holy Saviour were preached in the early months of 1733 in Tramonti, a mountainous region between Amalfi and Salerno in the heart of the Lattari peninsula. Campinola was the first centre to hear the new missionaries.

A typical village church in the mountains near Pagani where Alphonsus and his companions preached one of their first missions. Mission crosses which were erected at the close of the missions can be seen against the wall of the church on the left of the picture.

One of the magnificent carved pulpits which were a feature of the churches at the time of Alphonsus

The façade of the cathedral at Amalfi where Alphonsus preached one of his last missions. In the square at the foot of the steps he organised the burning of musical instruments which he held responsible for the irreligious spirit of the city.

Alphonsus directed his main missionary thrust towards the inhabitants of the Neapolitan countryside. They were the most pastorally neglected of the Bourbon kingdom. Their lifestyle has altered little in the intervening years.

Men and women still work together in the fields, and the women bring their children with them as they did in the time of Alphonsus. Infants are left in their Moses baskets while their mothers work.

MEDULLA

THEOLOGIÆ MORALIS

HERM. BUSEMBAUM
Soc. JESU Theologi.

ACCEDUNT

Nicolai Propositiones ad hanc usque diem 1749 proscriptæ ;

Quarum & Index ad libri calcem texitur, & suis in locis mentio fit opportuna.

Adduntur in fine Tractatus, qui desiderabatur de Sanctæ Cruciatæ Bulla, & Casus reservati in Bulla Cœnæ.

PATAVII, MDCCXXXVII.
Ex Typographia Seminarii.
Apud Joannem Manfrè.
SUPERIORUM PERMISSU, & PRIVILEGIO.

The frontispiece of the 1737 edition of the Medulla Theologiae Moralis of Herman Busenbaum, which Alphonsus used as the basis of his Adnotationes or Annotations, his first major theological publication in 1748

The title page of the first edition of Alphonsus' Moral Theology. Half way down the page it is stated that it was written for the instruction of the young clerics of the Congregation of the Most Holy Saviour.

MEDULLA
THEOLOGIÆ MORALIS
R. P. HERMANNI BUSEMBAUM
SOCIETATIS JESU THEOLOGI ;
CUM ADNOTATIONIBUS
PER REVERENDUM PATREM
D. ALPHONSUM DE LIGORIO
RECTOREM MAJOREM CONGREGATIONIS SANCTISSIMI SALVATORIS
Adjunctis post Dubia, seu Articulos præfati Authoris, ubi operæ pretium visum fuit, juxta literas alphabetico ordine ibi interjectas.
ACCEDUNT IN CALCE LIBRI
Propositiones damnatæ ; Necnon omnes EPISTOLÆ ENCYCLICÆ, ET PONTIFICIA DECRETA mores spectantia
SS. D. N. BENEDICTI PAPÆ XIV.
Quæ insuper omnia propriis in locis opportunè adnotantur ; unà cum duobus uberrimis Indicibus,
AD USUM JUVENUM PRÆFATÆ CONGREGATIONIS.
OPUS DICATUM
ILLUSTRISSIMO, ET REVERENDISSIMO DOMINO
D. JOSEPHO NICOLAI
ARCHIEPISCOPO COMSANO, SANCTISSIMI DOMINI NOSTRI PRÆLATO DOMESTICO, AC PONTIFICIO SOLIO ASSISTENTI, BARONI OPPIDORUM SANTI-ANDREÆ, ET SANCTI-MENNÆ, ATQUE UTILI DOMINO FEUDI PALIROTUNDI.

* * * *
* * *
*

NEAPOLI M. D. CC. XLVIII.
APUD ALEXIUM PELLECHIUM
SUPERIORUM PERMISSU.
EXPENSIS D. JOANNIS OLIVERII.
Si vende nella Libraria del Signor D. Filippo Porcelli a S. Ligouro, e dal Signor Bartolomeo d'Anria sotto il Campanaro di S. Lorenzo.

and they have repaid you with ingratitude. You have terrified them with chastisements — or rather — I should say with threats. You threatened them with a plague epidemic but then did not send it; you threatened them with the sufferings of war but then these sufferings have fallen on others rather than on your people; you threatened them with death under the destruction of the earthquake but instead you destroyed the buildings but did not inflict death on the people.

And Lord, what has been their response? Nothing; they have become worse than before. What now do you wish me, Lord, to say to them? If you wish me to tell them what I feel I will tell them to prepare themselves for all the punishments they deserve; I shall tell them that they should no longer seek or hope for compassion and pardon because they no longer deserve it. Lord, do you wish me to speak to them in this way?

No, dear friends, no, you ungrateful sinners to whom I address these words especially. God does not wish me to speak to you of justice and punishments but of peace and pardon if you will only stop offending him.

The sermon was then divided into three parts dealing with the patience, the mercy and the love of God for all sinners and especially for the sinners of Foggia. Examples and stories from the experience of the saints and other missionaries helped to demonstrate this mercy in action. The sermon was in total contrast to the fear-inspiring type of sermon characteristic of many of the popular preachers of the time. If ever there was perfect justification for such an approach in an opening mission sermon it was here in Foggia where the evil reputation of the city and the memory of the earthquake provided the ideal setting. But such an approach was not for Alphonsus. He placed before a people steeped in sin and forgetful of God, the image of their God as a tender Father calling his children to accept the offer of his love. The call of God to his people was incarnate in his Son, Jesus Christ, whose death and resurrection were the source of true christian liberty and life. Sermons on such aspects of religion as death, judgment and hell—the last things—were to follow but they were not to erase the fundamental orientation of God as a loving Father, but rather to motivate the sinner to return to his Father's house. And if the fear of damnation failed to move the unrepentant sinner there was always the emotional appeal of the sermon on Our Lady, the *Madonna*, to soften the incorrigibility of the Neapolitan sinner. Only when Alphonsus' missionary approach was taken out of its Neapolitan context and psychology and brought across the Alps after his death was the terror element exaggerated to the extent that it became undeservedly synonymous with his approach.

The mission closed on 6 January 1746 amid scenes of religious enthusiasm which the bishop recalled two years later as he reported to Rome on the condition of his diocese. 'Missions', he said, 'do not make people impeccable but it is only the frequent repetition of missions with their sermons and frequentation of the sacraments and their instructions which can arrest their decline into sin and all forms of materialism.' Not all were so enthusiastic. A contemporary report recounts how one unfortunate visitor arrived from Calabria to indulge in the joys of city life for a while only to find the whole city absorbed by the mission and its activities. 'When the devil will these missioners leave the place?' he demanded in frustration.[13]

Benedict XIV had explicitly mentioned the renewal of convent life as one of the purposes of the general mission throughout the Kingdom. The Cardinal had accordingly recommended that the missioners pay special attention to this aspect of their apostolic activities. During the mission in Foggia Alphonsus preached the spiritual exercises in two of the convents of the city, both following a mitigated form of the Rule of the Franciscan *Clarissae*. Both convents were opulent, catering for the education of the children of the upper classes and apparently very much in need of reform; their educational apostolate made them more an active order, a *conservatorio*, rather then a strict contemplative group. All the usual abuses of the time were present, violation of enclosure, laxity in the matter of poverty, lavish entertainments of every description in the convent reception rooms, lack of silence and consequently of commitment to prayer. The root of much of the disorder was to be found incredibly in an extraordinary attachment, common to many of the convents of the Kingdom, to a florid and unliturgical form of music known as *canto figurato*. Apart from the unliturgical nature of the music — which perhaps could be overlooked except by purists — the performance of this type of music became as elaborate as the presentation of an opera in Naples. In fact the convent could become a miniature opera house. Professors of music and, using this as a pretext, others who were anything but professorial, were summoned to instruct the choirs and individual sisters blessed with the gift of a good voice, which many Neapolitans were. Lavish presentations followed in which one convent vied with another; each year's entertainment had to surpass the previous one.

These entertainments and the expenditure involved were a cause of grave scandal to the ordinary people. The abuse reached its climax at what should have been the most prayerful of convent ceremonies, religious profession. Caffarello, the renowned *castrato*, was in constant demand at this time for ceremonies of religious reception and profession. The daughter of the duke of Monteleone refused to enter the convent chosen for her by her father unless Caffarello sang at her reception. He was lured from his home in Calabria for an enormous sum and thrilled the congregation with an operatic rendering of the Salve Regina which satisfied the determined young novice as she began her religious novitiate. The abuse was most widespread during the musical displays of Holy Week, when the re-enactment of the christian mysteries in the convents faded into the background and the week took on the character of an operatic festival more than anything else. It was not unusual for the congregation at the ceremonies not only to applaud but to stand up and shout Bravo! Bravo! at the conclusion of a solo motet performed by one of the sisters, something more in keeping with the hired *claquers* of an opera house than a liturgical ceremony.[14]

During the course of his retreat Alphonsus attacked the two abuses of the *canto figurato* and the scandalous expenses connected with it. He determined that something should be done in the matter. The Mother Abbess was totally unimpressed and took his remarks in very bad part. However she bowed her head in submission knowing that time was on her side and that when the storm of the mission had subsided, things could revert to what they were before. News of this fictitious submission was communicated to Alphonsus while he was still in Foggia. He felt obliged in conscience to make clear his position and addressed an open letter to the Mother Abbess and all her religious:

> Very Reverend Mother Abbess and Reverend Sisters,
>
> I had the very great honour, despite my demerits, of being of service to your community by preaching the spiritual exercises. Out of concern for the truth and for the unburdening of my conscience I think it well to make known to you clearly in this letter what I laid down about the *canto figurato* and the expenditure of the officials of the community as a result.
>
> As regards the *canto figurato* I say that it is not suitable for religious in general and much less for cloistered nuns. And this is laid down expressly in the Rules of all religious orders. And if the *canto figurato* is still in use in some convents it is considered an abuse. For if one considers the circumstances connected with it, it is morally impossible for it not to occasion sin, on account of the disturbances, the vanity, the distractions, the expense, the inobservance of Rule which it occasions, not to mention other abuses which inevitably arise from it, both inside and outside the convent. And the sins which arise can be of greater or lesser gravity in proportion to the scandal which flows from it all. According to reports here in Foggia the scandal has been considerable.
>
> As regards the expenditure of the officials I said that a letter of the Sacred Congregation of 26 January 1742 contains and lays down a positive command to all religious officials that they should not incur the least expense or give the smallest gift on the occasion of convent feasts . . . [15]

Alphonsus then went on to show from canonical sources the force of this decree as well as the canonical penalties attached to the violation of these norms, which included dismissal from office and the loss of the right of voting and being voted for in convent elections. But the abbess was unimpressed by this marshalling of threats and continued on her uncanonical way undeterred. She apparently abandoned for a while the offending canto and then secretly applied to the relevant Sacred Congregation in Rome for permission to restore it, without of course giving an objective explanation of the issue at stake. Two of the sisters, disturbed at the subterfuge, contacted Alphonsus back in Deliceto. He urged them to write at length to the Roman authorities giving a true picture of the situation. He sent them an outline of the protocol to be employed and advised them to despatch their letters secretly through Maria Celeste Crostarosa, to avoid interception by the ever vigilant Abbess. He allowed them to mention his name to Crostarosa in justification of their action. Some time afterwards Sister Maria Poppa, one of the nuns in question, began to fear the possible consequences of her actions; Mother Abbess was a redoubtable figure. Alphonsus wrote to encourage her to live with the possible consequences of her action:

> I received your letter which was full of fears and human respect. What a fine Spouse of Jesus Christ you are to fear persecution for the love of Christ! What you did was a good action and now you regret it! Do you not realise that it is a fault to regret doing a good deed? But you say you will be persecuted for it. Amen. You ought to rejoice at this and to desire it and not to be afraid of it. "Happy are those who are persecuted for justice's sake." I should like to see you always persecuted by the world for the love of Jesus Christ. . . . For goodness sake never let me hear of similar pusillanimity from you again or I shall doubt if I will see you in heaven. Say the same to Sister Maria Crocifissa and do as I wrote you. Pray for me.

We do not know if the two nuns were of sufficiently stern mettle to confront the Mother Abbess or what the conclusion of the saga was. The matter disappears from Alphonsus' correspondence. Perhaps some future researcher will come across the relevant documents in a Foggia archive.

– IV –

The success of the mission in Apulia resonated throughout the Kingdom. Inevitably there were pressing requests not only for missions but also for foundations. The most pressing came from Conza, where the archbishop was Giuseppe de Nicolai, to whom Alphonsus was to dedicate the first edition of his *Moral Theology*. Conza is situated in the very heart of the Appenines to the south west of Apulia and was the sort of abandoned area which should have appealed immediately to Alphonsus. The people there, to use his own words, resembled wild beasts — *fiere selvaggie* — more than human beings endowed with reason.[16] The invitation came during the mission in Foggia with the offer of another deserted sanctuary, this time known as Materdomini on a mountain top overlooking the town of Caposele at the head of the Sele river which flows south into the Mediterranean below Salerno. Initially Alphonsus rejected the invitation out of hand; he was anxious to consolidate the three existing foundations of Ciorani, Pagani and Deliceto before venturing further afield. Villani was of the opposite opinion and persuaded Alphonsus to preach at least one mission at Caposele before coming to a final decision. After preaching the renewal of the missions in Foggia and Accadia, Alphonsus set off for Caposele with Villani and three others in May 1746 when Irpinia with its breathtaking mountain scenery — one of the most wonderful experiences in all the south of Italy — was at its most enthralling. During the mission, the archbishop of Conza came to Calabritto on the peak of the mountain next to Caposele some twelve kilometres distance by road. Alphonsus rode over to pay his respects and to discuss the question of a possible foundation. He arrived at the *palazzo* of the local lord, where the bishop was staying, around siesta time and rather than disturb the household he went into the domestic chapel beside the palace to recite his breviary. The family chaplain roughly ordered him out. The sight of what purported to be a priest with his poor clothes and beard was anything but reassuring. 'Yesterday one altar cloth was stolen from here and we don't wish to lose another.' Alphonsus departed and finished the recitation of his breviary in the open air where he waited until it was time to send word to the archbishop of his presence. The embarrassment of the chaplain was considerable when the bishop warmly welcomed the Neapolitan *patrician* whom he had mistaken for a beggar. He made amends, however, by recounting this story against himself at the initial process for the introduction of Alphonsus' cause.

After his visit with the archbishop Alphonsus went to see the deserted sanctuary of Materdomini; in many respects it was a repeat of the situation at Deliceto. The fact that the building had been deserted for some time and was situated outside the town recommended it to him for the usual reason that there was less likelihood that the presence of the Fathers would arouse the jealousy of the local clergy, numerous as usual, but pastorally inactive. In the deserted church Alphonsus sat down at the organ and with his companions sang the litany of Loreto. The meagre accommodation of just six rooms requiring considerable repair before they could become habitable made Alphonsus hesitate at the prospect of further outlay of money but the fertile field for missionary activity in the diocese of Conza and its six suffragan dioceses all accessible from Caposele outweighed the obstacles. On Trinity Sunday 4 June 1746 the new foundation was agreed upon. The news was greeted by the people with bonfires and the discharge of musketry while the local feudal gentry, the Prince de Rota and the Princess di Sanfelice offered free materials from their estates for the restoration of the house. The local inhabitants recalled that some twenty years earlier the provincial of the Franciscans from Naples, Fra Giovanni della Croce, had refused an offer of a foundation there for his Alcantrine reform, prophesying that the sanctuary was not destined for them but for another order of missioners who would take charge of it years later.

Alphonsus left Materdomini shortly afterwards but was back again a few months later to preach the novena in preparation for the feast of Our Lady's Nativity on 8 September. He was sufficiently satisfied with the way negotiations were proceeding to petition the King for approval. The favourable outcome was communicated to Alphonsus in November with a secret warning that no more foundations were to be established since the royal tolerance was now exhausted. The permission contained the usual restriction that there was no question of establishing a religious house, just a secular dwelling for secular priests engaged in the giving of missions. Sportelli lost no time in organising a series of missions throughout the diocese and the work was in full swing by the time permission arrived from Rome for the Fathers to take possession of the sanctuary, which they did in August 1747 with Sportelli as superior. Alphonsus sent him two companions, the delightful Father Francesco Garzillo and Brother Gaspar Corvino. Garzillo, a recent recruit, had requested admission to the congregation during the Foggia mission at the age of fifty-five. Alphonsus accepted him and professed him after a brief novitiate in Deliceto. Garzillo was unable to undertake the rough missionary journeys but was invaluable as the permanent member of any community he was assigned to. He developed considerable skill as a carpenter and exercised a permanent apostolate in the confessional in the little church of the sanctuary of Materdomini. From his days as a Canon he still smoked his pipe and sent a request to Alphonsus some days before Christmas 1747 for further supplies of tobacco, to which Brother Gaspar added his own request for more snuff. The gentle Garzillo always refused to accept any position of responsibility referring to himself as nothing more than ballast for the ship. He asked to be excused from attendance at Chapters, declaring his acceptance beforehand of whatever was decided. He was one of those delightful characters whose evident humanity and good humour was a perfect foil for the grimness of many of his companions.[17]

– V –

Alphonsus' father died during the mission at Troia. After the failure of Alphonsus' first efforts at Scala, Don Giuseppe had not interfered in any way with the priestly activity of his son, knowing well that such interference was not only resented but would also be fruitless. Nevertheless the thought of a bishopric for Alphonsus had not left his mind. Within a few years of the arrival of the Bourbon king in 1734 Don Giuseppe had regained some influence in Court circles where, in reality, bishops were appointed. He began to sound out the possibilities of a suitable bishopric and when he found that the prospects were encouraging he had the temerity to write to Alphonsus to that effect at Ciorani. The reply was chilling. Alphonsus addressed his father in the formal reverential and half military style *Gnore mio*, in use at the time:

> As regards the matter of the bishopric, my dear Sir, please do not mention it to me again, if you do not wish to displease me very much. I am determined to renounce even the archbishopric of Naples itself were you to succeed in securing it for me, in order to devote myself to this great work to which Jesus Christ has called me. If I were to abandon this work I would consider myself on the road to damnation since I would be neglecting the call of God. Therefore I ask you not to bring up the matter again and now all the more so since it is one of the rules of our congregation that we must renounce bishoprics and all such honours.
>
> I do not omit to pray for you to our Lord. Bless me always that I

may continue faithful in the service of God to whom I owe everything. I remain your humble servant and ask your blessing.

Don Giuseppe's irascible bad humour was now vented on the youngest of the family, Don Hercules, who soon found life with his father intolerable; he was less well able to stand up to it and assert his independence than Alphonsus had been. In October 1737 Alphonsus was in Naples preaching a mission in the basilica of the Holy Spirit for the Apostolic Missions. One morning Hercules presented himself almost in tears of desperation caused by the hurtful moods of his father who was refusing to speak to him. Taking up his pen in his brother's defence with the daring of one who had personally experienced his father's black humours, Alphonsus confronted Don Giuseppe as he may never have been confronted before:

My dear Sir,

For heaven's sake will you have a little more consideration for your son. This morning he came to me here in Naples in tears because he is almost at the end of his tether with your black humours. My God, do you wish to drive him to desperation until he throws himself into a well or takes some other drastic action?

For heaven's sake, put an end to your black humours at table. Show some consideration for him since the unfortunate man is now married and living on the outskirts of Naples with little opportunity for relaxation. Be careful that you do not drive him to some desperate action; be particularly kind to him since he is so unwell at the moment. Never forget that he is your son and not just a dog. You should show more consideration for him than you do for your money and your property. Remember that when you show charity to your own flesh and blood the Lord will make it up to you in other ways. Let bygones be bygones.

I ask you, dear Sir, to endeavour to live more in union with God than you do, to go to confession more frequently; when Jesus Christ comes there is no more time to set your accounts in order. Remember that you are now well advanced in age [he was only in his 67th year]. Who knows how much time you have left here on earth? And the end will come whether you wish it or not. I pray for you every morning at Mass since I fear very much indeed for your eternal salvation (*temo molto della vostra salute eterna*). My hope is that Our Lady will help you but Our Lady without your Excellency can do nothing.

Alphonsus need not have had any worry about the eternal salvation of his father's soul. He probably underestimated the fundamental goodness hidden under that rough military exterior, which time purified to allow the real christian goodness to reveal itself. Helped by Father Rossi, Don Giuseppe mellowed considerably.

He sent Alphonsus from time to time some special delicacies, especially cocoa, commonly referred to at the time as the 'American drink' or *cioccolata*, which was widely recommended for every sort of illness. It was regarded as the infallible remedy when one was in weak health or out of sorts. 'I received your very welcome letter with the gift of chocolate, for which I am very grateful,' wrote Alphonsus from Ciorani to his father: 'I am well, thank God and go tomorrow to Salerno to preach the retreat to the clergy. Things here are just the same. If you wish to buy some lives of the saints for your reading, the life of St Aloysius which has just recently been published, the life of St Philip Neri and, if you can get it, the life of St Pascal Baylon or St Peter of Alcantara. You should buy a little book called *The Eternal Truths* by Rossignoli or the *Eternal Maxims* by Cattaneo.'

Don Giuseppe's last years were passed in great peace, with all his fretful anxieties about family prestige assuaged. He had come to the realisation that there was more to life than that and perhaps even acknowledged to himself — worldly-wise that he was — that the extraordinary path his eldest son had chosen would bring greater renown to the family name than he had ever contemplated. He loved to visit Ciorani, to make an enclosed retreat there and then to spend some time with the community among whom he was particularly attached to Father Rossi, whose turbulent spirit had brought him, too, into conflict with Alphonsus. He even expressed a wish to remain there in any capacity, either as a Brother of the Congregation or as a gardener. Whether this was a reflection of difficulties he may have had with his wife who grew more scrupulous and agitated towards the end of her life, we do not know. But Alphonsus refused to allow it on the plea that his father's duty to his family and home were paramount, but no doubt he was also influenced by his knowledge of the unpredictable temper of Don Giuseppe and the embarrassing situations which could so easily arise as a result. Towards the end of 1745 it was obvious that Don Giuseppe was near the end of his life. Alphonsus was away in Deliceto totally engaged with the foundation there and the missions. His brother, Don Cajetan, the priest of the cathedral was, however, on hand to render all spiritual assistance and Alphonsus dispatched Father Rossi from Ciorani to be with his father for the last few days. The end came peacefully on Wednesday 17 November. Alphonsus' reaction to the news during the mission in Troia, we have already seen.[18]

The death of Don Giuseppe opened a brief but revealing chapter in the story of Alphonsus' involvement with his family. In his Will Don Giuseppe left Alphonsus the sum of 100 ducats, fifty specified for the building at Ciorani and fifty to be disposed of as he wished himself. During his father's life-time Alphonsus had not claimed the full annual income of 150 ducats which was due to him as part of his patrimony; he had been content with 36 ducats on condition that after his father's death he would receive the whole amount annually. Don Hercules had other ideas, however. Relieved of the burden of his father and sharing no little of his parsimony, he was not over anxious to execute all the provisions of his father's Will, knowing full well that the money destined for Alphonsus would find its way inevitably to the Missionaries of the Most Holy Saviour. He cavalierly suggested that Alphonsus should be satisfied with just 42 ducats annually by way of patrimony in settlement of all claims against his father's estate and should waive the 100 ducats bequeathed to him in his Will. Particularly infuriating for Alphonsus was the fact that Hercules took the whole matter for granted, presenting Alphonsus with what amounted to a declaration that this was all he was getting and that was the end of it. Considerable correspondence must have passed between them which has not come down to us. But the final letter from Hercules was the last straw; the most generous concession he was prepared to offer was that when Alphonsus was in dire need he could make representations to him and he would be helped. To add injury to insult he made some references to the demands of brotherly love. The effect this letter had on Alphonsus can be judged by the reply:

> I have read your last letter in which you tell me in effect that when I am in need you will come to my assistance.
>
> Brother dear, this is not the way to get me to arrive at a compromise with you; rather it is the sure way to make me take you straight to law. And I tell you once more that I do not want to go to law but I well might since I am only seeking what is mine by right. And I assure you that I would only have to put in an appearance in the Courts to get the 150 ducats annually with the rest as well.
>
> At least you could have written to me in some such way as this — 'I would like you, my brother, to agree to leave me with so much'. But instead the idea of writing to state and to prove, as it were, that the 150 ducats do not belong to me, is going a bit too far.
>
> My father did not leave the 100 ducats to me personally but to the Congregation, 50 for the building at Ciorani, 50 to be disposed of as I thought best. And do you think that on account of this 100 ducats my father wished me to waive the claim to my annual income of 150 ducats and just to be satisfied with 42? The 100 ducats are a special legacy from the Will and the 150 are due to me by legal agreements drawn up years ago . . .
>
> You are fortunate that you are dealing with me. If you had to deal with Father Sarnelli who took his father to law to secure his patrimony or our own two sisters, Sisters Marianna and Maria Louisa who took our father to law during his lifetime and won a decree against him for their patrimony, you would not be talking as you are.
>
> I have been patient and tolerant up to the present so as not to upset you but you may yet drive me to take certain steps which I would find altogether repugnant.
>
> So now, brother, if you do not want me to go to law and if you do not wish to treat me as if I were not a member of the family but a bastard — *se non volete trattarmi da bastardo* — let me know one way or the other what you are prepared to give me annually so that I can settle my own accounts . . .
>
> I propose to give you back 42 ducats of the 150 due to me annually. Do you consider that too little? And so brother, I beg you for the love of Our Lady not to write to me in such a way again. . . . Don't annoy

me any further. As regards the 100 ducats, if you have not got them at
the moment, do not get them for me by borrowing at interest. Just let
me have what I have suggested as my annual income. This is the most
important thing so that you and I can live in peace.[19]

The fury of this reply made Hercules come to an immediate agreement and the whole matter was settled by the end of February 1746, three months after Don Giuseppe's death. Alphonsus settled for 72 ducats per year, less than half of what was due to him, but on condition that Hercules undertook to be of service to the Congregation when Alphonsus had need of an agent in Naples for business purposes. And the final word to Hercules was 'Be good and be sure to make the spiritual exercises during Holy Week with the Vincentian Fathers and do not omit to go to Confession and Communion.' Relations between the two brothers, the eldest and the youngest of the family, were never again seriously disturbed. Alphonsus treated Hercules more like a son than a brother and was as considerate as he could be to his wife and his children for whom he had a special affection. Unfortunately Hercules never seemed to enjoy real happiness in his married life.

– VI –

During 1745 Alphonsus was fully occupied with the preaching of missions, the affairs of the Congregation and in particular the negotiations in connection with the foundations at Ciorani, Pagani, Deliceto and Materdomini. To these must be added the flood of letters and memorials which flowed from his pen to members of the congregation, to nuns he was directing, to various influential persons whose support for his missionary society he enlisted. It is almost incredible how he could have found time for everything; not even the fact that at some time he took a vow never to waste a moment of time seems an adequate explanation. And still not satisfied he was now about to launch out into the writing and publication of books.

Alphonsus had already published some slight devotional pamphlets as far back as 1728 and the *capelle serotine*; they were mainly simple meditations, prayers and hymns to be sung on missions. A collection of meditations and prayers which he wrote in preparation for the feast of St Teresa of Avila appeared anonymously about 1743. However, the first publication with which his name is immediately connected was the book of meditations and prayers for a daily visit to the Blessed Sacrament, and to the Mother of God. The work had its origins in an effort to provide his novices and students at Ciorani with a manual of prayers for their visit to the Blessed Sacrament which was part of their daily spiritual exercises. At first there was a set of seven meditations and accompanying prayers, one for each day of the week but these were then expanded to provide one for each day of the month. From use among the students the booklet came to be used by the lay retreatants; the next step was publication. Having passed the ecclesiastical censor in Naples the first printed edition of the work appeared in 1745, paid for by Giovanni Olivieri. No copy of this first edition has, unfortunately, survived. With some slight alterations edition followed edition, year after year, until the booklet took on a life of its own; its popularity, totally unexpected, was immense. Within a few years it was published in Rome and then in Venice and some thirty years before Alphonsus' death was to be found in translations throughout Europe. Perhaps no other work, with the possible exception of *The Imitation of Christ*, has ever had such an effect on devotional practice throughout the whole Catholic world.[20]

At the same time Alphonsus was preparing for publication a series of instructions for bishops on the exercise of their pastoral duties. It was not a subject which was overworked nor were there many prepared to run the risk which any criticism, however implicit, of the Neapolitan hierarchy might entail for their own ecclesiastical careers. Alphonsus was uniquely equipped for the task; twenty years of missionary experience had brought him into the closest contact with the pastoral condition of many dioceses throughout the Kingdom; most of the bishops he knew personally before their appointment, others he was familiar with from meeting them in the course of missions or during the retreats he preached to their clergy. He had, moreover, by now achieved a standing in the ecclesiastical world which would prevent accusations of presumptuous temerity being levelled against him. Above all he possessed that apostolic freedom of spirit which prompted him to say what he thought regardless of the consequences if he felt that the salvation of souls or the good of the Church was in question. And yet he could write it all so inoffensively:

> I have noticed in twenty years of missionary experience that many matters never come to the notice of bishops. Therefore, prompted solely by the glory of Jesus Christ, I have attempted to note down here briefly some important considerations which may be of assistance to them in the exercise of the principal duties of their office. I also wish to describe the means which they should employ to secure the spiritual welfare of their flocks. This has been my sole purpose in writing these reflections.
>
> I shall set down the duties of bishops and the means of carrying them out in just two chapters. And I hope that with God's help these poor pages will be read with some profit at least on account of their brevity. If only their author were to be taken into account, they would not merit even to be considered.

The purpose of the booklet was to remind bishops of their responsibility as pastors of souls; it was not sufficient for them to be men of exemplary christian conduct if they were not wholly dedicated to the pastoral welfare of their people. A bishop had to pay particular attention to six points: his seminary, the students for ordination, his priests, his parish priests, his vicars and diocesan officials and finally the convents of the diocese which were under his care. On all these points Alphonsus had some practical considerations to put forward which give us an excellent picture of the life of the Church in certain areas of the Kingdom. The second chapter dealt with the means the bishop should employ to fulfil his pastoral duties, prayer, good example, residence in his diocese — still a problem in Naples — canonical visitation, missions, diocesan synods, a readiness to listen to good advice, accessibility to his people and finally the correction of those whose lives gave scandal. In the section on good example he reminded the bishops of their duty to be meek and humble and to show an example in their own lives of apostolic poverty and simplicity. He did not forget to mention the danger of bishops' getting out of touch with reality and deciding everything without taking the advice of others. 'The bishop who thinks that he does not need the advice of others in order to rule his diocese,' he wrote, quoting the bishop of Terme, 'must either be God or a brute among men — *bestia fra gli uomini*.' He suggested too that the bishops should be more accessible to their people, they should be ready to receive them at any time. And perhaps with the memory of his own experiences in certain dioceses he advised that 'he should instruct his servants to introduce anyone who comes and especially the parish priests since they are the ones who are busiest and who have many important matters to deal with. If once they are refused admission to the bishop they will not be anxious to come again and will excuse themselves on the pretext that it is impossible to see the bishop and as a result, souls and God's glory will suffer. He must listen to and deal with others with all courtesy. He is the father of his flock and therefore he should treat his people as if they were members of his family and not just vassals or serfs.'

In the section on missions Alphonsus was at his most eloquent and insistent:

> He who has not had the experience of missions and of hearing confessions on missions cannot understand how much good they do. In the first place, the Word of God is broken to the people in a certain ordered plan, and in such a way that it is hardly possible not to be converted to God as a result. As well as this, one can almost feel the presence of God during a mission and the special assistance He gives in so many ways.
>
> But, my God, what do some say? Missions disturb consciences! Therefore it would be better, according to them, to leave the poor sinners in their deplorable state without any qualms of conscience — the surest sign of their damnation. Consciences are disturbed? But it is precisely the duty of pastors of souls to awaken the conscience of those who are asleep in sin so that they may be aroused to a realisation of the danger in which they live and so return to God.
>
> And there is no better way of achieving this than a mission. It is precisely for this reason that we see Hell use all its force to prevent missions, using for this purpose a type of parish priest who in order to prevent himself and his deficiencies being shown up, seeks under other pretexts to prevent the holding of missions. But it is the duty of

bishops to remedy this defect by sending missioners to those very places where he knows the parish priest has neglected to have a mission. And the bishop should not in these cases wait for a request from the local municipality.[21]

The pamphlet for bishops was approved by the Neapolitan censor and printed there in 1745. Alphonsus sent a copy to all the bishops of the Kingdom. From the bishop of Molfetta on the Adriatic coast near Bari came a humble letter of thanks with a well-taken plea for sympathy and understanding; maybe too it was a very subtle defence of bishops:

> I have read with great profit the reflections on the good government by bishops which your Reverence with such great zeal, prudence and learning has just published and which you had the kindness to send me with your very welcome letter. In all this you have shown great charity towards me and indeed towards all the bishops; you have endeavoured to help us by your writings in the difficulties in which we find ourselves as a result of the serious responsibilities we have shouldered. You are like St Bernard and his beloved pupil, later his venerated Pontiff, for whom he wrote *De Consideratione*.
>
> I am sure this great charity of yours will be accompanied by your gracious sympathy and understanding. As a result of your twenty years of experience as a missioner with bishops and with the people, you will undoubtedly know how easy it all is in theory. And you will appreciate how universal is the good will and the good intentions of the bishops and yet at the same time how difficult is the practice taking into account these calamitous times. Were it not for confidence in the infinite mercy and understanding of the Eternal Shepherd, every bishop would resign his office. I have shouldered this burden for over thirty years with such great fear and terror that I ask your Reverence to help me by your prayers just as you have favoured me by sending me your book. I consider it a most precious gift which I shall treasure as one of my most valued possessions. So I thank you sincerely and offer myself to serve you in any way I can.

The *Riflessioni utili a' Vescovi* or *Reflections useful for Bishops* — there was only ever one English translation — was the first fruits of Alphonsus' long missionary experience. He was already occupied with more important problems in the realm of moral theology and preparing such writings for publication.

– VII –

Despite the well-known attitude of the Bourbon Government Alphonsus was keen from the very outset on securing royal approbation for his missionary society. This view must also have been shared by Falcoia since the first attempts in this direction were made in 1736, just two years after the arrival of Charles III. An approach was made through the good offices of Father

Fiorillo to the marquis of Montealegre, the influential Secretary of State and a member of the original retinue who had accompanied the King from Spain. Alphonsus drew up the requisite description of the missionary *adunanza* — a neutral term was essential to avoid any suspicion of a new religious society — with an outline of its purpose and Rule. But the approach was altogether premature and nothing came of it. After Falcoia's death and his election as Rector Major in 1743, Alphonsus determined to negotiate for royal approval in the face of opposition from some of his colleagues who considered it altogether too risky. He complied with the royal edict of 1740 and sought permission for the three houses at Pagani, Deliceto and Materdomini; Ciorani, established before the publication of the royal decree, did not require it. But permission for individual residences and churches did not include royal approbation for the missionary society as a whole and a decree could dissolve the society at a moment's notice, Ciorani included.

Despite the decided lack of enthusiasm of some of his colleagues who thought it better to let sleeping dogs lie, Alphonsus was determined to follow his own instincts in the matter. He arrived in Naples in June 1747, accompanied by Brother Francis Tartaglione, determined to push the matter to a conclusion, one way or the other. They stayed once again with Giovanni Olivieri near the church of Santa Catarina à Formello; despite the fact that Giovanni's sister was now one of the *beatelle* and wearing a religious habit and had taken the religious name of Sister Angela, she had not quite conquered all the old Adam — or Eve — in her, since she confessed to Father Tannoia later that she had spied on Alphonsus through the keyhole to watch him at his prayers and that she searched through his bags to see for herself the instruments of penance he had brought with him.[22] Alphonsus had arrived at what he felt was a propitious moment when the King and his ministers were in benign humour at the birth of the Queen's third child and first son, the unfortunate Prince Philip, duke of Calabria. It was not for a considerable time later that it became clear that he was severely mentally handicapped and unfit to succeed to the throne. The round of festivities following the birth continued for months and it was in this climate of euphoria that Alphonsus went from minister to minister, from influential friend to influential friend arguing the case for royal approval of his new missionary society. He soon realised the difficulty of his task; even the Marquis Brancone, who had secured royal approval for the three houses, was less inclined to support approval of the congregation as a whole. However, the fact that his brother had recently been appointed a bishop through royal intervention made him somewhat more amenable. Nevertheless, Alphonsus saw that his main hope lay with his long-time friend and fellow missioner, the Jesuit, Father Francesco Pepe, who had ready access to the royal presence at all times.

The unanimous advice of his friends was not to request approval for his missionary society as a religious order, the very mention of which would provoke the worst possible reaction from the King and his ministers. With this in mind, and tutored by Cardinal Spinelli, Alphonsus drew up a synopsis of the Rule for presentation to the King, deliberately substituting the word 'oath' for the 'vow' of perseverance, lest the very word 'vow', almost synonymous with religious orders, should arouse suspicion. In the light of what was to happen over thirty years later, when, amongst other alterations, a similar substitution of 'oath' for 'vow' in the episode of the *Regolamento* brought untold suffering on Alphonsus and temporary chaos to his Congregation, it will be well to remember that this question of 'vows' bedevilled the congregation from the very beginning. From the outset, it would appear that Alphonsus was willing to accept the substitution in order to secure something more precious, namely legal stability for his congregation. Once the Bourbon government was determined to persist in its refusal to approve anything in the nature of a new religious order, a compromise on the lines of the *Regolamento* was inevitable if Alphonsus' missionary society was to continue in existence. It was just unfortunate that when the inevitable happened and alterations were made in the Pontifical Rule, the distressing fact should have been used by some members of the Congregation as an opportunity to achieve their own unworthy purposes. But all this was still in the future.

The interminable round of interviews, the letter writing, the advice he was receiving from his consultors who were at a distance and above all the interminable flow of suggestions emanating from Villani at Ciorani, ultimately got on Alphonsus' nerves. Accusations that he was acting on his own, and that the whole exercise was ill-conceived, irritated him beyond endurance. He wanted to hear no more complaints and he would tolerate no further criticism of the efforts in which he was engaged. He wrote from Naples:

> I tell you the truth were it not for the sake of the Congregation I would throw everything up and lock myself in a cell in Ciorani without bothering any further. But I can't do it in conscience.
>
> Consider well the position at the moment. There is good hope. Brancone has taken the matter up seriously, the King is well disposed, more so now since Father Pepe talked to him. Even the Cappellano Maggiore is inclined to help us. But, of course, the climate can change, and with it the opportunity will go as well.
>
> In these circumstances do you really believe it is prudent to bide our time? I tell you before Jesus Christ that if this vital matter goes against us, there will be no further remedy. I call it a *vital affair* because the whole stability of the Congregation depends on it. All your fears are frivolous — the greatest fear is that the Congregation without the King's approval will not have stability and may well end up by fading out.
>
> Before God, I am leaving no stone unturned; it won't be my fault if I fail. I am not saying this because I wish to act the founder or behave as a despot. You see all the doubts I have had and all the advice I have sought from others. When you see that everything is being done after

> mature consideration and with all discretion, you should not begin to put obstacles in the way.
>
> I pray that the Lord will not destroy this work on account of my sins and I ask you to continue your prayers.

Charles III was inclined to grant the royal approval. He suggested that if the Pope were to agree to suppress some insignificant convent or congregation in Naples, of which there were several, his approval together with the Pope's could be granted almost simultaneously to the missionaries of the Most Holy Saviour. But the final decision lay with the Cappellano Maggiore, Mons. Celestino Galiani, to whom Alphonsus now presented a memorial petitioning royal approval. The contrast between the two men could not have seen more startling. Galiani, aged sixty-six, a member of the Celestine Order, was a typical philo-jansenistic ecclesiastic of the Neapolitan *settecento*, intellectual, diplomatic, playing off pope against king and church against state, never declaring himself fully, cursed by the regalists as an arch papalist, condemned by Benedict XIV for undermining the Concordat of 1741. His morals were externally, at least, above reproach but his outlook was totally worldly. He weighed the archbishopric of Taranto, which would have brought him in a revenue of 10,000 ducats, against the office of Cappellano Maggiore, with a nominal income of only 3,000 but where the possibilities of lucrative patronage were almost unlimited. It was for this man that Alphonsus in his memorial painted a picture of abandoned souls in the country areas of the kingdom, parishes without a mission for over thirty years, the shortage of workers in this field of apostolic endeavour and the necessity of priests who would associate themselves with these unlettered peasants and would talk to them in a language they could understand. Surprisingly, Galiani was not at all unfavourable, due perhaps to the very definite interest he knew the King was taking in the work of the missions. Then when the way ahead seemed clear the whole situation was suddenly complicated by two totally unconnected events, the death of the archbishop of Palermo in Sicily and the re-appearance of Don Vincente Mannarini from the far-off days in Scala.

The death of the archbishop of Palermo, Mons. Domenico Rossi, in the first week of July, left the royal court with a diocese of great importance to fill. It was the first see of the Kingdom of the Two Sicilies where the King himself, according to custom dating back to Norman times, had been crowned. The situation in Palermo was complicated by many conflicting interests and the position called for a candidate outside all factions and of irreproachable integrity. The King, who was clever enough to recognise the genuine article when he saw it, thought immediately of Alphonsus as the perfect choice. The report shocked Alphonsus; a sort of nervous hysteria gripped him and led him back to the King's ministers and especially Brancone to beseech them to dissuade the King from his intention. He dashed off a letter to his spiritual director, Father Cafaro at Deliceto, begging for his prayers. One cannot but help thinking of the confrontation that would have taken place had Don Giuseppe been alive to see his life's dream for his son within his grasp and being rejected. Alphonsus enlisted the intercession of all his friends from Cardinal Spinelli down to Father Pepe to avert the catastrophe. His plea was always the same — 'There is no lack of aspirants to the mitre but it is difficult to find missioners for the neglected areas of the Kingdom.' Finally the Cappellano Maggiore decided to sacrifice himself and to offer himself — at the instigation of his relatives, he added — for the vacancy. The King relented and agreed not to force the mitre on a reluctant candidate; the danger for Alphonsus passed.

Then something occurred which offered an even more insidious menace; it came in the person of Don Vincenzo Mannarini, whose Congregation of the Most Blessed Sacrament had struck roots in Calabria. His work had been cited publicly as one of the glories of the province when the young prince Philip, heir to the throne, was formally proclaimed duke of Calabria. Mannarini was also held in high esteem in Rome where his advice was sought concerning several matters of ecclesiastical import in those areas. More important still, he enjoyed a considerable amount of support from the Cappellano Maggiore. Mannarini now proposed to Galiani and to Alphonsus that their two institutes should unite, with Alphonsus as superior of both; royal approval would follow and Rome's would not be long delayed. Alphonsus had no hesitation in rejecting the proposal out of hand; the two institutes had developed along different lines since their foundation. Above all, there were the two important questions of schools and the acceptance of foundations in the centre of cities. On neither point was Alphonsus prepared to compromise.

But the proposal was attractive nonetheless. Was sacrificing the distinctive character of his own congregation in a few points too great a price to pay for royal approval and an unassailable legal status in the kingdom? Should he refuse the union and thereby run the risk of being refused approval or worse, face suppression? He suffered agony as he weighed up the pros and cons and read the letters of advice from his consultors in Ciorani and Pagani. Then a third course suggested itself, involving the mildest of external deceptions. Should he agree to the union and, once the royal approval was a fact, allow Mannarini and his followers to go their way while he went his? But the likely complications were unthinkable — which institute in that eventuality had in fact been approved, theirs or his? Which Rule were they to follow?

All during the heats of July and August the discussions and rounds of interviews continued; five times the Cappellano Maggiore refused to give him audience. Once the heat was so great that he was on the point of fainting as he reached Brancone's palace. His companion and secretary, the young Father Celestino de Robertis, heard him pray, 'Jesus, give me strength. I want to give you glory with every step I take.'[23] Rebuffs and even insults were the order of the day. The wife of the ambassador to the court of Madrid, seeing him in a waiting room, referred to him as 'one of those wretched Calabrians', the worst possible insult to a Neapolitan patrician.

Eventually Alphonsus succeeded in getting an audience of the King. The news arrived unexpectedly while he was reciting his breviary in the cloister of the Dominican church of Santa Catarina, summoning him to an immediate interview. Leaving his breviary and engaging a carriage, he arrived at the royal palace unshaven. The young King was exceedingly gracious, intensely interested in the work being done by Alphonsus and his missionaries. He expressed himself all in favour of the new congregation but left the final decision to his ministers.

Alphonsus was at the end of his strength, unable to sleep, emotionally exhausted. 'I am totally shattered from dealing with all these ministers' — nothing can quite render the force of the fine Neapolitan phrase he used: *sono crepato in trattar con questi ministri*, literally, burst asunder. 'I am fed up with life itself. I feel as if I have a well of poison within me and I cannot go on any longer. I should just love to run away but unfortunately there is no escape for me from Naples. I must remain until the matter is put to a vote.'

On 22 August the decision of the Cappellano Maggiore was sent to the Council of State for ratification — the unification of the two institutes, under the name of the Most Holy Saviour, with Alphonsus de Liguori as supreme head, together with the approval of the Rules. Mannarini had momentarily triumphed, Alphonsus was in deep depression. Fortunately the decision had to be confirmed by the Council of State where Alphonsus had concentrated his efforts. On 23 August the Council of State rejected the proposals of the Cappellano Maggiore. The King then decided that the position should remain as it was.

The decision was conveyed to Alphonsus on 25 August by Brancone who softened the blow by conveying to him a message of personal esteem from the King. It was a bitter disappointment after months of effort but at least the disaster of forced union with Mannarini or immediate suppression had been avoided. He went back to his lodgings with Olivieri and all he could say was 'the Will of God'. On the following two mornings he celebrated Mass in the church of the Oratorians, where memories of his boyhood must surely have flooded in on him. And then the reaction set in. The precariousness of the legal position of the Congregation became clear. Had he jeopardised it further by his untimely efforts for approval? Had his advisers been right all the time when they warned him against taking any steps in Naples? Was the dissolution of his society now only a matter of time? All these doubts crowded into his mind, bringing him once more to the verge of a nervous breakdown. He was constantly on edge. During Mass in the church of the Oratorians with Father de Robertis serving him, he turned round to distribute Holy Communion. A gentleman in the congregation did not go on his knees. In a loud voice, with the Sacred Host in his hands, Alphonsus said 'There is someone here who refuses to go on his knees.' His temper got the better of him; standing was not at that time, nor even now, an attitude of disrespect in those parts of Italy. The gentleman in question came round to the sacristy afterwards to enquire who the priest in question was. When told that it was Alphonsus de Liguori he graciously left without making any further trouble.[24]

Brancone was, in Alphonus' highly nervous state, his only support. Brancone was able to calm his fears and assure him that the position was not as desperate as he seemed to think. The three houses of Pagani, Deliceto and Materdomini had the formal signed approval of the King; nothing could touch these. And he was able to renew the royal assurance to Alphonsus that the work of the missions had full support and approval and that the royal favour was more valuable than all the opposition of the Ministers or the Cappellano Maggiore. With these assurances Alphonsus returned to face his colleagues in what should have been the peace of Ciorani.

Part Two

The Paths of the Lord

1743–1762

CHAPTER NINE

THE THEOLOGIAN FROM OUT THE WOODS 1745–1750

– I –

Several pastoral problems connected with the ministry of the confessional had been occupying Alphonsus' attention for years. Of these the one he had most frequently encountered was the practice, mainly among men, of cursing the dead, a form of blasphemy widespread in the country areas of the Kingdom of Naples. Blasphemy, the direct and intentional insulting of God and his saints, is a sin which up to recent times has been almost the preserve of Latin people, who vent their anger, in a paroxysm of rage, on God and His creatures. In Apulia and Irpinia it took the form of cursing the dead, either in general or the particular relatives of some person one wished to offend seriously. Authentic blasphemy, always a grave offence against God, fell into the category of reserved sins in most dioceses — that is, a sin the forgiveness of which the bishop 'reserved' to himself or to some few priests of the diocese, in an attempt to highlight its seriousness. During a mission special faculties were usually given to the missioners to deal with such cases.

From his own experience of the people and his knowledge of their mentality, Alphonsus began to suspect that this habit, however reprobate, was not in fact directed in any way against God and His creatures — in so far as they were his creatures and gifted with His grace. Rather was it directed against the mortal remains and consequently the relatives of the dead. Disrespectful certainly, and deserving of condemnation, *mannaggia i morti* still did not possess the grave malice of blasphemy. Perhaps in the majority of cases it was not a grave sin at all. This had important consequences for pastoral practice on the missions. Alphonsus gradually became convinced that the practice had been judged according to altogether too rigorous principles and with no real psychological understanding of what lay at its root among the unlettered and unsophisticated country folk. He sought for confirmation of his opinion in the classical treatises of theology but nowhere found the problem adequately dealt with, though there were certain encouraging hints to be found in the writings of some of the 'local' Neapolitan theologians whom he had known personally, such as Sarnelli, Canon Jorio and Canon Giuseppi Sparano. He decided to commit his own views to paper. In the moments he could snatch from the missions and the various other matters to which he had to attend, he prepared a short treatise on the matter, outlining his fresh approach. He then circulated the work to the three main missionary societies in Naples and to the religious orders engaged in the missionary apostolate. Most of the societies paid him the compliment of discussing his opinion in their moral theology academies. They informed him, one by one, that his arguments had convinced them that his analysis was correct and that they were agreed that cursing the dead was not the sin of blasphemy. The Pavone missioners under the direction of the Society of Jesus went further still, urging him to put his opinion to the bishops of the Kingdom and even to announce it prudently to the people on the missions; while the habit should be eradicated, the consciences of the people were not to be left in error. Encouraged by the generally favourable reaction, Alphonsus decided to publish the dissertation, which he did the same year. No copy of this first edition, the first fruits of his moral writings, has come down to us though the treatise itself is well known from its inclusion later in his *Moral Theology*.[1]

The effect of the treatise was soon evident. Missioners began to follow it in practice while the sin itself, the cursing of the dead, gradually disappeared from the diocesan lists of reserved sins. There was, however, one stridently dissenting voice, which introduced Alphonsus to the less edifying aspects of theological controversies; he experienced for the first time the truth of the theological axiom, *theologus theologo lupus*, which means that theologians attack each other like wolves. From Bari, a Dominican, under the pseudonym of *Ciriaco Criseo*, took issue with him. Abandoning the serene atmosphere of reason and authority, he launched into a fierce personal attack in a treatise published a short while later in Rome. 'Who are you', demanded the Dominican, 'to set your self up as a lawgiver and master of theology from out the woods' — referring, of course, to the woods of Deliceto, an argument lacking in any great theological content. The author accused Alphonsus of being an 'innovator', always a crime to some, no matter whether the innovation was good or bad. He accused him of citing neither St Thomas nor St Augustine, but of relying on men whose opinions were not worth a straw, little men of sixth-rate minds and members of insignificant missionary congregations composed of 'vagabonds', which was rather unkind to the Apostolic Missions, the Pii Operai and the Vincentians. However he kept his best adjectives for Alphonsus himself, ignorant, stupid and rash, *indoctus, stultus et temerarius*. Not satisfied with this personal onslaught, the pseudonymous author turned his attention to the Missionaries of the Most Holy Saviour, mixing ridicule with calumny. They were good for nothing except teaching hymns to women and children — the writer had obviously never attempted this task himself or he would not have spoken so disparagingly of it. He accused them of preaching that no one could be saved without the practice of mental prayer, that the rosary and the Our Father were to be discarded. Furthermore, they were guilty of resurrecting some form of Quietism. The final accusation was the most intriguing of all: they were 'illegal' since they had not the approval of Rome.

The small circle of those interested in theological debates followed the controversy with interest; from the tone and the list of accusations in the Dominican's letter it promised to be both a protracted and an unpleasant one. The Nuncio in Naples sent a copy of both publications to the Pope, Benedict XIV, who was intensely interested in theological discussions. He studied the case and agreed with the views put forward by Alphonsus, seeking at the same time confirmation of his view from the Prefect of Studies at the Collegio di Propaganda Fide, Father Thomas Sergio of the Pii Operai. Fearing that the controversy would get out of control, he instructed the Nuncio in Naples to calm things down, which was done through the Dominicans' Minister General for the Dominican and through the bishop of Bovino, the ordinary of the diocese in which Deliceto was situated.

Alphonsus was particularly pained by the fact that his adversary was a Dominican, an order 'for which he had the greatest veneration' to use his own words. He had no wish to continue the controversy for his own personal vindication but he considered it necessary to come to the defence of the good name of his missionary society, quoting the example of St Ignatius Loyola who submitted to the Holy See a defence of his young society against accusations brought by some religious in Salamanca. Alphonsus inserted in his first major publication, the *Adnotationes in Busenbaum*, which appeared in 1748, a dignified defence of his Congregation. The Apologia was also printed separately, and the Nuncio once again forwarded a copy to the Pope. There is a quiet dignity about it, in complete contrast to the tone of the accusations:

> I cannot omit to clear myself and my companions of the iniquitous calumnies which my adversary heaped upon us so undeservedly. He can look to his own conscience as regards the motives which inspired his efforts to defame us. My only interest is to clear myself and my companions of the calumnies which were so injuriously laid against us since our reputation is so necessary for the work we do, preaching the Word of God for the spiritual welfare of souls.

Alphonsus dealt, one by one, with the accusations made by the Dominican, demonstrating their falsity:

> It is true that up to the present we have not received the approbation of the Holy See, as our adversary casts up against us. Up to the present

> on account of our small numbers we did not judge it expedient to petition the Pope for approval of our society. But now since we have grown and continue to increase through the divine mercy and since we have won the approval of so many bishops and those who seek the glory of God, we hope in a short while to lay our petition before the present Holy Father for the approval of our Institute and to secure it, which is our dearest wish. The Holy Father has very much at heart the work of the missions in the Lord's Vineyard as we can see from his recent encyclical letter in which he encouraged the work of the missions throughout this whole Kingdom and entrusted the task to his Eminence Cardinal Spinelli. He, in his turn, out of zeal for the salvation of souls, honoured us by selecting our Congregation for missions in many areas and provinces.

There was a sense of genuine pride in the tone of the conclusion:

> It is now fifteen years since our Congregation was founded and already we have laboured through innumerable areas of six provinces of the Kingdom — not as our adversary suggests, uninvited — but rather, invited or sent by the local bishop. And my one regret is that I am unable to accede to the desires of many bishops who wish to have foundations in their dioceses, especially the bishops of Brindisi, Aquila, Cassano and Caiazzo. Since we are not sufficiently numerous at the moment I have had to reply to them gratefully that it would not be right to spread ourselves over more houses than the four we have at the moment. And I do not mention the repeated demands we receive for missions every day from bishops; if we had twice our numbers we still would not be able to cope with them.
>
> I do not say all this in any spirit of boasting but for the glory of God and for the due praise of our young Congregation so that it will not suffer any injury to its good name in those places where we are already engaged in giving missions. Such detraction seemed to be the aim of the author of the letter concerning me. I trust that as a result of this reply our good name will be vindicated, all the more so since the author expressly declares that what he wrote against us he did not experience at first hand but that it was recounted to him by others.[2]

– *II* –

The publication of the paper on the morality of the cursing of the dead was the prelude to Alphonsus' first major publication in the discipline of moral theology. For nearly fourteen years he had been engaged in collecting material for a text-book which would provide a convenient manual of study for the members of his missionary society. He taught moral theology for several months in Ciorani and Deliceto and experienced at first hand the need for a suitable text for his students. Although, at the outset, the majority of the new recruits to the congregation were ordained priests, he was acutely aware of the inadequacy of their theological formation in general and particularly in the area of moral theology and confessional practice — an area which he considered of vital importance for his missioners, who were expected to be specialists in that ministry. Moreover, after the death of Falcoia it had been decided to accept non-ordained candidates which made the proper study of moral theology more imperative than ever. Alphonsus devoted most of his time to the study of the classical theological authors, sifting their opinions, weighing their authority. Despite the poverty of the early foundations when there was no money at times for the bare necessities of life, he still endeavoured to secure the latest publications for the libraries of the houses. The foundation at Deliceto was fortunate in that the founder, Canon Casati, donated his theologically valuable library to the Fathers. The study of moral theology took pride of place in the various houses and attendance at the weekly academy of moral discussion was obligatory. The results of this emphasis, which Alphonsus insisted upon, were soon evident in the reputation which his missioners achieved for their competence in the area of moral theology; it was one of the points in their favour passed on from bishop to bishop.[3]

When Alphonsus finally set himself the task of preparing a text-book in moral theology for his students he adopted the expedient of taking an established manual and re-editing it with his own comments and additions. For this purpose he finally selected the *Medulla Theologiae* of Father Herman Busenbaum, a Westphalian Jesuit whose work had first appeared a hundred years before, in 1650. The choice was not a haphazard one, as if any existing text-book would have served equally well as a foundation for the theological outline which Alphonsus envisaged. The *Medulla* was well known in Italian seminaries even though it was not the one, as we have seen, which was used by Torni in Naples nor consequently the one which Alphonsus himself had studied as a student for the priesthood. Nearly 200 editions of the work had appeared throughout Europe and Cardinal Orsini, later Pope Benedict XIII, had insisted on it as the standard work of moral theology throughout his own diocese of Beneventum, with whose priests and their practice Alphonsus would have been familiar. But apart from its reputation the work commended itself to Alphonsus, as he explicitly states in his preface, on account of its brevity and its practical nature which made it an excellent manual for the initiation of priests into the confessional ministry. It was a practical rather than a speculative work, with its question and answer method and then the application of the answers to the solution of practical cases — the classical methodology of seventeenth-century casuistry. Above all, it was balanced in its judgments, neither too lax nor too strict even though some propositions upheld by Busenbaum had not escaped condemnation by Popes Alexander VII and Innocent XI. Although Alphonsus was at pains to insist that he was mainly interested in the order of the material and not in the doctrine proposed, the book had the great merit in his eyes of not imposing serious obligations where none existed.[4]

Alphonsus began his annotations in Ciorani in one of the small cells looking out over the valley, with his books of reference piled up on his table and on the floor. Before him on the desk he kept his Crucifix and a picture of the Mother of Good Counsel; the version of 1737 which he used is still to be seen with his annotations and comments in the Church of the Immaculata in Catanzaro in the very south of Italy. From 1742 onwards the tempo of his work increased as he spent eight, nine and even ten hours a day on the preparation of his work for the printers. Every line was written out laboriously by hand. When he left Ciorani for Deliceto and the missionary campaigns in Apulia, he took the manuscripts with him to continue the work among the woods of Deliceto. There, with the aid of Canon Casati's books, the work progressed. The winter of 1745 to 1746 was extremely severe; the valley was thick with snow, the piercing *tramontana* whistled down from the Appenines through the windows of the house which did not not yet possess the luxury of glass but had oiled paper in the frames instead. The water in the hand-basins in the rooms froze at night, and the novices — Fathers Landi and Tannoia among them — recalled visiting Alphonsus in his room where he had his Neapolitan *scaldino* or heating iron beside him, to warm his fingers as he wrote.

While he had his novices and students primarily in mind, he wished at the same time to have a unified approach among his missioners as they worked together on the missions. Not merely was there need to rethink the accepted approach to questions such as the cursing of the dead, there was a variety of other social habits such as family vendettas, cohabitation of those engaged to be married, which had to be addressed and for which appropriate moral norms had to be laid down. The manuscript was completed by the end of 1746. From being a small-sized compact volume of some five hundred pages, Busenbaum's *Medulla* had grown to nearly three times its original size; it would emerge from the printers as an octavo volume of a thousand pages with newspaper-small print. Alphonsus added some appendices to the text, a defence of the doctrine of the Immaculate Conception of the Blessed Virgin, a treatise on Papal Infallibility and on the Pope's supremacy over an ecumenical council. The preparation of these additions delayed the final text before it was submitted to the ecclesiastical censors and then in January 1748 to the royal censors, for permission to print. Both were forthcoming with an interesting comment from the royal censor to the effect that the author had been able 'to render to Caesar the things that are Caesar's'. The much imposed-upon Giovanni Olivieri once again undertook to finance the publication.

Alphonsus arrived in Naples in January 1748; with the exception of a few fleeting visits to Ciorani and Pagani, he was to be based there for the next six months. He had to fulfil a number of preaching engagements, as well as seeing his theology through the printers. Brancone, furthermore, had suggested that another effort at securing royal approval would not be out of order. All these commitments gave legitimacy to what was possibly the underlying motive for his presence in the capital for so long; he wished to be near his mother who was now nearing eighty years of age and was suffering great distress from scruples and anxieties of conscience. For the greater part of this sojourn in Naples he stayed with her.[5]

He accepted Brancone's suggestion at its face value. Persistence was essential if anything was to be achieved with the Bourbon Court and so with Mannarini safely out of the way, he was able to make his pleas unhampered by the complications of a second missionary society. Once more the tiring round of visits to the various Ministers of State began. In the interval the marchese Fogliano had replaced Montealegre as prime minister but he was too lazy to take any interest in such a matter. Power had passed in reality into the hands of Tanucci, and Alphonsus was advised that he should concentrate his efforts in this quarter. Tanucci was first approached through Canon Matteo Testa, Alphonsus' missionary companion during the Naples general mission seven years earlier. He was the one cleric Tanucci numbered among his friends at the time. Next followed the usual routine of drawing up a formal petition to the King; by this time the composition of such documents must have been second nature to Alphonsus. He could not have been too hopeful of the outcome after the bitter disappointment of the previous year; at the same time he could not afford to neglect any effort which might possibly bring the matter to a successful conclusion.

And then the unpredictable happened. Whatever chance there may have been of a successful outcome was shattered by a most absurd incident which not only prejudiced the whole affair but destroyed any benevolence the King and Tanucci were prepared to show Alphonsus. In the tenth Visit to the Blessed Sacrament Alphonsus had written a short meditation on the accessibility of our Lord in the Blessed Sacrament; we can approach Him directly without any intermediary, without the tiresome protocol and difficulties surrounding audience with the great ones of this world. The idea was not original nor the result, in any way, of his own personal experiences; it was taken directly from a reflection to be found in the life of St Teresa of Avila.[6] An anonymous informer reported the offending reflection to Tanucci. So sensitive was the legalist climate of the Court that the reference was regarded as critical of the King and unwarranted, especially since Alphonsus had already been granted audience of Charles and had assured his Majesty of his loyal esteem. The Court buzzed with news that the author would be severely punished, probably exiled as an example to others. Fortunately, Brancone was able to assure the Minister that there was nothing sinister behind the reflection nor was any reference, however remotely implicit, intended to the situation existing in Naples. Cardinal Spinelli was also enlisted to assure the King that there was no personal insult and that Alphonsus deeply appreciated his Majesty's graciousness in receiving him so cordially. The storm in a tea-cup abated but the good will and any inclination to concede the request had vanished. Basing himself on the decision of the previous August Tanucci simply returned an unfavourable verdict and the Council of State followed suit. Once more the petition for royal approval was rejected.

While all this was taking place in Court circles Alphonsus was, at the same time, seeing his *Adnotationes* through the press. The printing was completed by September but then the binder refused to bind the volumes unless he received payment in advance — from his point of view, a wise precaution. Towards the end of the year, however, the work was finally ready for distribution. Alphonsus sent complimentary copies to a number of bishops; he presented one, artistically bound *à la francesa*, to Cardinal Spinelli, and awaited reaction with a degree of apprehension after the reaction to his pamphlet on cursing the dead. But he need not have feared. From Bari, Taranto, Molfetta and many other dioceses favourable verdicts arrived, swelling to a chorus of approval for the work. Of more importance were the opinions of the accepted theologians of Naples itself, whose disapproval of the work could have had serious consequences. Jorio, Sparano and Coppola, the foremost theological names in the diocese, were enthusiastic in their praise with only two reservations, a practical one from Jorio that he considered the price excessive, and the other from Sparano who considered one opinion too lax. He felt that Alphonsus was prepared to allow too great freedom to feminine vanity in the matter of *décolletage*, which is all the more remarkable since it was an area in which Alphonsus might have been expected to show himself excessively rigid.[7]

In the event, Alphonsus was himself the severest critic of this, his first major effort in the field of moral theology. He felt he had rushed prematurely into print and that certain questions had not received adequate treatment; he now considered the order faulty, the very aspect of the work which had attracted him to Busenbaum in the first place. He set himself, as before, to work in between missions to perfect the *Adnotationes*, and the second edition appeared some seven years later, this time in two volumes, dedicated to Pope Benedict XIV. The title still kept the reference to the *Medulla* of Busenbaum — this was not to disappear completely until the sixth edition in 1767 — but already the work had developed into an original effort altogether distinct from the work of the Jesuit theologian and Alphonsus could without scruple claim full paternity.[8]

And so he was nearly sixty years of age — maybe there is a valuable lesson here — when he found himself, through the accident of wishing to help his own missionary students, an accepted authority in the field of moral theology, where, without any doubt, he was to make his greatest contribution to the life of the Church. His intellectual preparation had been more than adequate, his years of practical experience on the missions of incomparable value in appreciating human goodness on the one hand and sympathising with human frailty on the other. His spiritual life and hours of prayer gave him a perception which comes only from the indwelling presence of the Spirit of God. And whatever may have been the extent of his own personal scruples, his judgment in dealing with a variety of conflicting opinions and the opposing trends of laxity and rigorism was calm and balanced. His genius lay in the area of practical conduct, what was to be the decision in the circumstances of both place and time. And he was not afraid to reconsider whatever position he had adopted and to alter it if necessary in the light of further study and more mature reflection. His missionary career may have been coming to an end but a whole new field of apostolic endeavour in moral theology was opening up before him.

– III –

In his defence of his Congregation in reply to his Dominican critic, Alphonsus stated that he had hesitated to apply to Rome for approval until their members were sufficiently numerous to warrant such a step. When they took their first vow of stability in Ciorani in 1740 they numbered nine, five Fathers and four Brothers. After that and more particularly after the death of Falcoia in 1743, their numbers began to increase steadily if not spectacularly; the yearly intake of vocations was on average three. The majority of these were clerics at least in major orders but Alphonsus succeeded in 1743 in securing the admission of suitable candidates even if they were not sub-deacons, provided they were at least eighteen years of age. The emotional difficulties which so many Neapolitans experienced in leaving their families were matched many times by the unwillingness of their families to allow them to join. Candidates needed to be possessed of great determination in order to follow their vocation to the new missionary society which was now very much in the public awareness; very unfavourable reports of its frightening rigidity and asceticism were circulated by those who had left and returned home. Father Paul Cafaro, no weakling, struggled for five years against the opposition of his family and his bishop until finally he left without informing them. His brother followed him to Barra where he began his novitiate on the Spinelli missions in Naples, and heaped abuse on Alphonsus; his bishop met him some time later and, not deigning to leave his carriage, forbade him ever again to set foot in the diocese. Carmelo Antonio Fiocchi, a deacon of twenty-two, struggled for over a year with his father, a highly placed civil servant, before he summoned up courage to leave home to join. From Ciorani he wrote to appease his father's anger:

> If the greatest honour for a nobleman of the Kingdom is to offer his son for the protection of the King and for the defence of the realm, then there is no higher honour for a father than to give his son for the service of Jesus Christ and for the spread of his Kingdom. *Deus vult militares*. Here we are, fighting for the cause of God. Courage, father, and acceptance. I am determined not to make peace with the devil, the enemy of my vocation.

But the father was not easily dissuaded from his opposition. He obtained a royal decree forcing his son to leave Ciorani and reconsider the whole matter in a monastery in Salerno, away from the influence of Alphonsus. There the family besieged him with entreaties not to abandon them; his resistance, however, was able for the strain and, finally, fortified in his resolution he returned to Ciorani and worked as a missioner until his death in 1776.

Such was the story of nearly all the vocations during those early heroic years and the firmness of young Fiocchi had to be matched by nearly every young man who presented himself at the novitiate. Biagio Amarante had to escape from his home secretly at night; Father Lorenzo de Antonio was followed from his house by members of his family holding on grimly to the reins of the horse. Father Geronimo Ferraro, a priest aged thirty-one and a professor in the seminary at Conza, was followed to Deliceto by his sister, who arrived at the house almost at the same time as he did. For two days she refused to leave until the Fathers smuggled Don Geronimo secretly from the monastery at night and, by forced marches, led him over the mountains to Ciorani.

These hard-won gains, however, were offset both by continuing defections and by death. The first member of the congregation to die was the delicate Brother Gaudiello who died in April 1742 proudly proclaiming that he was going to heaven as the standard bearer for his companions. Then in 1744 the first missionary priest died, Sarnelli, who continued to regard himself as a member despite his permanent residence in Naples. The following year he was followed to the grave by the eager Vito Curzio, one of the old guard and of whose total commitment to the congregation there could not be the slightest doubt. His death in September 1745 from malaria, just thirteen years after his arrival in Scala, left a void in Alphonsus' life and brought back memories of those early days on the mountain when they were both struggling towards a goal which had not been clearly revealed to them. As Alphonsus sang the funeral Mass in the little community church at Deliceto, he wept visibly at the loss of one who had shared all the hardships of the early years in loyalty and devotion.

With the number of members approaching thirty, Alphonsus turned his thoughts to the question of Roman approval; when Torni, some fourteen years earlier, had mentioned his hope that the new missionary society would secure approval in Rome it had seemed totally unrealistic. The work of drawing up a definitive draft of the Rules had continued steadily since the Ciorani Assembly following Falcoia's death. There were varying formulations in existence; one form or other of the Rule had been submitted to each of the local ordinaries who had accepted foundations in their dioceses. As well as these, various outlines and copies of particular decrees were circulating as well. The task of collating the various formulations and producing an agreed text was not an easy one nor always marked by agreement between Alphonsus and his colleagues. Differences of opinion emerged from the very beginning, just as Falcoia had foreseen, and reached something of a climax at a gathering of some members in Ciorani in October 1746. A bronchial catarrh kept Alphonsus confined to bed in Deliceto though the likelihood is that his illness was diplomatic and his reluctance to take part was motivated by his opposition to some of the ideas which he knew were being proposed.[9]

The principal area of disagreement concerned Alphonsus' office as Rector Major and the exercise of his authority. Falcoia had insisted — motivated by memories of the difficulties in his own Congregation — that the Rector Major should be elected for life and have virtually unlimited powers. Alphonsus was aware that there was a degree of dissatisfaction with this concept among certain of the members who were planning to restrict the exercise of the Rector Major's powers at the caucus meeting in Ciorani. He was quite upset at the direction the drafting of the Rule was taking in regard to the position of the Rector Major and at the fact that he had not been kept fully informed of everything that was being proposed. He threatened to resign. Villani bore the brunt of his displeasure:

> My dear Don Andrea,
>
> I am annoyed with you. You could well have confided in me what was happening while you were free to do so, knowing the esteem that I have for you. . . . If the Rector Major cannot give a dispensation in this matter, this is equivalent to restricting his powers, thus throwing over-board the whole principle of government left us by Mons. Falcoia, namely government by one sole head, just like the Church, *governo per un capo solo, a forma della Chiesa*.
>
> As far as I am concerned myself, I desire and have always desired — and much more so now in the present state of things — to remain in a corner just to observe and to serve the Congregation. I accepted the government of the Congregation through obedience and it is only that which is keeping me there since in attending to the Congregation I have little time for my soul, burdened as I am with a thousand cares.
>
> But if I see that our unity is going to be compromised I shall do everything I can to resign, promising at the same time to serve the Congregation with the same devotion as before. If they are going to destroy the basic principle of the Congregation's government and multiply rules it would be better for me to resign and allow a new Rector Major more in keeping with their ideas to take over.
>
> I wish all this to be kept secret. Mention it to nobody except Don Saverio Rossi to whom you can read this letter since it saves me duplicating one to him.
>
> I ask you in confidence to arrange with your usual prudence to dissolve this gathering as inoffensively as you can; it can be reconvened later. In my opinion the devil has already made considerable inroads among the group. It is only by the grace of God that nothing has been finalised up to the present because if they do accept the points in question I assure you there will be considerable trouble as a result.

The letter to Villani, whose conduct in this matter and later on in the critical affair of the *Regolamento* was not above reproach, had the desired effect; the gathering at Ciorani was dissolved. To make doubly sure, Alphonsus instructed Sportelli to leave the meeting at once for Naples under the pretext of dealing with the affairs of the Materdomini foundation.[10]

The seeds of much of the sufferings which marked Alphonsus' declining years were sown during this early period. As well as the external difficulties arising from the regalism of the Bourbon government there were more serious internal divisions which impaired the congregational unity necessary to face the Bourbon threat. While many of these divisions may have sprung from personal ambition and incompatible personalities, the root of the problem lay in the dissatisfaction which many genuinely experienced at the fact that the Rector Major's office was for life, that Alphonsus had remained in the office during his episcopate and that he was not prepared to resign even at the advanced age of eighty-five.

Alphonsus was totally convinced of the advantages of the Rector Major's office being for life; fidelity to this decision of Falcoia became a matter of conscience for him. Lest there should be any doubt in the matter, he committed his views to paper. Besides the arguments which he used in his letter to Villani, quoted above, he argued that periodic changes of Rector Major would be detrimental to observance and would inevitably lead to relaxation since not every candidate for the office 'would be equally zealous in this regard'. But his main argument — and in this he may have known his colleagues better than we do — was that perpetuity of tenure would remove all opportunity for ambition.

> At times, members of congregations, in order to secure their own personal advancement, elect the less zealous candidate while the superior himself is tempted to close his eyes to the defects of his subjects in order not to lose their votes. And add to this cliques that are formed at the time of elections, the intrigues that take place, and the promises that are made etc. Prayer goes by the board, silence goes, charity and obedience decline and anyway, no one pays much attention to a superior who is going out of office.
>
> This is one of the reasons why observance flourishes during the lifetime of a founder — he is in control for the whole period of his life. But after his death when superiors are elected just for a determined period, the spirit deteriorates.

The example of the Society of Jesus for whom he had the very highest regard carried great weight with him; their strength stemmed from the fact that their General was elected for life.

The intensity of Alphonsus' feelings in this matter may be gauged from the conclusion of his memorial: 'And so for the attention of those who will succeed after my death, I leave in writing, and I burden their consciences, that they should never even contemplate altering the system of electing the Rector Major for life. Otherwise they will have to render an account to God for the insoluble problems and for the spiritual relaxation that will follow'.[11]

The work of finalising the formulation of the Rule continued despite the temporary set-back caused by the unofficial Ciorani meeting. 'Another validly constituted meeting was convened for the following October 1747 when the final touches were given to the Rule leaving the way open for an approach to Rome. The Rector Major's authority survived unimpaired and his office was for life, but the opposition still remained unconvinced.

– *IV* –

Failure to secure approval in Naples had only strengthened Alphonsus' determination to secure approval in Rome. A chance meeting in Naples with

Mons. Giuseppi Maria Puoti, a native of the diocese of St Agatha of the Goths, where Alphonsus was later to be the bishop, and a private secretary to Benedict XIV opened up possibilities for success. Having explored the matter with the help of Puoti and been instructed in the correct procedure, Alphonsus drew up a memorial to the Pope which the secretary promised to deliver to him personally on his return to Rome in March 1748, thus obviating the danger of having his petition blocked by some official at the very outset.

By 1748 Alphonsus was fully conscious of the fact that he was in the process of establishing a new missionary family in the Church. He was convinced the work was from God and that he was nothing more than the inadequate instrument of this purpose. His vision of his congregation had both evolved and matured since Falcoia's death. He saw that it had already taken on a distinctive existence and that it would have its own place in the Church, a modest one, unlike the central position occupied by the great religious families such as the Dominicans and Jesuits. Lest any of his followers might have illusions of grandeur he constantly referred to his society as 'this least of all Congregations'.

He had no difficulty in delineating what he envisaged the Congregation to be. Its houses would be situated outside the centres of population; it would work in the most neglected dioceses which other missionary groups seldom visited; it would minister to the country people most neglected pastorally and preach to them in a simple direct way; it would instruct them in the rudiments of the truths of religion and administer the sacrament of penance in a way that would remove the prevalent abuse of sacrilegious confessions. And when some time had elapsed after a mission, the missioners would return for a few days to preach a 'renewal', directed at consolidating the good already achieved. His horizons then, were those of the Kingdom of Naples and its people, specifically those in the countryside. It was only as the years passed by that these horizons were broadened to extend beyond the Bourbon world of the Two Sicilies. Inherent in his missionary society's commitment to evangelisation was indeed a willingness to go overseas at the command of the Pope but that missionary dynamic was secondary and latent during the early years; expansion outside Italy was not initially even a dream. And when it did take place it was due more to an act of providence in the arrival of the Moravian-born Clement Hofbauer than to any expansion planned by Alphonsus from Pagani.

Alphonsus' memorial about the Congregation was presented to Benedict XIV in the spring of 1748; the Pope on reading it sent it to the Congregation of the Council, thus setting in motion the long process of examination and check which precedes the approval of new religious institutes and their rules. The Prefect of the Council, Cardinal Gentili, after a preliminary discussion with his assessors, returned the memorial to Cardinal Spinelli in Naples *pro informatione* and for his own vote before God on the new congregation and its rules. Having been informed of the developments, Alphonsus sent the Cardinal a copy of the Rules which had been sanctioned by the Ciorani meeting. The Cardinal in turn passed them on to his theologians and canon lawyers for examination. Among the examiners were Alphonsus' former professor and his missionary companions, archbishop Torni, Canon Nicholas Borgia, later archbishop of Cava and Canon Testa, all from the Apostolic Missions. Alphonsus had been wise, despite all the pressure from Falcoia, not to offend Spinelli in any way or to sever his links with the Apostolic Missions. Their benevolence was critical for him at this juncture.[12]

Alphonsus sought to anticipate the objections against the establishment of a new religious congregation which Spinelli would certainly put forward, knowing the attitude of the Court and the guarantees given in the Concordat with the Holy See. In a memorial to the Cardinal, Alphonsus repeated his arguments:

> It will probably cause surprise to hear that we are seeking approval from the Holy See for a new Institute since there are so many other religious orders, congregations and institutes in the Church already. There are those who would say that it would be better to suppress some of the existing ones or reform them rather than attempt to establish a new one. But the surprise will cease when the purpose and scope of this new institute is fully explained and when one examines the success with which the Lord has blessed its efforts up to the present. Furthermore, similar opposition has always marked the establishment of new religious families which have sprung up in the last centuries, the Theatines, the Jesuits, the Pii Operai. And yet the Holy See, inspired by the Holy Spirit, has not hesitated to approve them. The results bear witness to the great benefit which each of these societies has contributed to the Church of God.'

Next followed a well-argued paragraph on the objection that all congregations begin with great fervour but then decline from their original high standards:

> The answer to this is first, that many institutes *have* preserved their fervour and *still* preserve their fervour. Even though it may not be quite up to the standard with which they began still it is of such a degree that even now it is of great benefit to the Church both for the example of their religious lives and for the work they do for others.
>
> And then we must never forget that we cannot alter the nature of all human endeavour; as a result of the human condition everything begins with fervour and then declines. Water, the further it travels from its source, the more turbid and murky it becomes. But God who loves his own glory and who is certainly the first founder of all these institutes, has thought it good to dispose things in such a way that not only is the Church, his Spouse, clothed in a variety of differently coloured garments but these new institutes, beginning with great fervour, supply for the deficiencies of the old ones that may be falling away. And

this initial fervour, generally speaking, is maintained for a number of centuries to the immense good of the members of the Congregation and of the People of God. What would happen in a vineyard if the old vines were not regularly replaced by new ones? The old ones would dry up, there would be no new ones and that would be the end of the vineyard.[13]

Whatever hesitations the Cardinal may have had were dispelled not only by this *apologia* but also by the favourable reports of his three assessors. In October 1748 Spinelli signed a most laudatory memorial to the Congregation of the Council in favour of Alphonsus and the new congregation. 'In the last five years we have personally seen how valuable is their ministry', he wrote, making at the same time a few minor suggestions concerning points of the Rule as well as mitigating some of the ascetical practices. He then forwarded the Rule to Rome.

Alphonsus was by this time too well experienced in court procedures to leave his Rule and Congregation to make their own way through the various Roman processes which preceded approval; a man on the spot was vitally necessary. Just as he had personally attended to securing royal approval in the Court at Naples, he should in the ordinary course of events have gone to Rome himself to supervise the progress there. But his health was unequal to the long journey in the difficult weather at the end of the year so he had to entrust the work to one of the Fathers. His first choice was in all probability Sportelli who, however, was in failing health himself, aggravated by the hardships he had endured in his efforts to consolidate the foundation at Materdomini. He would be dead within eighteen months. Fathers Margotta and Celestine de Robertis who had worked for Alphonsus in Naples, both very capable, were either too young or too recently admitted to the congregation. Finally Father Villani was chosen, and Brother Tartaglione, Alphonsus' own companion in Naples, was assigned to accompany him. Villani at the time was Master of Novices in Ciorani. Unsophisticated in the ways of diplomacy, he was not too easily impressed by rank or titles, totally devoid of human respect and somewhat in the nature of an innocent abroad. But he learnt quickly. He may not have been the ideal choice for such delicate negotiations as the approval of the Rule and Congregation demanded but he was sufficiently humble to acknowledge that he was quite capable of ruining everything and so was ready to accept advice from others wiser than himself.

Villani and Tartaglione left Naples by hired coach for Rome on 9 November 1748, a good augury, according to Villani, for the success of their mission on two accounts — it was a Saturday, the day dedicated to Our Lady and it was also the anniversary of the foundation of the Congregation, sixteen years before. They had no suitable travelling bags but managed to borrow one from Olivieri who was promised an immediate replacement from Father Garzillo, a relic of his more opulent days as a canon. They got their passports after some difficulty. The journey took five days. In order to eke out their money they dined on cheese, bread, *castagne* and wine on the side of the road, using the inns for sleeping only. Once through the customs check on their entrance to Rome, they found lodgings adjacent to the Basilian monastery in the street of the same name running into the Piazza Barberini. Since it was the feast of St Stanislaus Kostka their first visit on arrival was to the church of Sant' Andrea al Quirinale to visit the body of the saint and the cell in which he died. Across the road from that beautiful Bernini church was the Quirinal Palace, the residence of the Pope; they had the good fortune to see him leave to pay a visit to the church in Rome where the Forty Hours devotions were in progress.[14]

Influential contacts in the Eternal City were considered essential to the successful outcome of the mission and among the first whom Villani was instructed to contact was a young Basilian monk, abate Giuseppe Muscari from Calabria. He was a typical example of the Neapolitan career cleric, at once clever, voluble in his protestations of piety, ingratiating, and above all ambitious. He was in some ways another Tosques, this time in a Basilian habit, and was to cause just as much trouble. He had joined the Latin section of the Basilians in his native Calabria. From there he was sent to their monastery situated between Pagani and Ciorani where he became well known to Alphonsus and his colleagues. In 1745 he was sent to Rome as prior, where the following year, not without some efforts on his own part, he was designated abbot of Santa Maria de Patire in Calabria, a titular position which allowed him to remain in Rome as Definitor General of his order and secretary to the Superior General. Here he cultivated the influential in the ecclesiastical world. Restless and harbouring a deep dissatisfaction with his vocation as a Basilian monk, he was to play a sinister role in the history of the Missionaries of the Most Holy Saviour.

Among the other contacts figuring on Villani's list were the Fathers of the Pii Operai who had a house at Santa Maria ai Monti, a stone's throw from the Colosseum. Villani quickly realised he had to tread warily here. A certain jealousy of Alphonsus and his colleagues had developed among a section of these missionaries inspired by their aversion for their own ex-superior general, Mons. Falcoia; opposed to him during his life, they were anything but enthusiastic for the missionary society he had established. While outwardly friendly their protestations of assistance were not as authentic as they appeared to be. There was, however, one genuine friend among them, the young Francesco Sanseverino who had been professed by Alphonsus himself in Deliceto in 1744. Soon afterwards his health deteriorated and he was forced to leave. From Naples he went to Rome and there entered the novitiate of the Pii Operai. After his ordination to the priesthood during his novitiate, he was appointed to work in the Congregation of Bishops and Regulars and he was there when Villani arrived to open negotiations with this congregation. Sanseverino never lost his admiration for Alphonsus and the congregation and was to repay fully any debt he owed by his support. He could well claim that Roman approval for his old congregation was in large measure due to his efforts.

Villani found it difficult to acclimatise himself to life in Rome. Even though Naples was larger and three times more populous, he felt like a fish out of water in his new surroundings. 'Things are quite different here from what one would imagine,' he wrote. 'I have great need of your prayers. In Rome one must move very cautiously. You can trust no one and you must be suspicious of everybody. There is not a shadow of the simplicity of Jesus Christ left here.' He went to St Peter's which took his breath away: 'I don't think there is another temple in the world like it,' he declared ingenuously. When he got down to the real purpose of his visit he experienced total frustration. There was the endless round of interviews, the interminable talk getting him nowhere, being passed on endlessly from one official to another. His Neapolitan accent — his *larga bocca*, as the Romans called it — showed him up as a stranger to the ways of pontifical Rome. During the first week he thought he would go mad and he hinted unpleasantly, 'here everybody talks a lot and one would need a sack of money, but we are poor'. Gradually, however, he adjusted. He realised to his horror that in his simplicity he had worn his heart on his sleeve; he had spoken too much and to too many. His long list of introductions, instead of helping him, had been counter-productive. Everybody knew what he was in Rome for and was talking about it. His reception by Mons. Amato, Secretary of Briefs, from whom much had been hoped, proved disappointing. Only gradually did he become aware that Amato was in league with the Pii Operai whose views on the new institute he shared. But at least Villani had learnt the important lesson that he should make doubly sure whom he was talking to in future and then say as little as possible. He was dismayed to learn that the Passionist Fathers, who were in Rome on a similar quest for their own Congregation, had encountered opposition from at least five other well-established religious orders and in the end all they had succeeded in getting was the initial *decretum laudis* from the Pope.

The first proposal of the Basilian Muscari was for Villani to go directly to the Holy Father and present the petition to him personally. Wiser counsels indicated that any short-circuiting of the Sacred Congregation of the Council who had ultimately to deal with the petition would only create enemies where as yet there were none. This piece of excellent advice came from the Procurator General of the Vincentians, Father Lomellini, who was well versed in Roman protocol. Guided by him, Villani presented the report of Cardinal Spinelli and the draft of the proposed Rules of the new congregation to the Congregation of the Council, together with a dossier of laudatory letters from various Neapolitan bishops. The first reactions were favourable though certain directions of the Rule were branded as childish and treated more or less as a joke, to the great annoyance of Villani who hastened to assure Alphonsus back in Pagani that he would give his life for the smallest point.

The Cardinal Prefect of the Congregation of the Council, Gentili, a priest of deep apostolic sensibility, was sufficiently impressed initially to designate one of his fellow members of the Council to act as *ponens* of the petition. Villani had set his heart on Cardinal Orsini for no other reason than the fact that he was a family friend of the Liguoris and his father had secured a rich benefice for Don Cajetan, Alphonsus' brother. But Orsini's familiarity with religious rules was at best peripheral; after the death of his wife he was promoted a cardinal by Benedict XIV out of esteem for his uncle, the late Pope Benedict XIII. Orsini only accepted the cardinalate on condition that he would not have to receive Major Orders lest the death of his two children should necessitate a second marriage to perpetuate the family name.

Gentili opted instead for Cardinal Besozzi, the Cistercian Cardinal, and titular of Santa Croce in Gerusalemme, an excellent choice as it turned out. Orsini recommended the new institute to Besozzi who, however, announced that he was not going to be influenced by any pressure one way or the other and would make his decision on the intrinsic merits of the new congregation and its Rules. Negotiations were now progressing so smoothly that Villani reported to Alphonsus that he could almost see the hand of God directing affairs. Alphonsus ordered special prayers to be recited in the four communities and a special penitential regime was established for the duration of Villani's mission.

Villani's main efforts were now directed at preventing the examination of the Rule from falling into the hands of the Pii Operai, but, to his horror, this is precisely what happened. Cardinal Besozzi was greatly impressed by the Rules as presented to him but realised that certain alterations would have to be made. An immediate change was the substitution of the word 'Redeemer' for 'Saviour', apparently to distinguish the members of the congregation from the Canons Regular of the Most Holy Saviour which was the official title of the Canons of the Lateran Basilica. Moreover, the draft as presented to him had grown up around twelve virtues, one for each month of the year, which gave the Rule an ascetical rather than a canonical approach, which in those days was not acceptable. In order to bring the Rule within the accepted canonical format Besozzi entrusted the reformulation to Father Thomas Sergio of the Pii Operai, one of the most highly esteemed theologians in Rome, the same to whom Pope Benedict had sent Alphonsus' treatise on the cursing of the dead. The choice of Sergio was a disaster in Villani's eyes and his dismay was increased when Sergio informed him, in the best Roman tradition, that the work of revision would take years and that in the meantime it would be better for him to return to Naples. A more sensitive man might well have accepted the inevitable but not Villani. He had no intention of returning to Naples and certainly not at the suggestion of a member of the Pii Operai, one section of whom, he was now convinced, were leagued in conspiracy against the congregation. He had one faithful ally among them — the ex-novice, Sanseverino, who was, by remarkable coincidence, Sergio's secretary. Together they worked at the reformulation of the Rule, guided by Sanseverino's expertise from dealing with similar cases. They assured Sergio that they would submit the final draft to him for his approval so that he could present it as his own achievement. As well, Villani presented him with personal copies of Alphonsus' publications and particularly the *Adnotationes* of Busenbaum. The offerings worked wonders and Sergio was satisfied to allow the revision to go ahead under his nominal direction though in actual fact it was carried through by Sanseverino, Villani and the ever-present abate Muscari.

The trio worked tirelessly all through December and the Christmas festivities; the revision was completed by the middle of January. On the eighteenth Cardinal Besozzi signed his formal approval in his residence at Santa Croce, declaring that he would sacrifice his life's blood on behalf of the new Congregation. The new formulation of the Rule had now to be approved by the thirty or so Cardinals who made up the Congregation of the Council. A further round of visits to each of the Cardinals, soliciting their *placet* for the approbation of the Rule which was due to come before them at their next plenary session on 25 January, now began. Villani was tireless and persistent; his greatest assets, he reported to Alphonsus, were his legs and an iron constitution which allowed him to trudge round Rome and wait patiently in the ante-rooms of Cardinals from morning to night on nothing more substantial than bread and cheese.

In the meantime Cardinal Besozzi sent his signed approval to be drawn up in curial form by his *auditor*, the abate Puzzolani, prior to presenting it to the meeting of the Cardinals of the Council. Puzzolani, whether maliciously or not we shall never know, restricted the approbation and the canonical existence of the new Congregation to the Kingdom of Naples. It was by the merest chance that Besozzi noticed the offending insertion and had time to order its deletion before leaving Rome for Civitavecchia, entrusting the formal reading of his favourable *votum* for approbation at the next meeting of the Council to his secretary, Mons. Furietti. On Saturday morning 25 January 1749 the Cardinals met in the Quirinal to discuss, among a host of other affairs, the approbation of the Congregation of the Most Holy Redeemer, as it had now become. Brother Tartaglione, who had shared the labours of the last three months, took up a post of vantage in a room adjoining the meeting hall while Villani went across to the church of Sant'Andrea al Quirinale to pray for the successful outcome of the deliberations. Shortly after noon the meeting broke up with most of the business unfinished; among the items not considered was the approbation of the Congregation. Tartaglione came across the street from the palace to convey the news to Villani. Disappointed but still determined, Villani knew there was one way left. Since the approval of the Cardinals was already assured and the only missing element was their formal consent, the decree could still be signed by the Cardinal Prefect in his own residence and ante-dated to the formal meeting of the session of the Council. It was an accepted curial *modus agendi* and a widely practised stratagem to offset the delays of a cumbersome body like the Congregation of the Council. Villani betook himself at once to Cardinal Orsini, begging him to present the decree personally to Cardinal Gentili, the Prefect, in his residence the following Monday. Orsini agreed. Villani had completed a letter to Alphonsus over the week-end detailing the sequence of events and was arranging for its despatch by courier on Tuesday morning 28 January when Orsini's valet arrived with a note conveying the news that Gentili had signed the decree of approval of the Congregation and its Rules. Without waiting to write another letter, Villani inserted between the first two lines of his letter, 'Gloria

Patri'. The Congregation has been approved. This very instant a servant of Cardinal Orsini has just brought me the news.' Villani signed himself *Andrea Villani del SS. Redentore*, the first member in the history of the Congregation canonically entitled to do so.[15]

Alphonsus was in Ciorani when Villani's letter arrived. Opening the despatch from Rome the words 'Gloria Patri' caught his eyes and he read the two lines. Immediately he rang the community bell and summoned the whole community, Fathers, Students, Brothers and Novices, to the church where they sang a *Te Deum* in thanksgiving. Taking as his text the words of psalm 80, 'Visit this vine, Lord, and protect it, the vine your right hand has planted', he urged all to the perfect observance of the Rules which the Church had just approved. He ordered prayers of thanksgiving with special fasts and penances in each house. For himself, he kept repeating, as he wrote to Villani, *Nunc dimitis servum tuum, Domine* — he had nothing further to live for if God wished to call him. It took a long while for the full import of it all to sink in, '*Neppure ora arrivo a credere*,' 'I can hardly believe it yet'.

But the last act in the dramatic sequence of events in Rome was not played out yet. Four weeks were to elapse before the decree of the Council, dated 25 January 1749, was sent to the Datary and presented to the Pope for his signature; only then would the decision have legal effect. 'Here in Rome', wrote Villani, now wise to the deviousness of ecclesiastical bureaucracy, 'ships can be wrecked even in the harbour.' The news of the approbation of the fledgling missionary congregation brought a new wave of opposition; certain members of the Pii Operai came from Naples to enlist the support of the Spanish ambassador to the Holy See, Cardinal Portocarrero, in an effort to set aside the decree or at least to diminish its force. As the Brief was being drawn up in the Datary the phrase, '*caeterum non intendimus supradictum institutum in aliquo approbare*' — 'however we do not intend in any way to approve the aforementioned institute' — was inserted. This restrictive clause, which allowed for the approval of the Rules and Constitutions but not the institute itself, had already found its way into the *summarium* which had been submitted to the Pope and signed by him before being returned to the minutante's office for final drafting. Fortunately the unauthorised insertion was spotted in time by Muscari—one of the few achievements for which he can be thanked. Villani had his suspicions at whose instigation the restrictive clause had been inserted, an insidious manoeuvre which would have robbed the papal approval of much of its value. Together they approached Cardinal Passionei, Secretary of Briefs, who if not himself enthusiastic about the approval of new religious orders was yet sufficiently upright not to tolerate unauthorised tampering with the decisions of the Cardinal Prefect of the Congregation of the Council. The abbate Fiori, the official responsible for inserting the offending clause, pleaded that such had been, up to this, the official *stylus curiae* in these matters and that the same restrictions had been employed in the case of the Passionist Fathers some time before. The Cardinal himself erased the restrictive insertion.

Villani and Muscari left nothing to the integrity of the curial officials from then onwards; they personally supervised the drawing up of the Brief in the curial office. Villani wrote that he was in constant fear until he had the Brief, signed and sealed, in his own hands. The saga ended on Wednesday 26 February 1749 when Villani received the Papal Brief, *Ad Pastoralis Dignitatis Fastigium*, which the Pope had signed the previous day and sealed with the seal of the Fisherman in red wax in St Mary Major's. 'Now we can say that our Congregation is really approved and not before', was Villani's comment.

The success of Villani's efforts and the extent of the approbation he had received was a source of much discussion in ecclesiastical circles in Rome. The whole process had taken just over three months though the majority of observers had held out little hope for them when they arrived. Mannarini had been to Rome some time before on a similar errand and, despite his numerous houses and several influential friends, had returned to Calabria empty-handed. Villani and Tartaglione had a final audience of Pope Benedict XIV to express their thanks before setting out for Loreto on a pilgrimage of thanksgiving to the Mother of God, leaving Muscari to attend to the printing of fifty copies of the precious Brief. As Villani left the city the ungracious parting message of Mons. Filippo Pirelli, one of the consistorial advocates, was ringing in his ears, 'Other religious orders were able to maintain their fervour for the space of about one hundred years; you should endeavour to preserve yours for at least fifty.'

– V –

If Villani brought back with him from Rome papal approval for the new Congregation and its Rules and Constitutions, he also brought back a less desirable acquisition in the person of the abate Muscari. There are many bewildering incidents in the history of the origins of the Redemptorists from the happenings in the convent at Scala to the intrigues of Don Silvestro Tosques but they all fall into the category of the normal compared with the story of Muscari. He had long been dissatisfied with his vocation as a Basilian, and this dissatisfaction was due in part, according to himself, to serious divisions in the Order which he described dramatically as a 'miniature hell', but even more to his own restless ambition. He found it impossible to settle down in peace. He had wanted to join the Vincentians and when this failed — they were more discerning than Alphonsus — he set his heart on the new Congregation which he had supported in Rome. While Villani was still in Rome, Muscari made the Spiritual Exercises in the Jesuit Noviceship in the city; he confided his difficulties to the spiritual director whose discernment of the situation concluded by advising Muscari to leave the Basilians and join the Redemptorists. The first inkling of such a development was conveyed to Alphonsus by Villani from Rome under the most inviolable secrecy in December 1748. Villani was enthusiastic at the prospect; Muscari had convinced him that he was guided by the highest of spiritual motives. Moreover, his assistance in the approval of the Rule had placed the whole Congregation under a deep debt of gratitude to him which would make refusal to accept him unthinkable.

Alphonsus did not share the enthusiasm of Villani and moreover, one of the more sensible decisions of the Chapter meeting of 1747 was to forbid reception of candidates from other orders. But the abate was nothing if not persistent and persuasive. He kept up pressure from Rome relentlessly, begging Alphonsus *per viscera Jesu Christi* to receive him. It was a remarkable aberration of judgment on Alphonsus' part that he finally acceded to the request. Muscari then approached the Pope for the necessary canonical dispensation which was granted. The way was now clear for Muscari to return to Ciorani to commence his novitiate. But then the most incredible incident in the whole affair took place. Since the papal dispensation for the transfer from the Basilians to the Redemptorists would have no legal force in Naples without the royal *exequatur*, which could not be taken for granted, Muscari's plan was to don the Redemptorist habit in Rome and arrive in Ciorani as a fully-fledged member of the Congregation. To compound his original error of judgment Alphonsus, by his powers as Rector Major, dispensed him from the novitiate and designated Cardinal Orsini to receive the vows of the former abbot as a Redemptorist. The strange ceremony took place in St Peter's near the *Confessio* on 1 June 1749 in the presence of the Cardinal and two notaries. A few days later, on fire with zeal for his new Order, and already planning great developments, Muscari arrived in Ciorani bringing the printed copies of the Rule. Alphonsus received him with all deference as his spiritual son; had he any forebodings of the havoc the abbot would cause in his thirty months of membership?

Since the newly approved Rule had to be formally accepted by all, Alphonsus convoked an extraordinary assembly of the professed Fathers and Students to meet in Ciorani on 1 October 1749. According to the minutes of what has come to be accepted as the first General Chapter of the Congregation of the Most Holy Redeemer, the delegates were conscious that their presence marked the birthday of their society in an ecclesiastical sense. Tannoia states that the delegates spent three days in silence and prayer before the Chapter opened, a fact which is not mentioned in either the official Acts of the Assembly or in the more detailed account given by Father Landi who was its President. There was general agreement that the Rector Major's Consultors and all others officials including the local superiors should resign, thus allowing for new elections and new appointments as the case might be. But what about the office of the Rector Major? Here there were a number of complications.[16]

Due to a nice piece of diplomacy on the part of Villani the Papal Brief explicitly stated that 'the aforesaid Alphonsus was Rector Major for life'. Behind this insertion lay the fact that for some time Alphonsus had secretly been considering resigning his office. When the definite news of the successful outcome of the Roman negotiations reached him in the famous 'Gloria Patri' letter at the end of January, he immediately intimated his intention to Villani. He was painfully aware of the volume of criticism being raised against him; more to the point, he was tired, weary and discouraged. Much of the criticism may not have centred on himself personally but on the fact that his office was for life; Alphonsus, as we have seen, totally supported the decision of Falcoia in this matter. Others were equally opposed to it. The negotiations for the approval of the Rule provided an opportunity for discussion on this point to come out into the open; it became so widespread that Alphonsus urged Villani to pay special attention to it in the consultations he was having. Villani determined to leave nothing to chance. Besides securing papal approval for the life-tenure of the Rector Major, he was now determined to secure papal confirmation of the fact that Alphonsus *was* Rector Major for life. Needless to say he was totally opposed to any idea of Alphonsus' resignation:

> God wills that your Paternity [the accepted form of address to the Rector Major] should carry this Cross until your death; to refuse to do so would go against the Will of God. Just at the very moment when this frail bark of ours requires a reliable Captain, you begin to complain. *Pazienza*. The Lord will assist us. Why should we lose heart when we know that this is the Lord's work? *Padre Mio*, have courage; don't lose heart. Now is the time to be daring. Clearly the Lord is looking after us in a special way and you must realise this from your own experience. Once more I say to you, have courage. Pay no attention to the displeasure of others, sufficient that the Lord is pleased. His greater glory is all that matters.

This was the background to the clause which Villani succeeded in having inserted into the second paragraph of the Brief of Approbation, 'the aforesaid Alphonsus (de Liguori) is the elected and designated Rector Major for life'. The insertion was meant to serve a dual purpose; it highlighted the fact that the office was for life and at the same time it was intended to deflect Alphonsus from any thoughts of resigning and the other members from expressing any further opposition to him.

But Villani reckoned without Muscari. On his arrival in Ciorani as a member of the Chapter, Muscari set himself up as the canonical expert; his Roman experience and his familiarity with the praxis of the Roman Curia gave him a special aura among some of the Chapter members. What he had to say was accepted more readily than it should have been; he, for his part, seemed to revel in the intrigue of it all. He queried the interpretation of the reference to Alphonsus in the Papal Brief as Rector Major for life. According to him it merely referred to a fact which existed and did not in any way formally designate or confirm him for the future. On the other hand those with a different interpretation held that Alphonsus was just what the Brief stated, Rector Major for life and that was that. Muscari's interpretation was certainly tenable and may even have been the correct one but in the light of his conduct at a later date his scruples can perhaps be traced to other than canonical subtleties. However, the damage had been done; the differing interpretations had compromised the situation to the extent that only a new election would allow the position of Rector Major to be put beyond challenge. There was no opposition to this course from Alphonsus.

On the morning of 1 October, Mass of the Holy Spirit was celebrated at which Father Cafaro preached; exposition of the Blessed Sacrament followed for a short while before the delegates assembled in the Chapter hall. Alphonsus, on his knees before the Assembly, begged pardon for his faults of government and resigned his office as Rector Major into the hands of the delegates, upon which all the superiors and officials followed suit. Then the youngest of the Fathers, Giuseppe Landi, whose account of the pre-ceedings is a vital source of information for us, was proposed and elected as President of the Assembly to prevent undue importance being attached to the first voting. One by one, beginning with Alphonsus, the delegates indicated their acceptance of the Brief of Approbation of Benedict XIV and renewed their vows in accordance with the prescriptions of what was now called the Pontifical Rule.

The next important business was the election of the new Rector Major. A group proposed that the election should be postponed for some days to allow further consultation to take place; the majority wished it to take place without delay. Landi's account leaves us in no doubt about the climate of the meeting: 'the devil gets into Chapters and elections and goes around sowing discord'. The senior Fathers, recounts Landi, realised what was afoot under the pretext of further consultation and the danger that threatened; they may have lost the decision regarding the interpretation of Alphonsus' position as contained in the Papal Brief, but they were not going to provide more time for any further mischief to surface. 'Delay in proceeding to the election of the new Rector Major could cause harm to the Congregation and greatly disturb the Chapter itself, since any delay would allow the devil to make his presence felt among the delegates, causing dissensions and untold disturbances.' Landi as President accepted this submission of what he styled the sanior pars of the Assembly and announced the election of the Rector Major for the afternoon of the same day.

The Chapter assembled in the Community oratory at the appointed time. The Veni Creator Spiritus was intoned and after the usual formalities the twenty-five delegates, which included the professed students but not the Brothers, proceeded to the election of the Rector Major in accordance with the provisions of the newly approved Rule, in other words, a superior for life elected by a two thirds majority. On the first scrutiny Alphonsus received twenty-three of the total twenty-five votes cast. One of the two votes which he did not receive was certainly his own; whose was the other must remain, like the results of his first election, the secret of history. Could it have been Muscari's? From the result of the voting it would seem that whatever talk there may have been of replacing Alphonsus with another candidate had little basis in fact; maybe his most committed supporters — Mazzini, Villani, Rossi and Cafaro — saw conspiracies where there were none.

According to Tannoia who was present, the Chapter was dominated by Muscari; he was the expert whose word was law. Villani in due course was elected Assistant to Alphonsus, Cafaro followed as consultor secretary. Since there were to be six consultors in all, this left four vacancies to be filled. Sportelli, Mazzini and Rossi were duly elected and then, incredibly, the enthusiasm of the delegates led them into the crowning indiscretion. They elected Muscari as one of Alphonsus' counsellors, a decision which they very soon came to regret.

Chapter Ten

Building The Edifice
1749–1762

– I –

From the point of view of the Bourbon administration, the Ciorani Chapter, following on papal approbation, was illegal, its prescriptions void. The election of Alphonsus as Rector Major, his appointment of local superiors, the regulations for the reception of candidates and their formation, the decrees concerning the preaching of missions were all enacted in virtue of a papal brief which had not been registered in the Royal Chancellery and had not received the royal *exequatur*. In the secret articles of the concordat of 1741 the King had undertaken to execute freely and without delay all Bulls, Briefs and Rescripts emanating from the Pontifical Court and its tribunals. But this solemn undertaking remained by and large a dead letter, and Tanucci and his colleagues soon realised that withholding the royal *exequatur* was a powerful weapon in their struggle against Roman influence. For an ecclesiastical association such as the missionaries of the Most Holy Redeemer to act in virtue of a Roman decision which had not received royal assent was punishable by suppression. In fact, since the Papal brief approving the Congregation was not to receive the royal assent in the lifetime of Alphonsus, every corporate act of the Congregation was technically illegal. Consequently, any member of the Congregation who wished to do so could appeal to the King against a decision of his superiors, challenge the legality of his position and have his orders set aside. Some did, and others threatened to do so; at times it was only the more powerful influence of Alphonsus with the King's ministers which prevented a royal decree in favour of some Father who, for example, had been changed from one house to another and objected to going. The possibility of appeal to the King was held like a sword over every superior and over Alphonsus himself. Finally, after years of what amounted to virtual blackmail he was forced to face the threat head-on in a circular letter to all the houses when this menace was at its most threatening:

If they begin to write I also have pen and ink. It is my duty to fulfil the intentions of God and of the King by keeping those subjects who are fit for the work of the missions and by sending away those who are found to be useless and even hurtful for this work. I am the sole director of this society of missionary priests and this too is the wish of the sovereign. I have no doubt that he will more willingly listen to my truthful representations than to the appeal of the intractable and discontented.[1]

The news of the success which had attended Alphonsus' efforts in Rome brought a generous letter of congratulations from Mannarini. The old longing for reunion was still strong in him and he broached the matter once more, this time with the bait that his powerful connections at Court would be instrumental in securing the royal *exequatur*. Full of hope, Mannarini came to Ciorani in a final effort to induce Alphonsus to go along with the idea. Having consulted widely among his colleagues, Alphonsus was able to inform him, once and for all, that there could be no question of uniting their two societies. And so ended the last attempt of Mannarini to repair the divisions of Scala.[2]

Alphonsus gauged the temper of the royal court sufficiently accurately to be pessimistic about the prospects of securing the royal *exequatur*; Villani, on whom the triumphant outcome of his Roman negotiations had had a heady effect, foresaw little difficulty. 'We shall get the *exequatur* easily,' he wrote to Alphonsus from Rome. But Alphonsus was correct in his assessment. Brancone advised him that there was little prospect of securing the *exequatur* for a missionary society which the King and his ministers had refused to approve some months before. So he decided to leave well enough alone and to throw himself into the work of the missions and his writings. Within a few months, however, another of those absurd incidents, which so characterised the Bourbon regime in Naples, took place, necessitating immediate action. In March 1751, the King was hunting in Tremoleto, in the neighbourhood of Deliceto in one of the twelve royal hunting reserves. From a hill, the King saw the Redemptorist monastery of Santa Maria della Consolazione in the distance. Asking whose castle it was, he was informed that it was a house of the missioners of Father Alphonsus de Liguori. The informant added, for good measure, that the Fathers had just inherited a fortune of 60,000 ducats, a statement which was completely false as his Majesty could have verified if he had taken the trouble to visit what was popularly known in the Congregation at the time as the 'house of cold and hunger'. No doubt the royal companion — more than likely a member of the local Maffei family which was later to bring the Congregation to the verge of destruction — had his own malevolent motives for retailing the false rumour to the King, whose reaction was predictable and immediate. 'They are scarcely founded and they are now just like all the others.' Within a few weeks of his return to Naples, the King ordered a full investigation into the charges. The news cast a deep gloom over Alphonsus; the whole incident had been so unfortunate and the possible consequences so serious that he really feared for the existence of his society. Once again he recalled the example of St Ignatius: 'God wishes the Congregation to expand not as a result of royal favour but as a result of poverty, persecution and insults. St Ignatius rejoiced when he saw his young society suffering contradictions and hardships.'

All during 1751 fear of suppression gripped the Congregation; Alphonsus ordered special prayers to be recited in the four communities to avert disaster. He drew up a memorandum which listed the fixed annual revenues of the four houses from the deeds of foundation — 300 ducats per year in Deliceto, 500 each in Ciorani and Caposele, and no fixed income at all in Pagani — a total of 1,300 ducats which was less than the recent increase in salary accorded to the marquis Tanucci. The royal commission, set up to investigate the revenues of the four houses, and presided over by Alphonsus' old card-playing friend, Baldassare Cito, duly confirmed Alphonsus' depositions.[3] When the findings were communicated to the King in September 1752 he was reluctant to believe the truth and appeared disappointed that he had not succeeded in uncovering a grave ecclesiastical scandal. In a meeting of the Council of State he spoke vehemently against Alphonsus and his missionaries. As a result, Alphonsus was summoned to Naples where he found the outlook for the Congregation critical in the extreme. Brancone, who knew the temper of the King, suggested to Alphonsus that he should immediately offer to close two of the houses as a gesture to assuage the royal anger. So wrathful had the King shown himself that had it not been for the protection of Brancone, a royal decree dissolving the Congregation would already have been issued.

Once again Alphonsus took up residence in Naples to begin the tiresome rounds of his friends, enlisting their support with the King. He went first to the Jesuit, Father Pepe, only to find that his influence at Court had suffered considerably and that he no longer was the power with Charles III that he had been. More serious still was the fact that the case of the Redemptorists had been passed to the President of the Consiglio di Santa Chiara, the anti-roman and anti-clerical tribunal *par excellence*, under the control of the marquis Fraggianni, a typical enlightenment figure with no religious sentiment whatsoever, despite the fact that he had a daughter a Poor Clare. Referred to as Papa Nicola, he greeted Alphonsus insultingly: 'Do not come to me with your gibberish. Tell it to old women.' He did not even invite him to be seated. Alphonsus said simply, 'Marquis, I recommend to you the cause of Jesus Christ,' to which the marquis replied, 'Jesus Christ has nothing whatsoever to do with the Royal Council Chamber.' Alphonsus then attempted to approach the marquis through their mutual friend, the bishop of Bovino, Mons. Lucci. To Lucci, Fraggianni explained the root of his opposition. The missionaries of Father Liguori were like the Jesuits; they begin to grow powerful, little by little, and then are never satisfied. But the real reason for refusing the royal *exequatur* was the obsession with church property which possessed the King and his ministers. Alphonsus protested that money or property did not interest him or his missionaries; they would be more than satisfied if they could live unchallenged with a roof over their heads and with sufficient to eat to sustain life and their work. And such was all they eventually got.

It was Brancone who saved the day. Through his influence the King finally agreed that the work of the missions should continue; there would be no question of suppressing the Congregation. At the same time Bourbon policy in the matter of Church property and the wealth of religious orders would have to be respected. Together, Brancone and Alphonsus worked out an agreement which entailed considerable concessions on the part of the Congregation and a considerable derogation from the full canonical effects of papal approval. But it was better to make concessions than to lose all. On 9 December 1752, a royal decree permitted the 'Missionary Priests under the direction of Don Alfonso de Liguori' to continue to exist on a number of conditions. Their corporate existence as a religious body was not to be recognised; they were to remain a group of secular priests living together, subject to the bishops of the different dioceses. They were not entitled either to acquire or possess property in common. Whatever property or foundations they had already acquired — and an inventory of these was contained at the end of the decree — was to be administered by the bishops of the dioceses where the houses were situated, under the supervision of the local civil officials. The bishops were to allot to each member of the community — to a maximum of nineteen, twelve fathers and seven brothers — the sum of two carlins a day from the revenues of the property. Whatever remained was to be distributed by the bishops to the poor of their dioceses. Finally, if the missionaries ceased to exist, the property was to be disposed of and all funds distributed among the poor. 'Under these conditions and none other, the King permits the aforesaid priests to live together in the four houses of Ciorani, Materdomini, Deliceto and Pagani and not in any others, provided that they live together as secular priests under the jurisdiction of the local ordinaries since the King does not consider their houses as colleges or religious communities.'

It is an indication of the gravity of the situation that this decree of partial confiscation and the grant of a daily maintenance allowance of what equalled the ordinary wages of a liveried footman, was regarded by Alphonsus as a triumph. The nuncio reported to Rome that the missionaries were not 'discontented with the terms of the royal decree'. A few weeks later Alphonsus wrote to a friend who had helped during this difficult period:

> I thank you sincerely for the favour you have shown to this poor persecuted little flock of Jesus Christ. The storm which hell has raised against us has been severe but the Lord has made things issue favourably for us. The King, who was somewhat against us at the beginning, is now favourably disposed. It is true that the royal decree has imposed certain limitations on us but we are satisfied since, at least, the work is approved and stabilised, which was the most important point of all. For the rest, if we remain poor and behave ourselves, God will not be wanting.[4]

The decree of 1752 was full of significance for the future. Some form of legal recognition in the Kingdom of Naples had been secured at the heavy cost of important canonical rights which papal approbation had conferred. Basically, the corporate legal existence of the Congregation of the Most Holy Redeemer, which had been approved in Rome as a canonical religious body, was not recognised; it could not own or acquire property. Gifts or legacies in favour of the Congregation as a corporate entity were invalid; instead, each member of the Congregation was legally entitled to retain his own property and revenue, thus setting aside important provisions of the rule of Benedict XIV and opening the way to serious controversy in the future in the matter of canonical poverty. Congregational property and revenues were to be administered by the bishops of the dioceses, thus subjecting the Congregation to the jurisdiction of the hierarchy in a relationship not envisaged by the Pontifical Rule. Finally, the decree stated that the members were to live together as secular priests, more or less as the members of the Apostolic Missions in Naples might live together, thus negativing the religious community aspect which Alphonsus had envisaged for his followers. The four houses were to be simply residences where secular priests lived together and were in no legal sense to be regarded as religious communities. In the light of what was to happen some thirty years later when a further royal decree under Charles III's son and successor, Ferdinand, went one step further and imposed a royal rule in place of the Pontifical Rule, the decree of 1752 set a pattern of dissimulation which anticipated the tragic situation of the closing decade of Alphonsus' life. Externally, the Congregation after 1752 conformed to the legal norms laid down by the Bourbon Court; internally it hoped to be able to continue to follow the prescriptions of the Roman rule provided, of course, that no disgruntled member was to report the deception to the royal officials. This double-think, which continued for thirty years, was to create a climate which prepared the way for the *Regolamento*. Whatever his attitude may have been during the *Regolamento* crisis, Alphonsus did not hesitate in 1752 to waive fundamental canonical rights — at least externally — in order to secure some measure of legal security from the Bourbons. And in contrast to the drastic action taken by Pope Pius VI in very similar circumstances thirty years later, neither the papal nuncio in Naples nor Pope Benedict XIV in Rome found anything reprehensible in the course of action which Alphonsus followed in 1752. In an age of despotic regalism and anti-curial feeling, the Congregation had to make the best of a difficult situation; better to continue to exist and do some good than to stand on one's canonical rights and be suppressed.

The following year, 1753, Alphonsus, incredibly, contemplated a further attempt to obtain the royal *exequatur*. The King had contacted him about the possibility of undertaking the reform of a small religious congregation of men, which would have entailed absorbing them into the Congregation; it was, in point of fact, meant to be a painless method of suppression. Even though he had to refuse the request with all the graciousness he could summon, the new contact with the King awakened once more the hope of securing the royal approbation. Alphonsus was convinced that if he could only talk personally with the King, explain that he was completely satisfied with the financial arrangements of the previous year, that his missioners did not wish to possess any property whatsoever beyond what was sufficient to live on, the King would surely agree to granting the royal approbation. But to get to the King was the problem. He had recently refused all audiences and even Brancone failed to arrange a meeting for Alphonsus. Undaunted, Alphonsus decided to approach the Queen, Maria Amalia.

The Queen was a personal friend of Mother Mary Angela, the prioress and reformer of the Carmelites of Capua, who also happened to be a penitent of Alphonsus. Moreover, the Queen went frequently to Capua to spend the whole day with Mother Angela, away from the suffocating atmosphere of the Court, discussing her problems of husband and children with the prioress; they would talk for hours together in private. Alphonsus determined to enlist the support of his penitent. If she could succeed in interesting Maria Amalia in the matter of the royal approbation for the Redemptorists, then the Queen would be able to wring the permission from her husband, however reluctant he might otherwise be. In July 1753, Alphonsus wrote to Mother Angela to enlist her support, informing her that 'it may well be that the Lord has arranged for you to become so influential with the Queen, not merely for the benefit of your own reform programme, but for other matters which pertain to his glory as well.' Unfortunately, the hunting season intervened before the whole plot could be fully set up and Alphonsus realised that it was a totally unfavourable time to give the Queen the memorial he was drafting; the King would not be interested and the Queen would probably mislay it anyway. So he bided his time. In the autumn, he took up the scheme again and Mother Angela agreed to play her part. Through a friend inside the Court, Alphonsus arranged for the Prioress to be notified in good time of the Queen's next visit. When he was sure of that, he would at once present the original of the Papal Brief and a memorial to the Court, so that the Queen's representations to the King and the petition from Alphonsus would coincide. There were two essential elements in the plot — the first, that Mother Angela should be convinced about her role and, secondly, that Maria Amalia should be so well briefed and so worked up to a determination to secure her husband's consent, that there could be no possibility of failure. Alphonsus feared that if he allowed the original of the Papal Brief to fall into the hands of the King's ministers without assurances of a successful outcome, he might never get it back and so would lose everything. 'If Mother Angela speaks in an unenthusiastic sort of way to the Queen and if the Queen promises in a half-hearted sort of way, it is no good at all. In that case, as I said before, I would not risk the Brief.'[5]

Alphonsus next endeavoured to enlist the support of the Pope. On sending Benedict XIV the first volume of the second edition of his Moral Theology, which had appeared that year, Alphonsus begged him to use his influence with Charles III on behalf of the Redemptorists. But Benedict was as much in difficulties with the Bourbon Court as he was himself; the Pope rightly felt that any intervention on his part would serve for nothing more than to provide a further opportunity for the King to snub the Holy See. All he could offer were his prayers that God would change the heart of Charles and his advisers. Eventually, nothing came of all the schemes, letter writing and plans. Whether it was that Mother Angela was not able to excite sufficient enthusiasm on the Queen's part or whether the Queen simply refused, we do not know. But one thing is certain; the favourable climate for granting the royal *exequatur* was not created. More and more, Alphonsus became convinced that God did not wish his Congregation to receive royal approval during his lifetime — it was all due to his sins and God wished to humble his pride. Only two years after his death did the Bourbons of Naples, on the eve of revolution and exile, grant a favour which would have crowned a lifetime of effort on behalf of his missionary Congregation.

– II –

After the Chapter of 1749 Alphonsus appointed Muscari to Pagani to supervise the studies of the twelve or so students there, who were preparing for ordination under the spiritual guidance of Father Mazzini. The Chapter had made an effort to reorganise the studies. Those whose early training in the humanities was considered deficient, were to continue their studies of the classics until they attained the required standard. Purchot's *Institutiones* was to be the philosophy textbook, an extraordinary choice since the book was widely criticised in France, its country of origin, as a mixture of Descartes and Malebranche. The suggestion had come from Muscari who, besides everything else, had set himself up as an expert on philosophy; as a young Basilian he had composed several philosophical tracts. Alphonsus suggested the *Compendium* of Isaac Herbert for dogmatic theology and his own annotations of Busenbaum for moral theology and confessional practice.

Muscari undertook his teaching assignment with something less than selfless dedication. His undoubted intellectual gifts were not balanced by any depth of virtue and his lack of spiritual formation in the Congregation soon manifested itself. He began to ridicule the ascetical practices which he found in use among his new confreres — different, no doubt, from those to which he was accustomed as a Basilian. The harm that his general attitude and conduct were doing to the students made Father Mazzini, the Rector of the House of Studies, uneasy, but the ex-abbot was not amenable to correction nor would he accept that he was in any way at fault. The dissensions came quickly to the ears of Alphonsus in Ciorani, who, under the pretext of getting him to preach the spiritual exercises to the Ordinandi at Ciorani, removed Muscari from his position as professor and director of Studies. At once, Alphonsus' consultors, Villani, Cafaro and Fiocchi, rose to Muscari's defence; surprisingly, Alphonsus listened to their pleas, removed Mazzini from Pagani to Deliceto and installed Muscari in Pagani, this time in complete control of the students. It was one of those errors of judgment of character which occurred time and time again in his life.

Despite the upgrading of his position, Muscari found it impossible to settle down as a Redemptorist. And his dissatisfaction soon communicated itself to the students. He began to discuss with his favourites among them the possibility of founding a new religious order for the evangelisation of Mongolia, China and Paraguay in that order. His dreams of a new religious order on purely foreign missionary lines upset the students to the extent of disturbing their studies and turning them against the apostolate of the missions at home in the Kingdom of Naples. The students were again in turmoil and it was obvious that Muscari would have to be removed. Alphonsus sought a suitable pretext. From the time of Villani's visit to Rome there had been a proposal to establish a foundation in the Eternal City, so, in September 1751, Alphonsus determined to entrust the task to Muscari, assigning one of the most promising of the young missioners, Father Bernard Tortora, to accompany him. Muscari was initially flattered at the prospect but, after a little reflection, was shrewd enough to discern the real purpose behind the move. While outwardly preparing for the journey to Rome, he was secretly planning to leave the Congregation, taking four of the Pagani students with him, and another from the Chinese College in Naples, where he had also been active. In great secrecy he drew up a long document attacking the Congregation of the Most Holy Redeemer and its superiors, which he induced the four students to sign; he claimed that serious abuses of religious observance existed.

Quite by chance, indications of what was afoot came to Alphonsus' notice in Ciorani. Immediately he summoned his council to discuss the situation, and proposed the expulsion of Muscari. His advisers were incredulous and unwilling to take such drastic action against one who was, like themselves, a member of the Rector Major's council. They even challenged the Rector Major's right to act thus, accusing him at the same time of being both authoritarian and arrogant. The heated discussion continued for hours and it was only next morning that all was revealed when the four students presented themselves to Alphonsus, ready to leave and demanding their dispensation. With all the kindness of a father he entreated them to remain but no reasoning could shake their determination. Eventually, he went on his knees before them, asking what harm he had ever done to them, or what harm the Congregation had ever caused them. But not even this dramatic gesture could alter their purpose; Muscari's indoctrination had been too thorough. Although Alphonsus finally refused to dispense them from their vows they left. There was now no disagreement about the decision to be taken about Muscari; his expulsion was unanimously decided upon, but, before the decision could be conveyed to him, he left Pagani for his old Basilian monastery a few miles distant, from where he sent word that he wished to have whatever books and belongings he had brought with him.

Alphonsus took considerable pains with the letter which he sent to Muscari on 15 October; a rough draft, still preserved, bears witness to the careful preparation which went into one of the most moving letters of his whole correspondence:

My most esteemed Don Giuseppe,

For two nights I have been unable to sleep with the thought of the ruin you have brought to this poor Congregation which you esteemed so highly before you entered, and which you have hated so intensely since then. I could not believe that you would be instrumental in causing four young men to abandon their vocations, but from what I learnt from their own lips and from other sources, there is no escaping that conclusion.

I am not going to waste time going into details: it would be pointless and would only cause you displeasure. You know, Don Giuseppe, how greatly I loved you and esteemed you before you became one of us.

You know what I did to honour you with those small tokens of esteem which a poor Congregation like ours can give. I entrusted to your care from the very beginning the most precious treasure of the Congregation, its young men. To give you greater peace in your work I changed Father Mazzini from Pagani, a man of such high repute among us and of such edification. I appointed you a professor and kept you as one, and finally made you director and spiritual guide of the students — but, all the time, I must now confess, with certain misgivings.

Your Reverence may well say that nothing really has happened — well, here is that nothing! Four young men who were so many angels beforehand have now been changed into so many living furies, even though I besought them with all tenderness and affection, even to the extent of going on my knees at their feet, to postpone just for three days, their precipitous departure from our Congregation. I valued these young men as the apple of my eye, because, truthfully, they were as good as gold and always behaved admirably. Their humility and submissiveness gave edification to us all. But yesterday morning even your Reverence would have been scandalised to hear the disrespect and arrogance with which they spoke to me and others, the threats they made against the Congregation, going so far as to announce that they would appeal to the King against me, because, as they said, I was keeping them by force since I would not dispense them from their vows. My God! they themselves bound themselves to Jesus Christ and now they say I am keeping them by force! Why did I not dispense them at once from their vows? Because I love them and had compassion on them and saw that they were abandoning their vocation as a result of a temptation of the devil.

But enough. There is no point in annoying you any more since I realise that every word I write must pain you. Neither I nor the Congregation deserved the treatment you have meted out to us. I pardon you and I beg of Jesus Christ to forgive you since I still love and esteem you. I pray that Our Lady will make you realise one day — if you do not do so already — the evil you have done in damaging the Congregation and in harming these four young men and that she will bring you to weep for your conduct as you should. Nobody says anything further against you except that you have betrayed the Congregation and that, the very stones cry out.

Your Reverence has written to say that you will not do any further harm to the Congregation but that you will endeavour to help it. I beg of you once more not to harm the Congregation, because, in doing so, you would give great displeasure to Jesus Christ. Here, we have no other interest than to suffer and toil for Jesus Christ, for poor souls, and you know that well yourself. I fear that from this day forward when you hear the Congregation of the Most Holy Redeemer mentioned the devil will make you think that it should be the object of your greatest hate and will suggest to you that you should discredit it, in every possible way, in order to justify your conduct. Father Giuseppe, do not do it. I write to you from my heart and with tears in my eyes. I can only hope that once your anger against me and my advisers has cooled, you will show by your conduct that you have renewed that affection and benevolence which you formerly had for us.[6]

The departure of Muscari and the possible damage he could cause to the Congregation, despite his assurances to the contrary, terrified Alphonsus; the royal investigation into the Congregation's finances following on the King's hunting expedition in the neighbourhood of Deliceto was under way. He conjured up all the possible reprisals that Muscari in his vindictiveness might take against the Congregation, first with the King and his ministers, then with the Pope in Rome. On 13 October, the day following the discovery of Muscari's intentions, he sent Father Celestino de Robertis to Naples, to inform Brancone of all that had taken place and to put him on his guard if Muscari or one of the students had recourse to the King against the Congregation. De Robertis was instructed to explain to Brancone the point on which they were most vulnerable, namely, that even though they had elected a Rector Major and appointed superiors according to the Rule approved in Rome, this had all been done secretly but not in any way in defiance of his Majesty or his ministers who had not yet granted the *exequatur*. So intense were Alphonsus' fears that he instructed de Robertis to contact Brancone at any cost; if he was out of Naples he was to hire a coach to follow him, regardless of expense. Letters to Sanseverino and Cardinal Spinelli in Rome followed immediately to prevent any harm to the Congregation from that quarter. Spinelli's reply was reassuring. Sanseverino was shocked beyond belief by the news and, having reported to Cardinal Besozzi, he was able to assure Alphonsus that there was nothing to fear; Rome would support whatever action he had taken.[7]

But Alphonsus need not have worried. Muscari may have been a vain, ambitious man but he was not vindictive. He never spoke disparagingly of the Redemptorists. When he applied to the King of Naples for the *exequatur* for the papal dispensation which allowed him to return to the Basilians, he alleged that after three years in the Congregation his health was shattered and he had to leave. He went back to his full abbatial dignity among his Basilian brethren and threw himself, with great enthusiasm, into a dispute — whether theological or canonical it can be left to others to decide — as to whether the abbatial office was not more honourable than that of a mere canonry. After some time, he resumed his ministry of preaching and for twenty-five years was one of the most colourful figures in the pulpits of Calabria and Sicily, where his abbatial robes — he had a special indult to wear them in public — became a familiar sight. Towards the end of his life he became abbot of Grottaferrata outside Rome and remained a genuine admirer of Alphonsus' writings, especially his moral theology, which he strenuously defended.

Within a few weeks of Muscari's departure with the four students, Alphonsus addressed one of his first circular letters to the Fathers and Brothers of the Congregation. This practice, which began with a letter in July of the same year, was to become a feature of his government of the Congregation. There were twelve letters in all, occasioned by some event affecting all the members, some sad departure from the ranks of the Congregation, some crisis which threatened its very existence, or by the necessity for a clarion call to more perfect religious observance. When he wrote in November 1751 he made no explicit reference to Muscari but his purpose was clear:

> My dear Brothers,
>
> You know that I am not upset when I hear that one of my confreres has been called by God from this life. Of course, I feel it, since I am flesh and blood but in reality I rejoice because I am certain that one who dies in the Congregation is certainly saved. Nor am I distressed when I learn that someone, on account of his defects, has left the Congregation. Rather am I delighted that the Congregation is rid of a diseased sheep which could infect all the others. Nor do persecutions worry me — rather, they give me courage because if we behave ourselves as we ought, I am certain the Lord will not desert us. But what really terrifies me is when I learn of someone who is not obedient and makes light of the Rules.

With the departure of Muscari, calm returned to the House of Studies at Pagani. Father Mazzini, whom Alphonsus had sacrificed to placate the abbot, came back from his exile in Deliceto while the young Alexander de Meo, the most brilliant of all the early Fathers, took over the chair of theology. Then, within a short while, Alphonsus himself left Ciorani to take up residence at Pagani which was more convenient to Naples and a more suitable centre for the general administration of the Congregation. His presence helped to stabilise the students after the traumatic eighteen months of Muscari's sojourn among them.

– III –

Alphonsus' difficulties with the Bourbon régime were typical of the restrictions experienced by the Church throughout the Kingdom. Cardinal Spinelli, whose royalist sympathies were well known, and whose readiness to make concessions to Charles and Tanucci had earned him the unpopularity of the more militant church group, ultimately found conditions intolerable. As a response to the flood of errors circulating in Naples, he was finally driven to take action in a number of cases which were completely within his jurisdiction. But his actions aroused the fury of the regalists, some, even among the clergy and the bishops who branded his pastoral measures as smacking of the worst days of the Spanish Inquisition. Despite his protestations to the King that his one concern was for purity of doctrine and the extirpation of error with no anti-royalist prejudice whatsoever, Charles III, at the instigation of Tanucci, published a series of decrees which formalised the incursion of the Bourbon administration into matters of purely ecclesiastical competence. Bishops, for instance, were forbidden to proceed in matters of doctrine against any ecclesiastic without the authorisation of the King and his ministers; no church could be built without royal permission — this, in the name of the poor, by the very same monarch who lavished millions on the royal palaces at Capodimonte, Portici, Caserta, and on the opera house of San Carlo. Finally, the Cardinal, finding his position untenable, departed unceremoniously for Rome at the end of 1749, leaving the church of Naples without its pastor. The whole affair was a bitter disappointment for Benedict XIV, who had been as conciliatory as he could with the Neapolitan court.

The absence of an archbishop proved disastrous for the diocese of Naples. From all sides, requests went to Rome to Spinelli, begging him to return to attend to the spiritual needs of his diocese — from the different missionary and religious societies, from ecclesiastics of influence like Father Pepe. To this chorus Alphonsus added his voice in a forceful letter; where the interest of souls was in question he was fearless. He challenged Spinelli's conscience since there was a well-grounded suspicion that Spinelli's motives for not returning were connected basically with his fear of compromising the political fortunes of his relatives:

> I trust that your Eminence is not going to abandon the Church in Naples. Do you know what I would like to be able to do? Even though I am a poor ignorant nobody (*un povero sciocco*) I would like to have the opportunity of speaking with your Eminence's confessor and make him understand the grave harm your absence is causing and which will increase with your continuing absence. For my part, I think that it is the sins of the people which are preventing your Eminence and your confessor from realising this.[8]

The necessity of praying for the spiritual welfare of the capital became a recurring theme in Alphonsus' letters from now on, as he witnessed the public decline of morality and the loss of fervour among the clergy. 'Pray especially for Naples', he asked his penitent, Mother Mary of Jesus, a Carmelite of Ripacandida, 'where, according to reports, there are now many atheists who deny the existence of God.' After five years of exile Spinelli finally handed his resignation to the King in February 1754, and, a few weeks later, the Pope announced the translation of archbishop Antonio Sersale from Taranto to fill the vacancy, creating him a cardinal at the same time. No sooner was the new Cardinal Archbishop enthroned in his see than Alphonsus wrote to him from Pagani; they had been companions in the Apostolic Missions for many years and had conducted missions together throughout the Kingdom:

Your Eminence,

Since my health does not allow me at the moment to do anything more, I am writing this letter to greet you as an old friend and now, your son and subject. There is no need for me to assure your Eminence of the joy I felt at the announcement of the election of the most worthy person of your Eminence to the government of the Church of Naples. But you can imagine it yourself.

I regret that your Eminence will no longer find the clergy of Naples as you left them; you will find, instead, a clergy in ruins, and as a consequence, the people in ruins as well. You will find, in particular, that the spirit of those presenting themselves for ordination has deteriorated. Still worse is the condition of the three congregations of missionary priests through whose efforts, for so many years, the standard of the Neapolitan clergy was maintained until they became an example for the whole Kingdom and indeed, one could say, for the whole world. Now, it would move you to tears, to see how these congregations have declined.

I trust that Jesus Christ has sent your Eminence here to remedy the whole situation. I hope to see realised once more the days of St Charles Borromeo who preached to the people of Milan with such profit. I look forward to seeing your Eminence preach to the people of Naples in the same way. Who can describe the good the preaching of the pastor of the flock achieves? Your Eminence was such an excellent preacher in your early days as a missioner. Now, I say, I hope to have the consolation of knowing that you are preaching once more in Naples.

Pardon my boldness, but I have no other motive in writing all this than the glory of Jesus Christ. Your Eminence would do great good if you ordered a mission to be held throughout Naples and if you were to preach yourself in at least two or three places. This is important during the first years of your episcopacy. And you should even give the spiritual exercises to the assembled clergy, urging them to be assiduous in attending the clergy conferences and observing the rules of their clerical societies. Exhort them also to continue their zeal for the missions since the whole Kingdom was helped by the missions given by the Naples clergy.

And make those for ordination understand well that they must either show signs of a genuine vocation or they should remove their soutanes. The Church is shedding tears over the ruin caused to her because many are admitted to ordination without true vocations. Make them understand further that your Eminence will not admit them to ordination unless they have been well tested, not merely in their knowledge, which is important certainly, but, also, in their conduct and their ecclesiastical spirit, which is more important still.[9]

Sersale received this letter with humility. He went personally soon afterwards to Pagani, accompanied by the bishop of Cava, Mons. Borgia, and the bishop-elect of Amalfi, Mons. Antonio Puoti, to consult with Alphonsus on the affairs of his diocese and of the Church in the Kingdom of Naples in general. From now until his declining years, Alphonsus was, by far, the most influential priest in the whole of the Kingdom, one whose advice was sought on all sides and on every problem by Cardinals, bishops, ministers of the Court as well as by priests and nuns whose consciences he directed.

The troubled state of church-state relations existing in Naples and the possibility that at any moment the government in anger or, out of mere caprice, might create serious problems for the Congregation determined Alphonsus to seek a foundation outside the area of Bourbon influence; he felt that at any moment Tanucci, whose opposition to religious orders had become an obsession, might strike. As early as 1751, he had set his mind on a foundation in the papal states — the appointment of Muscari was not altogether a subterfuge to secure his removal from the house of studies — but his great friend, Mons. Borgia of Cava, urged him strongly to go to Beneventum instead. The duchy of Beneventum had been a papal enclave for centuries and though geographically situated right in the heart of the Kingdom of Naples, it was free from Bourbon influence; the Fathers from Beneventum could conveniently be employed on the missions in Naples as well. The archbishop of Beneventum, Mons. Pacca, a prelate of great holiness of life, was enthusiastic about welcoming the missionaries to his diocese. A foundation was agreed upon in the little mountain town of Sant'Angelo à Cupolo, less than ten miles from the episcopal city. While the new monastery was in course of construction, the archbishop placed a summer residence, belonging to Cardinal Orsini, at the disposal of the missionaries and here, in April 1755, Father Villani and Brother Gennaro Nola took up residence. Villani and his companions began their ministry of preaching and hearing confessions in the local churches until such time as their own monastery and church were completed. The archbishop considered the presence of the Redemptorist missionaries 'a special disposition of providence'. As a sign of his esteem, he brought all the necessary canonical documents in connection with the foundation to Pagani personally, to assure Alphonsus of his favour, begging him at the same time to lead a group of his missioners to Beneventum in November. Alphonsus could not refuse the request despite the fact that he was physically exhausted. The foundation, which marked the escape of his Congregation from the clutches of the Bourbons, depended both on the goodwill of the archbishop and the missionary success of the Fathers. Although they had conducted missions in the diocese on previous occasions, this was the first time they had been summoned to conduct a general mission in the episcopal city itself, which, up to that time, had been a Jesuit preserve.

The summer of 1755 was memorable for the deaths of some of Alphonsus' closest friends. At the end of August, Father Pagano, who had guided his steps towards God for so many years with such gentleness and tact, died at the age of eighty-five, in Naples; a few weeks later word came from Foggia of the death of Mother Celeste Crostarosa, whose visions at Scala had been instrumental in bringing the Congregation of the Most holy Redeemer into existence. And then in October, Brother Gerard Majella died at Caposele, acclaimed on all sides as a saint and a miracle-worker. Although they had never lived for long together in the same community and had met, in fact, only a few times, Alphonsus was well aware of his reputation and called him a modern St Paschal Baylon. He immediately set in motion the machinery for collecting the facts of his life with a view to the introduction of his cause.

But these losses were slight compared with the news of the serious illness of his mother which reached him on the eve of his departure for Beneventum. He had gathered twenty of his own Congregation and two diocesan priests to begin the missionary campaign. Having instructed the missioners to proceed to Beneventum he immediately left for Naples. No matter how important was the mission in Beneventum for the future of his Congregation, or his obligation to Mons. Pacca, his first duty lay with his mother. In Naples, he spent three days at her bedside, praying with her, consoling her in her anxieties and scruples of conscience. Both Cajetan and Hercules were also present and to Cajetan he confided her last days. He also left Brother Francis Tartaglione in the house to be of any assistance he could. The archbishop sent his own carriage to Naples for Alphonsus to bring him to Beneventum when his family duty was completed. Alphonsus opened the mission in the cathedral on Sunday 16 November and asked the congregation to pray for his mother in her final illness. Hercules kept him informed of her condition and to his great joy he learnt that her scruples, which had so tormented her, were calmed; her conscience was at peace. A few days later, a courier from Naples brought the news that his mother had died. He informed his companions very calmly of the fact as they sat down at table. '*Sia lodato Gesù Cristo*, my mother has gone to heaven.' And he asked them to be good enough to celebrate Mass next morning for the repose of her soul.[10]

The Beneventum mission was crowned with success; the zeal of the missioners, their assiduity in the confessionals, were a revelation to both clergy and people. 'Beneventum did not realise until then what zealous men really were, nor the power of God's grace working through them.' Even the Pope heard about the phenomenal success of the work and sent his congratulations personally through Cardinal Orsini. The success of the mission confirmed the archbishop in his wish for a Redemptorist foundation. Work on the new monastery and church at Sant'Angelo continued under the guidance of the Brothers, one of whom, tragically, lost his life in an accident on the site. At times, Alphonsus allowed the novices and students to join the work, which took four years to complete. Finally on 1 September 1760 the new building was ready to receive its first formal community of some twenty Redemptorists — the first foundation where they could live and work, free from the tensions of life created for them by the Bourbons.

The Beneventum mission of 1755 marked the climax of Alphonsus' missionary career; it also showed clear indications that his missionary powers were declining. His voice could not be heard throughout the cathedral. In each of the three succeeding missionary seasons he was to lead a team of missioners for general missions in Amalfi, Salerno and Nola but it was evident to all that his health and his voice were no longer equal to the strain, and at Nola in 1759 he had finally to concede that his days of major missionary effort in the cathedral pulpits and in the confessionals were at an end. His health, which had never been robust, had stood up to the ever increasing demands he made on it until the winter of 1744 when he fell ill in Deliceto. The severity of the winter there and the rigorous conditions in the house, due to lack of income, proved too much for his congenital chest weakness. He took to bed with a serious bronchial catarrh and a high fever which left him severely debilitated. A similar illness manifested itself again in 1746 and in 1748, in a more serious form, when he fell ill in Naples during the negotiations in connection with royal approbation for the Rule. From this time onwards, these same illnesses recur each year in varying degrees of severity and no year was to pass in which he had not to take to bed for some time, either with a fever or acute inflammation of the lungs. 'As soon as winter sets in, my bronchitis reappears; Lent is the worst time of all for me,' he wrote in reply to a preaching invitation from Cardinal Sersale. Each year the attacks became more acute and the after-effects more debilitating, his voice in particular losing its power and resonance. He was convinced that, in this weak state of health, his death could not be far off and from now on he made frequent references in his letters to his approaching end. 'I am now old and in bad health and my day of account is drawing nigh,' he wrote in August 1754 — he was not quite fifty-eight. After his death it was claimed for him by a number of witnesses that he was favoured with the gift of foretelling the future. Fortunately this claim was not made in connection with foretelling the time of his own death, in which he was as much as forty years wide of the mark.

In January 1756, with the arrival of a particularly severe winter, Alphonsus fell ill in Pagani; his lung condition did not yield to the usual treatment, possibly due to his exhaustion after the missionary efforts in Beneventum. In April, he suffered a relapse and fears were expressed for his recovery. Villani was summoned from Sant'Angelo to be in the house in case of his death and to assume the reins of government. He was, at the same time, Alphonsus' director of conscience. During Holy Week it seemed to Alphonsus that his death was imminent and the thought of dying during the week of the liturgical commemoration of Our Lord's Passion and Death was a special consolation for him. At his own request, the prayers for the dying were read to him, and some passages from the work of Father Gisolfi on the joys of heaven. He was at perfect peace, absolutely resigned and united with the sufferings of Jesus. He told the Fathers that he had no worries or anxieties of conscience; as regards his sins, he trusted in the mercy of God that they had been pardoned. The sole worry that disturbed him for a while — only to be firmly dispelled as a temptation — was that in moral theology he had become a Probabilist. The medical crisis passed and Alphonsus was pronounced out of danger, but the convalescence proved long and tedious. For months afterwards, he found it difficult to study or write. Even by the middle of November he had not shaken off the effects of this illness when he set out at the head of a group of fourteen missioners to evangelise Amalfi and the surrounding villages, a nostalgic return to where it had all begun twenty-five years earlier.

The mission proved difficult. Alphonsus delivered some of the strongest sermons he had ever preached, in order to get the message of the mission across to the people who were not readily receptive. He preached the *sentimenti* in the streets where the local prostitutes lived; he appeared in the pulpit with a halter round his neck in the guise of a criminal before God; he led the men in a ceremony of self-flagellation for their sins. In his sermons he inveighed against the prevalent evils of scandals and family feuds, and summoned eight of the wealthiest families to a ceremony of public reconciliation in the cathedral, in an effort to establish an atmosphere of peace in the parish. He felt that the unrestrained life of pleasure and amusement for which Amalfi was a byword was at the root of much of the irreligious spirit of the place. He succeeded in getting many of the young men and girls of the city to bring their musical instruments — the *tamburi* and the *calascione*, both of arabic origin — along to the square, where they were burnt in public. A delighted father, Don Giro di Afflitto, recounted how he, personally, brought along the two *tamburi* of his daughters, who had refused to hand them over.

Alphonsus spent long hours in the confessional, as, indeed, did all his companions. He was hearing confessions in the chapel of the Immaculate Conception when one of those incidents took place which could only happen in southern Italy. A woman confessed to him that, in order to cure her son of a mild form of epilepsy, she had sought the advice of a fortune teller, who told her that if she swallowed some of the water into which her son fell during his attacks, as well as casting it over her shoulder, the boy would be cured. She carried out the instructions of the gypsy. Alphonsus remonstrated with her for her superstition, and told her to go away and meditate on her lack of faith, and then return for absolution. Next morning his confessional was crowded as usual, when along came the woman accompanied by her very irate eldest daughter, a *beatella*, Sister Dorothea. She took Alphonsus to task for deferring absolution for her mother — and did so all in public and with absolutely no inhibitions. Furthermore, she insisted, despite the crowd of penitents who surrounded his box, that Alphonsus should deal with her mother first and grant her absolution without further delay — *ecco la mamma; fatela passare*. Capitulation was the only prudent course and the penitent of the previous day was immediately granted absolution. The events of this famous mission passed into the folklore of the area. At the various processes in preparation for his canonisation, witnesses from Amalfi came forward to recount these and other stories of what had occurred. It was claimed that Alphonsus prophesied vocations to the priesthood and religious life for some, and early death for others. When he preached on Our Lady it was said that he was raised from the pulpit in ecstasy and a ray of light shone from the face of the statue of the Mother of God and played around his countenance. He was surrounded by people begging for miracles; they cut pieces from his soutane as relics and took everything that they could lay their hands on, down to his precious snuff-box.

Two years later, in 1758, Alphonsus led a team of about twenty missioners to Salerno, invited there as a result of the enthusiastic reports of the Amalfi mission. In the vast cathedral of San Matteo in Salerno, his voice could not be heard in the aisles and side chapels beyond the pulpit. Many of the Fathers with him made no secret of their displeasure that he continued to assign the night sermon to himself; the priests of the cathedral were dissatisfied while Father Biagio Amarante, the most powerfully-voiced missioner of the Kingdom, was straining at the leash to replace him. But, it was argued by others, Alphonsus was now preaching more by his presence than with his voice; the effect of his presence in the pulpit was such that the confessionals were besieged by penitents who admitted that they were moved to sorrow by his very appearance. Even Father Rizzo, the most articulate member of the group in his demands that Alphonsus should not be allowed to monopolise the *Predica Grande*, was the first to acknowledge the effect of his presence in the pulpit, judging by the harvest they reaped in the confessional. But there was no gainsaying the very clear signs that Alphonsus' missionary career was coming to an end. The following year, 1759, he led his missionary colleagues for the last time in a formal general mission, appropriately enough in the cathedral of Nola, a city which was known to be the grave of many a missionary reputation. Alphonsus had preached there on many different occasions with varying degrees of success. The people were demanding in their expectations of visiting missioners, and Alphonsus was the first to admit that the novena he preached there in 1756, in honour of the Immaculate Conception, had been a failure. The memory of this debacle remained so fresh among the missioners that the novena of the Immaculate Conception in Nola was regarded as the one apostolic assignment to be avoided at all costs. On his arrival in Nola at the head of a large missionary group in February 1759, Alphonsus assigned the evening sermon to himself. But after a few days it became clear, even to himself, that he was unequal to the task and Father Amarante, who had hoped to replace him at Salerno, was given the task on this occasion. Alphonsus went to a smaller church where he preached to a select group of nobles and military officers. He had led his missioners for the last time and preached his last formal *Predica Grande*. Although he continued to undertake individual preaching engagements, especially in Naples and more particularly to special groups such as the university students and military officers, his days as a missioner in the sense of leading some twenty Fathers in a general missionary offensive were over. He was sixty-three and the years had taken their toll.

– IV –

In 1752 Don Giuseppe Jorio, superior of the Pavone missionary society in Naples, received a request for his missioners to undertake a mission in Monteforte in Irpinia, which he was unable to accept. He replied to the mayor of the town who had requested the mission, recommending Alphonsus: 'Don Alphonsus de Liguori is the foremost missioner of the Kingdom, for his knowledge and holiness of life, as well as for his other qualifications.' For over thirty years Alphonsus had dedicated his life to every type of missionary work throughout Naples and the country areas of the Kingdom; his experience was unrivalled and he had come to occupy a position of eminence in this pastoral field which no one could challenge. In a century which produced great popular missionary preachers such as Francis Jerome, Leonard of Port Maurice, Louis Grignion de Montfort and Paul of the Cross, he takes his place among the greatest.

The main outline of Neapolitan missionary methods had been well established by the time Alphonsus began his priestly ministry with the Apostolic Missions. However, he soon came to experience the inadequacies of the system he had inherited. Consequently, from the very outset of his own missionary efforts with his Scala companions, he found himself cast in the role of an innovator, a fact which was at the root of much of the early opposition from the established missionary societies. With Roman approval for his missionary society a reality in 1749, it became imperative to codify the system which had evolved among his followers during the previous twenty years. The Chapter of 1749 set the process in motion, and Alphonsus carried it on over the next ten years, constantly seeking suggestions from his companions out of their shared experiences in the mission academies held in the four houses. There were in existence, as well, a number of excellent missionary handbooks, describing missionary techniques with which Alphonsus and his companions would have been familiar and, among them, the classic work of Philip de Muro, a colleague of bishop Falcoia, *Il Missionario Istruito*. Alphonsus planned a separate missionary handbook for his own priests and, more specifically, for the young priests of the Congregation, to initiate them into a method which was at once distinctive and reflected the spirit of the Congregation. By 1760, his ideas had crystallised sufficiently for him to publish '*Brevi Istruzione degli Exercizi di Missione colle sue Regole e Pratiche*', 'The Exercises of the Missions' — his definitive work on the theology and practice of Redemptorist mission preaching. In his introduction he readily admitted — as he often did to an exaggerated degree — his debt to other writers and especially to de Mura, but no protestations can minimise the originality of what he wrote.[11]

Alphonsus saw a mission as a great pastoral instrument for the reform of the lives of the faithful and for the maintenance of their fervour. If he announced the purpose of the mission as the conversion of sinners, he did not do so in any narrow context; he understood conversion to mean not only the reconciliation of the inveterate sinner, but also the deepening of christian life, the fuller understanding of the christian message, and that firmer adhesion to Christ which resulted from the mission exercises. For him, a mission was the continuation, in the locality visited by the missioners, of the work of Christ the Redeemer in all its facets. He was convinced that missions, as an activity of the apostolate, were not merely something useful, a spiritual luxury, but that they were necessary and not only for country districts — even though these would be given priority — but for large centres of population such as Naples, Salerno, Foggia and Beneventum, as well. The simple preaching of the word of God, the wealth of doctrinal instruction and advice for the living of one's christian life in whatever life-situation one found oneself, the frequentation of the sacraments in the course of the mission, all combined, in his view, to prepare Christians to co-operate with the action of God's grace in their lives. He was totally convinced that this extraordinary proclamation of the Word of God was worthy of any sacrifice.

Much of what he wrote and legislated for reflected, inevitably, the religious and social conditions peculiar to Bourbon Naples and which would not have applied in other regions of Europe, perhaps, not even in other areas of Italy. One of these was the problem of sacrilegious confessions. Alphonsus stated 'that this was an abuse which was widespread in small country areas and which sends many souls to their damnation'. The arrival of a group of priests unacquainted with the people, removed one of the greatest psychological obstacles to the fruitful reception of the sacrament of penance. The ministry of the confessional was central to the success of the mission. Alphonsus urged the Fathers to be mild and patient with the people in the confessional — this was the pervading spirit of all his moral writings. If the Fathers grew tired and their nerves were on edge they were to leave the confessional and walk around for a short while rather than risk losing their tempers. He urged them never to discourage sinners in any way; the function of the confessor was rather to encourage people in every way, no matter how deep they may have been sunk in sin. He laid down that the confessors should be available in the confessionals during a mission for seven hours a day and he frequently went round the church to see that they were in attendance. His own patience in the confessional was remarkable; it was there that he achieved his greatest triumphs over his natural impetuosity and irritability. It is revealing that he described the confessional as *una lima sorda*, a file which silently but painfully smooths the irritability of one's character. At the end of his missionary career he claimed that he could not remember ever having dismissed a penitent without granting absolution.[12] While his preference was for those in serious sin who had grave need of the ministrations of an understanding confessor, he also knew the value of this sacrament for those who were endeavouring to lead a life of close union with God. Some of his confreres were not slow to chide him for the amount of time he was prepared to devote to the confessions of women. His reply was to the point:

> I do not say as some do — and in this they go to extremes — that it is a waste of time to devote oneself to the cultivation of pious women. I say that it is a work very pleasing to God to guide souls to perfection and for this reason I exhort and beg priests that when they come across someone, man or woman, who lives free from serious sin and is inclined to piety, they should do all they can to help them along the road of divine love in which consists all holiness.[13]

To those who objected that missions did not achieve lasting results, that people lapsed back rapidly into the same vices which the missioners had endeavoured to eradicate, Alphonsus replied, 'Whoever has had experience in these matters knows full well how many family feuds are healed during a mission, how many evil practices are rooted out, how much restitution is made, how much hatred is dispelled and, above all, how many sacriligeous confessions are rectified. Many return to God and persevere in grace until the end of their lives; and many others, if they do relapse into their old sinful ways, at least persevere for some time, perform their Easter duties and, as a result of the grace of the mission, confess their sins before death.'

Since he envisaged a mission as a continuation of the work of Redemption he insisted that the missioners should enter the place where the mission was to be preached, inspired by only one motive, the salvation of souls. He saw his missioners, as he expressed it, in the vanguard of the Lord's army, the shock troops against the forces of Hell. They were to be prepared to face all dangers and even death itself, in the service of Christ, who gave the supreme example of charity. Patient tolerance of the difficult conditions which they encountered in the villages was the minimum requirement. The poverty they experienced, the conditions in which they had to live, the cold in the churches, the ignorance and uncouthness of many of the people, the unpleasantness of dealing with them, demanded great sacrifices; ministering to the '*procuoi*' — the word used among the missionaries to designate the wandering herdsmen of southern Italy — called for constant heroism. Some of their experiences were hardly credible. On one occasion, Alphonsus and his companions buried the dead of a village, carrying them to the graveyard on their shoulders. Another incident, which Alphonsus himself related to one of the Fathers on his return to the monastery, was of such a nature that the Father would not dare commit it to writing. Later, he tantalisingly referred to it simply as 'Alphonsus recounted one incident to me which deprived me of sleep for several nights'. On account of the primitive conditions prevailing in the rural areas, Alphonsus emphasised to his companions that much of the benefit which it was hoped to achieve, would be negatived if the missioners did not enjoy both the sympathy and the respect of the people. They were not to appear among them as ecclesiastical lords or aristocrats, hence the importance of the poverty of their dress. *Milorderia* — a word Alphonsus used frequently — in dressing was to be avoided at all costs. They were not to travel by luxury coaches which were part of the trappings of the nobility. If the place to be missionised was near, the Fathers walked to it; if it was at some distance, they went on horseback. Alphonsus himself usually rode side-saddle, *al femminile*; when on occasions he drove in a *galesso*, a modest single-seated conveyance widely used by ordinary people, some of his colleagues complained and demanded similar privileges for themselves. The journey was interspersed by silence and prayer and at times by the singing of hymns. As they neared the place for the mission, the crucifix was raised aloft at the head of the missionary cavalcade, the litany of Our Lady was recited and, as they entered the parish, the Benedictus hymn. On arrival at the church they went immediately to the Blessed Sacrament and as the people usually followed them, one of the missioners would take advantage of this to address them in the name of the whole missionary band. As occasion offered, they might stop in the village *piazza* or at the intersection of the streets to begin the *sentimenti* introducing the mission and its purpose.

The missioners went in large groups, at times more than twenty together; eleven or twelve was the ordinary complement. In this was included, however, a Brother who attended to the material needs of the missioners, and, on certain occasions, novices and students who recited the Rosary or taught catechism to the children under the supervision of the Fathers. Young Bernard Apice was so successful in his catechising when he accompanied the Fathers on a mission to Gragnano, near his home town of Castellamare, that he was granted the privilege of preaching to the children. The missioners lodged in a house or building placed at their disposal by the local municipality — who frequently engaged and remunerated the missioners — or by the local bishop or clergy. Where they stayed became, in all but name, a temporary 'monastery'; as many of the religious exercises such as the recitation of the breviary, meditation in common, reading at meals, as were compatible with the proper conduct of the mission, were continued. In the social conditions that prevailed the conduct of the missioners was closely scrutinised; it was imperative that no breath of scandal should attach to them. In a mission in Ferino, a priest from Naples, accompanying the missioners, was slightly free in his relations with some of the local 'devout women' designated to assist the missioners. In the intriguing phrase of Father Zampoli he became *un poco domesticato*. Alphonsus was aware of his conduct and refused to take him along again. He was particularly rigorous in his insistence on the simplicity of the missioners' table during their stay; the food was to be the simple food of the people with no exceptions made for luxuries of any description. If the priests of the place wished to share the missioners' table they were also to share the missioners' fare which, in many instances, guaranteed that they dined alone. The standard of food on the missions was one of the points about which Alphonsus seems to have developed a definite complex; another, as we shall see, was the use of an ornate style of preaching. He allowed a simple *minestra di cicorie* or *rapa*, followed by un *bolito di carne* or some ordinary dish such as *castagne cotte* but nothing further. The very sight of any form of *dolce* (dessert) on the missioners' table enraged him. His reasoning was that if the people imagined for one moment that the missioners were living in luxury and eating delicacies, they would be scandalised. Chicken, he held in particular horror — apparently in rural areas it was regarded as the food of the nobility. In Saragnano, the Fathers were served on one occasion with a local dish of minced chicken, *polli spezzati*, known in dialect as *teano*, which he sent back, untouched, to the dismay of the missioners; even the ubiquitous Neapolitan *pizza* met a similar fate on several occasions.

Alphonsus recommended that there should be a mission every three years and not merely in the large centres of population but also in the very smallest *casale* or *frazione*. This he insisted on, against the practice of the other missionary societies who held their missions in one main centre, summoning the people from the smaller centres to attend. It was a cardinal point in his method that the missioners should go to the people and not vice versa. During the course of the mission in a large centre, or sometimes at the end of it, three or four Fathers went to the smaller centres to preach and to hear the confessions of the people. It was these isolated centres, hidden away in the mountains with their own local priest, which needed, most of all, the presence of a visiting missioner. The mission season began with the coming of the gentle autumn rains after the harvest and continued right through the Christmas season until the heats of June made further missionary work impossible. In certain churches there was a break during Lent if the parish had a foundation to provide a special Lenten preacher, which was another problem area.

The various functions of the mission were distributed among the Fathers according to seniority and their personal gifts. First in prestige, if not in importance, came the *Predica Grande* or evening sermon followed by the *catechismo grande* or formal instruction of the people which, in Alphonsus' opinion, was of paramount importance. The recitation of the rosary was often entrusted to one of the students or novices or to the preachers of the *fervorino* after the sermon. There was also the exercise of the morning meditation with the people, as well as the preaching of the spiritual exercises to the clergy and to the sisters of whatever convents happened to be in the district. And it often happened that some Father was brought along with no specific function beyond — according to the quaint explanation of the chronicler — that of giving good example; Father Giovanni Rizzo, as often as not, found himself cast in this role. As the missionary cavalcade made its entry into the village the church bells rang out and in some places, according to their civil status the sound of cannon was heard as well. There were parishes, of course, where the reception was less than cordial, due to the fact that the inspiration for the arrival of the missioners came either from the bishop or the local municipal authorities against the wishes of the local clergy. In Santa Tecla and in Conca, in the diocese of Salerno, the parish clergy declared that there was no room to accommodate the missioners and refused to receive them or give them hospitality. Undismayed, Alphonsus, who had been directed by the bishop to preach the mission, took up residence in the few rooms attached to the sacristy of the church. Another irate pastor met them threateningly with a club in hand. Alphonsus, unperturbed, continued to ride towards the church, singing the Litanies and with the Crucifix held aloft. But, in the generality of cases, the welcome was cordial. Alphonsus was insistent that the missioners were to greet the people with all courtesy and to raise their hats in response to their salutations. 'In this way', he declared, 'you will attract the people very much and gain their confidence — especially of the country folk, who are not accustomed to being taken notice of by persons of higher social rank than themselves. Reply to their greetings by saying '*sia lodato Gesù e Maria* (praised be Jesus and Mary). And if, by chance, we are not saints at home in the monastery, let us show ourselves to be such outside it, not, indeed, to deceive or to be hypocrites, but in order that, by our example, all those we evangelise may give themselves to God'.[14]

To bring the exercises of the mission to the attention of the people as well as to encourage them to attend, the missionaries went around the villages during the early days of the mission, preaching short exhortations in the market square or in isolated localities. At night they went around again in procession, with Crucifix and lighted torches, chanting the Litany of Our Lady, stopping before taverns or wherever the men of the village were likely to be gathered, preaching to them the necessity of penance and conversion — the *sentimenti di notte*. This was to last no more than fifteen minutes and concluded on the last night with the *sentenza terribile*, a warning to those who refused the occasion of grace, of the terrible consequences of their obduracy. From experience the missioners knew that it was only after these *sentimenti di notte* had been preached for four or five consecutive days that the mission began to take hold of the people. A dramatic variant of the *sentimenti di notte* was used only in particularly tough areas where the people showed themselves indifferent to the exercises of the mission. Without allowing their presence to be known, the missioners stationed themselves at vantage points throughout the village; when they were at their posts an insistent ringing of the church bells startled the people and gave the signal for the various missioners to preach the *sentimenti di semina* — a stern warning of the judgments of God against those who refused to listen to his voice during the mission. A short while later a further ringing of the bells signalled the end of the *semina*, leaving the last phrases of the *sentenza terribile* echoing in the silence of the night.

A considerable amount of mission time was devoted to the doctrinal instruction of the people, who were often ignorant of the very fundamentals of the faith. There were places where Alphonsus and his companions found it necessary to enquire of those who came to confess, whether they knew the bare minimum of the creed, sufficient for the valid reception of the sacrament. The catechetical instruction of the young people and a special series of sermons for them took place during the day; it was quite common for the missioners to find young adults in their twenties who had not made their first Communion. Catechetical instruction of the adults was reserved for the evenings when they had finished the labours of the day, usually in the fields. Alphonsus regarded the catechetical element as of paramount importance, more important than the main sermon of the night. He told his young missioners, as he initiated them into mission practice, that it was more important to instruct the people than to preach to them; a good mission catechist showed a rarer talent than a thunderous preacher.[15] A mission was, for the great majority of the ordinary uneducated rural inhabitants, the sole opportunity of learning the truths of religion. This doctrinal instruction consequently took on a predominantly practical approach with the emphasis firmly on those moral imperatives necessary for the conduct of their lives as Christians — prayer, the sanctification of the day, the avoidance of the occasions of sin and especially the widespread practice among those who were engaged to be married, of living together before the marriage was celebrated. This abuse and the immorality to which it gave rise was the object of the fiercest condemnation from all ecclesiastical authorities throughout the Kingdom; the sin was reserved in every diocese. Naturally, this problem formed an important part of the missionary preaching and moral instruction of Alphonsus and his companions. Interestingly, their strongest condemnation was reserved for parents, whose anxiety to secure their daughters' marriage outran their interest in their spiritual welfare.[16]

The night sermon or *Predica Grande* lasted, on occasion, for nearly an hour and a half; the themes included the great eschatological realities of Death, Judgment, Hell and Heaven. But contrary to his posthumous reputation, Alphonsus consciously broke away from the 'terror' tradition of the Neapolitan mission, by insisting that on every mission, no matter how short, there should always be sermons or at least sections of sermons centring on the Love of God, the Passion of Jesus Christ, Prayer, and the Patronage of Our Lady. His main innovation as a missioner was to de-emphasise the terror element — the *verberare terroribus* of St Augustine — which was a living tradition in eighteenth-century Italy and nowhere more so than in Naples. He was well aware of the grace of the 'fear of the Lord'; at times, it was the only means of awakening those whose lives had been spent in sin. It was an initial step on the path to friendship with God, at times a very necessary step, and one which no other consideration might have been able to achieve. Maybe it could also be argued that it was particularly suited to the Neapolitan psychology which could be easily moved on the one hand and was ready to discount much of what had been said, on the other. Despite the fact that he had been trained himself in the Neapolitan tradition, Alphonsus came to realise that conversions based wholly on fear were not lasting unless they continued on the firmer foundation of the love of God:

> On a mission, the sermons on judgment, hell, etc. are useful. They inspire fear and even terror and, of course, they cause a great stir. But conversions merely from this terror do not last — these motives are soon forgotten. But whoever is converted through consideration of the

> love of Jesus Christ, their conversion is more genuine and lasting. Fear will not achieve what love cannot achieve. Sometimes a sermon which causes fear can be dismissed with a shrug of the shoulder but one spark of the love of God is sufficient to burn up everything else.'[17]

He laid it down as a principle for his missioners that the test of the genuine preacher was to leave his congregation inflamed with the love of God after *every* sermon, even those on the great Eternal Truths:

> Even in the sermons which inspire fear, such as the justice of God and the number of sins, one should always be careful not to dishearten sinners but always to leave them with motives of confidence for pardon.'[18]

His own two favourite themes were hatred for sin and love for Jesus Christ. As a motive for enkindling the love of God in the hearts of the congregation during a mission, he used the Passion of Our Lord, a sermon which he never omitted and which he recommended earnestly to his colleagues. As a bishop, he sent a circular letter to all the superiors of his own congregation as well as to the superiors of the various missionary bodies working in his diocese, urging them all to insist in their sermons on the love we should have for Jesus Crucified. With this in mind, he commissioned a large realistic painting of the Crucifixion from an artist in Naples; since the painter failed to measure up to his expectations, Alphonsus personally added more realistic touches of blood and torn flesh which left little to the imagination. His purpose was to portray in painting the words of scripture about Our Lord being covered with wounds for love of us. He then had several copies made and distributed to the houses for the use of the different missionary groups. Towards the end of the mission, the painting was carried through the church for the veneration of the people and then brought to the pulpit in a solemn procession while a Father preached a *ferverino* on the love of Jesus Christ as shown in his Passion. Alphonsus understood well the psychology of his Neapolitans, their emotional reactions, their tenderness. It became axiomatic among the missioners that if some sinner resisted the grace of the mission during the early days of preaching he would repent infallibly after the crucifix ceremony — *dopo il Crocifisso*.

To envisage a mission merely in terms of the confessional or to see it mainly as promoting the minimum of religious practice demanded by the observance of the commandments of God and of the Church — worthy though such achievements may be — is to do scant justice to Alphonsus' concept of what a mission should be. His idea was to make a mission a complete work of spiritual renewal, hence the emphasis he placed on the exercises of the 'devout life'. The *vita devota* was the great speciality of the Pii Operai and very dear to Falcoia. Alphonsus and his missionaries were to widen its scope considerably and to allot more time to it than had been customary. The very first General Chapter in 1743 highlighted the importance to be placed on the exercises of the 'Devout Life' in the mission preaching of the Congregation. By 1760, Alphonsus had perfected his concept of this aspect of a mission; he altered much of what he had inherited from Falcoia and, at the same time, added considerably to it. In the first place, the exercises of the 'Devout Life' were no longer to be an afterthought, an addition to the mission, as it were, after the formal closing. They were to be integrated into the mission itself; the mission would not be complete without them. 'I maintain', he wrote, 'that the *exercizio della Vita Devota* is most useful because one is dealing with the means of perseverance and with inflaming hearts with love towards Jesus Crucified.'[19]

The main feature of the 'vita devota' was mental prayer. The people were first instructed on how to reflect on some aspect of the life of Our Lord and then to pray, in their own words, for their own needs. This instruction took place on two or three occasions, usually in the evening before the sermon. Then came the actual practice, the meditation made in common, directed by a priest from the pulpit. Alphonsus introduced this meditation in common from the earliest years of his missions. He had to overcome considerable difficulties, mainly due to lack of co-operation from the local clergy, who, to excuse their own lack of zeal, pleaded that this exercise was beyond the spiritual capacity of their people. To the meditation on the mysteries of Christ's life from the Incarnation to the Passion, Alphonsus then added the practice of a formal daily visit to the Blessed Sacrament in which he urged the use of his own book of *Visits*. He promoted special devotions in church on Thursdays in honour of the Blessed Sacrament; for those who could not come to church, he suggested that the church bells should be rung, that the people should place lighted candles in the windows of their homes and recite together the *Tantum Ergo* or some other hymn in honour of Our Lord in the Blessed Sacrament. The practice of a daily visit to the Blessed Sacrament and the use of his book of *Visits* soon spread throughout the whole Kingdom. From there, in the footsteps of the members of his Congregation, it spread throughout the whole Church, becoming in the 150 years after his death, a characteristic aspect of Catholic devotion. The final element of the 'Devout Life' was the establishing of sodalities for different sections of the people — priests, young women, men, the nobility. All this convincingly contradicts those who assert, without any research into the past, that mission preaching constituted a mutilated form of Christianity; indeed, the opposite was true.

The Neapolitans were an emotional and demonstrative people who loved externals, processions, statues, lights and incense. In church they were totally uninhibited, following the preacher's exposition with expressions of their approval, breaking into tears at the description of Our Lord's sufferings, groaning and sighing as he enumerated their sins which had crucified their Saviour. A powerful preacher could work them up to any heights of emotion he wished. There were, as a consequence, a number of quite macabre ceremonies in use throughout the missions in Bourbon Naples, styled *pandette*, which are almost unintelligible to non-Latin peoples, and which provided a rich source of ridicule and cynicism for non-Catholic tourists from northern Europe on the Grand Tour in the eighteenth century.

During the sermon on Death, for example, the preacher would bring a skull into the pulpit which he used as a visual aid and which he apostrophised dramatically; during the sermon on Hell the lights were extinguished and a painting of a condemned soul was carried in procession throughout the church between blazing torches and was finally placed beside the preacher in the pulpit, where all could see it. Then, there were the penitential processions in which the people walked in penitential garb with ashes on their heads and, at times, a noose around their necks, to signify that by their sins they were no better than common criminals. And the practice of self-flagellation for men during the mission was still in common use. All these were the stock-in-trade of an authentic Neapolitan mission. Alphonsus was cautious in the use of these ceremonies, leaving the decision to the superior of the mission on each occasion. He was known to have employed the death's head and the noose only on particularly difficult missions. He forbade, in general, the ceremony of the cursing of unrepentant sinners, when the preacher, wearing a black stole, holding in his hand a burning torch and employing the high-pitched third tone of the Neapolitan preacher, would call down maledictions from heaven on the unrepentant. This terrifying ceremony found little favour with the majority of his missionary companions but he permitted its use and even recommended it in quite exceptional circumstances. He felt that it could be used both in Santa Maria à Capua and Marcianise where the sin of blasphemy had become an inveterate public scandal. Instead of this ceremony he usually followed the example of Father Sarnelli and adopted the equally exotic practice of the *strascino di lingua*, in which the men made crosses on the floor of the church with their tongues, in reparation for their sins of blasphemy. More easily intelligible was the ceremony for the Reconciliation of enemies and of families whose feuds were public knowledge and a cause of scandal to the christian community. After a special sermon, the *sentimento di pace*, preached by the *padre paciere*, one of the missioners specially designated for this purpose, the feuding factions were brought together in front of the Crucifix and, before the assembled Congregation, forgave each other and embraced in a sign of peace.

– V –

Sacred eloquence in Naples in the eighteenth-century had not escaped the effects of the baroque movement in art, literature and architecture. The florid style, the rich decoration, the unregulated exuberance which characterised the baroque altars of Bernini and Pozzo, had their counterpart in the language and style used in the pulpits of eighteenth-century France, Spain and Italy. The artificial style of preaching which had already evoked a strong reaction in the north of Italy, was still in its hey-day in Bourbon Naples. At its worst, the sermon no longer had any meaning as an explanation of the Gospel message; it had become the vehicle for a display of literary virtuosity, of mastery of phrase and figures of speech, for the use of 'new' words intelligible only to the initiated and which were in the process of being 'canonised' as proper speech by the literary academies, and especially, by the self-appointed monitor of the whole of Italy, the *Accademia della Crusca* in Florence. The *Crusca* advocated the use of words mostly from fourteenth-century Tuscany, thus placing its language beyond the comprehension of the Neapolitan peasant and *lazzaroni*.[20]

The reaction in the north of Italy to this desecration of the pulpit was headed by Father Paul Segneri, S.J., who objected to the pulpit becoming a vehicle for language reform, and the church a literary salon, where the sophisticated assembled to taste the delights of literary ingenuity and of choice Cruscan language, more or less in the same spirit with which they would have attended the literary salons in Paris or Florence. This style of oratory was at its height during the early years of Alphonsus' priestly ministry; his first sermon, as a deacon, on the Good Shepherd, which was banal in its simplicity, was a declaration of his refusal to become part of the movement. The classical occasions for a display of oratorical brilliance were panegyrics and the Lenten sermons, the *Quaresima*; Lent was the liturgical period for which the fashionable preachers waited and prepared. The *quaresimalisti*, or Lenten preachers, were chosen with as much care as the *prima donnas* of the San Carlo; the competition was almost as unrestrained. Some religious orders added certain external solemnities to the designation of their respective preachers, as if they were performing sacred rites of mystical import. The announcement of the names in the various churches of the city took on the aspect of who could provide the greatest attraction, somewhat in the manner of modern film companies outdoing each other in advertising their main protagonists. In certain cities, theatres closed during Lent, not out of a spirit of penance, but because they could not compete with the attraction of the Lenten preachers. Rich foundations, endowing the Lenten courses, abounded in Naples, making them valuable prizes, jealously sought after by the top preachers. This, then, was the background to Alphonsus' decision to forbid his colleagues to preach panygyrics and above all, the Lenten courses. In the first place, they would have been tempted to preach in an affected style and, secondly, they would have aroused the opposition of the clergy thus deprived of a rich source of income.

On these occasions, the antics of the preacher were studied down to the least detail, the modulation of the voice betrayed no personal religious feeling nor imparted any shared religious experience to the congregation; tropes, literary figures, conceits, metaphors, tumbled over one another in a bewildering display. The greatest exponent of this style of preaching was the Capuchin, Father Bernardo Maria Giacchi, whose sermons were published in Venice, shortly after his death in 1744, quickly running into several editions. As we read them now, we realise that we are in a totally different atmosphere from any we know, where little is said in paragraph after paragraph of vapid rhetoric, where strange words, which one could only guess to be some form of Italian, abound, and where there is no application to everyday conduct and just the bare minimum of doctrinal content. The words and language are all. Giacchi became the model for the aspiring young fashionable preachers in Naples and threatened to infect all sections of the ecclesiastical world, even the Apostolic Missions, which had been seen as the strongest bastion against this desecration of the pulpit.

Alphonsus set himself resolutely against this style of preaching. He was not a pioneer in this, as some have made him out to be, but he was one of the strongest supporters of the movement away from Giacchi and, eventually, he became, through his writings and his example, the dominant influence in ridding the pulpits of Naples of this type of oratory. He even disliked the over dramatic style of preaching, with sudden changes of pitch and volume — 'at one moment shouting to the point of breaking a blood vessel, the next, whispering inaudibly'. For him, this style lacked that dignity which should characterise the minister of Christ as he preached the Word of God. He advocated clarity of diction so that the congregation could follow what was said without difficulty. His own style of preaching was completely personal, more a conversation than a formal sermon, and there were few who could rival him in achieving this intimate contact with his congregation. 'We must try to preach as if we were conversing with somebody in a room, urging them to some good work or relating an incident. In this way we preach in a familiar style, without false tones and we preach with results.' Ultimately, he adopted the word 'apostolic' to describe the style he advocated. He did experiment with the famous 'third tone', that artificial inflection of the voice towards the end of sentences, which was characteristic of a certain style of Neapolitan preaching right up to the end of the last century, but Falcoia expressed strong disapproval, with the result that Alphonsus abandoned it and recommended to his own followers that they should abandon it too, but not with much success.

With the exception of the great churches of Naples and the cathedrals such as Salerno and Amalfi, the majority of the churches in which Alphonsus and his missioners preached in the course of their journeys, were small rural churches, at once intimate and easy to be heard in. They were ideally suited to his familiar style. Among his colleagues, Alphonsus' preaching could not compare for vigour with that of Biagio Amarante or Bernard Apice, both of whom were gifted with tremendous voices which resounded through the largest cathedrals of the kingdom. Amarante, who was impatient of Alphonsus' feeble efforts in Beneventum and Salerno and who replaced him finally at Nola, was the classical missioner. He thundered from the pulpit as his voice boomed throughout the largest cathedral. He preached with such whole-heartedness and vigour that, at the end of his sermon, he seemed almost to faint in the pulpit from exhaustion. He perspired profusely, with the result that his soutane appeared, according to Father Landi, 'as if it had been placed in a river'. Highly strung and nervous during his sermon, he was known even to vomit in the pulpit. He spent eight months of each year on the missions and, after a brief return to his monastery, left it immediately for the hot baths at Ischia to recuperate his strength for the next missionary campaign. He died at the early age of forty.

Alphonsus's sermons were simple and eminently practical. He spoke to the people in language they understood, using turns of phrases and expressions in their own local dialect with which they were familiar. Here lay his particular genius as a missioner — 'one must lose oneself in the spirit of the people when preaching to them, otherwise, you get as far as their ears, but you do not touch their hearts'. On one occasion as he was initiating his students into the composition and delivery of sermons, one of them employed a word which was Cruscan in origin. 'All right,' said Alphonsus, 'but do you think that the poor old women on the missions — *le femminnelle* — will understand your Cruscan expression?' If his criterion was not *le femminnelle* then it was *Sabatiello*, the John Doe of Naples.[21] The remarkable effect of his sermons on the people was not due to any tricks of oratory or to pomposity of language or, indeed, to anything extraordinary in what he said; there only remained the obvious sincerity and his authentic holiness of life which christian people could discern by some special power.

Reaction to his preaching varied, of course. Archbishop Pacca of Beneventum came to hear him preach in the cathedral, and expressed considerable disappointment that he could find nothing remarkable in his performance; others, like the visitor from Bari who heard him preach in the basilica of the Spirito Santo in Naples, felt that they had been listening to St Paul. Before ascending the pulpit he spent a long while in prayer, usually in the house where the missioners were staying; to these prayers he frequently added the use of the discipline to bring down God's blessing on what he was to say. And, when the sermon was over, he spent some time in prayer again.

Simplicity, however, and popular expression which Alphonsus advocated so strongly, were never to be made an excuse for roughness or vulgarity of language; he utterly condemned *le parole goffe*. He was careful never to offend the susceptibilities of his congregation in any way and he never descended to vituperation. He forbade his followers to use certain expressions which were the common currency of missioners, as they launched out in attack on sinners — they were never to address them as 'evil' or 'wicked' or call them 'nothing more than baptised Turks', or possessed 'of souls black as pitch', *scellerati, turco battezzato, anima di pece*. He even composed a short Tuscan grammar to help his young missioners preach, not merely simply and in an apostolic manner, but in a grammatically acceptable manner as well. It is arguable, at the same time, that he developed a fixation about preaching style which two well documented incidents illustrate. On the occasion of a visit to Naples in 1747, he was invited, by the superior of the Apostolic Missions, to address the members on the simple apostolic style of preaching which, by their Rule and tradition, they were bound to employ. The influence of Giacchi was already evident among some of the younger priests. He launched out into an attack on Giacchi and what he stood for. 'I hope he saved his soul and I hope to God that he does not have to lament his vanity in purgatory until the day of judgment.' These remarks about Giacchi, who had died just three years before, were greeted with considerable disapproval by a section of his listeners. Eight days later, Alphonsus was back again with the Apostolic Missions, and spoke with even greater vigour on the same point: 'Some of you, I hear, believed I referred to them when I condemned the florid style and method of preaching of Don Giacchi. I considered for a while confessing it, but I did not do so since I realised I have no purpose of amendment,' and he then proceeded to confirm what he had said on the previous occasion.

Something similar took place a few years later in the small church in Pagani, when Father Alexander de Meo was called upon, at short notice, to preach the Saturday sermon on Our Lady, as a replacement for Alphonsus who was indisposed. De Meo lost himself somewhat in a display of learning as he showed how, even before her birth, Mary had been foretold by the oracular utterings of the Sibyls and the Argonauts, which may indeed have been true but was somewhat lost on the country folk of Pagani. Unfortunately for the preacher, Alphonsus entered the gallery of the church just in time to hear mention of the Sibyls; he was appalled. His anger increased as the sermon progressed until he was unable to control himself any longer. He dispatched one of the Brothers down to the church, to summon De Meo from the pulpit. To add to this public humiliation, he ordered De Meo to spend three days in retreat and forbade him to celebrate Mass during them. Both of these incidents were strongly urged against Alphonsus during the process of his canonisation. They are certainly two of the least attractive incidents of his life and none of the attempts made to excuse his conduct, and even to present it in a positive light, carries much conviction. It would have been better to admit simply that on both occasions his anger got the upper hand and that his actions could not be justified. Perhaps, after all, he did confess them, or, at least, should have.[22]

The pulpit in eighteenth-century Italy was a centre of interest in a way which we find it impossible to understand; it was the centre of religious, dramatic and literary experiences for the people and therefore rivalled the theatre and the opera house. In many ways it occupied a position in social life which is held in our contemporary society by the cinema and television screens, with the result that 'pulpit matters' were as much a subject for discussion and critique as cinematic productions are today. Incredibly, the whole question of oratorical style provoked passionate discussion and polemical writings which developed into a major controversy in the middle of the eighteenth-century. The great weight of reputable scholars was on the side of a simple, apostolic, intelligible style of preaching as the only one fitting for the pulpit. In 1750, in a posthumous work, Father Ludovico Muratori of Modena, reputedly the most learned man in Italy, strongly defended the apostolic style, much to the delight of Alphonsus, who, though he dared to cross swords with him on other theological points, quoted him with full approval in his *Exercises of the Missions*. Alphonsus' remarks did not please the professor of Rhetoric and Greek in Gaeta, Father Bandiera, who was at first a Jesuit but later a Servite. He was an ardent admirer of the Cruscan and all it stood for; he even spent hours in the futile exercise of transposing the sermons of Father Paul Segneri from their original Italian 'dialect' into the 'new' Cruscan, and publishing the two versions side by side. Bandiera dared to criticise explicitly Alphonsus' defence of the simple style of preaching. For him, one of the purposes of preaching was to delight the ears of the listeners with the perfection of the choice of words, the roundness of phrases, the rhythm and music of language. A sermon from him became, as it were, a symphony in words, a source not of personal conversion or religious experience but of aesthetic pleasure such as might have been sought in the theatre. Typically, Alphonsus was unable to allow the challenge to go unanswered. Within a few months of learning of Bandiera's criticism he published in Naples *Letter to a Fellow Religious*, in which he insisted on the necessity of preaching the Word of God in a simple apostolic style, intelligible to all, even the most unlettered among the congregation. The 'Letter' was, of course, a literary stratagem to refute Bandiera:

> O God, what a shame it is to see religious ascend the pulpit — even religious belonging to reformed orders — wearing their religious habit, the badge of their mortified lives and the sign that they are aflame with zeal for souls and, as a result, the congregation eagerly expects from them words and thoughts inspired by Divine Love. And then, all they hear is a conglomeration of literary virtuosity, descriptions, balanced phrases and other trivialities, delivered with pomposity and rounded phrases. And, of course, the greater part of the audience understands very little of the sermon and takes away no benefit whatsoever. What a tragedy it is to see so many ordinary people going to these sermons in order to learn what they should do to save their souls, and after listening to the preacher for more than an hour and a half, they find they have learnt nothing. They return home as empty as they arrived and disgusted with themselves for wasting all that time in listening to a sermon which they did not understand.
>
> Muratori says in his book, that he saw country folk listening to a panegyric with their mouths open but he saw clearly that they did not understand as much as one word of it all. And what is the result? These unfortunates, once they realise that what is being preached is beyond them, conceive an aversion for the church and sermons, refuse to attend any more and so remain rooted more firmly than before in their spiritual miseries.[23]

To secure the maximum impact from this 'Letter' Alphonsus sent a copy to all the bishops of the Kingdom, expressing the hope that they would bring it to the notice of their clergy and especially of the *quaresimalisti*, though he was not too hopeful that these would alter their ways:

> My Lord,
>
> Out of compassion for so many unfortunate people who attend church to listen to sermons but get little or no benefit from them since preachers speak in such a florid and involved style and refuse, as they say, to lower themselves to preach the Word of God to the people

according to their capacity to understand, I have printed the present *Letter*, which I have the honour of forwarding to you.

I ask you to deign to glance at it and then to ask your priests, who are appointed to the ministry of preaching, to study it. Please send it to the religious houses in your diocese, urging the superiors to get their subjects, especially those engaged in the ministry of preaching, to read it.

And I beg you to get the Lenten and Advent preachers, in particular, to study it. I know they arrive with their sermons already prepared but who knows but, that on reading this, they may alter something in the future, when they realise the great account they will have to render to God if they do not make themselves intelligible to the ordinary person in their sermons.

CHAPTER ELEVEN

THE THEOLOGICAL WARS 1749–1762

– I –

Those same thirteen years following the papal approbation of his missionary congregation, which witnessed the climax of Alphonsus' missionary efforts, saw the emergence of another side of his apostolic activity. Between 1749 and his consecration as a bishop in 1762 he published over forty-four different works, including his *Moral Theology* and its companion volumes. It is an incredible output, even taking into consideration that he was assisted by a group of his colleagues. And when we take into account that he was at the same time preaching missions and retreats, arranging new foundations, carrying on the ordinary work of the daily administration of his religious order in the face of enormous difficulties, maintaining a voluminous correspondence, and was seriously ill for long periods, we can gain some idea of his spirit of work and his capacity for it. All of his literary activity, in the broadest meaning of that term, was at the service of souls; his writings were as much a part of his apostolate as his preaching in the mountains of Irpinia or his retreats to priests and nuns in Naples. Several times he expressed the hope that his writings would continue to speak and work for the salvation of souls when he could no longer work for them himself.

As a young priest he began to collect his own library of theological works; when he founded his missionary group he had very much at heart the establishment of libraries of ecclesiastical significance in each house. His ideal for his followers was that they should be eager to continue their theological study and to spend their lives among books. The amount of money spent on libraries at a time when the revenues of the houses were totally inadequate, is a measure of his priorities; during his lifetime, the house at Pagani alone spent over 15,000 ducats on books. He set the example of incessant study and he possessed the rare talent of being able to avail of every free moment between other occupations. On missions he took with him the latest publication on theology and when he was able to snatch a few moments from the confessional, he was to be found studying or writing. He claimed that he kept up to date with all the latest developments in every branch of the ecclesiastical sciences, a boast which he made publicly and without fear of contradiction in his *Adnotationes* to Busenbaum and in the *Glories of Mary*. He sent to Naples on learning of any new theological publication, whether orthodox or controversial, and eventually he had his agents, in both Venice and Rome, to forward such works to him. His own publishers, too, Remondini of Venice, eventually kept him supplied with the latest publications and reviews. He availed himself of his visits to Naples — usually to the court or to one of the Ministries — to study in the great libraries of the city; with note-book in hand he was seen in the libraries of the Vincentians, the Oratorians, and of the two Jesuit Houses of the Gesù Nuovo and the Gesù Vecchio. When he was permitted to borrow books from these libraries he scrupulously kept a list to make sure he returned them — a practice to be highly recommended. He read with his pen — his quill — in his hand, taking notes. He had a phenomenal memory for scripture references and for the writings of the Fathers, for incidents from the lives of the saints and the advice they gave. With this went a facility for recall which enabled him to use what he had read to explain or prove his point. Not indeed, that his quotations were always accurate, or word for word, but he was more careful on this point in his theological works and works of controversy than in his purely ascetical and devotional writings. In these latter works he was very often satisfied with the popular collections of quotations from the Fathers and lives of the saints which went under the titles of *Catena*, *Selva* or *Prontuario* and which did not always have the scientific accuracy demanded by modern standards of scholarship.[1]

Since writing was, for him, an apostolic activity he surrounded it, like his preaching, with prayer; much of his Moral Theology was written on his knees. He often studied and wrote for as long as eight or nine hours daily. Yet, not even this assiduity nor his resolution not to waste a moment of time would have enabled him to achieve his phenomenal output unaided; he was assisted in his work by a whole group of collaborators. Father Angelo Ruscigno worked with him in preparing the second edition of his Moral Theology until tubercolosis caused his early death in 1755. Father Pascal Amendolara succeeded him until the same disease carried him to the grave some years later. At various times, Fathers Ferrara, Caione, and the great de Meo worked side by side with him, checking references, studying particularly difficult points in reply to some adversary — at times, even, composing whole tracts, which Alphonsus would then adapt to his own purposes. Willing hands among the students, too, Nigro, Criscuoli, Reale and de Paola came to his study to copy out in more legible script a manuscript which he had completed or to take down one which he dictated to them from his notes. De Paola frequently translated into Latin a manuscript which Alphonsus had prepared in Italian since his Latin was altogether more elegant than Alphonsus' own. On occasions Alphonsus found it necessary to simplify it.

Alphonsus' practice was to make a number of copies of each manuscript all, of course, in long-hand — since he never knew what fate awaited them at the hands of the different censors or by using the precarious expedient of dispatching them by courier to the printers in Naples or Venice. He was enthusiastic in his commendation of what he had written. One work was 'small but juicy' *piccolo ma tutto sugo*, another was a 'golden little volume', and so on. At the same time he contracted most of the occupational diseases of authors — he vented his wrath on the carelessness of printers, he was never content with the final appearance of the finished product, he blatantly played one publisher off against another, he advised those who ventured into print to be ready to be torn asunder. His sanctity and the apostolic motives which prompted his writings did not eradicate any of these endearing human characteristics. In his early days as an author he had the humiliating experience of having to finance the publication of his works and since his own resources were inadequate, friends like Giovanni Olivieri or Don Letizia, from the old *capelle serotine* days, had to come to his assistance. Significantly absent from the list were his own brothers, Cajetan and Hercules. But when the publishers began to realise that his works could be a source of profit to themselves, the twenty or so of them in the capital fought for any manuscript he was ready to send them. They drove Alphonsus to desperation; he called them 'beggars, *pezzenti*', negligent, unskilled and with no respect for authors' rights or the accuracy of his ideas. Indeed, once a work was printed and published in the city, it was fair game for other printers to pirate editions without reference to the author or the original publisher. The *Glories of Mary* was pirated by one well-known printing brigand, Signore Stasi; Alphonsus was enraged at the standard of the work, as he told Stasi in no uncertain terms; it was, he claimed, a down-right disgrace, *vituperio*. And he was then pirated by Migliaccio. When he transferred the publishing of his works to the more reputable Remondini of Venice, the Neapolitan publishers took their revenge by refusing to stock his works or advance their sales in any way. Enraged, Alphonsus, as any self-respecting author would, referred to them as 'those blessed booksellers of Naples, *questi benedetti libraii di Napoli*'. They were the only ones who could drive him to the verge of imprecations![2]

Fortunately, he was completely uninterested in the financial side of his publishing transactions. His sole interest was in the spiritual good he felt his writings could achieve. Many of the works he published in Naples were disposed of below the cost of production. He received no money from his Venetian publisher, Remondini, when he transferred the bulk of his work there but, in return, Remondini, sent him a number of free copies of everything published. Later, by mutual agreement, Alphonsus appointed Father Ferrara and Brother Tartaglione to take up residence in Naples to attend to the sale of Remondini's publications on the understanding that they were given forty per cent commission on their sales.

One of the major complications in connection with the publication of books in Naples was the arbitrariness of the official censorships, both ecclesiastical and royal. For its part, the Bourbon government was extremely sensitive concerning anything remotely touching the royal prerogatives. Alphonsus had to be extremely careful in some of his works not even to mention papal jurisdiction lest this should be interpreted by the royal censors as derogating in some way from the royal omnicompetence. The archiepiscopal curia usually entrusted the censorship of books from the ecclesiastical angle to some of the diocesan or regular clergy of the city; the office of the Cappellano Maggiore, who dealt with the civil censorship, entrusted the revision of works for publication to one of the university professors. Within a few years, the censors began to arrogate to themselves powers which did not belong to their office; they took it upon themselves to refuse publication to works merely because they contained opinions with which they did not agree. Among the ecclesiastical censors there were very definite philo-jansenist and anti-papal tendencies, while the university professors, educated in an atmosphere of regalism, were anxious to curry favour by discovering cryptic anti-royalism in everything from visits to the Blessed Sacrament to Sunday sermons.

Censorship became an instrument of repression. Difficult as things were in the early years of Charles III's reign such difficulties increased enormously as the years went by until they reached intolerable limits after his departure for Spain in 1759. Then, royal decrees prohibited the publishing of books even outside the Kingdom without royal approval, under pain of banishment or two years in the galleys. Alphonsus lived under considerable tension as a consequence of his connections with the Venetian firm of Remondini. There was the further inconvenience caused by the censorship exercised at the Neapolitan frontiers, ostensibly for the purpose of preventing pernicious literature from England, France, Holland and Switzerland from entering the Kingdom. In reality, it was an administrative stratagem to prevent anti-regalist or pro-papal writings from reaching Naples. French and English 'Enlightenment' publications flooded in unchecked. Alphonsus, well-known for his pro-Roman views, was a marked man. He was forced to display remarkable ingenuity and to risk considerable danger in order to get some of his publications through the customs. His reply to the Dominican, Patuzzi, concerning Probabilism, which was printed in Venice, had to be smuggled in, since the Dominicans had secured a royal decree forbidding circulation of the work in Naples. On instructions, Remondini sent the packet containing the publication to the chaplain of the royal fort of Manfredonia on the Adriatic coast in Apulia, Don Scipio Sabatelli, whose despatches would not have been tampered with. From there, the chaplain sent them on secretly to his friend, Alphonsus.

The fact that the main centre for the publication of his books was in Venice caused Alphonsus considerable anxiety. First of all, the manuscript, one of the two or three copies he had made, or on occasions, corrected text of some work already printed in Naples, had to be boxed, either in Pagani or, at a later date, in the diocese of Sant'Agatha. The container was then dispatched to Venice, by way of Foggia to Manfredonia and from there by sea to Venice; on occasions an alternative route by the via Appia to Rome and then overland to Venice, was used, depending on the season and the courier service available. Whichever way the parcel went, it was accompanied by many prayers. The likelihood of its being lost en route was considerable, hence one of the reasons for making two or three copies. Delays due to weather conditions or to the capricious humours of the postal officials were normal. For weeks on end, Alphonsus would hear nothing after dispatching his manuscript. He suffered agonies while they were in transit and he made everybody else suffer with him. Prayers and sacrifices were doubled until he received news of their safe arrival:

> This morning, while at table, I got your esteemed letter with the news that my *Dissertatio* had arrived safely. All I could do was to get up from table and go on my knees to thank the Blessed Virgin for the safe arrival of the packet. I was very anxious about it, fearing lest I should have to do the whole thing over again with all the fatigue which it cost me.

A packet containing a supply of the *The True Spouse* and one hundred copies of a moral pamphlet failed to arrive:

> I can get no word of the whereabouts of the *Spouses* and the hundred copies of the *Apology for Probabilism*. The fishes must have eaten them by this time. Would you please make enquiries of the ship on which they were despatched.

According to the editors of the critical edition of the works of Alphonsus as many as ten works of a devotional nature may have been lost in transit from Naples to Venice and never saw the light of day.[3]

– II –

Much of what Alphonsus wrote can only be understood against the background of the various theological and philosophical trends which were manifesting themselves at the time. The middle of the eighteenth century witnessed a ferment of new ideas and new attitudes, not merely in the intellectual world where the dechristianisation of European thought and the growth of agnosticism and practical atheism became apparent, but also within the Church itself. The theological controversies of the sixteenth and seventeenth centuries, centred round Bishop Jansen of Ypres and his *Augustinus*, resulted in a variety of tendencies which, for lack of a more appropriate term, is still loosely styled Jansenism. In the last stages of its evolution, Jansenism spread into Italy, where the number of integral Jansenists — those who followed the theological doctrines of the *Augustinus* — were few, but where Jansenist attitudes were clearly in evidence in theology, asceticism, spirituality and devotional practice. In moral theology the Jansenists were Rigorists. In its pastoral application this attitude manifested itself in the frequency with which Jansenist confessors refused absolution to penitents or, at least, automatically deferred it for considerable periods of time, and in the demanding conditions they laid down for the reception of Holy Communion.

As a result, Communion became a rare event in christian practice. In the matter of personal devotion they professed an intellectual determination to seek the 'true primitive spirit of devotion', which meant, in effect, a decided suspicion of anything remotely resembling personal warmth and affective piety. Their great fear was what they styled 'superstition', which, for them, became any manifestation of popular piety; they rejected anything which seemed to smack of the external, anything which seemed to come from a warm and affectionate heart. On a broader front, they showed a lack of enthusiasm for papal prerogatives through a mixture of Gallicanism and Regalism. Naturalism replaced supernatural asceticism.

Besides moral theology, their main quarrel was is the area of Marian piety. Taking their cue from the Ninth Provincial Letter of Pascal, they rejected 'indiscreet piety' and this they discovered on all sides in Italian devotion to the Mother of God. One would not wish to claim that all popular manifestations of Marian devotion in Italy, and particularly in the Kingdom of Naples, were beyond criticism but it was one thing to prune these popular devotions of their indecorous elements and another to abolish them altogether. In their anxiety to preserve 'discretion' in their devotions, even the doctrine of the Immaculate Conception became a pious exaggeration. Our Lady's Mediation, her Assumption into heaven, her role of protectress, found no place in their theological or devotional repertoire. Similar reserves were displayed by these advocates of well-regulated piety towards devotion to the Sacred Heart of Our Saviour, which had received a new impetus through the revelations of Margaret Mary Alacoque in the Visitation convent of Paray-le-Monial and which was popularised by one section of the Jesuits. The advocates of this devotion were branded as Nestorians or more insultingly still, as '*cordicoli*' or '*alicoquisti*'.

The most eminent representative of this spirit in Italy was the altogether worthy and zealous priest, Don Ludovico Antonio Muratori, provost of Santa Maria della Pomposa of Modena, the leading intellectual in ecclesiastical circles in Italy and perhaps even in Europe, and whose name is forever linked to the 'Muratorian Fragment'. His critical acumen and his indefatigable researches illumined many important pages both of church history and biblical criticism, but he feared the effect of Italian popular piety on the intellectual and critical atmosphere in which he gloried. From 1714 until 1747 he published a number of monograms with this general orientation, ending with his best known work, *Della Regolata Devozione dei Christiani*, *Well Regulated Devotion*, under the pseudonym of Lamindo Pritanio, as if he was, somehow, ashamed to admit paternity. In it he expressed his doubts about the doctrine of the Immaculate Conception, denied Our Lady's Mediation, attacked certain devotional practices, such as the *voto di sangue*, disagreed with the recitation of the Litany of Loreto during the exposition of the Most Blessed Sacrament, and the excessive emphasis on the Mother of God in sermons for the feast of the Annunciation and during Advent.

These trends would probably have made little impact were it not that the movement had its eminent supporters in Rome, even among the Cardinals.

It is an indication of the strength of the movement that there were those who claimed — falsely, indeed — that Benedict XIV shared their views. The recognised head of the movement in Rome was Mons. Giovanni Bottari, an ecclesiastic of vast culture and personal charm, director of the Vatican Library and a renowned historiographer and archaeologist, as well as a member of the Cruscan Academy. His apartment was the centre where kindred spirits met for discussions; connected with him were a number of clerics throughout the peninsula who shared the same outlook on theological, ascetical and devotional attitudes. In this virtually philo-jansenist academy, all the leaders of the movement were to be found, among them at least three eminent Neapolitan ecclesiastics, all acquaintances of Alphonsus, Andrea Serrao and Giuseppe Capecelatro, who later became archbishops of Potenza and Taranto respectively, and canon Giuseppe Simeoli, professor of theology both in the Naples seminary and in the university, the censor of several of Alphonsus' works and the one who caused him most annoyance. They were all, in Alphonsus' phrase, *amici del partito*, 'members of the Party'. They were all totally opposed to everything Alphonsus stood for and practised — from defence of papal prerogatives to devotion to Our Lady and the traditional practices of asceticism. Also connected with Bottari was an influential group of Oratorians from the Valicella in Rome and a group of Augustinians under Father Xavier Vasques. Linked to them by correspondence was Muratori and the leaders of the movement in both Florence and Brescia. Included, too, amongst the group was a formidable phalanx of theologians, Orsi an Augustinian, Alberto Capobianco, a diocesan professor from Naples, and an imposing array of Dominicans: Concina, Patuzzi and Sacco, all of whom, in one way or another, ranged themselves against Alphonsus and what he stood for in theology. One of Alphonsus' practical books in moral theology, intended for rural confessors, *Il Confessore Diretto*, was sent to Capobianco as censor. 'I have been allotted a very peculiar censor in Naples,' he commented, 'and to tell the truth, he has very little understanding of moral theology. From the very beginning he began to object to many points unreasonably.' The Patriarch of this whole underground movement in Rome was the enigmatical figure of Cardinal Passionei, the same who had signed the Brief of Approbation of the new missionary society of the Redemptorists in 1749 and who, by his integrity, had frustrated the final attempt to restrict the papal decision. In their secret correspondence, the inner circle of the philo-jansenists referred to him as the 'Prior'.

The Bottari circle harboured considerable reservations in their attitude to papal infallibility and jurisdiction, clearly indicating that they accepted certain tenets of Gallicanism and Regalism. Tanucci and Mons. Bottari were in constant communication — in fact, Bottari seems to have played the role of Roman spy for the Neapolitan regalist, advising him of every nuance of Roman attitudes to the Bourbon claims and pretensions. There was one attitude, however, which was common to all these men, no matter how they might differ on other points. They were united in their shared hatred of the Society of Jesus. One wonders, at times, if their theological attitudes were not, in the first place, anti-Jesuit and only secondly, based on other premises. They were anti-Probabilists in moral theology because Probabilism was to a large extent favoured by Jesuit theologians; they were against devotion to the Sacred Heart because the Jesuits had made it their preserve; they were opposed to papal supremacy in both its doctrinal and practical aspects since they saw in the Jesuits the archdefenders of the papacy. Without their influence inside the Church, it is debatable if the Bourbons and their allies throughout Europe, would have succeeded in destroying the Society of Jesus and securing its papal suppression. Jesuit baiting was the acceptable ecclesiastical sport at the time among this group, giving rise to all types of calumnies, innuendoes and pasquinades for which Rome was famous:

> O vos qui cum Jesu itis
> Ne eatis cum Jesuitis.[4]

Bottari could not stand the very sight of a Jesuit; for him to meet one on the streets of Rome was to incur the risk of a stroke. His opposition to the canonisation of Cardinal Bellarmine, delayed it for nearly 200 years.

On every aspect of church life from rigorism to papal infallibility Alphonsus found himself in the opposing camp to the Jansenists. Whether he consciously set himself the task of leading the movement to counteract their influence is open to discussion among his biographers but there is no denying the fact that on every single point he took issue with them. Certainly in Naples, during his lifetime, he was recognised as the centre of the anti-jansenist movement. As a result, he suffered considerable harassment. Canon Simeoli, a friend of Tanucci, put every possible obstacle he could in the way of the publication of his works in the capital. His moral theology was branded as being nothing more than a copy of Jesuit theology with the result that the opposition reserved for Jesuit writings was equally directed towards his; when Jesuit theological works were publicly burnt in Lisbon, the works of Alphonsus were added to the pile. This explains why, later on, he had to plead so strongly for independent judgment on what he had written and the practical decisions he advocated in moral problems. He made it clear that he was not a Jesuit theologian masquerading under another name but an independent theologian whose opinions differed in many points from those of the main body of Jesuit moralists, much as he respected and revered them.

– III –

In 1750 after nearly twenty years of study and reflection Alphonsus saw the publication in Naples of his work on the Mother of God, *Le Glorie di Maria*, The Glories of Mary. As was only to be expected, his manuscript had encountered considerable difficulties in its passage through the censor's office. The idea of writing a book about the Mother of God had been with him from the earliest years of his priesthood, due in no small degree, to his friendship with the Neapolitan mariologist, Father Francis Pepe, S.J. Among the many causes to which Pepe had devoted his pastoral activities was the spread of devotion to the Immaculate Conception of Our Lady. In the square in front of the Jesuit Church of the Gesù Nuovo in Naples rises the Giuglia dell'Immaculata, the obelisk in honour of this privilege of Our Lady, erected as a result of public subscriptions by Father Pepe in 1747, to rival that which had already been erected in Rome in the piazza di Spagna. Pepe became the guide for Alphonsus in his study of the Church's teaching and practice concerning Mary's part in the whole divine economy of salvation. Alphonsus spent years reading the writings of the Fathers; he studied the theologians of the past, especially St Bernard, and visited the Marian shrines within easy reach during his missionary campaigns. As he formed his mind in the school of tradition and absorbed the *sensus fidelium*, he often discussed the weight of different opinions with Pepe, who wrote to him in the summer of 1734:

> There is a great difference in the order of sanctity between Jesus and Our Lady, certainly for the reason you give, namely that Jesus has it by *right* while Our Lady has it by *favour*. However, as well as that, there is also the fact that Jesus has it as *Head*, while Our Lady has it as *Neck*, and through the merits of her Son, who possesses the substantial holiness of the Hypostatic Union.
>
> You can certainly mention, without any scruple, Our Lady's infinite degree of grace since this opinion is defended by theologians such as Father Cristoforo Vega in his *Theologia Mariana* and is confirmed by the authority of the Fathers of the Church, St Bonaventure, St Anselm, Epiphanius, Damian, Bernardine of Siena, St Bernard, Denis the Carthusian and many others.
>
> Do not hesitate to have your work printed and all for the glory of the Mother of God.

The work, however, did not see the light for some sixteen years; in the meantime Alphonsus continued to note the sayings of the Fathers and theologians of the Church in their references to Our Lady. He gradually matured his theology of Our Lady in his mission sermons and in the novenas he preached in preparation for her feasts. By the end of 1748 he had accumulated a considerable amount of material which he began to organise for publication. The framework of the book was provided by the prayer, *Salve Regina*, the Hail Holy Queen, which he took as the basic text for commentary. In the first section there are ten chapters on just two fundamental themes — the goodness and the power of the Mother of God. Flowing from these came the notion of Mary as Queen of Mercy, Mother of the Faithful, Hope of Abandoned Sinners, Pledge of Salvation, Help in Spiritual Dangers and Gate of Heaven. Around these themes, Alphonsus wove a pattern at once devotional, exhortatory and prayerful but always soundly theological. Having completed his commentary on the *Salve Regina*, he devoted the second part of the work to nine discourses for the principal feasts of Our Lady during the year, together with considerations on Our Lady's Sorrows, and a study of the virtues of which she gave an example during her life. The work concluded with a series of prayers and practices of devotion in her honour.

The Glories of Mary did not originate in any polemical spirit, neither as an attack on Jansenism nor more specifically as a rebuttal of the mariological reserve of Muratori, although in the course of years it became associated with both. The book was, in the first place, an offering from a devout child of Mary to his spiritual Mother, as Alphonsus protested in his preface. More significantly still, it was dedicated to Christ the Redeemer, as a token of 'love for Him and His Mother'; to set it up as an effort to detract from the omnipotent salvific action of Christ in the mystery of salvation, is totally unwarranted. Alphonsus saw it as an effort to nourish genuine devotion to the Mother of God among the faithful and at the same time he intended it as a theological source-book which would provide priests with readily available material for their meditations and their sermons. It was, in short, what all his other works were, a missionary book, aimed, primarily, at the salvation and sanctification of souls. And Alphonsus was careful to declare in the opening pages that if some of his assertions seemed 'too advanced or unclear', they were to be interpreted in the light of sound theology and the teaching of the Holy Roman Catholic Church.

One must, of course, make some reference to an aspect of the book which, unfortunately, is too often the only aspect of it that is remembered and which has tended to discredit the work as a whole. At the end of each chapter of the first part of the work and occasionally in the text itself there are stories or 'examples' to illustrate aspects of devotion to Our Lady, taken indiscriminately from popular history or legends, without the slightest critical preoccupation. It is not a little surprising that even in this sophisticated age when we are so accustomed to understanding things in their historical context, we fail to appreciate so obvious a literary form as that of the *esempi*, so dear to seventeenth and eighteenth century writers and preachers. Alphonsus was a man of his time and country, a man of his contemporary theological culture, which he was able to transcend in so many ways but which he conformed to in others. Among the most popular expressions of devotion to the Mother of God at the time — and to the saints as well — were the Saturday evening sermons in her honour which would include a story or 'miraculous' occurrence, illustrating her powers of intercession with her Son. In Rome, the sermon and narration of a miracle in the Gesù in honour of the Mother of God was a social as well as a devotional event in the life of the city. The special preachers, like Fathers Bovio and Santocanale were as renowned in their own day as the Lenten preachers in Notre Dame in Paris in a later century. And who is to say that they were not as effective in their own way in leading their congregation to prayer and devotion? Naples did not lag behind the Eternal City in any way and the Saturday sermons of Father Pepe, among others, under the patronage of his Majesty King Charles III and frequently graced by the royal presence, with the narration of miracles attributed to the Mother of God, were as much a feature of devotional life in the city as in Rome. One has only to read Father Pepe's *Discorsi in lode di Maria Santissima per Tutti Sabbati dell' Anno*, published in 1756 with its fund of *esempi* at the conclusion of every discourse, to catch the authentic atmosphere of a literary form, no longer in general use, and which we tend now to judge by false criteria. The people who listened to the examples in the pulpits of Rome and Naples and other Italian cities did not trouble to ask themselves were they historically true, or did they really happen; they did not even feel that their credulity was being taken for granted. Instead, the narrative fixed in their minds a truth deeper than any historical event; the ordinary listener in Rome and Naples was sufficiently sophisticated to be able to appreciate the purpose of the literary figure just as we can appreciate the purpose of the parable of the Prodigal Son without questioning whether Palestinian swine-food was fit for human consumption. There was an extensive library of collections of these 'esempi' available to preachers from which Alphonsus borrowed freely; just how reserved he was in his choice of examples can be judged by comparing them with some of those quoted by Father Pepe.[5]

Beneath the apparently devotional form of *The Glories of Mary* lies a rich mine of sound theological teaching on the Mother of God. As a positive contribution to the mariological section of theology, it marked a decisive stage in the doctrinal evolution of the doctrine of Our Lady's Immaculate Conception. At the very time that Alphonsus was stating his views that the doctrine was certain teaching and could be the subject of a doctrinal definition, Mons. Bottari was formally advising Benedict XIV:

> Since the bible does not speak of the Immaculate Conception and since the tradition of more than three centuries is contrary to it, this doctrine could not be proclaimed as a doctrine of faith by any Pope. Whoever wishes can believe this doctrine out of reverence for the Mother of God. However, it would be entirely unlawful to give one's life for this devotion or belief which is without any divine foundation.

Alphonsus' instinct rested on surer theological foundations. His understanding of the living tradition of the Church as manifested in the christian sense of the faithful and in the argument drawn from the liturgy, convinced him. It was under the influence of Alphonsus and his writings that the way was finally cleared for the definition of the Immaculate Conception some hundred years later.

The main theological impact of *The Glories of Mary*, however, was in the doctrine of Our Lady's Mediation of graces; Alphonsus proclaimed his belief in the providential role entrusted to the Mother of Jesus in the distribution of the graces of salvation. He was not the first to formulate Mary's intercessory function, which is common to all God's saints, but he developed it with great clarity. If, in the case of the doctrine of the Immaculate Conception, he was content to base his main line of argument on the belief and practice of the faithful, as well as on the liturgical practice of the Church, in this case he altered his approach. Admitting that the approved devotional practice of the Church as well as the devotional practice of the faithful were both orientated to the truth of this doctrine, he sought to underpin it with a sound theological line of reasoning. Indeed, the main lines of theological argument still used in modern expositions of this point of view are all to be found in what he wrote.[6]

Pusey's accusation of Mariolatry against Alphonsus is well known. Newman, on the other hand, with a finer hermeneutical sense, was able to point out how necessary it is to understand the background against which Alphonsus wrote and for whom. He wrote for Neapolitans and in an idiom they would understand.[7] His work was, first of all, a book of devotion for Neapolitans for whom the word 'Mamma' with its delightful variations such as 'mammina' and 'mammucia' means so much. They had no inhibitions in using this same word, even its diminutives, in connection with the Mother of God — a display of affection which would be intensely embarrassing for northern temperaments. When Father Pepe wrote to Alphonsus in 1734 he congratulated him on labouring so zealously for the 'glory of Jesus and Mamma', a quite unacceptable expression for non-Latin temperaments, no matter how tenderly loving towards the Mother of God. But beneath all this 'Neapolitanism', which it should not be beyond modern criticism to penetrate, lies a sound theological content which places this work at the beginning of the whole modern mariological movement and makes it the last great European classic written in honour of the Mother of God.

The publication of *The Glories of Mary* coincided with a renewal of interest in the works of Father Muratori, who had died at the beginning of the same year, 1750. Alphonsus had no polemical purpose in mind as he steered his work with difficulty through the Neapolitan censors and in the book itself he studiously avoided attacking those theologians opposed to the views he defended. Once, however, in the course of the first part of the work, when dealing with the mediation of graces, Alphonsus referred with considerable deference to the provost of Modena:

> The proposition that whatever graces we receive from the Lord come to us by means of Mary, does not please a great deal a certain modern writer. Despite the fact that he has written with great learning and piety on true and false devotion, nevertheless, when speaking about devotion to the Mother of God, he is very reluctant to accord her the honour which St Germanus, St Anselm, St John Damascene, St Bonaventure, St Antoninus, St Bernardine of Siena, the Venerable Abbot of Celles and so many other doctors of the church have no hesitation in granting her. These men have no difficulty in declaring, for the reasons I have stated, that the intercession of Our Lady is not only useful but also necessary.[8]

With the theological atmosphere so charged at the time, this single reference to Muratori was sufficient to spark off strong reaction. Two Sicilian Jesuits, Fathers Plaza and Maurici, were chasing the ghost of Muratori at the time, and the whole tone of Alphonsus' work seemed to indicate that he was in their camp. Without waiting for the official biography of Muratori to appear, an Augustinian, Father Ambrosio Manchi, rushed into the fray under the pseudonym of Lamindo Pritanio Redivivo. While his main shafts were directed against the Jesuits, Alphonsus was included as one of the latest opponents of Muratori and three whole sections were devoted to rebutting what Alphonsus had written about him.

He shared too in the general vituperation: 'their writings and their names merit nothing more than stygian darkness. Their impertinence, in daring to censure and calumniate, shows that they must have read the works of Muratori in their sleep and that their writings were composed in their dreams.' Alphonsus was accused specifically of attributing to Muratori statements which he had not made. However, Manchi, as we shall see, merely used *The Glories of Mary* to launch a quite vicious attack on Alphonsus' *Moral Theology* for its laxity; it 'quite nauseated him'. The harm that it would do, especially since it was intended for the education of the young members of the Congregation, appalled him. And the harmful effects were all the more insidious on account of Alphonsus' reputation for holiness.[9]

Alphonsus replied to this attack in the second edition of *The Glories of Mary* which appeared in Naples in 1756. The controversy was of some help in boosting the sales and the work went rapidly into several editions in Naples within ten years of its first publication. The Venetian's printing houses were eager to cash in on the popularity of the work and several of them requested permission to reprint it. But Alphonsus wished to remain loyal to Remondini who in 1760 had a compact two-volume pocket edition ready for distribution. From Venice the work escaped the confines of Italy. The first German translation appeared in Augsburg a few years later and a Spanish translation followed in Valencia. There must be something remarkable in a work which, within 200 years of its first publication, has been translated into over eighty different languages and appeared in 800 known editions.

– IV –

Father Manchi, kept his bitterest attack, in the best Neapolitan vituperative style, for Alphonsus' *Moral Theology*:

> Why should you feel so strongly against Pritanium (Muratori) and others in a matter about which one can be mistaken with impunity — namely, whether a certain privilege can be attributed to the Virgin Mary — when in moral matters which are concerned with avoiding sin (a matter of the highest importance) you should be so easy and benign in your attitude as to overstep the limits of indulgence? I have studied your *Adnotationes in Busenbaum* a little, but I was so nauseated by their spirit of indulgence that I put the book away at once.
>
> I was greatly distressed to read that you proposed to train the young men of your Congregation — as you admitted yourself — with such a work, while there are much sounder moral theologies available with

which to initiate these young evangelical labourers, who are destined, later, to guide the consciences of the faithful.

But what I deplore, most of all, is that since you have a reputation for piety, your opinions are esteemed as if they fell from heaven. They are being followed, without anxiety, on no other authority than the reputed piety of the Doctor who teaches them. I have heard that there are those in Naples who swallow everything you say in your *Adnotationes* and put these opinions into practice. Many of these opinions, indeed, the majority of them, would need to be reviewed.

In 1753 you prefixed to the second edition of your work a list of propositions which you re-examined more carefully. Thanks be to God! You give a list of questions which you reconsidered; you should have reconsidered a lot more as well. And it would have been better for you to have omitted altogether some of the opinions which you reconsidered.

Father Manchi's attack is easily explained. Three years after the publication of *The Glories of Mary*, the second edition of the *Moral Theology* appeared in Naples. During the five years that separated the second edition from the first publication of the *Adnotationes* in 1748, Alphonsus was able to reconsider some of the opinions he had followed initially. He discussed many problems with Fathers Jorio and Sparano, both, like himself, widely experienced in pastoral problems affecting the Kingdom of Naples. One such was the question of the holiness of life required for a cleric prior to ordination, on which he published a short dissertation in 1751, altering a more benign opinion he had followed in 1748. His second thoughts on the matter, which were of special relevance in Naples on account of the excessive number of clergy, found wide acceptance and were inserted by Pope Benedict XIV in a subsequent edition of his own work on diocesan synods. Encouraged by the reactions to the publication of his *Moral Theology*, Alphonsus decided to remodel the *Adnotationes* and to transform it from being a commentary on the Jesuit's manual to a complete moral theology with his own personal imprint. The revision took years, entailing severe restrictions on his other activities. To Mother Mary of Jesus in the Carmelite convent of Ripacandida, who sent him a cry of distress to visit her, he replied in December 1751:

> Sorella mia,
>
> It is altogether out of the question for me to go to see you, at least for the present. Besides the fact that I cannot undertake such journeys any more on account of the condition of my health, I am preparing a work for the printers for confessors, which I cannot leave for one moment, this year. As a result, I never leave the house.[10]

When the revision of the first volume was complete, Alphonsus thought of dedicating it to the Pope whose interest in all pastoral problems he had experienced. Through the good offices once more of Father Sanseverino, he was informed that the Holy Father was willing to permit the dedication and, at the same time Sanseverino warned that the dedicatory letter should be couched in the best of Latin — *purezza di Latino*. Due to the slowness of the printers the first volume did not appear until 1753, but when it did, it was more elegantly printed and with larger type on better paper. This time Busenbaum was relegated to a secondary place in the title and the work appeared as the *Moral Theology of Alphonsus de Liguori, Rector Major of the Congregation of the Most Holy Redeemer*. The dedicatory epistle to the Pope was sufficiently elegant to make it difficult to understand in places but with Alphonsus' own introductory letter to the reader which followed, we are definitely back in another climate where clarity and not elegance is the main characteristic. His purpose in writing this work was to steer a middle course between too great laxity and too great rigidity, to be adequate in his treatment of questions and at the same time not to be diffuse. He prefaced the first volume with a list of 58 opinions which he had altered in the course of the intervening years and the second volume with almost a similar number. Excessive indulgence on the one hand only allowed the sinner to fall deeper into his evil ways, while extreme rigidity, which saw in every counsel a strict precept, only multiplied sins and obligations until human nature was driven to despair. To arrive at this middle course, this balance of judgment, Alphonsus claimed that he had endeavoured in every case to weigh the evidence with absolute objectivity, to put aside his personal prejudices. The result is a work of great serenity of judgment, of remarkable calmness and a delicately balanced equilibrium, all resulting from his mastery of theory and his sympathetic understanding of all the circumstances of the human condition.

Pope Benedict XIV expressed his pleasure with the work in a letter from St Mary Major's on 15 July 1755:

> Having paged through your work on Moral Theology which is dedicated to Us and for which we express Our special gratitude, I can say that Our first impressions are very favourable. The work is certain to be well received universally and to be of considerable benefit to the faithful. We will continue to study the work as the opportunity arises and We hope that what We read will be as good as what we have already studied.

The *Moral Theology* sold as rapidly as it emerged from the printing presses in Naples. There was a delay of two years between the appearance of the first and second volume which cannot altogether be blamed on the printers. When finally the second volume appeared in the early summer of 1755 it was eagerly bought up; a few weeks later Alphonsus had only a few copies still available.

The success of the work brought a request from Remondini in Venice to publish the work there; Alphonsus readily agreed, though the question of the ecclesiastical censor worried him:[11]

> I ask you not to give the work to be censored by any theologian of the Rigid school — as for the most part, the Dominicans are today. This is not my way of thinking since I have endeavoured to steer a middle course. It would be all to the good if you could find a Jesuit Father for the task since they are, in all truth, masters of moral theology. The Jesuits here in Naples have praised my book, even in public; only a

few have declared that in some points I have been very strict. But, as I say, I prefer a middle course.

Remondini was only too pleased to accommodate Alphonsus on this point since his own relations with the Society of Jesus were cordial and it was probably a Jesuit, in the first place, who drew his attention to the desirability of publishing the work of this new Neapolitan theologian. The publisher was on particularly intimate terms with Father Zaccaria, a well-known theologian and librarian of the Este Library. The suggestion of Zaccaria as a possible censor gave Alphonsus immediate satisfaction:

> I am pleased that you will have the work examined by a Jesuit Father. If it had been a Dominican Father of the school of Concina, he would attack me for being too lax in many of the opinions I have followed. For the most part I have followed the opinions of the Jesuit Fathers and not those of the Dominicans, since I have found the Jesuit opinions to be neither too broad nor too rigid, but well balanced. And if, in places, I hold some strict opinion against some Jesuit writer, I do so, perhaps, on the authority of some other Jesuit writer. I admit that I have learnt from the Jesuits whatever little I have written. They have been and are, as I always say, the masters of moral theology. It is not at all true, as some Rigorists say, that the Jesuit writers follow one another like sheep. In many cases one writer holds the opposite of another. And so, I have made up my own mind, as appeared best to my conscience. If on occasions, I have not considered some Jesuit opinions as probable, I have not expressly condemned them.
>
> So you need not fear that I am very strict or too lax. I ask you to read this letter to the revisor so that he may understand the method I have followed; I am a Probabilist and *not* a Probabiliorist nor a Rigorist.
>
> Have any Jesuit you wish, then, revise my work. And I would be very pleased if Father Zaccaria could give a look over it since from his writings I judge him to be a very learned man and well-balanced in his opinions, neither lax nor rigorous.

Father Zaccaria, praised by Alphonsus so highly, did, in fact, revise his work before its publication in Venice. He was just forty at the time. His fine intelligence marked him out as one of the most eminent Jesuits of his generation, a theologian, patrologist and historian. The *Adnotationes* to Busenbaum had not altogether pleased him initially — many of the opinions appeared too lax but the new edition of the work with about a hundred changes of opinions, had adjusted the balance to his satisfaction. Not merely did he agree to revise the work for the printers, he offered to associate himself with it by writing a historical introduction, which Alphonsus gladly accepted. Thus began a friendship between the two men, so different in personalities but united in mutual esteem. When the Jesuit went to Naples a few years later to examine the libraries, he met Alphonsus on several occasions, who declared him a man of 'considerable charm'.

Remondini's edition of the *Moral Theology* appeared in Venice in the middle of 1757 in three folio volumes with the long introductory dissertation by Father Zaccaria on the history and development of casuistry. The news that the work was to be published in folio-size dismayed Alphonsus at first, since he regarded this format as unwieldy and an obstacle to its general use by the clergy. The excellence of the paper and the quality of the printing were, however, some compensation. Due to Zaccaria's influence, the name of Busenbaum figured once again in the most prominent place; it was the *Moral Theology of Herman Busenbaum* and the monograph of the Society of Jesus was at the foot of the page. The Jesuits had virtually appropriated the work.[12] In a gracious letter of dedication, Zaccaria showed his admiration for Alphonsus, *viro doctissimo*:

> It is a source of great wonder to me, that you, whose work on moral theology has been so highly esteemed by the Roman Pontiff, the learned Benedict XIV, should have such a humble opinion of yourself that you should be unwilling to allow Remondini to publish the third edition of your work without a dissertation of mine by way of introduction.
>
> But since your wish has to be obeyed, lest I should seem to show any lack of appreciation for your benevolence towards my religious family, the Society of Jesus, and of the honour which would accrue to me as a result, there is no one else to whom I could possibly dedicate this Dissertation except yourself.

With the publication of the second Neapolitan edition and the first edition outside Naples, Alphonsus' *Moral Theology* had assumed its own decisive characteristics and individuality. Publication in Venice assured its spread throughout Europe. Within his own lifetime, nine editions were published; within a century of his death there were over seventy further editions throughout Europe. It had been his endeavour to steer a middle course between the two prevailing extremes of Laxity on the one hand and Rigorism on the other. He took his stand firmly against the dominant climate of Rigorism in which he had been trained. His reaction — or rather revolt, for revolt it was — aroused the suspicions of many of the established theologians of the time. Jorio in Naples was hesitant at first, Zaccaria in Venice was opposed, Lamindus Pritanius Redivus was aghast; the Dominicans, led by Concina and Patuzzi, headed a formidable opposition. The stand Alphonsus took was all the more remarkable when we realise that it imperilled the future of his young missionary congregation and the missionary work to which he had devoted his life. The so-called 'lax' doctrine which he favoured was intended mainly for the young men of his congregation and was to be the norm for their pastoral practice. In the prevailing climate this was tantamount to jeopardising their whole future. It was a risk which only one of his reputation for learning and personal holiness of life could have afforded to take.

THE THEOLOGICAL WARS 1749–1762

– V –

By the end of the seventeenth century, moral theologians were embroiled in controversies connected with the proper formation of one's conscience, or, to put it simply, on how to choose what course of action to follow as a Christian, in certain given circumstances. In the process of forming one's conscience correctly, there frequently occurs the necessity of weighing up probabilities; some arguments indicate one course of action as the correct one, other arguments seem to favour the opposite. In this state of conscience, one is, according to theologians, technically 'in doubt', with one's judgment, suspended, as it were, between two courses of action, one of which might be, in some way, against God's law. Consequently, for fear of offending God, one cannot follow either course without further clarification. In the great majority of cases, however, there is little difficulty in resolving the issue — the arguments for one side so outweigh the arguments on the other that it is quite clear which course one has to follow. But human probabilities are not always so conveniently clear-cut; at times, opposing arguments can appear almost evenly balanced. The problem then is, how can one come to a decision which respects both one's God-given liberty of choice and one's duty to God?

This speculative problem, which did not disappear until a different orientation of moral theology began to impose itself within the last hundred years, was clearly enunciated as early as 1577, by the Dominican theologian, Bartholomew Medina, when he wrote, 'It seems to me that it is lawful to follow a probable opinion, even though the opposite opinion is *more* probable.' The controversy unleashed by this statement gave rise to a flood of theological literature and tended to dominate all other aspects of moral theology for decades. By the middle of the seventeenth century, theologians were divided into two main and bitterly opposed schools, the Probabilists, who followed Medina, and the Probabiliorists, that is, those who insisted that the more probable opinion should be followed at all times. At the instigation of Pope Alexander VII in 1656, the Dominican theologians, led by Father Billuart, became the great exponents of this attitude, while the Jesuits, in the main, rallied to the defence of Probabilism.

Unfortunately, the controversy was not confined within these acceptable limits. In the first place, some theologians recklessly brought Probabilism into disrepute by pushing it to outrageous extremes, declaring that if an opinion possessed even the slightest degree of probability from whatever source, it could safely become the norm of one's christian conduct. Then, by way of reaction, the pendulum swung to the opposite extreme of Rigorism, which, while not specifically Jansenist in its origins, became closely identified with it. The Rigorist theologians, mainly in France and the Netherlands, insisted that when opinions were divided between liberty of choice and the obligation of the law, one is always bound to follow the opinion in favour of the obligation. Many of the Probabiliorists too — Dominicans, in the main — had, by now, come to insist to such an extent on the obligation of the law that they became indistinguishable from the out-and-out Rigorists and were tarred with the same brush. And while theologians argued, it was, as always, the ordinary faithful who suffered most. Had the controversies been confined to the 'schools', little harm might have resulted, but the theoretical differences were carried over into practice, with serious pastoral consequences. The extreme Probabilists, seeking to uphold the freedom of the christian conscience from an excess of law, opened the way to considerable laxity of conduct, while the Rigorists, the Jansenists and the out-and-out Probabiliorists, who argued for the rights of law, became so extreme in their views that they imposed impossible burdens on the faithful, who, as a consequence, kept away in fear, if not in despair, from the frequentation of the sacraments of Penance and the Eucharist.

By the time Alphonsus began his theological studies the position had stabilised somewhat, though the controversy still raged as fiercely as ever. Probabilism, tarnished by the imputation of laxity, was in decline; Probabiliorism which easily deteriorated into Rigorism was in the ascendant, and had become the accepted approach of many bishops and confessors in their pastoral ministry. But, above all, there was an atmosphere of confusion as theologians, with their genius for complicating matters, continued to categorise opinions as certain, probable, less probable, more probable, equally probable and, unbelievably, probably probable. There was an air of barely concealed frustration with all these theological subtleties. Was it not possible to draw up a moral system which would respect the imperatives of the christian gospel on the one hand and, on the other, would take into sympathetic consideration the weakness of fallen human-nature, as well as the life-situations of the ordinary faithful? It was here precisely that the genius of Alphonsus was to find its greatest challenge.

Alphonsus was plunged into this theological morass as a student with the Apostolic Missions; his introduction to moral theology was, as we have seen, in the Probabiliorist or Rigorist school. The prevailing theological climate in the seminary was reflected in the use of Genet's theology as the official text book. Cardinal Spinelli was proud to report to Rome the steps he had taken to prevent any infiltration of the more benign teaching. Though the 'official' teaching was Rigorist there was, however a strong under-current of opinion supporting aspects of the Probabilist school — at least, unofficially. Canon Torni, whom Alphonsus referred to publicly in his *Adnotationes*, as his 'most learned and illustrious mentor', was, according to the latest research, a Probabilist at heart, while outwardly adhering to the official Genet line. There was no doubt whatever about where Father Pagano stood. He was an out-and-out Probabilist, who held that it was a prudent norm of christian conduct to follow a solidly probable opinion in favour of liberty, even in face of another opposing opinion, *more probable still*, in favour of an obligation. Alphonsus thus began his priestly life with a theological outlook differing in many ways from those of his two principal mentors, Torni and Pagano — a significant indication of his stubborn independence of character.

In 1756, Alphonsus wrote to Remondini in a letter about his *Moral Theology* the magic words, 'I am a Probabilist'. This simple declaration represented an intellectual conversion which entailed twenty years of great personal suffering, anxieties of conscience and, above all, extensive study. He was fortunate that he had Pagano to advise him in the early years and then Canon Torni, but most decisively of all, at a later stage, the highly respected Neapolitan theologian, Canon Giuseppe Jorio. Sportelli was one of the first to insist that he should be prepared to follow a probable opinion even against a more probable one — at least, that is what Alphonsus entered carefully into his personal note-book — '*di seguitare la probabile in concursu probabilioris*'. Following on this came an obedience regarding his own spiritual life, not to worry any further about whether his spiritual directors had been Probabilists or not, a scruple which must surely be unique in the history of that affliction. It is clear that the scruple referred to advice he had received from Pagano.[13]

It took Alphonsus over twenty-five years to work out the speculative side of the problem to his own satisfaction and to devise a system which could not be assailed either on theoretical or pastoral grounds. He published eleven separate dissertations during his lifetime on the whole question of conscience formation in moral theology. His first was in 1749, in favour of the moderate use of a probable opinion in face of a more probable one. This initial study, tentative in many ways, and published anonymously, was replaced six years later in 1755, by a completely re-worked exposé of the whole matter. Despite his verdict that the whole controversy had 'aroused more invective than good reason', he realised at the same time that the problem was of importance in determining which direction Catholic moral teaching was going to take, whether the supporters of Rigorism or Laxism would triumph, at least speculatively, either of which outcome would have been calamitous. The dire consequences of Jansenist confessional practice he had experienced himself at first hand on the missions. But the dissertation of 1755 was still not the last word for him. In 1762 an entirely fresh treatment brought further precision of thought and this was incorporated into the later editions of his *Moral Theology* from 1764 onwards. This was the dissertation which brought down on his head the wrath of the opposing theologians and developed into the violent controversy with the famous Dominican, Patuzzi, who launched his counter-offensive in 1764. But, by then, Alphonsus was a bishop and the controversy belongs to his years in Sant'Agatha of the Goths.[14]

Alphonsus' *Moral Theology* reflected his deep pastoral solicitude for souls which he expressed very clearly:

> It is not my intention when writing about *Moral Theology* which deals with human conduct, to present you with a discussion on human acts which is full of scholastic questions. Since my purpose is the salvation of souls — yours and others — I am going to deal only with the more important questions with which you should be familiar as the basis for

conduct. If I did otherwise would I not be wasting my time in writing, and you, your time in reading, such useless things?[15]

His main purpose was not to present moral theology in its scientific structure but to provide his young missionaries and priests in general with sound moral doctrine and safe guidance for their ministry as confessors and directors of souls. In other words, he set himself to produce, not a speculative manual, but a pastoral one. To say that Alphonsus was essentially a pastoral theologian with an eye firmly fixed on human conduct in everyday life, writing with particular relevance to social conditions in Bourbon Naples, is not to belittle him as a theologian on the one hand or to disparage speculative theologians on the other. Both have their functions which are complementary. Alphonsus looked constantly to *practice* or, as he wrote, to *pratica*, that is to theology as it affected the daily life and conduct of every category of Christian — pope, bishop, priest, religious, judge, doctor, teacher, hairdresser, peasant, the educated and the unlettered.

His genius lay in his ability to translate theory into practice, into acceptable norms at once balanced and prudent, which would lead souls securely to God. His charism was his *feel* for things, his human understanding. Many moral theologians writing in his day were no longer equipped with this essential requisite; they had almost ceased to be human beings. They lost themselves in the web of their own speculations, calculating probabilities with little reference to unredeemed human nature. Alphonsus, on the contrary, conceived of moral theology as something human, made for human beings. He considered every opinion in itself, in the first place, but then more specifically in its relation to souls, whose struggle in the circumstances of their daily lives he appreciated so well. And he devoted himself to the study and writing of moral theology not from any desire for controversy but to understand and to make others understand as well, how one should behave for the salvation of one's soul.

It is impossible to appreciate Alphonsus' work as a moral theologian unless we consider, side by side with the folio volumes of his major work, their two indispensable companions, each of them known, confusingly, as Pratica, though separated in point of fact by two years in their dates of publication. The first, *Pratica del Confessore per ben esercitare il suo ministero*, freely translated as the *Confessor's Guide to the correct Pastoral Exercise of his Ministry*, was printed in Italian in 1755, as an appendix to the second Neapolitan edition of the *Moral Theology*, as a concession to those rural confessors whose Latin was defective. Here, in a popular manual and easily accessible in the vernacular, Alphonsus was able to outline his ideal of the confessor — one who was well versed in the principles of moral theology, but possessing also the holiness of life required to sustain him in the discharge of this ministry, a holiness of life centred on prayer and daily meditation on the Scriptures. The confessor was to be a kind father, characterised by charity and christian courtesy; he was to be at the disposal of his penitent in every way, even to speaking dialect with him, to gain his confidence and his good will. He was to be at the same time a doctor of souls, skilled in prescribing remedies for the ills of sinful humanity, both as regards present conduct and future perseverance. For Alphonsus, moral theology was the most demanding of sciences, and the office of confessor the highest exercise of charity.

His practical advice to confessors in these volumes intended for the ordinary 'general practitioner', reveals a remarkable familiarity with social habits throughout the Kingdom. The custom of male hairdressers for women, for example, met with his considerable displeasure — it was a 'cursed practice recently introduced by the Devil himself'. He considered it a proximate occasion of sin for the men involved except, perhaps, for those who had been so employed for a considerable time and were thus inured to possible temptation. But what about the ladies? Were they at fault to seek the services of male hairdressers, particularly if they were young? Alphonsus broached the point only to refuse to discuss it further, since his information was that, where the custom had been established, the ladies in question still went to Confession and Communion, apparently without scruple on their part or admonition from their confessors. But he urged the ladies and their confessors to look into the matter in all honesty. It was his belief that women of delicate conscience would be satisfied with the services of female hairdressers, even though they might not be up to the technical standard of their male counterparts. In quite a different area of conduct, his advice to confessors was not to be over enthusiastic when young girls expressed a wish to enter a convent; they were to be particularly on their guard if they proposed to consecrate their lives to God in virginity while remaining at home. They were to be vigilant, too, never to allow young ladies to take reading lessons from young men and, much less, writing lessons — if such situations did not constitute occasions of sin, they were certainly very dangerous. And a final admonition warned confessors not to permit young girls to wander aimlessly from church to church under pretext of 'praying', rather than remaining at home assisting their parents in their domestic chores.

But he did not envisage the confessor merely as the minister of forgiveness, as if his only function was to absolve the penitent correctly and impose the appropriate satisfaction. There was much more to it than that. The confessor was to guide the soul to God, to help him to lead the christian life to the full by the frequentation of the sacraments, by instructing him in the way of union with God in prayer which at times could even lead on to the graces of contemplation. The confessor had to experience these things for himself in the first place, so as to be able to advise his penitents from his own experience. And with this in mind, Alphonsus appended for the confessor a guide for spiritual souls including a treatise on contemplation, on mortification, the frequentation of the sacraments and especially of Holy Communion. Then he outlined the approach to be taken with certain types of penitents — the poor, the ignorant, the peasant, the dying, children, adolescents, those with vocations to the priesthood or the religious life, those in doubt about their vocations, those afflicted, as he had been himself, with scruples, the deaf and the dumb and finally those possessed by the devil. His knowledge of human nature in all its manifestations was phenomenal.

To appreciate the merit of Alphonsus' *Pratica* one has only to compare it with the contemporary work of the Dominican, Father Concina, whose *Istruzione dei Confessori* was published in Venice in 1753. He, too, wrote after thirty years of pastoral experience and demanded the 'benignity of Jesus Christ in the confessor but not that benignity which some modern casuists have invented'. His anti-Probabilist obsession ruined the whole approach of his work. Father Zaccaria — who may not have been completely objective — compared them both:

> The *Pratica* of Father Liguori is replete with unction, full of charity, sweetness and moderation. The *Istruzione* of Concina breathes fury, passion, sternness and fanaticism. In the former, one can see the theologian of discretion in search of the salvation of souls, in the second, the unbalanced moralist who drives the faithful to desperation. The first proceeds methodically, opens the way and marks the road to repentance with equilibrium and balance. The second is nothing more than a medley, confused and with unbalanced opinions which make confession an odious burden. Blessings on the devout and learned author of the *Pratica*.

Despite the publication of his major work, first in Naples and then in Venice, followed by the *Pratica*, Alphonsus was still not satisfied that he had done enough to revive moral theology among the clergy. He thought of the many priests throughout the kingdom for whom the price and size of the two folio volumes would be a deterrent and whose inadequate knowledge of Latin would discourage them further. He decided to reduce the two large volumes to a more compact form which would make his theology accessible to the ordinary priest. At the same time, the new work would have to be sufficiently complete to equip priests who had studied it, with a general competence in the whole field of moral theology. Alphonsus determined that the compendium should appear in Italian and not in Latin. This initiative he first checked out with the Congregation of the Index in Rome, who indicated that he could go ahead without fear, provided that certain delicate matters would still be written in Latin. Early in 1757, Alphonsus had the work virtually completed; by the summer of that same year, the first sections of the work were already with the printers in Naples and in the spring of the following year, 1758, the work appeared in three handy-sized volumes, entitled *Istruzione e Pratica per un confessore*. The work was a vernacular compendium of all that was contained in the two-volume work to which was added the first *Pratica* of 1755 as the last chapter. Alphonsus had foreseen a ready market for this latest work; it would sell by thousands, he believed. And, he was proved correct. The work was bought up immediately in Naples and throughout the length of the Kingdom. Within a few weeks the first edition was sold out. The *Compendium* or the *Pratica Grande*, to distinguish it from its shorter predecessor, became a runaway best-seller.[16]

Remondini, for once, had misread the situation. He was opposed to the idea of publishing what would, in effect, be a concise manual of moral theology in the vernacular rather than in Latin, believing that the use of Italian would greatly restrict the sales. He informed Alphonsus that the work would have to be translated into Latin before he could consider publishing it. But the success of the work in Naples surprised him, and he determined to cash in on its success by requesting permission to bring out an Italian edition right away. At the same time he asked Alphonsus to arrange for a Latin translation. The very thought of the labour involved was daunting but having enlisted the assistance of a group of helpers among the Fathers and the students, Alphonsus set himself to the task. With the help of Father Ferrara, his main assistant, the work, which he originally reckoned would take nearly two years, was completed by October 1758 and the manuscript was en route by way of Rome to Venice. The news of the impending publication of the Latin compendium brought enquiries from bishops and rectors of seminaries anxious to use it. All through the winter of 1758 and the spring of 1759, Alphonsus kept up a constant stream of letters to Remondini, reminding him of the demand for the Latin edition and urging him to expedite its publication. By the time the seminaries resumed work in the autumn of 1759 the Latin compendium under the title of *Homo Apostolicus* was ready. Alphonsus introduced it as the text-book for the students in Pagani. But the pressure on Remondini to rush publication resulted in a text full of typographical errors which brought down on his head the wrath of Alphonsus. 'The work is so full of errors it would turn your stomach.' These, however, were corrected in subsequent editions, which followed rapidly, and the success of the Latin version was only slightly less than that of the Italian.

Such was the popularity of the *Homo Apostolicus* that pirate editions soon made their appearance. Alphonsus had warned Remondini of this possibility urging him to take out a 'privilegio' at once — a publisher's expedient somewhat similar to our copyright. But Remondini neglected the precaution and too late realised that he was losing the monopoly of this important work. His complaint to Alphonsus in the matter did not meet with a very sympathetic reception:

> Signor Giambattista mio,
>
> Do you think I can stop these publishers from reprinting whatever they wish to? Am I the King? It is the King's business to keep the publishers under control, not mine. However, if you have any copies of the *Pratica* in stock, please send them on at once and have no doubt they will easily be disposed of, since they are in continual demand. For heaven's sake do not complain any more of this business because there is nothing I can do to remedy the matter.[17]

With the trilogy now successfully published—the fundamental work of the *Moral Theology*, the small *Pratica* and then the *Compendium* or *Homo Apostolicus* in both Italian and Latin editions, Alphonsus' own contribution to moral theology was completed. He continued to revise his moral writings incessantly as the works went into edition after edition. Even as a bishop he found time to correct and make additions to what he had written, until age and increasing infirmities made further study impossible for him.[18]

– VI –

The spread of the ideas of the Enlightenment to Italy opened up for Alphonsus a further field of apostolic endeavour. While he worried about the trends in the field of devotional and moral writings he was still more disturbed by the flood of atheistic and irreligious literature making its way into Naples from France and England. The frantic efforts of the Roman authorities to prevent the infiltration of the new ideas by means of the Congregation of the Index were proving futile. The Enlightenment, which made a god of Reason, considered revealed religion with its beliefs and practices as nothing more than outmoded absurdities which were being skillfully exploited to keep the people in submission. The only concession the new ideas were prepared to make to religion was a vague type of Deism, which, in the words of Dean Swift, was a religion 'which contained nothing that cannot easily be comprehended by the weakest noodle.' Faith in divine revelation was abandoned, belief in a body of revealed truths rejected, the supernatural discarded, authority in religious matters ridiculed. The herald of the whole movement was the *Historical and Critical Dictionary* of Peter Bayle, the first volume of which appeared as early as 1697. Virulent in its attack on the dogmas of revealed religion, it was an open defence of atheism by the son of a Huguenot pastor who had received his education from the Jesuits. Nothing was spared his irreverent attacks, the Bible, the priesthood, celibacy; miracles and relics were especially ridiculed.

And where Bayle left off, Voltaire took over. Two years older than Alphonsus — he was born in 1694 — he succeeded in making the attack on religion fashionable. Where up to his time it had been attacked and sneered at in private in intellectual circles, he dared to jeer at religion and its manifestations on a broad public front. Even though he was not an atheist himself — as he said, atheism is the vice of clever people, just as superstition is the vice of fools — his satirical attacks did more to discredit religion than all the writings of Bayle. Hard on the heels of Voltaire, came the various volumes of the *Encyclopedia*, financed by Madame Geoffrin in Paris; its thirty-five volumes, the first of which appeared in 1751 and the last in 1776, became the infallible source-book of free thought and irreligion. The various contributors united to prove that the idea of God was altogether unscientific, life after death an illusion, the existence of the human soul, made in the likeness of God, a myth. It all added up to making Christianity nothing more than a great fiction, a tissue of superstitions. There was no supernatural foundation for the principles of basic morality; only some vague form of natural morality survived.

The new ideas spread inevitably to Naples, the second Paris, aping in everything the fashions of the French capital. Just as Caserta was to be the new Versailles so the philosophical salons of Naples were to challenge those of Paris for their intellectual sophistication. Voltaire saw at once the importance of establishing a centre in Bourbon Naples from which the new ideas could conveniently make their way throughout the whole peninsula. French bookshops were opened in Naples, the works of the Enlightenment authors circulated freely among university students, the clergy, and even breached the walls of monastic libraries.

Women, too, Alphonsus complained, were reading them. He was all too painfully aware of the extent to which the new ideas were prevalent among all sections of the literate classes in the Kingdom. He lamented the fact that these ideas had penetrated into 'nostra Italia' and 'nostra Napoli'; he was appalled at the havoc they were causing to the piety and devotion of both clergy and laity. 'Naples is ruined,' he lamented, 'no one goes to confession any longer, no one listens to sermons; everyone discusses theology and make what they like of Scripture, dogma and the commandments.' The irreligious climate, the palpable atmosphere of unbelief caused him extreme anguish. The whole outlook was totally alien to his own faith in God's revelation in Christ Jesus, and in the Church, his love for the Word of God in the Scriptures, his understanding of God and his benign Providence, his devotion to Our Lady and the saints. He discussed the threat to the faith of so many Neapolitans with Cardinal Sersale, but the Cardinal, who was a pastoral disaster, either did not seem to be aware of the danger or was unwilling to take any steps to counteract the intellectual poison which was undermining the faith of his flock.[19] Unable to enlist episcopal support Alphonsus decided to take up his pen in an effort to stem the tide of impiety; he was not prepared to permit the false teachings to claim victory by default.

Side by side with his study of moral theology he now concentrated on the study of the main tenets of the Enlightenment writers, both French and English, from Bayle, Voltaire, and Rousseau to Spinoza, Hobbes, Locke and Berkeley. The French authors he read in the original, the English authors he studied in French or Italian translations, and, at a further remove, in the various outlines of their teaching contained in other apologetic writers such as Valsecchi, the Dominican. He applied to Rome to the Congregation of the Index, and even to the Pope personally, for permission to read condemned publications. From the mass of literature which was circulating he made a synthesis of the errors he wished to refute; nowhere else are his remarkable powers of synthesis and simplification better exemplified. He gathered the various errors together under three main headings, materialism, deism and finally the errors of those who denied that the Catholic Church was the one true Church. His purpose was clear. Since others were not prepared to make some effort to stem the tide of unbelief, he would do all he could to counteract the 'pernicious poison'. He wrote for believers so that they would be strengthened in their beliefs and encouraged to give thanks to God for their faith:

You who love Jesus Christ, please consider the persecution that the Church is suffering from the host of unbelievers, who, not content with damning their own souls, are endeavouring through their writings and teachings to pervert others who will accompany them to perdition. To this end they are spreading their poisonous books everywhere, even here in our own Italy, where they are being read by unfortunate young people, either out of curiosity for new ideas or from a desire for greater freedom in their conduct. Having partaken of the poison, they then abandon themselves to every sort of unworthy behaviour.

You who have any zeal for the good of our Faith should give yourselves totally to preaching, advising, admonishing and proclaiming the dangers that exist until this great pestilence is extirpated. You may well object that human endeavour is inadequate for the task. I agree with you. We need the help of God. But does that mean that we are to remain idle ourselves, doing nothing more than deploring and wringing our hands at the damage being inflicted on the Church? . . . here is what we can and must do. We must preach, admonish, instruct, make known the dangers and at the same time pray to God, begging Him incessantly, importuning him with our tears to put an end to the damage that is being done to souls at the present time.[20]

In all, Alphonsus published five major apologetic works between 1756 and 1773, the first two while he was in Pagani, the others during his years as a bishop in Sant'Agatha of the Goths. But the works must be considered as a whole even though this entails anticipating his years as a bishop. His first publication in this new genre appeared in 1756 entitled *Against the Errors of Modern Unbelievers called Materialists and Deists*, in which he specifically mentions his intention of refuting the errors of Spinoza, Leibniz and his disciple Wolff, Hobbes, Locke and Berkeley in England and Bayle and Voltaire in France. This was followed six years later by *The Truth of the Faith as evidenced by the Motives of Credibility*. Neither of these works made much impact on the situation in either Naples or Italy and were not reprinted in Alphonsus' lifetime. Remondini could not be cajoled to add the *Errors of Modern Unbelievers* to his list of publications. Alphonsus considered the work on the *Motives of Credibility* a 'golden little book'. However, both these efforts were nothing more than his opening salvoes in this new field of apologetics. He continued his study and five years later in 1767 — he was by then a bishop — he completed the task of uniting both these works under the title of *The Truth of the Faith*. This was a major work on which he claimed he had 'sweated blood'; it ran to over six hundred pages and went into at least four editions during his lifetime. It enjoyed considerable success as a source book against the literature of the Enlightenment in Italy and represents his main contribution to the Church's response to these particular errors. Three other works during his episcopacy completed his list of publications in this type of polemical literature: an account of the teaching of the Council of Trent aimed mainly at the errors of Luther and Calvin, a history of all the heresies in the life of the Church under the title of *The Triumph of the Church*, which was dedicated to Tanucci and finally, a pamphlet-sized work in 1773 on the truth of Divine Revelation, directed once again against Voltaire and the Deists.

These works are certainly a tribute to his zeal; assessment of their merit as apologetic works is more difficult. Their impact on the English-speaking world was minimal, and only two of them were ever translated into that language. In the first place, they were mainly syntheses of other works which Alphonsus had studied; he used the word *raccolta* or 'source-book' in describing them himself. The extent of his reading was, by any standards, remarkable, the extent of his knowledge, encyclopedic. He showed familiarity with everything from anthropology to the Scriptures, from classical literature, philosophy, mythology to oriental religions, biblical history and theology. He wrote unashamedly from the point of view of one who believed, whose faith was unshakable and who had integrated all the problems which troubled his opponents — evil, suffering, death, eternity, revelation, the existence of a supreme being, and knowledge itself — into a satisfactory whole. His gift of simplifying the most abstruse problem was obvious and his writing, always powerful, reached considerable literary heights time and time again, though it suffers considerably in translation:

> Formerly, unbelievers wished to remain anonymous rather than appear irreligious and stupid. If they professed errors in matters of faith, they did not dare to flaunt their unbelief. But modern unbelievers make no secret of it; shamelessly they boast of their freedom to believe what they like about God and religion so as to display themselves as daring spirits and devoid of prejudice. And so they destroy every law and norm of correct living. Once belief in God as a rewarder of good and punisher of evil is destroyed, once the imperatives of religion disappear, the human person is reduced to the level of the beast, indeed, even lower. The senses control reason, what is right is determined by one's own pleasure, what is just by one's self-interest, one's honour is vindicated by vendetta. In a word, whatever is evil becomes good, simply because it appears useful and pleasurable.[21]

He was totally of his time in his attitude to those who were branded as heretics and unbelievers. Their names were prefaced with various adjectives from 'impious' to 'depraved' and their opinions held up to ridicule and compromised by reference to their disedifying lives. Spinoza and Mohammed were major victims of this unfortunate contemporary technique. Spinoza had no religion; the Jewish name given to him by his parents was Baruch, which in translation meant *benedetto*. It would have been more appropriate if he had been named *maledetto*, commented Alphonsus ungraciously 'since he was an out-and-out atheist who fashioned a religion and a God to suit his own caprices'. To complete the picture, Alphonsus added that he lived a disedifying bohemian life and died of tuberculosis, having attracted few followers for his theories. A similar mixture of personal abuse and ridicule was meted out to the Deists. George Berkeley, whom modern philosophers regard with considerable respect, was summarily dismissed as unworthy of being taken seriously; his whole theory of *idealism* was simply ridiculous, a judgment, which had Alphonsus but known, was shared by Dr Johnson who styled Berkeley's theories 'sheer nonsense'. The tolerance and respect for the great religions of the world which has characterised Christianity since the Second Vatican Council was undreamt of in his day and Alphonsus was totally of his time in the account he gave of the Jewish and Mohammedan religions. The one concession which he was prepared to make and which was, in itself, theologically perceptive was contained in an *obiter dictum* when he concluded, 'Revelation is necessary and no other religion has received it besides the christian religion, at least in its fullness.'

Alphonsus' contribution to the evolution of fundamental theology and to the theological tracts on Revelation and the Church was a positive one without being brilliantly original; some would claim that he gave Italy its first treatise on fundamental theology. His apologetic method, however, would enlist little support today but it was typical of its time and, to a certain extent, effective for the readers he had in mind. There are times, however, in these publications when his simple piety — one hesitates to call it credulity — gets the upper hand, as for example, when he adduces the relics of St Nicholas of Bari, the liquefaction of the blood of St John the Baptist, of St Stephen and St Pantaleone in monasteries in Naples and Ravenna as evidence of the existence of miracles in the Church. Of course, the liquefaction of the blood of St Januarius in Naples merits a special treatment of its own and a detailed refutation of those who, even then, attempted to discount the miraculous nature of whatever takes place. We can easily, too, detect the limitations of theological understanding on several points which prevailed at the time and nowhere more so than on the question of the evolution of dogma. A few lines was all he was able to write in reply to the difficulty that the Church had enlarged the deposit of faith by various definitions throughout the centuries. He was at his most assured, however, when he wrote on the infallibility of the Church in its teachings on matters of faith and morals. From the infallibility of the Church he moved confidently on to the position of the Pope, his supremacy and the infallible nature of his teaching charism in certain circumstances. In this context he dealt with the theories of Wycliffe and the errors of the Conciliar Movement. He devoted more than a quarter of this whole work to the section on the Papacy; this was the area of ecclesiology which he had most at heart and where his teaching was most insistent. It was also the doctrine for which he was 'prepared to give his life' and where his influence was to be dominant right up to the celebration of the first Vatican Council. When it was brought to his notice that one of his confreres in the Congregation, following the teaching of Giovenino, denied the infallibility of the Pope, he wrote to him that he was scandalised that an *Italian* priest — as distinct from a *French* priest — would hold such an opinion. He begged him at least, to keep his opinion to himself, lest the students of the Congregation should be affected by the same error.[22]

– VII –

The damage caused by the writers of the Enlightenment was, to a large extent, restricted to the educated and the intellectuals; more pernicious was the threat from the Jansenists in the area of popular devotion and piety since this affected the vast majority of the ordinary faithful. Alphonsus abhorred the cold Jansenist spirit which deprived christian piety of its warmth, spontaneity and tenderness. Jansenist spirituality painted a picture of God as a severe task-master ready to condemn, watching for the slightest infringement of his law; their model was the Master in the parable of the coins, 'Master, I knew you to be a hard man' (Matt. 25.24). The road to the Kingdom was not merely straight and narrow but was reserved for the few, who, almost in desperation, prostrated themselves before the great majesty of God. There was no place for loving contact with the person of Jesus in his Sacraments, no audience of the Father in familiar prayer. Anything which enkindled tenderness in one's relationship with the forgiving Father of the Parable of the Prodigal Son was frowned upon. The loving kindness of God manifested in the mysteries of the Incarnation, the passion of Christ, and the Blessed Sacrament was neglected. And, needless to say, devotion to the Sacred Heart of Jesus was particularly calculated to anger them.

The principal battles against Jansenism were not fought in the theological lecture halls or in the learned tomes of theology, rather were they fought to the bitter end in the practices of popular devotions and in the popular manuals of prayers and piety. The corrosive spirit of Jansenism was finally eradicated through the persistence of the ordinary faithful in their simple devotions to the saints, to the Mother of God and to the love of God as manifested in the mysteries of the Incarnation, Passion and Death of His only Son. Alphonsus soon discerned where the main struggle was centred and he was not prepared to allow the Jansenist offensive to go unopposed. During this same period, some fifteen books of different sizes flowed from his pen in his efforts to maintain the fervour of the ordinary lay person's devotion. His themes were predictable, prayer in all its aspects, devotion to the Infant Jesus in the mystery of the Incarnation, devotion to the Passion and the Way of the Cross, meditation on the great truths of faith, devotion to the saints and, above all, to the Mother of God. It seemed as if he felt that the whole defence of authentic christian piety devolved on him alone, that he stood as the sole bulwark against the insidious menace of the whole Jansenist system.

He realised that the question of prayer was of primary importance. Having published a delightful devotional book on the art of conversing continually with God, based on a French original, Alphonsus then produced a short pamphlet on the necessity of prayer in the christian life, both of which were in the nature of preparation for a major work which he published in 1759, *Del Gran Mezzo della Preghiera per Conseguire la Salute eterna e tutte le Grazie che desideriamo da Dio*, known in English simply as *Prayer, the Great Means of Salvation*. The work, in two parts, was once again the fruit of years of theological study and of practical experience gained in the preaching of missions. The seventeenth and eighteenth centuries were filled with the war of theologians over the mystery of grace and of God's assistance to his creatures in their actions; it is one of the oldest, certainly one of the most intractable, of theological problems, in which all the great names from Augustine onwards have been involved. The controversy, at all times lively, seemed to lose all balance towards the end of the sixteenth century with the publication of the Jesuit, Louis de Molino's work on grace. In desperation, the Pope could do nothing more than impose an embargo of silence on all the participants. But the whole question came to life again, with the Jansenists' teaching on predestination, man's freewill and the infallibility of grace.

Alphonsus' reaction as a pastoral priest and above all as a missioner was one of dismay that so vital a section of teaching as God's salvific Will for his people, his assistance to them in their temptations and the power of His grace, should be so clouded by the theological wars of the schools. The errors of Jansenism were threatening the whole mystery of salvation, not merely in theory, but also in practice, in the everyday life of the ordinary faithful. The wealth of speculation and the various theories in this whole area were a luxury that the ordinary Christian could ill afford — he needed something clear and simple while the theologians could be left to their speculations about predestination and God's foreknowledge. For Alphonsus the important thing was the basic essential elements of christian teaching which could be preached to the people, insisted upon and instilled into their consciousness as a sure guide to conduct — God's will to save all creatures, the fact that He gives to all the graces necessary for the salvation of their souls, our essential liberty in the matter of salvation and the fact that Jesus died on the Cross for all. He saw that the key to unravelling the whole problem, from the pastoral point of view, at least, lay in one word, prayer — prayer to God for the graces necessary for salvation. Herein lay the unifying pastoral principle which transcended conflicting speculations and provided secure norms of conduct for the ordinary person. The evolution of his thought was gradual, built up over the years of his missionary experience and particularly by his participation in the campaign of prayer launched in the diocese of Naples by Father Sarnelli and Cardinal Spinelli. It was as a result of his growing conviction that prayer was the pastoral key to the whole problem of God's grace, that he introduced the innovation of a special sermon on prayer into the mission repertoire.

Alphonsus' approach to the problem was fully formulated by 1757; by December of the following year he had completed the manuscript of *Prayer, the Great means of Salvation*. Early in March 1759, the work, of some four hundred pages, came from the printers in Naples. Alphonsus sent a copy at once to Remondini and within a year the work had gone into two editions with the Venetian publishers. The work, which Alphonsus styled 'theological-ascetical', was divided into two parts, the first dealing with various aspects of prayer itself, the second, more speculative, dealing with the fact that God gives the grace of prayer to everybody and the manner in which his grace operates. Alphonsus showed his familiarity with all the problems which had preoccupied the minds of theologians for centuries; he expressed his own opinions and his preference for certain solutions, according to a completely eclectic plan. His purpose was pastoral and here his argument was simple. There existed, as all admitted, ordinary grace which was sufficient to enable everybody to pray. With prayer every other grace was obtainable — even to carry out the most difficult of the divine commandments and to fulfil all one's christian obligations. The pastoral solution then, to centuries of theological speculation lay here. God gives to all the grace necessary to pray; prayer can obtain from God all other graces, even those which are special and are not, as it were, on general issue from the divine goodness. Throughout the whole work there is the authentic ring of christian optimism which praises at once the divine goodness of God, and at the same time, prevents us sinful creatures from falling into despair, unable to overcome the obstacles to our salvation, arising from ourselves and the world around us. We are responsible for our salvation and if we lose our souls there is no point in cursing Adam or original sin or our temptations and least of all God Himself. The key is prayer to God for the assistance of His grace. It was all succinctly contained in the Italian jingle, repeated over and over again until not even the most illiterate could forget it:

> Dal mundo, inferno e carne
> Al mal sei spinto
> Prega, prega se vuoi
> Non essere vinto[23]

In his assessment of his writings, Alphonsus gave this small volume a place apart:

> I have published many books of devotion but I do not think I have composed any work as useful as this present one. If it were possible for me to do so, I would print as many copies as there are inhabitants on this earth and present a copy to each so that they might understand the necessity of praying in order to save their souls. There is nothing that preachers, confessors and authors should insist on more than the necessity of prayer.

In his anxiety to carry out this wish he insisted with Remondini on a give-away price for the book. When supplies reached him, he despatched them as quickly as possible throughout Naples and also to Rome and Sicily. Reprinted time and time again in Alphonsus's lifetime until he could not keep track of the editions, the influence of the work was immense. After his death it went into hundreds of editions in numerous languages until it came to occupy a secure place among the great christian classics of popular theology.[24]

If Alphonsus' works on prayer played a considerable part in stemming the Jansenist spirit in Italy and later throughout the whole christian world they were supported in their task by a series of simple devotional works from his pen which were calculated to infuriate the Jansenists — they were 'worthless little books of stupid piety' (*ses méchants petits livres de piété inepte*), as they styled them in their anger. In the forefront was the *Apparecchio alla Morte*, the *Preparation for Death*, a series of simple meditations on the great eternal verities, death, judgment, eternity, hell and heaven. The book, like so many of its predecessors, had a dual purpose, to provide a source book for preachers on missions and also as a handy book of meditations and spiritual reading. One has only to compare these meditations with those on similar themes from the pens of his Jansenist contemporaries to appreciate the difference of approach. Not one single meditation in the *Preparation for Death* ends without a prayer for the love of God and for the grace of perseverance in that love; every meditation is shot through with genuine christian optimism. Of all his works this was the one most pirated. It became the national meditation book of Italy; it was the favourite spiritual book of Daniel O'Connell, the Irish national hero and it was also in the hands of the dying mystic, St Gemma Galgani.

The same year, 1758, that saw the publication of the *Preparation for Death*, also saw the publication of meditations and novenas in honour of the Child Jesus, of St Joseph and finally a novena in honour of the Sacred Heart.

This last had an interesting history. It had its origin in a special course of sermons Alphonsus had preached earlier in the year in Nola. His interest in the increasingly popular devotion to the Sacred Heart went back many years. He had familiarised himself with the life and revelations of Margaret Mary Alacoque of Paray-le-Monial. In fact, the concluding visits in the book of Visits to the Blessed Sacrament were largely inspired by her spirituality. Alphonsus prefaced his short work on the Sacred Heart with a precise doctrinal mise-au-point.[25] He was personally convinced that the devotion was based on sound theological principles and that Margaret Mary was the providential instrument of God in securing its formal acceptance in the Church's liturgy. Despite the fact that Benedict XIV, surrounded by his philo-jansenist advisers, was hesitant in the matter, Alphonsus in his preaching ministry had persisted in urging the devotion from the pulpit; this was one of the resolutions he entered in his personal note-book at the end of his retreat in August 1752. He had pictures of the Sacred Heart printed according to the suggestions of Margaret Mary, who was not then canonised. He tried, unsuccessfully, to enlist episcopal support for a petition to the Pope for the official establishment of the liturgical feast. The publication of this small devotional work played a considerable part in overcoming the final obstacles to the establishment of the feast in the Church's calendar. His brief doctrinal introduction, in which he quoted with approval the work of Muratori, clarified the true nature of the object of the devotion to general satisfaction.

The work filled the Jansenists with fury. Just when they imagined that they had securely closed the door to any further liturgical advance of this devotion, Alphonsus' short treatise restated with new force and theological clarity the arguments in its favour; the 'Alacoquisti' were making their presence felt again. With the accession of Cardinal Rezzonico as Pope Clement XIII the same year, the whole attitude of the papacy changed; petitions for the establishment of the liturgical feast poured into Rome from all over Europe until the Pope finally acceded to the request in January 1765. In the meantime Alphonsus had become a bishop and the news delighted him; he was among the first to establish the feast in his diocese the very same year. The Jansenisers never forgave him for his support for this 'outlandish, incoherent, pharisaical, false, superstitious and nestorian devotion to the heart of flesh of Jesus Christ which had its origins in the hallucinations of the visionary Alacoque'.

Chapter Twelve

Among The Brethren
1749–1762

– I –

The stability provided by the papal approbation of 1749 and the restricted measure of royal approval secured in the decree of 1752 were reflected in the remarkable growth of the Congregation. There were some thirty-five members in 1749 when Alphonsus petitioned the Holy Father for approval; thirteen years later when he left as bishop-designate of Sant'Agatha of the Goths, the number had increased to nearly 150, and there were twenty novices in Ciorani. Moreover, a papal decree of 1757 granted to the Congregation canonical privileges similar to those enjoyed by several other missionary groups such as the Pii Operai, the Fathers of Christian Doctrine and the Oratorians, thereby greatly facilitating the work of the Congregation and confirming the high esteem in which it was held in Rome. The twenty-fifth anniversary of the foundation in Scala that same year passed without any celebration — at least there are no references to any festivities in all the documents and letters that are extant. With the acceptance of the foundation in Beneventum, there were now five houses, four under Bourbon jurisdiction and one in the freer atmosphere of the papal enclave. Requests for foundations were frequent, four from Calabria, one in the Basilicata near Matera, and there were concerted efforts to lure the missioners back to Villa degli Schiavi, but, by royal decree, no further foundation was permitted in the Bourbon jurisdiction. More important than the numerical increase was the high esteem in which the Redemptorist missionaries were held throughout the Kingdom, even in the anti-clerical circles of the Court; they were regarded as the least objectionable of all the clergy. The bishop of Lettere, Mons. Giannini, declared that he was on familiar terms with the lawyers of Naples who spoke disparagingly of every type of cleric and religious community, but never once dared utter a word against the Congregation of the Most Holy Redeemer, and he added,

'I have also confirmed this same thing in my experience on the missions throughout the Kingdom.'[1] In his letter and talks to the members of the Congregation, Alphonsus insisted on the importance of maintaining this high reputation, rooted more than anything else in the esteem with which he himself was regarded. He warned them at the same time of the precarious nature of their existence; the slightest misdemeanour on the part of any member of the Congregation could have serious consequences in the Bourbon Court, ever on the watch for some incident with which to manifest its anti-clerical orientation and to bait the Pope.

In 1756 Alphonsus was able to fulfil a long cherished wish to send a group of missioners down to the spiritually abandoned region of the two Calabrias. The project had been in his mind even back in the days of Scala when he planned with Donato and Mannarini to evangelise those regions which were certainly in need of their ministry. The subsequent division, the fewness of subjects, the increasing calls for their services nearer to Naples, all made the realisation of the project impossible. In November 1756, a year after the general mission in Beneventum, Alphonsus dispatched the first group of missioners to Calabria. The journey took eight days. The campaign opened with the mission of Maratea in the bay of Policastro, and continued from village to village with enormous enthusiasm, Cassano, Aieta, Mormanno, Scalea, Castelluccio, Tortora. Crowds flocked to the missions; they besieged the confessionals. 'What a crime it is', wrote back young Father Peter Paul Blasucci, in the enthusiasm of his first general missionary outing, 'to see the people longing to have confessors and there are none; we are so few we cannot hear them all.' Few of the local Calabrian clergy showed any interest in this tiresome ministry; the great majority of them were not even theologically qualified to do so. Those who promised their co-operation failed to put in an appearance though the spiritual exercises preached by the missioners to the numerous clerics of the area did something to remedy the situation.

The Fathers were hailed on their return to Pagani as missionary heroes. Alphonsus was ready to listen interminably to the accounts of their exploits, the conversions, and the necessity of restraining the Calabrians rather than encouraging them. Blasucci was eager to fill the novitiate in Ciorani with young Calabrians, who he announced, were vivacious, intelligent and well mannered; Alphonsus was more circumspect. The following year another missionary band was back in Calabria where scenes similar to those of the previous year were repeated. From the diocese of Cassano the missioners ventured further south into the mountains to evangelise those strange ethnic groups of Calabrian Greeks and Albanians in the ancient Lombard and Saracen towns of Saracena, San Basile, Lungro and Firmo, where the inhabitants spoke their own unique dialect and used a semi-oriental liturgy. This second expedition was even more fruitful than the first. The missioners found a people spiritually neglected but avid for all the spiritual ministrations they could provide. In their anxiety to benefit from the temporary sojourn of the missioners, many remained away from home all night, sleeping in the precincts of the church to make sure of getting to confession. The spiritual climate of the area altered considerably as the missioners instructed the people doctrinally, taught them how to pray and to sanctify their simple peasant lives, instructing them in the frequentation of the sacraments, in the method of visiting the Blessed Sacrament, putting an end to public scandals and reconciling feuds and family vendettas which had lasted for years. At least four foundations were offered. On their own initiative the civil and ecclesiastical authorities of Policastro, Cutri, Normanno and San Giovanni in Fiore, presented their requests personally to the Royal Court, pointing out the necessity for apostolic labourers such as the Redemptorists, and offering to the missioners one of the many suppressed monasteries of the area. But to no avail; the attitude of the Court had stiffened and not even Alphonsus could wring a reluctant assent from them.

In 1758 the possibility of fulfilling another project very dear to Alphonsus presented itself — the possibility of accepting a foreign missionary commitment. In the early years of his priesthood he had felt called to commit himself to this apostolate. When it was made clear to him that his work for the moment, at least, lay in Naples, the attraction lingered on and was shared by his colleagues. In the initial drafts of the Rule before Roman approbation, all the priests were to bind themselves by vow at the age of thirty-three to dedicate their lives to evangelisation overseas at the command of the Holy Father, a prescription which was suppressed at the instigation of Cardinal Spinelli as superfluous. But the desire to consecrate their active lives to the foreign missions continued to be shared by many of the priests and from time to time, in a rush of fervour, some individuals volunteered for this work. In 1752 the novices in Ciorani, carried away by their youthful zeal, petitioned Alphonsus to be designated for the conversion of Japan:

> We feel a burning desire to shed our blood and to give our lives for Jesus Christ in Japan, and to save those poor souls redeemed by the blood of Our Saviour. For the love of Jesus Christ and of the Mother of God and for the love of souls which prompted your Paternity to found this Congregation, we beg you to grant us the privilege of going to those foreign lands, not indeed now, but in due time. In the meantime, we beg your Paternity to direct our Superiors to humiliate us, despise us and make us suffer . . .

The final request from these enthusiastic novices was more than likely superfluous and the letter drew this reply from Alphonsus:

> My dear sons,
>
> As long as you show me plainly that you have the true spirit of a foreign missionary I will have no difficulty in designating you for this work. But this spirit cannot be gauged just by bearing humiliations imposed on you for this purpose, but by bearing whatever humiliations come your way, with patience. Humiliations of your own choosing, or when you know they are imposed merely for a purpose, are of little benefit.

And so from this day onwards, behave yourselves so that no one will be able to cast up to you — 'so you are the one who wished to go to Japan!' Every day, especially at Holy Communion, pray for me to Jesus Christ and convey this same request to all the novices.

Your Brother, Alfonso of the Most Holy Redeemer.[2]

In the summer of 1758 Alphonsus received an invitation from the Propaganda Fide to send missionaries to Mesopotamia in the Middle East, to work among the Nestorians. Since 1756, Cardinal Spinelli had been Prefect of Propaganda and the dire need of missionaries in that area brought back to his mind the missionary aspirations of Alphonsus and his colleagues. The news of the invitation was, for some reason, conveyed to the five communities by a circular letter written by Father Fabrizio Cimino on behalf of Alphonsus. Cimino, a young priest of twenty-five at the time, and later to be saddled with the odium of the *Regolamento*, was acting as Alphonsus' secretary. The fact that Alphonsus himself did not attend personally to the invitation or convey the exciting news to the communities, may well be an indication of his less than total enthusiasm for the project. At any rate, letters of reply came from all ranks and ages in the Congregation; men like Father Margotta, whose active days were past, volunteered; the response from the younger men was overwhelming as was, of course, the response of the students and novices. But the whole project came to nothing. One of the conditions demanded by Propaganda was that the proposed missionaries should formally leave their institute and work under Propaganda as secular priests without religious vows — a condition which was totally unacceptable to Alphonsus. So the negotiations collapsed.[3]

The disappointment at the failure of the Nestorian project was compensated for, a few years later, by the opening of the first Redemptorist house in Sicily. The negotiations, which began in 1756, were protracted. In the first place, Alphonsus found himself faced with the concerted opposition of his consultors who were utterly opposed to the foundation. Then, to his surprise and frustration, he encountered, for the first time, the considerable reluctance of the brethren to leave Naples. Their enthusiasm for missionary endeavour evaporated before the reality of Sicily. Twenty years later this reluctance was still in evidence. It required forty days of prayer, he was to state, in scarcely concealed annoyance, to get one of the brethren to accept an assignment to the new foundation in the Papal States, a hundred kilometres or so north of Naples, '*perchè ognuno non si vuol partire da Mamma*, no one wants to leave Mamma.' Though the consultors remained opposed to the Sicilian foundation, Alphonsus stubbornly persisted in his purpose and after five years his determination bore fruit. In 1761 a foundation at Agrigento on the south coast of the island was agreed upon and four Fathers, Peter Paul Blasucci, Bernard Apice, Michelangelo Perrotta and Dominic Caputo with Brother Pasquale, agreed to undertake the mission. The four Fathers had all just turned thirty and were quite junior in the Congregation, ample evidence of the lack of enthusiasm among the older generation for the new missionary venture. Alphonsus addressed them before their departure. They were going as apostles to the Kingdom of Sicily to give glory to God and to Jesus Christ, the Divine Redeemer and to their spiritual Mother, the Congregation of the Most Holy Redeemer, by means of the good example of their lives and by their preaching. He recommended to them faithfulness to their Rule, obedience to their superiors and to the bishop of Agrigento, the father and benefactor of the foundation. He inculcated a spirit of mutual charity, humility and zeal for the salvation of souls, since the purpose of the foundation was to bring spiritual assistance to the poor people of the area who were deprived of spiritual ministrations where missioners were few.[4]

There was as much excitement and preparation as if the group had, in fact, been setting out for the Far East in the footsteps of Francis Xavier by way of the Cape of Good Hope. They left by boat from Naples only to be driven back three times by storms; on the last occasion the storm was so severe that they had to run for shelter north of the bay and were saved from shipwreck, according to the account of Tannoia, more by the prayers of the missionaries than by the skill of the crew. A few days later, the adventurers arrived back in Pagani. Apice had fallen seriously ill and received the Last Sacraments. Father Francesco Pentimalli, who had arrived in Pagani unexpectedly from Sant'Angelo, was assigned to take his place (Apice and two others joined them in Sicily the following year). Without further delay the newly constituted group set off again; this time taking the land route down the coast through Calabria — Pentimalli's native province — and the Basilicata. At Reggio Calabria, in sight of Sicily, they were forbidden to cross to Messina due to an outbreak of plague and were obliged to spend some time in quarantine. At the suggestion of Father Pentimalli, who was just fifty, they went back to his home at Santa Eufemia to await clearance for the rest of the journey. There, after ten days in the happiness of his first family reunion for many years, Pentimalli contracted a fever and died within a week. Hell, it seemed, was conspiring against the new foundation and the consultors may well have experienced a thrill of satisfaction that their opposition had been endorsed. Finally, on 11 December, nearly three months after they first set out from Pagani, the missionary band, now reduced to four members, arrived at Agrigento to begin their work as missionaries on the island. The undertaking, which continued to suffer its share of vicissitudes was, however, visibly blessed in many ways from the outset. One of the last reports Alphonsus received, before news of his election as bishop came from Rome, was a letter of gratitude from the bishop of Agrigento at the close of the first mission preached by the Redemptorists beyond the mainland of Italy:

> I assure your Reverence that the Fathers have given the highest satisfaction to all classes of the faithful. I have experienced the greatest pleasure in seeing my flock crowd to the church to hear their preaching. During the coming Lent, they have planned to preach the spiritual exercises to the various sections of the population. On my own behalf

I wish to tell you that I am most content with these good Fathers whose one interest is the salvation of souls and who edify the whole city by their exemplary lives. I trust that these few lines will serve as a consolation to your Reverence.[5]

– II –

Alphonsus' spiritual life settled down to a normal rhythm in Pagani during the years preceding his elevation to the episcopate. Father Paul Cafaro, who was inclined to be unfeeling and rather ruthless in his treatment of penitents, was his spiritual director for ten years from 1753. Few of his penitents persevered under his direction for as long as Alphonsus, though Alphonsus made no reference to this aspect of his director when he published an account of his life some years afterwards. After Cafaro's death in 1753, Alphonsus chose Villani as his spiritual director and when Villani went a few years later to the new foundation of Sant' Angelo à Cupolo, Father Mazzini stepped into his shoes. Alphonsus' practices of piety and his penances had been standardised well before this, with the result that the succession of directors did not alter to any great extent the pattern of his life. Villani and Mazzini, however, were both of gentler dispositions and less rigorous than Cafaro, a fact which Alphonsus would have found reflected in their direction. His serious scruples were to a large extent under control; his strict adhesion to the norms laid down over the years by his confessors from Pagano to Mazzini had succeeded in calming the anxieties of the early years. But he still needed reassurance. He entered in his note-book on 15 August 1753 that Villani had confirmed all the instructions given him by Cafaro; on 14 July 1759 he recorded that Mazzini in turn had confirmed all the instructions of his previous confessors beginning with Pagano, and that this was to hold good until his death — *sino alla morte*. Above all, he was not to go back on decisions he had made in the past.

In Pagani, his normal day began half-an-hour before the community was called; he spent the time in prayer in his room before going down to the choir for morning meditation with the community. He then returned to his room where he recited the morning office with one of the Fathers or students who came to accompany him — a reminder of days when his private recitation of the breviary was beset with scruples. After this, he began his study or his writing, to which he attended for the next five hours or so until mid-day, when he celebrated Mass in a chapel next to his room. At Mass he was slow, tediously so for those who assisted him, although later in life he became more normal in this regard. One morning Brother Nicholas told him to get another server as he was too busy to spend all the time required with him. While the community was in the refectory at their midday meal, Alphonsus spent the time in thanksgiving in the oratory and when the community had finished their meal he dined with those who had served or read at table. He then joined the community for the short period of recreation which remained. During the hour of siesta—or in summer, an hour and a half — he usually visited the Blessed Sacrament or went to his room to work; as he moved about the monastery he took off his shoes so as not to disturb the brethren. He finally lay down on his bed for about half-an-hour.[6]

The afternoon began with some spiritual reading and half-an-hour of prayer, then back to study and writing. A short time before the *Ave Maria* — which varied according to the season of the year — he went out into the garden, where he sometimes attended to the flowers or weeded the beds. After a further community meditation, he went to his room again, while the community went to the refectory to dine. As at midday, he dined when the community had finished its meal and then joined them once more for a part of the evening recreation and night prayers. It was a day of great simplicity, divided between prayer and study.

Equally simple were his practices of devotion, the recitation of the rosary, the Way of the Cross every day, usually during siesta time, or after night prayers. His devotion to the Mother of God made him take a vow to recite the rosary every day; to this he added the practice of three Hail Marys, morning and night, which he recommended to the people in his preaching and writings. He recited the five psalms in honour of the name of Mary which, at the time, were attributed to St Bonaventure. He wore the scapulars of Our Lady of Mount Carmel and of Our Lady of Dolours and he was enrolled in the Rosary confraternity of the Dominican Fathers. Saturday was a day of special devotion to the Mother of God; it was also the day of his weekly confession. At table on Saturdays he practised some special acts of self-denial in Our Lady's honour, abstaining from fruit and for many years he did not eat at supper at all on that day. Up to 1750, he fasted on bread and water on Saturdays, but his health began to fail and on Sunday morning he felt, according to his own words, more dead than alive, with the result that he had to abandon that practice and partake of a more or less normal midday meal. Cafaro wisely commuted the Saturday fast to just one course of fruit and an extra half-hour of spiritual reading which was easily absorbed into his normal routine of study. He always spent the recreation period of Saturday night in the presence of the Blessed Sacrament, and on that day he usually washed up with the Brothers in the kitchen, decked out in an apron.

He cultivated right throughout his life a great devotion to the saints. He read their lives until they became, as it were, his living companions, so easily could he quote from their writings and refer to incidents in their lives. It would be difficult to say who was his favourite saint; he changed as the years went by. Early on in his life, his great models were Teresa of Avila, Francis de Sales and John of the Cross. Later, he was enthusiastic about Aloysius Gonzaga, then the Franciscans, Francis of Assisi, Anthony of Padua, Peter of Alcantara and Paschal Baylon. He was a faithful member of the Franciscan Third Order, wore the scapular faithfully and, as a Tertiary, recited the Office and observed the special fasts.

He bound himself by 'vows', some eight or nine of them in all, to perform certain acts of piety such as reciting the rosary each day, going to confession on Saturdays, not to eat fruit on certain days. The most important of these, however, was the 'vow' not to squander a moment of time, or, perhaps, to put it positively, always to be occupied in some aspect of his ministry such as prayer, study, preaching. All the witnesses of his life speak of this vow and they were accustomed to refer to it in his presence when his scrupulous interpretation of it placed an excessive strain on his physical or mental health. But we do not know when exactly he made it or in what precise terms. According to the testimony of others he was always occupied, never really just 'doing nothing', though this did not exclude joining in community recreation, taking a siesta, going into the garden for relaxation, or, of course, playing the clavichord. However, as the postulator of the cause pointed out at the process of beatification, these were not 'vows' in the strict theological or canonical sense, binding under pain of grave sin. He made only two such vows of which we know, namely, not to abandon the work of the Congregation when his companions left him in Scala in 1733, and, secondly, not to abandon Mons. Falcoia as his director of conscience. The other 'vows' were really resolutions and more or less reminders to himself of the standards he wished to maintain.[7]

His external penances make strange reading today but they were the normal ascetical currency of the century in which he lived and indeed for long afterwards. The food in the houses was very far from being luxurious; it was the normal menu of the ordinary people at the time, though Alphonsus was insistent that it should be both adequate and well presented. He was accustomed to sprinkle bitter herbs on his food to make it less palatable — powdered aloes, myhrr and wormwood. He kept a small box—like a snuff box — with these herbs, on his person and when he thought he was not being observed, he sprinkled them on his meals. The house cats were more selective than he was. On several occasions when a portion of what he had left on his plate was later given to the cats they refused to eat, not being partial, obviously, to the taste of bitter herbs. On certain days each week he took his midday meal on his knees and, on occasion, added to this the bizarre practice of wearing a stone tied round his neck in the guise of a criminal. Early on in his priestly life he did not drink wine but later, under directions from Falcoia and his directors, he used it sparingly, considerably diluted with water. The regime of self-inflicted penances which he undertook early in life he continued faithfully down through the years and it was an area in which he had to be restrained. All his directors, and especially Falcoia, warned him of the danger of excess in these practices but his obedience in the matter was total and he had explicit permission for whatever penances of this nature he performed with the exception of very few occasions. He used the discipline every day, sometimes twice. He wore spiked chains known as *cilices* — an adaptation of the hair-shirt — for some time each day next to the skin. These practices were then in vogue, and would not have been regarded as exceptional — still less, eccentric. He, in turn, recommended their use to his penitents and detailed the principles governing their use in his spiritual writings for priests and religious and more particularly 'for those who wished to be directed in the way of perfection'.[8] While staying on one occasion in Naples with Hercules, he was found slumped on the floor where he had fainted. Brother Francis summoned the doctor and as they put him to bed they found that he was wearing the *cilices*. His main worry on recovery was that his secret had been discovered. One day Brother Peter Paul came across Alphonsus' hair-shirt which had iron spikes woven through it. Out of curiosity he decided to experiment secretly himself but the experiment did not last very long for he found it quite unbearable and he removed it as quickly as he could. He described the experience as 'hell'.

Alphonsus' simplicity in the matter of food was matched by his poverty in his clothes, which irritated Hercules considerably. He purchased most of his clothes in the *Giudecca*, the second-hand clothes market in Naples. His soutanes, which he bought there, were usually cast-off Jesuit soutanes which he wore patched and cleaned until the tailor at Pagani refused to have anything more to do with them. His most cherished possession was his travelling cloak which he had for years; it, too, came from the *Giudecca* but was of different religious provenance — it was a cast-off Franciscan cloak which he had dyed black — in the words of his contemporaries, *cappotto da Franciscano tinto nero*. His shoes were those of the ordinary artisan, *scarpe all'Apostolica*, serviceable and sometimes with an iron buckle. The poverty he affected in his dress did not find general acceptance; bishops and priests — his own among them — commented adversely. One bishop complained to Villani that while the other members of the congregation were at least respectable, Alphonsus was nothing better than a bundle of rags. He had, it would seem, developed a mild form of obsession in the matter as an antidote to the danger of vanity in his life and also as a reaction against the foppishness of the 'society' clergy who affected, in his own chosen phrase, *la milorderia nell'vestire*. He inveighed against clerical vanity in his preaching to priests. He adopted a similar attitude in the matter of a beard; they were gradually going out of fashion and the new style — especially among the more sophisticated clergy — was to be clean-shaven. Predictably, he refused to follow the new fashion; at most, he agreed to keep his beard trimmed with a scissors, an operation which he performed himself with no great skill. Trimming the beard had developed, at the time, into a highly technical operation. According to the professionals, it had to be done from east to west and from north to south, or as the Neapolitans claimed, *da Levante a Ponente, dal Settentrione a Mezzogiorno*, leaving the beard smoothly even all over and flowing. Alphonsus attacked his beard with complete disregard for any such refinements as was immediately recognisable from the results, making him at times a source of amusement or annoyance to others. When he arrived to preach the clergy retreat in the diocese of Sarno, the bishop, Mons.de Novellis, objected strongly to his appearance and without further ceremony sent for his barber; Alphonsus submitted without objection. A similar incident occurred in Lettere where the bishop, Mons. Giannini, insisted that he shave off his beard before preaching a mission in his diocese. Besides these occasions which are well documented, Alphonsus agreed to shave his beard before going to Rome for his episcopal consecration and on another occasion when, as bishop, he dined with King Ferdinand IV in the royal palace.

His greatest triumph, however, over these years was the increasing affability he was able to show exteriorly; this did not come easily to him. There were very sharp edges to his character which, uncontrolled, would have made him intolerable both as a colleague and, above all, as a superior. His affability, which caused people to compare him with Francis de Sales — on whom he did, in fact, model much of his conduct — was only achieved at the cost of great effort. His natural sharpness of manner, his bad temper and touchiness were the constant object of his self-control. Time and time again in the process of canonisation reference is made to his *'temperamento bilioso'*, to his irascibility; it recurs like a chorus in the evidence of those who knew him intimately. But he well knew his own character defects, as much from having them pointed out to him by his directors, as from his own self-examination. In this he was much more truthful than his early biographers who wished to portray him as already perfect. 'Everyone has his defects and I more than anybody,' he wrote to Father Caione in August 1753. 'If the biographers of the saints would write of their defects as well as of their virtues, their biographies would be more voluminous,' was a comment of his which he wrote to one of the novices and which can well be applied to his own case. When one of the canons of his cathedral remonstrated with him at a later date for remaining silent when publicly insulted by one of his priests, his reply revealed his efforts, 'for so many years I have worked to acquire patience and self-control and do you wish to make me lose it all?'[9]

The key to much of his conduct was his effort to overcome his natural pride and vanity, that *stima propria* which he shared with all his Neapolitan confrères. This national character trait was the main object of his attack. He refused to speak of the nobility of his family; when he spoke of them at all, it was to disparage their titles of nobility and to emphasise their poverty. When the censors, in approving his works for publication, mentioned the nobility of the author he invariably retorted that it would be better for them to approve the doctrinal content of his writings rather than his family lineage. He refused to take advantage of the family name to gain admission to audience either of court officials or bishops but took his turn simply with others when a word as to who he was would have opened doors to him at once. He waited in the ante-chambers with the ordinary suppliant for Brancone, Spinelli and the other bishops and officials throughout the Kingdom. He would request the *maestri-di-camera* who received him, lackeys, who were all deference to the nobility and much less gracious to the lower strata of society, to inform his Lordship that a priest wished to speak with him, refusing at the same time to give his name. His poor clothes were a sufficient disguise for his social status. When he went to Cerreto to visit Mons. Gentile, the bishop, the footman, one Pasquale, was sweeping the ante-chamber and dismissed him rather abruptly, telling him to wait. Alphonsus sat down and the footman continued his work, sweeping indiscriminately right under the seat where Alphonsus was sitting. For a Neapolitan nobleman to tolerate such an indignity would have been unthinkable. Finally, the servant asked the priest his name, which meant nothing to him, and then went leisurely to inform the bishop that one Don Alfonso de Liguori wished to speak with him. To the amazement of the servant, the bishop prepared to receive his visitor suitably; instead of instructing the footman to show Don Alfonso in, he went personally to receive him into his private study. Alphonsus was equally careful not to cast himself in the role of founder of the Congregation. When this was referred to in his presence, he immediately replied that he was not the founder but that Falcoia was. When a priest asking him a favour, rather imprudently wrote that he was an example to all, he replied by letter, 'Padre mio carissimo, I can only declare that so far from being a saint I am nothing more than a poor sinner. I tremble at the account I shall have to give to God for my unfaithful co-operation with all his merciful graces.' Once in Naples he overheard himself referred to as the 'servant of God'. Annoyed, he replied, 'And who else should we serve if not God?'[10]

He was in constant demand during these years as a spiritual director and adviser at all levels. There was a stream of visitors to Pagani seeking guidance in difficulties concerning vocation and other spiritual problems. Bishops consulted him on their pastoral problems, on moral theology, on their dealings with the government. He received an average of about five hundred letters a year at this time. When he went to Naples there were often up to thirty or forty people waiting to see him either in the house where he was lodging or in some church, or in the case of nuns, in their convent chapel. He was prodigal of his time and endeavoured to make himself readily available. His particular gift was a remarkable memory for each one's problems as if he carried them neatly indexed in his mind. All this posed problems for his vanity; he warned in his writings of the dangers of 'wishing to play the role of master in the spiritual life', a reflection of the personal struggle in which he was engaged. Around 1753, Cardinal Orsini came to Pagani to visit him. In the presence of others he exclaimed when Alphonsus appeared, 'Don Alfonso, I have come all the way from Rome to consult you.' Obviously the remark remained in Alphonus' mind to be used by the devil as a source of temptation to self-conceit and self-importance. When the Cardinal left, Alphonsus went up to the attic of the monastery and inflicted upon himself a severe self-flagellation to blood which disabled him for some days, an indiscretion which the Promotor of the Faith urged strongly against him at the process of beatification. But the Promotor of the Cause had little difficulty in adducing by way of rebuttal the well-known example of St Benedict rolling himself in thorns or nettles to overcome his lustful desires, so that the 'sufferings of the body would obliterate in his soul the sin of the mind.'[11]

Equally questionable to our present-day way of thinking are the well-documented examples of the numerous occasions when, apparently, to redress the burden of his vanity, Alphonus pretended to be ignorant or 'simple', This was his invariable response to those who, he felt, came to see him out of curiosity and without any real problem to be solved. Many such visitors left completely disappointed at his apparent childishness or even worse; some departed to ridicule his stupidity. His great horror was a fear of making a parade of his learning, of setting himself up as a source of knowledge and advice for others. His stratagems to avoid this were transparent. At times he endeavoured to put into the mouth of his interviewer the opinion which he wished to give, so as to make it appear to come from the person himself. When asked an opinion in the presence of others, he frequently took up a book from his table, pretending to quote from it the advice which he was giving, as if he himself had nothing at all to do with it. More disconcerting still and embarrassing for his colleagues, was his readiness to appear foolish, even uneducated, when he felt that he was in danger from his vanity. One Saturday night in Pagani there was an élite congregation of government officials, high-ranking military personnel, clerics and the local nobility present to hear him preach on the Mother of God. The occasion called for some special effort on his part. Instead of rising to the occasion he deliberately preached a very ordinary sermon in the plainest and most unadorned language; the community was thoroughly embarrassed. 'A child would have done as well', one of the Fathers commented. The expectant congregation left in disgust, disappointed because of what they now saw as the exaggerated reputation which Alphonsus enjoyed. Once again the Promotor of the Faith, who seems to have been eminently sensible, urged this incident against his canonisation, considering it an altogether imprudent act of mistaken piety. But his case fell to the ground when it was adduced in rebuttal that Francis de Sales had done precisely the same in the presence of the Queen of France in order to humble his vanity and to mortify the curiosity of his royal auditor. After all, Our Lord had refused to satisfy the curiosity of Herod by working a miracle to show his divine power.

The advice given to Alphonus years before, by both Pagano and Falcoia, to walk in the path of confidence in God's love and to abandon the way of fear and terror, had borne fruit. The characteristic note of his spirituality had become his complete abandonment to the will of God. God had become for him a kind and loving Father, disposing of the events of his life in loving wisdom. He no longer spoke of submitting himself to the dispositions of providence; seldom, either, of conforming his will to that of God. Now he preferred to speak of *uniformity*, as if his own will no longer existed, but was one with that of his Creator. One of the Fathers read in his personal manual of prayers a slip of paper containing prayers of love and trust in God which he had composed for himself. As a result, he was able to show an outward sense of happiness and general amiability which concealed the interior desolation and aridity of spirit which, as far as we can divine from the reports of his confessors, was the normal condition of his soul. He confided to his good friend, Don Giuseppe Jorio, that he experienced nothing but spiritual aridity and dryness of soul in his spiritual life, none of the consolations which he experienced in his early years as a seminarian and a young priest. When one of the novices wrote to him explaining that he was suffering from great aridity of spirit, with no sensible consolations in his devotions, Alphonsus consoled him with the phrase, *febbraio secco, massaro ricco*, a dry spring brings a rich harvest.

He practised to the full the reticence characteristic of the saints about their spiritual lives. Not merely did he use all possible stratagems to hide his practices of mortification but he was extremely slow to speak of his interior life or of the graces and favours which God granted him. This reticence about the things of God he inculcated in others, telling them to be silent about the action of God in their souls, to guard well the secret of God's dealings with them. Of his own mystic gifts he never spoke. Early in 1762 Father Angelo Verdesca entered his room in Pagani to recite the canonical hours with him, only to find him with his arms extended in prayer, his eyes fixed on heaven and his whole body raised some inches from the ground. Verdesca had entered silently and knelt beside him, as he recounted afterwards, for the space of a quarter of an hour. Finally with a deep sigh and with the repetition of the words, 'My God, My God,' Alphonsus came to his senses again. The presence of the Father caused him extreme embarrassment and he commanded him not to tell what he had seen to anybody.[12]

Alphonsus had few human interests, if any; politics, archaeology, literature, seem to have had no attraction for him. He was in no sense a humanist or a *litterateur* though he was tolerant enough to allow his colleagues like De Meo and Tannoia to pursue their intellectual interests. 'Saints are not literary men, they do not love the classics and they do not write Tales,' wrote Cardinal Newman. For Alphonsus, everything seemed to be centred in God — if he painted, it was only sacred subjects, if he wrote or read, it was always from the pastoral view-point and not from any human interest. His verse was just to sing of God and the mysteries of religion while his music was mainly hymns. The great archeological excavations which Charles III had organised at Pompei, and a few years later, at Herculaneum, and which brought tourists from beyond the Alps flocking to Naples to see the art treasures of ancient Rome and Greece, awakened not the slightest interest in him.[13] He passed the excavations and the museum in the Royal Palace at Portici as if they did not exist. While giving a retreat at Nola he was prevailed upon to visit the local Museum which hosted many classical art treasures, but it totally failed to interest him. He regretted the visit and the time it involved, prompting him to say afterwards that if all the museums in the world were gathered together, he could not envisage taking one step to visit them.

His relaxation was his clavicord but even here his repertoire consisted mainly of hymns to the Madonna, or to the Bambino Gesù or to Christ in his Passion, many of them composed by himself and based on the melodies of Neapolitan folk-tunes. Like all Neapolitans, he had music in his heart; it was part and parcel of him. Like the ordinary peasant of the Kingdom he could say 'If I do not sing I will die.' He was completely in his element on a mission when he was singing with the people and teaching them one of his own compositions, *O Bella mia Speranza, Gesù Mio, con dure funi*, or *Tu scendi dalle Stelle*, which are still 'prayed' by the country people of southern Italy

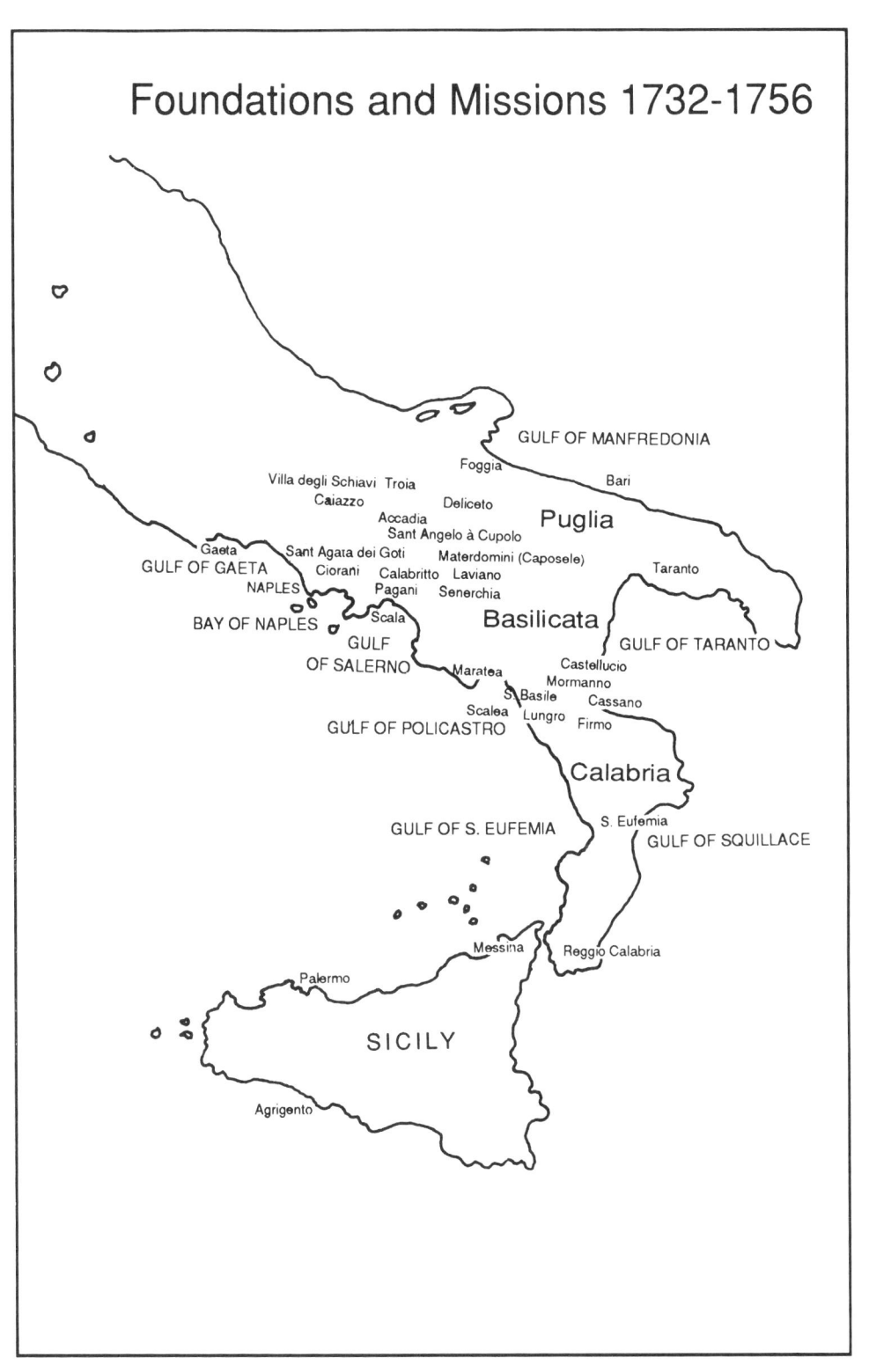

THEOLOGIA
MORALIS
ILLUSTRISSIMI AC REVERENDISSIMI
D. ALPHONSI DE LIGORIO
EPISCOPI S. AGATHÆ GOTHORUM,
ET RECTORIS MAJORIS CONGREGATIONIS SS. REDEMPTORIS,

ADJUNCTA IN CALCE PERUTILI INSTRUCTIONE
AD PRAXIM CONFESSARIORUM,
UNA CUM

ILLUSTRISSIMI AC REVERENDISSIMI
JOANNIS DOMINICI MANSI ARCHIEPISCOPI LUCENSIS
EPITOME DOCTRINÆ MORALIS, ET CANONICÆ
Ex Operibus Benedicti XIV.

Nunc primum ab eodem Auctore plurimis additamentis illuftrata, & pluribus in locis correcta

ACCEDIT ETIAM
PRÆSTANTISSIMI THEOLOGI
DISSERTATIO PROLEGOMENA
De Cafuifticæ Theologiæ originibus, locis, atque præftantia.

EDITIO SEXTA NOVISSIMA,
IN QUA PRÆTER EA OMNIA, QUÆ IN CÆTERIS ADDITA FUERE,
NUNC PRIMUM

Auctor ipfe plura reformavit, aliquibus fententiis clarius explicatis, aliis de novo additis, aliis re melius perpenfa immutatis, plurefque Tractatus nunquam antea editos, & novas animadverfiones magni ponderis adjecit.

TOMUS PRIMUS.

ROMÆ,
MDCCLXVII.
SUMPTIBUS REMONDINIANIS.
SUPERIORUM PERMISSU, AC PRIVILEGIO.

The title page of the sixth edition of Alphonsus' Moral Theology *published in Rome in 1767 in three folio volumes. It was the first complete edition of* Moral Theology *with no reference to Busenbaum on the title page.*

A page of the original manuscript of the Glories of Mary *in the handwriting of Alphonsus*

The church and monastery of Ciorani built on the estate of Baron Sarnelli. Here the members of the missionary society took religious vows for the first time and elected Alphonsus as the first Rector Major. To his considerable displeasure the missionaries were known for many years as the Cioranisti.

The Pontifical Basilica at Pagani where the remains of St Alphonsus de Liguori are venerated. He died in the monastery to the right of the Basilica.

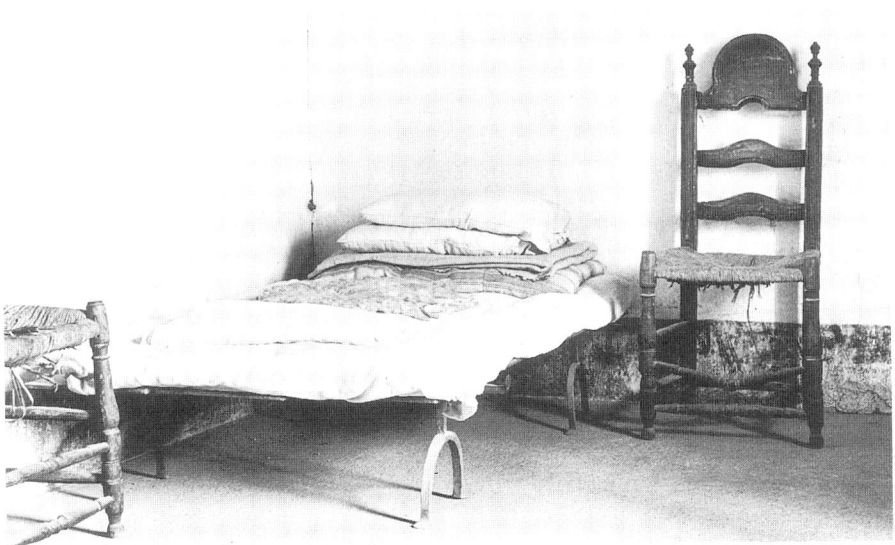

An angle of the room in Pagani where Alphonsus died, with a contemporary bed and chairs

The city of Deliceto in the heart of the Appenines, viewed from the Redemptorist monastery of Our Lady of Consolation

The Redemptorist monastery of Deliceto is today a training centre of young men. The doorway to the far left of the building still has the title S. Maria Consolationis 1750 carved on the architrave.

In Alphonsus' episcopal city of Sant' Agatha of the Goths as one approaches from the direction of Maddaloni, the tower and cupola of the Cathedral can be seen to the left.

A view of the episcopal city of Sant' Agatha of the Goths with Monte Taburno in the background. When his resignation was accepted in 1775, Alphonsus said he felt as if the whole weight of the mountain had been removed from his shoulders.

where the *anima meridionale* still prays in song. When he came to the sacristy to celebrate Mass, after a morning of study in his room, he would often prepare himself for the liturgy by singing quietly a hymn in honour of God or the Madonna.[14]

– III –

According to the Rule approved by Benedict XIV, Alphonsus as superior — his title was Rector Major — had virtually absolute authority in the internal government of the Congregation. He appointed all the important officials in each house, from the superior down to his advisors; he could also remove them at his pleasure and they did not have a defined canonical term of office. He could dismiss members from the Congregation and the exercise of these powers was unrestricted. He had, according to the prescriptions of the Rule, his consultors whom he was *bound* to meet once a month to discuss important matters, but it was stated explicitly that he was not bound to follow their advice — nor did he, as the Agrigento foundation amply demonstrates. The consultors' function, was, in the main, purely consultative. And this authority was for life. Furthermore, it was stated that the superior's principal duty was to maintain the observance of the Rule and it was laid down, lest there be any doubt in the matter, that 'he was to punish transgressors severely, especially if they are superiors, without any respect of persons'.

An unpleasant feature of Neapolitan religious life at the time was the system of secret informers. It was an accepted administrative practice for a superior, especially at higher level, to designate, in total secrecy, a member of the community distinct from the superior himself, to keep him informed of what was happening. This 'official' was to pay particular attention to the area of observance of the Rule and even the superior of the community was to come under scrutiny in this regard. This practice was further extended to the missions with the result that there was, more often than not, one of these 'spies' included among each large mission band. As a consequence, Alphonsus found himself fully informed of everything that took place, every movement and utterance of the members of the different communities, their peculiarities, their slightest misdemeanours, their least indisposition. Nothing was left unreported — De Paola had an attack of 'gleet', De Robertis and Villani were not getting on well together, young Corrado hated having to remain at home in the monastery, the student Nigro had bowel trouble, while de Michele was looking anything but well. Whatever may have been the motivation behind this system and despite the attempts to justify it with some specious spiritual arguments, it was the cause of considerable tension, creating an unhealthy atmosphere of fear and suspicion in the communities. Several times in his letters Alphonsus had to assure some members who had written to him in distress that they had not, in fact, been 'reported' and that Father So-and-So was not one of the secret inspectors. In the hands of someone less considerate or less tolerant of the foibles of human nature, this distasteful practice could have proved totally destructive of community life among the brethren.

Many aspects of the exercise of authority in religious communities at the time were calculated to encourage the worst manifestations of authoritarianism in superiors. Exceptional spiritual qualities and a degree of psychological equilibrium were required to transcend it all. Judging on the available evidence, Alphonsus as a superior succeeded to a remarkable degree and better than most of his colleagues, certainly in the period before his appointment as bishop. He was determined that his regime would be anything but dictatorial; he laid it down for himself that amiability and a general spirit of *dolcezza* was to characterise his dealings with members of the Congregation. The authoritarian and peremptory style adopted by the otherwise excellent Peter Paul Blasucci was not for him — in the Neapolitan phraseology of the time, he rejected the *commando musulmano*.[15] Judged by the criterion which he laid down for himself he must be regarded as an understanding, patient and benign superior. He knew his fellow Neapolitans inside out, understood their psychology, their humours, strengths and weaknesses. He knew when to placate, when to threaten, when to close his eyes to what was happening. His usual approach was to explain to the subject the position or difficulty in which he was placed or the fact that he had nobody else on whom he could call. Before he had time to proceed further, the subject, flattered by the confidence and his apparent indispensability, was ready to accept with alacrity whatever followed. He made it appear to the member of the Congregation that, far from being commanded by obedience to do something, he was in fact, doing the superior a favour, an approach which seldom failed. Father de Meo, a brilliant writer and preacher, had a pathological dread of being appointed a superior, even of a mission group — a reluctance which was not shared by all his confreres. On one occasion Alphonsus found himself in the position of having to insist, which he did by letter but in such a manner that De Meo could not refuse:

> Your Reverence is by far the most senior of all the Fathers on this occasion. Furthermore, you are the most experienced in giving missions and the most sought after and applauded by those who will be attending. I ask you then, out of love for the Mother of God, to be so good as to take on the position of superior on this occasion. Please do not disappoint me, since, before God, I think it the best thing.

Flattered, De Meo overcame his repugnance where a curt command would have brought voluble protests and possibly no results. At the same time, these stratagems did not destroy Alphonsus' integrity in his relations with his brethren. One always knew where one stood with him. One of the shrewdest of those who lived with him admired this characteristic particularly. 'Although he was superior of us all,' wrote Father Dominic Caputo, 'he was not, in any way, a politician; his government was sincere and kind, without descending to deception or double-dealing.'[16]

His main task as superior, especially in those early years, was to give the Congregation a sense of identity, a defined sense of mission, and a characteristic spirituality. He watched over the growth of the Congregation and the formation of the members, with the love of a mother for her family. No one could challenge his claim to have loved the members of the Congregation more 'than I loved my brothers and my own mother'. However, this was only what was expected of him:

> Be assured my brothers, that I love each one of you after God as my only love on this earth; and I offer for each of you from this moment, my blood and my life: for you, who are young, may do much for the glory of God but as for me, who am old and ill and useless, what more service can I render? God demands this of me in my office more than anything else.

His constant effort was to make himself available to the members of the Congregation at any time; they were free to write to him, to visit him and he assured them that when it was a question of assisting one of his brethren he would leave everything. He was under no obligation whatever, he insisted, to publish books but he was under an obligation to devote his time to his confreres. And he assured them that he would only spend whatever time he had over from attending to the members of the Congregation in the task of writing and publishing. This concern for his confrères was not always reciprocated. He received many offensive and insulting letters from them — some anonymous — taking him to task for what he had done. These letters pained him considerably, though he consoled himself with the thought that even if he were as gentle as Francis of Assisi he would still have to suffer this unmerited personal abuse.[17]

He took particular delight in spending time with the novices and students, talking to them of his experiences as a missioner and of his early days in Naples, his struggle for the priesthood and the beginnings of the Congregation. It was from their recollections that much of the account of the early years has been reconstructed. To the novices and students he was able to express the ideals of personal holiness of life which he wished to see prevailing in the Congregation. 'You must learn to walk well from the very beginning in the way of christian perfection,' he told them at one of the clothing ceremonies at which he officiated. One young man told Alphonsus that he came to the Congregation to save his soul. 'You can do that outside' was the reply, 'but if you wish to come to us it must be in order to sanctify yourself.' He demanded of those in the process of formation the complete dedication of their lives to the service of God and a willingness to correct whatever was defective in their characters. And if they did not measure up to these standards he had no scruple in dismissing them. Father Picone, the Master of Novices, was so worried about the responsibility of guiding the novices that he asked to be allowed to return to the missions. Alphonsus wrote to encourage him and to give some norms for his office:

> I hope your Reverence will continue to work with great courage and confidence in God. Do not be upset that there are some who grow cold in their fervour and leave. Help all of them as much as you can

> but let me know who is lacking in the necessary qualities and lacks the proper spirit and I will send him away. Let those who want to stay, stay. Only those who are prepared to suffer and who wish to dedicate themselves totally to the work of their perfection should be allowed to remain.
>
> You may read this letter to the novices and tell them that those who have not this spirit are not suitable for our Congregation. At the moment we have sufficient subjects and we have no need of subjects who are lacking in fervour. Among other things, see to it that they learn to obey. Tell them, that, above all, we do not want those who are rough-mouthed, *duro di bocca*, inordinately attached to their parents and full of their own importance, *stima propria*.[18]

For the benefit of the young religious of the Congregation he wrote three small treatises concerning vocation to the religious life, *Avvisi spettanti alla vocazione religiosa*, which he later adapted and published for religious in general but which in their origins were intended for the young members of his own missionary group. Despite the fact that they became the accepted classical works on vocation in general and on religious vocations in particular for more than 150 years, they bear unmistakable indications of their place and circumstances of origin. They need to be interpreted in the light of the quite unique social conditions existing in Bourbon Naples.[19]

Against the background of the extraordinary opposition to the religious life prevalent in Neapolitan society, Alphonsus placed before the young men the importance of following their religious vocation, which he saw as a special invitation from God to follow the way of the gospel counsels. So many obstacles were placed in the way of Neapolitan youth who wished to consecrate their lives to God in the religious state, that it amounted to a serious ecclesiastical abuse. Parents were prepared to go to any length rather than allow their sons to become religious — recourse to the King, threats, even imprisonment. The accepted wisdom in Naples was, *prete in familia, si; religioso, no* — a priest living at home with one's family, yes; a religious, certainly not. Francesco de Paola's vocation was strongly opposed by his family who enlisted the support of their diocesan bishop. For two years the struggle continued until de Paola fled to the novitiate. Alphonsus feared that the bishop would take reprisals by reporting the matter to the King, so he contacted Brancone in the hope of negativing whatever action the bishop and the King contemplated. But the bishop, instead of protesting to the Royal Court, deprived Alphonsus and his missionaries of diocesan faculties, and refused to allow them to minister in his diocese. This was an unusual reaction, since in nearly every case where the parents brought their objections to the monarch, the predictable outcome was banishment of the candidate to a monastery of Benedictines or Minims where his case would be investigated by the local ordinary, who was then charged with reporting back to the Court.[20]

In 1755 young Luigi Capuano presented himself at the novitiate in Ciorani where he was received with great delight. Immediately his parents raised a storm to secure his return. They threatened to present a memorial to the King for his 'release'. Presuming that events would take their normal course Alphonsus wrote a remarkable letter to the young novice:

> My dear Brother,
>
> Summon up courage! I am confident that God expects great things of you since Hell creates such a disturbance to draw you away from your vocation.
> It will, perhaps, happen as I have warned you, that you will have to go by order of the King to some monastery to be examined in regard to your intention. Recommend yourself to the Mother of God and fear nothing.
> Your relatives will undoubtedly then come to the monastery to tempt you, and the monks themselves will do the devil's work in order to appease your father and mother. They will represent to you that it is a matter of conscience for you if you thus bring ruin upon them.
> Pay no attention to such scruples; if your parents wish to be ruined it will be their own fault. Inform them, that, in order to please them, you cannot imperil your eternal salvation by losing your vocation. Of this there is no doubt. Be assured that after this trial in the monastery, your relatives will no longer annoy you.
> One more important point. If you go to the monastery do not believe what some of the monks will tell you. They have been won over by your relatives and they will give you a thousand reasons to induce you to return home. If this happens, be careful not to listen to them. Be certain they only wish to deceive you. So the moment they begin to do the Devil's work, dismiss them politely. Do not attempt to answer them because they will be able to confuse you. The best thing is not to answer but to inform them simply that you will recommend yourself to God in order to find out His Will for you. Get rid of them in this way . . . [21]

Parental objections to religious vocations made secrecy about one's intentions in the matter an absolute imperative. Dealing with the means of securing one's vocation, Alphonsus advised keeping one's determination secret from the family circles:

> Speaking in general, one should keep one's vocation secret from everybody except one's spiritual director, since, nowadays, people have no scruple about telling young people who wish to become religious that one can serve God everywhere and even in the world. And the amazing thing is that such advice comes even from priests and in some cases even from religious. . . . Of course, one can serve God anywhere but not the person genuinely called by God to the religious life and who refuses to follow a vocation through mere caprice. Only with difficulty will such a person lead a good life and serve God.[22]

But even with this secrecy one's parents still remained the great enemies of one's vocation. Alphonsus could well remember the difficulties which his own father caused him. When he quoted the example of his uncle, his mother's brother, Mons. Cavalieri, there are clear biographical echoes of his own story as well:

> We read in the life of Mons. Cavalieri, bishop of Troia, that his father, though a pious man in many ways, did everything in his power to prevent his son from joining the Congregation of the Pii Operai. He even went so far as to arraign his son before an ecclesiastical court. And how many other fathers, also men of prayer and piety, have there not been who in similar circumstances were changed out of all recognition, as if they were possessed by devils? Hell seems to me never to be so powerful as when it attempts to prevent those who feel themselves called by God to the religious life, from following their vocation.

The struggle to foster vocations for the Congregation encountered difficulties from other sources as well. As a result of the decree of 1752 candidates for the novitiate were required to possess a patrimony, otherwise they could not be ordained. This royal prescription was clearly intended to reduce the number of ordinations and it achieved its purpose, since many parents, faced with the necessity of providing marriage dowries for their daughters, were unable to provide a patrimony for their sons as well. As a consequence, Alphonsus was forced to turn away many excellent young men who presented themselves to enter the Congregation but did not possess a patrimony; in some cases he was able to help financially either from his own resources or by representing the need to some of his friends. Many young men came to the novitiate with no more possessions than the clothes they wore. Later, when two foundations were made in the Papal States, Alphonsus investigated the possibility of sending his students there for ordination in an effort to circumvent the Bourbon decree.

The sick were the object of his special care. He showed them every possible attention, visited them or wrote to them to encourage them to bear their illnesses with spiritual benefit to themselves. He saw to it that the doctor was called in time, no matter what expense was entailed. To impress superiors who may have been anxious about the expense involved, he told them in a striking phrase, that they were to sell the very chalices from the church, if necessary, to provide for the sick brethren. 'The sick are not a burden to us,' he replied to one who made such a suggestion, 'they are a blessing since they maintain us by their prayers, the good example of their sufferings and by their own acts of virtue.' He set the example himself. He sent the sick from house to house for a change of air, he sent them to take the waters and the hot baths — the *terme* and the *stufe* — at Ischia, Pozzuoli, Telese and Castellamare, which were the fashionable cures at the time and entailed considerable financial outlay. Only when he found that the change-of-air cure was a pretext for spending time with one's family did he grow more cautious in this matter. He saw to it that the sick were provided with special food; he often examined personally what the infirmarian was bringing to the sick room. On the general mission in Salerno Father Agostino fell ill; Alphonsus insisted that he should remain in bed and he ordered chocolate for him for ten days.

Some of the brethren, however, attempted to take advantage of his well-known kindness to the sick — with amusing results. In the cold winter months in Pagani, some of the community remained in bed in the morning on the pretext of feeling unwell — an indisposition which disappeared as the morning advanced; the patient showed no signs of illness by the time of the midday meal. Eventually this reached epidemic proportions and Alphonsus felt he had to act. When he was certain of the dubious nature of the illness which kept one of the Fathers in bed and absent from morning office, Alphonsus went to the Brother Infirmarian during meditation, told him to instruct the Father to remain in bed on a strict fasting diet and to bring him a glass of cold water for his breakfast. He repeated this remedy on a number of occasions when fictitious illnesses rescued a member of the community from early rising or some equally unpleasant duty, with the result that the bout of imaginary illnesses faded rapidly.

Alphonsus showed special concern for the community at Deliceto where the income was extremely meagre and where the rigours of the climate, especially in winter, made severe demands on one's health. When conditions became temporarily intolerable he removed successively the novices and students from the house. He secretly sent as much money as he could to Deliceto to supplement their resources, begging the superior not to let the other houses know of it and above all, not to inform Father Rossi, the bursar in Ciorani, since he was constantly seeking extra funds for his own community. Caposele, too, found it increasingly difficult to survive on its revenues and was forced, like Deliceto, to appeal for subsidies. Alphonsus developed a wry sense of humour about it all. On one occasion begging letters arrived at the same time from each of these communities. He showed them to Father Blasucci who happened to be in his room at the time. 'My official title is Rector Major', he said, 'but I should really be styled superior of a group of beggars dying of hunger.' The problem of the students' health constituted a major concern for him as well; there could be no joking about that. The scourge of tuberculosis was rife in the Kingdom of Naples and seven promising students died of it within a period of eight years from 1751 to 1759. Inevitably, the good name of the Congregation suffered; it gained a reputation not only for excessive austerity but also for a lack of care for the health of the members, especially the novices and students, adding a further reason for parental objections to joining the Congregation. Whatever may have been the austerity of their lives, due to lack of income, the charge of neglect of the health of the members was cruelly untrue.

Alphonsus was insistent that the standard of food in the houses should be that of the ordinary people. At the same time, he was determined that this should not be made an excuse for any lack of quality. The harassed bursar of Pagani from time to time embarked on a regime of economy reflecting his financial difficulties. For one particularly difficult period the daily meal of the community was a *minestra* whose main ingredient was nothing more substantial than *coccuze*, a species of marrow, which grew in abundance in the garden; he absolutely refused to buy anything more sustaining. The last straw came at Easter when a generous supply of pastries was handed in at the monastery by way of a gift. The bursar was miserly with them and doled them out so slowly to the community that the main fare was now *minestra di cuccozze* and stale pastries. Unable to keep his patience any longer, Alphonsus publicly reprimanded the bursar in the dining hall, declaring that the members of the Congregation were not pigs but children of the Congregation who deserved better. Meanness disgusted him — 'What was the good', he wrote to the Rector of Caposele, 'to build outside and tear down inside by depriving the community of substantial meals?'[23]

– IV –

The houses of the Congregation quickly established a reputation among bishops and people for faithful observance of the Rule. Alphonsus consistently inculcated this aspect of religious life for his followers but never to the extent of being unbending and inflexible. He was much more reasonable than Villani, for example: 'I want observance but not rigidity', was his formula. Not everybody possessed that delicate balance in relation to following the prescriptions of the Rule which was part of Alphonsus' charism both as a theologian and as a superior. He never forgot that he had suffered from that very same spirit of rigid legalism when he was a member of the Apostolic Missions on the occasion of the first novena he had preached in Foggia. Villani, particularly, was inclined to adhere unimaginatively to the letter of the law. 'You must be zealous for regular observance but not to the extent of falling into the opposite extreme,' Alphonsus wrote to him. 'The Constitutions are not the Ten Commandments; there are cases in which it will be necessary to dispense them and if you do not do so, you are acting incorrectly.' A remarkable example of the contrast between them as superiors came in the case of young Father Criscuoli. He was not yet thirty when he was of some spiritual assistance to a Sister Illuminata Garzillo in a convent at Lauro near Avellino. Keeping rigidly to the letter of the law, Villani, the local Rector, refused to allow Criscuoli to correspond with the nun, who had continued to seek his advice in her spiritual difficulties. The case was appealed to Alphonsus who had no hesitation in setting aside Villani's decision:

> It is true that members of the Congregation, and especially our young priests, are not permitted to undertake the direction of nuns. But it is not forbidden to give them advice from time to time, especially when they are at a distance. In a word, it is our duty to minister to souls and especially to religious in difficulties. All the more so, when she is at some distance. There are exceptions to every rule in case of necessity, otherwise, every rule would become unjust.

So, having considered the serious need of the nun in question, I have decided before God to write to Father Criscuoli that when the nun writes to him for advice he is free to reply, provided that it does not happen too frequently.[24]

Alphonsus' great gift as a superior lay in this flexibility of approach and his ability to adapt himself to each one's temperament. He approached a mild temperament in one way; he handled a temperament as irascible as his own, quite differently. He took into consideration, too, the spiritual qualities of his subjects, showing more human consideration for one not as far advanced in the external practice of virtue as another. When he felt that he should bring some matter to the notice of a member of the Congregation he bided his time for a suitable opportunity, often waiting for weeks on end. Knowing the explosive temperaments of the men he was dealing with and his own irascibility, he trained himself to wait until both he and they had calmed down. Then he endeavoured to speak to them with calmness and reasonableness. His colleagues used to compare favourably his manner of correcting with the harshness of Blasucci. And yet there were times, all through his life, when his hasty temperament got the better of him and made others suffer unjustly; but he had the humility to admit his fault and beg their pardon. There was a dramatic example of this on the occasion of a mission preached by two Fathers from Pagani in the neighbouring churches of Nocera. Word came to Alphonsus that the mission was a failure due to the carelessness of the missioners; they preached too long, there was confusion about the times of the different exercises and they began the services before the people arrived. The report upset him considerably; it preyed on his mind and without sufficient reflection or investigation he went down to where the Fathers were preaching. In the first church where Father Vacca had already begun his sermon, Alphonsus called him down from the pulpit and then addressed the people himself. He did the same in the second church where he found Father Carlo Gayano well into his sermon. When the Fathers returned to Pagani at the conclusion of the mission he rebuked them publicly and placed them on retreat in rigorous silence. When they had all calmed down, the Fathers pointed out to Alphonsus that he had been totally misinformed; he could only rue his hasty action, admit that he had been mistaken and ask their pardon.

His knowledge of the psychology of his confreres was remarkable. Villani suggested that Father de Paola should be appointed Master of Novices. De Paola suffered from the *malattia della casa*, the classical occupational disease of Neapolitan and other missioners — he was ill when at home in the monastery, in excellent health and spirit when on missions:

> Yes, Father de Paola would be a good choice for Master of Novices but I see one difficulty. As Master he will not be able to go out on the missions and when de Paola does not go out he gets upset and goes off colour. However, appoint him and when you see he is getting restless, put someone else in his place. I think Father Michele de Michele would also be good and perhaps even better than him.[25]

Father Francesco Margotta, the rector of Caposele, was another excellent missioner who suffered from a restless spirit, he always had to be doing something with the result that he undertook too much and was seldom at home. His moods, too, were famous in the folklore of those early years. Alphonsus had to take him to task:

> I know that your Reverence does not wish me to treat you with kid gloves or that I should deal with you in the matter of obedience as if you were a subject of little virtue and no back-bone — as I have so often to deal with others. I believe that your Reverence has high ideals and that you wish to do whatever gives most pleasure to God; you can judge my high regard for you from my conduct towards you.[26]

With this introduction, Alphonsus then went on to point out to him, in a Neapolitan colloquialism, that 'he had taken on too many cats to comb' and that the house and community at Caposele were suffering as a result.

Father Tannoia, too, needed to be reminded of certain aspects of his conduct. On account of his poor health he had been ordained without completing his full course of moral theology. Despite this, Alphonsus appointed him superior of Deliceto where, hopefully, he would have adequate time to complete his studies. At Deliceto, however, Tannoia threw himself into building, the study of local history and the works of Cassian, and Alexander Natalis — anything, except his moral theology. Alphonsus had to lay down the law:

> I would prefer to see your Reverence study my book on moral theology for half-an-hour a day, so that you would be able to hear confessions rather than hear that you are studying Cassian or Alexander Natalis. Do you want to remain all your life without hearing confessions despite the fact that you have plenty of intelligence?
>
> Listen to me! There is a good deal of laziness and lackadaisical attitude in your make-up. Study, I tell you, those tracts which deal with the commandments, sin, penance, censures, charity, conscience and laws. In a word, all those sections which you have not yet studied. I am not giving you an obedience to do so, but do it when you can.[27]

Assigning members of the Congregation to different houses was a complex task, dictated to a large extent by the knowledge of which Fathers would get on well together and, more important still, which members of the Congregation could live with certain superiors. Villani and Celestino de Robertis, both admirable men, could not tolerate each other; Cafaro and Sanseverino found each other quite uncongenial. Alphonsus was at his wits' end at times to keep them at a safe distance from each other. Changing a subject from one community to another was always a problem for him lest he should cause unnecessary pain. He always prefaced a change of community with a short flattering introduction as to his high opinion of the subject's virtue or the great need that the community had of him; at times, too, he appointed the Father he was changing to some office which would sweeten the pill.

Deliceto came to be regarded as the Siberia of the four houses and a change there was nearly always unwelcome even though Alphonsus considered it, from every point of view, the ideal missionary house. When assigned there from Pagani, Father Pasquale Capriolo made no move to go. Alphonsus pretended not to notice the reluctance to take up the assignment. Then, one afternoon as they assembled in choir for prayers, Alphonsus said to him, 'When does your Reverence think of going to Deliceto? You know they need you there since I have appointed you assistant to the Rector.' That was all that was needed to speed Capriolo on his way. Alphonsus was fully aware of the fact that there were certain persons about whom nothing could be done; the community just had to put up with them and make the best of it. Father Caione, the superior of Caposele, complained that he had in his community a Father whose interests were centred more on the spiritual welfare of his confreres than on his own conduct. He was critical of everything, considered the standard of observance in the community poor, and believed that everybody except himself was inobservant. The only remedy Alphonsus could suggest was simply to put up with the pest.

> Speaking in general I must say that these critical spirits, provided that they do not go too far and do not assume authority they do not possess, are useful in a community, because they keep us all on our toes. Father Ferrara, for example, does not endear himself to his confrères with his constant complaints, but I tell you, in all truth, he is a great help to me in keeping the edge on observance. In community life we just have to put up with these 'bitter mouthfuls', *bocconi amari*, — all things work together unto good.[28]

The slender incomes of the various houses was a source of constant anxiety. Alphonsus' letters are full of references to gifts of money and other unexpected sources of income which he endeavoured to spread around from community to community, according to need. In this connection he was constantly at logger-heads with the various superiors of houses who could not resist the inclination to build. He called it 'the stone disease', the *mal di pietro*, which was all the more worrying, since it was generally at the expense of food and clothing for the community. He warned Father Caione at Caposele:

> There is no doubt that all superiors are eaten up with the desire to build so that everyone will see what they have done. I am letting you know this so that you will not annoy me in this matter. Make sure that clothes and suitable food are not lacking in the community on account of the expenses incurred in building. I cannot say that I am altogether satisfied with your obedience in this respect. For charity's sake, put out of your mind, for the moment, all thought of building and all other expenses which are not absolutely necessary and let things remain as they are.[29]

He was equally annoyed that many of the Fathers set themselves up as specialists in architecture. He had engaged the Cimafonte brothers, two of the most reputable architects in Naples, to design the monasteries, churches and retreat houses. But many of the superiors and some of the communities preferred their own ideas to those of the Cimafontes. At one time, the community at Deliceto was in uproar over differing opinions concerning the building of the monastery there. 'I tell you', Alphonsus insisted to Villani at Deliceto, 'as I have always told you before, that whenever there is some doubt you are to follow the directions of the architects and not what the Fathers say. They are supposed to have studied moral theology and not architecture.'

– V –

Towards the end of his life, when severe internal problems threatened to destroy the Congregation, Alphonsus, in an emotional outburst, declared:

> I love each of you, my brothers, more than a brother of the flesh; and when one leaves the Congregation I experience unspeakable pain; but when I see that the wound has become gangrene and that caustic is necessary, I must apply it, however much pain it may cause me.

Though the statement is his own, it is a totally verifiable verdict on his dealings with the members of the Congregation. He had great sympathy with those who were suffering in any way and especially with those who were going through periods of special difficulty regarding their vocation or their spiritual life. It was a considerable tribute to him that more often than not he was the first to whom the person in question had recourse.

Brother Gaspar Corvino in Ciorani was experiencing great temptations against his vocation. The ordinary duties of attending to the cleanliness of the house and particularly washing up after meals seemed to him an insupportable humiliation. Alphonsus divined the struggle that was going on. He said nothing but appeared in the scullery each day for many weeks beside Gaspar, washing up and drying the table equipment with whatever skill he could muster. The lesson was not lost on Gaspar who found new strength from the example and overcame his difficulties. He died at the age of eighty-three having spent over fifty years in the house at Sant' Angelo in Beneventum where he testified to the influence this action of Alphonsus had on his perseverance.

The subtlety of approach which solved Brother Gaspar's problems was replaced by a good dose of bantering in the case of Father Giuseppe Melchionna, a nephew of the difficult Father Ferrara. Young Melchionna was just a few years ordained when he was assailed in Deliceto with severe temptations against his vocation. He got the idea into his head that he was in Deliceto by way of punishment — Deliceto had acquired the reputation of being a place of banishment for some offence or other. Melchionna, who lacked a sense of humour and was, moreover, of the depressive type, like his uncle, convinced himself that he was really in prison and for no fault of which he was aware. His confreres did not help by seizing on his lack of humour to tease him interminably. He eventually developed such a total complex in the matter that he sat down and wrote a letter to Alphonsus which fairly burnt up the paper and ended with something in the nature of an ultimatum to be recalled from Deliceto at once or he would leave the Congregation. Alphonsus gauged the situation perfectly. He realised that this was not a case of malice, but rather an example of a man's imagination getting the better of him; it was a case for humour and patience:

> Yes, certainly, tell Father Rector, in my name, to send you here to Pagani as soon as he can manage.
>
> Did you ever hear the story of St Paul the hermit and St Anthony? Anthony begged him to open the door for him or he would die at the entrance. Paul opened the door and then said, 'That's a nice way to ask for something, by threatening dire consequences.' And I say the same to you. I have great sympathy for your imaginings. Are you dreaming? Whoever put it into your head that you were sent to Deliceto as a punishment? I do not see why the confreres should tease you like this.
>
> 'Otherwise I will ask for my dispensation' you write. You may write for it if you wish, but who do you think is going to give it to you? *O Master George*, you are only wasting your time' [Master George was the favourite colloquial expression in Neapolitan dialect for somebody 'doing the big man']
>
> Anyway do not worry. I shall not let your uncle know of your letter. But, for heaven's sake, when you write the next time do not display such fury. If I didn't know you so well, I would have sent you the quickest horse I could find to take you out of the Congregation. Anyway, come as quickly as you can; I am looking forward to seeing you.
>
> And, at the same time, I want you to realise that there are other reasons besides faults which necessitate the change of subjects from house to house. I repeat, I appreciate that it was not really you who wrote but your bad humour. Next time, please tell your bad humour to write with a little bit more civility and discretion.[30]

Young Bernard Apice, from Gragnano near Castellamare, was another who owed his perseverance as a Redemptorist missioner to Alphonsus's patience and understanding. Apice was one of the most promising young men to be ordained in the Congregation in the years immediately following Roman approbation. Full of intelligence, deeply pious and with considerable natural talents as a preacher, he was, at the same time, hot-tempered, excitable and unpredictable. He was constantly in trouble during his formative years, though his misdeeds were always immediately atoned for and his fundamental goodness transparent; he was the classical *enfant terrible*. On more than one occasion when his impulsiveness had betrayed him into some indiscretion — always, unfortunately, in full sight of one of the older members — Alphonsus' consultors recommended that he should be sent away. Alphonsus was reluctant to do so although he admitted 'this young man is driving me to desperation'; instead he corrected him — *dolcemente* — with the result that Apice kept out of his way and avoided Pagani, where Alphonsus was in residence, as much as he could. Assigned to Caposele, he found unlimited scope there for his great energy and missionary gifts. But, after some time, he grew dissatisfied and requested a change to Deliceto from which most of his contemporaries wished to escape. Alphonsus went to great lengths to humour him:

> It is clear to me that this is not the Will of God for you but a temptation of the devil, since I know the good you are doing where you are. If you go to Deliceto what good will you do there? Father Cafaro tells me that everything seems black to you where you are, but if you leave yourself in the hands of obedience everything will become white for you. I beg you to calm yourself with the thought of the Will of God, otherwise, you will be unhappy no matter where you are.
>
> Anyway, write to me, telling me honestly what does not please you about where you are at the moment so that I might be persuaded to change you if I think fit . . .
>
> My dear Don Bernard, you know how well disposed towards you I have always been and indeed still am. Please put yourself at ease since it upsets me just to hear that you are upset.[31]

But Apice's indiscretions continued; no one knew what he would do next. Finally, Alphonsus gave him one last chance. He told him plainly that he was both frivolous and mixed-up and that another indiscretion and he was gone. The reality sunk in at last. Apice matured out of all recognition. Alphonsus chose him to accompany him on the vital mission in Salerno and, to the amazement of everybody, especially his consultors, included him in the pioneer group for Sicily where he came into his own as a missioner and superior. Alphonsus' intuition had been proved correct once again and Apice fully justified his faith in him, developing into a magnificent missioner both in Sicily and Naples and eventually challenging Alphonsus' own reputation as one of the most sought after preachers in the Kingdom. His early death at the age of forty-one, with a reputation for great holiness of life, was a deep personal sorrow for Alphonsus without whose support Apice would never have survived in the Congregation.[32]

Following on papal approval, Alphonsus was faced with the problem of how to deal with those who wished to be dispensed from their vows and it took several years before a coherent policy evolved. His initial reaction was to grant an immediate dispensation from the vows of religion and the oath of perseverance in the Congregation, to those who requested it. His leniency in the matter did not meet with the approval of his consultors who felt that this readiness to allow those who had joined to leave, was inflicting considerable harm on the general *morale* of the members. It soon became obvious that there were those who requested their dispensation without sufficient reason; at the first sign of difficulty in their chosen vocation, they asked freedom to return home. Alphonsus' attitude changed; he grew increasingly reluctant to dispense the members from their commitments without making every effort to get them to alter their decision. He went to considerable trouble to bring them to a different frame of mind. Finally, he warned them of the consequences which would follow from their decision, among them a possible danger to their eternal salvation, which, at first sight, may seem unduly alarmist to our mentality. But the possibility may not have been so outrageous as it seems. Alphonsus was speaking, in the first place, of those who left out of some passing whim or other. On their departure from the Congregation, they returned to their homes with no intention of pursuing their priestly ministry; there, they often lived lives of idleness or engaged in some occupation out of keeping with their priesthood. Whatever good resolutions they may have had at their departure, they quickly succumbed to the atmosphere of home and native village. Prayer was abandoned, they neglected to celebrate Mass; in a word, they joined that clerical proletariat which was such a sad feature of the Church in Bourbon Naples. Alphonsus and his companions had so many experiences of such cases in their mission ministry that it was not unreasonable for him in the circumstances of the time to warn those leaving the Congregation without good reason, that they were jeopardising their eternal salvation.

The new policy of making departure from the Congregation difficult brought with it, in turn, its own problems. Within a few years of taking his vows, one Francesco Manfredonia requested his freedom; Alphonsus refused, making every effort at the same time to persuade him to change his mind. Baulked by this approach, Manfredonia simply took his leave, believing that his dispensation would follow; it was a direct challenge to Alphonsus, who determined that this type of blackmail would not succeed — 'Those who attempt to leave without a genuine reason would have to face up to the fact that this meant they would have to leave in mortal sin.' Manfredonia was finally persuaded to return to Ciorani where Alphonsus gave instructions that he was to be treated kindly even though he had to undergo a penitential regime to make amends for his waywardness. Despite his best efforts, it ultimately became clear that Francesco Manfredonia was not destined for the Congregation and, the following year, Alphonsus granted him his dispensation without difficulty.

A further refinement of this canonical blackmail was attempted by Vicenzo Tomangi from Avellino, which became a *cause célèbre* among the brethren. Within a few months of his profession Tomangi decided to leave the Congregation. Realising that he would be unable to secure a dispensation from Alphonsus, he determined to extort his expulsion by outrageous conduct; he felt it would be as good a way as any of securing his liberty. He disregarded the Rule, refused to study, was openly defiant of authority. When the matter was reported to him, Alphonsus saw that he was being publicly challenged; he made it quite clear to Tomangi that he would not succeed in blackmailing him into granting a dispensation. Unable to handle the situation, Father Blasucci, the Prefect of Students, determined to land the problem right in Alphonsus' lap by sending the recalcitrant Tomangi to Pagani. When Alphonsus got wind of the Prefect's intention he was furious; he forbade

Blasucci to send the student to him. If Tomangi wished to write, well and good, but if he wrote requesting a dispensation from his vows which he had so recently taken, Alphonsus threatened to tear up the letter on receipt of it. In an effort to help him to come to a better frame of mind he transferred Tomangi to Caposele, but with no result. Unable to secure his dispensation, Tamongi determined to resort to the ultimate expedient of running away, but not before he had found some of the Fathers prepared to abet him in his decision. Aware of the moral and canonical consequences of becoming in canonical terms, a 'fugitive', Tomangi secured absolution from his excommunication from one of the Fathers — apparently Father Fiocchi — on condition that he applied formally, at the same time, to Alphonsus for his dispensation. When word reached Pagani, Alphonsus exploded in anger and frustration. His letter to the superior of Caposele speaks for itself:

> My God, what do I hear has taken place in your house? I understand that with the consent of many of you, Tomangi has been absolved on condition that he requests his dispensation. But he had already asked me for it a thousand times, so it was quite superfluous for you to have imposed this obligation. In a word, what he was not able to get from Rome, he has got from you. I have been very upset by what I have heard. What need was there for you to get involved in such a delicate matter which concerns the very survival of the Congregation? . . .
>
> Dispensation? I shall never give a dispensation to those who leave the Congregation without previously getting a dispensation from me unless they first return to the Congregation and perform whatever penance is imposed on them. Only then will I consider what should be done in the matter. And this is the procedure which every Rector Major should adhere to, if he does not wish to lose his soul and destroy the Congregation. I have already advised the Cardinal Penitentiary in Rome of my attitude and if he should decide to grant the dispensation against my wishes I am determined to write again and again to the Holy Father himself. But the community at Caposele has granted the dispensation which the Roman Penitentiary has refused!
>
> Please communicate this letter to all the Fathers of the community and especially to those who gave the advice. I also request your Reverence, according to your prudence, to communicate at least the substance of this letter to the young men and Brothers, so that this example shall not be the cause of the ruin of others. And I am particularly anxious that you make sure the contents come to the notice of Father Fiocchi . . .[33]

The last thing that Alphonsus wanted to do was to dismiss anyone from the Congregation and yet he had to face up to the painful duty on many occasions with all sections of the Congregation, Fathers, as well as clerical Students and Brothers. While the process of dismissal was less complicated canonically at that time than it has now become, Alphonsus made every effort to avoid taking the final and, for him, irrevocable step. He allowed adequate time for correction and improvement; only when this did not ensue did he resort to the ultimate sanction of dismissal. He was infinitely tolerant of ordinary human failures — far beyond what his consultors advised — as the example of Bernard Apice well demonstrates, but he was equally ruthless in dismissing subjects for behaviour which he felt to be harmful to others or to the good name of the Congregation. He learnt that one of the novices was having a corrupting influence on his companions in the novitiate; despite the fact that he was the nephew of a bishop, Alphonsus dismissed him at once, informing the novice master that the novice in question could do more harm than 'ten heretics or one hundred devils'.

He was particularly insistent in the matter of obedience. He soon learnt that, for many of his subjects, unquestioning acceptance of a command was out of the question; a command was not something to be obeyed, but rather, something to be discussed. His circular letters to the houses are full of exhortations to obedience at all levels. In 1758 he addressed a special letter to all the Fathers — which was not to be shown to the students lest they be scandalised — in which he took them severely to task for their failures in this matter; their conduct had caused him great displeasure, *disgusti*. On at least four occasions during these years he was forced to take drastic action in cases of disobedience. Father Mateo Criscuoli for example, had just returned from a mission when his superior requested him to undertake another preaching engagement. He refused; a second request some time later met with a cold calculated refusal. That very evening, having examined the incident, Alphonsus presented him with his dismissal from the Congregation. A member of the Pagani community who was changed to Ciorani, refused to go; he pleaded that he had to remain in Pagani in order to direct some law case in which his family was engaged in Naples. His refusal was absolute. The following morning while he was celebrating Mass, Alphonsus got one of the Brothers to bring his travelling cloak and his belongings to the front hall. When the Father in question had finished celebrating Mass, Alphonsus informed him that he had been dismissed from the Congregation and that he would find his belongings at the monastery door waiting for him.

Once a member of the Congregation had been dispensed from his vows or dismissed, Alphonsus was extremely loath to reverse his decision and allow him to return. There are, at most, only five exceptions to his practice in this matter and three of them concern the re-admission of those who had left as students; the only priest to be re-admitted to vows in the Congregation was professed on his death-bed. There are incidents recorded during those years when some, who had been dispensed or dismissed, regretted their behaviour and petitioned to return, even going so far as to invoke, on their knees before Alphonsus, the name of the Madonna. But to no avail. Father Genovesi, who had been dismissed in 1752 for obdurate disobedience tried as hard as he could to return to the Congregation, urging on Alphonsus the example of the remorse of conscience which the Provincial of the Jesuits reputedly experienced on his death-bed at the thought of those he had dismissed from the Society. Alphonsus's reply made no concession to this plea: 'Father Manulio was worried at the end of his life when he thought of the subjects he had dismissed from the Society of Jesus. I, on the other hand, if I were to die this minute, would have no other worry than that of having been too indulgent and of not having dismissed from the Congregation, at once, subjects who showed little spirit of edification.'[34]

– VI –

During the years he spent at Pagani, Alphonsus addressed the community each week at their Chapter meeting. The outline of these talks have been preserved for us thanks to the extensive notes made by members of the community. The conferences concentrated on the fundamental virtues of the religious life as it was lived at the time. After the imitation of Jesus Christ which was basic to the spirituality of the Congregation, strict adherence to the minutest prescriptions of the Rule was paramount. The talks were neither theoretical nor doctrinal but were directly related to practice, the daily conduct of the Fathers and Brothers, both at home and on the missions. There was nothing pretentious in what he had to say, nothing beyond insistence on the importance of sanctifying the ordinary details of their lives from the moment of awakening in the morning until they retired at night, silence, prayer, acts of humility, study, the good intention, love for the Congregation to which God had called them, and, inevitably, their spirit of obedience to superiors and to the Rule. His language was unadorned, full of dialect phrases and references, delivered as if he were talking rather than preaching or lecturing:

> In your case, my brothers, what does loving God with your whole heart mean? It means that a member of the Congregation, one of the Fathers, for instance, or one of the Brothers or one of the Novices, observe faithfully our Rule. That he maintains himself in complete recollection during the day, that he does not leave his room without necessity, that he does not speak in time or places of silence, that he receives with humility the corrections of his superiors, that he loves being despised as the saints did, or at least, that he bears this patiently. It means that he should be a great lover of mortification, both internal and external, especially at table, if the food does not please him. That he bears the sufferings God sends him, that he leaves himself like clay in the potter's hands and that he can at least overcome himself to the extent of not being deliberately disobedient. This is the programme for you.[35]

At times his talks revealed his own spiritual struggles; vanity, for example, figured largely in what he had to say. Speaking of the intention with which the missioners should engage in their ministry, he warned:

> How often can it happen that some unworthy motive, such as human respect, self-satisfaction, desire for praise or reputation, seeking for

one's self part of the glory which belongs only to God, will deprive the missioner of all the merits of his efforts. Vainglory is such an insidious thief, as one master of the spiritual life warns us, that before we are even aware of his presence, he has deprived us of all that we had hoped to merit. And do not believe that vainglory is a temptation just for those who are beginners in the spiritual life; no, it is a temptation to which even those far advanced in the ways of the spirit, are liable. St Gregory admitted that although it was his intention when writing his books to work only for the glory of God, nevertheless, on occasions, some tinge of vainglory entered into what he did. In the same way, how many there are who go to preach or to hear confessions apparently for the glory of God and then are assailed by some desire to be praised or to be seen by others.[36]

He did not spare the members of the Congregation in the way he castigated their failings but he used the universally accepted technique of including himself among the failures by saying 'and I am including myself in all this'.

On Thursdays the community gathered to discuss some spiritual topic; in accordance with the tradition established years before in Scala, there was an air of informality and good humour about these particular meetings. The subjects chosen for discussion were simple and practical: 'What are the motives and the means to help us to do our every action well?', 'Is it right for a member of the Congregation to desire to be employed in the work of the missions and even to request to be so employed?', 'Besides the virtues of faith, hope and charity, what virtue is the most important for a missioner?' Alphonsus usually presided and then summed up with a practical sense of humour. In July 1752 the community discussed the problem, 'What should a religious do to live happily in his religious order and to receive the grace of the Holy Spirit?' One by one various spiritual expedients were discussed — humility, observance of Rule, etc. In his summing up, Alphonsus suggested that the best way of being happy as a Redemptorist in those days was to possess '*Musso di porcellone, Spalle di asinello*', which meant, to have the mouth of a piglet for the food that was served and the shoulders of a mule for the burdens that were being imposed. And then he added something which came from his heart and of which his own life was the best example, the importance of loving the Congregation. It is impossible, he said, without this affection, to be contented as a member of the Congregation, and he quoted the old Latin tag, '*qui amat ranam, ranam putat esse Dianam*', which meant in the context that one who loved the Congregation considered it to be the most wonderful thing in existence. 'I should like to see this love for the Congregation in every member; he who does not possess it, will live unhappily and will make others unhappy too or he will leave after some time. I am always afraid for the future of those who do not possess this affection.'[37]

The defection of Muscari in 1751 provoked from Alphonsus his first circular letter to the members of the Congregation. Between that year and his departure for his diocese, eleven years later, he addressed at least ten other letters to the Fathers, students, Brothers and novices, constituting a remarkable testimony to his hopes and fears for his society of missioners. Amongst the members, there was a mixture of considerable heroism on the one hand and considerable mediocrity, declining at times to quite reprehensible behaviour, on the other. He put before them the necessity of setting a high standard in those early years; 'God has called us to this Congregation, especially now in its early years, to sanctify ourselves; whoever wishes to save his soul in the Congregation, without attending to his sanctification, I do not know whether he will save it at all or not.' He had much to contend with. There were many who did not share his high ideals and found the standards he set for them too difficult. There were others whose lives and conduct caused him great sorrow. It is against this background that we must interpret these letters, at one time threatening, at another, flattering, coaxing. He played on every emotion in the whole range of their characters and all for the one purpose of inspiring them to live up to that standard of heroism and total dedication which he set for himself and expected of them. The themes varied only slightly — obedience, poverty, fervour, observance of the Rule. It is important to appreciate that these circulars were not written as a formal legacy for the future but to deal with very particular problems in very special circumstances. To take them out of their context, as has been done, is unfair both to them and to Alphonsus himself. He was writing for those who knew him, who shared his volubility and his ardent temperament, those for whom the superlative was the normal form of the adjective and who were ready to discount many of his threats. They knew that he did not mean what he said to be taken literally. Translated literally, and taken out of their Neapolitan context, these writings appear to be the outpourings of a man in great anger, threatening, calling down chastisements from heaven, warning them that he would accuse them before the Tribunal of God. The Promotor Fidei objected at the process of canonisation to Alphonsus' way of expressing himself to his Neapolitan brethren: 'He who has no love for the Congregation and no respect for the Rule has no love for God either. What is the Congregation? What is the Rule? — they are Jesus Christ' But the objections were easily answered when it was explained that Alphonsus was not speaking in precise theological terms but was using the colourful and living idiom of Neapolitan conversation.[38]

But if he was prepared to find fault with his brethren for their conduct he was equally ready to rise to their defence. Baron Giffoni wrote to Alphonsus complaining of the action of one of the Fathers on a mission; it was alleged that he had apparently lost his patience to the extent of striking someone. Alphonsus replied on 7 June 1761:

Most esteemed Lord,

Your letter has reopened the wound caused me a few days ago by news of the incident about which you wrote to me. The Father in question has written to me himself, asking pardon for his fault and expressing his willingness to perform penance for it. I have always insisted with the Fathers that they should never as much as harbour a thought of striking even the children to whom they give religious instruction on the missions. What has happened has pained not only me but every one of the community as well.

My dear Baron, what has happened cannot be excused but when all is said and done, the members of the Congregation are only human. On the other hand, speaking generally, they give edification wherever they go and I know, for a fact, that many are impressed by them. I myself and all the other superiors are incessantly on our guard to root out the noxious weeds which, on account of our human condition, are always springing up on this earth of ours. I trust that the Congregation is the work of God and that He will preserve it as His own. But, if it is not the work of God, then I do not wish it to continue and I pray Him to put an end to it right away.

I am grateful for your letter since it affords me an opportunity of giving a strong warning to all on this matter. I want you to know that those who are incorrigible are not tolerated in our midst, even those whose defects may not be very serious. They are dismissed. A short while ago, three were dismissed on this very principle.

With profound reverence and declaring myself the very humble and devoted servant of your Excellency,

Alfonso de Liguori of the Most Holy Redeemer.[39]

Chapter Thirteen

Zeal for the Lord's House 1749–1762

- I -

By the year 1759, Ferdinand VI, King of Spain and half-brother of Charles III of Naples, had declined into complete imbecility; Elizabeth Farnese, his stepmother and real mother of Charles, took over as Regent. On 10 August of the same year the King died and Charles of Naples succeeded to the Spanish throne on 11 September to the tremendous joy of his mother. The next problem was to settle the succession to the throne of Naples where the prospect of the departure of Charles filled the people with dismay and was full of import for the Church in the Kingdom in general and for Alphonsus and his Congregation in particular. Charles had been the first 'native' monarch, one whom the Neapolitans were prepared to claim as their own and not as the representative of a foreign power. His youthful queen, Maria Amalia, had given birth to four daughters in succession, all of whom died as infants. In 1747 their first son, Philip, duke of Calabria was born, to be followed in succeeding years by Charles Anthony and then by Ferdinand, whom his parents, now with a surplus of male heirs, thoughtfully destined for an ecclesiastical career — a Cardinal, after all, was the next best thing to a King or a Prince. But Philip, duke of Calabria, developed into an incurable epileptic and already gave indications of inheriting his Spanish grandfather's imbecility. At any rate, a panel of experts was assembled in Naples and decided unanimously that the thirteen-year-old child was unfit to reign. So the second son, Charles, was then declared Prince of the Asturias and heir apparent to the Spanish throne; he would, therefore, have to leave Naples with his parents for his new home and kingdom which he had never seen. That left Ferdinand, whose ecclesiastical career had now to be abandoned. Aged eight, he was declared King of the Two Sicilies in succession to his father. On 6 October 1759, Charles girded on the same sword of Louis XIV on him which he had received himself nearly thirty years earlier when he had left Spain to claim the Two Sicilies for the Bourbons. With a heroic sense of duty, worthy of a nobler cause, Charles and Maria Amalia set sail from Naples, leaving their youngest son behind them and the Kingdom under the control of a Regency Council.[1]

Alphonsus hoped that Tanucci would follow his royal master to Spain; instead, he remained in Naples to dominate the Regency Council and become, in effect, Viceroy of his Spanish master. He was the faithful mouthpiece of Charles with whom he corresponded at length once a week; his heart, he said, was Bourbon and the new King of Spain trusted him completely. Tanucci acted with his usual astuteness. As guardian of the young King Ferdinand, his first move was to restrict the influence of the Jesuits on his education. Queen Maria Amalia had planned to appoint her own confessor, the German Jesuit, Father Germano Cardel, as the boy's confessor. He was already making valiant efforts to teach him Latin, French and German — a task beyond human achievement and the boy never succeeded in learning a word of any of these languages. The manoeuvre of Tanucci succeeded in blocking the Queen's wishes. Instead of the Jesuit, Mons. Benito Latilla, bishop of Avellino, Abbot General of the Canons of the Lateran, an able politician and, for some time, a member of the newly established Freemason Lodge in Naples, was appointed to instruct and direct the young King's conscience. Father Cardel found himself assigned to minister spiritually to the pilgrims at the shrine of Loreto. Deprived of his parents, surrounded by courtiers, young Ferdinand's upbringing proved disastrous. Despite his native intelligence, no intellectual cultivation of his mind was possible. His religious training was equally defective as his later life amply demonstrated. He became a royal boor in every sense, interested only in hunting and fishing with the *lazzaroni* of Naples, and in general horse-play and buffoonery. Ambassadors at the royal court reported that he had not matured beyond the age of ten.

The departure of Charles coincided with a general deterioration in the moral atmosphere of the Court and an increase in the now deeply rooted spirit of the Enlightenment. It augured badly for Alphonsus and his missioners who were to find themselves more and more at the mercy of Tanucci. Even the young King began to resent his minister's influence, calling him 'a bear that walks on two feet'. His appointees were all in positions of vital importance. The arch-Gallican, Marquis Fraggianni, became head of the Council of Santa Chiara, while the Marquis Carlo de Marco, a 'declamatory Jansenist', according to Tanucci, took over the Council of Ecclesiastical Affairs on the departure of Brancone, Alphonsus' friend and penitent. Both of these appointments had serious consequences for the future of the Church and religious orders in Naples.[2]

The first to experience the winds of anti-clericalism blowing throughout Europe were the Jesuits. In 1757 an attempt was made to assassinate Louis

XV of France. The search for the accomplices of the assassin, Damiens, led the secret police to, above all things, the *Medulla Theologica* of Busenbaum, who, like most theologians before him, treated of the age-old problem of the morality of tyrannicide. In his teaching, the police, to their delight, found, as they thought, the speculative basis for the assassination attempt. In a wave of anti-Jesuit feeling and royalist sympathy, the *Medulla*, as well as the *Moral Theologies* of La Croix and Zaccaria, were publicly burnt in Toulouse with as much feeling as if the days of the Albigensians had returned. Alphonsus' well-known friendship with the Jesuits in Naples, and the fact that his *Moral Theology* had been published as a commentary on the *Medulla*, served to tar him with the same brush. After hasty consultation with Father Zaccaria in Naples and a series of letters to his publisher Remondini, Alphonsus arranged to excise from his work the sections dealing with tyrannicide and the lawfulness of duels for a point of honour — the first, out of fear of offending the susceptibilities of the French authorities, and the second, out of fear of incurring the wrath of Pombal in Portugal, whose royal master, King Joseph I. was addicted to the sport of private duels — which he invariably won.

In 1758 Pombal initiated his all-out attack on the Jesuits in his territory. Pope Benedict XIV was forced to appoint Cardinal Saldanha, Patriarch of Lisbon, as apostolic visitor of the Jesuits Houses in Portugal, which was equivalent to signing their death warrant. It was small compensation that the Pope, on the day before his death, signed the decree of beatification of the Neapolitan Jesuit and prophet of Alphonsus' future greatness, Francis Jerome, which was greeted by the anti-Jesuit faction with the gospel phrase, *in finem dilexit eos*. The following year, Pombal decreed the confiscation of all Jesuit property in the territory and colonies of 'His Most Faithful Majesty', and the expulsion of all Jesuits from the country, eleven hundred of whom arrived in Città Vecchia in search of sanctuary. The news sent a thrill of delight through the courts of Europe and their expulsion from France, Spain and Naples was now only a matter of convenient opportunity. Tanucci, whose anti-Jesuit feeling had reached irrational proportions, now saw the way open for similar action in Naples; the Lisbon decree, he wrote, was the only one to be expected of a conscientious government.

Alphonsus followed the fortunes of the Jesuits as if he were personally involved; he was eager for any item of news he could get. He expressed his conviction to Mons. Borgia, bishop of Cava, during a discussion in Pagani, that the royal courts, which had been so assiduously cultivated by members of the Society, would end up by destroying them. Nevertheless, the news of the suppression in Portugal, when it came, was a terrible shock to him; he wrote at once to the Rector of the Jesuits in Naples, Father Pasquale de Matteis:

> I have been much pained by the news from Portugal. Everyone who has come to visit me has brought nothing but sad news in the matter. Some were clearly delighted at what has taken place, but I, for my

part, have regretted it as much as if it had happened to my own Congregation. I was consoled to learn from your Reverence's letter of the spirit of constancy which has marked even those who were not professed; this is a sure sign that the Spirit of God reigns among you.

I believe that the Lord will bring great glory from this persecution to Himself and great good eventually to the Society. From other sources, I know that the Pope and the majority of the Cardinals are very much on the side of the Society.[3]

The campaign of vilification against the Jesuits now gained momentum, even in ecclesiastical circles. Every possible calumny was uttered and published against them and was as readily believed. The injustice of the whole campaign wounded Alphonsus deeply and he made no secret of his support for the Society; their value to the Church was his main argument. He demanded of those who joined in the campaign that the Society should not be condemned, without being given an opportunity of speaking in its own defence. As the flood of anti-Jesuit literature increased in Naples, the fact that the Society made no effort to counteract the charges brought against its members, filled him with serious misgivings. If the accusations were false, why were they not refuted? Could it be that they were true? Or worse still, was it conceivable that the Society was actually defending the very accusations alleged against them? The climax came with the publication of the infamous *Mémoires* of Father Norbert Curel, alias l'Abbé Platel, a one-time Capuchin from Lorraine. On his return from the missions in China, Curel published very damaging charges against the Society, claiming that he had the approbation of Pope Benedict XIV, who, however, immediately retorted by having the work condemned by the Holy Office, at a session over which he presided personally. The work, translated into several European languages, became a best-seller. The situation was sufficiently serious for Alphonsus to address an urgent letter to Father Lorenzo Ricci, the General of the Society, in Rome:

> Although I have not the good fortune of belonging to the Society of Jesus I esteem it as much as if I were a member. Seeing it now so much under attack as a result of the calumnies reported in Father Norbert's book — even though it is on the Index — I have begged the members of the Society, especially those in your Houses here in Naples, for a reply which can be put in the hands of University graduates, who, it appears, cannot now get their degrees unless they add to the chorus of Jesuit-baiting.
>
> Pardon my boldness, your Paternity. Your Society has been placed in the Church for the general welfare of christianity and we are all aware of the good which it has achieved, and still achieves, throughout the world, for the last two hundred years. Now that good name is under attack from your enemies, using Father Norbert's book which is to be found everywhere and which, as your Paternity is fully aware, recounts the most shocking events. Since no refutation of these charges

has been forthcoming, we are faced with a dilemma — either these charges are false and then why don't the Jesuits reply to them and make the truth known to all? Or they are true and then why don't superiors punish the perpetrators and condemn the events? Or is it that they are defending them? Besides what has been said about Malabar and China, other shocking imputations have been brought forward and I almost die of shame when I hear them.

For the honour then of the Society and for the glory of God, I feel myself constrained to write to you to give directions where they are needed so that these charges will be answered and the whole position clarified. It is, in my opinion, imperative that this be done. I have heard that a reply to Father Norbert has already appeared in France. Your Paternity should have it reprinted either in Rome itself or here in Naples.

Pardon me again, I beg you, if I have overstepped the bounds in any way in this letter. The love I have for the Society has constrained me to write to you. As for myself, I am of no importance, but I want you to understand that I have always been loud in my praise of the Society.'4

But nothing could stem the anti-Jesuit tide in Europe. Pope Clement XIII was forced to permit the civil trial of the Jesuits in Lisbon, culminating in 1761 in the execution of Father Gabriel Malagrida. Alphonsus felt personally each blow aimed against the Society and he began to have forebodings that a similar fate, of perhaps less dramatic proportions, awaited his own missionary society in Naples.

– II –

Alphonsus' ministry to the priests of the Kingdom of Naples began within a few months of his ordination to the priesthood when Cardinal Pignatelli instructed him to preach the spiritual exercises to his priests. With the expansion of his missionary apostolate outside the confines of the capital, he found abundant scope for his zeal among the clergy. He insisted that the spiritual exercises should be preached during every mission to the priests and clerics of the locality; a Father was to be specially designated for this ministry, while the clergy were to be assembled in whatever church or oratory was available, separate from the laity. There were three main areas which called for attention, the low spiritual level of priestly lives, the ignorance of theology and general priestly learning, and finally, the lack of zeal and pastoral interest. The hierarchy of the Kingdom was as concerned at the situation as was Alphonsus. When the bishop of Montemarano, Mons. Innocenzio Sanseverino, wrote to Alphonsus to thank him for his *Moral Theology* he poured out to him his distress at the ignorance of moral theology among his clergy. They had to be implored to hear confessions. The bishop admitted that he had been compelled to force some of his priests, ignorant of theology as they were, to hear confessions rather than allow his people to be deprived of this sacrament. For this reason, among others, the burdens of his episcopate were becoming intolerable; the previous two months had almost brought him to the end of his tether and only a course of asses' milk had helped him to keep going. The sad state of the clergy, and especially the rural clergy, which Alphonsus had experienced for himself in the course of his missionary campaigns, offended every priestly ideal he had drawn up for himself. He was appalled at meeting priests who never wore clerical dress, whose hair was waved with 'hot irons', who wore wigs heavily powdered with cypress powder, which fell on the corporal during Mass, who either associated with the proletariat in gaming and drinking, or aped the aristocracy in their foppishness and lack of religious spirit. Their lives were a scandal to the ordinary faithful.

All these abuses are referred to in his retreats to priests. Alphonsus had no illusion about the difficulty of the task confronting him in his efforts to raise the standard of priestly life and holiness throughout the Kingdom. With the diocesan organisation so inadequate, the spiritual exercises preached to the local clergy as part of a wider missionary effort in the area were virtually the only occasion available to many priests for a personal conversion experience. A retreat, made privately or with others, in a religious retreat house which Alphonsus advocated strongly and which he catered for in the four houses of his own Congregation, demanded a special effort which the majority of the rural clergy were not prepared to make. Alphonsus' verdict on his ministry to priests was at once realistic and pessimistic: 'It requires a miracle for a priest who has been leading a sinful life to be converted by making the spiritual exercises and the same holds good for the improvement of those whose lives have been tepid. And my experience is that these miracles rarely take place.'[5] His approach to priests is clear from the outline programme he drew up in 1756 for all the Fathers of the Congregation who found themselves engaged in this apostolate. He emphasised from the outset that the priests, no matter how indecorous their lives might be, should be treated with the respect due to their sacerdotal dignity. The approach of the retreat director was to be one of humility in an endeavour to win the clergy to a better frame of mind, rather than to alienate them by attacking them. He forbade the Fathers to preach on the difficulty which a priest would experience in saving his soul if he had entered the priesthood from unworthy motives and without a true vocation, as was the common practice of retreat preachers from other missionary orders. Such a lecture — suitable certainly for seminaries — did nothing more than depress the unfortunate clerics who found themselves in that situation; since they were ordained there was nothing that could be done about it except to adopt a positive approach and encourage them to lead holy lives. At most, Alphonsus would allow the preacher to refer in a passing way to the fact that one who had entered the priesthood from unworthy motives should now make a special effort to lead an even stricter life than others. His general approach was to lead them to love Jesus Christ and then to teach them how to pray and to insist that they devote time each day to mental prayer.[6]

As well as sermons or talks of an exhortatory nature, the retreat was meant to emphasise doctrinal and practical matters as well. Two specific instructions were never to be omitted, the first, on how to hear confessions, and the second, on the correct celebration of Mass. The instruction on confession Alphonsus considered the most important of the whole retreat. He wrote a full instruction on the subject himself and sent it to all the houses so that the Fathers would have a model to follow; he suggested that the instruction might even be given twice. Next in importance came the practical instruction in the rubrics of the celebration of the Eucharist, with insistence on the necessity of preparation and thanksgiving. There were many priests in Naples who, according to the reports of the Nuncio to Rome, never celebrated Mass or recited the breviary; the position was considerably worse in the rural areas. And where these priestly duties were discharged, there were those whose celebration of the Mass was so slipshod that they did not observe even the minimum of liturgical decorum. The speed with which they celebrated was at once a scandal to the faithful and a true reflection of their lack of faith and reverence; Mass had become for them nothing more than a ritual performance, discharged as rapidly as possible, to entitle them to the financial offering attached. The same was true of the speed with which they discharged — it could hardly be styled, prayed — the recitation of the Divine Office.

Having insisted on the proper celebration of the Eucharist and the prayerful recitation of the breviary, Alphonsus then proceeded to present to the priests a rule of life to which he devoted several lectures. Their day was to begin, he suggested, with half-an-hour's prayer, followed by the recitation of the appropriate part of their breviary, then by the celebration of Mass. The rest of the morning was to be spent in the works of the ministry or in the study of theology. In the afternoon there should be spiritual reading, recitation of the breviary, and a walk with some companion or the performance of some pastoral duty such as visiting the sick and those confined to their homes. This was to be followed by a visit to the Blessed Sacrament, the recitation of the rosary, a further half-hour of prayer and a final period of study. One day a month was to be passed in special recollection and each year they were to make the spiritual exercises in some religious house of retreats. This rule of life, *Regolamento di vita per un sacerdote secolare*, was the very least he was prepared to accept. He then complemented it with a further outline of a rule of life for those who aspired to the perfection of priestly holiness, *Regole di spirito per un sacerdote che attende alla perfezione*. Here he proposed a life of prayer, of separation from secular interests and human affections as well as positive ideals of self-denial and mortification. It was an outline which made little compromise with human nature and which showed the high degree of spirituality he expected from those who were so often lacking even in the bare minimum.[7]

Having preached to priests all over the Kingdom of Naples, Alphonsus, as was now his usual practice, set about publishing the vast amount of material concerning all aspects of priestly life which he had accumulated in the course of his ministry to them. In 1760 came the *Selva* — an accepted term for an anthology — which was ostensibly a source book of sermons and instructions for those engaged in the ministry of preaching to priests but was, in point of fact, a convenient *vademecum* for priests for their own meditations and spiritual reading. It contained, by way of appendix, the two *Rules of Life* which had become central to Alphonsus' efforts to raise the standard of priestly conduct. Its popularity was immediate. Reprinted time and time again, it spread throughout the dioceses of Italy as the accepted manual of priestly devotion. Within twenty years of its publication in Italian and while Alphonsus was still in St Agatha of the Goths, he was thrilled to hear that it had been translated into German; within a few years of his death it was translated into all the other major European languages, thus ensuring that it gradually became normative for priestly spirituality and practice for the greater part of the nineteenth century. Hard on the heels of the Selva came the publication of *La Messa e l'Officio Strapazzati — The Mass and the Divine Office Hurriedly Said —* which completed his first series of publications for the renewal of priestly life in Bourbon Naples. A few years later, during the first half of his episcopacy, he completed and published a handbook on the correct rubrics of the Mass, *Delle Ceremonie della Messa*, intended mainly for the priests of his diocese but which contained as well a second series of meditations and prayers for each day of the week to be used by priests by way of preparation for and thanksgiving after the celebration of Mass. While the little volume on the ceremonies of the Mass made only minor impact, the prayers and meditations took on a life of their own and continued to be reprinted separately or included in manuals of devotion. Right up to the present day when different theological emphases have brought changes in Eucharistic spirituality, different versions of these prayers and meditations have become the universally treasured patrimony of the world's clergy, including popes, bishops, priests and saints, among them the Curé of Ars.[8]

The accepted means of guaranteeing the spiritual welfare of the mass of the unattached clergy at the time was to enroll them in a clerical sodality or *Congrega*, corresponding in modern times, to a *Pia Unio*. On the occasion of the mission preached in Vignola, near Nola, in 1760, the missioners established a new clerical sodality in the town with a *Rule of Life* drawn up by Alphonsus which was identical with the norms he laid down in the appendix to the *Selva*. The priests of the sodality were to meet once a week; they were to be especially zealous in hearing confessions, never refusing when requested. On feast days, at least five hours were to be set aside for this ministry. They were to devote an hour and a half each day to the study of moral theology. Besides choosing a spiritual director, each member was to be careful not to dress in a foppish manner nor to wear wigs or long dressed hair. They were to avoid, in a word, *milorderia* in dressing — it had now become Alphonsus' favourite word in this context — which would make them more of courtiers than priests. And finally, they were not to spend their time in the village piazza with the men and women of the place in idle gossip; above all they were to avoid the wine shops and taverns. One can gauge how different was the clerical world of that time when it was laid down that, at their weekly meeting, the members should wear on their head a crown of thorns as an act of devotion in honour of the Sacred Heart.[9]

The difficulty of achieving a renewal of priestly life after ordination, to which Alphonsus referred again and again, brought him to the realisation that the real reform of the clergy had to begin in the seminaries. In his letter for bishops he had stressed the priority they should give to their seminaries, with the result that he was in constant demand for retreats to their seminarians. Time and time again he was invited back to the seminarians in Naples, Aversa, Sarno and Nola. Nola, where he was a familiar figure, provided one of the most bizarre experiences of his whole missionary career. He was asked to preach at the opening of the new seminary there, built, at great expense, by the court architect, Vanvitelli, and then to follow the inaugural ceremony with a retreat. The grandiose building had attracted some very undesirable candidates. Discipline reached such a low level that a plot was hatched — and fortunately foiled — to murder the vice-rector. The place, apparently, had more in common with a convict settlement than an ecclesiastical training college. From the first moment of Alphonus' appearance, the students laughed at him, openly mimicking him, his gestures, his sermons. Driven to desperation, Alphonsus determined to preach on the General Judgment. Leaving the predella of the altar from where he had been addressing the students, he secured immediate silence by asking, at the top of his voice, was there one amongst his listeners, damned? Holding his crucifix in one hand and a lighted candle in the other, he went through the chapel from seat to seat, repeating the question and praying the Lord to be enlightened as to who among them were destined for the fires of hell. The effect can only be imagined. Four ring-leaders of the conspiracy were identified and left immediately; others were publicly dismissed. The whole dramatic performance had the desired effect and some kind of religious climate was re-established which allowed the retreat to continue. Though he had forbidden his colleagues to preach on the evil of unworthy motives for entering the priesthood, he had no hesitation in stressing the point to seminarians. Quite the contrary; it was a theme to which he returned time and time again during the course of his retreats to them. When the retreat at Nola was over, he drew up a new rule for the seminary there, which he had printed immediately on his return to Pagani, and which he sent to all the bishops of the Kingdom, many of whom adopted it for their dioceses. In succeeding years, the Rule appeared as an appendix to the *Selva*.[10]

By 1760 Alphonsus had completed his work for the clergy of the Kingdom, from bishops and priests to seminarians. Having preached to them he had published his sermons and instructions to continue what he had begun in the pulpit. His efforts were compared to those of St Vincent de Paul in France and he earned the reputation of playing just as significant part in the reform of the Neapolitan clergy as Charles Borromeo had done in Milan. Yet he was a reformer within the constraints of the existing established system of the Neapolitan Church with all its pre-Trent characteristics. It would take the political upheavals at the end of the century and the pontificate of Pius IX before the Neapolitan Church succeeded in casting off its medieval peculiarities.

– III –

Parallel to Alphonsus' ministry to priests went his ministry to the nuns of the Kingdom. This too began immediately after his ordination and his earliest extant letters are to convents. Besides being invited to investigate the revelations at Scala he had already preached the spiritual exercises to the Benedictine sisters in Polignano in Apulia, on his missionary journeys with the Apostolic Missions. When he later initiated his missionary preaching with his own companions from Scala in Tramonte in 1733, he devoted special attention to the nuns in Pocara. After his first visit there, he sent the sisters a consignment of books, separating them into three sections, specifically suitable for personal meditation, private spiritual reading and public reading in the refectory. This initial interest and involvement with sisters he maintained right through his active ministry, preaching the spiritual exercises, undertaking to direct an ever-increasing number, visiting them and replying to their letters with infinite patience. From all over the Kingdom, nuns wrote to him for spiritual guidance. No matter how busy he was he replied, often at great length, writing letters which, in point of fact, were short treatises on prayer or norms of conduct or some other aspect of the spiritual life.

Whether on a mission, engaged in preparing his latest work for the printers, in Naples in the throes of delicate negotiations with the Bourbon authorities for the survival of his Congregation, or later as a bishop in his diocese, he was never too busy to help some nun in her convent far from the consolation of having a priest who could deal with her difficulties with competence and understanding. His attitude was expressed clearly to Mother Teresa, a Carmelite of Ripacandida; 'Whenever you have a special problem write to me the salient aspects of the problem and I will steal whatever time I can — as I do now — to reply. But it will be just a few words, since I have not a moment to spare.'[11] Actually, his replies to Ripacandida frequently ran into many pages.

Like most other aspects of ecclesiastical organisation in the Kingdom, convent life in Naples had its own unique features both spiritually and socially, some edifying, others, quite bewildering, to say the least. The convent population ran into many thousands — there were over 3,000 nuns in the city of Naples alone — many of whom were there without any authentic religious vocation and consequently without any real religious motivation in their lives. As in the case of the clergy, we get the striking contrast between lives of admirable holiness and, at times, heroic sanctity, side by side with others of scandalous luxury and worldliness. There were many who lived in the convents with their own personal servants and for whom the monasteries were nothing more than first-class hotel accommodation. The vast majority of the convents of the Kingdom were nominally contemplative with strict enclosure and all that went with it; the active sisterhoods which have characterised the post-French Revolution Church were just beginning to make their appearance. The necessity of renewal of the religious life was obvious to all the church authorities in Naples for over a hundred years and figured largely in successive synodal discussions but never seemed to issue in anything more tangible than the tightening of regulations concerning enclosure.[12]

One remarkable aspect of the convent system was the fact that the majority of the so-called contemplative convents were, at the same time, boarding schools where the daughters of the aristocracy and the lesser nobility, while still only children, were placed to be educated and reared until they were ready for marriage as arranged by their parents. The age of admission for these *educande*, as they were called, varied. The general age was twelve to fourteen but children as young as five were admitted with a routine papal dispensation; Alphonsus' two sisters were five and nine respectively when they became *educande*. The educational regime varied considerably from the sophistication of the Francophile Visitation convent and the aristocratic cultural level of the Spanish Santa Maria della Concezione to the more plebian convents such as San Girolamo, San Marcellino and the Cappuccinelli, patronised by members of the Liguori family. The *educande* or 'boarders' — often referred to in legal documents as *vergini in capillis* — commonly wore some form of religious habit which they received at entry at a reception ceremony and were, in many convents, addressed as 'sister' as well. They had to possess either a dowry providing a sufficient yearly income or else contract for a yearly fee which varied with the social rating of the convent. In Pocara, in Tramonte, the fee was thirty-six ducats a year; in San Girolamo where Alphonsus' sisters went, the pension was over sixty ducats, while in the aristocratic convents like Santa Chiara and the Visitation it reached astronomical figures. Even though the *educande* were bound by canon law to have their own section of the convent, separate from the sisters, they still followed the rule of the convent just like the professed; they came to Office in choir, observed the rules of silence and of enclosure. During their time in the convent they were not allowed to return home and were subject to the same restrictions in the matter of visitors at what was called the 'grille' or the 'grate' as the professed nuns. In due course, the parents were expected to summon their daughters home for some months to prepare them for the marriage celebration which had been arranged for them. They were allowed to remain in the convent until they were twenty-one, or in some convents until they were twenty-six, by which time it was felt that their parents' efforts to arrange suitable nuptials for them had failed and they would have to fend for themselves in the world. The alternative, of course, was to join the convent. If a girl expressed a wish to follow this vocation — and the pressure on her to do so in many cases must have been considerable — she was bound to leave the convent for some months and live 'in the world' before she could be either lawfully or validly received as a religious postulant. Despite this minimum safeguard, which was at least some attempt at assuring liberty and maturity of choice, many young women found themselves in enclosed orders without the slightest indication of a genuine vocation and where they lived virtually incarcerated, if not completely frustrated. While a dowry was essential for religious profession, a convent dowry was considerably less expensive than a suitable marriage dowry, with the result that daughters of the impecunious lesser nobility very often had little choice.

This rather disturbing picture highlights another aspect of convent life at the time. The convent population was composed almost exclusively of the children of the nobility; the uneducated children of the lower classes of society as well as the young women of the countryside found the consecrated life closed to them. At most, they could enter as servants of their social betters, accepting at the same time the status of a *conversa* or lay-sister, with religious vows certainly, but whose main duties were to wait on the needs of the professed nobility. And just as the church hierarchy, from cardinal to bishop, provided careers for the sons of the nobility so, equally, superiorship of the opulent and aristocratic convents became the preserve of their daughters. The Caraccioli, Sersali, Pignatelli and the Orsini were nearly always found as the superioresses of the aristocratic Neapolitan convents; the highest office that Alphonsus' sister Maria Louisa was able to attain was that of counsellor, which did give her some slight distinction as a member of the convent cabinet.

The high number of forced vocations together with the fact that convents also became places of refuge for aristocratic ladies whose husbands had abandoned them, make it easy to appreciate how the standards of religious life deteriorated. Just as there was need for reform among the clergy, so there existed a long catalogue of abuses throughout the convents which demanded attention, even though abuses in the convents were regarded with greater tolerance by society at large and by the Bourbon court in particular. The young ladies forced behind convent walls were not disposed to lead religious lives of great asceticism and they took their revenge by gradually transforming their convents into the most pleasant ladies' clubs imaginable. The aristocrats of Santa Chiara in Naples, where there were over 350 'sisters', made their convent cloister and refectory — over one hundred yards long and with a fountain and a fish-pond in the centre — into a gem of ceramic art, designed and executed by Vaccaro, where the great master of the *mattonelle* depicted, for the love-lorn nuns, scenes of idyllic love and profane social life. The wealth of many convents, the magnificence of their buildings and the extent of their property, especially in the very heart of Naples, did not arouse the anger of the Court as much as the few hectares of vineyards possessed by Alphonsus and his missionary companions. In many cases, the nuns lived more like society women than religious. As well as their personal servants, they were in continuous contact with their relatives and friends whom they entertained lavishly in the convent reception rooms. Prayer and penance, the basis of the contemplative ideal, were to a large extent absent from their lives. What should have been houses of silence, prayer and self-denial became, in Alphonsus' own words — which may seem harsh but which he repeated several times in his letters — *serragli* of 'caged females'. It was well known in Naples that on more than one occasion tension built up in some convents to such a pitch that opposing factions engaged in hand-to-hand fighting. Alphonsus was called in on one such occasion to help establish a truce.

Much of the social life of the convents centred round the musical festivals which the convents arranged throughout the year and which were often financed by the wealthier members of the community. Tourists from northern Europe and ambassadors accredited to the Bourbon Court, vied with each other to secure invitations to what were intended to be religious celebrations, but became purely secular occasions. We have seen what immediate action Alphonsus took when he encountered this abuse in the convents of Foggia. An equally fertile source of relaxation of religious observance were the banquets given each year by those nuns who held offices in the community such as sacristan, cellarer, bursar. On these occasions, the nun invited her friends and the convent benefactors, together with some important local personage — the more important the better — and her reputation, as well as the reputation of her family, was measured by the magnificence of the banquet. This abuse which had defied the decrees of Popes, Cardinals and Apostolic Visitors — and we can add Alphonsus' own efforts — was only finally eradicated by a royal decree of 1779 by King Ferdinand IV. Alphonsus' own niece, Teresa, the daughter of his brother Hercules, found, when she opened her father's Will, that besides her dowry and her share of the family inheritance, he had assigned her a considerable sum to provide for the banquet she would have to finance if and when she became a nun.[13]

Alphonsus believed wholeheartedly in the value of a life consecrated to God and insisted that nuns who lived their religious lives as they should, were the 'most illustrious section of the church of Jesus Christ'. At the same time, he was fully aware of the prevalent abuses; when he published his reflections for bishops in 1745 he devoted one entire section to the bishop's duty to remedy the sad condition of the convents. Predictably he himself endeavoured to remedy whatever abuses he could by his preaching and finally by his writings, just as he had done for the clergy. Once again it must be pointed out that all his efforts at reform of convent life were within the existing structures; he showed no inclination to alter what was established and still less did he propose any new forms of religious life. Basic to the whole situation, as he found it, was the lack of genuine religious vocations. He began by burdening the conscience of bishops with the obligation of seeing to it that only those with an authentic call from God should be allowed to enter convents. This simple reform would have entailed a revolution both in society and in church life had it succeeded.

> It is the misfortune of our times that so many enter convents more from the wishes of their parents or for some other purpose, than from a desire to consecrate their lives wholly to God and His service. The result is that there are so many convents devoid of any real religious spirit. Relaxation grows from day to day. We must eradicate the abuse at its source. The bishops, therefore, should examine the young girl with all diligence, before her clothing ceremony, away from the other sisters,

and not as a mere formality, but with the determination of discerning the truth as to why she wishes to become a religious. Is she being forced into it by her parents or the Sisters themselves? And, if he does not discern an authentic vocation to the religious state, he should be adamant in refusing to allow her to take the religious habit.[14]

One by one he outlined the various abuses, suggested the appropriate remedies and ended by suggesting that bishops should limit the number of nuns in each convent of their dioceses — a startling enough proposal: 'where there is a crowd, it is difficult to have good observance', was his reasoning. And he could not resist his final suggestion to the bishops that only priests of exemplary life and well qualified, should be allowed to preach the spiritual exercises to sisters, otherwise it would be better for the sisters to make their retreats in private.

Throughout his life, Alphonsus was in constant demand as director of the spiritual exercises to nuns; there were few convents where he had not preached and he returned to many of them on several occasions. He directed the spiritual exercises in the convent of Santa Chiara in Nocera on at least six occasions. His approach was quite personal. At times, he began his conference to the sisters by singing a spiritual canticle to move them to fervour and devotion — an expedient which it would be foolhardy for the majority of retreat masters to emulate. His gifts of discernment and, at times, of prophetic insights, greatly impressed many of the superioresses. In the same convent of Santa Chiara, the Abbess brought him one of the *educande*, Donna Felicita Calenda, a talented young lady and daughter of the Governor of Ischia, whom the Abbess was anxious to encourage to join the convent, since she possessed a beautiful singing voice which would have been invaluable for the musical life of the convent. Known as *Felice* in her family circle, she was called *Vittoria* in the convent — *Felice nel mondo, Vittoria nel chiostro*. To the great disappointment of the Mother Abbess, Alphonsus informed her mysteriously that the young lady in question would belong neither to the world nor to the cloister. A short while afterwards she met with a serious accident with the result that she spent fifty years at home, paralysed, on a steel frame, belonging 'neither to the world nor to the convent'. Of course, his ideas did not always meet with approval any more than they had done even in the convent in Scala. He was invited to preach the spiritual exercises in a convent at Cava near Salerno. He found, as was only to be expected, the usual list of abuses but the last straw was the fact that the Mother Superior kept a pet poodle in her room which she brought down to choir where he kept guard as she presided, at the chanting of the Office. Greatly daring, Alphonsus attacked the abuse. The superioress, determined to keep her canine companion, appealed to the local bishop, who supported her. Alphonsus refused to continue the retreat, packed his few belongings and left. He had seen enough to convince himself that the convent was relaxed beyond reform. He announced publicly that it was a doomed ship, *una barca scassata*, and would soon founder as, in point of fact, happened some years later.[15]

His disillusionment with the level of holiness of life in convents throughout Bourbon Naples is evident in many of his letters:

> I would like to see all nuns sanctify themselves since they have so many graces available to them, but my God, what a miserable thing it is to see so many nuns and so few saintly ones among them.[16]

To a young *educanda* who was contemplating entering the convent where she had spent her adolescence, he wrote exhorting her to choose some other place:

> More than ever now, I recommend you to choose some other convent because the one you are in is more like a *serraglio* of worldly women than a convent of religious. But be of good heart. Jesus Christ wishes you to sanctify yourself and you will be much happier in another convent than all these nuns where you are, with their entertainments and their dissipated lives. Jesus Christ alone can make you happy. Everything else is only deceit.[17]

When he pronounced his mature verdict on the state of the convents to which he had ministered for nearly forty years it was anything but complimentary:

> For the rest, I would have you know, that with a few exceptions, all the convents in my experience are like your own, relaxed in observance and full of division and bickering.[18]

The standards he set for nuns were very high and he was uncompromising in the demands he made on them — total commitment to the Lord, complete detachment from the world they had left and their friends, faithfulness in prayer, a willingness to suffer, a deep spirit of humility and an uncompromising spirit of mortification. The regime of corporal austerities which he outlined for them made little concession to the weakness of human nature. To a nun who wrote informing him of the religious profession of her sister, he replied:

> I rejoice at the espousals of your sister with Jesus Christ. You who are already His Spouse, love him as a bride should, that is, do everything for him out of love, forgetful of yourself, without seeking either spiritual or human consolation.

When a nun wrote to him requesting him to offer Mass for the recovery of her health, he urged her to greater resignation:

> Tomorrow I shall say Mass for you. But I tell you that Our Lady will not obtain your request for you because you pray without resignation. You should seek first of all *resignation* rather than restoration of health. If you sought a spirit of willingness to suffer or even restoration to health with a spirit of acceptance of whatever God wills, then you would have a better chance of obtaining both.
>
> Now, you are to do as I tell you. Pray from now onwards for *patienza*, not only in times of ill health but also when you are despised and thought little of by others. What better way can there be of accumulating treasure

in heaven than by suffering just as Jesus Christ suffered. You must suffer and be despised and be prepared to suffer alone without even the sympathy of others.

He warned the nuns who wrote to him that they should place all their affections in Jesus Christ to whom they had consecrated their lives. Inordinate attachments became a constant theme in his letters to sisters, perhaps with the memory of Crostarosa still in his mind. One nun wrote lamenting that she had not seen him on the occasion of his last visit to Naples: 'I want you to learn to direct all your affections towards that Infinite Goodness who alone merits all our love.' When a sister wrote anxiously to him during one of his illnesses his reply was slightly ungracious:

> You should not have been upset at my illness. Every human affection which is immoderate, even though above reproach from every other aspect, is an obstacle to our love for Jesus Christ. If you wish to belong wholly to Jesus Christ you must not worry about whether I am well or ill; it is sufficient that Jesus Christ, who merits all your love, should be with you.

And yet even in this matter of affection he could be surprising: his balance of judgment is evident in a short reply he wrote to a nun who admitted to him a slight tenderness for her confessor:

> I believe that it is necessary to have a well-ordered affection for your confessor since, in this way, you will more easily obey him in what he recommends and will not in any way give him displeasure. For the rest, look upon him just as one who helps you in the important matter of the eternal salvation of your soul, and live then in such complete indifference that if he is changed you will be immediately ready to accept whatever God wishes for you in the matter.[19]

The human side of his character revealed in his dealings with nuns is intriguing. From his letters it is clear that he was perfectly relaxed and at ease with them. Apart from the spiritual message which his letters contained there was also a discernible lightness of touch, a gentle inoffensive humour uniquely characteristic of this section of his correspondence. And while he pretended to be outraged on occasions at their unreasonable demands, he gave in ultimately. The incident with Sister Mary Archangela Lipo in the convent at Monticchio in the diocese of Massalubrense at the tip of the Lipari peninsula was typical. She insisted on having Father Bernard Apice as her confessor; he was the key to her eternal salvation, according to herself. When he was unable to answer her call since he was detained for some time on special assignment in Gaeta, she demanded of Alphonsus that he should instruct him to come at once; she would brook no excuses. Alphonsus, more incredulous than angry at her outrageous demands, decided to send her Father de Robertis instead:

> So the position quite simply is that if Father Apice were to die, your only

hope of salvation would disappear. At the moment he is in Gaeta and cannot leave; I wanted him here myself and did not get him.

Now, out of consideration for your soul I am sending you from here another of our Fathers, Celestino de Robertis. He is an excellent priest, and in no way inferior to Father Apice. Get Faculties for him at once from the bishop so that he can hear your confession. Tell him all your scruples and worries.

I want you to know that I need Father de Robertis here with me but out of consideration for you I am sending him to you at great inconvenience. So make use of him while you have him. And if you do not agree to manifest your conscience to him after all the trouble I have gone to in order to get him to you, then don't dare, on any account, to ask me ever again to send you Father Apice (or any other Father, for that matter), since I simply won't answer you.

So let this Father know all your worries as quickly as you can and allow him to leave since I need him here with me. What a right mess it would be if I had to send Fathers to every monastery where they had preached during a mission, to settle the scruples of nuns . . . [20]

His nun acquaintances continually sent him gifts, mainly of fruit, cakes and sweetmeats. On nearly every occasion he felt bound to protest that they should not do so; he threatened that he was tempted to send them back or else refuse to write to the sisters in question any more. But the nuns accepted his protestations for the ritual refusals they were and the gifts continued to arrive. He thanked one of his penitents for the box of pomegranates she had sent him — they were just the thing for one of his relations who was coming to visit him from Naples. As for himself, she should know well that he rarely partook of such luxuries which were good for neither soul nor body. He was delighted with a present of *mostacciuoli*, a type of spiced cake characteristic of Christmas celebrations in Naples, and with the *graffioli*, a special type of cherry preserved in sugar, though he felt bound to say that he would have preferred the cherries without the sugar, the syrup upset his stomach. When one of his penitents addressed him as *Vostra Signoria Illustrissima*, a courtly title, Your Most Illustrious Lordship, he chided her gently: 'First of all, I say to you, my dear daughter, do not use the title V.S. Ill. when you write to me; it will be sufficient to say *Vostra Reverenza* out of respect for the priesthood which I unworthily bear.' He unashamedly recommended his own devotional books to them, being careful to let them know where they could be purchased. He instructed them to keep his letters safely and to re-read them when they were depressed since they could not expect him to write at length on the same problems again and again; it is thanks to this direction that so many of his letters to sisters have survived.

He possessed a special charism for counselling nuns who were suffering either physically or spiritually. And he was at his most assured in dealing with scruples as so many of his letters clearly demonstrate. Here he had his own personal experiences to draw on and the directions he gave to his penitents were identical with the instructions he had received himself. His advice was clear and direct, uncompromisingly so at times, and he insisted on absolute obedience no matter how repugnant some of his penitents may have found his decisions. The scrupulous nun he directed in the convent at Fisciano near Salerno was to continue to receive Communion even if she believed that she had consented to every possible temptation; she was to communicate even if she believed she was committing a sacrilege. His instructions to Sister Maria Giovanna of the aristocratic Sparano family was nothing if not forceful: 'I fear this may be God's last call to you. You are on the brink and the alternatives are "either a saint or buried in Hell". God certainly wishes you to be a saint.'[21]

The very first penitent he directed into a convent was Sister Mary Magdalen of the Crucified whom he met during his ministry at the Chinese College — he was, she declared, so kind to her, *tutto dolce*. After some years in the convent of Santa Maria Maddelena sopra Gesù e Maria in Naples, she fell victim to a mysterious illness which confined her to bed, paralysed, for over forty years. Each time he went to Naples he visited her and he wrote frequently to her as well. Unfortunately, she destroyed his letters as an act of detachment — it is difficult not to resist the conclusion that this was at his instigation — and only one of the long series has survived:

> I have read your letter. I think your only remedy in all your troubles is to abandon yourself completely to the Will of God, wishing neither for good health nor spiritual consolation but only complete submission to His good pleasure. This is the greatest peace that a soul who really loves God can experience in this life. So in all your desolation of spirit repeat over and over again, "My God, I wish only what pleases you". And will you say this prayer not only for yourself but for me also so that I too may do His Will in all things. And I shall do the same for you. I bless you.[22]

His most famous penitent was Sister Brianna of the aristocratic Carafa family, whom he met for the first time when he gave the spiritual exercises in the convent of San Marcellino in 1759. Dissatisfied with her life, she contemplated leaving this convent for the eremitical life in the *Eremo*, the hermitage founded by Sister Orsola Benincasa. After a lengthy period of discernment when the matter was considered even by the archbishop of Naples, Alphonsus decided that she should remain where she was and for years he guided her through great spiritual difficulties, encouraging her to persevere in the singular way of holiness to which, he was sure, God was calling her. She grew very attached to him and his departure after his visits to see her in Naples left her feeling lonely.' 'My departure', he assured her, 'is only the departure of a creature. We should only be disconsolate at the thought that God would leave us. The Lord wills that I should support you with my prayers which I do and not with my presence.' When Alphonsus' niece, Teresa, finally decided to join a convent, she entered San Marcellino, where Sister Brianna was present to assist her in the first difficult years.

Alphonsus had a special affection for the Carmelite sisters of the Teresian reform and he lavished his special care on these convents. His interest in Teresa of Avila dated back to the early years of his priesthood when he set himself to study her life and writings; her teaching on detachment and union with God, he made his own. When, two years after his ordination, St John of the Cross was canonised, he immersed himself in the writings of this Carmelite mystic and reformer as well. He recommended his writings to his penitents, especially his Carmelite penitents, choosing specifically that section of the beginning of *Notte oscure* dealing with the seven fundamental sins. One of his earliest publications — what has, in fact, come to be regarded as his first 'book' in the strict sense — was a work on the life and spiritual teaching of Teresa of Avila.[23] He expressed a hope that after his death this little work would continue his apostolate among his beloved Carmelite sisters and all his life he continued to draw inspiration from these two Carmelite doctors for his own spiritual advancement and to equip himself for the spiritual direction of his Carmelite penitents.

Sister Maria Giovanni della Croce, a nun of exceptional holiness of life in the Carmelite convent at Camigliano near Caiazzo, became his spiritual child while he was at Villa degli Schiavi in the early days of the Congregation. Soon after her entry into Carmel he undertook the direction of her spiritual life and outlined a special rule of life for her in her early days in the cloister. He continued to correspond with her for forty years. On one occasion when she wished to discuss some matter with him which could not safely be entrusted to a letter, she sent a horse and carriage to bring him to the convent. He informed her when he was leaving Villa and insisted that she continue to write to him — 'I am now leaving here for another foundation we have made in the diocese of Salerno, at Ciorani. Nonetheless I wish to continue to help you as far as I can, so continue to write to me.'

Under his direction Sister Maria Giovanni progressed to a very intimate degree of union with God though at the inevitable cost of great desolation of soul. His letters to her clearly revealed his own experience:

> Be satisfied now with having Our Lord in your heart even though you do not have him in your eyes. Offer this desolation — than which there cannot be any greater for those who love Jesus, a desolation which Our Lord Himself suffered on the Cross — to God. But what good are you if you cannot suffer for God as your own St John of the Cross said? And it was St Philip Neri who said that the greatest cross in the world is not to have a cross. He also said that that person has little love for Jesus Christ who does not wish to suffer for him. When you are deepest in your desolation lift up your heart to Our Lord with a sigh and say to Him, "My Spouse, I do not seek for your consolation but only for yourself." And try to experience that suffering which St Aloysius experienced which made him a veritable martyr of love — namely that he was not able to love God as much as he knew God deserved to be loved.

> Be careful in everything, whether trouble or desolation, to offer it to Jesus. How happy, I am, dear daughter, to hear of your desolation in prayer and at the same time of your perseverance. Continue all this time to make acts of union of your will with the Will of God.
>
> If you were to realise that all was well with you in your relations with God where would there be any place for suffering? Suffering would be paradise! Try to regain your peace at once in your desolation and persevere in your prayers and in your spiritual exercises despite all the tedium you feel and even though everything seems to you to be lost. *Lascia fare à Gesù*, allow Jesus to do as he wishes with you.
>
> And even though you are in desolation of spirit, endeavour to be in good humour with the Sisters, and to speak to them with all sweetness; make a great effort on this point . . . And at the same time recognise yourself before God — even more than before those to whom you speak — for that miserable creature that you are and worthy of all disrespect; do not even reply to any thoughts of vainglory.[24]

There were those among his colleagues who viewed with something less than approval the attention Alphonsus lavished on sisters but he was personally fully convinced of the importance of this pastoral ministry. The majority of nuns were dependent on the convent confessors for guidance in their spiritual lives and, as often as not, these confessors had little interest in the spiritual progress of their penitents; they were, at any rate, insufficiently equipped theologically for the task. There was therefore an element of self-justification in what Alphonsus wrote on this whole question. As a consequence, the preaching of the spiritual exercises in convents especially in rural districts, came to assume considerable importance in the developing apostolate of the Congregation. Besides urging his colleagues to prepare themselves adequately for this ministry, which they were not to undertake before the age of thirty, he included in the *Pratica del Confessore* of 1755, a special chapter for those confessors who found themselves designated as confessors to convents of nuns:

> The ministry of leading spiritual souls along the path to holiness, so that they may belong wholly to the Lord, is a ministry which gives great pleasure to God. One perfect soul is of more value in his sight than a thousand imperfect ones. So, when the confessor realises that his penitent is leading a life free from serious sin he should do all in his power to lead that soul along the way of perfection and divine love. He should point out how much God deserves our love and the gratitude we owe to Jesus Christ who has loved us to the point of dying for us. And at the same time, he should show them also the danger in which souls, called by God to a life of holiness and perfection, may find themselves if they disregard this invitation.

He divided this instruction into three sections, the first, on the various stages of prayer, the second on the spirit and practice of mortification and self-denial which should characterise the spiritual soul, the third on the frequentation of the sacraments. His advice on prayer began with a simple outline of a method of making mental prayer and then continued with a treatise on the various stages of contemplation, of union with God, including the mystical marriage of the soul with our Lord. Based on the teaching of Teresa of Avila, and relying on John of the Cross for those sections dealing with the different stages of purification which the soul experiences in her journey to God, Alphonsus revealed not only his mastery of the theology and psychology of prayer but his personal experience of the highest mystical states; he wrote with the authentic stamp of one who had experienced what he described. And finally, he urged confessors to allow the nuns to communicate daily — advice which he had to put forward with long justifying explanations, on account of the prevalent Jansenistic spirit and practice. He was only too aware that there were priests who refused Communion to those who wished to communicate daily — even to nuns; his own approach was quite the opposite:

> Would to God, I say in conclusion, that there were very many more of these souls, whom Rigorists style irreverent and presumptuous, who communicate frequently and even daily, inspired by a genuine desire of overcoming their faults and advancing in the love of God.

Finally, rather than leave anything to chance, he provided the confessor with a clear and simple *Rule of Life for a Religious who wishes to be directed along the Path of Perfection to God*.[25]

Alphonsus practice in the matter of spiritual direction of sisters was first of all to lead them along the path of holiness by insisting on faithfulness to their Rule and the observance of the vows. His direction was practical in the sense that he dealt with the ordinary details of religious life and the different religious exercises; he knew Neapolitan convent life, with all its problems, inside out. In his directions concerning prayer he was careful to begin with the basic principles, at times to the disappointment of those who too readily imagined they possessed the mystical gifts of infused contemplation. However, it is clear from his writings and from his letters, that he certainly met with nuns who were graced with mystical gifts from God and these he led gently along to the highest states of union with God with a deftness of discernment which came from his own depth of prayer and his familiarity with the mystical teaching of the Carmelite doctors. He was careful, however, not to reveal to penitents that they possessed the graces of higher forms of prayer; he refused even to allow them to discuss these higher states with him. Instead, he warned them of the dangers of becoming preoccupied with visions and personal revelations; he was ever on his guard that they might fall victims to vanity or self-deception. The more convinced he was that one of his penitents was favoured with mystical graces the more did he demand of them in the way of humility, detachment from their own inclinations, and readiness to obey the instructions of their spiritual directors. He was at his best in encouraging those who, under the purifying action of God in their lives, were suffering aridities, trials, darkness and temptations. Only when he was assured of the genuine mystical experiences of his penitents, did he introduce them to the study of both St Teresa and St John of the Cross, marking out for them the sections they were to read, forbidding them at the same time to read further than was appropriate for their own degree of prayer and union with God. For the pseudo-mystics, there was the ever-present likelihood of dangerous illusions; these he forbade to think about their state of prayer, but rather to persevere in their acts of humility, their awareness of their own nothingness and in the increase of their abandonment to the Lord.[26]

The inevitable outcome of Alphonsus' ministry to nuns, his conferences, his letters, the relevant instructions in his moral writings, was a book for nuns to complement the works he had already published for bishops and priests. He had been collecting suitable material for years and it only remained for him, with the help of his colleagues, to assemble it in presentable form. He was more than usually careful, however, in his preparation of the book, knowing how critical his principal readers would be. He worked hard at enriching its style and presentation and when it was completed he expressed himself satisfied that it was the most polished of all his spiritual works, a sound *vademecum* of everything that reputable masters had written for the sanctification of nuns. The news that such a work was projected aroused considerable interest and such was the demand for it that the Naples publisher begged to be allowed to publish the first volume even before Alphonsus and his amanuenses had completed the second. By 1761 the two volumes of *La Vera Sposa di Gesù Cristo, The True Spouse of Jesus Christ*, had appeared in Naples; the same year they were also published by Remondini in Venice. The demand for them exceeded expectations; within a few years, Alphonsus could inform his Venetian publisher that every convent in Naples was full of them. It was his hope, he wrote to a nun to whom he sent a copy, 'that it will preach for me when I am dead since at the moment I am not able to preach'.[27] Three years after its appearance in print in Naples, the work was translated into German; long before his canonisation in 1839 the work had appeared in the four main European languages and had made its way into virtually every convent of the English, French and Spanish speaking world. In Ireland, Catherine McAuley was familiar with it during her own initiation into religious life and as she established her Sisters of Mercy. It succeeded in determining convent spirituality throughout the nineteenth century in a way Alphonsus could never have envisaged or perhaps even intended. Only with the second Vatican Council has the search for a spirituality of the active religious life for women broken free from the constraints and practices of a spirituality primarily intended for the contemplative monasteries of Bourbon Naples.

The work, however, remains an illuminating social commentary on many aspects of convent life and spirituality in Naples at the time. One section, for example, deals with the problem of a nun who finds herself in a convent against her will, due to pressure, perhaps even physical, from her parents or relatives. Faced with a situation which cannot have been altogether rare, Alphonsus makes it clear in the first place that he would not have allowed her to enter the convent in these circumstances had he been her director of conscience. But instead of advising her to leave or questioning the validity of the vows she had taken under duress, he goes on to encourage her to make a virtue out of necessity. If the Devil — very much a reality in the religion of those days — had engineered her presence in the convent to bring about her spiritual ruin, she was to turn it to her sanctification: 'Give yourself wholeheartedly to God and you will be happier than all the princesses and queens of the world.'

In this he was perhaps following St Francis de Sales who had given the same advice. And then he quoted the example of one Blessed Giacinta Marescotti of Viterbo who was placed in a convent by her parents against her will and who lived for some ten years like a caged lioness. Converted to a better frame of mind she then gave herself to God completely and died twenty-four years later after a religious life of great heroism which brought her to the honours of the altar.

More startling still was the section in the very opening chapter on the unhappiness of married women, not just some of them, but *all* of them. Alphonsus began by praising the value of virginity consecrated to God in the religious life and the happiness, despite the inherent sacrifices, which this life brings to those who embrace it. In contrast, he painted a picture of marital unhappiness in just four pointed paragraphs which, if it in any way was a true reflection of the reality at the time, makes distressing reading; the picture was one of unrelieved misery and suffering. He describes demanding husbands shouting abusively at their wives if their slightest wish was not carried out at once and to the letter — one wonders if this was an echo from his childhood — and children making incessant demands on their mothers, driving them to distraction. To reinforce the authenticity of this picture of unhappy married life, he stated categorically that *all* married couples without exception lead lives full of misery and unhappiness — *e dico tutte senza eccezione*. And he was prepared to stand over this statement based on his years of missionary experience. When he came to the spiritual lives of married women, the picture was equally negative and discouraging. It was virtually impossible for a married woman to achieve any degree of spirituality — the only paradigm of holiness for them was an approximation to martyrdom, and those who achieved this in their married lives were as rare as '*mosche bianche*', white flies. It is all a far cry from the genuine spirituality of married life today.[28]

The book also gave him an opportunity to unburden himself at some length on the question of *canto figurato* which still ranked as a major abuse in convents. What he had to say was quite personal:

> Let me now say something about music and the singing of nuns. In itself singing in church is a good thing because in this way we praise God. But in the singing of nuns I firmly believe that there is more thought

of vanity and the Devil than of God. Someone will say to me, what harm is there in singing? What harm is there? I tell you that there is, first of all, waste of time and a lot of time. Music is an art and unless one is a master of it, it not merely does not give pleasure but even annoys. In the second place, it is the cause of a thousand distractions, occasions for vanity, disturbance and irreverence in church. How much irreverence is there not in certain convents during Holy Week when the nuns sing the Lessons. Gentlemen come, not out of devotion but to hear such a nun sing and then when she has concluded he cries out in a loud voice 'Brava', just as if he were in a theatre ... Do you really think that a nun who sings solo in this *canto figurato* inspires any devotion in the gentlemen who hear her? I, for one, do not believe it; temptations, yes, but devotion, no! And in the third place, this singing can even be an occasion of losing one's soul since nuns must take lessons in singing from music professors, at times, quite young, and it is not difficult to imagine that with the familiarity the Devil will gain much.

Now do not think that I am an enemy of music. I like music very much and before I became a priest I spent a considerable amount of time at it — it would have been much better if I had spent it loving God instead — nor do I disapprove of Plain Chant for nuns. But I repeat, *canto figurato*, sung solo by a nun, is absolutely improper.[29]

– IV –

Towards the end of 1761, a great sense of fatigue came over Alphonsus; the incredible activity of the previous thirteen years, the recurring bouts of illness, had taken their toll. Writing became a torture for him and he decided that he would write nothing more. 'I am old now,' — he was sixty-five — 'and my head is not what it used to be.' At most, he would collect all he had written and arrange for a final complete edition of his works. He had become noticeably deaf and his mind was occupied by the thought of approaching death. He believed his life's work was completed and that his main task now was to prepare himself for his last journey to God. On New Year's Day in 1762, he preached in the church in Pagani, taking as his text the words of the letter to the Romans, 'the just man lives by faith'. The sermon was a strange medley of ideas, as if it had not been logically worked out, beginning with a description of the christian life as the life of God communicated to us by grace, then moving on to the exercise of faith in the ordinary affairs of one's life and concluding with a practical exhortation drawn from the ending of one year and the beginning of another:

> We are now at the end of 1761; today the New Year of 1762 has begun. How many saw the beginning of the year that has just gone but did not live to see its end! We should give thanks to God that we are allowed to see its conclusion. But do we know whether we shall see the conclusion of this year? Many, certainly, will not see it. Who knows if we shall not

be amongst this number? A year must dawn for us which will be our last.

We should awaken our faith and strive for the remainder of our lives to live according to the maxims of our faith. Why should we wait until death overtakes us and finds us living according to the maxims of the world? Let us awaken our faith to realise that this earth is not our true home but that we are merely here as pilgrims.

Our faith will give us confidence in our difficulties, teaching us that whoever prays will be saved. May our faith make us always live with the thought of eternity, keeping ever before our eyes this great thought — everything in this world comes to an end, whether it be prosperity or adversity, eternity alone never comes to an end.'[30]

Within a few months the first demands of this spirit of faith would be made on himself.

Part Three

Reaping the Harvest in Life and Death

1762–1787

Chapter Fourteen

A Mitre in the Caudine Forks 1762

- I -

On 11 February 1762, news reached Pagani of the death of Monsignor Flaminio Danza, bishop of St Agatha of the Goths. It came as something of a shock since the bishop was well known to the Fathers of the Congregation who had preached several missions in his diocese. Following the burial of Mons. Danza in the magnificent marble tomb which he had already prepared for himself in his cathedral in the episcopal city of St Agatha, the Vicar Capitular, Mons. Francesco Rainone, ordered prayers throughout the diocese for divine guidance in the appointment of a successor. A triduum of Exposition of the Blessed Sacrament was held in the cathedral and the professor of Theology in the diocesan seminary, the Dominican, Father Tomasso Maria Caputo, preached three sermons on the qualities required in their new bishop, *santo, dotto, zelante*, holiness, learning and zeal. The episcopal revenues were sufficiently large to make the position attractive, and, according to a contemporary account, many priests of the diocese and surrounding areas considered themselves totally identifiable with the model of Caputo's sermon and, accordingly, worthy of being chosen as the 'spouse of the widowed church of St Agatha'. At least seventy candidates offered themselves in one way or another to make the sacrifice entailed in accepting the mitre of the diocese, some from as far away as Brindisi. It was the rush of candidates for the office which prompted the Pope, Clement XIII to ask Cardinal Spinelli to seek a neutral candidate, a proposal which was supported by the Nuncio in Naples and the Neapolitan ecclesiastics at the Roman Curia, Cardinals Orsini and Castelli. Their determination was strengthened by the fact that St Agatha was one of the few remaining dioceses in the

Kingdom which could be filled by the Holy See without reference to the Bourbon Court.¹

On Tuesday 9 March an official from the Nunciature in Naples arrived at Pagani; he was brought to the room where Alphonsus was and introduced himself with the words, 'I have the honour of declaring myself the servant of your Excellency. You have been made bishop of St Agatha of the Goths.' Alphonsus smiled, reacting as if the whole thing was some sort of joke. Then the messenger handed him a letter from Mons. Andrea Negrone, *Uditore* of Clement XIII, whose function it was to convey to bishops-elect the news of their appointments:

> I have the honour to convey to you, by reason of my office, the news that his Holiness has deigned to choose you for the bishopric of St Agatha of the Goths, vacant through the death of Monsignor Flaminio Danza. In accordance with the decision of his Holiness, your Excellency will make arrangements to come here to Rome for the usual examination and for your appointment to be afterwards published in Consistory.

A personal letter from the Nuncio in Naples, Mons. Locatelli, who was mainly responsible for the appointment, conveyed his congratulations:²

> It is with the greatest personal satisfaction that I forward to your Paternity, in obedience to the commands of his Holiness, the enclosed letter of Mons. Uditore in which you are informed of your appointment as bishop of St Agatha of the Goths. In making this appointment which is so conducive to the service of God and the spiritual profit of the diocese, his Holiness has been prompted by the knowledge of your ecclesiastical spirit, your solid piety and your profound learning. The appointment is a source of great joy to me and I assure you of my readiness to serve you in any way possible.
>
> With the expression of my deepest esteem and respect, I have the honour to remain, your servant,
> Giuseppe Locatelli, archbishop of Carthage.

The news came as a terrible shock to Alphonsus; his reaction was immediate. Within an hour he had drawn up a letter outlining his reason for being unable to accept the nomination, while, at the same time, expressing his gratitude for the honour conferred on him. When this was done he recovered his good humour and considered the whole matter finished with. He dismissed the memory of it with a joke. 'It only cost me an hour to frame the refusal but it cost me four ducats for the messenger.' Alphonsus had developed a psychological and almost physical repugnance to being made a bishop which verged on the obsessive. This was altogether distinct from any spiritual motive of humility or sense of unworthiness or even fear of succumbing to human ambition or vanity. The phobia had developed since his early days as a priest in reaction to his father's ambitions on his behalf. He confided to his confessor that the two greatest efforts he ever had to make to overcome himself, were, first, when his father tried to dissuade him from becoming a cleric, and secondly, when he was appointed a bishop: 'In this last case I had to struggle against my natural repugnance since I was obliged to accept something which I did not want on account of the terror I felt at the responsibility of the office and the rigours of the judgment of God.'[3] In his early years as a priest, he manifested his fears to his spiritual director Father Pagano, who was much more anxious that he should renounce the possibility of a canonry, a pastoral cul-de-sac, rather than a bishopric. He was clever enough to insist with Alphonsus that there should be no further discussion of the matter until such an appointment actually materialised. As the years went by, Alphonsus felt that the danger had passed and he was sufficiently at ease with himself in the matter, to confide to his good friend, bishop Borgia of Cava, that one of the greatest benefits of being a member of his missionary congregation was avoiding the danger of being made a bishop. Such a fate, he was honest enough to inform Borgia, would have been inevitable had he remained a priest at home in Naples. Even Pagano, he sensed, was in favour of it.

The nuncio in Naples conveyed Alphonsus' refusal without delay to the Papal Secretary of State, Cardinal Torregiani, sending on his letter — which unfortunately has never been found — with a covering letter from himself, in which he made no effort to conceal his disappointment at the turn of events:

> The great satisfaction which I experienced yesterday on receipt of the notification from Mons. Uditore, of the appointment of Don Alfonso de Liguori as bishop of St Agatha of the Goths, on account of his excellent qualities which are well known to your Excellency, is the measure of my disgust at his refusal, which I have to convey to your Eminence with this letter. The reasons which he gives for his action are his advanced age, his declining health, the necessity of not relinquishing the direction of his young and exceedingly important Congregation, together with the vow prescribed by their Constitutions which have been approved by the Holy See, of not accepting ecclesiastical dignities. On account of the high esteem in which he is regarded here, this appointment by his Holiness would have won universal approval, though I doubt whether those who were displeased with his vindication of the Church's right to ban books, would have been equally satisfied.[4]

Alphonsus' refusal occasioned considerable perplexity in Roman circles since offers of bishoprics usually met with a ready, if not always, supernatural acceptance. He had, moreover, despatched a message to Cardinal Spinelli by special courier, imploring him to support his refusal; he had also enlisted the support of Borgia of Cava for the same purpose. Under this pressure, Spinelli decided not to force the nomination on such unwilling shoulders and communicated his attitude to the Pope, who acquiesced. On Sunday 14 March, those who were in the inner circles at Rome took it for granted that there was no question of proceeding with the appointment. Then, early on Monday morning, the Pope sent for Mons. Negrone and ordered him to forward to Alphonsus a formal precept of obedience to accept the appointment without further opposition. The background to the Pope's decision was described two days later in a letter from the abate Bruni, Cardinal Spinelli's secretary, to the bishop of Cava, regretting that he had been unable to secure the release of Alphonsus from the burden of the episcopate:

> Now, as regards padre Don Alfonso. I adore the inscrutable designs of God. At first, the Pope was inclined to accept the refusal. But the other morning, on his own initiative, inspired by what spirit, I do not know, he instructed Mons. Uditore to impose a formal precept of obedience and I know that he has despatched letters to this effect to the Nuncio in Naples. To Mons. Uditore who asked him some questions or other about the decision, the Pope simply replied, "It is my wish," and assumed all the air of a Pope in doing so. Cardinal Spinelli, astounded at this unusual turn of events, could only bow his head and say, "It is God's will."[5]

There was no delay in executing the Pope's wishes. On Tuesday 16 March, letters were despatched to the Nuncio in Naples. On Friday 19th, the feast of St Joseph, the Nuncio, with an unmistakable air of triumph in his letter informed Alphonsus in Pagani of the Pope's decision:

> 'It is my duty to send you for the second time a letter from the Uditore of his Holiness in the matter of your election to the bishopric of St Agatha of the Goths. From it you will see that it is the expressed wish of the Holy Father that you should accept this bishopric and, to this effect, he has freed you from the Vow which you took in your Congregation. There is nothing I need to add to what the Uditore has informed you on behalf of his Holiness. I am persuaded that your Excellency will hear in the words of the visible Head of the Church the call of the Invisible Head and, in consequence, will bow your head in submission to the Divine Will.
>
> However, I permit myself the liberty of saying that since everyone knows well that your Excellency did not seek the bishopric, and that, in a most edifying way, you also went so far as to refuse it when it was offered to you, they would be equally convinced that to persevere in your opposition would be to resist the decree of God. Your Excellency can have no idea of what the Lord will achieve through you and of the good which will result from your appointment both for the diocese and your Congregation. Humanly speaking, everything possible was done to make the reasons you adduced, prevail. The *Uditore* put them before the Holy Father and I expressed my opinion that they were reasonable, particularly the fact of your advanced years and declining health. And still, notwithstanding all this, his Holiness persisted in his determination. There is no escaping the conclusion that the decision clearly comes from the Father of Light since the Holy Father is specially

assisted by the Holy Spirit in matters concerning the welfare of the Church.

My purpose in putting all this before you has been to anticipate any further objection on your part. I trust that you will accept the divine call and give clear proof of your resignation to the wishes of the Vicar of Christ. I await your reply to forward it to the *Uditore* by tomorrow's courier.

During all this time Alphonsus in Pagani had increased his prayers and his penances to make sure that his refusal could be accepted. On Saturday 13 March he preached as usual to the people in the church, enlisting their prayers on his behalf. He begged them to recommend him to Our Lord and the Mother of God that he might be delivered from the great trial that faced him. Jokingly he said, 'They wish to give me a wife in my old age,' referring to the liturgical concept that a bishop is wedded to his diocese in love and faithfulness.[6] When the courier from the Nunciature arrived at the monastery in Pagani for the second time, he first met Father Paravento to whom he announced that he was looking for Father de Liguori since the Holy Father did not wish to accept his refusal of the bishopric. Paravento, fearing the effect the news might have on Alphonsus himself, summoned Father Mazzini, who, in turn sent for the Rector of the house, Father Fabricio Cimino who, from this time onwards, looms large in Alphonsus' life. Cimino, as was the wont of rectors in those days, somewhat irregularly took it upon himself to open the dispatch packet with the enclosed letters. Together they went to Alphonsus' room. Mazzini asked him dramatically to go on his knees and all together recited an *Ave* to the Mother of God. Mazzini then quite simply informed him that the Pope had not been willing to accept his refusal and had, instead, insisted that he should accept the bishopric. Alphonsus' reaction was simple. '*Gloria Patri*. God, then, wishes me to be a bishop and so I wish it too.'

With the courier's return to Naples with Alphonsus' formal written acceptance of his appointment, word was sent to Rome that the Pope's wishes had been obeyed. From there the *Uditore* conveyed the Pope's satisfaction at his submission:

> His Holiness has learnt with intense pleasure that your Excellency has submitted your will to his expressed wishes and that you are now resigned, and agree to accept the bishopric of St Agatha of the Goths. His Holiness is, moreover, confident that this act of submission and of your obedience to the Will of God, will draw down an abundance of those graces and strength necessary for the carrying out of your duty in the diocese.[7]

Alphonsus' acceptance of the Pope's wishes had only been achieved at great cost to himself. Not merely did the prospect of the bishopric terrify him psychologically, but he came to regard it as a punishment for his sins. He believed he was being banished from the Congregation. And the thought of the responsibilities he was to assume began to haunt him. Suddenly it all became too much for him, and for the second time, one of those strange psycho-somatic illnesses to which he was occasionally subject, took hold of him. On Sunday morning — ironically enough, it was Laetare Sunday of Lent — he ran a burning fever and took to bed seriously ill. During the week, his condition gave cause for alarm and he received Holy Viaticum. From Lettere, Cava and Nocera itself, the bishops were summoned to visit him and encourage him. Slowly he regained self-control and serenity in face of his appointment, and with these, his health began to improve. A week later, having secured Rome's permission not to travel during the rigorous weather of March, he began to make preparations for his journey to the Eternal City and his consecration — as it was then referred to — as a bishop.

The news of his brother's appointment filled Hercules with delight; it opened up considerable prospects for the family. Cajetan's reaction, on the other hand, does not figure in any of the correspondence at the time nor did he accompany his brother to Rome for his episcopal ordination, as one might have imagined. Alphonsus arranged with Hercules for a loan of some 4,000 ducats for expenses in connection with his appointment, which he contracted to repay at the prevailing rate of interest over a number of years. Hercules threw himself enthusiastically into the necessary arrangements. In accordance with his idea of episcopal dignity, he suggested that he could purchase a splendid carriage, even though second hand, from the Marquis of Valva, at a reasonable price but, to his considerable disappointment Alphonsus insisted that he could acquire his predecessor's carriage more economically from the diocese. 'You are delighted at what has happened,' he wrote to Hercules (signing himself, despite all his protestations, 'your affectionate brother, Alphonsus, bishop-elect of St Agatha,') 'while all I have done is weep. How could they have given me a bishopric in my old age? Blessed be the Will of God who wishes to make a martyr of me in my last years of life. I have lost sleep, appetite and am almost stupid at the thought that the Pope, who never imposes this command to accept a bishopric, should have done so in my case.'[8]

On Holy Saturday 10 April, he preached his farewell in Pagani. He asked the thronged congregation in the little church to pray for him, assuring them, at the same time, that he was not saying *addio* since he would return one day to die in their midst. Newly shaved in deference to the wishes of his episcopal colleagues of Nocera and Cava, and the requirements of Roman etiquette, and with a whole outfit of new clothes, which included a new soutane and a pair of shoes with plain buckles which were to last him for the next twenty-six years, he left Pagani by coach on Easter Sunday morning for Naples. Among his belongings were his instruments of penance which he continued to use while in Rome right up to the eve of his ordination.[9] He appeared in excellent health and in great good humour, joking about his appointment. On the way to Naples he called to visit his friends, the Gargano family in Torre Annunciata, laughingly telling them that 'when the Holy Father sees that I am only a bag of bones he will send me back to my monastery to die in the midst of my brethern.' In Naples, he stayed with Hercules, having arranged with him for some rooms on the ground floor of the family palazzo to be put at his disposal where he could receive the inevitable round of visitors paying him their respects. The week in Naples was spent in visits to his old clerical friends at the Chinese College and the various missionary societies with whom he had worked. There were also the formal visits of protocol, expected of a bishop-elect, to the Papal Nuncio, the Cardinal, the Cappellano Maggiore and the Council of Regents. At a more personal level, he visited the various convents where he had preached and where the many nuns he directed requested him to celebrate Mass. He was careful not to omit to visit Sister Mary Magdalen whose vocation he had discerned as a young girl in the Chinese College and who had been an invalid in her convent since the age of nineteen. His mood fluctuated between depression and expressions of self-depreciation. To Sister Maria Rosa Graziani in the convent of the Most Holy Rosary, he joked about his appearance: 'now that I am about to be made a bishop, I shall be called *Illustrissimo*. But when I go into the presence of the Holy Father and he sees how crippled and deformed I am, he will declare, "Oh, no. A mitre would not sit well on you," and will send me home with all possible honours.'

On Monday 19 April, Alphonsus left for Rome by coach accompanied by Father Villani and two representatives from the diocese, as well as one Domenico Antonio Janella, the late bishop's butler, whom he was considering for re-employment as his own personal servant. They travelled along the Appian Way through Sermoneta, Castel Ginnetti to Velletri from where they went to pay their respects to Cardinal Spinelli. Alphonsus still harboured a slight hope that the Cardinal might yet intervene with the Pope for his release but Spinelli was adamant in his refusal to re-open the question; he found Alphonsus' attitude tiresome. On Sunday 25 April, Alphonsus and his companions entered Rome by the Porta Maggiore and passing St John Lateran and the Colosseum, went directly to the monastery of Santa Maria dei Monti, one of the Roman houses of the Pii Operai, where they were to stay. Alphonsus' first visit was to St Peter's where he prayed at the *confessio*. Since the Pope had left for Città Vecchia and would not be back for some days, Alphonsus decided to make a pilgrimage to Loreto. On Wednesday 28 April the party left for Loreto in the Marches of Ancona, and remained there for three days. On his return to Rome, Alphonsus was granted an audience of Clement XIII who assured him that obedience would work miracles. For an hour and a half they remained together discussing the state of the Church in the Bourbon Kingdom of Naples. This was the first of many audiences to which the Pope summoned Alphonsus for consultation about a variety of questions from the situation of the Jesuits in the Kingdom, the work of the Encyclopedists, the practice of Frequent Communion and devotion to the Sacred Heart.

Six weeks were to elapse before all arrangements for his episcopal ordination were completed. In the meantime he visited the basilicas, the Vatican Library and the small church of St Sebastian on the Aventine where St Leonard of

Port Maurice, the great Francican missionary, had lived and died, and where his body was buried. There was a constant stream of visitors to see him at Santa Maria dei Monti, among them Father Ricci, the General of the Jesuits, who came on at least three occasions to discuss with him the growing opposition of the Courts of Europe which clearly threatened the very existence of the Society. Most of the invitations to dine with personages of importance, Alphonsus was able to decline, but he was unable to turn down an invitation from Cardinal Orsini, the Neapolitan ambassador in Rome, who had always been one of his greatest admirers and a strong supporter of his missionary Congregation. On his arrival at the Orsini palace in his ordinary Redemptorist missionary habit — even though it was a new one — the attendant doubted whether he would be received since he was not wearing formal clerical dress as befitted the occasion. Alphonsus explained to Orsini that he came in the only soutane he possessed and regretted if his clothes did not meet with his approval. The Cardinal only laughed and received him with all graciousness. But as the weeks passed by Alphonsus found his way in Rome beginning to pall. 'It seems to me like a thousand years until I can get out of Rome, and get away from so many receptions, even though everybody treats me with great kindness. *Le mancie*, the 'tips' one has to give here, would bleed you to death. True, there are magnificent receptions but magnificent "tips" have to be given as well.'[10]

On 11 June, nearly seven weeks after his arrival in Rome, Alphonsus presented himself at the Quirinal Palace for the formal theological examination which, in those days, preceded the public announcement of the appointment of a new bishop. The Pope presided with Cardinals Galli, Orsini and Antonelli, assisted by the formal synodal examiners. After the ritual questioning the proceedings were enlivened somewhat by a question from the Master of the Sacred Palace, Father Ricchini, O.P. who asked Alphonsus, not perhaps without a touch of malice, to deal with the question in the *Summa* of St Thomas, whether it is lawful to seek to be made a bishop. Alphonsus excused himself on the plea that he had not heard the question correctly but Cardinal Galli was quick to turn to the Pope saying, out loud, that there is no one deafer than the one who does not wish to hear. As he left the examination hall Alphonsus turned to Clement XIII and said, 'Holy Father, since you have deigned to appoint me as a bishop, please pray for me to the Lord that in my office I may not compromise the eternal salvation of my soul.'[11]

On Sunday 20 June, Cardinal Ferdinand Rossi, assisted by bishops Gorgoni and Giordani ordained Alphonsus a bishop in the Dominican basilica of Santa Maria sopra Minerva, in a side-chapel dedicated to the Most Holy Redeemer. The following morning, the new bishop celebrated his first Mass at the magnificent baroque altar of St Aloysius in the Jesuit church of St Ignatius; that same afternoon, after a farewell audience of the Holy Father, he left for Naples, having refused indignantly to petition — as was the custom — for an Indult to wear the *Soli Deo*, a bishop's skull-cap, during the celebration of the Eucharist. 'Am I to pay twenty-five scudi for the privilege of being bad-mannered to Our Lord in the Blessed Sacrament.'[12] He spent the first night of his return journey in Frascati in the palace of Prince Buoncompagni and the next day took the route by way of Valmonte and Ferentino through Monte Cassino and Capua. Don Hercules came to Aversa to meet him and to accompany him back to Naples to the family home. In Naples the same pattern of visits which had to be made prior to his ordination were repeated, formal visits to the Council of Regents, to Tanucci and the Marquis Carlo de Marco, Minister for Justice and Ecclesiastical Affairs. Tanucci made clear his annoyance that Alphonsus had accepted the bishopric of St Agatha offered to him by the Pope, despite having refused the more attractive see of Palermo, offered to him by the King. The Council of Regents granted the Royal Exequatur to the Papal decree appointing Alphonsus bishop of St Agatha without further demur, and the new bishop dined formally with the boy King. More significantly for the future, Alphonsus established a sincere friendship with De Marco which was important for the smooth government of his diocese. When Alphonsus pointed out to De Marco that he was going to a diocese where there were serious ecclesiastical abuses, and where his efforts to right the situation would inevitably meet with serious opposition and appeals to the King, De Marco assured him that he could always count on the support of the Court when this was necessary, a fact which was to be verified again and again in the coming years. The social visits to the various convents and missionary societies were repeated and there was a special visit to the convent of San Girolamo where his two sisters were members of the community.

Many of the priests from the diocese now came to be introduced to their new bishop. There were a number of them living in Naples, some under the pretext of further studies, others engaged as tutors or in commerce, one was practising as a medical doctor, others in more indecorous occupations. One ill-advised diocesan presented himself to his new bishop, dressed, not in clerical clothes but in the latest fashion with elaborately buckled shoes and — one of Alphonsus' *bêtes-noires* — in a flowing wig, finely combed and powdered. Alphonsus expressed his disapproval in no uncertain terms: 'Those shoes are unsuited for a priest, that wig with the waves does not become you. If you, as a priest, are to serve as a model for the laity and yet titivate yourself in such way, what excesses can you not expect from them?' Word was soon back in the diocese about what could be expected of their new bishop. A final visit to Cardinal Sersale in Torre Annunziata and another visit to the Gargano family, where he remained overnight and celebrated Mass for them in their private oratory, brought Alphonsus' stay in Naples to an end. He then set out for Pagani. The Fathers met him a few miles out at the village of San Lorenzo and brought him back in triumph to the monastery. His weeks of freedom from the monastic routine, the change of air and surroundings, the exercise he had taken, all contributed to a marked improvement in his health; he looked a new man, rejuvenated and with colour in his cheeks. He may not have found his episcopal dignity so repugnant after all.

– II –

The main purpose behind this final visit to Pagani before making his formal entry into his diocese, was to finalise arrangements for the future government of the Congregation. The problem had, to some extent, been resolved, since his six General Consultors had decided to petition the Holy See to allow him to continue as Rector Major during his episcopate but with the obligation of appointing a Vicar-General to take immediate control of affairs. This decision of the consultors was confirmed by informal meetings and voting in the various communities. The decision was dictated as much by self-interest as anything else. The Redemptorist missionary Congregation had become virtually synonymous with Alphonsus de Liguori; it depended on him to such an extent that its existence was unthinkable without him. Indeed, it was common talk in Naples that it would cease to exist on his death. With his departure as bishop, a similar outcome could not be ruled out.[13]

The process leading up to the consultors' decision is less than fully documented. One contemporary account claimed that their initial decision was taken without Alphonsus' knowledge, a claim which any acquaintance with the tightly-knit nature of the Congregation at the time, and the constant flow of information which made its way to Alphonsus, would put beyond the realms of credibility. Be this as it may, he would certainly have been aware of what was taking place when the consultors decided to seek the opinion of the communities. Accounts of only two of these informal community gatherings have come down to us, those of Pagani and Deliceto, where there was at least one dissenting voice. Unfortunately, we have no indication of Alphonsus' reaction to this decision on the part of his consultors — whether he acquiesced without a murmur, or whether he protested. And there is something highly suspicious in Villani's claim, in his petition to the Holy See, that there was no dissenting voice, *unanimiter et nemine discrepante*. We have evidence that there was, in fact, at least one. The matter is important since the whole process was later called into question from the canonical point of view, when dissatisfaction with the dual authority of the Rector Major and his Vicar reached a climax. The seeds of dissensions for the future were being well and truly scattered.

Villani presented his petition to the Sacred Congregation of Bishops and Regulars in Rome on 25 May in the name of 'all the Consultors and Communities of the Congregation', some four weeks before the date for the episcopal ordination. The request was granted by the Roman authorities, apparently without any difficulty. By virtue of the Roman decision, Alphonsus was empowered to choose a Vicar General from among the members of his Congregation, 'with the same full and complete powers which he now holds as Rector Major but with the obligation of depending on, and taking the advice of, the said Rector Major in all matters of importance — *di rilievo e conseguenza* — such, for example, as the foundation of another house, the closing of a house, or the dismissal of a member from the Congregation'. In Pagani, Alphonsus chose Villani as his Vicar General, a choice which had been a foregone conclusion. Villani was to retain the office for the next eighteen years until he was forced to resign in the midst of the chaos and acrimony of the *Regolamento* crisis in the summer of 1780.

Besides settling Congregational affairs, Alphonsus was able to complete his own episcopal 'family' during the weeks after his return from Rome. It was the accepted practice at the time that important diocesan officials could be chosen from outside the diocese. As his Vicar General, Alphonsus chose Mons. Giovanni Nicola Rubino from the diocese of Conza, a priest of just thirty-seven years of age, who remained with him all during the thirteen years of his episcopate and who was less than enthusiastic about him when his cause of canonisation was introduced. As his own personal secretary and confessor he chose Father Felix Verzella, a priest of the diocese of Nusco, near Avellino. After his ordination in 1752, Verzella visited Alphonsus in Pagani on Holy Saturday, to seek his advice and blessing. He never forgot that meeting. Alphonsus, then at the height of his powers as a missioner, spoke to him of his obligation as a priest and ended with words which burnt themselves into the young priest's memory: 'May the Lord preserve you from ever celebrating Mass in the state of mortal sin. All your life be assiduous in study and prayer.' Verzella was actually making a retreat in the Redemptorist house of Sant'Angelo when he received the invitation to become the new bishop's personal secretary, a position which he filled loyally for over eleven years until he retired back to his diocese. Another member of the episcopal retinue also made his appearance at this time. The choice of his predessor's butler, Domenico, had not proved a happy experience and on his return from Rome Alphonsus dismissed both him and the coachman. In their place came Alessio Pollio, a young Neapolitan of twenty years, by trade a shoemaker. He became Alphonsus's factotum and was to devote his whole life to the bishop and end his life as a Brother in the Congregation after the death of his wife.

Alphonsus set 8 July for his departure to take possession of his diocese. He sent Verzella on in front of him, with two Redemptorist Brothers, Francis Anthony and Leonard Cicchetti, who had instructions to bring his straw mattress with them. Many of the confreres advised him strongly against taking official possession of the diocese at the very height of the summer heats, urging him to delay the departure until the beginning of autumn or late summer at earliest. But increasing scruples about the obligation of residence drove him to insist on his immediate departure. Early on the morning of that Thursday he said good-bye to the assembled community at the door of the monastery at Pagani and headed for Naples: 'The Lord has not judged me worthy of continuing to live in your midst. I am going into exile from your company and from the Congregation. Please do not forget me.' And then he assured them that he would return to die amongst them and to leave his mortal remains in the church of St Michael.[14]

– III –

The diocese of St Agatha of the Goths, in the ecclesiastical province of

Beneventum, occupied the historic territory of the Samnites. To the north and west, it was bounded by the rivers Calore and the Volturno, while its southern confines were traced out roughly by the old via Appia which ran from Maddaloni through Santa Maria à Vico through the Caudine Forks and Arpaia, on to the ancient Samnite town of Caudium, the modern Montesarchio. Early in the fifth century, the Goths had occupied this territory, hence the name, while the Lombards concentrated on neighbouring Beneventum and Irpinia. The diocese of St Agatha, which traced its origins to its first bishop, Manelfredo, in the last quarter of the tenth century, and had a population of about thirty to forty thousand souls, formed the feudal territories of powerful families, the most famous — or infamous — of whom were the dukes of Carafa of Maddaloni and the Principe della Riccia of Airola. The Bourbon reforms had not yet succeeded in depriving Carafa of the control of justice in these territories and he had still power of life and death as well as the lucrative privilege of collecting and administering taxes. With the exception of the episcopal city of St Agatha and four other centres of population, Airola, Arienzo, Durazzano and Frasso, the inhabitants of the diocese consisted of mainly rural population, living on the *masserie* or estates of their feudal lords, and occupied in tending the vineyards, olive plantations, orchards and corn crops of their masters. As bishop of the diocese Alphonsus found himself part of the whole feudal system and, *ex officio*, a baron of the Kingdom of Naples with the responsibility of appointing a civil governor for the area. Socially, the diocese was totally typical of the *ancien régime*, with the life style of its inhabitants virtually incomprehensible to our way of thinking. The long tradition of the faith in the area went back, some claimed, with more enthusiasm than historical justification, to the preaching of St Peter on his journey from Brindisi to Rome. Pride of place, however, among its succession of bishops went undoubtedly to Felice Peretti, later Cardinal, and ultimately, Sixtus V, the Pope of the Spanish Armada and the Vulgate.[15]

On Sunday 11 July, Alphonsus left Naples for his diocese, accompanied in his coach by Father Margotta and driven by his new factotum, Alessio Pollio. Following the bishop in a second carriage came Father Maione and Don Hercules. The bishop of Caserta, Mons. Albertini, through whose diocese they had to pass, welcomed the new bishop and accompanied the cavalcade to the confines of his diocese which bordered St Agatha of the Goths at the Valle di Maddaloni. From there, Alphonsus drove through Bagnoli to his episcopal city.

The news of his appointment had been received with very mixed feelings in the diocese, according to the testimony of Don Giovanni Battista di Luccia, who was a senior seminarian at the time. But there was no evidence of this in the welcome prepared for him at St Agatha. Alphonsus left his carriage at the entrance to the city and walked through the crowds to the cathedral where he was met in the cortile of the episcopal palace by the assembled Chapter. When he had vested for the solemn procession to the cathedral, it was discovered that he did not possess an episcopal hat so one of the clerics removed the hat hanging over the tomb of his predecessor Mons. Danza. After the liturgical formalities and the intoning of the *Te Deum* the bells of the city rang out in welcome. The Blessed Sacrament was exposed and Alphonsus addressed the congregation of priests and laity. He had not been sent by God for his own pleasure or satisfaction but in order to help the faithful of the diocese to save their souls, by his sweat and his labours. And, accordingly, he did not come with the desire of commanding but with the intention of being the servant of all. He asked the clergy to assist him, as far as they could, in carrying his burden. During his address, a violent bout of coughing assailed him and one of the canons in the choir remarked quite audibly to his neighbour, 'Let us get ready to receive another bishop. If another cough like this afflicts Mons. de Liguori, he will certainly die.' The remark made its way back to the bishop who enjoyed the joke and replied, 'Let the canon look to himself since I shall see the whole of the present Chapter completely renewed.' Back in the sacristy, Alphonsus addressed the clergy alone. 'I had hoped to end my days in a cell in my Congregation but God, to whom be praise forever, has chosen me in His Providence to be your father and your shepherd. As long as you behave worthily and show yourselves dutiful members of my flock I shall certainly show myself to be a true father to you all and a loving shepherd. But if, on the other hand, you do not behave as sons you shall find me one who punishes severely and, where my powers do not succeed, I shall have no hesitation in calling in the powers of the State.' Brother Leonard is the source of this information. He listened at the door of the sacristy to the bishop's address and felt no embarrassment in recounting it as evidence at the Ordinary Process years later.[16]

There was a clear indication of the spirit of the new administration when Alphonsus with the clergy and the local nobility returned to the episcopal palace. His secretary, Verzella, who had been in the diocese for some days preparing the liturgical reception, had also prepared a banquet for the guests according to the accepted style. Furthermore, the rooms of the palace were full of gifts from the nobility, clergy and convents of nuns throughout the diocese, fruits, cheeses, wines and assorted delicacies. The luxury of it all dismayed Alphonsus. As regards the banquet there was nothing he could do and it went ahead as arranged, but he warned Verzella that on no account was there ever to be a repetition. 'May the Lord forgive you on this occasion. I have not come to the diocese to throw banquets for my friends. In my house, there must be no niggardliness but, equally, there must be no luxury. We are living among so many poor, some of whom die of starvation. How can we regale ourselves with banquets.' When the time came for him to retire for the night the luxury of his sleeping apartments startled him. He asked Brother Leonard if he had installed his straw bed from Pagani, according to his instructions, which the Brother had been unable to do on account of opposition from the Chapter, who had their own idea of the furnishings of a bishop's bedroom. He solved the problem for the first night by insisting that Hercules should occupy the episcopal apartment, while he went off by himself to an unprepared room where he slept on empty sacking on the floor. Next day, after his formal visit to the seminary, where he received an address of welcome, as well as poems in Italian, Latin and Greek, he faced the problem of the gifts, which were still arriving. Very determinedly, he insisted that they should all be returned to the donors with his thanks, and a plea to them to understand that it was his inflexible rule not to accept gifts on any account while bishop. When he returned the supply of pork which the archpriest of Frasso, who remained a thorn in his side right through his episcopate, had sent to the palace, Alphonsus endeavoured to explain the reason for his action:

> I thank you sincerely for the wild boar you so kindly sent to me. Please do not take it ill that I am returning it to you. You will understand that it is a principle with me not to accept gifts from any source. I ask you to consider the gift as accepted and I trust you will enjoy it yourself.[17]

Alphonsus' action was not due to any boorishness or lack of gratitude on his part but rather to a determination to preserve his liberty and independence, from the very outset, in the difficult task of reforming the diocese with which he had been charged by Papal mandate. He wished to be under no obligation to anyone, either lay or cleric, so as to be able to deal with them all equally, on the basis of their merits and conduct, not their wealth or power or their generosity towards himself personally. There was also, as we shall see, an underlying scruple in the matter of canonical simony which troubled him all through his episcopacy. And, finally, he was living among a peasant people with whom he wished to associate himself as bishop, just as he had done as a missioner. His purpose was to distance himself from the accepted pattern of the 'Lord Bishop', the ecclesiastical counterpart of the feudal nobleman. He wished to be the poor apostolic bishop, living among his people without luxury and with no display of riches in his style of life, dress, food and lodging. It is not without significance that on this first occasion when he returned the gifts he made an exception for the artistic arrangement of flowers which the Carmelite nuns of Frasso sent him for the altar of his private oratory.[18]

– IV –

Alphonsus was now faced with the challenge of putting into practice what he had outlined for bishops in his *Reflessioni utili a 'Vescovi* of 1745; had he foreseen that he would end up one himself, he might have been less cavalier in his advice. At any rate, the challenge facing him was to make the transition from theory to practice. In the official proclamation of his appointment, Alphonsus' conscience was charged with the obligation of supplying his cathedral church with the liturgical vestments which it lacked and with the appointment of a Canon Penitentiary to the Chapter. But there were far more urgent pastoral problems than these awaiting him; even contemporaries were ready to add that the diocese was, in the strictest sense, in need of reform. Conditions had deteriorated under the episcopacy of Mons. Danza, whose own life was morally irreproachable, but whose pastoral zeal was sadly lacking. He was certainly unequal to the task of the spiritual renewal of his diocese which possessed all the worst features of ecclesiastical life in the Kingdom of Naples at the time. For a population of about 39,000 souls, there were at least 350 diocesan priests, not counting priests of the diocese who lived in Naples or elsewhere, most of them employed in secular professions. And this number did not include religious priests in eleven monasteries. There were over a hundred priests living in or around the episcopal city of St Agatha itself, with a population of not more than 7000. In Arienzo, there were 120 priests for fewer than 10,000 inhabitants. Few of these clergy had any pastoral interest and fewer still practised any form of authentic priestly spirituality. There were, of course, the same glaring contrasts which were to be met with throughout the Kingdom at the time, priests of exemplary life, well-educated and cultured, fully versed in theology and adequately equipped for their pastoral activities. But there were others, the majority, indeed, ordained without the least sign of a sacerdotal vocation and with no interest in it either, ignorant not merely of the fundamentals of theology but devoid of even a basic education, virtually illiterate, who had never been sufficiently instructed in the rubrics of the Mass, and whose lives were, at best, spent in the least scandalous forms of idleness such as gambling and drinking in the local taverns — and at worst, in every form of licentiousness. Many had been appointed to their benefices through bribery or the use of improper influence and so were, canonically, irregular. Their main interest was money and freedom from state taxation. Besides the inadequate parochial organisation throughout the diocese, there were hundreds of confraternities, pious societies and *congreghe*, the heritage of the piety and devotion of the past, with their own churches and oratories and, more important still, their own revenues. These were independent of episcopal control. Appointment of priests to these churches and the allocation of revenues were often in the hands of the members themselves or of some powerful family, like the Rainone family, to which the archdeacon of the cathedral chapter belonged. The noblest ambition of scores of clerics was to secure appointment, by any means at their disposal, to one of these benefices, where an adequate income was assured and where the obligations were, at most, a weekly Mass and attendance at the meetings of the members of the sodality. Preaching and the burdensome duty of hearing confessions were none of their concern.[19]

The state of the clergy was reflected in the religious condition of the ordinary people. Naturally good, but with a religious sentiment which all too easily deteriorated into superstition, their great lack was instruction in the very fundamentals of their faith. Many of them, even though baptised, had insufficient knowledge of the truths of religion to receive the sacraments validly. In the realm of sexual morality there was considerable promiscuity. There was also the custom whereby those intending to get married, lived together, a custom inveterately rooted throughout the diocese and was not merely connived at, but actively arranged by parents, especially mothers, for their daughters. Strangely for a rural community, prostitution was rife while drunkenness and violence characterised many of the traditional festivals held throughout the year.

Alphonsus had prepared himself well to deal with the problems which faced him in the diocese. He had informed himself fully and had planned his course of action accordingly. There was to be no period of initial inactivity, no hesitation in addressing the most pressing problems. Four matters, in particular, had to be dealt with. Within a few hours of his arrival, indeed as part of the inauguration ceremony, he announced a mission for St Agatha to begin the following Sunday and which would be extended during the autumn months and into the following year, 1763, throughout the diocese. This showed a determination to face up immediately to the cases of public immorality which were known to exist in the very shadow of his palace, involving the most powerful families as well as some of his own highly placed clergy. He would, as we have seen, return all gifts sent to him on the occasion of taking possession of his diocese, and finally, he would address a letter to his clergy clearly stating his policy and the areas on which his government would concentrate its energies.

The letter was composed, printed and dispatched within three weeks. In this — his first *Ad Clerum* — he used his full formal title, 'Alfonso Maria de Liguori, bishop of St Agatha of the Goths and Suessula, Baron of the Castle of Bagnoli, and Rector Major of the Congregation of the Most Holy Redeemer'. He recommended to his priests the correct rubrical and reverential celebration of Mass, declaring his intention to watch out for this personally when he could be present; if not, he would use 'his spies' — *sara continua ed esatta la nostra attenzione in osservare e spiare il modo come si celebrano le Messe*. Next came a long section on the obligation of preaching the Word of God and, above all, the necessity of preaching in a simple style and according to the capacity of the congregation to understand what was said. He used his favourite expression — to preach *all'aspostolica ed alla populare* — and he made sure to include explicitly the Lenten preachers in his exhortation. His final point must have come as a great shock to many of his clergy. He warned them not to attempt to use influence with him, from any source, to secure advancement in the diocese, or to obtain benefices and still less to make him admit a candidate to ordination. 'Let those who attempt to use influence in these matters know that they are *ipso facto* considered unworthy of ordination, preferment or a benefice.' The uncompromising message was clear, 'the personal merit of the candidate was the only recommendation he would consider'. This was no empty threat as his clergy were to experience before long.[20]

Alphonsus took advantage of the general mission in St Agatha and throughout the diocese to face the problem of public concubinage. Very powerful families were involved, as well as high-ranking clergy, even members of the metropolitan Chapter. The whole credibility of his episcopal ministry was at stake if he refused to face the issue as Danza had done. Moreover, it was vital that action should be taken in the episcopal city itself and without delay; from there, word would spread throughout the diocese. Assisted by his two Redemptorist missioners, Fathers Margotta and Maione, and calling in confessors from outside the city, Alphonsus opened the mission on the Sunday following his arrival. In the pulpit he recovered all his old fire, which had seemed to desert him in his last years in Pagani. He preached with extraordinary vehemence on Hell, wearing a black stole and with a flaming torch in his hand, denounced the evils of blasphemy and concubinage; he was no less explicit in his sermons to the clergy. St Agatha had witnessed nothing like it in living memory, certainly not in the days of his ineffectual predecessor. Alphonsus was determined that, when every other remedy had been tried and failed, the scandalous lives of powerful and well-known citizens should be denounced in public and the same legal penalties applied which were enforced for the ordinary citizen.

Alphonsus' action in invoking the full rigours of the law on those who violated the norms of public morality must be considered in the light of the legal and social conditions prevailing at the time. Under a law enacted by Charles III and re-enacted by his son Ferdinand IV, prostitution, concubinage and adultery were criminal offences punishable by whipping and banishment. Tanucci, whose own married life was above reproach, had no sympathy with any loosening of public morality and he insisted on the strict enforcement of these laws — but unfortunately, more so in the provinces than in Court circles in Naples. It was quite common throughout the provinces for prostitutes to be whipped in the local jails and then banished to some other part of the Kingdom; it was the accepted practice throughout the whole region which embraced the diocese of St Agatha. However repugnant it may be to our sensitivities, Alphonsus, as bishop, was within his rights in handing over to the civil authorities those whose lives offended the legal norms of public morality, and he made it public that he was prepared to do so, without fear of the consequences, in all cases which did not yield to his prayerful entreaties. His line of action was first to approach those whose lives were a source of public scandal and to beg them to alter their ways. On occasions he resorted to private prayers and penances in order to bring the delinquents to amend. Since he was well aware that, in the majority of cases, the women were more sinned against than sinning, and that poverty was very often the real reason for their immorality, he was prepared to provide them with a regular monthly income from the episcopal revenues to enable them to break with their immoral living. Only when all these efforts failed did he resort to the civil authorities so that the law could take its course, as happened in the case of one Carmina Graziano whom he handed over to the duke of Maddaloni to be imprisoned, whipped and banished:

> Your Excellency,
>
> I have learnt to my great sorrow that in Colonna, a frazione (village) near St Agatha, a young woman, Carmina Graziano, who, for some time, was known for her piety, has now become a young devil and has opened a house of ill-fame in that village which is the ruin of the young men of the place, as well as of St Agatha. Only your Excellency has the power

of remedying this situation by denouncing her to the Governor and having her banished from St Agatha. All my efforts to convert her have gone unheeded. They say that in large cities these women must be tolerated, but, in country areas and small towns, such people cannot be tolerated since they are the ruin of young men and even, at times, of whole families.

For myself, I have no further hope of doing anything more in the matter beyond seeking the assistance of your Excellency who has such zeal for the glory of God and for the welfare of your vassals. I anxiously await your favour in this matter and remain, etc.[21]

During the mission in St Agatha Alphonsus had to deal with two of the most embarrassing cases of public immorality in the diocese, involving priest relations of the archdeacon of the Chapter, Don Francesco Rainone, an influential figure whom he had to consult in the ordinary administration of affairs. As a result of Alphonsus' efforts, Dom Giacomo Rainone ended his immoral liaison and began a life of penance for the scandal he had given. Don Giuseppi Rainone, the archdeacon's brother, however, was a more blatant example. He was living in open concubinage with a married woman, Elizabetta Conti. The unfortunate woman expressed her conversion dramatically by demanding pardon publicly from the pulpit of one of the churches. Her dispositions, however, were not shared by her lover, who persuaded her to resume their illicit relationship. Alphonsus faced both the archdeacon and his wayward brother, who publicly threatened to shoot him if he proceeded any further with the matter. Having exhausted his prayers, penances and entreaties, Alphonsus, despite the influence of the archdeacon, formally handed the matter over to the civil authorities in Naples where both Tanucci and De Marco rallied to his support. Following the issue of a royal decree, Elizabetta was imprisoned and whipped in Montefuscoli, while Rainone escaped to Caiazzo. Eleven years later the unfortunate woman returned to St Agatha, poor and abandoned. Alphonsus granted her a monthly pension of six carlins to support her in her poverty, on condition that she gave no further scandal.[22]

Having faced up to the power of the Rainone family, Alphonsus now had to confront an even more serious challenge from the anger of the Petti family. Don Marco Petti, one of the canons of the Chapter, had been living in concubinage for over sixteen years when Alphonsus arrived. The Petti were more powerful even than the Rainone clan, and had publicly defied the half-hearted efforts of Mons. Danza. Petti had lost all sense of his priestly obligations and was known to have two mistresses. He even paraded his three illegitimate children publicly in the streets. And to Alphonsus' horror, he continued to celebrate Mass. Alphonsus sent for the canon and exhorted him in as friendly a manner as possible to change his life. He invited him to come to live in the episcopal palace away from the occasions of sin. The canon refused, but suggested he would build a hermitage for himself on his considerable estates, where he would live a hermit's life of retirement in prayer and penance. Alphonsus was unimpressed; the hermitage would be fine, he replied, were it not for the *eremitessa*. He knew his canon only too well. Despite his efforts the canon refused to alter his ways. Alphonsus proceeded to draw up the required accusatory citation which he forwarded to the King, with the necessary proofs and legal testimonies. On 2 October 1762, a royal decree ordered the arrest and imprisonment of the offending canon. On the morning of 18 October, a detail of soldiers from the *Udienza* of Montefusco arrested the canon in the public square of St Agatha, watched by a considerable crowd. He was imprisoned, first in the episcopal prison, but since it was an insecure place of confinement, he was brought to the regional prison a few days later. Alphonsus spent the day of the arrest in prayer and penance. When the news of the successful arrest reached him, he thanked God for the removal of the scandal. Some weeks later, on securities from the family, Petti was returned to the episcopal prison where Alphonsus visited him and gave him a spiritual book to read. The Royal Tribunal in Naples upheld the action of the bishop when the family brought an action to the Royal Court for the release of the canon. The following August 1763, he retired to a monastery where he led a life of penance for the scandal he had given. Some years later, Alphonsus secured for him the consolation of being allowed to celebrate Mass once more, though in private, and he brought him to live with him for some time in the palace. To complete the healing of the scandal, Alphonsus was able to unite the woman with her husband and arranged for financial support for the upkeep of her illegitimate children.[23]

The action of their new bishop in his episcopal city was a good indication to the rest of the diocese of what they, in their turn, could expect. With the coming of the winter months, the general mission spread throughout the diocese. Even though he had employed his own Redemptorist companions in St Agatha, he felt it would be more prudent not to use them on this first round of missions in the other areas of the diocese, lest they should be regarded by the clergy as the bishop's agents to report back personally to him. Moreover, there were several foundations in different parishes to fund missions to be given by the Society of Jesus and he asked the Jesuit superiors to designate capable missioners for these places. He then invited the Pii Operai, Dominicans, Franciscans, and Capuchins as well as the missioners of other missionary societies in Naples to play their part. Twenty Pavone Fathers arrived for the mission in Airola.[24] While he kept overall direction in his own hands, he appointed his great friend and fellow-theologian, Don Giuseppe Jorio, in whom he had full confidence, to immediate control. His own first cousin on his mother's side, Father Frederico Cavalieri, was included among the missioners sent by the Dominican provincial. Alphonsus insisted on a special instruction for the assembled confessors before giving his approval; they were to avoid rigorism as much as laxity in their approach and were to be kind and gentle in their dealings with penitents. Similar indoctrination was provided for the preachers; they were each given a copy of his pamphlet on the correct method of preaching '*all apostolica*', taken mainly from the *Selva*. The Lenten preachers, especially those chosen independently of the bishop by the local feudal noblemen or municipality, were specially examined before being granted jurisdiction to preach and hear confessions.[25]

A great longing came over him to be in the pulpit once again — he described it as *prurito* — and he insisted on preaching on several occasions during the campaign, wearing his Redemptorist habit with the pectoral cross as the only sign of his episcopal rank. Throughout the winter months and into the spring of 1763, despite the cold and snow, the rhythm of the missionary activity continued in the presence of the bishop. To those who objected that he was putting excessive strain on himself he replied that the example of seeing their bishop present was as good as a special sermon for the faithful. Arienzo, Santa Maria à Vico, Airola, Luzzano, Bucciano, Pastorano, Frasso, Durazzano, Cervino and Forchia were all evangelised with the bishop present at one mission exercise or another. Preaching in his presence was always a strain, as the missioners waited for his reactions, but they had been well briefed beforehand and knew what was expected of them, as regards both style and content. Only twice, is it recorded, was he angry at what he heard. In the church of the Annunziata in Airola, the preacher, Father Cafarano, used the new Cruscan language as he preached on the evils which flow from venial sin. Alphonsus clearly suffered agonies as he sat on the episcopal throne in the sanctuary; his appearance made clear the struggle he was undergoing not to call the preacher down from the pulpit. Afterwards, Alphonsus informed him that such sermons were a betrayal of Jesus Christ and the people. 'In these missions, I am looking for you to deal with major problems and not with minor ones. You could well have remained in Naples and I cannot think that you are free from serious guilt in all this.'[26] Something similar occurred on the occasion of a special celebration of the feast of the Sacred Heart in Arienzo, in the presence of the archbishop of Amalfi, Mons. Puoti, and civil dignitaries from Naples. Father Giuseppi Margillo, a member of the Pii Operai, delivered a most florid panegyric. Making no attempt to disguise his displeasure at what he heard, Alphonsus deliberately turned his chair away from the pulpit and the preacher, and faced the Blessed Sacrament, where he spent the rest of the sermon apparently in prayer. 'I would never have believed', he complained to Margillo, 'that a missionary would have so betrayed the Word of God. Had you been a member of my Congregation, I would have had no hesitation in calling you down from the pulpit, as I have done before.'[27]

Not all the parish priests gave the missions their whole-hearted co-operation; some of them regarded the whole pastoral stratagem of the new bishop as both disturbing and, in some way, a reflection on themselves. In this, they may well have been correct. Many of them used every possible excuse to avoid receiving the missioners — there was no room to accommodate them, the parish revenues were inadequate for the expenses involved. Alphonsus had to threaten and cajole until his wishes were carried out. As regards expenses, he pointed out that the missioners would attend to their own and, where this was not possible, he would see to it from the episcopal revenues; he would sell his mitre, he assured one priest, if necessary, to reimburse him. Don Francesco di Filippo, the archpriest of Frasso, to whom Alphonsus had returned the gift of wild boar, proved particularly difficult. His main church was clearly too small to accommodate the crowds, so Alphonsus suggested that the mission should be conducted each day in two or three churches, if necessary. Di Filippo raised every possible objection. A long series of letters resulted, entailing the exercise of great patience on Alphonsus' part. When at last he brought the parish priest to accept his decision regarding the number of churches to be used, the missioners refused to fall in with his arrangements on account of the jealousy which would arise between the different preachers of the Predica Grande on the same night. Only when this problem was resolved was the mission able to proceed.

– V –

Following on the round of missions which had initiated the work of the spiritual restoration of his diocese, Alphonsus decided to make a pastoral visitation of the diocese. This was the most important task of a bishop — at least that was his opinion when he wrote his *Reflessioni utili a 'Vescovi* — little realising that he was laying down norms by which he would be judged himself. His diocese was sufficiently small to allow him to visit personally every parish within the period of two years stipulated by the Council of Trent. In each area the Visitation lasted as long as was necessary for him to familiarise himself with every aspect of ecclesiastical life and to make the necessary dispositions to correct whatever abuses existed. At times, he spent over two weeks in a parish, turning the Visitation into a sort of personal mission preached by himself. He was usually accompanied by his Vicar General, Don Rubino, as well as his secretary Verzella, his personal servant Alessio, and one of the Redemptorist Brothers. They went together by coach as far as possible, and then by horseback into the more inaccessible parts of the diocese where the roads made coach travel impossible. On one occasion near Frasso, when one of the landowners expressed his astonishment at seeing the bishop arriving for Visitation on some type of mule, Alphonsus jokingly quoted the verse of psalm twenty, 'Hi in curribus, et hi in equis; nos autem in nomine Domini' — some trust in chariots or horses, but we in the name of the Lord — but the point was probably lost on the Baron of Frasso. On the way, the episcopal party recited the rosary and prayed to the Angel Guardian of the parish for a blessing on the work. The journeys were not without risk; on the journey from Durazzano to Frasso, the coach broke down three times. The third time it overturned, throwing Alphonsus violently to the ground, dislocating his wrist. When he arrived in Arpaia for the Visitation at noon, the assembled clergy remonstrated with him for travelling by horse-back, rather than by coach. Just at that moment a chicken vendor passed by on foot with a column of chicken baskets on his head. Pointing to him, Alphonsus asked, 'Which of us travelled more comfortably, me on horse-back, or that man on foot, with the load on his head?'

His example was as much part of the Visitation as his examination of the clergy and the state of the parish. He invariably insisted on choosing for himself the worst apartment of those placed at their disposal, on some threadbare pretext such as a large room being bad for his asthma. He continued to follow the regime which he established for himself in St Agatha, the same order of the day, the same prayers, the same meagre fare and the same corporal austerities, which he never abandoned, no matter where he went. He brought his mattress with him and had it filled with straw where he was lodging for the night. Only after a formal obedience from Villani did he agree to abandon this practice, after his serious illness. He was particularly insistent that he should pay for the expenses of the Visitation out of episcopal revenues. Any type of gift was immediately refused or returned to the donor, on the plea that the Sacred Canons were adamant on this point, and incapable of any other interpretation. His authority on this matter was the work on *Episcopal Visitations* of Giuseppe Crispino, bishop of Bisceglie on the Adriatic coast; it was the standard Neapolitan work on the subject. He quoted it to his priests *ad nauseam* until it became something of a joke among them. One of his closest friends in the diocese, Don Giovanni Manco of Airola, sent him some local *ricottella* for breakfast on the occasion of a Visitation in his parish, which Alphonsus promptly returned. Don Giovanni, offended, complained to the bishop who pointed out to him the relevant section in Crispino on the matter of gifts. Furious, Don Giovanni exploded, '*mannaggia Crispino*, well, damn Crispino, anyway!'

The Visitation was organised to involve both clergy and laity. It opened with a sermon from Alphonsus. If his arrival had not been adequately announced beforehand, he had the church bells rung; on occasions, in rural areas where the inhabitants were working in the fields, he sent Alessio and Brother Francis Anthony with hand bells to summon them to church. His themes were always the same, the eternal truths, the love of God, the necessity of prayer, the avoidance of the occasions of sin, devotion to the Blessed Sacrament and Our Lady. Each day he gathered the children of the parish to catechise them and was, more often than not, appalled at their ignorance. He fixed times at which he would be in the confessional if the people wished to confess to him. In the diocese, the custom prevailed of administering the sacrament of Confirmation at the age of seven or eight, even before the first reception of Holy Communion, unlike the custom in Naples, of postponing it to the age of manhood, as happened with Alphonsus himself. So, during the Visitation, considerable time was allotted to the administration of this sacrament. On one occasion, Alphonsus insisted on taking a mule right up into the mountains near Forchia, to administer Confirmation to an old man who was dying. As far as the laity were concerned, his main effort was to establish in every parish a solid rhythm of daily devotional practice. He insisted that the priests of the place should celebrate Mass for the inhabitants in the church each day, and he introduced the practice of daily mental prayer, according to the simple method he had devised for the missions. He was adamant, moreover, that the churches should be re-opened in the evening for the daily visit to the Blessed Sacrament in common. He laid down that this exercise should take place at a suitable time, according to the different seasons of the year, to allow the men, women and children to get back from their work in the fields before the church bells summoned them to visit the Lord in the Blessed Sacrament. He conducted the visit himself as often as he could, using the little book he had composed years ago in Ciorani for his students and the retreatants. He taught the people to sing hymns with him, examine their consciences and say their night prayers. Soon this practice was introduced in every single parish of the diocese without exception, and wherever he was, in St Agatha or anywhere else in the diocese, Alphonsus came down to conduct the visit himself. It all added up to a revolution in pastoral practice and met with considerable opposition from the clergy who now found the burden of their ministry considerably increased. But the bishop was insistent that his arrangements should be implemented without any question of exceptions being made.

The key to diocesan renewal clearly lay with the clergy, or as the accepted ecclesiastical wisdom at the time put it, *omne malum a clero*. Having set in motion his efforts to put an end to public scandals involving the clergy — and there were at least ten major examples to be dealt with — Alphonsus soon came to realise than an enormous effort on his part was needed, as well as unlimited patience, if he was to raise his priests to the level he expected of them. From the experience of his Visitations, he was under no illusions concerning the difficulty of the task confronting him. His ideal was a pastoral clergy, whose main interest would be the salvation of souls by means of their ministry, and whose ministry would not be impaired through their ignorance of theology or be voided by the scandal of their private lives. He explained to them that the sacrament of Holy Orders gave them power over the sacramental presence of Christ in the Eucharist and also power over his Mystical Body. If the priest was going to avail himself of the first in celebrating Mass, why should he not dedicate his life to the second, by hearing confessions, directing souls along the path of holiness, teaching them the elements of doctrine, and announcing the gospel tidings through their preaching, all very basic, but revolutionary and strange in the diocese of St Agatha in the middle of the eighteenth century. These ideals explain many of the incidents in his dealings with the priests. Don Donato Truppi, a subdeacon, lived and worked in Naples. Alphonsus recalled him to the diocese to be ordained to begin his pastoral ministry. Truppi agreed to ordination but made clear, at the same time, that he had no intention of spending his life in work for souls. 'Why do you agree to be ordained if you are not ready to dedicate your life to helping souls in your own diocese?' was Alphonsus's reply, which contained an ultimatum which had to be faced by Don Donato. It was an eye-opener for him, since, like many others, he had become a cleric without the slightest pastoral orientation. Alphonsus' ultimatum revealed to him a meaning and practice of priesthood which, up to that moment, he had never even considered.

The outcome of the bishop's intervention in a somewhat similar incident was more successful. He succeeded in getting one of his priests, Don

Marcantonio di Ambrosio, to return to the diocese from Naples where he had been practising medicine for eighteen years. At their first interview, Ambrosio refused the invitation to return to assume his pastoral responsibilities among his people. Taking off his glasses and standing up to his full height, Alphonsus warned him that if he returned to Naples he would lose his clientele, his life and, perhaps, his immortal soul. Moved by the sincerity of the appeal, and not a little frightened by what seemed to be in the nature of a prophecy, Ambrosio returned to the diocese. Shortly afterwards, Naples was ravaged by a plague epidemic. Most of Ambrosio's clients perished in the epidemic and many of his medical colleagues lost their lives. Against the opposition of his Curia, Alphonsus, at a later stage, appointed Ambrosio a Canon of the Chapter of Arienzo where he laboured zealously for the salvation of souls and lived to testify to his encounter with his bishop and to tell the story of his conversion to priestly ministry. During his periods of illness in the diocese, Alphonsus agreed to call in the former doctor on a number of occasions as a medical consultant.[28]

Alphonsus found that the most effective means at his disposal for the renewal of the priestly life of those already ordained, were the priestly sodalities, or fraternities, known as *congreghe*, which already existed in the diocese but needed to be revitalised. He insisted that they should be reactivated and he made faithful attendance and participation a condition of any diocesan appointment — a subtle but infallible means of compulsion. The sodalities began to meet regularly each week, the Divine Office was faithfully recited and there were weekly study seminars in theology, preaching and the rubrics of the Mass. He attended these meetings regularly himself, both in St Agatha and later in Arienzo; when on Visitation he made a point of never missing a meeting. When indisposed, he arranged for the meetings to be held in his residence, so that he could be present. He drew up a list of moral questions to be studied through the course of the year, printing them in the diocesan calendar and having them circulated to all his priests. He instructed them to purchase a set of Moral Theology books and when some refused to do so, he made them a present of his own works, so that they should have no excuse for theological ignorance. On Visitation, he examined the clergy in theology and if he considered their knowledge inadequate he deprived them of sacramental jurisdiction until they had improved their acquaintance with moral principles. His intellectual tolerance was never more in evidence than during these theological discussions. He never imposed his opinions and encouraged those who wished to disagree with him, to explain their reasons for doing so, despite being fully aware, at the same time, that the motivation for disagreeing was, frequently, more a perverse wish to take issue with the bishop rather than any great theological insight.[29]

Next in importance for Alphonsus, came the proper celebration of the Eucharist. Ignorance of the basic rubrics, indecent haste and general uncleanliness were evident on all sides, and were a scandal to the faith and devotion of the ordinary people. Alphonsus found the whole situation intolerable. At the opening of the mission in Santa Maria à Vico, he gathered the clergy together and gave them a practical demonstration of the rubrics of the Mass, emphasising the decorum and devotion which he demanded of them in the celebration of the Eucharistic mysteries. There were priests who took less than fifteen minutes to say Mass, not due to any fluency of movement or mastery of Latin, but simply to their complete ignorance of rubrical procedure. Eventually, he was driven to forbid many of his priests to celebrate at all, until they had totally re-studied the rubrics, and he imposed a canonical suspension, ipso facto, on any priests who celebrated Mass in less than a quarter of an hour. One newly ordained priest was so badly instructed in the rubrics that Alphonsus insisted on finding out the name of his mentor. He summoned Don Domenico Propallo, the priest in question, and found, to his horror, that it was a classical case of the blind leading the blind. The result was that both pupil and master had to undergo a course in rubrics and a formal examination before they were allowed to celebrate Mass again. One inveterate offender in Airola spent the rest of his days without saying Mass rather than exchange his own method of celebrating for the rubrics of the Roman Rite.[30]

– VI –

Alphonsus' dealings with his priests presents an intriguing study in personal relationships between a bishop and his clergy. He was always at their disposal, and he made it clear that they were to come to see him whenever they wished, without formality. If he was otherwise engaged — in writing perhaps — he immediately left what he had in hand to receive them; they always had precedence over anything or anyone else. Despite the fact that he had the unpleasant task of restoring ecclesiastical discipline throughout the diocese, his priests came to recognise his essential kindness. He visited them when they were ill, he was prepared to do whatever was in his power to help them in their difficulties. At the various canonisation processes, the priests who lived under him, even those who suffered temporarily for the immorality of their lives, came forward to testify to his fundamental *umanità*, to use their own word for his human understanding and kindness.[31] In his personal encounters with them, he was deferential and gentle, insisting that they should sit down and talk to him at their ease. He endeavoured to remove any trace of the feudal relationship between lord and vassal which the hierarchy of Bourbon Naples had assimilated. He knew all his priests personally and had a private notebook in which he noted whatever he wished to remember about them, their needs, their merits and in certain cases, their demerits.

It was Alphonsus' misfortune to have in his diocese a high proportion of clergy whose life-style offended every accepted clerical convention. And it is important to appreciate fully the degree of scandal their lives gave in that very enclosed and unsophisticated rural society; there was no way their conduct could be tolerated. Two examples will illustrate the problems the bishop had to face. There was Don Antonio Nanciello of Frasso, who spent most of his time drinking and gambling in the village. In his drunken rages, which were the usual outcome of his conduct, he had attacked and seriously injured a number of people. And in each case he was known to have celebrated Mass the following day. Don Giuseppi de Luca from Bucciano, whose conduct had driven even Mons. Danza to have him imprisoned for five years, returned to the diocese soon after Alphonsus' arrival. He abandoned all clerical pretence and, armed with a shot-gun and a stiletto, resumed his life of debauchery and banditry. Alphonsus had no option but to set in motion a second civil process against him; a short while later, the unfortunate priest was found one morning murdered. Despite the number of similar examples which recurred all through his episcopate and which Alphonsus had to deal with, the image of him as an episcopal tyrant, narrow and intolerant, is totally false. His dealings with his priests were characterised by kindness and an understanding compassion for sinful human nature. He summoned his erring clergy to his presence and did everything in his power to get them to amend, offering to keep them with him in his residence for as long as they wished to remain. One unfortunate priest, who had resisted all approaches to get him to amend his life, was summoned to the bishop's palace in St Agatha for one last effort. At the entrance to Alphonsus' study, where the bishop was expecting him, he found a large crucifix laid on the ground across the threshold. Alphonsus said to him quietly, as he hesitated to enter, 'Come along and be sure to trample it underfoot, since it would not be the first time you have trampled Our Lord under your feet'.[32] If he was convinced of their determination to amend their ways, he sent them to make a retreat in one of the Redemptorist houses, usually Sant'Angelo à Cupolo, which was in the metropolitan See. He was prepared to give them every opportunity to rehabilitate themselves and he was ready to reinstate them in their ministry if at all possible. Only as a last resort did he initiate a formal canonical process against them, first of all, in his own episcopal court. If this failed, and the public scandal continued, he considered himself obliged to hand the matter over to the state officials to be dealt with in a civil action which could result in banishment from the diocese and a period of imprisonment in some civil jail.

The greatest tribute to Alphonsus' humanity was paid by his priests who insisted that they preferred to be dealt with summarily by him in person in any matter which would ordinarily have been processed through the episcopal court. Never once during his whole episcopate was there an appeal from his decision to the metropolitan in Beneventum, a remarkable record which speaks for itself, when we consider the Neapolitan's love for litigation in any court, whether civil or ecclesiastical. There were occasions when Alphonsus' leniency to offending clergy did not meet with general approval. The case of Don Giuseppi Farace is a typical example. A priest of Moiano, he had been charged both in the episcopal court and in the civil court by the husband of a woman with whom he had an illicit relationship. Determined to amend his ways, he went to Alphonsus and convinced him of the sincerity of his conversion. Alphonsus sent for the curial process, and, in the man's presence, tore it up and then undertook to have the civil process cancelled as well, to the considerable displeasure of the offended husband.[33] The ultimate verdict on Alphonsus' leniency can be left to one of his less edifying clerics, Don Giuseppi Tofano, who had been imprisoned for several months at the bishop's instigation, first of all in the civil jail in Casandrino, and then in the more forbidding Castello D'Ischia. Due to the intercession of the Principe di Ricca, he was released, on condition that he presented himself to the bishop in St Agatha, formally begged pardon and promised to amend his life. But instead of humbly begging pardon, Don Giuseppe took the opportunity of berating the bishop for the injury he had done him, and of declaring that he was bound in conscience to make reparation to him for what he had suffered. Without a word of reply, Alphonsus got up and gave the enraged cleric a copy of his book of meditations, *The Way of Salvation*, which he had composed with the clergy of St Agatha principally in mind. 'With this gift I shall make retribution for all the injury I have done you,' remarked Alphonsus. It is to the credit of Don Giuseppe that, incredulous and shocked as he was, he was able, at the same time, to see the humour of the whole situation. He declared that Alphonsus was certainly a saintly bishop but a bit of a fool, *ciuccio*, as well. Properly interpreted, it was a subtle assessment of Alphonsus' conduct.[34]

Alphonsus was insistent on ensuring that the canonical norms of clerical decorum were observed. He forbade gambling and public drinking to his clergy. Clerical dress was a major item of concern and he insisted on the wearing of both the clerical tonsure and the ankle-length soutane, though he was reasonable enough to realise that the long soutane was totally impracticable in rural areas during the rain and snow of the winter months. From 1 November to 1 April, alternative dress was permitted to those priests actively engaged in pastoral ministry in rural areas. There was another problem which exercised Italian bishops at the time, from the Pope down. Some clerics, imitating the court fashion in hair styles, wore their hair flowing down over their ears and reaching to their shoulders, *allo nazareno*, as it was called. Those with less abundant growth supplied for their deficiency by wearing waved and powdered wigs. Papal decrees had forbidden both these customs for years, and the majority of canonists at the time considered the prohibition a serious one. Benedict XIV went further by forbidding clerics to dye their hair; the colour of the hair, he laid down, should correspond to the age of the cleric, since 'neither chestnut-coloured hair nor blond, is natural for old men'. Dispensations from these papal ordinances had to be obtained fom Rome. Petitions for dispensations poured in, on the plea, among others, that a wig was necessary for one's health. 'There is a great flow of priests to our Palace', recounted Benedict XIV, with gentle humour, 'accompanied by barbers who describe to us the various diseases of their clients. One comes along with a depressed and worried countenance to explain that there is a priest who suffers from a disease of the head which, in some way, affects his stomach.' As bishop of his diocese, Alphonsus quite simply enforced the canonical norms. He forbade his priests to wear their hair long, insisted on the tonsure and forbade the wearing of wigs. When Don Domenico Mauro, an otherwise exemplary priest, came to visit him, nicely wigged and powdered, Alphonsus removed the wig from his head, cut it to pieces with a scissors and placed it in water to complete the destruction! There was considerable amusement at the process of canonisation over this incident when the Promotor of the Faith expressed his view that the bishop's action was altogether too hasty and drastic. When one of his clerics presented himself for ordination in Durazzano with his hair *allo Nazareno*, Alphonsus refused to ordain him until the local barber had deprived him of his tresses. Despite the tears of the cleric, Alphonsus was adamant.[35]

Alphonsus realised that the main weapon at his disposal for the reform of his clergy was his power of appointment to benefices; here was the one place where he could insist on the necessary qualities that a priest should possess — personal integrity of life, adequate theological learning, and, above all, active zeal for the salvation of souls. Even though many of the benefices at his disposal did not include the obligation of active pastoral ministry — this was a fundamental reform which only the total social upheaval at the end of the century would make possible — Alphonsus was not prepared to appoint to them priests who were not, to some degree, pastorally motivated. When a benefice fell vacant, his practice was to set up a board of examiners to assess the merits of the candidates, at which he usually presided himself. At the conclusion of the various phases of the *concursus*, he appointed the candidate whose qualifications were the most acceptable from every point of view. While theological knowledge and personal integrity of life were indispensable, the deciding factor was always pastoral zeal. No outside influence, whether from King or Prince, could move him to provide with a benefice a cleric who was not, beyond all doubt, the most worthy candidate; on this he was absolutely inflexible. Time and time again he was threatened by angry and disappointed candidates. Some threatened to report him to the King, others said they would take revenge on him by violence. Nothing, however, could move him. The civil authorities of St Agatha itself, spurred on by some disappointed clerics, delated him to the King because he had not always provided natives of the city to vacant canonries in the cathedral Chapter. Alphonsus answered the accusations by pointing out that there was no obligation whatsoever on him to restrict the appointments to the natives of St Agatha; they were open to all the priests of the diocese, provided they were otherwise worthy of the appointment, a stand in which the king's ministers upheld him. Even the powerful Principe de Ricca failed to have his protégé appointed to a vacant parish. 'Your candidate', wrote Alphonsus, 'was not, in my opinion, suitable for the office of parish priest. When he gets older and has more experience and gives proof of his qualities, I shall not fail to appoint him.'[36]

The root of the problem lay in the fact that these ecclesiastical appointments were sought, not from pastoral motives, but for the economic benefits they brought with them. Quite simply, it was a question of money, social advancement and the freedom from taxation to be secured through the possession of a rich benefice by the clerical member of the family. Alphonsus' criterion, on the other hand, was the salvation of souls. When a canonry fell vacant in the cathedral Chapter, Don Francesco Sarracino, the mansionary of the Chapter — that is, with duties of choir but without pastoral responsibilities — presented himself for promotion. He had been acting for years as personal secretary and economo to the Conte di Cerreto, brother of the duke of Maddaloni. Until the vacancy occurred, Alphonsus had never even seen him. Unashamed, Don Francesco presented himself and urged his claim as a matter of justice; he was the senior mansionary. Alphonsus replied that he had never once seen him in the cathedral. Since he had served the Prince of Cerreto so faithfully why did he not ask him to make him a canon? 'Don Francesco mio, give up your position as secretary and come here and serve the cathedral or I shall deprive you even of your benefice as mansionary.' When another unworthy candidate requested a benefice, 'out of love for Our Lady', Alphonsus wrote back that it was precisely out of love for Our Lady that he was refusing to appoint him.[37]

Alphonsus demanded wholehearted commitment to their ministry from those he appointed to the pastoral care of souls. To his dismay he found that some of his parish clergy spent a considerable amount of time absent from their parishes, living on their revenues. Don Vicenzo Parillo in Dugenta was absent from his parish for considerable periods of time, under the pretext that the air was bad for him. Alphonsus, to the pastor's dismay, forced him to resign, replacing him at the same time with another priest more zealous for the spiritual welfare of his flock. Don Liberato Razzano, a parish priest in one of the parishes of St Agatha itself, had no interest in pastoral work and less aptitude for it. He had already failed to secure a canonry in a concursus and, having brought his father along with him to remonstrate with and threaten the bishop, he left his parish and went to live at home, though still claiming parish revenues. In order to safeguard his reputation, Alphonsus suddenly promoted him a mansionary in the cathedral Chapter, a canonry to which the care of souls was not attached. Don Liberato missed the point of his promotion completely, and objected that he was unable to sing and therefore could not chant the Office. Succintly, Alphonsus replied, 'I don't mind whether you can sing or not; my obligation is to see to the spiritual welfare of the souls in your parish.'[38]

– VII –

Alphonsus' efforts to improve the general standard of his clergy met with a certain degree of success; he was to express some satisfaction with them in his first Report to Rome, even though he was to state explicitly that 'they could be better'. However, he was conscious of the fact that there was only a certain amount he could achieve with those who were already ordained and settled in the diocese, so he concentrated his attention right away on his seminarians. The seminary building, which connected with one angle of the episcopal palace, was in poor repair; Alphonsus saw no alternative to a major reconstruction programme. Under the direction of the Cimafonte brothers, the work began, and the seminarians were temporarily housed in one wing of the palace. The reconstruction of the seminary was strongly opposed by the Chapter who formally protested about the expense involved. Since he believed that what he was doing was essential to secure a supply of pastorally orientated priests for his diocese, this opposition did not in any way deflect Alphonsus from his purpose, though at a later date difficulties arose which delayed the completion of the work. He never had the pleasure, as bishop, of seeing his new seminary solemnly blessed and inaugurated.[39]

More important than the material structure was the calibre of the seminarians themselves. In October 1762, some months after his arrival, he sent them all home under the pretext of a vacation and the reconstruction of the seminary. He then made them all re-apply individually for readmission, thus giving him the oppportunity of weeding out those he considered unsuitable. On their return, the students found the whole orientation of their studies altered; everything was now geared to the formation of a pastoral clergy, whose main priestly interests were to be centred on preaching the Word of God and hearing confessions. Seminary training was no longer meant to qualify them for tutorships in Naples or as economic secretaries to feudal Lords. The *Homo Apostolicus* became the new manual of moral theology while Tourneley was chosen for Dogma. From the very outset of their studies, the bishop insisted that they should receive a positive training for their preaching ministry. He gave them his own small publication on rhetoric to train them in the composition of sermons and this was followed by practical exercises in declamation, until they were gradually initiated into his method of simple, apostolic preaching. The students became fully alive to his insistence on simplicity, and on the use of words and phrases which could easily be understood by the unlettered peasants of the diocese, to whom they would be ministering. It was well known that, time and time again, some of the senior clerics would deliberately insert difficult words and polished phrases into the compositions they had to deliver in Alphonsus' presence, just to enjoy his immediate reaction of outrage; he was never able to avoid rising to the bait. He was insistent on a standard of intellectual achievement and culture necessary for a minimum of clerical decorum. At the same time, he was sympathetic towards those whose other gifts compensated for their lack of scholastic ability, particularly since it was difficult to find priests for certain unattractive areas of the diocese. Dugenta, for example, was regarded as particularly unhealthy and was avoided by every cleric of the diocese who was not a native. When a young man presented himself at the seminary from Dugenta, Alphonsus was delighted, since it would guarantee a priest for an area where no one else was willing to minister. Unfortunately, as the contemporary report expressed it, the young man was of *scarso talento*, which apparently was a flattering description of his intellectual calibre. Alphonsus decided to examine him personally. His first question was, 'What is the meaning of the Latin word, Ego?' When the young man found this too much for him, Alphonsus had to admit that there was no question of admitting him to the seminary though he declared, at the same time, that in the light of the pastoral needs of Dugenta, he would have been prepared to ordain him had he been capable of mastering the formula of sacramental absolution.

As part of his effort to renew the whole seminary atmosphere, Alphonsus drew up a new set of rules on the lines of what he had prepared years before for the seminary in Nola. They were to be read in the refectory each Saturday. Confession and Communion were to be received every two weeks; in special cases, with the permission of one's confessor, once a week or, in exceptional cases, more frequently still. There was a special day of recollection and prayer once a month, with the spiritual exercises preached each year. The sad examples of public immorality among the clergy which greeted Alphonsus on his arrival in the diocese, determined him to take whatever steps he could to prevent a recurrence of similar scandals among the priests he hoped to ordain for the diocese. The number of students whose moral conduct, whether in the seminary or at home, gave rise to anxieties for their future celibacy, was considerable. Those whose conduct was discovered to be defective in this matter were immediately asked to leave, even though, on occasions, this entailed dismissing students already in Minor and Major Orders. Any example of levity such as gave rise to doubts about a student's ability — or desire — to lead a celibate life, met with immediate reaction. Nothing could move Alphonsus to ordain a student who failed in this area of priestly formation, neither patronage, influence, or debt of gratitude. The Count of Cerreto argued interminably with him in an effort to persuade him to ordain one such candidate, but in vain. He refused to ordain Don Pasquale Ianotti, a subdeacon, whose failure in celibacy only became known on the eve of his ordination. The Chapter and persons of considerable influence united to bring every possible pressure to bear on the bishop to alter his decision, but in vain. Ianotti finally left the diocese in disgust, and became a soldier in the Bourbon army. When Alphonsus heard of this, he wrote to the Inspector General, secured Ianotti's release, and brought him back to the diocese where he appointed him sacristan in the cathedral but resolutely refused ever to ordain him.[40]

Alphonsus was reluctant to ordain any candidate for the diocese who had not completed his course of studies under his own eyes in the diocesan seminary; free-lance seminarians who studied in Naples, refusing to come to the seminary in St Agatha on the pretext that they found the air there unsalubrious, had to face a rigorous examination from the bishop on every aspect of their lives and studies, resulting, more often than not, in a verdict of unsuitability. Alphonsus was prepared, however, to make an exception for the students from the town of Airola since, according to the accepted wisdom in the diocese, they were unable to tolerate the humid air of the episcopal city. But even they were not permitted to go to Naples. Alphonsus established a special sodality for them in their native town, with a strict rule of life and a course of study similar to that of the seminary. He placed the candidates under the direction of an excellent priest, Dom Pascale Bartolini, and only on his sworn testimony would be agree to ordain the candidates from Airola.

The seminary became the apple of his eye. He loved to visit the seminarians in class and joke with them. They were free to come to him with their problems if they wished. He saw to the quality of their food, especially at times of examinations, at which he presided personally. He once passed the remark that he did not wish to have with him the type of examiner who used the examination to overwhelm and terrify the students. He had a delicate task in dealing with the Rector of the seminary, Mons. Cacciapuoti, who was eighty years of age and had been rector for over fifty years; he was greatly loved by all. Alphonsus had to replace him, which he succeeded in doing only with considerable difficulty and in the face of widespread opposition. The new rector was Father Thomas Caputo, a Dominican, who transformed the seminary into a very worthy establishment. As the time of ordination approached, Alphonsus usually sent the students to St Angelo à Cupola to make their ordination retreat. He insisted that the days of priesthood and first Mass should be spent in prayer and recollection and on no account would he allow his newly ordained priests to return home for the celebration of their first Mass. One candidate for ordination, Don Custode Troisi, whose family were preparing elaborate celebrations for the occasion, was ordained by him in secret before the appointed time, and was sworn to secrecy as well. After ordination in the bishop's oratory, Alphonsus kept him in the palace for several days where he celebrated Mass each day for the bishop. Only then did he allow him to return home to his parents for the local celebrations.[41]

– VIII –

As a result of his experiences during the Visitation of the diocese, Alphonsus was appalled at the material condition of many of the churches; they were dirty, badly in need of repair, while the sacred vessels and liturgical vestments were equally neglected. In Arienzo, the churches of St Agnes and St Stephen were in danger of collapse. Worse still was the condition of the church of St Andrew in Dugenta. The situation was all the more scandalous since, in the majority of cases, the revenues of the benefices were substantial and the shameful condition of the buildings was due, quite simply, to the avarice of the local incumbent and his reluctance to spend church revenues on their upkeep. The most discouraging aspect of the whole situation for Alphonus was the indifference of the people, added to their reluctance to contribute in any way; clerical exactions and avarice over the years had deprived them of any pride or interest in the sad condition of their churches. A further problem throughout the diocese was the location of the churches and the existing parish boundaries. Growth in population in certain areas had left a great number of people without a church in close proximity, providing one more excuse for neglect of Mass attendance and frequent reception of the sacraments. Even missions, when preached only in the central church, were unable to make an impact on the lives of very considerable numbers scattered throughout the diocese in isolated hamlets. It was clear that there would have to be an extensive programme of church building as well as maintenance, accompanied by a re-drawing of parish boundaries. Alphonsus' vision was to provide a church with an active, pastorally-minded priest in each area of population, even if there was already in existence a central parish or collegiate church but at some inconvenient distance from centres of population; this was particularly urgent in isolated rural and mountainous districts. But it was to prove a heart-breaking task with his best endeavours for the spiritual welfare of his flock frustrated again and again by the opposition of his clergy, the apathy of the people and the interference of the Bourbon officials in Naples.

Alphonsus tackled the problem initially in St Agatha itself, where he established three new parishes to cater for new centres of population on the fringes of the city. He encountered considerable opposition from the existing parish incumbents on account of the loss of income which this entailed for them, and little compensating enthusiasm from those he was appointing to the new centres, on account of the meagre income which would initially be theirs. A similar reform had been contemplated thirty years before by the bishop at the time, Mons. Muzio Gaeta, who had, however, capitulated before the opposition of the clergy. This time there was no retreat on the part of the bishop; he was determined to demonstrate in St Agatha itself, what he intended to achieve throughout the rest of the diocese. But the opposition was not easily deflected. Frasso was the classic example, providing a paradigm for nearly every other parish. Here a second church and a redivision of parish boundaries were urgently called for. But the parish incumbent, Francis de Filippo, as cantankerous a creature as one could imagine, opposed Alphonsus in every way. Neither discussion nor threats had any effect on him; appeals to the decrees of the Council of Trent and their binding force in conscience, made no impact. Finally, Alphonsus, in desperation, simply informed him that a decision to establish a separate parish and build a new church had been taken. Not to be outdone, de Filippo formally appealed the matter to the King's Council, thereby automatically preventing Alphonsus from proceeding with his plans and entailing months of legal wrangling in Naples. Faced with the prospect of interminable delays as a result of the pastor's tactics, Alphonus could only settle for the expedient of establishing a permanent curate in the outlying area and guaranteeing him a salary independent of the parish revenues.

The parish clergy learned quickly from one another, and opposition to the bishop's plans for the pastoral reorganisation of the diocese followed the pattern which had been so effective in Frasso. When, for example, Alphonsus proposed a filial church in Pastorano to relieve the situation in the main centre at Bucciano, the local clergy first agreed, then opposed the scheme and finally appealed to the King against it, thereby automatically halting the bishop's plans. The same thing happened again and again. Alphonsus planned to centre a new parish round the ruined church of St Thomas the Apostle on the outskirts of Arienzo, to cater for the growing population of farming families on the feudal estates of the duke of Maddaloni. The parish incumbent, Don Vincenzo Mauro, who up to that time had paid scant attention to the church and had allowed it to sink into disrepair and disuse, suddenly expressed intense interest in it and refused to cede his rights in the matter. Alphonsus was stymied again. Nor, on occasions, were the people any more co-operative either.

On the slopes of Monte Tairano, for example, there were four isolated villages with a combined population of nearly 800 souls, nominally ministered to from Arienzo, but which were, in point of fact, pastorally abandoned. Alphonsus, after his Visitation of the area, proposed to build them a small church in the most central area of Crisci. He succeeded in securing a site, and made a considerable contribution from episcopal funds to set the work in progress. But the population were less than enthusiastic and refused to support the work financially. The project had to be abandoned for lack of funds and when Alphonsus retired from the diocese, the walls, which had reached no more than shoulder height, were stark evidence of how his building plans had been frustrated. With his church building projects he failed more often than he succeeded, and he had to settle, in nearly every case, for a solution which he regarded as second best from the pastoral point of view.

Not all his efforts, however, came to naught; two building projects remained as monuments to his pastoral vision, the church of St Nicholas in Vico and the *campanile* for the church of the Annunziata in Airola. In the populous area round Santa Maria à Vico the small church with accommodation for only 300 people was totally inadequate for the population of about 4,000. Alphonsus discussed the need for a new church with the local clergy and municipality. To persuade the priests to cede a portion of their revenues was an almost impossible task; a grant from the municipality was altogether easier to get. Despite the opposition of the clergy, the work was begun under the direction of the Cimafonte brothers. Alphonsus laid the foundation stone on the feast of St Joseph in 1763. Just when everything seemed to be progressing smoothly a royal decree abolished church tithes throughout the Kingdom. Sensing a golden opportunity, the population of Vico refused to contribute further to the erection of the church and brought the bishop to court in Naples to complain of the financial burden he was imposing on them. The case, fortunately, came before Alphonsus' card-playing friend of their student days, Don Baldassare Cito, who re-imposed the tithes on that area until the church building was completed. In such a climate, it was not surprising that the building took years to complete and was not finished when Alphonsus retired from the diocese in 1775. But at least by then he could claim that he had completed the work of restoration of the cathedral in St Agatha, as he had been instructed to do in the decree of his appointment, and had been able to consecrate it solemnly in 1763.

– IX –

Alphonsus realised that catechetical instruction of the largely illiterate faithful should be a pastoral priority for his diocese. He insisted that every pastorally active priest in the diocese should concentrate on this aspect of their ministry; they were never to neglect to instruct the congregation in the very rudiments of the faith at Mass on Sundays and Holy days. With this in mind, he drew up a scheme of doctrinal instructions to be followed, beginning with the Sign of the Cross, the Creed, the Our Father and Hail Mary, then the Ten Commandments and church precepts, followed by a simple instruction on the number and nature of the Sacraments and ending with the christian acts of Faith, Hope and Charity. In order to make sure that the faithful were sufficiently instructed in these essentials, he arranged that they should be examined before the sacrament of Marriage, and at Easter, before their paschal confession and communion. Only on showing a certificate to this effect from their pastor, could they be given absolution. Parents and employers were under strict obligation to send those in their charge to the christian doctrine instruction before Mass each Sunday; if they neglected to do so, they themselves were not to be admitted to the sacraments.[42]

Alphonsus was scrupulous about his obligation as bishop to preach to his people; his attitude on this point was not always appreciated by his clergy. What he said to the people was always simple and direct; his themes were nearly always hatred of sin and love of Jesus Christ. On Fridays in Lent he went to the church of the Franciscans in St Agatha to preach on Our Lord's Passion where he delighted in leading the congregation in singing one of his own hymns on the sufferings of Our Saviour, such as *O Fieri Flagelli*, just as he had done on the missions. On Sundays, he went from parish to parish throughout the diocese where he preached at Vespers, having advised the priest in charge the evening before by special courier of his intended visit. If he found the attendance poor, he refused to begin the service until the Brother or the sacristan had gone round the village with a hand-bell to summon the people to church. On occasions his conscience troubled him. Once when he saw a crowd gathered in front of the church of the Annunziata in Airola as he passed in his carriage, he grew agitated. He had gone some distance when he decided to return to preach to them. The Vicar General, who accompanied him, objected. 'Who knows but that God has determined that some soul will be saved by means of this sermon?' was his reply. And he returned to the church where he preached for nearly an hour. The parish priest of San Felice à Cancello came to him for the necessary faculties for a special preacher for a triduum in preparation for the feast of the Holy Cross. To his great embarrassment, Alphonsus said he would go himself. Don Pasquale, hoping to dissuade the bishop from his intent, pointed out that this was a special occasion and the bishop would not have time to prepare suitable sermons. 'Don't worry,' Alphonsus assured him, 'the Cross and mortal sin are one and the same thing.' Despite the cool welcome from Don Pasquale, Alphonsus preached for three days on the Passion of Christ, caused by the sin of the world.[43]

As bishop, Alphonsus succeeded in establishing a pattern of devotional practice for his flock which was totally predictable. There was the common visit to the Blessed Sacrament and Our Lady each evening; Saturdays were set aside for special devotions in honour of the Mother of God, consisting of a sermon and Benediction of the Blessed Sacrament; he insisted that it was his privilege to preach this sermon whenever he could. To complete the exercises of piety for his flock he established special devotions on the first Monday of the month for the souls in Purgatory, on Wednesdays in honour of St Joseph and once a month, the exercises in preparation for Death, all of which became the accepted practices in the churches of his Congregation as it spread throughout the world after his death. Popular devotions, however, could lead on occasions to serious abuses. He had to forbid midnight Mass in Arienzo and the neighbouring churches due to public immorality; the churches were not to be opened until five o'clock on Christmas morning. The feast of St Mark, on 25 April was the occasion of a pilgrimage to a sanctuary overlooking Arienzo. The Rogation Procession, as it was known, was a christianisation of a pagan festival and the original nature of the communal celebration was very much in evidence. The statue of St Mark was carried in procession followed by a motley gathering of people from as far away as Acerra, Nola, Caserta and Maddaloni. Besides the commercialisation of the celebration, the feast had lost its religious character, with one contemporary account referring to the drunken brawls, violence, even murder and the sexual promiscuity which characterised it. Alphonsus, with considerable courage, suppressed the celebration of the Rogation Days in its existing form, forbade the procession to the mountain, confined the religious celebrations to the forenoon in the parish church, after which the church was closed. The feast lost its popularity immediately. One wine vendor, who found himself deprived of his biggest source of revenue at one stroke, appealed to the King for the re-establishment of the celebration in its old form but without success. There was something similar in the Fusaro, the marshlands south of the diocese between Maddaloni and Acerra, where hundreds of men and women migrated during the summer months to cure the flax and hemp which was cultivated there. They slept in the open air, giving rise to considerable promiscuity; there was a large influx of prostitutes for the season and the immorality of the place was proverbial. Most of the area was outside the borders of his diocese though Alphonsus knew that many of his diocesans were involved. He endeavoured to do whatever he could to put an end to the abuses, urging his brother bishops in the neighbouring dioceses to take action. But the situation was beyond their control and the recurring immorality remained a source of great sorrow and scruple to Alphonsus during the whole of his episcopate.

Alphonsus felt a personal responsibility for every sin committed in the diocese and a corresponding obligation of conscience to remove the root of the evil. He was aware that much of the sexual immorality which he found amongst the people was due to the prevailing social conditions and to the poverty in which they lived. The state of the prisoners in the communal jail in Arienzo, for example, with men and women confined together, appalled him. There was absolutely no provision for their spiritual needs. Through his representations to the duke of Maddaloni he secured a separate section of the prison for females. He visited the prison as often as he could, especially when he took up the residence in Arienzo, preached to the inmates and sent them whatever money he could afford every Saturday to buy special food and whatever else would alleviate the conditions in which they were confined. After considerable effort, he obtained permission for the erection of a chapel for them; he appointed a chaplain who celebrated Mass and gave regular instructions — a remarkable advance for those days.[44]

During his episcopacy he established what was virtually a one-man social welfare service to alleviate the moral consequences of the poverty of many of his people. It was his firm belief that the episcopal revenues belonged by right to the poor; he often quoted the injunction of Pope Gregory the Great that the first duty of a pastor was to attend to the upkeep of his poor. With the assistance of the clergy, he drew up a register of poor families, assigning them a weekly allowance; Brother Francis Anthony was his almoner. His annual outlay for the poor came to more than his outlay for his own support and that of the upkeep of the episcopal palace and his episcopal 'family'. His particular concern was for those whose economic condition led them to sin — girls living in illicit unions through lack of a marriage dowry; women whose poverty led them to seek bare subsistence from a life of vice. He regularly made up the dowries for young girls so that they could marry honourably. Women of evil life, whose only reason for their conduct was economic necessity, he supported, provided they first abandoned their sinful ways. It became a saying in the diocese that those of evil life were the most favoured by the bishop, which was indeed true. When a woman in St Agatha challenged him publicly with the fact in the cathedral — possibly because she had been refused alms — he replied as gently as he could, 'Figlia mia, I would like to help everyone, but I just cannot manage it. I help some in a special way in order to take them away from sin.' The poor loved him and talked with him much more than did the rich and the feudal lords of the diocese.[45]

He frequently sent to Naples those he was able to rescue from their evil way of life, to live for at least some period of rehabilitation, in one of the *conservatorios* established in the city for that purpose; there, he followed them with clothes and money for their maintenance. Typical of his concern was the case of a young girl whom he persuaded to go to the Conservatorio della Monaca di Ligno in Naples, in order to remove her from the influence of her mother, whose poverty had driven her to prostitution. After some time, he succeeded in rehabilitating the mother as well, and provided her with a regular monthly income sufficient to support herself and her daughter. Alphonsus then decided to bring the daughter back from Naples. In order to provide her with a suitable outfit, he wrote to a priest friend in Naples:

Don Salvatore mio,

I sent for the mother of that child in Naples and she seems to me to be a good woman though utterly destitute. I have decided to send her to Naples to get her daughter so that they can now live here together and I have promised her a monthly allowance for them both. But I hear that the child has nothing to wear and must be fitted out from head to foot.

I ask you then to do me the favour of providing her with a complete outfit at my expense but with as little extravagance as you can manage. She will need, first of all, two vests, new ones. A veil for her head and a shoulder shawl. Then a shirt, frocks of twill, blouse, cardigan and two pairs of shoes and socks.

These need not all be new since the expense would be excessive. You could look round in the *Giudecca* to see what you can get second-hand. At the same time, make sure that they are all in good condition, otherwise they will not last and I shall have to do the same thing all over again.

Were it not that I can rely on your charity I would not dream of imposing these burdens on you. Will you please fix it up with Brother Francis Anthony and then let me know how much money I have to send you. When the child is fully supplied with her clothes I shall send her mother to bring her home. I recommend this work of charity to you.[46]

Housing conditions throughout the diocese, with whole families living in one room with only one bed, greatly upset him on account of the danger to morals. He felt obliged to arrange separate sleeping accommodation for the children of poor families whenever it was in his power to do so. Not everyone agreed with what he was doing, and one of the canons of the Chapter ventured to suggest to him that he should leave things as they were; human nature has its own reserves. His immediate reply was that he felt bound in conscience as a bishop to prevent as many sins as he possibly could, no matter what others thought or the inconvenience to himself as bishop.[47]

– X –

In July 1765 Alphonsus completed three years as a bishop in his diocese. To comply with the canonical norms he had to send a full account to the Sacred Congregation of the Council in Rome on the state of his diocese and of his own stewardship since becoming a bishop. He sent a twenty-page account of every aspect of the diocese, written in excellent Latin to his procurator in Rome, Don Giovanni Maria Puoti, brother of his friend, the archbishop of Amalfi, who presented it to the Cardinal Prefect. It was a calm, matter-of-fact document, emphasising the positive aspects of the religious state of the diocese; nothing was exaggerated, nothing suppressed. It captured something of that balance of judgment and honesty which characterised his moral writings. Only in one area did he admit failure and that was in the matter of holding a diocesan synod. The bishop admitted that he was aware of his obligation but, at the same time, he was equally aware that summoning a synod might well cause more problems than it solved. In the first place, as a result of Bourbon legislation, permission of the Court was needed. Then, the results of the synod had to be presented for examination and ratification by the Ministry of Ecclesiastical Affairs. Alphonsus was only too well aware that many of his priests were prepared to utilise every opportunity provided by regalism to challenge his decisions and even his authority. To hold a synod in the prevailing political climate was to open a can of worms. And yet his conscience troubled him. He consulted his fellow bishops and two clerical friends in Naples, whose opinions he valued, Jorio and Fatigati, head of the Chinese College. The advice he received helped to calm his scruples somewhat and he came to the conclusion that what he could achieve by holding a synod would be achieved with less dangerous consequences by episcopal decrees. At the same time, he felt bound to explain the matter fully to the Roman authorities and await their verdict.[48]

Within a few months, the Congregation of the Council acknowledged Alphonsus' report. They were fulsome in their praise. There was nothing more to be done for the spiritual and temporal welfare of his diocese than he was doing; he deserved every possible commendation. In the matter of the synod, the Congregation expressed their understanding of the position; they were fully aware of what Alphonsus meant when he used the phrase 'in the present climate'.[49] But, rather than cede the fact of a *fait accompli* to the Bourbons, Rome felt obliged to repeat the ritual encouragement to the bishop to hold his diocesan synod if at all possible, which it never was during his thirteen years in the diocese.[50]

Chapter Fifteen

The Care of All the Churches 1762–1770

- I -

The episcopal palace in St Agatha was a vast building resembling in many ways a barracks; Alphonsus occupied only one small section of it. Living with him, as was then the custom, was the 'episcopal family' Giovanni Nicola Rubino, the thirty-seven-year-old priest from the diocese of Conza who was his Vicar General, Verzella, his secretary; one or two Redemptorist Brothers — Francis Anthony and Romito for most of the time; Alessio Pollio, his personal servant and factotum; a Redemptorist Father, if one could be persuaded to stay; and his kitchen staff, consisting of a chef and his young assistant. Alphonsus insisted on the furniture being ordinary. He did not keep any of the rich furniture belonging to his predecessor; he got rid of the gilt chairs and mirrors which had given the place an air of opulence. He installed, instead, a few simple tables, cane chairs, and ordinary beds. From the sale of his predecessor's furniture he stuccoed the atrium of the cathedral. Gradually the palace began to take on the aspect of an austere monastery. In keeping with this was the food. He maintained the same standard in the matter of food which he had set for himself on the missions and for the same reasons — the ordinary *minestra* followed by the ordinary food of the people, who knew all about the episcopal menu, since Alphonsus, with this in mind, insisted that the chef should purchase all his culinary requirements from the people in the public market. Not all the members of his household willingly accepted the standard of living he insisted on; there was much grumbling from the Vicar General in particular and from Verzella. On the occasion of a visit, the Dominican Prior, Father Canti, was courageous enough to say that if the bishop did not wish to eat, at least others did.

Alphonsus did agree to special arrangements on certain occasions, such, for example, as the visits of Mons. Puoti, archbishop of Amalfi and Mons. Albertini from the neighbouring diocese of Caserta, and of his penitent, the Duchess of Bovino, but even on these occasions he insisted that there should be nothing in the nature of a sumptuous banquet. On these and similar occasions Verzella often succeeded in getting the chef to raise the standard beyond what Alphonsus had laid down; Alphonsus afterwards invariably remonstrated with him, insisting that the table of a bishop was not the table of a prince. It was this social sensitivity which was at the root of his episcopal poverty. Apart from any ascetical motives which he realised were valid only for himself, he had a genuine scruple about spending, as he said, the money of the poor. He was not only the father of the poor, but also their *econome*: 'I do not know how I could in conscience eat several dishes, prepared from the blood of the poor, when they have not even enough bread for themselves.'[1] It did not help matters for Rubino and Verzella that the chef, euphemistically referred to as '*maestro*', was totally inadequate. They strove with might and main to have him dismissed on one plea or another, but Alphonsus refused. When he eventually retired from the diocese back to Pagani, the first official act of the episcopal curia, even before the appointment of a successor, was to dismiss the '*maestro*'.

A similar spirit of poverty was reflected in his clothes. As a bishop, he continued to wear his Redemptorist missionary soutane with a small pectoral cross. He refused to wear silk. The wife of Alessio attended to his laundry requirements and ultimately found herself complaining that his garments were coming to pieces in her hands. Within a few days of his arrival in the diocese — actually while the General Mission was taking place in St Agatha — he was troubled by severe toothache. The canons of the cathedral, not yet familiar with his 'style', arranged to summon dental assistance from Naples. Alphonsus rejected the idea out of hand, insisting instead on the local practitioner. The archdeacon Rainone, with considerable reluctance summoned one Mastro Nicodemo from Santa Maria à Vico. The appointment had to be early in the morning since by evening the 'dentist' was in no fit condition for his professional activities. Nicodemo arrived and carried out the extraction without any form of anaesthetic, while Alphonsus clutched a crucifix. That left him with only one tooth, which distorted his articulation to such an extent that Nicodemo was summoned again a few days later to repeat the operation, leaving Alphonsus toothless for the rest of his life. Verzella, looking to the future, is reported to have preserved one of these teeth as a relic and to have had it formally authenticated by a notary and the canons of the Chapter.[2] Alphonsus altered the Redemptorist routine he had established for himself in Pagani, as little as possible, even insisting for years on making his bed each morning until ill-health put an end to this. His day was ordered just as it had been as a religious. Brother Francis Anthony called him. Even though he would probably already have been awake, this was an essential part of the routine and relationship with the Brother. When he had dressed he spent half-an-hour in meditation, then recited part of his breviary, followed by Mass at which he was assisted by his secretary. Then he, in turn, assisted Verzella at his Mass in thanksgiving. His morning was mostly occupied in giving audiences and in attending to the business of the diocese; his priests, as we have seen, had immediate access to him. But equally so had his people and he made the poorest sit down which was totally against the feudal protocol of the time. He dined at midday with the whole episcopal family. At meals there was reading, usually of some book of church history. After lunch he took a short siesta, then spent some time in reading a spiritual book, and finished his breviary before going for a short drive in his carriage. He returned in time for the visit to the Blessed Sacrament and then resumed his work of study or writing. The rosary with the household finished the day officially and then he took his supper. Afterwards he often worked in his study until midnight. When he retired to bed he read for some time by the light of a candle, usually *The Glories of Mary*. The monastic regime was not at all pleasing to Verzella or the Vicar General and even his Redemptorist brethren found it very wearying. Brother Francis Anthony lost his temper on one occasion and complained to Alphonsus that they were all in perpetual motion, without proper time for eating or sleeping and that he wished he could get away from it all back to one of the Redemptorist monasteries.

The bishop's sensitivity as regards the episcopal standard of living was heightened within a few months of his arrival in the diocese by a severe famine which was widespread throughout the Kingdom and hit the diocese with particular severity. The scarcity of grain became evident during the winter of 1763 with the result that flour and bread, the staple food of the poor, increased enormously in price, and finally became unobtainable until international relief made supplies available during the following summer of 1764. As soon as the effects of the famine began to manifest themselves in St Agatha, the bishop's palace became a centre of relief for the victims. Alphonsus immediately gave whatever money he had available to buy grain, *fave* and *fagioli* for those who were in need; he borrowed until the money lenders refused him further credit. Following the example of his fellow bishops in Naples and Avellino, he sold the silver dinner service and cutlery from the palace and then the episcopal ring which he had been given by Mons. Giannini, and his pectoral cross. Despite the objections of the canons he disposed of his carriage and horses in Naples — they were bought by Hercules. Whatever is in the palace belongs to the poor, Alphonsus declared. The Christmas of 1763 saw the sufferings of the poor reach a peak and the opening months of 1764 brought no relief. Hercules and the Jesuits in Naples were generous in sending whatever they could, even though their city too was experiencing similar difficulties. With papal approval Alphonsus mortgaged certain episcopal property and made over certain episcopal revenues to the municipality to enable them to buy grain for the poor. To his disappointment, the canons of the cathedral Chapter refused to sell certain items of church silver from the Treasury to bring relief to the starving. The palace itself was placed on iron rations and the bishop formally appealed to all the monasteries to reduce their own standard of living in order to help the poor. To one less than enthusiastic superior who refused to contribute further to the relief fund on the plea that his first duty was to his religious community, Alphonsus replied, 'When you became a monk you promised to live a life of poverty and penance and not to fill your belly to overflowing, *per emperti la pancia e saziarti*.' And all this time the granaries of the local feudal lord, the duke of Maddaloni, were full of grain reserved for sale at exorbitant prices in Naples. At the request of the local municipality of St Agatha, Alphonsus begged the duke to release his grain to the local inhabitants, assuring him that he would receive the same price as in Naples. 'I fear there will be a revolution unless something is done and already there have been riots among the poor, *plebaglia*,' he wrote at the end of January. His predictions proved correct. Despite his pleas and the efforts he made, there were riots in St Agatha and Arienzo during the following months, with crowds of up to a thousand rampaging through the streets, ringing the church bells to summon the people and shooting off muskets into the air. Alphonsus spent sleepless nights in the palace; he gave the unfortunate mayor of the city refuge to rescue him from the fury of the mob. Armed with authorisation from the provincial governor, Maddaloni called in the troops to quell the riots and to deal with the ring-leaders. Once again Alphonsus intervened, first with the duke, and then with the central authorities in Montefusco in an effort to prevent reprisal against the leaders. Gradually, with the improvement of the supply situation, tempers cooled and an uneasy peace was restored. But the first riots of the Revolution had taken place in Bourbon Naples; the writing was on the wall for the *ancien régime*, even in Naples.[3]

The episcopal revenues of the diocese were quite adequate to maintain the bishop and his Curia in considerable comfort, if he had wished. St Agatha's was in the first twenty as regards income among the 130 dioceses of the Kingdom, hence the rush of candidates anxious to secure the bishopric. But the revenues declined steadily during Alphonsus' episcopate. He reduced all taxes for curial transactions and dispensed them entirely where the poor were concerned. Refusing to accept the norms suggested by the metropolitan of Benevento, he reduced all episcopal impositions to the bare minimum of the so-called *tassa Innocenziana*. When it was objected that this way of acting prejudiced the freedom of his successors, the argument carried little weight with him. He replied that it was for him to do as he wished and 'whoever comes after me can make his own decisions.'[4]

– II –

Alphonsus' health began to give cause for anxiety soon after his arrival in St Agatha; it could have been foreseen as an inevitable consequence of his frenetic activity. He fell ill with the usual bronchial condition in 1763; he was unable to shake it off and he had to spend a few days in Pagani in the summer to convalesce, much as he disliked having to leave the diocese. His asthma was now a permanent condition which improved with the summer but returned with the cold and damp of autumn. After the severe winter which characterised the early months of 1765, confining him to the palace and aggravating his bronchitis, Alphonsus began to think seriously of tendering his resignation as bishop. He had always kept the possibility of doing so in the back of his mind since Cardinal Spinelli had mentioned it to him in Rome, more as an *obiter dictum* in an attempt to overcome his reluctance to accept the bishopric than anything else. The possibility of resigning now became a matter of conscience for him and all his scrupulosity or delicacy of conscience, whichever one wishes to call it, began to manifest itself. His natural inclination was to return to his monastery in Pagani, away from the daily burdens of his office, but he realised at once that this was not in itself a sufficient reason to seek his release. His appointment was clearly the will of God and there would need to be some equally clear indication that it was the will of God that he should resign.

He approached the problem as he would have done with any other problem of conduct in his *Moral Theology*. He began with St Thomas's treatment of the question and then moved on to Pope Benedict XIV's guidelines in the matter. He confided his thoughts to Villani and Tannoia, asking them for their opinions and then to get the opinions of certain Neapolitan moralists as well, the Vincentians, Fathers Porcara and Giovanni Alasi Fatigati, the superior of the Chinese College, and Father de Mateis, a Jesuit. His problem was which course of action was for the greater glory of God? The facility with which the two Vincentians dismissed his anxieties about seeking the glory of God did nothing to assuage his anxieties. Their solution was admirably simple and practical — let him tender his resignation; if it was accepted there would be no further ground for worry. They were not inclined to consider whether there were any objective grounds for resigning in the first place, or not. Not satisfied with the replies he had received, Alphonsus drew up for himself as objective a statement of the position as he could manage, and submitted it, this time, to Father Giannicola Chiesa, an Augustinian in the church of San Giovanni à Carbonara in Naples. Had he but realised it, he was reverting to the pattern of conduct he had fashioned for himself thirty-five years before, when he sought advice from so many quarters about leaving Naples to initiate a missionary Congregation at Scala.

> The anxieties which I feel in the midst of so many affairs, the scruples of conscience which continually distress me, make me wish to enjoy the peace of retirement. But I do not wish my monastic cell in Pagani to be turned into a hell by the thought that I freed myself from my office against the Will of God.
>
> I am certain that three years ago God wished me to become a bishop. Now, in order to renounce it, I must also be morally certain that God does not wish me to continue.
>
> Here is my position . . . I am certainly old since in September I shall complete my sixty-ninth year. It is also true that I am in bad health,

especially on account of the bronchial condition which I get every year. Yet, for all that, it seems to me that my office does not suffer in any way. I see to the examination for Faculties and for the Ordinandi, both as regards their theological knowledge and their moral conduct. In point of fact, as regards their theological knowledge I am considerably more demanding than others. I do not neglect anything in the matter of public scandals in the diocese but endeavour to root them out without any human consideration. As regards diocesan appointments, I appoint only those who are the most worthy, even though in this way I make more enemies than friends. True, in the winter I am not able to go out to visit the diocese but I do that in the summer for four or five months. In the winter I do not venture out, but I discharge all the business, examinations, confidential letters, etc. since my head is not affected. Even though I cannot write much with my own hands I have Brother Francis Anthony who is absolutely trustworthy.

Since this is the position as I see it, I do not think that I can offer my resignation without scruple on the grounds that I am unable to perform my duties, either on account of my old age, or of my bad health. This is precisely why I am continually agitated about the matter. I would love to be free of all worries and difficulties and so much unpleasantness. But I seem to hear, 'If you love me, feed my sheep,' and then it does not matter whether I die or suffer agony. It is the worry of whether it is the Will of God for me to resign or not, which causes me the greatest distress.[5]

Despite the fact that he came down clearly in his own analysis in favour of the opinion that there was no objective reason for him to tender his resignation, the result of the consultation was that he felt free in conscience to forward his resignation to Rome in June 1765; the decisive factor had been the advice and encouragement of his great episcopal confidant, bishop Nicholas Borgia, now transferred to the neighbouring diocese of Aversa. While waiting on the reply from Rome, he set out as usual on his visitation of the diocese and he was not too hopeful of the outcome as he confided to Villani from Airola.[6] Moreover, he had just learnt that Rome had refused to accept the resignation of the bishop of Lettere, who was over eighty, and in Alphonsus' own words, was nothing more than a skeleton, *è un vero cadavere*. His premonitions were correct. A few weeks later the reply of Clement XIII instructed him to continue his work for the salvation of souls in the diocese. That same will of God, insisted the Roman reply, which had elevated him to the bishopric would continue to assist him with light and strength in the government of the diocese. Alphonsus' reaction was immediate and predictable; the will of God was plain.[7]

Following the rejection of his resignation Alphonsus decided to change his residence from St Agatha to Arienzo. He tried everything to avoid the change but the doctors insisted that the humid atmosphere and the mists from the slopes of Monte Taburno were killing him; it was imperative for him to move to the more healthy atmosphere of Arienzo where, in fact, his immediate predecessor had mainly resided. At the end of October 1765 Alphonsus left St Agatha to the great disappointment of the inhabitants. He knew himself that he would miss the seminary and the seminarians in a special way and he expressed forebodings that the moral tone of the city, which he had done so much to improve, would decline again with his absence.[8] But the doctors were adamant. Within a few months of establishing himself in the episcopal residence attached to the collegiate church of Sant'Andrea in Arienzo and after a course of asses' milk, his health improved considerably, but it proved not to be lasting. The following summer, in August 1766, he fell seriously ill and was anointed.

The change to Arienzo entailed no alteration in his life-style either at home or throughout the diocese. He continued to follow the same pattern of prayer and ascetical practices as in Sant'Agatha; when he had to suspend some penitential practice on account of illness he requested permission to resume it from Villani when he felt well again. He still wished to have a companion with him for the recitation of his breviary but this became more and more difficult since he recited the psalms so slowly that every member of the household dreaded the ordeal. Verzella used to say that he would rather die than be asked to recite the breviary with Monsignor. Alphonsus was aware of the fact that he was hard to live with and that there was increasing difficulty in getting one of the Fathers of his own Congregation to come to stay with him. Father Angelo Maione, who was later to play a major role in the *Regolamento* crisis, seemed the ideal candidate for the position. He was retiring, prayerful, could be relied upon not to get involved in diocesan politics and had good judgment. Besides, he was a competent preacher and theologian, who could help in the theological examination of candidates for ordination and appointment to benefices. But even he could not endure it more than a year and wrote secretly to Villani to recall him to one of the Redemptorist houses; anywhere would be more tolerable than the bishop's palace. The news upset Alphonsus considerably. He needed a companion who would 'counsel me in the difficulties and scruples which beset me every day; I am surrounded by troubles on all sides.'[9] Villani too must have been at his wits' end since Alphonsus was proving difficult to satisfy and made it clear that he would not accept just anybody; he went so far as to exclude a number of possible candidates by name.

Towards the end of 1766 Alphonsus wrote an intriguing letter to the Pope, referring once again to the possibility of his resignation and suggesting the name of his successor. The news of his offer to resign had become public and from all sides candidates for the See began to press their claims, none of whom appealed to him as ideal. His favourite candidate, if his resignation were to be accepted, was Mons. Antonio Puoti, archbishop of Amalfi, whose health suffered greatly from the sea air. And despite his absolute refusal to consider any recommendations made to him personally in his diocese, Alphonsus had no scruple in recommending his friend to the Pope:

> Holy Father,
>
> Since the Lord has sent me another serious illness causing me to be

anointed in August, I beg you once more to accept my resignation as bishop of St Agatha of the Goths. I am now in my seventy-first year and every spring I am forced to remain indoors on account of a chronic lung condition.

And since I would like the little good the Lord has been willing to accomplish through me in this diocese to be maintained, I petition your Holiness to translate to this diocese, Mons. Puoti of Amalfi, whose health cannot tolerate the sea air of his diocese. However, if your Holiness wishes to name some other prelate to this diocese, I have no objection to offering my resignation.

Therefore, if your Holiness is willing to accept my resignation I will submit it unconditionally into your hands. But if, on the other hand, you think I should continue to govern this diocese despite my age and my infirmities, I am willing even to die bearing this burden in order to do the Will of God. I await the wishes of your Holiness.[10]

Alphonsus never settled down to enjoy his episcopate as he advised others to enjoy their priesthood. He complained unceasingly of his responsibilities, of the judgment he would have to face, of the problems of the diocese. These are recurring themes in his letters to Hercules, in his communications with his episcopal colleagues, in his letters of direction to his penitents and to converts. Finally, his protestations cease to convince or to make any impact; as evidence of virtue they are ambivalent. It was almost as if he felt he had to be continually bewailing the burden of his episcopate lest anyone should imagine that he was enjoying it or at least had come to terms with it. One can be excused for feeling that he would have presented a more authentic christian witness if he had accepted his responsibilities and carried out the ministry entrusted to him without further lamentations. But in the last analysis, it all had little to do with virtue and everything to do with his psychology and temperament.

He made great efforts, however, to overcome his temperament in other areas. He succeeded in bringing his outbursts of temper under control, even when publicly insulted, which was not altogether a rare occurrence; it was even urged against him that by tolerating these personal insults he was failing in his duty to vindicate the episcopal dignity. Very few signs of his old impatience manifested themselves. His priests became more and more aware of his serenity, of the general air of peace which pervaded his whole outward comportment. Gone, too, were the peevishness, the old sharpness of manner; he became more human and more tolerant. He loved animals and got quite upset if he heard of their being mistreated. He kept a cat which he called 'Mohamet', allowing him to be with him at meals and in his bedroom. There were times when he could see the humour in a situation which before would have outraged him. On one occasion, realising that certain officials, whose attendance in church was a rare event, were present he preached a very powerful sermon on sin and worked up the whole congregation to considerable depths of repentance; some were in tears. When

Alphonsus stopped, the emotion was tangible in the silence of the church. The parish priest then intoned the opening stanza of the *Tantum Ergo* in such outrageous dissonance that the whole congregation exploded in laughter. 'My God', said Alphonsus later in the sacristy, to the offending cleric, 'I struggled for over half-an-hour to make them cry and you, just by opening your mouth once, made them all laugh and destroyed everything I had achieved.'

There was much to exercise his patience. Many whose scandalous lives he had censured, both clerics and laity, did all in their power to revenge themselves on him. He was reported to the King and the royal Ministers; others directed their complaints to Rome where there was a constant stream of complaints against him. He absolutely refused to take action against his accusers; on the contrary, he went out of his way to be kind and even to show special consideration to those who had calumniated him. A cleric who had calumniated him to the King, presented himself at the concursus for a benefice. The Board of Examiners reported to Alphonsus that they could not decide between him and another candidate. Alphonsus immediately gave his casting vote to his accuser. And this was not an isolated incident. When Don Carlo di Marco, the Minister for Religious Affairs, ascertained the falsity of accusations made against the bishop by one of his priests, he determined to take action against him. He was dissuaded from doing so by Alphonsus himself, who said, 'I have deserved much more than this; may the Lord bless him.' When a priest requested to be appointed to the cure of souls Alphonsus told him that he would most certainly arrange this provided he studied moral theology and prepared himself for the pastoral ministry. As a gesture of goodwill he presented him with a copy of the latest Italian edition of his *Pratica*. Enraged, the priest threw the book on the floor and with an insulting remark stormed from the room. Some irate clerics called him *birbo* to his face, perhaps the modern word *phoney* renders it most accurately. In more lurid language still, he was told that he was not even fit to be in charge of turkeys, *pinti*. More seriously, his life was threatened physically, in every instance by men whose public concubinage he had denounced. Only the timely arrival of Alessio saved him from injury when he was physically attacked in the Palace by an irate victim of his condemnation. On another occasion his carriage was stoned as he drove along. 'If they wish to kill me, let them do so. But if God does not permit it, all their efforts will be in vain. I do not wish to fail in my obligations.'

The archpriest of Arienzo, where Alphonsus was now living, did not see eye to eye with the bishop. Alphonsus was pontificating in the church of the *Annunziata* there on Holy Saturday. In accordance with the prescriptions of the rubrics he had given instructions that the bells of the other churches were not to be rung until the bells of the Annunziata announced that the bishop had intoned the Paschal *Gloria*. The archpriest, a short distance away in his collegiate church of Sant'Andrea, decided to challenge the bishop by commencing his own celebration some time earlier, and ordering his bells to ring out a considerable time before the bells of the *Annunziata*. The public insult was missed by no one. Despite the promptings of his episcopal family, Alphonsus refused to vindicate his personal honour and when the archpriest later came to apologise, he received him with the greatest affability and passed the whole incident off as a joke.

Alphonsus was fully aware that his government did not meet with universal approval. Even his colleagues in the episcopate, whose lives were silently reproached by the life-style of the bishop of Sant'Agatha, joined in the chorus of complaints against him. They objected to his poverty, to the way he dressed, to the fact that he went around without the accustomed retinue. He overheard one of the bishops complaining that he was, in fact, disgracing the episcopate. For his part, Alphonsus felt obliged in conscience to write to some of them recalling them to their duties, especially on the point of residing in their dioceses, and such letters were seen as a liberty which was not much appreciated. The saddest feature of his episcopate, however, must have been the lack of loyalty of his Vicar General whom he had chosen specially to assist him. It became well known in ecclesiastical circles that Rubino had formally criticised Alphonsus to the Nuncio and also to the Pope. Moreover, he had deceived Alphonsus into giving his brother a lucrative benefice, which he was well aware was reserved to papal grant. When Alphonsus queried the point, Rubino assured him that there was no such reservation. Two of Alphonsus' most loyal friends, Puoti of Amalfi and Borgia of Cava were fully aware of Rubino's disloyalty, and counselled Alphonsus to dismiss him from the diocese. But Alphonsus refused to take any such action against his Vicar General. On the contrary, it later transpired that he had — with that lack of critical assessment which sometimes marked his dealings — recommended him at least twice for bishoprics in the dioceses of Marsico and Sora. At the process of beatification Rubino could find nothing positive to say in favour of his bishop; he had lived with him for thirteen years and his verdict was that he could not see any manifestation of sanctity in his life, *non so cosa di positivo della di lui vita spirituale*. As the years went by even Verzella began to lose patience. As the bishop's infirmities multiplied, the secretary began to speak roughly to him and to treat him with scant respect. Unable to tolerate the boredom of the episcopal residence, he sought relief in frequenting the local convents of sisters, much to the annoyance of Alphonsus. When Alphonsus challenged him on the matter, Verzella decided that it was better for him to return to his own diocese, which he did in 1773, leaving Alphonsus to rely more and more on his Redemptorist confreres for the last two years of his episcopate.[11]

He still continued to struggle against what he considered was his personal vanity. He refused to accept the title *Eccelenza* which was in common use when addressing bishops. He insisted that the title *Illustrissimo*, used by the Church was sufficient, even though Verzella objected, pointing out that this was used for nearly everybody in the diocese, even for the barber — who was also the dentist. Alphonsus admitted that he was seriously assailed by temptations to vanity when he was being incensed by the deacon at a Pontifical Mass in Arienzo and he immediately confessed the matter to his

[405]

confessor. His scruples still worried him but they centred less on his own personal life and sexual problems than on his responsibilities as bishop. He felt oppressed by a sense of responsibility for the salvation of souls entrusted to his pastoral charge. 'God help us,' he said to Mons. Albertini of Caserta, 'if one soul is lost through our fault.' When some scruple got the better of him during Mass he would call his secretary and ask him to note it down and remind him of the matter after Mass. One morning during the celebration of the Eucharist he got quite agitated about some important document. At the Lavabo of the Mass he summoned Verzella to look for it. He remained at the side of the altar for nearly fifteen minutes while all this was in progress. Only when Verzella returned to reassure him that the document was safe did he continue in peace. In Arienzo his medical advisers ordered him to eat meat during Lent. He refused to accept their word for it and insisted that the instructions should be given to him in writing. He would then send the document to the parish priest of whatever parish he happened to be in, for the necessary dispensation. Despite the fact that he was told that all this was quite unnecessary and that the doctors' decision was valid for the rest of his life, he stubbornly refused to alter his procedure and demanded a fresh medical declaration each year.[12]

– III –

All during his episcopate Alphonsus maintained the closest relations with his youngest brother Hercules. His other brother, Cajetan, was well settled into his rich benefice at the cathedral in Naples and there is no evidence that he even once visited his brother in St Agatha. He is mentioned only in passing in Alphonsus' correspondence. Alphonsus did not easily forget Hercules' generosity in lending him sufficient funds to equip himself for his bishopric, or his support during the famine, even though he was slow in repaying his debts. Payments readily promised had to be spread out over the whole thirteen years of the episcopate. Alphonsus was intensely interested in every move that Hercules made. The great disappointment was that his marriage to the altogether admirable Donna Rachele was childless, though she had five children by her previous marriage; the Liguori family line was faced with extinction. At the end of October 1762, a few months after the bishop's arrival in his diocese, Donna Rachele died, and, within a week, Hercules — he was fifty-five — began to contemplate a second marriage. The very same letter which requested Alphonsus to celebrate Mass for the soul of Donna Rachele contained his thoughts on the possibility of a second marriage. Alphonsus replied at length, counselling him on every point:

> My advice to you is to choose a lady of blameless morals and not light-headed since you are well-on in years. If she is just a young girl who wishes to spend her whole time in Naples and go out each evening to some soirée, she will quickly pick up with a *cicisbeo* as is now the fashion.
>
> He will then come to your house to visit her, with the result that you will see little of her. And then you will be faced with the alternative

of sending her away to a convent or of remaining in a continual state of anxiety, and what is worst of all, anxiety of conscience. So it would be preferable if she were of less noble birth and with less fortune rather than let yourself in for so much worry. Make it quite clear then from the outset, both to the lady and her family that you have not the means of keeping her always in Naples [Hercules was living in Marianella on the outskirts of the city] and that you yourself are not keen on social evenings and such things.

Please consider what I have written to you, otherwise you might be troubled for the rest of your life both in mind and in your conscience.'[13]

Within a few weeks Hercules was able to report that he already had several attractive offers of marriage. Alphonsus was worried and urged him to proceed cautiously:

Choose the one who will cause you the least anxiety since in these days society ladies make no secret of having several 'husbands'. And don't forget that young women are more attached to men of their own age than to men of advanced years like yourself. The desire to be courted turns their heads.

And, by the way, now that you are alone in the house, dispense with the young maid servants for the moment. The devil always remains a devil. With the danger so near and the lack of surveillance I myself would be afraid of falling.[14]

Alphonsus was dismayed over the coming months by the fact that Hercules seemed to get carried away by the prospect of marrying a rich member of the higher nobility; he warned him, in nautical terms, not 'to open his sails too wide'. In other words, Hercules, in Alphonsus' view, was moving above his station, despite the fact 'that the family position is little altered from what it was'. Hercules finally made the choice of Donna Marianna Capano Orsini, the princess of Pollica and countess of Celso — titles were of little significance — a young lady of quite modest means who had been educated in the convent of Donna Romita. The marriage was celebrated in March 1763. Alphonsus was unable to officiate on account of the time of year and his diocesan commitments. Hercules who always had financial problems, was in dire need of money for the wedding expenses; his bride's dowry of 5,000 ducats was not available in cash. He put pressure on Alphonsus to repay the loan which he had made to him on his appointment as bishop. If he did not have funds available, Hercules suggested that he could sell whatever grain was in the episcopal granaries. But Alphonsus had nothing to give him; as for the grain, he would have to wait until the spring of the following year to sell it if he were to make any money from the transaction. In point of fact, it was already clear that he would have to dispose of the grain to assist the poor during the famine:

I want you to understand that when I sell the grain I shall give you what I can but if you want something immediately, you will have to send me to prison in order to get a carlin from me. You have my sympathy since you cannot realise at once the dowry your bride is bringing with her. And I appreciate that you have considerable outlay at the same time. How unfortunate it is that your marriage and my appointment should have come so close together.[15]

As a wedding present, Alphonsus sent the bride a picture of the Madonna. Hercules, with some reason, made no secret of the fact that he did not consider this an adequate present from a bishop. Soon after the marriage the bridal couple came to visit in Sant'Agatha. Hercules felt that the occasion would be an ideal opportunity for his brother to remedy the inadequacy of his wedding gift, but the most that was forthcoming was a bouquet of flowers: 'Do you wish me to deprive the poor in order to make a present to my relatives?' Fortunately, the nuns, knowing the spartan regime of the palace, sent in special food for the guests, causing Alphonsus no little anxiety.[16]

Donna Marianna soon became attached to her brother-in-law and confided to him the worries and scruples of conscience which tormented her and which later caused her complete mental breakdown. She very much enjoyed staying with the bishop — her convent upbringing probably made her more at home there than in Marianella with her husband. As a result the couple showed no great inclination to return to Naples from Sant' Agatha. Finally Alphonsus had to intimate to them as diplomatically as possible that he felt they had overstayed their welcome: 'I should very much like to have you stay longer with me but it is impossible since the money I am spending belongs to the Church and so must be given to the poor.'[17] Hercules' great wish was for a son to carry on the family name. In July 1764, Marianna gave birth to her first child, a daughter, Teresa, who was baptised by Cajetan. In the autumn of the following year, 1765, she became pregnant again and Hercules brought her to Alphonsus at Airola where he was on Visitation, staying in the palace of the Principe della Riccia. He asked the bishop for a special blessing that the child might be the long-desired son and heir to the family name. The humour of the situation did not escape Alphonsus, who joked with Don Pietro Truppi who was present — 'Do you hear what my brother wishes me to do, as if this power were included in my pastoral faculties?'[18] It is recorded that on this occasion Alphonsus took off his glasses before sitting down to listen to his sister-in-law's scruples, which were increasing all the time. He insisted that Don Truppi should be present at the interview, though not within hearing distance. Possibly to comply with the canonical prescription concerning the necessity of a *crates* between priest and female penitent during confession, he held a handkerchief to his face as Marianna leaned towards him. When she moved closer Alphonsus moved his chair away from her until they gradually found themselves on the opposite side of the room.[19]

In April 1766, Donna Marianna gave birth to twin boys in Marianella to the great delight of her husband. The following year, 1767, the last member of the family was born on 5 August. The event coincided with Alphonsus' last visit to Naples to save his Redemptorist Congregation from legal suppression by the Bourbons, with the result that he was able to baptise his youngest nephew in the parish church at Marianella and call him by his own name, Alfonso Maria. By this time, Marianna's mental health had deteriorated irretrievably; she lapsed into deep suicidal depression and had to be kept under constant observation. Alphonsus was deeply affected by his sister-in-law's illness and ordered prayers for her recovery to be recited throughout all the houses of the Congregation. He expressed his great admiration for her and encouraged Hercules to be patient and attentive to her in every possible way; 'She is suffering greatly, poor child, and it is not she, but her illness that makes her behave as she does.'[20] In an effort to console his brother, whose family life was shattered by the tragedy of his wife's illness, leaving him to attend to four young children under the age of five, Alphonsus invited Hercules to come to Arienzo in 1769. He was totally sympathetic and supportive, despite the fact that he himself had fallen victim to a severe illness which partially paralysed him and left him deformed for the rest of his life.

– IV –

Alphonsus' departure for his diocese in the summer of 1762 initiated a period of dual government for the Congregation which was to cause innumerable problems and was to be at the root of much of the chaos which characterised Alphonsus' last years. His appointment of Villani as his Vicar was the only choice he could have made; they understood each other perfectly and saw eye to eye on nearly every question. Furthermore, Villani was his spiritual director. The Congregation settled down to the new arrangement without apparent difficulty, though from later events it is clear that there already existed considerable areas of discontent among the Fathers. There were many who questioned the validity of the whole process leading to the confirmation of Alphonsus as Rector Major on his elevation to the episcopate. There were two lines of attack: one, that the process of consultation of the Fathers was not canonically correct; the second, that the process had not passed through the Bourbon curia in Naples. Without the *regium placet* the legal position of both Alphonsus and Villani and, as a consequence, the local superiors appointed by them, could easily be challenged. Nothing daunted, however, Villani took up the reins of government. In October 1762 he addressed his first circular letter to all the houses, thanking his confreres for their generous acceptance of his appointment — little did he realise the true position — and urging them to faithful observance of the Rule; an accompanying letter contained a reference to a number of areas to which he wished to draw special attention. From this time onwards, references to abuses creeping into the Congregation and to a general decline in observance, begin to multiply.[21]

The Rule of Benedict XIV prescribed the holding of a General Chapter every nine years and one was therefore due about this time. Alphonsus made no secret of his reluctance to summon a Chapter, for the same reasons that prevented him holding a Synod in his diocese. According to the regalist legislation he would need the authorisation of the Cappellano Maggiore and all decisions would have to be submitted to that office for confirmation. But Tannoia goes out of his way to make clear that psychologically Alphonsus had little love for General Chapters; rather, he dreaded them and feared their consequences and did everything in his power to prevent them being held. Both by inclination and theory he was totally in favour of single monarchial government. 'A member of the Congregation who couldn't open his mouth outside the Chapter and wouldn't be worth paying attention to anyway, suddenly becomes a Solomon in Chapter and with his negative vote can upset everything,' was his verdict on his Chapter experiences. Even the gentle Mazzini had his misgivings and expressed his belief that 'all the demons of Hell are let loose in Chapters'.[22]

Faced with the inevitability of holding a Chapter, Alphonsus and Villani discussed the matter at length. Circumstances were not ideal — the famine, which had spread throughout the Kingdom, was just ending; there was pestilence in Naples. Alphonsus was totally occupied with the affairs of his diocese. He suggested holding the Chapter in Benevento to obviate any clash with the Bourbon authorities and to anticipate any attack on the validity of a Chapter summoned without royal authorisation. For some reason which is difficult to fathom he proposed that Mons. Borgia of Cava should be present at the sessions. Finally it was agreed that the Chapter would convene in Pagani in September. Everything was to be done quietly so as not to draw the attention of the government to what was taking place. On the morning of 3 September 1764, Villani celebrated the Mass of the Holy Spirit for the opening of the Chapter in the presence of some twenty delegates. Alphonsus was present from the very first day. Within a few hours of assembling there was clear evidence of widespread dissensions. The validity of the election of certain members of the Chapter was called into question. Then the more fundamental differences surfaced. Was the Papal Brief confirming Alphonsus as Rector Major validly obtained? Did his consultors at that time not cease automatically to be consultors on his appointment as bishop? As the whole situation became more and more embroiled, the six consultors tendered to the Chapter their resignation, which was immediately accepted. The Chapter then proceeded to the election of their successors and with the logic typical of Chapters, proceeded to elect the same six members.

Following this unpropitious opening, the Chapter got down to its main work of codifying the details of Redemptorist life and ministry; the outline Rule, approved by Benedict XIV, had to be completed by specific decisions on matters which the Rule had dealt with in only general terms. This task was dominated by Father Tannoia, who had a particular genius for codifying every detail of life and conduct from the clothes to be worn on horseback to the number of snuff-boxes permitted to each member of the Congregation. The capitulars apparently got carried away by a desire to legislate for every possible situation with the result that the succinct ten-page document approved by Rome was expanded to thirty times its original size. The complete work, referred to disparagingly by a section of the brethren, as the Tannoia Constitutions, became an immediate sign of contradiction which would lead to serious division within a few years; it was never fully accepted by the houses in the Papal States. Alphonsus did not remain long at the Chapter meeting; by the third week of September he was back in his diocese clearly distressed at what was taking place among his missionary family and probably with forebodings for the future. The only intervention of his on record is his defence of the seven hours to be spent each day in hearing confessions during the missions.[23]

The Chapter of 1764 had serious consequences for the spirit and observance throughout the houses. The attack on the canonical validity of the Rule and Constitutions on the pretext that they had not yet been granted the royal exequatur, the claim that the Chapter itself was invalid for the same reason, the questioning of the validity of the appointment of all superiors from Alphonsus as Rector Major down to the local officials had seriously affected the morale of the members. By the following year, 1765, Villani and his council were distressed at what they considered the decline in every aspect of the Congregation's life: obedience to superiors, the practice of poverty, the study of theology and preparation of sermons, the typical simple, direct style of mission preaching, the observance of the Rules and Constitutions. The Congregation was on the verge of disintegration. In an attempt to restore morale and re-establish observance, Villani addressed a long Circular Letter to all the houses, and Mazzini led the consultors in Visitation in an effort to redress the situation. Then at the end of August 1765, Alphonsus intervened with a trenchant letter condemning the decline of fervour and expressing his determination to see that the original standards of prayer, preaching and observance were maintained; his tone was rather hectoring:

> I am very pained to think that the subjects of our Congregation have degenerated from their primitive spirit. . . . Do we wish to become like so many others who are a cause for scandal to the church rather than a cause of edification?
>
> I have sent for the Father Vicar, Don Andrea Villani, and I have declared to him that I wish to be informed of all the grave faults that are committed because I shall have every one of them punished by severe mortification and I shall order the expulsion of all those subjects that are found to be incorrigible. The Congregation has no need of a multitude of subjects, but it needs subjects who wish to become saints. It is sufficient that there remain ten that are animated by a true love of God.

Already the disadvantages of the dual government were obvious, and Alphonsus himself cannot escape a degree of blame. He publicly expressed his dissatisfaction with Villani's style of government and gave instructions which virtually undermined Villani's authority and credibility among the brethren:

> I have notified Father Villani that in his government he is too feeble and gentle. I have now laid down that I wish to be informed of all important happenings. I therefore beg each of you to make known to me all serious faults which Father Villani finds he cannot remedy. But I shall find a remedy and it is for this reason that the Lord spares my life.

And his concluding remarks were curiously unrestrained by any standards:

> I bless you all but only those who are well disposed. As for those who are not, who have not got these dispositions, if I do not curse them, it is because God will curse them and drive them out of the Congregation.[24]

Alphonsus now made a determined effort to maintain a firm hold on Congregational affairs. Despite his protestations that he had no intention of reducing Villani to the role of a scare-crow, *mazza vestita*, that is precisely what he did. He made it clear to Villani that he was displeased he was taking decisions in important matters without first referring them to him; this was not to happen again. At the same time he realised he had to be careful not to go too far in this direction lest Villani should resign. He even deceived himself to the extent that he could seriously write to one of the Fathers that it was his principle not to interfere in matters concerning the government of the Congregation and especially in matters concerning individuals. And, all the while, he was determining the personnel for various missions and reserving to himself the right of dismissing members of the Congregation without any reference to Villani. And when Villani and his consultors decided to dismiss the difficult Father Giuseppe Melchionna, Alphonsus refused to accept their decision and made this known publicly behind their backs. He forced the unfortunate Villani to alter his decisions on a number of occasions. He wrote a strong letter to Mazzini who was Rector of Ciorani, imposing a whole series of regulations on the community, the final one being that the members of the community as well as visiting Fathers were not to enter the workshop where Brother Mattia Fazzano repaired the clocks. Information poured into him from all sides; he was fully informed of every little tittle-tattle of gossip, much of which he would have been unable to verify from his diocese. Soon the members of the Congregation became adept at playing off one against the other, requesting permission from Alphonsus for something which Villani had refused and vice versa. The situation ultimately became intolerable and could not have continued. Either Alphonsus would have had to hand over the reins of government to Villani or Villani would have resigned. But these internal divisions which threatened the life of the Congregation from within were obliterated by the external threat of suppression which now came from the Bourbon court, where only the prestige of Alphonsus and his legal skill prevented his missionary Congregation from meeting the same fate as the Society of Jesus.[25]

– V –

The danger threatening the Congregation, and which became an ever-present feature of life until the *Regolamento* in 1780, began in the two houses of Ciorani and Deliceto and arose from the unlikely alliance of the Maffei and the Sarnelli families. The Fathers at Deliceto had endeavoured to remain on friendly terms with both the local inhabitants and the Maffei family, the traditional land-agents of the local feudal lord, the Prince of Castellaneta. It was a difficult balancing act. Francesco Maffei, the head of the family, had a totally unpredictable temperament and had several skirmishes with the community. Peace had been preserved, however, mainly through the friendly manners of Tannoia and the repeated insistence from Alphonsus that the community should keep aloof from all local quarrels. But by the year 1765, despite everyone's best efforts, Francesco Maffei was at logger-heads with the community at Deliceto; he was determined, moreover, to rid the locality entirely of the missionary community. With this in mind he drew up a long list of accusations against the Fathers which he presented to the Court. According to him, the missioners were amassing property and administering it in contravention of the Royal decrees. They were collecting large sums in alms which they then transferred out of the Kingdom to the house at St Angelo. And they had received certain privileges from Rome which had not been submitted to the Court for the royal *exequatur*. By an unfortunate coincidence the house at Ciorani was also the subject of litigation at the same time. The original members of the Sarnelli family whose generosity to Alphonsus and his missioners had enabled them to establish themselves at Ciorani in the first place, had all died. The new head of the family, Nicholas, was totally devoid of any similar good-will towards the missioners. He felt they had deprived him of a portion of his inheritance which he was determined to recover by fair means or foul. The routine pattern of attack was well established by this time. The unholy alliance of the Maffei and Sarnelli, united by a common desire to destroy the missionary Congregation of the Redemptorists, proved formidable. Their case was favourably received and made rapid headway in the Regency Council. Father Fiocchi, one of Villani's council, took up permanent residence in Naples in order to monitor every development in the case and report back to both Villani and Alphonsus.

Fear gripped the four communities in the Kingdom and there was a widely accepted feeling that suppression was only a matter of time. The general fatalistic air of *cui bono* that pervaded the Congregation further undermined religious observance. Alphonsus took occasion to blame the difficulties the Congregation was encountering on the decline of observance and lack of devotion to the Mother of God, when he wrote from Arienzo in October 1766:

> My dear Brothers in Jesus Christ,
>
> You see how the Lord visits us by sending us a multitude of tribulations and anxieties through our enemies who wish to see the Congregation suppressed. What the outcome will be, I do not know. God is chastising

us for the fact that regular observance has declined. Let us hope that His divine Mercy will not permit the destruction of our Congregation. . . . Let us endeavour to enlist Our Lady's protection in the present crisis by resuming the common Saturday fast in her honour in all the houses.[26]

The success of the Maffei-Sarnelli onslaught was due not so much to the intrinsic merits of their case but to the heightened anti-religious sentiment pervading the Royal Court at the time, which was channelled into securing the expulsion of the Society of Jesus and was then extended to all other religious groups, the Redemptorists included. Maffei and Sarnelli had struck at precisely the opportune moment.

The hatred of the Bourbons for the Society of Jesus had continued to intensify following their suppression in Portugal. In 1764 France followed suit, provoking an immediate response from Pope Clement XIII who issued a papal letter praising and defending the Society of Jesus. The document brought immense joy to Alphonsus who wrote at once to the Pope congratulating him on it. But anti-Jesuit feeling in Naples continued to grow and Alphonsus was aware that his own Congregation could not escape unscathed. Sarnelli cleverly took advantage of the anti-Jesuit sentiment to direct some of it on to the Redemptorists. He had succeeded in getting a copy of the Redemptorist Rule approved by Benedict XIV and claimed that it was in many respects nothing less than a copy of the Jesuit rule. Next he secured a deposition from the printer, Giuseppe di Domenico, that Alphonsus had the Pontifical Rule printed by him without royal approval. Then in April 1767, Charles III of Spain decreed the expulsion of the Jesuits, about 5,000 in all, from his dominions. The news caused Alphonsus immense distress; suppression in Naples would inevitably follow and the likelihood was that his own Congregation would be involved in the ruin. Fiocchi reported from Naples that even those whose theological sympathies lay with the members of the Society were equally the subject of government suspicion. Taking advantage of the fact that the Court had moved to Caserta, which was within reasonable distance of Arienzo, Alphonsus sought an audience of Tanucci and de Marco in an effort to negative the efforts of Maffei and Sarnelli. Tanucci was non-commital but de Marco promised to interest himself in the whole affair; it was the most that could be hoped for. A letter from Alphonsus to all the Fathers and Brothers stressed the dangers that threatened the Congregation:

> Let us unite ourselves with Jesus Christ. At the moment we are in great danger on account of the persecution we are suffering. Without the help of the Lord the Congregation will not be able to survive the crisis. And if we do not behave ourselves, Jesus Christ will abandon us . . . We are in great danger of being dissolved and sent back to our homes, which would be the greatest punishment the Lord could inflict on us.[27]

Under pressure from Villani and his consultors, Alphonsus determined to go personally to Naples. All the indications were that the court case would go against the Congregation and only Alphonsus through his personal influence could by some means or other prevent the ultimate disaster. Just when he had agreed to go he was struck down by an attack of fever and asthma which prevented him from sleeping at night. This bout of illness was brought on by his anxieties over the future of the Congregation. All he could do at the moment was to write at length to his friend, Baldassare Cito, President of the Council, imploring his support. Ten days later — it was mid-July 1767 — summoning all his courage, he set off for Naples to take control of the defence of his Congregation against the calumnies of Maffei and Sarnelli.[28]

Alphonsus was to remain in Naples for two months before returning to his diocese in the middle of September. He got down to work right away with Fathers Fiocchi and Corrado and the lawyers he had engaged, Don Gaetano Celano and Maestro Sabbatini. Together they drew up a lengthy memorial to Ferdinand IV rebutting the accusations levelled against him personally and against the Congregation. Alphonsus showed all his legal expertise as he outlined the facts of the case, going back over thirty years to 1735. Shamelessly he exploited the good will shown to his missioners by 'His Most Catholic Majesty', Ferdinand's father. He reminded the King of the good his missioners achieved by their preaching to His Majesty's soldiers and to prisoners in all the state jails, *carceri delle Udienze*. And his emotional conclusion was worth all the legal intricacies of the previous twenty pages:

> And so my poor companions and myself who are continually engaged in giving missions in the country districts of your Kingdom, humbly beseech your Royal protection for our little society. And we do so in a special way since we see ourselves assailed from many sides at once. I understand that certain individuals from Deliceto where we also have a house, have conspired with Baron Sarnelli to level the very same accusations against us, hoping, I presume, with their united forces to see us destroyed.
>
> However, we, relying on the piety of your Majesty, are confident of your Royal protection for the work of the Missions, especially in those abandoned country areas of the Kingdom where so many thousands of your Majesty's subjects live. The more faithful they are to God as a result of our missions, the more faithful servants will they also be of your Majesty.[29]

Alphonsus realised that the foundation in Sant'Angelo was the weak link in his defence; there they were supposed to have stored the 'immense wealth' they had transferred from the Kingdom of Naples. He concentrated every effort in rebutting this 'calumny'. Next he began the round of visits to every possible member of the Royal Court, pleading his case both on its legal merits and through the claims of friendship. Dressed in his Redemptorist habit with a simple pectoral cross, he presented himself in the ante-chambers of every person of influence in ecclesiastical, legal and court circles in Naples. All doors opened to him. His visit became in many respects a triumphant tour. Maffei and Sarnelli prosecuted the case with no less energy but they soon realised they were fighting a losing battle against the enormous influence Alphonsus was able to exercise. The first clear indication that the case was going against them came when an immediate verdict which they had hoped for was refused and their case was postponed to a later date; in Naples postponement was the usual prelude to failure.

With plenty of time now on his hands Alphonsus turned his visit into a virtual mission. He preached in church after church, a novena for the feast of St Vincent de Paul, the novena for the feast of the Assumption in the cathedral. He went to the Dominicans for the feast of St Dominic and spent considerable time in his favourite Carmelite church. He preached in more than twenty convents in the city, either at morning Mass or at Vespers before the Blessed Sacrament. He visited his sisters in the convent of San Girolamo where his sister Marianna was out of her mind with scruples; he urged her to obedience to her confessor but all to no avail. He went out to Marianella to baptise Hercules' last child whom he christened after himself, Alfonso Maria. But his most significant — and provocative — visits were to the Jesuits. Despite the fact that feelings against the Jesuits were running high and that it was accepted that suppression in the Kingdom could occur at any moment, he determined to show his support for the Society, fully aware that this public challenge to Bourbon policy could militate seriously against his defence in face of the legal challenge from Sarnelli. On the feast of St Ignatius he went to the *Gesù Nuovo* where he said Mass and presided at the evening celebrations in honour of the saint. The following day he went to the *Gesù Vecchio*. His action did not go unnoticed in court circles on the one hand nor was it ever forgotten to him by the grateful members of the Society on the other.[30]

The hearing of the charges brought by Sarnelli and Maffei against the Congregation was fixed finally for 11 September. The plaintiffs continued to present memorials to the Court which were immediately rebutted by the defendants' lawyers. For some reason, rumours of the imminent suppression of the Redemptorists spread throughout Naples; it was an anxious time. The communities increased their prayers and penances. Alphonsus gave instructions that special prayers were to be directed to the Angel Guardian of the marquis Francesco Vargas Macciucca, councillor of the Supreme Court of Santa Clara, who had emerged as the key figure in the final decision. His Angel Guardian would have to bring him to a favourable frame of mind if the case were to be won.[31] On the date fixed for the hearing of the case, Sarnelli and Maffei, for some inexplicable reason, failed to put in a personal appearance and their lawyers, no match for the top professionals Alphonsus had briefed and instructed personally, made no effort to proceed with the charges. The judges dismissed the charges as outlined but decreed that a full official investigation of every aspect of the case should be initiated under the direction of Cito, President of the Council. Alphonsus regarded the outcome as a victory. While the legal position of the Congregation was still precarious and the threat of dissolution was not removed, the communities could live in some peace and continue their missionary campaigns undisturbed.

Alphonsus bade farewell to Naples some days after the Court's decision, never to return. Perhaps he had a premonition that he would never again visit the city of his birth and of his brief professional career. Alexis Pollio is our source for the fact that one of his last visits was to the church of Our Lady of Ransom, where, nearly forty years before, he had signalled his intention of becoming a priest. On his return to Arienzo he addressed a letter to his friend Cito who was to head the investigation into the charges laid against the Congregation. In other legal systems this might well have laid him open to the charge of contempt or of interfering with the course of justice; in Bourbon Naples, it was apparently acceptable:

> I have complete faith in God that your Excellency is destined to free us from the persecution that is being waged against us and that the Lord will reward you appropriately for it, both in this life and in the next. In all my work with the Congregation of Missioners I had no ambition to gain the title of 'Founder'. My one purpose in everything was to set in motion a work pleasing to God. And now, after so many years, we can see how much glory has been given to God. This is the reason why I am certain that the Lord will reward all those who defend this work.[32]

Back in the diocese, Alphonsus took advantage of the crisis the Congregation had been through to write a circular letter to all the houses condemning the abuses which had been brought to his attention, and urging strict observance of the Rules and Constitutions. He expressed his horror at the fact that the simple missionary style of preaching was being abandoned, that the priests were vying with each other for preaching engagements and that their spirit of zeal and commitment to the work for souls was dwindling. Whatever likelihood there may have been that the defects — if they were really as serious as Alphonsus made them out to be — could have been remedied by the direct action of Villani and his council, the endless faultfinding which characterised Alphonsus' letters from the diocese, must have proved more annoying than encouraging to the brethren:

> And then you are upset at the persecution which the Congregation is suffering. As far as I am concerned, I fear more the faults of the confrères than all the persecutions, which are still continuing. If we keep on behaving as we are the Lord will abandon us and we shall see the Congregation and our houses go up in smoke . . .
>
> You already know I spent several months in Naples, where, thank God, I left things in a more or less satisfactory state from our point of view. But the storm was severe and the danger has not yet passed . . .[33]

The relief, in fact, was to be nothing more than a temporary respite.

– VI –

Within a few months of Alphonsus' return to the diocese, the final blow fell on the Jesuits. On 31 October 1767, King Ferdinand, under intense pressure from Tanucci, signed the expulsion order against them. By the end of November seventy houses of the Order had been suppressed and 1,500 Jesuits had been either expelled from the Kingdom or ordered to leave the Society and return to their homes. The news, which came as no surprise to Alphonsus, was still a considerable shock. Pope Clement XIII publicly expressed his dissatisfaction with the supine conduct of Cardinal Sersale in Naples and of Bishop Filippo Sanseverino, the Chaplain General and a member of Tanucci's cabinet. It is a measure of the tension which existed in Naples at the time and the fear that gripped other religious orders that there is no letter of sympathy from Alphonsus to his Jesuit colleagues, extant. He must certainly have written expressing his dismay but all such correspondence would have been destroyed lest it should have fallen into the hands of Tanucci and his specially appointed Committee of Abuses which oversaw the dispersal of the Jesuits and their property. We have no written evidence of his feelings beyond well-concealed and cryptic references from letters to his penitents in Naples.[34]

Alphonsus passed the winter months of 1767 house-bound in Arienzo. He looked forward to the summer of 1768 when he hoped to resume the Visitation of the diocese which he had been unable to complete on account of his sojourn in Naples in connection with the affairs of the Congregation. In the middle of May his health began to deteriorate. At first it was thought to be nothing more than his usual fever and bronchial attack. But then the fever was replaced by a sudden and severe pain in his hip which indicated the onset of some new malady distinct from anything he had previously experienced. The local doctor, Dr Nicola Ferrara, diagnosed arthritis and sciatica and prescribed the accepted remedies of hot poultices and blistering. Alphonsus joked that the only possible cure this time would be water and oil, water for the poultices and oil for the Last Anointing. Baffled by the suddenness and severity of the pain, Ferrara seriously considered 'firing' the hip, but was eventually content with the use of blister-paper and ointments, all of which proved of no avail. With his right leg virtually paralysed, Alphonsus was unable to move and had to remain night and day propped up in his chair. He had no option but to cancel all his engagements, the visitations he had planned, the preaching engagements he had undertaken in the diocese, the retreat to the clergy in Naples. The pain, at first localised in his hip, now moved right through his body, centring mainly in the cervical spine, forcing his head forward and downwards, until the point of his chin was pressed onto his chest. The pain was intense. He prayed ceaselessly, resigning himself to the will of God. 'Lord, whatever you wish, I wish too,' was the ejaculation which Verzella heard him repeating when alone.[35] The illness baffled Dr Ferrara who realised that he was faced with something more than the onset of the normal degenerative process of ageing; he recommended that specialists should be summoned from Naples but Alphonsus refused on his usual plea that as bishop he should be content with the medical skill available to him in the diocese. As a special concession he gave permission for Don Marcantonio di Ambrosio, now a canon in Arienzo, to be called in for consultation. Unable to write, he continued to dictate his letters to Villani and to his penitents, describing his illness with that wry sense of humour which disguised the reality of his sufferings. 'I am lying in the bed like a log of wood,' he wrote to Sister Brianna Caraffa. At times he grew discouraged and almost lost the will to live: 'I have almost lost heart to continue, but all the same, I am satisfied because it is the will of God,' he confided to Don Salvatore Tramontano in Naples.[36] Towards the end of June he experienced a slight remission; and was able to move around with the assistance of Verzella and Brother Francis Anthony. Towards the end of July he ventured into the pulpit of the church of the Annunziata in Arienzo to pray for rain during a novena in honour of St Anne. The strain was too much for him; he fell ill again. It was a complete relapse with all the same symptoms of severe osteo-arthritis, a high fever and unbearable pain in his hip and spine.

He was now critically ill. He was convinced that, this time, death was near at hand. He prepared himself for his last moment without any signs of anxiety or scruples and composed a series of ejaculations and acts of resignation which he entrusted to Father Caputo, the Dominican, who was to assist him in his last moments. He added a further codicil to his Will and arranged for Masses to be celebrated for his soul after his death. Preparations were made throughout the diocese for the celebration of his obsequies and St Agatha insisted that after the preliminary rites in Arienzo, his body should be brought back to the cathedral for the full final rites of the Church. From Pagani, Mazzini requested prayers. 'We are afraid Our Lord intends to take him to Himself. We are making novena after novena that he may recover and be spared to us for some time yet, if it be for God's glory and the good of souls.' Villani was sent for and on his own initiative summoned specialists from Naples to accompany him. They were appalled at what they found. Dr Dolci confirmed the diagnosis of osteo-arthritis which had manifested itself with insidious suddenness and had spread rapidly from the pelvic region along the whole length of the spine. The patient's whole body was deformed, twisted to one side, the neck bent forward with the chin being forced down on the chest. His beard and chin had broken the skin on his chest and a raw gaping wound was seriously infected. Instead of spreading, it was penetrating deeper and deeper into the chest. The specialists declared that it was gangrenous and was the source of an unpleasant odour. A high fever seemed to indicate that the infection had spread through the whole system.[37]

For six weeks Alphonsus lay between life and death. Twice he was anointed and the prayers for the dying recited. His sufferings were beyond description. The slightest movement caused him agony; he was unable to sleep. He sat propped up in bed with his head leaning forward on a table for support, until his forehead grew blistered. It was the very middle of summer and the heat was at its height. The provincial of the Alcantarine Franciscans, who came to visit him, thought immediately of the bibical descriptions of the sufferings of Job. Gradually the doctors brought his condition under control with the result that the danger of death passed. The wound in his chest was cleared of infection and began to heal. With the fever abated the doctors removed Alphonsus from his bed and allowed him to remain in his chair day and night, where he was more comfortable. At the end of August, he was able to dictate a letter of spiritual consolation to Sister Brianna Caraffa in Naples, whose spiritual sufferings evoked his sympathies:

> Now that I am able to reply to your letter, I do so. For some time I have been very ill. I received holy Viaticum several times and for some days I was very near to death. But now I am somewhat improved. The fever has left me. I am out of bed but only to find myself in a chair day and night with unceasing pain. I am telling you this only for the purpose that you will recommend me to Jesus Christ every day in your prayers that he will give me the grace to offer all this up to Him as I should . . . Here in my chair I shall pray for you and you, please, do not forget in your turn to obtain for me the grace of perfect resignation.[38]

Villani remained in Arienzo for nearly two months until he was confident that all danger had passed. By November Alphonsus was able to walk again but it was now quite clear that he would never be able to stand erect; his head would remain bent forward over his chest so that seen from behind he seemed to have no head. He continued to joke about his condition, playing on the several meanings of Neapolitan words and phrases. He said he was 'headless', *sto cionco*. 'I have been called *collo torto*, and now in fact I am one' — *collo torto* was an accepted Neapolitan colloquialism for a 'Holy Joe', one with his head always to one side praying. To one of his priests who asked him how he spent his day, he repeated a Neapolitan proverb, 'I spend my days shooting flies and my nights catching crabs.' His greatest problem was not from the pain of the arthritis but the fact that he was unable to sleep; there was no position in which he could find ease. His mind, however, was as alert as ever and he was soon able to read and to dictate. Letters continued to pour out from the palace to all his penitents as well as on diocesan and Congregational affairs. For over a year he was confined to the palace. Gradually he regained the power of his limbs sufficiently to be able to walk, at first with crutches and then with some assistance from others. Early in June 1769 he was able to venture out in his carriage. Each afternoon he was lifted into the coach and driven slowly down the road through the vineyards as far as Santa Maria à Vico to the church which was still in course of construction. The doctors insisted that he should take a glass of *rosolio*, a delicate and finely blended liqueur, each night before he retired to rest. But his great longing was to be able to celebrate Mass which he had been unable to do for over a year. The doctors said he would never be able to do so again, the main obstacle being his inability to drink from the Chalice. This problem had been solved for ordinary liquids by having drinking tubes made, first of wood and then of 'German' metal but he rejected the suggestion that he should have a tube of precious metal made specially to enable him to consume the Precious Blood. Finally the ingenuity of the local Augustinian Prior solved the problem for him. He suggested that, at the Communion of the Mass, Alphonsus should recline on a chair with his head back, thus enabling the Chalice to be ministered to him by an assistant priest.

Alphonsus experimented several times with water and having succeeded in drinking without spilling it, was confident enough to resume the celebration of Mass. He celebrated Mass for the first time for over a year on 27 August and that same evening, having been assisted into the pulpit, preached in the church of the Augustinians. As far as he was concerned his period of illness was at an end, though he was never to celebrate Mass in public again; even Mass in private, assisted by Verzella, demanded considerable effort: 'Thanks be to God, I am saying Mass every day but with considerable difficulty. At the end, I am all covered in perspiration.'[39]

This latest serious illness brought the question of his resignation as bishop to the surface once more. During the year he had been confined to the palace, and for many months to bed, he remained in control of affairs, administering the diocese mainly through his Vicar General, who was with him in Arienzo, and the archdeacon Rainone in St Agatha. Together they had planned the schedule of missions throughout the diocese, which took place as appointed. But discontent with his government increased and criticisms multiplied both in Naples and Rome. He was accused of neglecting the affairs of the diocese by devoting too much time to study, writing and the publication of his books. During his months of illness the diocese, it was claimed, was run by a clique of three, the Vicar General, the archdeacon and Verzella. The sources of many of the calumnies and criticisms were traced to the ten or so priests he had suspended from their ministry or even banished from the diocese for their conduct. No story was too wild to gain credence. The Pope, it was reported, regretted having appointed him in the first place — this, despite the fact that Clement XIII who had appointed him and refused his resignation, died in February 1769. As a result of his neglect of diocesan affairs, it was said, there was such chaos that one of his priests had baptised a goat — an old *canard* which surfaced regularly throughout the Kingdom and was now inevitably laid at Alphonsus' door. Villani and the Fathers kept their ears close to the ground and reported all ecclesiastical gossip back to Alphonsus; his good friend, Don Salvatore Tramontano, kept him well informed of whatever was circulating about him in the capital. Unlike the previous occasion when he was beset by scruples about his resignation, Alphonsus on this occasion vigorously defended his stewardship both to Villani and Tramontano. He wrote to Tramontano:

> As regards the diocese, I don't know what more I could do than I am doing. I never omit anything that has to be done, nor do I put it on the long finger. When there is a question of admonishing someone for his conduct or imposing sanctions, I attend to the matter immediately. However, you know yourself that it is impossible to silence those who are ill-disposed. With the exception of purely Curial matters for which I rely on my two Vicars, one here in Arienzo, the other in St Agatha, everything connected with the diocese passes through my hands. Despite all this, as soon as one weed is rooted out, another springs to life.
>
> I am resigned to the fact that it is impossible to put an end to all these complaints against me. Provided the Lord has no grounds for complaint,

> I am satisfied. As well as that it is a salutary experience, since it keeps me humble to see myself calumniated and discredited. I pray to the Lord that He will sanctify my detractors.[40]

Despite this bravado, Alphonsus took cognisance of the volume of criticism now being levelled against him. He consulted with Villani and then with several members of the hierarchy, some of whom would have been anxious to secure the succession to Sant' Agata, Mons. Puoti from Amalfi and a new candidate, Mons. Giuseppe Maria Foschi from Lucera in Apulia. But the main consideration now was not so much the question of Alphonsus' resignation or the choice of his successor as the distinct possibility that in the existing climate of relations between Naples and Rome Tanucci and his ministers were quite likely to refuse to grant the exequatur to the appointment of a new bishop, thus leaving the diocese in a worse condition than before. The outcome of all the discussion was that in January 1770 Alphonsus decided against submitting a formal resignation to the Pope. Instead he would simply represent his state of health and his capacity to attend to diocesan affairs and leave it to the Holy Father to decide whether he should submit his resignation or not. It was all a bit involved and did not demonstrate any great anxiety to be rid of the episcopal burden. In due course, Alphonsus requested Cardinal Castelli, Prefect of the Congregation of Propaganda in Rome to convey his message to the Pope. The reply from the new Pope, Clement XIV, was predictable. Alphonsus was to continue to govern the diocese of Sant' Agata, even from his bed, if need be. And that would be the case.[41]

Chapter Sixteen

The Return to Pagani
1775

- I -

The accusations against Alphonsus that he spent a considerable amount of time as a bishop in writing were quite true, but he believed that this did not, in any way, interfere with his administration of the diocese. For their bishop to devote so much of his time to study, research and writing was certainly an unfamiliar experience for the priests of Sant' Agata as it would have been for any of the dioceses of the Kingdom at the time. The years of Alphonsus' episcopate were characterised by feverish literary activity. During those thirteen years over fifty works came from his pen, ranging from serious theological investigation in the realm of moral theology through dogmatic and historical works on the Papacy and Councils, apologetic works on fundamental theology, pastoral works on frequent Communion, sermons, translations of the psalms, works of simple piety and devotion. The inspiration for this activity came mainly from his zeal for souls and from his vow never to waste a moment of time. Nothing could restrain him, neither his recurring illnesses nor the long periods he spent confined to bed or to his chair nor the fact that his sight was failing. On the other hand, since he seemed to have absolutely no extra-ecclesial interests and was even less interested in socialising or personal relaxation, he was able to devote every free moment to his writing. Difficult as he was to live with at any time, his commitment to writing must have driven his 'household' to near distraction. He required an amanuensis to write down what he wanted to say, researchers to provide and check references from the authors he quoted. He used the treatises on various subjects which his colleagues had prepared, and borrowed shamelessly from them; de Meo was the source of much of what he wrote on frequent Communion, Ferrara was the authority on the rubrics of the Mass, Mancusi provided the specialised material on the psalms. 'We all work together as a team', he declared.[1] And only when the manuscript was ready did the real activity begin. The work had to be dispatched to Naples to the Brother there who attended to Congregational affairs. First it had to be taken to the censors, both civil and ecclesiastical; then it had to be seen through the press for the initial printing; and when all this was completed, corrected copies had to be despatched to Remondini for the Venetian edition. The whole process involved an immense correspondence running into hundreds of letters. Little wonder that some of his clergy felt that their bishop's activity in this sphere was excessive, and that they should have latched on to it as a ground of criticism.

Alphonsus' main theological activity during his first years in the diocese was centred on a dissertation on the *Moderate Use of the Probable Opinion* which he had been working on for some time in Pagani. Within a few months of his arrival in Sant'Agatha, the work came off the press in Naples. Ever since his declaration that he was a Probabilist, he had been continually refining his understanding of the system, eliminating the excesses in its application which led many of its adherents into laxity. His thinking was evolving until he reached the stage where he could more correctly be styled an 'equiprobabilist' rather than an out-and-out Probabilist. Indeed a contemporary reading this dissertation commented that the author was abandoning probabilism. Alphonsus was proud of his latest work; it completely superseded his two previous attempts in 1749 and 1755 to draw up an adequate exposé of his understanding of the whole Probabilist system.[2] The development of his thought, however, did not satisfy his opponents. His moral writings were still anathema to the more rigorous school of theologians and this last treatise of 1762, published over the name of the bishop of Sant' Agatha of the Goths, could not be allowed to go unanswered. The stage was set for an intense theological skirmish to be conducted with unusual fury. The opening salvoes in the counter-attack were launched from Naples by the Dominican, Father Alberto Capobianco, financed, it was rumoured, by no less a public figure than Tanucci. Alphonsus was branded as an 'extremely lax casuist'. But the main thrust came when the redoubtable Father Giovanni Vicente Patuzzi was persuaded, under considerable pressure from Naples, to lead the attack, which he agreed to do, despite his failing health, under the pseudonym of Adelfo Dositeo.

Unfortunately for himself, Patuzzi chose Remondini as his publisher. As each section of his reply came off the press, Remondini sent it directly to Alphonsus in Sant' Agatha. Alphonsus was delighted at the subterfuge and swore absolute secrecy in the matter; as the pages arrived he had plenty of time to reflect on his reply. Patuzzi's work was completed and published in Venice towards the end of September; a few weeks later a special edition was hurried off the presses in Naples. Alphonsus had his reply ready by October only to find to his dismay that the Dominicans had at least temporarily blocked its publication in Naples and were endeavouring to forbid its entry into the Kingdom if Alphonsus succeeded in having it printed in Venice. 'Patuzzi has been able to attack me with every type of abuse and I am not to be allowed to defend my opinions.'[3] However, thanks to the connivance of

Remondini who was firmly on his side, Alphonsus' *Apology* in defence of his dissertation of 1762 and in reply to Patuzzi was in circulation by 1764 despite all the efforts of his Dominican opponents. Patuzzi, whose brilliance had earned him the title of the Italian Pascal, had, unfortunately, descended to personal abuse in his refutation of Alphonsus' work; his considerable theological competence would have been better served by a less personalised and abusive approach. Alphonsus' reply was on an altogether different level, though he was admittedly hurt by some of the personal references; 'If I did not deserve respect, at least my episcopal office did.' For all his gentleness he could still deal some telling blows. Patuzzi had denied the possibility of invincible ignorance of the natural law, an opinion which had serious consequence in the realm of moral guilt. With considerable glee Alphonsus pointed out to Patuzzi that a number of canonised saints, among them St Thomas Aquinas and St Bonaventure, held conflicting opinions on points of the natural law. It followed then, pointed out Alphonsus, that some of the authors were now in Hell on account of invincible ignorance and challenged him to say which ones.[4] He stole a march on his opponent by dedicating his work to Pope Clement and, as usual, he submitted what he had written to the judgment of the Holy See if anything he had written was not in conformity with the Gospel or the rules of christian prudence.[5]

The intensity of passion, bordering almost on the self-righteous, with which Alphonsus had come to believe in his moral system is evident from the emotional conclusion of his *Apology*:

> Have I then forsaken the world and renounced my freedom and embraced this Congregation of mine with its strict poverty and reduced myself to living as a poor missionary in a cramped bare cell — which I have left out of obedience — only to be damned? And for what? Only because I am not willing to retract an idea of mine and repudiate a system my opponents think I have already secretly admitted to be indefensible. Wouldn't I be mad? And all the more so when, by altering my opinion, I could win universal applause. Anti-probabilists would praise me to the skies for joining them, the Tutiorists would no longer consider me soft in the head, ridicule me as stubbornly laxist, and worse still, have a bad conscience in the matter. But I am consoled to think that when I die, which cannot be long delayed on account of my age and chronic ill-health, it is Jesus Christ, who knows one's secret depths, who will judge me and not my critics.
>
> I now repeat what I stated at the outset, that I do indeed tremble before the Judgment of God on account of my sins, but certainly not on account of the moral system I defend. I regard that system as certainly true, so that only the condemnation of the Church would make me change my mind. I would, of course, submit my judgment to the infallible authority of the Church and I would accept its decision even though I failed to see on what grounds it was based. So, too, if by any chance the Church should pronounce against my opinions after my death I

hereby declare that I retract and disapprove of all that the Church may condemn in my writings. But even though I am not a prophet I am convinced deep down in the centre of my being that the Church will never approve of the opinions of my opponents or rule that it is unlawful to use opinions other than those which are morally certain by virtue of a direct judgment.[6]

The controversy proved a godsend to the publishers and book-sellers. Not a copy of the warring pamphlets remained unsold. Replies and counter-replies followed each other in profusion. Bishops and professors of theology hastened to take sides; the irrepressible Muscari proudly entered the lists in defence of Alphonsus. But the passion soon went out of the controversy. Patuzzi regretted the tone he had adopted and like the gentleman he was, formally withdrew his personal abuse of Alphonsus; 'I retract it here and now and humbly crave your forgiveness with all the sincerity of my soul.' Alphonsus' *Apology* steadily gained ground and it was generally accepted that he had won a convincing victory in the theological exchanges. Alphonsus allowed himself a modest satisfaction in the outcome:

Many professors who have read my *Apology* declare that I have clarified an area of theology which was previously much confused. And to tell you the truth, even I was not satisfied with the arguments which the Probabilists adduced in favour of their system. I felt considerable unease that some of the arguments and principles they put forward, simply would not stand up under examination. I have heard from many sources that my Apology has been well received in Rome. What has surprised me beyond measure is that even certain semi-Jansenists have praised the work. It has been favourably received too in Sicily where Concina and Patuzzi were the leading lights. May all this redound to the glory of God who certainly abominates the excessive rigour that is so damaging to souls.[7]

When he learnt two years later that Patuzzi was bringing out an abridged edition of his theology, Alphonsus rather ungenerously commented to Remondini, 'I hear that Patuzzi is working hard to abbreviate his Moral Theology. His problem will be to find someone to put it into practice.'[8]

The death of Patuzzi in 1769 left Alphonsus and his moral system in undisputed possession of the moral field, at least in Italy. There were few of his theological opponents still ready to challenge the positions he had adopted. At the same time Alphonsus was constantly on the look-out for the slightest attack. Out of the blue, a 'fanatic' from Taranto in the south of Italy, one Don Pasquale Magli, a canon of Martina, had the temerity to break the silence, accusing Alphonsus of being a follower of Hobbes, Spinoza and, for good measure, Epicurus. Alphonsus was outraged; he wished to break into print at once to see off this new challenge. Villani and other members of the Congregation did everything in their power to calm him down and to persuade him to disregard this latest attack. They alleged that any further theological controversy could embroil the Congregation in further legal trouble, even causing its ruin. Their pleas may well have concealed a feeling that at the age of seventy-seven, Alphonsus' mental powers may not have been equal to the challenge. But Alphonsus was nothing if not stubborn. Magli proved to be no fool; his arguments were subtle and had a freshness about them which could not be disregarded. 'This fellow has made me sweat,' exclaimed Alphonsus as he endeavoured to come to terms with the new arguments. He felt that Magli had insulted him even more than Patuzzi and he regarded it as absolutely essential that 'as Bishop and Superior of the Congregation I should defend my honour as well as that of the Congregation and make it clear that we are neither Manichaeans nor followers of Hobbes, as Magli asserts'.[9] The result was a fifty-page *Dichiarazione del Sistema . . . intorno alla regola delle azioni morali*, published in 1774. It was the last formal theological publication from Alphonsus.[10]

The priests who complained that Alphonsus devoted too much time as a bishop to his writings would have been well advised to consider that much of what he wrote during those years was destined specifically for the priests and people of his diocese. Painfully aware of the inadequate theological formation of many of his clergy, especially as regards the ministry of the confessional, Alphonsus set himself right away on his arrival in Sant'Agatha to provide them with a precis of his *Moral Theology*, and in Italian. The work, under the title, *Il Confessore Diretto per le Confessioni della Gente di Compagna*, was ready in 1764 and he was satisfied that any priest who had mastered this synopsis would be sufficiently equipped for the confessional ministry, especially in rural areas.[11] Next he targeted the doctrinal ignorance of the people. He drew up a manual of catechetical instruction on the Ten Commandments and on the Sacraments to be used by his priests in their instruction of the faithful. He was engaged on a further project for his priests when he fell ill in the summer of 1768. All during those months he occupied himself with the preparation of a book on the correct celebration of Mass from the points of view of both external decorum and internal piety. The book, which was based on a manuscript of Father Ferrari, was the result of the combined efforts of Verzella, Rainone and the two Redemptorist Brothers. Having catered for the main aspects of his priests' ministry with works on confessional practice, catechetical instruction and the proper celebration of the Eucharist, it only remained to provide them with a model of sermons for their Sunday preaching. This work which he began after his illness in 1769, took him two years to complete, each sermon, he stated, occupied him for fifteen days. His collections of sermons for each Sunday of the year appeared in 1771 despite the considerable difficulties which the royal censors in Naples placed in its way; several passages were considered to be critical of the government. Regalist censors easily developed neurotic sensitivity in the area of Bourbon supremacy.

But it was for devotional works that the years of his episcopate were most remarkable. He had reached the age when he felt that he should no longer concentrate on works of serious scholarship but should devote his energies in the main to works of a devotional nature. In 1766 he published a book of meditations and spiritual advice, intended, in the first place, for the priests of his diocese, which he called *Via della Salute, The Way of Salvation*.[12] As was the practice in some Neapolitan dioceses, these meditations were read out in church at evening devotions. The work accordingly gained immense and immediate popularity. But despite its great success the *Way of Salvation* served merely as an introduction to the devotional classic which followed it within two years and which can rightly lay claim to be Alphonsus' spiritual masterpiece, *Pratica di amar Gesù Cristo*, or *The Practice of the Love of Jesus Christ* as it is commonly known in its English translation. Based on the text of the thirteenth chapter of St Paul's First Letter to the Corinthians it encapsulates all that is most typical in the spirituality of Alphonsus, his love for Jesus Christ in the mysteries of the Eucharist and His Passion, his acceptance of suffering and his conformity with the Will of God as the touchstone of sanctity, his complete detachment, *distacco*, from everything that could in the slightest degree come between himself and the love of God in Christ Jesus. The work was completed and ready for publication in June 1768, a few weeks before the illness that brought him to death's door and left him paralysed for life, struck him. The bishop's conduct during his illness, his resignation and his patient acceptance of pain, his willingness to suffer whatever the Lord permitted, translated this spiritual masterpiece into action, as it were, and was the essential proof that what Alphonsus wrote came from the depths of his own union with God and not from any literary facility. *The Practice of the Love of Jesus Christ* rapidly gained its place among the great classics of Catholic devotional spirituality. During Alphonsus' lifetime, edition followed edition. After his death it was translated not only into every European language but also into most of the languages of the Middle East, India, China, Malaysia, Vietnam and the Philippines. It has run into thousands of editions.[13]

– II –

During the last six or seven years of his episcopate Alphonsus became preoccupied with the theology of the Church in general and the position of the Papacy and the authority of General Councils in particular. Theologically, the Church had been under attack for over a century; the encroachment of the state on her traditional rights and activities, which went under various names from Gallicanism and Febronianism to Josephism was reflected in the writings and teaching of theologians throughout the universities of Europe. Before Alphonsus' death Italy itself would witness the affirmation of anti-papal ideas in the synod of Pistoia. While every prudent instinct told him that he should leave aside his formal works of research, his zeal for souls and his sense of the theological dangers menacing the Church got the better of his competence and of the scientific apparatus available to him. He now ventured into the realms of historical theology, publishing some five or six works which did little for his reputation and which a century later were considered to have damaged his chances of being declared a Doctor of the Church.

His first contribution to the Church-State debate was a vindication of the papal position against Febronius which he succeeded in printing anonymously despite the attention of the Bourbon secret police. Its impact, however, was minimal, since a mere handful of copies came from the press.[14] Next he undertook a refutation of Paolo Sarpi's *Storia del Concilio Tridentino*, which developed into a dogmatic explanation of the decrees of Trent, to which he added a theological outline of various aspects of the true nature of the infallibility of the Church. Pope Clement XIV was pleased to accept the dedication of the work. With his health somewhat improved, though he was still confined to his residence in Arienzo, Alphonsus allowed his zeal and enthusiasm to run away with him. He seemed to be obsessed with the need to write. Even Tannoia ventured to comment that he was 'intoxicated with zeal', *quasi ebbro di zelo*. He set himself to write a history of all the heresies which had afflicted the Church from the earliest days right down to his own time. The work, which he had planned to be contained within a reasonable framework, got completely out of hand, running finally to encyclopaedic proportions. An immediate problem arose with regard to the censor. Sensing that his work was open to considerable criticism Alphonsus was afraid of a censor 'who would find skins in eggs', in other words, find fault with minor inaccuracies.[15] Canon Simeoli was at a loss as to what to do with the work and one can sympathise with his dilemma. He felt that it was less than scientific and hesitated about granting permission to publish. Whether it was his prerogative as censor to evaluate the work or not, can be disputed. His reluctance, however, to grant permission may well have been a cover for the fact that he disagreed with some of the opinions expressed by Alphonsus in the course of the work. The final verdict, granting permission to print, damned the work with less than faint praise:

> I have admired the effort the author has expended in extracting from a host of writers, learned and pious rather than notable for their critical discrimination, a continuous history of all the ages, and in refuting heresies, old and new, not only with arguments of earlier commentators but also with reasons of his own. The resultant work is a tribute at times to his faith, at times to his mental acumen but always and everywhere to his piety.[16]

To add insult to injury, Simeoli ordered certain alterations to be made in the text, instructing the printers directly, rather than dealing with Alphonsus himself. Alphonsus was indignant on every score. He could not for the life of him imagine how there could be difficulties with the text. However, he was prepared to accept the corrections in order to see the work in print. But on the question of the supreme authority of the Pope, which Simeoli had queried, he was adamant. 'I am ready to give my life to defend the supreme authority of the Pope; if this is destroyed the whole authority of the Church collapses as well.' The less than complimentary comments of

Simeoli annoyed him greatly and he resorted to the predictable emotional outburst:

> To assert that I have written to convert rather than convince means that I have written more as a pious author than as a theologian. And to say that my reasons are less than convincing and that my opinions are dictated more by the heart than the head is really to discredit the whole work. It simply means that I have written more like an imbecile.

For a while he considered refusing to allow the work to be published at all. Reluctantly he agreed to allow it to go ahead but not before protesting: 'Whoever engages in publishing must be ready to be torn to pieces. If I had written this for my own glory and not for the glory of God, I would have given up long ago.'[17]

Despite all his protestations, Alphonsus pushed ahead feverishly with his publications. *The Victory of the Martyrs* appeared in 1775 coinciding with the papal acceptance of his resignation from the diocese. This time the work made no pretensions to scientific merit; it was quite simply an account of the martyrs of the Church from the earliest times to the Japanese martyrs of the sixteenth century. Its purpose was devotional with an underlying apologetic motive of demonstrating the divinity of the Church from the constancy of its martyrs. His last work in this genre, *La Fedeltà dei Vassali*, made even less pretensions to historical accuracy.[18] A quaint little work of some forty octavo pages, it advanced the theory that heads of state — at the time, all were Kings or Queens — should defend the rights of religion, the Catholic religion clearly, root out heresies and keep irreligious books from circulating in their territories, if they wished to secure the stability of their government. Accepted teaching on the separation of Church and State as well as the toleration of different religious beliefs has moved well beyond where Alphonsus was at the end of the eighteenth century, and some of his ideas make startling reading in these ecumenical days. For him Kings and Queens were still the ministers of God and His instruments for the salvation of souls; the whole purpose of their governments should be to secure the Glory of God. With this introduction he singled out 'models' of christian government which include some startling choices, Constantine, St Louis IX of France, St Stephen of Hungary, Charles Emmanuel, duke of Savoy, and most surprising of all, Louis XIV of France. Louis merited his place among the elite because he had revoked the Edict of Nantes which granted toleration to the Huguenots, 'King Louis, despite the opposition of the Calvinists, had the great courage to forbid the Huguenots to exercise their religion either in public or in private, under pain of imprisonment and confiscation of property.' Alphonsus was back in Pagani when the work appeared. It was published in Naples but caused no ripples in intellectual circles. Remondini showed no inclination to include it in the catalogue of his firm's publications and the reasons are not hard to find. Remarkably, it elicited no comment from Alphonsus himself in his letters as did his other works; it was as if the work were an after-thought immediately forgotten.

Still, there was a sequel to its publication which Alphonsus could not have foreseen. In 1778 the work was translated into French and sent to the kings of Spain, Portugal, Sardinia, the Empress Maria Teresa of Austria and to several other reigning princes and dukes. There is no record of their reaction but then there was nothing in the work to warn them of the revolutionary storm that was approaching

– III –

The Pope's reply in 1769 that he was to continue to govern his diocese even from his bed was sufficient to quieten Alphonsus' anxieties about his diocese. He continued to attend to diocesan affairs with the help of his secretary and vicars; he went on Visitation during the summer months even if this entailed being carried from his coach to the church or, on occasions not leaving the carriage at all. Reports to Rome were dispatched regularly; letters and instructions to his clergy continued to issue from his chancery, demonstrating that he was fully informed of everything that was happening throughout the diocese. He still insisted on preaching whenever he was able to be helped from his coach to the pulpit; like all old men, he became more and more prolix and his sermons lasted, at times, for over an hour. During the winter months he was totally confined to his residence and for considerable periods to his bed, with recurring attacks of bronchitis and asthma. The arthritic pains were unbearable at times. The curvature of his spine in the region of his neck became more and more accentuated and his head was permanently bent forward and sideways on his chest.

The situation in the Congregation, which had improved temporarily after his exertions in the summer of 1767 in Naples, now showed unmistakable signs of internal decline to which was added a renewed campaign against its continuing existence. The numbers leaving the Congregation increased considerably since many now believed that its days were numbered. Abuses multiplied. The Constitutions of 1764 were an increasing source of division with de Paola, Leggio and Landi leading the opposition to them. Though copied out by hand and distributed among the communities, they were regarded by many as null and void. Recourse to the Royal Court for vindication of offended dignity and against the decision of superiors became more frequent. The unfortunate results of the dual government were more and more in evidence. Alphonsus continued to write his circular letter to the brethren, urging them to observance and the deepening of their religious spirit — he wrote three in 1770 and one in 1771. Survival, he reminded them, depended ultimately on their religious spirit. 'A touch of pride could destroy us just as it has destroyed the Jesuits.'[19] A hard core of malcontents established themselves in Deliceto, making life for Tannoia, the supposed inspiration of the 1764 Constitutions, intolerable. Unable to continue, Tannoia resigned his office. Alphonsus immediately dispersed the offending group to other houses, where they continued their resistance. 'I have resolved to dismiss them all,' Alphonsus assured Tannoia. Then to make matters worse irregularities in the giving of missions threatened the very *raison d'être* of the Congregation, and Alphonsus reserved to himself the assignment of Fathers to missions outside the dioceses in which the houses existed — another diminution of Villani's authority. The emotional tone of his circular letters increased with the deepening of the problems affecting the Congregation; the letter of 1771 ended on a note of near hysteria:

> I give each one of you an obedience to recommend me in a special manner to Jesus Christ that he may grant me a good death, to which both by reason of my infirmities and of my age I am drawing near. I am already seventy-five years old and am nearly seventy-six. I hope to save my soul and I hope in the next world to treat with God on the affairs of the Congregation. But I say to each one that despises the advice that I have written here, that on the Day of Judgment he will have me for his first accuser before the Tribunal of Jesus Christ. For I have never ceased to warn you of these very same things and nevertheless I have seen many who have left the Congregation. I wait for them all on the Day of Judgment.[20]

He faced up to those who threatened to bring their grievances against him to the King:

> I shall show no human respect or fear for the threats of certain troublesome individuals who do not possess the Spirit of the Lord. If they begin to write to the King, I also have pen and ink. It is my duty to carry out the intentions of God and of the King by keeping those subjects who are suitable for maintaining the work of the missions and by expelling those who are found to be unsuited and even harmful for this purpose. I am the sole Director of this group of missionary priests and this too is clearly the wish of our Sovereign. I have no doubt his Majesty will more readily listen to my authentic representations to him rather than to the appeals of the troublesome and the discontented.[21]

By 1774 it was commonly said that the Congregation would not survive Alphonsus' death. Alphonsus retorted: 'As regards what people say about the Congregation that when I die it will die with me, I have only this reply. The Congregation is not my work; it is the work of God. He has kept it in existence for forty years and he will continue to maintain it.'[22]

Meanwhile Sarnelli and Maffei continued to press their case against Alphonsus and the Congregation; their aim was its total suppression. Alphonsus master-minded the defence against them. In the midst of all his other occupations he gave directions as to whom to contact in Naples, when to present a rebutting memorial to the Court, when to remain silent, 'as if we were not in existence'. Personal contacts, an appropriate gift at certain times, a congratulatory letter from Alphonsus on special occasions were all as important as the justice of one's case. Alphonsus was a past master in this whole area of personal influence and legal intrigue. His gifts of chocolate or preserved fruits always arrived at the correct psychological moment accompanied by the most gracious of complimentary letters. The most insidious aspect of the Sarnelli-Maffei attack was their attempt to brand Alphonsus as a confirmed Jesuitphile, a blind follower of their lax theology, while his Congregation was nothing more than Jesuits under a different name, with a similar form of government, and a total loyalty to the Papacy. No matter how much he tried, Alphonsus was never able to nail the lie, as far as the Bourbon Court was concerned, that he was nothing more than a Jesuit Tertiary. Despite his protestations that he differed from them in his moral teaching, that he was an independent theologian who followed his own conscience in the opinions he adopted, the fact that his first work had been published as annotations to the Jesuit Busenbaum haunted him all his life. The subtleties of his modified system of Probabilism, which distanced him from many Jesuit moralists, escaped both the malice of his accusers and the regalist outlook of the Bourbon government. 'Good God, how can it be said that we are propagating the doctrines of the Jesuits when I, who have written so extensively on these matters, have expressly censured the teaching of the Jesuits in Moral and Dogmatic Theology? Shall we be obliged to teach the doctrines of Jansenius, Quesnel and their followers to escape being called Jesuits?'[23]

The attack on the Congregation in Naples was followed by a similar attack in Sicily where the work of the Congregation had achieved considerable success under the inspired direction of Blasucci. Suddenly everything had changed; all the hatred centred on the Jesuits was now directed against Alphonsus and his missioners. Alphonsus now had to defend himself and his Moral Theology and his missioners in Sicily as well as in Naples. The struggle was exhausting and Alphonsus was grateful to Blasucci who bore the brunt of the Sicilian attack. Finally in 1772 Alphonsus summoned Blasucci back to Naples and after consultation with him ordered the Fathers to abandon the Sicilian foundation, a strategic move which later led to their return on more favourable terms.

But all was not gloom; there was one hopeful development. From Benevento the Redemptorist missioners had expanded their activities right up to the borders of the Papal States or to the Romagna, as the Neapolitans styled it. The next move was into the Papal States themselves where under the dynamic leadership of De Paola a series of successful missions were preached. The outcome was that a foundation was mooted in Scifelli, in the diocese of Veroli, not far from the famous Trappist monastery of Casamari and the episcopal city of Veroli itself. Alphonsus was enthusiastic; he was more than ever convinced that unless the Congregation moved beyond the confines of the Bourbon Kingdom of the Two Sicilies, it had no future. Mission succeeded mission in the diocese of Veroli until finally the missioners arrived in the episcopal city. The mission there exceeded all expectations, with the result that the bishop, Mons. Jacobini, invited the missioners to make a foundation in his diocese. Villani came up from Naples to conclude the negotiations and in April 1773 the final arrangements were settled for the foundation in Scifelli. Alphonsus was delighted. He wrote personally to the bishop to express his thanks and suggested that the new foundation should request a blessing on its ministry from the Pope. Alphonsus took the new foundation to his heart in a special way. But Mazzini and Tannoia made no secret of their opposition thus increasing the dissension and division between the Fathers in Naples and those in the Papal States. Ostensibly their opposition was based on the fact that there were not sufficient Fathers willing to work in the Papal States, 'at the very gates of Rome' as Mazzini expressed it. But personal animosity towards the powerful but difficult personality of De Paola was also a factor. His success as a missioner, his administrative talents, aroused considerable jealousy among his brethren.

Alphonsus was fully alive to the situation which was developing but he was equally convinced that a secure foothold outside the Kingdom was essential. 'In case of suppression, we can take refuge in Sant'Angelo and in Scifelli', he wrote to De Paola.[24] He had a vision of the future and of a new source of vocations which was not shared by others. He did everything in his power to nurture the new foundation. He sent De Paola as much money as he could muster from his personal income and from friends but secretly, as much to avoid exciting the jealousy of the Neapolitan houses as from fear of the Bourbon fiscal authorities. He assigned as many Fathers as he could to the foundation, he sent them books for their library and he plied De Paola with a stream of letters advising him on his conduct towards the bishop. He suggested a certain flexibility in the planning of missions and above all he urged De Paola to restrain the more abrasive aspects of his personality. He was anxious that he should establish a sound basis of observance of the Rule as the source of the community's pastoral ministry:

> The question of our survival depends in the first place on God and then on the way we behave ourselves. Let us then remain united with God, observant of our Rule, display charity towards all and sundry, bear patiently the difficult conditions in which we live.[25]

As regards De Paola himself, he wrote:

> I take this occasion to beg your Reverence to discharge the duties of Superior with all humility and affability, especially on the missions and to show the brethren the greatest charity. They have to bear many deprivations in their life-style, they are far from Naples and their families. You must be very kind and understanding with them. I repeat this advice designedly for I know your intentions are good and your personal conduct irreproachable. But on the other hand your health is poor, you suffer from hypocondria which tries the patience of the brethren. That was the only defect that was noticed in you when you were Superior in Sant' Angelo.

And when De Paola replied defensively, Alphonsus replied sympathetically at great length:

> I know that in dealing with subjects at the present time, one would need the patience of a saint. And even then that would not be enough. I pity poor Superiors at the moment. But what can we do more than help to steer the bark as best we can.[26]

Despite his defects, which were the shortcomings of his great qualities, De Paola succeeded, with the help of Alphonsus, in securing for the Redemptorists a secure foothold outside the Kingdom of the Bourbons.

In the midst of the negotiations in connection with Scifelli came the startling news of the papal suppression of the Society of Jesus. The papal decree of July 1773, *Dominus ac Redemptor*, had been drawn up for over a year waiting for the final signature of the Pope. Its existence was widely suspected even though every effort had been made to keep it a closely guarded secret; when the news finally became public the shock was not unexpected. Alphonsus' reaction when the news reached him is recorded for us at second hand by Tannoia. He stood rooted to the spot where he heard the news. For a considerable time no word escaped his lips. Finally he exclaimed, 'The Will of the Pope is the Will of God.' Some time later when Tannoia was present the question of the suppression came up for discussion. The Vicar General and some other members of the group criticised the papal action. Alphonsus put an end to the discussion by saying, 'What could the unfortunate Pope do in the circumstances when the crowned heads of Europe united to demand the destruction of the Society? The only course open to us is to adore in silence the inscrutable judgments of God and not utter a word. At the same time I am convinced that if only one Jesuit were to remain, he would be capable of bringing the Society back into existence.'[27] Alphonsus followed his own advice. There is only one oblique reference in his extant letters to the suppression; there is no other comment, no criticism of the papal action.

All during the early months of the year of the suppression, there were rumours that the Pope wished the Redemptorists to accept a foundation in Rome and there was a suggestion that they should be given the church of the Gesù, following on the departure of the Jesuits. Fathers Cimino and Maione were in Rome seeking an allocation of the available Jesuit funds for the foundation at Scifelli. The prospect appalled Alphonsus, grateful though he was for the high esteem in which Clement XIV held the Congregation. When the danger passed in August 1774, Alphonsus left Villani in no doubt as to what his attitude would have been had the Holy Father persisted with his plans:

> If the Pope had persisted with his intentions I should have written to him in the strongest terms possible to alter his decision, even though I should have had to face the united opposition of all the brethren.
>
> What would we be doing in Rome? It would have meant the destruction of our Congregation. If our missions are neglected and our Institute diverted from its purpose the Congregation would be finished. Nothing would remain but a *hircocervus* (a monster with two heads, half goat,

half deer). A thousand others in Rome could do what we would be doing and in the meantime what would become of our work? Our Congregation is made for the mountains and villages. As soon as we are in the midst of prelates, *cavalieri*, ladies and courtiers, then good-bye to the missions, good-bye to the country places. We would quickly become courtiers ourselves. I pray to Jesus Christ that he preserve us from such a fate.[28]

Within a few months of the publication of the decree of suppression of the Society of Jesus, Pope Clement XIV's health began to deteriorate. In the summer of 1774 he was deeply depressed, totally turned in on himself and the whole apparatus of papal administration slowed down. Mons. Rosetti, a native of the diocese of Sant' Agatha who paid a visit to Alphonsus in Arienzo in July 1774, brought him up to date on what was happening in Rome and confirmed everything that De Paola was writing from Scifelli. Alphonsus wrote to De Paola confirming that there was no prospect of further progress for the moment in the Papal States:

> The Holy Father is fearful about his approaching death which has been prophesied for the 16 July by the nun who is incarcerated in the fortress of Sant Angelo . . . I do not know what to say except, poor unfortunate Pope, harassed on all sides. And I pray for him that the Lord will help him. No wonder then that he does not deal with any business, doesn't even want to hear the word mentioned to him. And the question of another foundation is in limbo for the moment. The Holy Father is closed in on himself and does not want to hear about anything or anyone. You should pray very specially for the Pope and the Church at the moment.[29]

In point of fact Clement XIV had already begun his final weeks as Pope. He never recovered from the strain brought on by the problems arising from the suppression of the Jesuits. On 10 September 1774 he was taken seriously ill and brought to his residence at the Quirinal Palace where his personal entourage and his Franciscan brethren gathered to assist him in his last moments. On the evening of Wednesday 21 September it became clear that the end was near; next morning, Thursday, between 7 and 8 o'clock he breathed his last. At the same time, something remarkable was happening in the episcopal palace in Arienzo which later caused considerable discussion during the process of canonisation. On Wednesday morning, the same day that Clement XIV entered on his final hours in Rome. Alphonsus celebrated Mass as usual in his private chapel. Then completely breaking with his usual routine he seated himself in his chair and apparently slipped into some form of unconsciousness. The Vicar General, Rubino, gave instructions that he was not to be disturbed. All that day, Alphonsus, watched over by different members of his household, among them the faithful Alessio, remained in a kind of coma. He neither ate nor drank. This continued into the night and was soon the subject of conversation among the people in the town; word

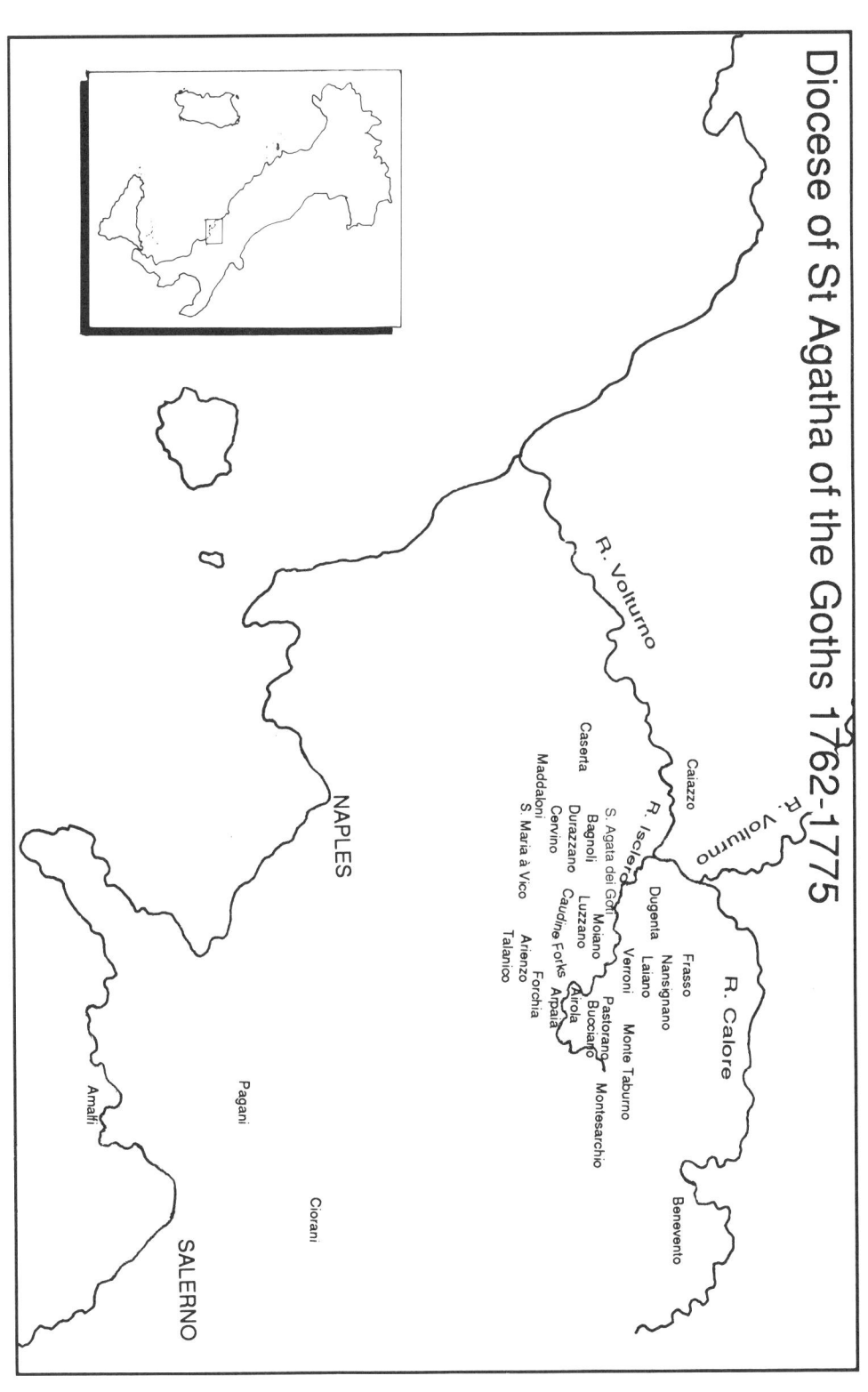

The statue of St Alphonsus in the piazza of Sant' Agatha of the Goths with the episcopal palace in the background

The plaque commemorating the nine years Alphonsus resided in his diocese at Arienzo. His health was unable to tolerate the dampness and cold of Sant' Agatha. The people formally complained to the king that Alphonsus had deserted his episcopal city.

Contemporary court portraits of Charles III of Naples and his queen Maria Amalia of Saxony

Charles III king of Naples 1734–1759 and king of Spain 1759–1788 by Goya. Two years before his death in 1788 Charles appointed Francisco Jose de Goya y Lucientes his official court painter.

Ferdinand IV of Naples (1759–1825) and his queen Maria Carolina of Austria, sister of Marie Antoinette

A contemporary caricature of the Marchese Bernardo Tanucci — in all but name the ruler of Naples during Alphonsus' lifetime

Estote parati, q.
qua hora non pu=
tatis filius ho=
minis veniet.

Memento homo, quia
pulvis es, et in pul=
verem reverteris

Sine intermissione ora.

Perfecta vita est morti
recordatio.

Fervor mortis contur=
bat me.

Biaggian.° Palep Nov.°
Jo Med.

REGOLAMENTO INTERIORE

Della Congregazione (*intitolata del SS. Redentore*)

De' Sacerdoti Secolari conviventi con Real beneplacito in quattro Case del Regno di Napoli,

Sotto la direzione di Monsig.

D. ALFONSO DE LIGUORI

Per attendere alle Missioni de' Paesi rurali, e della gente dispersa per le Campagne più abbandonata e destituta di spirituali soccorsi.

CAPO I.

Della direzione delle Missioni.

Riconoscendo quest'Adunanza di Missionarj la sua sussistenza, e fermezza nel Regno da due Reali Dispacci, uno cioè de' 19. Dicembre 1752., col quale si permise da S. M. C. lo stabilimento della medesima nelle quattro Case di Ciorani, Nocera de' Pagani, Caposele, ed Iliceto, sotto le condizioni in esso dichiarate, ed espresse; e l'altro de' 21. Agosto 1779., con cui fu dalla M. del Re N. S. approvata la pratica de' mezzi, che conducono al di lei durevole mantenimento, debbono pertanto queste due Sovrane determinazioni essere la base del presente Regolamento, e i due punti principali, che dovranno indispensabilmente osservarsi da ogni Congregato. Quindi si ne inserisce nel fine di esso il tenore, perchè tutti l'abbiano presente.

I. Il primo capo adunque di questo Regolamento interiore sarà, che tutti coloro, i quali pro tempore presederanno all' intera Congregazione, ed alle adunanze particolari delle mentovate quattro Case, dovranno procurare l'esatta osservanza di quello è prescritto ne' presodati Reali Dispacci, giusta la loro serie, continenza, e tenore, con rigettare dalla Congregazione i trasgressori. E di questo, come di cosa molto importante, ne saranno così gelosi i Superiori, che dovranno procedere contra i violatori con sommo rigore.

II. E poichè il fine della Reale concessione fu di doversi i Congregati impiegare nell'esercizio delle Sante Missioni, a questo si applicheranno principalmente tutti, senza potere accettare altre occupazioni distrattive; come di direzione di Seminarj, o di altri giovani particolari: di scuole, o studj, così pubblici, che privati: (ec-

The first three pages of a printed edition of the Regolamento. *The handwritten section is not part of the original text.*

even reached the Redemptoristine nuns in Sant'Agatha. Next morning Thursday, Alphonsus awoke as if nothing untoward had taken place, rang the bell for his assistants to come to him for Mass and when they expressed wonderment at what had taken place, he said simply, 'I was assisting at the deathbed of the Pope who has just passed away.' Within a few days details of the last moments of Clement XlV arrived in Arienzo to confirm the accuracy of what Alphonsus had said. At the process of canonisation the incident was dismissed by the Promoter of the Faith as of no significance; the 'ecstasy' was nothing more than a type of coma to which an old man of nearly eighty was susceptible. The mention of the death of the Pope was easily explained since it was expected from day to day. But the Postulator of the Cause on the other hand insisted that here was a clear example of the mystical gift of bilocation.[30]

The election of a successor to Clement XIV began to occupy Alphonsus' thoughts within a few weeks of the death of the Pope. He ordered prayers both in the Congregation and throughout the diocese for the guidance of the Holy Spirit in the Church. Cardinal Sersale of Naples was a candidate much spoken about as a distinct possibility; he had been among the front runners when Cardinal Ganganelli had secured election in 1769.

In the event of Sersale becoming Pope it was taken for granted in Naples that Simeoli, the ecclesiastical censor of so many of Alphonsus' writings, would be named a Cardinal. Not to lose an opportunity of ingratiating himself with a person of influence Alphonsus wrote a letter of unadulterated flattery to him in October 1774:

> It is commonly said that your Excellency will certainly be going to Rome and I hope to see you then with a soutane of a different colour. I do not wish to offend your modesty and humility and I speak only from a desire to see what is best for the Church. As it is at the moment, there is not one Cardinal in the whole College who is a theologian. Learned Cardinals are necessary for the Church since they are the advisers and assistants of the Holy Father. I repeat, I do not wish to offend your humility. Anyway, if you go to Rome please do not forget to recommend me in your Masses and ask Jesus Christ to grant me the grace of a good death which is very near. And if you do go to Rome, there is no doubt but that when you return again to Naples I will have turned to dust.[31]

Cardinal Giuseppi Maria Castelli, who would have been an excellent candidate himself were it not for the fact that he figured high on the list of Bourbon exclusions, requested Alphonsus to draw up a memorial outlining the abuses in the Church and among the clergy that needed special attention and the qualities required of a new Pope in order to be able to deal with them. The resulting document, to which Alphonsus immediately turned his attention, reflects a deeply pessimistic over-view. The Church was in a state of general relaxation and confusion at every level — Pope, bishops, religious, the secular clergy and the ordinary faithful. Among the bishops, few were animated with a genuine zeal for souls; religious were almost all, and indeed all, relaxed. Regular observance was lacking, obedience non-existent. The state of the secular clergy was even worse with the result that there was need for a general reform in order to correct the corrupt morals of society. Having sketched such a bleak picture Alphonsus made a plea for the election of a new Pope full of the Spirit of God, alive with zeal for the glory of God, fearlessly devoid of all human respect and totally independent of the governmental factions which endeavoured to influence Papal administration through their ambassadors. If a Pope were not elected who had only the glory of God before his eyes, then the position, critical as it was, would deteriorate further. The choice of new Cardinals should receive special attention, the accumulation of benefices should be ended, clear norms should be established to control the luxury and opulence of the hierarchy — the number of their servants, their entourage, their personal attendants, even the number of horses they maintained for their own personal use, should be determined, in an effort to put an end to the criticisms of the Church's enemies. Special care was necessary in the appointment of good bishops, men of personal holiness of life as well as intellectual competence. They should reside in their diocese and failure in this regard should result in their suspension or their replacement by apostolic vicars who would rectify their shortcomings. As regards religious, the new Pope should refuse to grant any privileges which would lessen regular observance, especially any relaxation in the matter of strict enclosure. Dispensations from the vows of religion should be greatly curtailed. Alphonsus ended with a prayer that the Lord would grant to his Church a Pastor full of his Spirit and capable of attending to the matters he had listed in his memorial.[32]

Whether the depressing memorial was ever introduced into the Conclave or not there is now no way of knowing. The conclave lasted for over four months until finally after two hundred and sixty-five scrutinies Cardinal Braschi emerged in February 1775 as the new Pope, Pius VI. In the meantime Alphonsus began a whole new round of consultations as to whether he should offer his resignation to the new Pope or not. Word had reached him that Simeoli had commented in private that he was giving scandal by not relinquishing his bishopric despite his old age and his infirmities. The discussions were interminable. Villani, Puoti of Amalfi, Borgia of Aversa were all contacted; all the same old arguments and scruples were rehearsed. Was he resigning out of love for himself, to be free of the burdens of office? Despite his physical deformities, his head was clear, *la testa, però, mi sta bene*. He was still able to attend to all the diocesan affairs. 'I root out every public scandal, invoking for this purpose the co-operation of the Court and of the police. My priests fear me since I punish them with justice. The seminary and the theological examinations have my full attention. All those I ordain are capable of hearing confessions and taking care of parishes. As regards the granting of benefices, I confer them only on the most worthy, after weighing the matter up a thousand times. And I am most particular with regards to the monasteries of nuns so that all may walk in the right path.'[33]

Turning to the question of the Congregation, which was still under attack from the Sarnelli-Maffei faction, he felt he could wield more influence in its favour as a residential bishop than as a retired one. After months of indecision Alphonsus finally sent his resignation to the new Pope with a covering letter at the same time to Cardinal Castelli, requesting his support to secure a favourable outcome. He confided to the Cardinal that his scruples continually tormented him. Showing that he was not entirely devoid of the wisdom of this world he requested, at the same time and through the appropriate channels, a generous pension in consideration of his advanced age, his infirmities and the need he would have in his retirement for servants, a carriage and horses among other things. As he put it with a mixture of shrewdness and humility, he felt that the diocese could well afford a pension higher than was his due since the diocesan revenues were more than two thousand seven hundred ducats a year.[34]

Pius VI had more important matters to occupy him than the incumbent of an insignificant diocese in the heart of the Kingdom of Naples. From what he could gather, Alphonsus' name alone was sufficient to rule the diocese, despite his age and his infirmities. His initial reaction was to reject the resignation but a chance audience with two Redemptorist missionaries returning from a missionary campaign in the Abruzzi, who painted a harrowing picture of Alphonsus' physical and psychological condition, moved him to free Alphonsus from the burden of governing his diocese. In May 1775 the news was conveyed to Alphonsus who thanked the Holy Father and sent him three of his spiritual books as a token of his appreciation. At the same time word came that the Holy Father had doubled the suggested pension. Finally some weeks later news arrived that Mons. Onofrio Rossi, bishop of Ischia, had been named to succeed him. No sooner had the name of his successor been made public than Alphonsus was beset with scruples as to whether he had taken the correct course of action. There was opposition to the appointment of Rossi on all sides. Alphonsus himself found it difficult to hide his disappointment at the choice and he began to fear that all his work of the previous thirteen years would be undone. When it then became clear that the Naples Court would not grant the exequatur to Rossi's appointment, Alphonsus offered to remain on in the diocese as bishop. But it was too late. The canonical formalities for the new appointment had already been set in motion and Rome was not prepared to reverse the process.

Alphonsus' departure from the diocese was arranged for 27 July. Protestations of sorrow at his departure multiplied during the intervening weeks, the most authentic coming from the poor who had always ready access to his charity. The canons of the Cathedral Chapter in Sant' Agatha came to Arienzo to pay their respects; even the troublesome archpriest of Frasso who had so often crossed swords with him expressed his regrets. On Thursday 27 July, accompanied by Villani and the Vicar General, Alphonsus set off for Pagani. On the road to Nola they recited together the Morning Hours of the breviary and then stopped at the seminary where Alphonsus, assisted by Villani, celebrated Mass. Having addressed the seminarians he departed in the afternoon for Pagani where a large crowd gathered to welcome his return among them. The following morning, Mons. Sanfelice, bishop of the diocese, came to pay his respects, delegating to him at the same time all the episcopal faculties at his disposal. It was exactly thirteen years since Alphonsus had left Pagani to assume the responsibilities of his episcopate. He had achieved nothing, he declared, *niente, niente, niente*. Any good that had been done in removing public scandals was due to the Marquis de Marco who had authorised the civil penalties. But now at any rate he could look forward to some years of peace and tranquility to prepare himself for death. If only he had known what lay ahead. [35]

Chapter Seventeen

The Regolamento 1775–1783

– I –

There was an immediate improvement in Alphonsus' health when, assured of the acceptance of his resignation, he began to prepare for his return to Pagani. There Fathers Villani and Mazzini insisted that he should have two connecting rooms in one of which he slept while the other doubled as a study and private chapel where he celebrated Mass. The rooms, on the second floor, looked onto the small garden where oranges, vines and tobacco plants were cultivated. He had no financial worries; the pension levied on the diocese by the Holy See had been increased by the royal authorities in Naples. A further pension, from the Collegio dei Dottori of the University of Naples augmented his income considerably. During the early months back in Pagani he was able to move around slowly, assisted, as in Arienzo, by Brother Francis Anthony Romito who continued to act as his secretary, and the ever faithful butler, Alessio Pollio, who was now provided with accommodation in the monastery adjacent to the bishop. After some time, however, Alphonsus was forced to make use of a wheel chair for comfort and as the years went by he became totally paralysed and was unable to move without it. The marks of the chair which scarred the jambs of the doors of his rooms are still visible. The local general practitioner, Dr Pignataro, was called in to assist in the establishment of a routine adapted to his state of health; obedience to medical advice was the easiest way of getting him to acquiesce in a regime which he would otherwise have resisted. He had his meals in his room, though he insisted on sharing the community fare. He was ordered to take a drive in his carriage each day which enabled him to visit some local churches and to converse with people — especially, children — along the way. There were occasions during the first year or so when he was able to preach on Saturdays in the small church; he even succeeded in giving talks in some adjacent convents and addressing the local sodalities of priests and laity. Very soon, however, these activities, entailing as they did, being assisted into the pulpit and in and out of his carriage, became impossible for him. He insisted on being brought down to the choir of the church to make his daily visit to the Blessed Sacrament; when it was suggested that he should stay in his room for this, he refused outright. Later on, the Way of the Cross was erected on the walls of the corridor so that he could pray from station to station without leaving his invalid's chair.[1]

Visitors came in increasing numbers to see him in his room — bishops, priests and, above all, children, for whom he had a special love; Alessio carried the small ones up to his room to be blessed. He became the spiritual counsellor of many of his fellow bishops. His former novice, Francesco Sanseverino, recalled that when he came to visit the old man in Pagani, Alphonsus' final words of advice were, 'Monsignor, I wish you every blessing for soul and body but above all I wish you intimate union with Jesus Christ.'[2] He had a special welcome for the younger members of the Congregation who had been professed since his departure for St Agatha and who had never met the founder of the society of missioners to which they belonged. With them he was at his most expansive, recounting his own early days and the beginnings of the Congregation, and urging them, at the same time, to holiness of life and the observance of Rule. There were moments when he appeared totally relaxed and happy in himself. One such occasion was in 1782 when the students succeeded in getting him to sit down and play for them at his old clavicord. When he finished he said with obvious satisfaction that he had come across authors who had written that there would be every kind of musical instruments in heaven. On occasions he joined the students at bowls in the garden. He enjoyed playing with the monastery dog named 'Bizzarro' at the entrance to the monastery until some scruple worried him and he denied himself even this pleasure. When he was seated on another occasion in the midst of a group of seminarians he described himself as an old owl in the midst of a flock of sparrows.[3]

It was predictable that he would want to continue writing, despite the strain this imposed on Brother Francis Anthony, Brother Michael Ilardo, the Brother in Naples, and on the Fathers of the community who had to search for the books he required and read out to him the relevant references. His failing sight now made reading extremely difficult for him; with arthritis in his fingers he was barely able to sign his name. Early in 1776 he announced to Remondini:

> I am now retired but cannot remain idle. So I have begun what will be quite an extensive volume, dealing with the particular and general judgment, purgatory, antichrist, the resurrection, the signs of the end of the world, the second coming of Jesus Christ as Judge, the future state of the damned and of the blessed, and the state of this world after the last judgment.

The work was to be entitled *A Theological-Moral Dissertation concerning Eternal Life*. He was full of enthusiasm for the idea and confident that the book would measure up to expectations.

> I synthesise everything and, as you know, I am all against longwindedness which is both boring and tedious. Nowadays people want books to be to the point as well as reliable. Judging by the section of the work which I have already completed this work will be just that. I am told that all my works have been praised for their clarity.[4]

The next problem, however, was the censor, Don Salvatore Ruggieri, who objected to views he expressed concerning Limbo. The usual confrontation ensued with Alphonsus refusing to yield an inch on what he considered to be the clear teaching of St Thomas Aquinas. He appealed directly to Simeoli for a different censor and wrote a long dissertation on the point for the erring Ruggieri. Finally both royal and ecclesiastical permission were forthcoming and the volume of over two hundred pages appeared that same year, 1776, both in Naples and Venice; it was the last work of any length from his pen.[5] More importantly, he was still able to maintain a close interest in the fortunes of his *Moral Theology*, which had run into seven editions; by 1776, a copy could not be bought in any of the book-shops of Naples:

> Of all the Moral Theologies on sale in Naples, mine is the one that sells the most and is most sought after by confessors, especially the last edition. And I am told that even in Rome my Moral Theology is the one most highly esteemed.[6]

With his collaborators, both in Pagani and in Remondini's publishing establishment in Venice, he set himself the task of preparing an eighth edition. His main object was to remove, once and for all, all traces of his connections with the Jesuits and what had come to be regarded throughout Europe as their lax system of probabilism. Anti-Jesuit feeling was still running so high that the slightest suspicion of being tarnished with Jesuit connections would have been sufficient to impair the good reputation of his work. He suppressed, for example, any mention of Busenbaum and even of the altogether reputable Zaccharia for fear of drawing upon his work the wrath of the anti-Jesuit lobby. In the autumn of 1779 in the midst of serious difficulties for the Congregation as a whole, he received the three volumes of the eighth edition of his Moral Theology. He was ecstatic:

> I can only say that with this latest edition, I can die content. On the other hand I would have died with disappointment if I had not seen this latest reprinting.[7]

– II –

Alphonsus had a presentiment on his retirement to Pagani that before long he would be fighting for the very existence of the Congregation. One of the main reasons, in fact, why he had hesitated to proffer his resignation to the new Pope Pius VI was his fear that, as a retired bishop, he would be less influential in defence of the Congregation. The unholy alliance of Maffei and Sarnelli continued its relentless campaign against the Cioranisti, adding new accusations as time went by and adapting them to the attitudes prevailing in both ecclesiastical and court circles. From 1770 onwards Alphonsus lived in a state of permanent tension as regards the continuing existence of the Congregation. He never knew what to expect from one day to the next. At one moment it seemed that suppression was inevitable, the next there was an indication from Tanucci or a friendly member of the government that the Congregation was safe and there was nothing to fear. With one of his consultors, Maione or Cimino or Fiocchi, based permanently in Naples to keep a watching brief Alphonsus was fully informed of every move that was taking place in legal and court circles against the Congregation and was ready to take immediate appropriate action.[8]

Towards the end of 1774 the expectation was that the case against the Congregation would come up for final decision in the middle of December. Opinions were divided as to the possible outcome but the Sarnelli lawyers had drawn up a very strong case and felt they could rely on the support of two of the most powerful voices in the government, the marchese Francesco Vargas Macciucca and the marchese d'Invitto. The main thrust of their complaints was that the Congregation had amassed considerable wealth, the sum of 70,000 ducats was suggested, and was, moreover, transferring it illegally into the Papal states. Alphonsus countered this accusation by briefing Tanucci's secretary at a private meeting in Arienzo, assuring him that the accusation was without foundation; he was certain that the secretary would convey the denial to his master. At the height of the crisis he summoned his most trusted advisers to meet him: Villani, Blasucci, Mazzini, Caione, Corrado, Maione and Cimino. The majority seemed to favour making some concessions to Sarnelli, even going so far as to suggest that the foundation at Ciorani should be abandoned in order to save the other three houses. Then, just as unexpectedly as the storm had blown up, the danger passed; the court deferred its decision to a later date. Taking advantage of the unexpected remission Alphonsus sought the support of every person of influence he could think of, from the Queen's confessor to Cardinal Sersale.[9]

Towards the end of 1775 Tanucci decided to put an end to the interminable litigation which had dragged on through the courts and the different royal ministries for nearly fifteen years. He decided to entrust the matter to the personal attention of the *Avvocato Fiscale*, Ferdinando de Leon; with this in mind he withdrew the case from the jurisdiction of the *Camera Reale* — a rather benign tribunal whose members were personally known to Alphonsus and favourably disposed — and entrusted it in January 1776 to the *Giunta degli Abusi*, the special tribunal which had dealt with the suppression of the Jesuits. A sense of foreboding spread throughout the Congregation; referral to the *Giunta* amounted almost to a death sentence and de Leon's attitudes were all too well known from decisions he had already put into execution. The news came as a great shock to Alphonsus, 'there remains no other hope for us now but God. And he is more powerful than Tanucci and all the others.' He wrote frantically to everybody he thought might be able to bring some influence to bear on their behalf, to Cardinal Banditi in Benevento, to Mons. Antonio Guettler, the Queen's confessor, to Father Cimino to contact the Princess di Ottaiano, to Mons. Bergamo, bishop of Gaeta. As a last desperate measure he suggested that one of his team of lawyers, Vivenzio, would use his influence with his brother who was doctor to the Royal Family. And he sent twelve carlins to the nuns at the convent of the Cappuccinelle, requesting them to make a novena to Our Lady with the recitation of her Litany each day. The key figure was still Tanucci. The fact that Tanucci now seemed determined to destroy the Congregation was the most terrifying aspect of the whole situation. Anything else Alphonsus felt he could deal with, so every effort would have to be made to deflect the marquis's intentions before the case got under way in the *Giunta*. The bishop of Gaeta felt that Alphonsus should go personally to the King; Alphonsus' reply reflects the general state of panic:

> Mons. Bergamo suggests that I should plead personally with his Majesty. I am certainly ready to sacrifice myself but I am deformed, (*cionco*), deaf, and I can also say, dumb, since I am unable to explain myself clearly. I cannot pronounce words properly and so what I say is not properly understood. I am not well and last night I had a bronchial attack (asthma). And the King would have to be contacted without delay. In the last analysis I am ready to go wherever the King is at this moment despite the severest weather. I am ready to drop dead, if necessary, in the middle of the road for the good of the Congregation. Since I have only a short while to live may God grant that I spend it for the glory of Jesus Christ.[10]

The threat of suppression highlighted the widespread dissatisfaction among the brethren with the administration of the Congregation. The problem centred in the first place on the dual control of Alphonsus as Rector Major for life and Villani as his Vicar General with equal authority.[11] There was the added complication that Villani now became the particular object of the united criticism of the brethren just as later these characteristic Neapolitan waves of opposition bore down heavily on de Paola, Maione, and Leggio. In the midst of all the anxiety about the real likelihood of the suppression of the Congregation, Alphonsus and Blasucci in the utmost secrecy discussed the possibility of getting another Vicar to replace Villani. Alphonsus proposed that the King should be asked to nominate an assistant to the Rector Major. It is hard to see the reasoning behind this suggestion beyond the fact that there seemed to be no canonical method of replacing him. At any rate, Blasucci, for a variety of reasons, rejected the proposal but not before he had the courage to make clear to Alphonsus that there was considerable dissatisfaction within the Congregation with the apparently unrestricted authority of the Rector Major and of the local superiors and the total ineffectiveness of the Rector Major's six consultors. He described authority in the Congregation as despotic and suggested that this was equally unacceptable to the Court where it seemed to be nothing more than a copy of the hated Jesuit system.

There was general expectation that Villani would resign his office on Alphonsus' return to Pagani but Villani was made of sterner stuff and made no move to relinquish an office which would now, with the Rector Major in residence, give rise to more complications than ever. Alphonsus, however, did not take long to impose his authority and to make it clear that he was in full control. Soon after his return to Pagani the mission season began and he took the opportunity of addressing a letter to the houses insisting on the necessity of fidelity to prayer, exact obedience and the observance of poverty. There was no lack of authority in the tone he adopted:

> If, my brothers, we conduct ourselves well, God will maintain us; if we do not, He will certainly destroy us. I am not sorry when a member of the Congregation is sick or even when he leaves us. To him I say, 'Good-bye to you.' But I am deeply grieved when my brethren fall into faults especially against obedience or poverty. Pray and have prayers said that God may protect us in the persecution through which we are passing and which is, at the moment, fiercer than ever. But I have confidence in Jesus Christ and in our Mother Mary that they will not abandon us.[12]

Maione too in Naples felt the full weight of Alphonsus' authority when he interpreted too freely some instructions he had been given. On top of this, he had the foolhardiness to suggest to Alphonsus that he should not write so many letters — a dangerous suggestion to make:

> Your reverence suggests that I would do better if I did not write so many letters. But what am I to do? I am the superior; if I were not I would leave it all to somebody else. But since I hold this office I should feel a scruple if I omitted to heed the lights I receive from God. God gives to superiors certain inspirations that he does not give to others and this is what makes me write so many letters.[13]

All during 1776 de Leon pursued his examination of the charges against the Congregation. While this gave rise to considerable anxiety, as we have seen, there were other events which presaged a more optimistic future. The Congregation had been invited back to Sicily and Alphonsus had readily agreed. Blasucci was already there with his missionary companions repeating their earlier triumphs. In the summer of 1776 another foundation was offered in the Papal States at Frosinone about sixty miles from Rome in the diocese of Veroli. Alphonsus had no hesitation in accepting and in doing so did not hide a certain disillusionment with his brethren in Naples:

> The houses in the Kingdom of Naples with the exception of Sant'Angelo a Cupolo are not able to provide stability for our Congregation. They do not form a body, as it were; they are only strung together. However,

we must support them as best we can at the moment. But to speak plainly, if the Congregation does not become established outside the Kingdom of Naples, then that is the end — it will never be a Congregation.[14]

He told Father de Paola whose efforts, not always appreciated by his Neapolitan brethren, had brought the Congregation to the Romagna, 'You have received from God the extraordinary vocation of spreading this Congregation. I am at the end of my life and it will be for you to give it stability when I am gone.'[15] Alphonsus made no secret of the fact that the houses in the Papal States, Scifelli and now Frosinone, were the apples of his eye and that he believed the Fathers there, and de Paola in particular, were the saviours of the Congregation. Moreover, he felt that the rule of Benedict XIV was being more faithfully observed there than in Naples though he made it clear in his new-found authority that he was going to leave no stone unturned to remedy that situation. To add to good news from Sicily and Frosinone, Cardinal Banditi in Benevento was urging Alphonsus to accept the church and residence of the Jesuits in his episcopal city. With the possibility of suppression increasing as the months went by, Alphonsus indicated his willingness to yield on the principle he had established of not accepting foundations in large centres of population. He agreed to take over the Gesù in Benevento and the foundation there was established in June 1777.

Meanwhile, reports leaked from de Leon's commission during the summer of 1776 confirmed Alphonsus' worst fears; the Avvocato Fiscale was intent on securing the suppression of the Congregation. But then, totally out of the blue, the whole scene changed. In October 1776 Tanucci fell from power, due mainly to the intrigues of the Queen, Maria Carolina, the one enemy Tanucci had made the fatal mistake of disregarding. In his place came the marchese della Sambuca, whose father was a devoted admirer of Alphonsus and an avid reader of his spiritual books. Alphonsus could hardly believe the news, it was *un fatto molto strepitoso*. There was now hope that all would be well, a fact that the Congregation's lawyer confirmed after a meeting with de Leon himself. 'I am happy because it now seems to me that the Madonna will help us to emerge successfully from this crisis,' was Alphonsus' verdict.[16] But there was still a long way to go.

In February 1777 de Leon issued his provisional report which amounted to a call for the suppression of the Congregation; all the hopes which had been built up in the previous months were shattered. The continuing existence of the Congregation in Naples was against the law; its Rule was nothing more than a carbon copy of the Jesuit rule with its unacceptable forms of obedience and despotic authority. Liguori's theology was nothing more than a rehash of Jesuit preaching. As a theologian he was more pernicious than Arius, a destroyer of morality, an enemy of the throne and a supporter of attempts against the very person of the King's Most Sacred Majesty. But the most remarkable section of the report was the concluding paragraph:

> Let your Majesty not imagine that you can halt the forward march of this Congregation without taking drastic action. Other similar Institutes have come into existence amid a thousand contradictions and so will this. It will simply bide its time until there comes a day when this present legal action will be considered a period of persecution and one of the glories of the Congregation. And my name, which merits nothing but oblivion, will earn some small renown in the life of Don Alfonso de Liguori as one of those of whom it was said that they were raised up by the devil to fight against the works of God.[17]

Alphonsus' initial reaction was to keep the news of de Leon's report from the houses of the Congregation but this proved impossible. Within days, the accusations contained in the Report were circulating throughout the whole ecclesiastical world in Naples. Rumours multiplied; the suppression of the Congregation was already a *fait accompli*, the royal dispatch containing the decree had already been drawn up. Alphonsus was galvanised into action in quite an extraordinary way which totally belied his eighty years. Never again during the remaining years of his life was his mind so clear, his decisions so definite. Pin-pointing the main danger, he mustered all the influence he could in Naples, to prevent the report being sent for consideration to the *Giunta degli Abusi* where justice might have been summary. Instead, he had it diverted to the *Camera Reale*, thus affording himself a breathing space to mount his counter-attack. He instructed de Paola to spread the word publicly that the rumour of imminent suppression was a complete lie concocted by the Sarnelli faction. 'Everything is under control and de Leon's report has been re-directed to the *Camera Reale*.' He ordered Blasucci to abandon his visitation of the houses in the Papal States and return to Pagani at once, where, with a team of his advisers, they set themselves to reply to the accusations in de Leon's report. Alphonsus himself worked far into the night despite his near blindness; when Night Prayers were recited and the community retired to rest, he was still to be found at his desk. He wondered if all the tension and activity might not precipitate a stroke. From the gathering in Pagani three lengthy memorials were addressed to the *Camera Reale* in rebuttal of the findings of de Leon's commission, one in answer to the charges against the Congregation, another in defence of Alphonsus' Moral System, and a personal defence of his conduct as Rector Major of the Congregation.[18]

From his office in Naples, Father Maione urged Alphonsus to come personally to the capital to plead his cause; his presence would be more effective than all the letters and memorials and the activity of his team of lawyers combined. But Alphonsus was adamant; there would be no further personal appearance in Naples. There was a wry humour in his letter as he conveyed his decision to Maione:

> Anyone who sees me in the state I am in at the moment, would never have the heart to ask me to come to Naples to visit the President (of the Camera Reale), the Cardinal, Sambuca and Paoletti. My arrival in

the city would do nothing more than attract a crowd of youngsters curious to find out if the occupant of the carriage were alive or dead . . . Sambuca would do nothing more than be amazed at the deformed shape of my neck and indeed of the rest of my body. And he would not be able to understand a word I say, because of the weakness of my head in putting my thoughts together and because I can barely pronounce my words properly . . .

Let us place ourselves in God's hands. He knows better than we do how to defend our cause which is more his than ours.[19]

As Alphonsus predicted, nothing happened in the *Camera Reale*. De Leon's report was duly placed before the members, who deferred any further decision. And gradually the whole atmosphere changed. Bishops and priests rallied to the support of the Fathers; requests for missions poured in from all sides and the Court was inundated with petitions for the continuing existence of the missionary congregation. Once again, the storm which had threatened to destroy everything, had blown over.

The improvement in the overall situation was then further enhanced by the most unexpected of coincidences. In 1778 King Ferdinand obtained from the Pope a Bull of Crusade to get money to equip his naval forces in their struggle against the Barbary pirates, who were an ever increasing menace along the Neapolitan coastline. Special religious favours were granted in the Papal Bull to those who contributed to the campaign. But the appeal failed to catch the imagination of the people with the result that the Crusade faced failure. The King's advisers suggested that he should enlist the help of the most popular and widely active group of missioners in the Kingdom, the 'Cioranisti', who were legally under threat of suppression. But Alphonsus' lawyers in Naples made it clear that if the King wished to employ these missioners to ensure the success of his crusade, he would have to regularise their position. Encouraged by the advice of many bishops and secretly assured by the marchese de Marco and Mons. Testa, the Cappellano Maggiore, of the changed atmosphere at court, Alphonsus formally sought royal approval for his Congregation at Easter 1779. On the 28 April the matter was entrusted to the office of the Cappellano Maggiore. Three weeks later he reported favourably to the King and on 21 August 1779 Ferdinand gave legal approval to the existence of the Congregation of the Most Holy Redeemer in the Kingdom of Naples, with the right to appoint superiors and to accept and educate the candidates for the work of the missions. Maione had worked wonders. Alphonsus was unable to read the text of the royal decree when it reached Pagani. Instead, Father Cimino read it to him, slowly, *posatamente*. When the reality came home to him Alphonsus could only exclaim 'Gloria Patri' and promise to celebrate three Masses in thanksgiving. In February 1777 the Congregation had been on the verge of destruction; two years later its legal existence was formally recognised by the King. 'I am feeling quite unwell,' Alphonsus wrote to Maione on hearing the news, 'but I assure you I shall die content if Jesus

Christ and the Madonna permit me to see peace restored to our communities as a result.'[20]

– III –

The royal decree of August 1779 had given the Redemptorists the legal right to exist in the Kingdom of Naples. For many that would have been sufficient to place the Congregation beyond the realm of any further royal vexation. But this would be to do less than justice to the subtleties of the Neapolitan legal mind. There still remained the question of the Rule of Benedict XIV. De Leon's report had explicitly found the Congregation guilty of following a Rule which had not received royal approbation — a serious charge which left the Congregation vulnerable to further legal challenges. Moreover, it was still possible for disaffected members of the Congregation to refuse to accept its binding force on the grounds that no Papal decree could be imposed in Naples unless, and until, it had received royal approbation. Alphonsus and his consultors believed that now was the time to proceed to secure approval of the Pontifical Rule; the idea was to strike while the iron was hot. At the same time, they were fully aware that certain aspects of the Rule would have to be adapted to meet the prejudices of the Bourbon court which had, by this time, established itself as the source of all ecclesiastical permissions, dispensations and regulations. Dispensation from prescriptions of Rule as well as from religious vows, permission to leave the cloister, judgment on internal dissensions in religious communities, derogation from decisions of major superiors outside the Kingdom, none of these were any longer referred to Rome. Instead, they were all available through the appropriate royal ministries in Naples. It had become quite the norm for the Court to supervise the re-drafting of religious Rules in accordance with its own ideas of religious life and government. In this way, for example, the Neapolitan Vincentians, never too amenable to their French superiors, had succeeded in gaining virtual independence and the right to choose their own rule of life.

Not only was Alphonsus fully aware of the proposal to submit the Rule of Benedict XIV to the Court for Royal approval, he was quite ready to accept whatever modifications would meet the humour of the King's Ministers and especially of the Cappellano Maggiore who had full control in this area, and was, in everything but name, the Neapolitan 'Pope'. The Cappellano Maggiore at the time was Monsignor Matteo Testa, who, as a youthful member of the Naples clergy, had accompanied Alphonsus in 1741 on the general mission ordered by Cardinal Spinelli. Regalist though he was, Alphonsus felt that he could be counted on to show considerable favour to his former missionary companions. In the light of the subsequent controversy which engulfed the Congregation and brought such suffering to Alphonsus, it is important from the outset to understand his approach in the matter; it was clear and consistent. He wanted to secure the Royal Exequatur for the Rule of Benedict XIV and, for this purpose, was prepared to accept certain modifications in it, if this proved necessary. This was the course he followed in 1752 when the royal decree of Charles III had granted official recognition to the four foundations already in existence. He had sacrificed important aspects of the Rule, especially in the matter of poverty and submission to episcopal jurisdiction in order to achieve it, and his diplomacy had met with at least the tacit approval of both Benedict XIV and his successor. But on this occasion he made a vital error. He neglected to inform Rome, or at least, the Nuncio in Naples of the course he was contemplating; had he done so, the whole *Regolamento* controversy might have been averted.

By the summer of 1779 the work of adapting the Rule of Benedict XIV to comply with the prejudices of the Bourbon Court was under way. Indeed, there are indications that it had been under consideration since as early as 1777 when his lawyers informed Alphonsus for the first time that Royal approval was at least a possibility provided certain concessions were made.[21] By late summer of 1779 Alphonsus and his consultors were ready to open formal discussions with the Cappellano Maggiore on the matter. Two of the consultors, Fabricio Cimino and Angelo Maione, both experienced in dealing with the Court, were authorised to undertake the negotiations. All of those involved bound themselves by oaths of secrecy not to divulge the slightest information concerning what was taking place for fear uninformed reports would jeopardise the outcome. This secrecy proved to be the second error which later poisoned the whole proceedings. Alphonsus' part in the details of the negotiations, was minimal. Despite his eighty-three years he was, for the most part, mentally alert and fully aware in general of what was contemplated. But he was ignorant of the details, which his consultors were careful to keep from him. Besides being deaf, his sight was considerably impaired, making it impossible for him to read more than a few consecutive sentences. He was unable to write, and even dictating letters of any length was increasingly beyond him. At most, he was able to express his ideas and, on occasions, decisions, which were then put into words for him by one of the consultors and written down by one of the secretaries. While his mental processes were still clear and were to remain so for the next two or three years, he was unable to sustain prolonged discussions. And he certainly was not the dominant figure among the consultors, who were increasingly prepared to act without reference to him. To facilitate the work of the two emissaries he provided them with a supply of blank sheets of paper with his signature appended at the bottom, thus enabling them to make representations in his name as if these had come personally and immediately from himself, even though, in point of fact, he might have had no knowledge of what was involved.

Despite the wall of secrecy which had been erected around the negotiations, or perhaps on account of the suspicions to which it gave rise, there was considerable uneasiness throughout the communities at what was happening. In July 1779 Tannoia, who had a genius for interfering in other people's business, challenged Maione to declare openly what concessions he was prepared to make. Rumours multiplied among the communities that major changes in the Rule were being contemplated and would be imposed directly from Naples. The communities at Caposele and Deliceto, the furthest from the centre of action, were the most disturbed, less at what alterations were being contemplated than because they were not being consulted. Early in September, Alphonsus, to contradict vehemently reports that he was prepared to tolerate major changes in the Pontifical Rule, declared that he would use all his efforts to see that the Rule was not changed in the slightest way.[22]

At the very time Alphonsus was writing these protestations in an effort to calm the communities, Maione and Cimino were hard at work with their trusted lawyer, and the Cappellano Maggiore, bringing the Rule of Benedict XIV into line with court thinking. By September, a rough outline was ready. Maione and Cimino brought it in great secrecy to Pagani where they showed it to the other consultors and to Alphonsus. Maione made no secret of the fact that he regarded Alphonsus as *scimunito*, senile; showing the proposed draft to him was the merest formality. Alphonsus made some effort to read the first page which dealt with the missions; unable to follow the text for more than a few lines and totally unaware of the changes that were contained in other sections of the document, he passed the text to Villani. Some would have it that Maione deliberately substituted an altogether different page from the one which began by asserting that the congregation existed in the Kingdom of Naples by virtue of the royal decrees of 1752 and 1779.

What took place with Villani will probably never be fully known. He certainly kept the document for three days; some assert that he did not even trouble to read it through. If he had, he would have been aware of the modifications being proposed — increased power for the consultors at the expense of the Rector Major, the substitution of oaths for the three vows of religion, alterations in the matter of poverty and the community of goods, the diminution of community autonomy vis-à-vis the local bishop. Whatever his precise reaction was, Maione must have succeeded in convincing him that nothing more could be extracted from a regalist government; it was either acceptance or suppression. Maybe Villani recalled his own visit to Rome thirty years before, when the Rule he brought from Naples was virtually rewritten by the Roman authorities. At any rate, he acquiesced and passed the whole matter off with Alphonsus by declaring that all was well. Fortified by the visit, Maione returned to Naples.

Meanwhile, the turmoil increased throughout the Congregation as rumours multiplied and no official information was forthcoming. Protests reached Alphonsus from all sides at Pagani. Unaware of what was happening behind his back, he continued to dictate letters to the various houses all during October, November and December, assuring them that there would be no change in the Rule. His denials, which must have been seen by the consultors, were categorical:

> I find it hard to believe that you would think for a moment that I am deceiving you, or that I would tell you lies or even that I have lost the

use of my senses to the extent that I would permit changes in the
Rule. I will say no more about this matter. But it pains me to hear
these rumours for I believe that they are the work of the devil to
create trouble in our midst. I repeat and affirm on my conscience that
nothing is being done contrary to the Rule or against the observances
existing in the communities. If you do not wish to believe me, what
more can I do?[23]

Tannoia was the most vociferous in expressing his misgivings, convinced
as he was, that Maione and Cimino could not be trusted. Despite all the
assurances from Alphonsus and Villani that there was nothing to fear, he
braved the rigours of winter to leave Deliceto for Pagani to find out at first
hand what was afoot. He discussed the whole matter with Alphonsus,
Villani and Mazzini, who were most reassuring. Still not satisfied, he went
to Naples to interview Maione and Cimino, where he came up against a
wall of silence which did nothing to allay his suspicions. The position simply
was that Maione and Cimino had assumed an independence in their actions
in Naples, which had not been contemplated when they were entrusted
with their commission. Their negotiations had taken on a dynamic of its
own as they discussed with the Cappellano Maggiore and the lawyers what
was acceptable to the court. They had imposed such absolute secrecy on
their negotiations that not only did Alphonsus not know what was on foot
but neither did Villani or Mazzini. With success in sight they continued
their work regardless of the opposition building up in the four communities
of the Kingdom, not to mention the anger and frustration which was
manifesting itself amongst the Fathers of the Papal States. For De Paola
and his companions the whole deceitful transaction was pushing their
tolerance of the government of the Congregation beyond breaking point.

The reworking of the Rule was completed by the end of the year to the
satisfaction of the Cappellano Maggiore who gave it his approval early in
January 1780; a few weeks later on 22 January it received the approval of
the Royal Council of Ministers. The text of the new 'Rule' is preserved in
the State Archives in Naples, written on some fourteen sheets of paper, five
of which have Alphonsus' signature at the bottom; the two-page accompanying letter addressed to 'His Royal Majesty from his faithful servant
prostrate before the Royal Throne' was signed on each page by Alphonsus.
Maione had made full use of the blank pages which Alphonsus had signed.
The formal dispatch from the office of Carlo de Marco announcing the
approval referred to the 'Chapters drawn up by Mons Don Alfonso de
Liguori for the internal government of his Congregation of Missioners'. An
addition to the decree suggested by Tanucci delayed the formal promulgation
of the document until 1 March. On that day the decree was signed and sent
to Alphonsus as Founder and Rector Major with instructions to enforce it.[24]

The 'new' Rule was entitled *Regolamento della Congregazione intitolata del
SS. Redentore*, thus giving it the name by which it has come to be known, the
Regolamento, to distinguish it from the Pontifical Rule of Benedict XIV.[25]

The document began with the controversial declaration that the society of missioners known as the Congregation of the Most Holy Redeemer owed its existence and continuing presence in the Kingdom of Naples to the royal decrees of 1752 and 1779, thereby refusing to admit its existence as a religious congregation in the Church, approved by Papal authority. The 'Rule' was divided into three sections: the giving of Missions, the spiritual norms to be followed by members of the Congregation, and finally, the government of the Congregation and the education and training of new members. In itself, it was quite an admirable document, demanding a very high standard of asceticism and spirituality. It left little to be desired either in its treatment of the missionary activity of the Congregation or in its form of government. There is nothing in it, with the exception of the opening declaration, which would not have received papal approval had it been presented in Rome as the rule of a new religious society. But it was flawed from the outset by the simple fact that it differed from the papally approved rule of Benedict XIV and that the alterations, acceptable in themselves, had a deeper significance. They represented a victory for Bourbon regalism over Papal authority in the Kingdom of Naples.

In the second section, dealing with the spiritual life of the members of the Congregation, the major change was the disappearance of the three vows of poverty, chastity and obedience. In their place, the *Regolamento* substituted oaths, since the King's Ministers were not prepared to tolerate religious vows. The formal vow of poverty disappeared and in its place there was an oath binding all the members to cede to their communities their income from Mass offerings, and the daily income granted to each member by the royal decree of 1752. But the members were permitted to retain the full ownership and use of their patrimonies. In a word, the community of goods and income, which Alphonsus had endeavoured to establish, disappeared, and in its place came a series of complicated decrees which only a Neapolitan lawyer could unravel, determining the use and disposal of personal property and money. More serious was the explicit declaration in paragraph fourteen of this section that each member was free to leave the Congregation if he wished to do so, while, on the other hand, the superior was granted authority to dismiss 'the disedifying, the disobedient, the inobservant and the incorrigible'. In the section on government there was a clear effort to increase the powers of the General Consultors and the Vicar at the expense of the Rector Major. The way was opened for the local bishop to have a part in the internal government of the local Redemptorist community. And finally, there was no mention of the holding of a General Chapter which, according to the Pontifical Rule, was to be convoked every nine years.[26]

The *Regolamento*, together with the royal decree imposing it on the members of the Congregation, was brought to Pagani from Naples by Father Gaspar Caione on Wednesday 8 March 1780. Alphonsus had been expecting the document ever since he had been informed in January that approval was imminent. He still had no idea what it contained, still less any suspicion that the Pontifical Rule had been recast and considerably altered in the process. He had tentatively planned for the community to renew their acceptance of the Rule on the approaching Good Friday. Since he had been more than usually unwell on the day that the dispatch arrived from Naples, Villani thought it wiser not to give him the packet until the following morning. That evening, however, the consultors decided to open the dispatch and examine the *Regolamento* for themselves. Tannoia, writing many years later after the traumatic experiences occasioned by the alterations to the Rule, is our main authority for the reaction in the community, and he had a thesis to prove. According to him there was general consternation among the consultors and the members of the community; they talked far into the night. To use Tannoia's own words 'the whole community was up in arms'. Next morning the text of the *Regolamento* was presented to Alphonsus. As he would have been unable to read the text for himself, it must have been explained to him. Tannoia paints a picture of his horrified reaction, bordering on hysteria. He reproached Villani bitterly, he blamed himself for his negligence, exclaimed that he had been deceived. He broke into tears, refused to eat, and was unable to sleep for several nights. Some members of the community feared that the strain would bring on a cerebral haemorrhage while others worried that he would not long survive the shock.[27]

When Tannoia wrote his account of Alphonsus' reaction to the *Regolamento* in the final section of his biography, a special papal commission had just declared that Alphonsus' conduct during the whole *Regolamento* controversy was not an obstacle to the cause of his canonisation, and that in the subsequent progress of the process, the matter was not to be re-opened. Under instructions from Blasucci, who was then Rector Major Tannoia had to be particularly careful in his account of events not to depart from the official line that Alphonsus had been deceived by his consultors and that he had nothing whatsoever to do with the changes introduced into the Rule of Benedict XIV.[28] Officially, Maione, and, to a lesser extent, Cimino, were cast in the role of villains and made bear the blame for capitulating to Bourbon regalism to the detriment of papal authority. There is no doubt that the *Regolamento* is mainly the work of Maione and Cimino in concert with Alphonsus' lawyers and the Cappellano Maggiore. But they were legitimately commissioned by Alphonsus and his consultors who had complete confidence in their competence and their integrity. From the precedent set in 1752 when Alphonsus, at the height of his powers, had made major concessions to the Bourbon government in order to obtain some measure of legal approval for the Congregation, they can not be faulted for their willingness to follow the same path in their own negotiations. It was precisely for this that they had been appointed. It may well be that they went too far in the concessions they had to make to Bourbon susceptibilities but it can be argued, at the same time, that they might not have been able to get away with making less. Mons. Testa was a powerful figure in royal circles and not easily deflected from his anti-Roman attitudes. Would Alphonsus himself, had he been capable of undertaking the negotiations, have been able to wrest any further concessions from the Court? It will all remain a matter of speculation, but the fact remains that the results of Maione and Cimino's efforts were to tear the Congregation asunder, bring it to the verge of total destruction and seriously to compromise Alphonsus' reputation with the Holy See.

– IV –

The immediate reaction to the *Regolamento* was one of total opposition, first of all from the community at Pagani and then right through the houses. The anger of the brethren which now manifested itself in their unlikely defence of the Rule of Benedict XIV was but a manifestation of the serious malaise which had been increasing for years and which was rooted in widespread dissatisfaction with the government of the Congregation. Many of the brethren believed that Alphonsus was in his dotage; orders and decisions emanating from him did not merit obedience since they were not his but those of one or other of the consultors. Villani attracted considerable criticism from all sides but the main opposition of the brethren now concentrated itself on Maione and Cimino who were considered to be the powers behind the throne, *les éminences grises* of the central government. Malicious tongues claimed — and Neapolitans yielded to none in this area — that Maione had been carried away by his appointment as consultor, that his plan, in any new arrangement, would be to enhance the position of the consultors at the expense of the Rector Major and that his ultimate objective was to secure that position for himself. Opposition, however, to the administration of the Congregation was at its most unrestrained among the Fathers of the Papal States, the *Statisti*, and was centred, once again, not so much on Alphonsus as on those around him, with Villani and Maione the main targets. Free to follow the Rule of Benedict XIV without any modifications, the *Statisti* prided themselves on being the authentic Redemptorists. Working in an altogether different climate from the oppressive atmosphere of the Bourbon Church, they wanted their independence as well as freedom to adapt their missionary techniques to the new environment. Neapolitans though they were — twenty years after the first foundation in Sant'Angelo à Cupolo, the Papal States had not attracted even one vocation to the Congregation — once they took up residence in the territory of the Pope, they adopted a superior attitude to their brethren in the Bourbon Kingdom and were less than understanding of the balancing act their confrères had to perform just to continue to exist. So, in the whole unsavoury story of the sufferings and defections caused by the *Regolamento*, it must be borne in mind that the document itself was not the sole cause of the dissensions which marked the final years of Alphonsus' life. But it was the occasion which sparked the explosion that had been building up for years. And the longer that anger had been contained the more destructive of harmony and brotherly charity was the final result.

In the unfolding saga of the *Regolamento*, from March 1780 onwards, the volume of letters, memoranda, petitions to the King, the Bourbon Court officials, to the Pope and the officials of the Congregation of Bishops and Regulars, as well as to influential figures in Naples, Rome and Benevento, grew to massive proportions. There were charges and counter-charges of deceit, lying, spying and the alteration of documents. The number of letters and petitions signed by Alphonsus which are still extant is considerable but how many of these he drew up himself, how many he dictated or inspired, or was even aware of their contents can, at best, only be surmised. He was more or less under the control of his advisers, who determined what course of action he should follow, and what letters he should sign. For a few years after 1780 he was to remain lucid and capable at least of following the main thread of events before his concentration lapsed but the full control and direction of affairs was clearly beyond him. With these reservations in mind we can follow the course of events.

Alphonsus' immediate reaction was to deprive Maione of his commission to negotiate in Naples. This he did with full legal formality, and appointed in his place Father Bartholomew Corrado to whom he entrusted a number of memoranda for the King, the marchese de Marco and the Cappellano Maggiore. He instructed Corrado to contradict the rumour spread by Maione in Naples that he was senile; he wanted it to be known that 'his head was still working, *mi aiuta ancora il cervello*'. At this stage, his letters, far from reflecting the hysterical outbursts described by Tannoia, were calm and reasonable. He admitted that there were several points of difficulty with the *Regolamento* and he agreed with the objections raised against it by the different members of the Congregation who had made representations to him. Each house was to discuss the matter, then elect two 'capable and edifying Fathers' to come to a general meeting in Pagani at a later date. Already, he assured them he had taken steps in Naples to secure alterations in the *Regolamento* as presented to them through Father Maione.[29] He went to considerable lengths to calm the Fathers in the Papal States. He exhorted Father Isidore Leggio, one of the dominant figures there, and the cause of much unpleasantness in the future, to remain faithful to the Rule of Benedict XIV but letting him know, at the same time, that certain concessions would have to be made in Naples to avoid challenging royal prerogatives. And the most important concession of all would have to be in the matter of the vows:

> We cannot secure everything that is in the Papal Rule; vows are simply out of the question. The King will not allow them. But we shall have an oath of obedience and this will be sufficient to maintain our way of life in internal matters.

Not every aspect of the changes proposed by Maione, however, were unacceptable to the *Statisti*; they were particularly pleased to see an attempt to curtail the authority of the Rector Major. But here Alphonsus rose at once to the defence of the Pontifical Rule:

> It is not true that the Rector Major can govern as he pleases. The Rule imposes many restrictions upon him . . . St Thomas states that

government in the hands of one man is more conducive to peace than in the hands of several. The reason is clear. Government by several persons facilitates the formation of cliques and cliques are the ruin of good government. If our six consultors were to have decisive votes we should soon have six parties.[30]

The opposition which the *Regolamento* had aroused and the personal abuse which was being heaped upon them, took Maione and Cimino by surprise. There were demands for their removal from office. They felt disowned and unwanted. Maione particularly felt himself an outcast. With great nobility of spirit Alphonsus opposed all efforts to depose him as a consultor; he came to his defence, crediting him with the best of intentions in what he had attempted to achieve. He invited him to return from Naples to whatever house he wished:

> Rest assured that for my part I love you as before and I shall show you this in practice. You will remain a consultor as you have been and you will give your opinion in all important matters concerning the Congregation. As regards your good name, leave that to me. My constant care will be to defend it before all and sundry, both confrères and strangers.[31]

But Maione was not going to capitulate so easily. Familiar with the way of the Court and still in possession of a number of blank sheets with Alphonsus' signature appended, he was already negotiating with the Cappellano Maggiore and even with the King himself for a royal decree putting an end to further discussion and formally imposing the *Regolamento*. Those who refused to accept were to be summarily expelled.

'He wishes,' declared Alphonsus, 'to make me the executioner of my own brethren.' Besides the signed pages Maione was also adequately supplied with funds from one of his admirers in Naples, which he used to good advantage to bribe his way into circles where he otherwise might have had difficulty in securing entry. His continuing presence in Naples posed a serious threat to Alphonsus and his efforts to secure alterations in the text of the *Regolamento* with the result that Alphonsus found himself having recourse to similar tactics to those being used against him. He informed his representatives in Naples that they were at liberty to remind those whose patronage they sought that Alphonsus would not be found lacking in generosity either.[32]

With the communities in the Kingdom of Naples in turmoil and the Fathers in the Papal States sensing a golden opportunity of asserting their independence, hopes for a solution to the problems were at first centred on the meeting to be held in Pagani in the middle of May, for which the Cappellano Maggiore had granted permission. But as the time drew near it it became clear that the proposed assembly would only aggravate the situation. Was the meeting to be a General Chapter as envisaged in the Rule of Benedict XIV? If so, the membership would be quite different from the proposed two delegates from each house. And if it was not to be regarded as a General Chapter, of which there was no mention in the *Regolamento*, what authority did it possess? It had been convened in the first place to allow the members of the communities to make known their reaction to the changes in the Pontifical Rule and to deal with the objection that it was being undemocratically imposed upon them. Since then it had come to be seen as a forum where the grievances against the Pagani administration could find expression and where demands could be made for the removal of the group around Alphonsus, and specifically of Maione and Cimino. The *Statisti*, shrewdly enough, were reluctant to participate lest they should become embroiled in purely Neapolitan quarrels. Some of the members of the communities in the Kingdom were equally opposed to the whole idea. Tannoia, for example, refused to accept his election as one of the representatives from Deliceto, and a Father in Pagani refused to take part in the assembly.

But the most ominous aspect of the whole situation was the fact that De Paola and his Procurator Leggio lost no time in bringing the whole affair to the notice of the Holy See. In the early months of 1780 they had stolen a march on their Neapolitan brethren by presenting their own very coloured version of events to the officials of the Congregation of Bishops and Regulars. In his representations to the Holy See De Paola did not confine himself to the problem of the *Regolamento*; he ranged widely over all the grievances of the Fathers in the Papal States. He declared that the election of Alphonsus as Rector Major for life in 1762 and its confirmation by the Chapter of 1764 were invalid, that the group of consultors around him in Pagani constituted an administration opposed to ministry in the Papal States, that they were unwilling, for their own selfish ends, to hold a General Chapter as laid down by Benedict XIV where these problems could be discussed, and that, finally, a new 'Rule' was being concocted and imposed upon them under fearful threats by Alphonsus. The obvious solution, he suggested, was to grant independence to the houses in the Papal States. Hard on the heels of De Paola's intervention came a memorial from Leggio — they concerted their efforts cleverly — in which he shamefully falsified the contents of a personal letter he had received from Alphonsus to give a false account of what was taking place in Naples. Leggio had embarked on his campaign of deceitful distortion which has earned him even greater opprobrium than the unfortunate Maione. Thus within a few months of the appearance of the *Regolamento* in Naples, what had begun as an internal Redemptorist problem, and should have been kept so, had been enlarged to involve the Holy See. Then, to make matters worse, a long memorial from Tannoia in Deliceto reached the Congregation of Bishops and Regulars confirming their initial reactions. Tannoia was irrationally opposed to the *Regolamento* and to its two principal instigators, Cimino and Maione; Cimino, in fact, was his personal *bête noire*, responsible, he believed, for leading Alphonsus into the whole *Regolamento* debacle. Misinformed, he further believed that Maione was in fact en route to Rome to secure Papal approbation for the changes in the Rule. With more passion and enthusiasm

than good sense he dashed off his letter to the Prefect of the Sacred
Congregation warning him to be on his guard against a request to be presented
to him by Maione on behalf of Alphonsus — Maione was still using the
signed blank pages. Tannoia's intervention, coming as it did from Naples
and containing a withering attack on the *pasticcio* (muddle) of the *Regolamento*
which had reduced what was once a flourishing religious Congregation
approved by the Pope to something less than a lay fraternity, convinced the
Cardinal Prefect that the matter was more serious than he had at first
believed and that definite action would have to be taken. Early in June the
matter was brought to the personal attention of Pope Pius VI himself and
the way was thus opened for years of painful misunderstanding, deceit and
great suffering.[33]

– V –

While prejudice against Alphonsus and his companions in Naples was
gradually building up in Rome, the Pagani consultation, for that was what
Alphonsus had in mind, got under way in the middle of May 1780. There
were sixteen delegates not counting Alphonsus and his consultors, Villani,
Mazzini, Cimino, Maione, Caione and another Liguori, no relation of
Alphonsus. Not all the delegates were to be present for the whole duration
of the meeting which lasted until the end of June. Alphonsus took very
little part in the sessions since he was unable to follow what was being said,
though he made two points clear, that he was unaware of the contents of
the *Regolamento* until it was placed in his hands and that he wished above all
to preserve the unity of the Congregation, come what may.[34] A contemporary account describes the sessions as 'tumultuous'; all the pent-up
dissatisfaction with the government of the Congregation immediately
surfaced. The consultors in particular and at times even Alphonsus himself
came in for considerable criticism. He was accused of acting with excessive
secrecy and of not listening to others. One delegate shouted at him that he
had founded the Congregation and had now destroyed it. 'I wonder,' he
concluded, 'can God forgive you this sin.' There were demands for the
whole administration to be removed from office.[35]

The Pagani gathering decided to open negotiations immediately with
the Cappellano Maggiore for alterations in some ten points in the text of
the *Regolamento*, the most sensitive being the question of vows, the alterations
in the practice of poverty and the lack of a vow of perseverance. For this
purpose two Fathers, Bartolomeo Corrado and Fabio de Buonapane, who had
no connection with the existing group of consultors or with the negotiations
for the *Regolamento*, were chosen. They had to be more or less compelled to
accept the commission. They set off for Naples towards the end of May
only to find that the Cappellano Maggiore and his officials were in no
humour to contemplate even the slightest concessions. For nearly three
weeks Corrado and Bonapane attempted to argue their case but without
success. They could sense the presence of Cimino and the lawyer Celano

behind the scenes, stiffening the resistance of the Cappellano Maggiore. In the second half of June they returned to Pagani with nothing to show for their exertions. There they found the assembly still in session though a few delegates had lost patience and had already departed. With a flurry of activity the delegates of the houses in the Kingdom of Naples proceeded to accept the *Regolamento* conditionally, *provided it was approved by the Holy See*.[36] This conditional acceptance was made verbally and not in writing or formally signed lest the Cappellano Maggiore would exact retribution. The assembly's next step was totally illegal. Alphonsus and his six consultors resigned their offices to allow the delegates to make a new beginning, Alphonsus being the only one to do so in writing. The delegates from the Papal States refused to vote or were not allowed to do so under the pretext that they would have needed royal authorisation. The remaining handful of delegates — only six according to one account — then proceeded to re-elect Alphonsus as Rector Major and to give him six consultors, Corrado, Tannoia, Blasucci, De Meo, Pavone and the only survivor from the previous group, Villani. Corrado, however, replaced him as Vicar General. It is difficult to imagine how the members of the assembly, all intelligent men and well versed in legal affairs, could have turned what was originally intended as nothing more than a consultative meeting, even though the delegates were expected to possess plenipotentiary powers, into an elective chapter which was invalid according to the Rule of Benedict XIV and for which there was no juridical basis in the new *Regolamento*. It was only one example of the chaos into which the *Regolamento* had plunged the whole Congregation.[37]

The Pagani assembly, far from securing a united response to the problem, caused by the *Regolamento*, only exacerbated the deep divisions already existing; the two sections of the Congregation, the four communities in the Kingdom and those in the Papal states were now virtually two distinct entities, mutually antagonistic. For their part Alphonsus and his new consultors set themselves immediately to secure the necessary modifications in the text of the *Regolamento*. It was to be a tiresome task entailing months of patient negotiations and necessitating interminable letters and interviews to muster the support of influential figures in the Bourbon administration. But this was nothing new, it had been the pattern of the Congregation's existence ever since its inception. De Paola and his entourage, on the other hand, returned home with a whole arsenal of new arguments against the Pagani administration, beginning with the claim that the Pagani elections were invalid and that Alphonsus was no longer the legitimate Rector Major. The first indications of the attitude of the Holy See went in favour of De Paola and Leggio. In response to representations which De Paola had made before going to Pagani, the Congregation of Bishops and Regulars informed the houses in the Papal States on 12 June, while the Pagani assembly was still in session, that they were not to accept the *Regolamento* but were to continue to follow the papally approved Rule of Benedict XIV. Once back in residence in Frosinone De Paola decided to press home his advantage which he did to good effect, ably assisted by his procurator Leggio, who by this time appears to have been driven by a pathological dislike, if not hatred, of Alphonsus and everything connected with his Neapolitan confrères; he referred to them insultingly as 'Alphonsus and his satraps'.[38] Orchestrated by De Paola, letters poured in to the Sacred Congregation from the Papal houses. Faced with an increasingly disputed and unharmonious situation, the Congregation decided to set in train a formal investigation under the presidency of Cardinal Tammaso Maria Ghilini as *relator*. The process then followed the accepted canonical routine of assembling all the relevant evidence. Rome requested the opinions of the two bishops of the dioceses in the Papal States where the Redemptorist houses were situated as well as a full report from the acting nuncio in Naples. As an interim measure but indicative of the way the wind was blowing, Rome took the immediate step of exempting the houses in the Papal States from the jurisdiction of the Rector Major and his consultors in Pagani.

De Paola and Leggio were anxious for a speedy outcome of the investigation as more likely to benefit their own plans, while Alphonsus and his advisers in Naples were content to play for time. Their hope was that Naples would agree to certain modifications in the *Regolamento* which Rome would then approve for the whole Congregation, thereby averting a division of the Congregation into two separate entities with two different Rules. But Alphonsus and his consultors failed totally to clarify their position with the Roman authorities; they were no match for Leggio who was on the spot and was as skilled in the ways of Roman diplomacy as Alphonsus was in his dealings with the Court in Naples. Alphonsus laboured under the serious disadvantage that letters from Naples took a long while to reach Rome and were subject to inspection by the Bourbon customs at the point of exit, hence the necessity for considerable caution and a certain amount of vagueness in Alphonsus' representations to the Holy See. Moreover, de Paola and Leggio played their cards very close to their chests, with the result that their intentions were never fully known in Pagani and could not easily be counteracted. In response to instructions from Rome the papal representative in Naples requested a full account from Alphonsus of everything that had taken place but neither of them appears to have treated the matter as urgent, thus allowing De Paola to press home his advantage in Rome. A letter from Alphonsus got through to Cardinal Carraciolo towards the end of August, promising to send two representatives to Rome at a later date to explain the position, and begging him at the same time to do everything in his power not to allow the Congregation to be divided into two distinct units. 'Some of my sons are waging war on me' he complained in sorrow, 'at my age, I did not expect such a gift from them.'[39] In point of fact he was gradually losing heart for the struggle; the effort to follow and counteract the various manoeuvres was more and more beyond him. That same month he summoned Blasucci back from Sicily and virtually handed over full responsibility for the future conduct of affairs to him, thus bypassing his consultors:

Will your Reverence examine the danger we are in and take whatever steps seem best to you. Otherwise I am afraid that everything will collapse. You must return here and then visit every one of the houses.

I am nothing more than a poor old decrepit man. I can hardly breathe and it is getting more difficult every day. It is essential to get to the King because it is the Cappellano Maggiore who has ruined us. I have done everything in my power to get him to desist from protecting the *Regolamento* drawn up by Maione, but without success. All I can say is *fiat voluntas tua*.[40]

While Alphonsus was requesting the Holy See not to take any action in the matter until his two representatives and the report of the Naples nunciature reached Rome, Leggio pressed relentlessly on. With scant regard for truth and with no scruple about the interpretation he gave to events, he presented a memorial to the Congregation of Bishops and Regulars in September 1780 which galvanised the Pope into action. In it he claimed that Alphonsus had fully examined the draft of the *Regolamento* and that it had been accepted by the Neapolitans. He omitted to mention that it had been accepted only conditionally and as the lesser of two evils. Since the superiors in the Kingdom were illegitimate, the houses in the Papal States were now leaderless, and so he petitioned the Pope to appoint a President for the houses in the Papal States who would then legitimately summon a General Chapter to make provision for the future.[41] The Holy See acted with unusual haste. Ignoring Alphonsus' plea for a delay in coming to a decision, Pope Pius VI took immediate action. By decree of 22 September 1780, he appointed Father De Paola President of the Redemptorist Houses in the Papal States, declaring at the same time that those houses in Naples which had accepted the *Regolamento* had 'ceased to be members of the Congregation and no longer enjoyed the favours and privileges granted to the Congregation by the Holy See.'[42] Two days later Fathers Tannoia and Gallo arrived from Pagani to put their side of the problem to the Roman authorities. But too late; the Pope's decision had been made and could not be reversed.

Leggio crowned his triumph with a sickening display of hypocrisy. He received Tannoia and Gallo with all possible show of friendliness. He protested that he had done everything possible to make clear to the Congregation of Bishops and Regulars and to the Holy Father himself, Alphonsus' total innocence in the whole affair. But in vain. The very mention of Alphonsus' name, according to Leggio, was displeasing to the Holy Father. At the same time he was careful not to allow the two envoys from Pagani out of his sight. He insisted on accompanying them to the officials of the Congregation who confirmed, as they were expected to, that there was no way the decision of the Holy Father could be reversed. Brutally, the Secretary of the Congregation informed Tannoia that Alphonsus was now 'cut off from the Congregation'. Leggio continually protested to Tannoia his love and respect for Alphonsus until one day, losing his temper in the heat of an argument, the mask slipped and he declared that Alphonsus by his conduct 'had gambled away the honours of the altar.'⁴³

Tannoia and Gallo arrived back in Pagani on 5 October. The news of the Holy See's decision was a bitter and totally unexpected blow. It amounted to the virtual canonical suppression of the Congregation in the Kingdom of Naples, even if this had not been directly intended. Not for one moment had the Neapolitans imagined that the Holy See would take such drastic action and with such haste, even before the report from the *chargé d'affaires* at the nunciature had arrived and before the Neapolitan delegates could be heard. The one alleviating feature of the situation however was that the decision was not irrevocable — it was *usque ad exitum causae* — that is, while the Holy See was building up a complete dossier on the situation under the direction of Cardinal Ghilini.⁴⁴ Villani was careful to break the news gently to Alphonsus, choosing the morning time when he was preparing to assist at Mass and receive Holy Communion, as the appropriate moment. Alphonsus received the news serenely. 'I only want what God wants. Provided I do not lose the grace of God nothing matters. If this is what the Pope decided, blessed be God.'⁴⁵ After assisting at Mass and communicating he went for his usual outing in the carriage with Alessio. In the course of the journey the reality of what had been decided came home to him and he became extremely agitated. He was the cause of it all; the Lord had destroyed the Congregation on account of his sins. There was no hope for his eternal salvation. Alessio cut short the outing and brought the old man home. Inside the monastery, Alphonsus broke into hysterical tears, shouting at the top of his voice that he was on the verge of despair. Villani and Mazzini were quickly on the scene to bring him to his room where they succeeded in calming him. He recovered control of himself gradually as he prayed aloud to Our Lady *'aiutame, Mamma mia: Gesù mio speranza mia. Non confundar in aeternum.'*⁴⁶

Two days after learning of the Papal decision, Alphonsus dictated a letter to De Paola; the sentiments are his though the wording is that of the secretary:

> Thanks be to God my head is now clear. I am pleased that the Fathers in the Papal States are now directly under the Holy Father and that your Reverence has been named as acting superior. Since it was the will of the Pope, you had to accept, so all is well.
>
> The Holy Father, no doubt, blames me for having accepted the royal *Regolamento*. If you get an opportunity through some friend, let him know that we were in danger of losing everything if we had not accepted. Then the Pope would certainly not condemn me.
>
> At a later date when the time is appropriate I hope to explain everything to him and to ask him for the favour which I hope for. I have not forgotten the affection which he has shown me, unworthy though I am. I hope to live and to die as a faithful servant of the Holy Father and of the Church. I beg you to find someone to plead my cause with the Pope. For the moment I am unable to write to him and

in the midst of all the difficulties in which I now find myself I can only resign myself to the Will of God.

Please do not omit to pray for me during Mass that I may die peacefully, for my end is very near. I have loved everyone of you very much. The Lord has willed this division. May His Holy Will be done.[47]

Pointedly he concluded his letter, not with his usual blessing, but by declaring that now it was for the Holy Father to bless them.

About two weeks later the long awaited report of Monsignor Severino Servanti, the papal *chargé d'affaires* in Naples, reached the Roman authorities. Servanti gave a full account of everything that had taken place from the foundation of the Congregation to the *Regolamento* and the holding of the Pagani assembly from May to June. In a telling phrase, he left it to the wisdom of the Cardinals to discern the motives behind the request of De Paola and Leggio for independence. For his part he implored the understanding of the Congregation of Bishops and Regulars on behalf of the Redemptorists to enable them to continue their work as one united religious group for the salvation of souls. If only Rome had delayed taking action until first Tannoia and Gallo, and then Servanti, had been able to explain the Neapolitan point of view, the division of the Congregation would probably never have taken place and Alphonsus would have been spared the considerable suffering of the final years of his life. But De Paola and Leggio were on the spot and made full use of their advantageous position.

– VI –

Alphonsus was to remain nominal superior of the Congregation for the next two years until he formally handed over all authority to Villani as Vicar General in 1783. At the same time he was fully aware of his dwindling influence over affairs, 'They pay no attention to me,' he complained in January 1781.[48] The history of events over these final two years is one of intrigue and deceit, of misunderstanding and suffering which makes fiction pale into normality. The decline of the Congregation in Naples after the *Regolamento* was immediately evident. A large number of priests and students left, some for the Papal States, principally Benevento, to continue their religious lives and missionary activity, others to return home to their families. From numbering nearly 120, the Congregation in Naples dwindled to just sixty; within a few months of the Papal decision of September 1780 there were no students left in the Naples section of the Congregation. For a while Alphonsus himself wrestled with his conscience as to whether he too was not under an obligation to go to Benevento where he could continue to live under the Papal rule. Only with difficulty was he dissuaded from this course on the plea that his departure would entail the total collapse of the missionary activity of his Fathers in the Kingdom, to the serious detriment of the salvation of souls.

For their part, the Fathers in Naples made every effort to prevent the widening of the breach between themselves and the Fathers in the Papal

States. A meeting was summoned for Benevento under the chairmanship of Cardinal Banditi and Mons. Bergamo of Gaeta, with a view to maintaining a united front in face of the mounting problems. But it came to nothing because De Paola refused to be present.[49] With Leggio, he was now negotiating in Rome for the appointment of a separate Rector Major in the Papal States, for which, of course, he would be the sole candidate. And at the very same time he was assuring Alphonsus in a personal letter that the Holy Father was prepared to confirm him as Rector Major of the houses, both in the Kingdom and in the Papal States, provided he could get a clear picture of what had taken place. There was considerable nobility in Alphonsus' reply:

> The Pope lets me hope that he will restore to me the office of Rector Major. This is not what I am troubled about. The decision that has hurt me is the withdrawal of the missionary faculties, without which we can do little for souls.[50]

However, taking De Paola at his word, Alphonsus determined to give the Holy Father a full account of the events leading to the Regolamento. Despite the prohibition to communicate with Rome without explicit royal permission, Alphonsus despatched his lengthy memorial directly to Pius VI in December 1780; it was the second attempt he had made to put his side of the story to the Roman authorities.[51] In his innocence he was directing his correspondence with the Roman authorities through De Paola, which meant in effect through Leggio, who immediately set about counteracting it. Too late Alphonsus and his advisers became aware of what Leggio was up to, and they immediately took steps to circumvent his activity. In February 1781, when the damage had already been done, they appointed a secular priest, Don Nicholas Matias Rossi to represent them with the Roman authorities, which brought their distrust of Leggio right out into the open. Alphonsus wrote first to Leggio begging him to desist from his efforts to frustrate the reunion of the two sections of the Congregation:

> I beg you, Father, to remember that if you continue to work for division among us and if you gain your purpose, I cannot imagine how you will ever enjoy one moment's peace for the rest of your life. The Congregation will be divided and it will not be possible to remedy the situation.[52]

After this direct appeal to the mischief-maker-in-chief, Alphonsus wrote to De Paola:

> Yes, it is true that I have engaged a procurator and a lawyer to attend to our interests in Rome. . . . I have done this solely for the purpose of proving to the Sacred Congregation of Bishops and Regulars and to the Holy Father that the *Regolamento* with its present modifications is in no way contrary in substance to the Rule of Benedict XIV. In all our dealings with the court of Naples we never had the slightest intention of deviating from the decisions delivered on this point by

the Sacred Congregation and the Holy Father himself. We have engaged our own Procurator because Father Leggio is continually intriguing with the Sacred Congregation and the Pope, as we know he is doing at this actual moment. If we had our own representative sooner, things would not have taken the turn they did. My dear Father Francesco, if you are in earnest about the union of the Congregation as you have so often expressed, then remove Father Leggio from Rome and let us sit down together to achieve reunion which is essential for the survival of the Congregation . . .

And he concluded the letter with a final appeal to De Paola's better instincts, 'If you truly love the Congregation and want to see it reunited, as I hope you do, recall Father Leggio and put an end to all the trouble he is causing.'[53]

While De Paola and Leggio were working feverishly in Rome for immediate action from the Roman authorities, Alphonsus and his consultors were patiently implementing a carefully conceived plan of action. Their efforts were concentrated on securing the emendation of the *Regolamento* to make it at least tolerable for those who had conscientious objections to it. All during the autumn months of 1780 the Pagani administration worked tirelessly through their agents and friends in Naples. In February of the following year 1781 their efforts were successful when a Royal Decree permitted the members of the Congregation to take an oath of poverty and of the common life, together with an oath of perseverance in the Congregation. Three of the most important demands of Alphonsus had thus been met to the great delight of the Neapolitan brethren; the community at Deliceto celebrated the news with a fireworks display. They believed that what had been obtained was little less than miraculous, due entirely to the intercession of the Madonna. There still remained, however, the question of vows, on which the office of the Cappellano Maggiore absolutely refused to make concessions. But Alphonsus was not unduly worried on this score. He was convinced that this point could be resolved satisfactorily since he was able to quote an important historical precedent. Less than a hundred years before, Pope Innocent XI, in somewhat similar circumstances, had allowed the Josephite Fathers to substitute oaths for the three vows of religion. Alphonsus was certain that Pius VI would follow this precedent thus depriving the *Statisti* of any pretext for a schism in the Congregation.[54] Convinced that nothing now stood in the way of the reunion of the two sections of the Congregation, and full of optimism, Alphonsus and his advisers instructed their procurator, Don Nicholas Rossi, to inform Cardinal Ghilini of the progress they had made with the Bourbon authorities. But their expectations were to be disappointed. De Paola and Leggio now revealed what had been their real intention all along. They were not prepared to agree to the reunion of the Congregation no matter what concessions Alphonsus succeeded in extorting from the Bourbon Court. Their goal was the independence of the Congregation in the Papal states and they were prepared to go to any lengths with the Roman authorities to secure it.[55]

While De Paola and Leggio were proving themselves less than co-operative in Rome, a further complication arose in Naples. Baron Sarnelli had reactivated his court case against the Redemptorists, adding to his accusations that the missioners of the Most Holy Redeemer were now refusing to accept the Rule approved by the court authorities — a further proof, if one were needed, of their opposition to royal decisions. To ward off any further investigation on the part of the Court and convinced that the modifications agreed to by the King had virtually removed any essential difference between the rule of Benedict XIV and the *Regolamento*, a circular, with Alphonsus' name appended, in May 1781 instructed the four communities in the Kingdom of Naples to adopt the *Regolamento*. In June 1781 the ceremony took place in the community at Pagani, with Alphonsus the first to pronounce his acceptance which he did, in very precise terms, duly recorded and verified by the Public Notary. It was a subtle formula which appeared to accept the *Regolamento* but at the same time was more a renewal of the vows of Benedict XIV than anything else.

> I bind myself to observe the contents of the Rules or *Regolamento*, now and in perpetuity and I swear to God to observe chastity, obedience and poverty, the common life and I bind myself to persevere . . . [56]

Confident that now all would be well Alphonsus and his advisers designated his Vicar Father Corrado together with Father De Leo to go to Rome to present a full account of everything that had taken place and to secure the reunion of the two sections of the Congregation.

The *Regolamento* saga now entered its final and most distressing chapter. Corrado and De Leo arrived in Rome early in June 1781; they set to work with a will. Long memorials, historical and canonical, defended Alphonsus and his actions in the whole matter. They claimed that everything contained in the Rule of Benedict XIV, with a few minor exceptions, was now included in the three royal decrees of August 1779, the *Regolamento* of March 1780 and the modifications secured in February 1781. In other words, Alphonsus had outfoxed the Court and won a famous victory over the Regalism of the Bourbon Court and the Cappellano Maggiore.[57] They were hardly able to conceal their triumphant expectations. But the two Neapolitans were no match for Leggio who countered their every move and succeeded in negativing their pleas for sympathetic understanding. While the Neapolitans wore their hearts on their sleeves and made the contents of their representations public, De Paola and Leggio kept their arguments to themselves with the result that Corrado and De Leo found themselves at a loss as to what arguments they should attempt to refute.[58] Leggio, on the other hand, knew precisely where to strike.

In July 1781 Leggio presented a memorial to the Holy See in which he demolished the Neapolitan submissions one by one.[59] It was a forceful document, logical and uncompromising. He began by asserting that the official version of what had taken place in Naples, namely that Alphonsus, due to his old age had been deceived by his advisers and that they had taken advantage of his infirmities, was false. The two decrees of 1752 and August 1779 provided the Congregation with every legal right needed to exist. He held, moreover, that these decrees amounted to the virtual *exequatur* of the Rule of Benedict XIV. The Congregation could elect its superiors, receive and train novices and students, dismiss the unsuitable. There was no necessity, he insisted, to take any further steps. To claim that after August 1779 the Congregation was still in danger of suppression was untrue, *poca sincera*. And it was also untrue to claim that Alphonsus entrusted the emendation of the Rule to just one individual who was personally responsible for the new *Regolamento*; he could not be exonerated from complicity with Cimino and Maione. Leggio quoted — out of context — from a letter of Alphonsus to himself of the previous August, in which Alphonsus admitted that he was ready to alter certain aspects of the Rule of Benedict XIV in order not to offend the King. Leggio's point was clear, Alphonsus knew what was at stake, and was ready to cede even on the point of vows. He could have forbidden any further negotiations along these lines had he wished but he had not done so. Instead, he agreed to the changes and insisted that all should accept them, even those in the Papal States. Leggio alleged that students who had left Naples to follow the Pontifical Rule in the Papal States had been threatened that when reunion eventually took place they would be made to pay for their infidelity. And he concluded by playing on Rome's detestation of regalism by branding the Neapolitan representative, De Leo, as a regalist, pure and simple, and Alphonsus' other advisers as macchiavellian.

From the point of view of the *Statisti*, Leggio's presentation was a masterpiece both of timing and argumentation. Just when it appeared that Alphonsus' position was beginning to be considered sympathetically and when the Holy See might have been disposed to make some concessions, Leggio's intervention proved decisive. A further piece of news proved disastrous for the Neapolitan case and hastened the final outcome. Word arrived in Rome that the houses in the Kingdom had formally accepted the *Regolamento*. Not merely had Alphonsus imposed the *Regolamento* but he had given those who did not wish to accept it forty days from 21 June to do so; if they refused they were *ipso facto* expelled from the Congregation and were no longer to be considered members. This provided just the opening De Paola needed. Before the Neapolitan emissaries could give an explanation of the background to this piece of information, Leggio rushed a new petition to the Congregation of Bishops and Regulars requesting an immediate decision to prevent a similar disaster befalling the houses in the Papal States, not that there was the slightest danger of this happening. But it was a shrewd scare tactic. Within a few days, on 24 August, Pius VI gave his reply. The decision of 22 September of the previous year was to remain in force and no further recourse to Rome was to be permitted. The matter was closed.[60] Victory lay with De Paola and Leggio and the *de facto* division of the Congregation into two sections was sanctioned by the Holy See. A few days later, having been rebuffed for weeks, due one suspects to the machinations of Leggio, Father De Leo succeeded in securing an audience of Pius VI. But it brought no consolation for the Fathers in Naples. The Pope declared that reasons of state, together with other considerations, prevented any change in the papal position. The final blow fell a few months later when a reply from the Holy See to a query from the bishop of Lettere outside Naples, maliciously requested by none other than Cimino, clarified the canonical positions of the Fathers who had accepted the *Regolamento*. As regards the privileges and canonical faculties the Fathers had received as members of the Congregation, they were now as if they had never received them. To use these faculties in their ministry as if they still possessed them would be to incur the appropriate canonical penalties. They were to look to their consciences in the matter.[61]

In Pagani, Alphonsus' health and mental alertness continued to decline. Each succeeding decision from Rome, together with the failure of all his representations, brought him increased sorrow. He became delirious at times, protesting that they were all still living by the Rule of Benedict XIV and so they must all still be members of the Congregation. No word of complaint or rebellion was heard to pass his lips; all he did was to resign himself to the will of God in repeated prayer.[62] Not everybody was as reticent in their judgment of the situation. From Rome, one of his ex-novices from Ciorani, Father Emilio Pacifici, who had secured a position in the Papal administration, wrote to him in the autumn of 1781 to console him in his distress at what had happened to his Congregation. His verdict was simple. He wrote: 'In plain language all that has happened is that your Reverence has lost four houses and four scoundrels [meaning, clearly, Cimino, Maione, de Paola and Leggio]. As for the houses, the Lord will provide; as for the scoundrels there are enough of them already in the world, God knows.'[63] Far from allowing himself the satisfaction of sharing these sentiments, Alphonsus reached heroic heights of generosity in his relations with those who in one way or another were responsible for the disaster which had befallen the Congregation. News of the success of the ministry of the Fathers in the Papal States and the extension of their apostolate beyond Rome to Gubbio and Spello in 'Sabine territory', as he called it, gave him as much delight as if it had been due to his own efforts. He was eager to hear every detail of their successes and pained when they appeared to ignore him and his position as Rector Major. The possibility of new foundations at Foligno and Gubbio and even Rome itself filled him with enthusiasm. Reports of fifteen and twenty novices was a source of special consolation because 'you will need all the members you can get to cope with the missions in these new foundations'. There was never a word of bitterness in anything he wrote, never the slightest recrimination. He seemed to live in a world far removed from the intrigues and dissensions all around him:

> Pray for me and for my companions that we may devote ourselves totally to the service of Jesus Christ. And pray that I may die a good death since it is now very near. And I pray that the Lord will make you grow in his love and that he will send you more foundations and more companions.

His special interest was still in the preaching of missions and he urged De Paola to be faithful to the system and the sermons which had proved so effective in the Kingdom. He recommended the preaching of the eternal truths and the sermon on prayer — 'I wrote a book for this very purpose' he recalled. And inevitably the Madonna was mentioned, 'make sure you preach on Our Lady in every mission.' His last letter to De Paola was in June 1782, clearly dictated by him, as is evident from the nature of the letter with its single-line staccato sentences, each making its own point:

> I thank your Reverence and your companions for remembering me in you prayers. And I, for my part, pray for you too.
>
> I thank you sincerely for directing that each of you will offer Mass for me on my death.
>
> Write to me whenever you can because your letters are a great consolation to me.
>
> I thank God that you make so much progress while I am coming to the end of my life humiliated. It is a sign, all the same, that God wishes to pardon my sins.[64]

And so the litany continued as he poured out his affection for those who had successfully separated themselves from him to go their own way and caused him so much suffering in the process. But the ways of Providence are mysterious. Were it not for the success of De Paola's efforts and the foundation he was to establish in Rome the following year, 1783, that restless hermit from Moravia, the future St Clement Mary Hofbauer, who was to be responsible for the spread of the Congregation throughout Europe and North America, would never have joined the Congregation of the Most Holy Redeemer.[65]

During 1782 relations between the two sections of the Congregation improved considerably, due in no small degree to the generous manner in which De Paola reciprocated Alphonsus' conciliatory spirit. He insisted, for example, that there should be a portrait of Alphonsus, 'their Founder and Father' in all the houses of the Papal States. He directed that a special Ave should be recited in each community at Night Prayer for the 'grace of a holy death for Monsignore Liguori'. One great sorrow, however, remained to torment Alphonsus, namely, the fact that the Holy Father was still displeased with him over the whole question of the *Regolamento*. 'For two years now, 'he wrote to one of the Cardinals in Rome, 'I have been greatly disturbed by the fact that, unwittingly, I appear to have offended the Holy Father.' He explained once more the difficult situation in which he found himself and the concessions he was forced to make to the Bourbon Court. 'I did not for a moment imagine that by so doing I would offend the Holy See, whose privileges I have always defended. On the contrary I felt that what I was doing was consonant with papal policy as outlined in a letter to me from Benedict XIV in 1755'. And then he made his appeal to the Cardinal:

> I wish before I die to obtain the forgiveness of the Holy Father for my mistake so that I die in peace. I hope to obtain this favour through the

good offices of your Eminence. And I ask for this forgiveness not only for myself but for my brothers in religion as well. I have been consoled to learn that your Eminence has, in your great kindness, expressed your support for me.

Included with this letter was a personal letter to the Holy Father which Alphonsus asked the Cardinal to present for him.[66]

The situation in Naples, meanwhile, began to improve gradually due to the fact that Mons. Testa, the Cappellano Maggiore, died in April 1782 to be succeeded by the gentle Benedictine, Isidoro Sanchez de Luna, archbishop of Salerno, a long-time admirer of Alphonsus and his missioners. Moreover, a considerable number of bishops rallied to the support of the Congregation. Living under the tensions created by Bourbon interference in Church affairs, they were able to appreciate better than Rome the constraints which had determined Alphonsus' course of action as regards the *Regolamento*.

The restraints placed upon the missionary activity of the Redemptorist missionaries by the Roman decisions had serious consequences for their dioceses, with the result, that one by one, they made known to the nuncio in Naples and directly to the Roman authorities themselves their dissatisfaction with the Pope's reaction. A chorus of protests came from the bishops of Capua, Amalfi, Matera, Conza, Salerno, Nola, Lacedogna, Bisaccia, Nusco, St Angelo dei Lombardi, and Bovino until the Holy See was forced to take notice. In April 1783 Rome restored all the privileges and missionary faculties to the Fathers of the Kingdom. In addition, the novitiate was re-opened in Ciorani and candidates were once again presenting themselves for admission. To crown the good news, the Sarnelli case finally collapsed and a court declaration of April 1783 put an end to the vexatious litigation of twenty years.

But the strain of the *Regolamento* had taken its toll. Alphonsus and his consultors in Pagani realised that he could no longer continue as Rector Major. The process of resigning the office and electing a successor was a complicated one in Naples at any time, but more so now than ever, due to the fact that the *Regolamento* had not catered for this eventuality.

The first step was to secure permission from the King for holding an assembly, which was obtained towards the end of 1782. Alphonsus waited until the following June before convoking the meeting for Ciorani at the end of July. There followed the inevitable dissensions which seemed to characterise every election in Naples. Ciorani's first effort to elect delegates was declared invalid. Further efforts failed to secure a valid election with the result that the community forfeited their right to be represented at the assembly held in their own house. A few days after formally convoking the Chapter, Alphonsus and his advisers decided to annul the whole proceedings since the election of delegates had given rise to such divisions among the brethren. Then under pressure from the various communities, this annulment was rescinded and the delegates finally met in Ciorani on 4 August 1783.

Alphonsus remained at Pagani and took no part in the assembly. He nominated Villani as President and delegated all his authority as Rector

Major to him, while the Chapter itself proceeded to elect Blasucci as its secretary. All the old faces re-appeared at the meeting, Mazzini, Tannoia, De Meo. The main business of the meeting was to choose a co-adjutor with right of succession to Alphonsus who wished to resign from all involvement in affairs and whose declining health was expected to lead to his death at any moment. In a strange reversal of normal procedure the Chapter first elected the Rector Major's six assistants, on 8 August, with the intention of electing Alphonsus' successor on the eve of the feast of the Assumption and celebrating his election on the feast itself. But matters did not go smoothly; after ten scrutinies no candidate emerged with the requisite number of votes with the result that the feast of the Assumption was spent in prayer and the Chapter resumed on the following day. Villani in his seventy-seventh year, emerged as the choice of the delegates with ten votes out of fifteen. He immediately took over as Rector Major and Alphonsus no longer concerned himself with any aspect of administration. As far as he was concerned, the long nightmare of the *Regolamento* was over.[67]

News of the convocation of the Ciorani assembly sounded a warning note to the administration in the Papal states. De Paola and Leggio stepped in at once to ensure that there would be no possibility of interference in their affairs. Leggio, with his usual skill, succeeded in convincing the Congregation of Bishops and Regulars to take the necessary action and on 4 July, a few weeks before the Ciorani Chapter assembled, a papal rescript appointed De Paola Rector Major of the houses in the Papal States, thus removing them completely from the jurisdiction of the Neapolitan section of the Congregation, a situation which was to remain unaltered until many years after Alphonsus' death. On 30 August a lengthy circular was sent to all the houses in the Kingdom of Naples containing the decisions of the Ciorani assembly, with a long list of reforms which needed to be implemented. The letter was signed by Alphonsus, even though he had nothing to do with drawing it up. It was the last occasion on which his signature was to appear on an official communication. The letter did not contain even one personal remark about himself or his health or his retirement. His anonymity was total as he retired into seclusion to prepare for death.

CHAPTER EIGHTEEN

WAITING ON THE LORD
1775–1787

– I –

After his retirement to Pagani, Alphonsus continued to demonstrate all his native Neapolitan interest in and affection for the members of his family. His main interest now was concentrated more and more on his nephews and niece, the children of Hercules by his second wife, whose mental health, as we have seen, eventually deteriorated completely leaving Hercules with the task of rearing his children. Teresa was sent at the age of seven to the Benedictine convent of Saints Marcellino and Festo, thus relieving her uncle in Pagani of any worries about her education. The education of the boys, Giuseppe and young Alfonso Maria, however, proved a major source of disagreement. Hercules had the ambition of a place for them among the royal pages at Court, only to face determined opposition from Alphonsus who feared the consequences of such a decision on the children's morals. Hercules, after considerable effort, finally succeeded in having them accepted in the *Collegio dei Nobili*, 'more on account of their uncle's holiness than on account of their father's noble blood', according to the wry comment of Tanucci who was still an informed commentator on social affairs in the capital.[1] As they grew older Hercules sought a place for them among the royal cadets, an élite corps of junior members of the nobility whose service in the royal entourage opened the way to successful careers. Once again, Alphonsus objected, though eventually, in frustration, he gave up any hope of influencing his brother's decision in the matter. 'You are their father and it is for you to do as you consider best, but I fear, that one day you will rue the consequences.'[2]

Hercules' next move was to arrange an appropriate marriage for Giuseppe. Although the boy was only thirteen at the time, Hercules saw in the eleven-year-old daughter of Signore Vespoli, a councillor of the Royal Chamber of Santa Clara, the ideal bride for his son. Alphonsus was appalled at the idea, especially at the thought of the moral dangers to which young 'Peppito' would be exposed if he got word of the proposed arrangement. Despite the fact that the problems of the *Regolamento* were now beginning to occupy all his time, Alphonsus summoned Hercules to Pagani. When the invitation was not taken up, he wrote him a number of letters counselling great prudence in the whole affair. Following on this, he invited his two nephews to come to see him in his rooms at Easter, and when this invitation, for some reason or other, did not produce the desired effect either, he wrote to them at great length in April 1780. He must have appreciated that some of his remarks were above their heads for he suggested that they should study carefully what he had written and seek an explanation of anything they did not understand. He was aware that they were not very assiduous in their studies, a fact, he said, which caused him great pain, because ignorance and laziness were the source of much sin and vicious conduct.[3] Five months later, in September, Hercules died unexpectedly, at the age of seventy-four. He had made his Will in favour of his children, having been assured by Alphonsus beforehand, that he did not wish to have any part of the Liguori estate.

Some four years after his father's death, young Giuseppe, barely eighteen, married Maria Guzman Sambiase, who brought with her a considerable dowry. The opulent young couple were very much part of the Neapolitan social scene and avid theatre goers. Within a few months of their marriage they visited Alphonsus in Pagani. He questioned them about their lifestyle, whether they frequented the opera and theatre and took part in social evenings and dances. In a word whether they took part in the fashionable round of what were known as *cavallereschi divertimenti*. Alphonsus had clearly been well briefed. Giuseppe and his bride were innocent enough to admit that nothing gave them greater pleasure. This admission elicited a long lecture from Alphonsus on the moral dangers inherent in such activities; he exhorted them to avoid such pastimes as occasions of sin which could lead to their eternal damnation. Only the love and service of God, he assured them, could bring them happiness in heaven. This visit to Pagani provided the background for the advice about saving his soul which Alphonsus, on his death-bed, three years later, gave to Giuseppe when he came to visit him for the last time.[4]

After the death of Hercules, Alphonsus felt added responsibility for his niece, Teresa, who was then sixteen. Through his penitent, Sister Brianna Caraffa, the superioress at the time, and a cousin who was a member of the community where Teresa was an *educanda*, he followed her development with interest. She possessed a beautiful singing voice which was heard to advantage in the chanting of the Divine Office. In her early years in the convent, Teresa had expressed a wish to become a nun, to the great delight of her uncle in Pagani; as she grew older, however, her resolution evaporated to his corresponding disappointment. He began to fear that she might even be contemplating marriage. From Pagani he wrote advising her against this at all costs:

My very dearest niece,

When your father was alive, you wrote to me expressing your intention of becoming a nun and this was a great consolation to me. Since his death, however, I have heard nothing further from you in the matter. I know that your father has left you an inheritance, but it constitutes only a meagre dowry. So, if you return to the world, your only option will be to marry some impecunious suitor.

I am anxious for your eternal salvation above all else, and it is for this reason that I point out to you that if you return to the world you could easily lose your soul. Society at the moment is corrupt. You would be tempted to offend God the very day following your departure from the convent.

I speak frankly since I know from experience that nowadays all married women are exposed to great temptations, and many of them succumb. And so I repeat, if you marry, you will soon lament having lost God.[5]

The corrupt morals of high society in Naples had been causing Alphonsus considerable worry for years. Time and time again in his correspondence, even to Hercules, he had condemned the fashionable practice of *cicisbeism*, which had become so characteristic of marriage in Bourbon Naples, that every married lady was expected to have her own *cicisbeo* or 'gentleman escort' who accompanied her wherever she went, out walking, at the theatre, even at Mass. Alphonsus developed a complex in the matter, to such an extent that in his later years, marriage and *cicisbeism* in Neapolitan society became for him one and the same thing.

Not satisfied with his letter to Teresa, he wrote in even stronger terms, a few days later, to her guardian, Don Pietro Gavotti:

I am very worried about my niece, Teresa, whose guardian you are. Some time ago she expressed a wish to become a nun, but she has now, apparently, abandoned the idea. I am afraid that she is even contemplating marriage. And this means that she could easily lose her soul.

Only with great difficulty can married ladies nowadays save their souls. The great majority of them live in sin on account of the numerous *cicisbeos* who collect around them to lure them into sin. I have already requested the priest, who is my niece's confessor, to encourage her in the direction of becoming a nun. And I ask you too, to do your part in this, since, in the corrupt time in which we live, if she marries, I shall regard her as lost.[6]

Alphonsus was next led to believe that it was the worldly-wise servants in the convent itself who were filling Teresa's mind with thoughts of marriage. He wrote at once to counteract the ideas they were putting into her head:

I beg you not to pay attention to anyone who wishes you to leave the convent and fling yourself into the merry-go-round of the world.[7] You would regret it the very next day. I am sending you another copy of the pamphlet which I gave you already, on the importance of saving your soul, which is the only thing that matters. Find a good spiritual director to advise you and talk the matter over with some edifying nun in the convent.[8]

The unfortunate girl was under considerable pressure from all sides to become a nun, from her uncle, the reputedly saintly bishop, her confessor, her guardian, and the nuns themselves. Finally, a letter from Alphonsus left her with little choice:

> I pray Jesus Christ to strengthen your intention of not returning to the world since it would be difficult for you to keep in the grace of God there. This is the advice I give to all young ladies like yourself who come here to consult me. I let them know that only with difficulty will they obtain eternal salvation if they lead their lives in the world, which is now so totally corrupt.
>
> It is my experience that women who become socialites at the moment, usually lose the grace of God. Do not, then, I beg you, abandon Jesus Christ for life in the world, since you would lose both Jesus Christ and your soul. By the grace of God, all my relations up to the present have died a good death and I hope to see them all one day in heaven. And I hope to be there too myself one day with you.[9]

In the summer of 1781, Teresa communicated to her uncle her decision to become a nun; she was just seventeen. Right through the *Regolamento* controversy, he kept up a constant stream of letters to her, as if her vocation were his sole preoccupation. He supervised every step she took. Early in 1782 she left the convent when her time as an educanda came to an end, and spent the ritual few months of freedom with the Duchess of Bovino, a long-time penitent of Alphonsus. His letters followed her even then. He encouraged her to make a 'total and perfect offering' of herself to Jesus Christ and advised her not to go to dances or take part in social evenings. Chaperoned by the Duchess, she visited Alphonsus in Pagani, where he presented her with a copy of his book of visits to the Blessed Sacrament and of the *Preparation for Death*. Teresa, however, had set her heart on a small picture of Our Lady of Good Counsel which Alphonsus kept always on his desk. He finally agreed to give it to her but only after the intervention of Father Villani, his director. After another period of hesitation about her vocation, Teresa was received into the convent in September 1782. She would have liked her uncle to be present at the ceremony but his health would not permit it. 'If the good Lord had allowed me to be present', he wrote to her, 'I would have done nothing more than weep tears of joy. But the Lord did not permit me this consolation.'[10] For the next two years he maintained a constant correspondence with her. She suffered greatly during her early years in the convent. She lost her voice and then went through recurring bouts of anorexia and depression, all indicative, perhaps, of how difficult she found it to come to terms with her vocation as a religious.

DON HERCULES MARIA DE LIGUORI, BROTHER OF SAINT ALPHONSUS

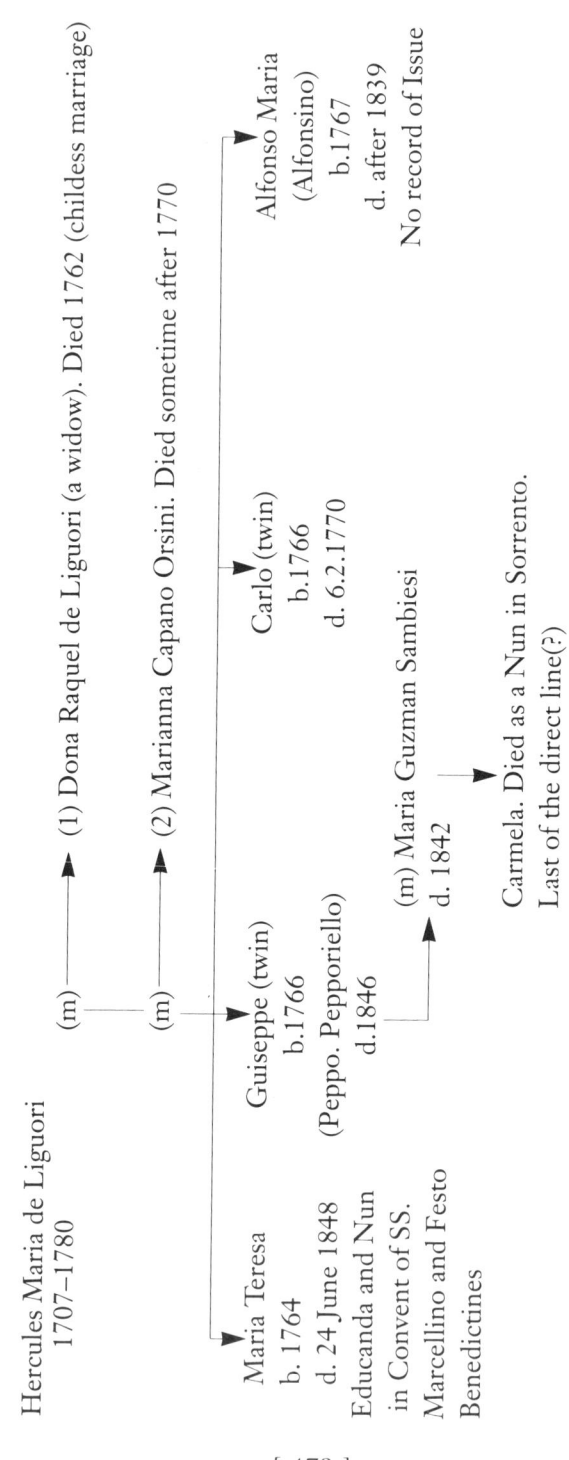

Rather than suggesting that she might have been happier outside the convent and married, Alphonsus' letters encouraged her to suffer with patience and to resign herself to the will of God — 'heaven was not made for the faint-hearted.'[11] Despite the suspicions one might have nowadays, about her freedom of choice and the maturity of her decision, Teresa remained faithful to her vocation as a nun and died in 1848 at the age of eighty-four, nine years after the canonisation of her uncle.

– II –

The death of his priest brother Cajetan in October 1784, left Alphonsus as the last surviving member of his family; he knew his own death could not be long delayed. His letters made increasing references to his approaching death, accompanied by requests for prayers that he might die in the grace of God. From his friends and especially from his niece, Teresa, he asked, too, for prayers that he might regain peace of conscience and that his scruples, which had returned to torment him, would disappear. His physical condition continued to deteriorate. His hearing and eyesight were both seriously impaired; to communicate with him, one had to shout. When assisting at Mass he could not hear the priest nor see the Host elevated at the Consecration. His arthritis worsened, with the result that the curvature of his spine and the deformity of his neck were both greatly accentuated. Prostate gland trouble developed causing him alternating bouts of retention of urine and incontinence. His phobia about not allowing himself to be touched, even for reasons of medical necessity, prevented his doctors from inserting a catheter to give him some relief. Instead, they were compelled to rely on the accepted remedies of hot poultices which were less effective and more painful. To these conditions was added a hernia, occasioned by a fall from his carriage; slight at first, it gradually extended itself until his medical attendants described it as *un enorme rottura*, which made walking impossible. He had to be lifted in and out of bed and confined to his wheel-chair, which he detested. There was an end to his drives in the carriage; the last time he left the house was in April 1784. Nor was he able to go down to the church or to the community oratory; his prayers were said in his own private chapel or in his wheel-chair, along the corridor, and, always, out loud. When he went to confession, which was once a week, he raised his voice so much that he could be heard in the adjacent rooms and even in the corridor. His confessions became almost public events. His usual confessor, Father Corsano, usually asked him to recite five Ave Marias by way of penance, to which he would invariably object as being too little. In November 1784, he celebrated Mass for the last time. He longed for death to come to put an end to his sufferings. On one occasion Father Lorenzo Negri surprised him in his room. He was sitting with his eyes on the crucifix and praying, 'Gesù mio, it seems to me a thousand years before I die and come to be with you in Paradise.' He had a small note-book which contained some prayers and devotions used by his mother which he had read to him from time to time.

Before his mental powers began to fade, he maintained his interest in whatever affected the welfare of the Church and religion. He talked about the Pope and his relations with the various states of Europe. He enquired about the situation of the Jesuits since their suppression, and followed with interest their continuing progress in Russia and Prussia. Nearer home, he was worried about the spread of Jansenism in Italy. He commented on the rise and fall of the King's Ministers in Naples from Tanucci to Sambuca to Caracciolo, and he was fully alive to the decline in the morals of the Court beginning with the King himself.[12] There was a constant stream of visitors to see him; he was widely spoken of as a 'saint'. Young priests came to seek a blessing on their ministry and a word of encouragement. With them he invariably insisted on the necessity for prayer. He urged them to show great kindness to sinners and to avoid severity in their ministry as confessors.

But the overall situation was far from ideal. In the testimony that they gave after his death, both Villani and Mazzini admitted that for the last five years of his life in Pagani, Alphonsus was a source of considerable trouble to the community. 'If his temptations and scruples were a very heavy cross for him, they were equally so for us for the last five years before his death.' His moods too were unpredictable. He could be kind and gracious one moment, and the next, demanding and impossible to satisfy. The real heroes were Brother Francis Anthony and Alessio, now a professed Brother in the Congregation, who looked after him from morning to night.[13] They read to him from spiritual books, often his own, recited the rosary with him, assisted him in his visits to the Blessed Sacrament. There were times when he tried their patience to its limits; to use Mazzini's words, they were 'martyrs of patience'. In course of time, they developed their own strategems to deal with him. They found that the magic words were 'obedience' and the 'will of God', which they consequently made use of to the full. When he proved difficult or un-co-operative, the mention of the necessity of obeying the superior's direction or of submitting oneself to the will of God, brought immediate compliance. There was considerable arguing and resistance when he had to be washed in bed; only Brother Francis Anthony and Alessio were allowed to touch him on these occasions. To get him to allow them to change his undergarments required major discussions and the invocation of the authority of superiors.[14]

At the process of canonisation in Rome there were lengthy arguments about the state of Alphonsus' mental health during the last five or so years of his life. The Promotor of the Faith argued forcefully that Alphonsus during this time was totally senile and consequently not responsible for his actions or what he said. The Promotor of the Cause, on the other hand, was equally insistent that he retained full possession of his faculties, that he was mentally alert and balanced, and that his judgment was unaffected. If he appeared stupid and foolish at times in what he said or did, it was because he deliberately allowed himself to appear so — a particularly Italian characteristic among the saints, Francis of Assisi and Philip Neri being cited as significant examples.[15] Furthermore, it was alleged that Alphonsus acted in that manner quite deliberately in order to counteract his natural inclination to vanity and self-esteem. Whatever the truth of the matter, there is no doubt that Alphonsus was greatly distressed mentally, for considerable periods during the last years of his life. His scruples, as we have seen, had reasserted themselves on his return to Pagani from the diocese, but were kept more or less under control for a time by obedience to clear directions from Villani and Mazzini. They released him from any obligation in the matter of the 'vows' he had made during his earlier years concerning prayers, acts of penance and certain devotional practices. They forbade him in the strongest terms to confess worries from the past and all their instructions were duly entered in another small personal note-book similar to the ones he had from his early years as a priest.[16] However, despite the best efforts of his directors, his mental anxieties were beyond control and reached distressing intensity in the five years immediately preceding his death; there were times when he seemed, literally, 'out of his mind'. He imagined that the devil appeared to him in several guises declaring that he was damned. He would burst into tears and cry out for help at the top of his voice, repeating acts of confidence in Our Lord and the intercession of the Madonna. In an attempt to put an end to these temptations to despair, he dictated a formal declaration to Brother Francis Anthony which the Brother wrote down and signed: 'Although I have always been uncertain and troubled by doubts, now, however, on 15 October 1785, abandoning myself into the hands of Jesus Christ, I declare my firm hope of saving my soul through the merits of Jesus Christ and the intercession of Our Lady. And I hope shortly to thank them in Paradise.' On occasions, he grew so agitated during the night that he called out for Alessio or Francis Anthony to summon Villani or Mazzini from their beds to deal with his scruples. 'He multiplied scruple after scruple,' said Villani. When Villani and Mazzini, in desperation, finally decided that they would not leave their beds during the night no matter how distressed he was, Alphonsus made the night attendant write out his problem, and then bring it to one of the confessors who was requested to write out his decision which the Brother would then read to him and calm would be temporarily restored.[17] After some time, Alessio and Francis Anthony learnt to leave his room and return after an appropriate delay with a reassuring answer from some Father they pretended to have consulted. When his anxieties became unbearable he screamed at the top of his voice and cried like a child; he could be heard right through the monastery. Sometimes he threatened to throw himself out of a window. He was warned that if he did not make a greater effort to deal with his scruples, he would die mad. Annoyed, he replied, 'And if God wants me to die mad, why should I object?'[18]

No aspect of his life or conduct was exempt from scruples. They extended even to his writings. For a period, he worried that his works were full of errors and were leading people astray, even to damnation. He was tortured by the thought that there was no way open to him to obtain pardon for these errors which were jeopardising his own eternal salvation as well as others. On the point of receiving Communion during Mass, he often drew back as he struggled with some scruple; he would interrupt the celebrant again and again to ask him about some imaginary sin he had committed. One celebrant, finding himself in this situation, shouted at him, 'Monsignor, how long are you going to keep the Lord waiting in the ante-room for you?'[19]

But it was in the area of sexuality that his scruples were the most distressing. His sensitivity in this area, which had been with him from adolescence, increased considerably during these last five years and gave rise to temptations which were described and discussed without any inhibitions during the canonisation process. Nothing was left to the imagination. On one occasion when a young boy was among a group of visitors who came to visit him, he refused to allow him to kiss his hand, the normal expression of reverence for a bishop. Alphonsus explained that 'those who lead a secluded life are particularly liable to sexual temptations and that includes the old as well as the young.' 'He suffered hallucinations of a sexual nature, imagining at one time that he was engaged to be married, reliving, apparently, the efforts his father made to arrange suitable brides for him in his adolescence. On another occasion he imagined that he saw a young woman enter his room to lead him into sin. He disturbed the whole house when he accused the Brother at the monastery door of allowing a young lady to violate the enclosure. Another time he imagined that a priest, whom he recognised, entered his room to argue that masturbation was something quite natural and not in any way sinful, and who then proceeded to do so in front of him. Alphonsus recoiled in horror and shouted out for someone to come to assist him.[20] But the most distressing experience of all was the occasion when he felt as if an invisible hand was forcing him to sexual self-abuse, resulting in a violent sexual arousal on his part, which was witnessed by those who were at his bedside, and about which Villani gave explicit evidence.[21] So persistent were his temptations in the area of sexuality that, just as he had done in the area of confidence in God, he insisted on formally renewing his commitment to celibate chastity, which he did on 15 September 1785 in the presence of Father Mazzini. The declaration was in writing and was witnessed by Mazzini, 'I, Alfonso Maria de Liguori have made a vow of chastity in honour of Our Lady in the presence of Father Giovanni Mazzini and I am ready to die a thousand times, rather than fail in this vow.'[22]

The Promotor of the Faith was quite matter-of-fact in his reaction to the evidence relating to the sexual temptations which Alphonsus suffered in his last years. He was of the opinion that they were more or less to be expected in an old man whose life had been spent dealing with every aspect of human sexuality in his missionary and confessional ministry, as well as in his writings. He accepted, too, the testimonies of the various witnesses that Alphonsus resisted with all his power and was consequently without fault. But he was not prepared to accept the theory of demoniacal influence put forward as an explanation by the Promotor of the Cause and he insisted on a further detailed examination of the whole matter. When this was completed and the question had been fully discussed again, he was satisfied that the heroic virtue of the venerable bishop of St Agatha shone forth in all its splendour in the midst of these distressing temptations.[23]

– III –

Alphonsus celebrated his ninetieth birthday in September 1786; it was to be his last. During the following months his strength ebbed rapidly and he wasted away until he was nothing more than skin and bone, *un cadavere parlante*, his colleagues described him. He was confined to bed for most of the time, though Brother Francis Anthony and Alessio lifted him onto his chair to provide some relief from the pain caused by extensive bedsores. He prayed incessantly and had moments of alertness, recognising what was said to him and, at times, recognising those who came to see him. At night, he talked out loud in his sleep. Brother Raffaele, who took his turn to be with him, noted that he seemed to be back on the missions, hearing confessions. He consoled a penitent by telling him that if he had confessed all his sins with confidence in the mercy of God, he could be certain of God's forgiveness. He recited acts of love and sorrow for the penitent to repeat after him. On another occasion, he reproached the penitent for approaching confession without sorrow or any intention of amending his life. 'Do you want to go to eternal damnation; you and your confessor?' And then he encouraged the penitent to pray to the Madonna who was now his last chance of salvation.[24]

As the months of 1787 went by, he grew more and more peaceful; by July it was evident to all that he was no longer agitated by his scruples or temptations. An air of serenity surrounded him. Each day Mass was celebrated in the room adjoining his bedroom and he received Communion with fervour. His condition continued unaltered until the middle of July when a high fever, accompanied by severe dysentry, indicated that the end could not be long delayed. Three days later he lapsed into light unconsciousness. Father Vincent Magaldi, who makes this sole appearance in his life, heard his confession and gave him General Absolution. From then on the members of the community, as well as representatives from the other houses, watched continually at his bed-side. Tannoia declared that he did not leave him for more than an instant during those last days. The local physician, Dr Francesco Desiderio, was in constant attendance and summoned two medical consultants from Naples. But there was nothing they could do. Gangrene had set in and the urinary tract had virtually ceased to function; the patient was in advanced stages of uremia accompanied by considerable pain. It was a slight compensation that his hearing seemed to have improved somewhat, and he more easily recognised what was being said to him and, at times, was able to reply. When shown a picture of Brother Gerard whose reputation for working miracles was even then recognised, he said, 'Even he cannot cure me now.'[25] On 23 July he was anointed by Father Nichola Mansione, rector of the house, and two days later he received Holy Communion as Viaticum. A few days later he was unable to swallow and could no longer receive Communion. He blessed all who asked him and he mentioned particularly the Pope, the King, his ministers, generals and judges, all the members of the Congregation, including a special mention of those in the Papal States. He recognised his nephew

Giuseppe, who came from Naples with his wife, and he whispered to him 'save your soul', an incident which was to become part of the stock-in-trade of preachers.

As the end approached the stream of visitors, which included bishops from the neighbouring dioceses, increased. Word had spread throughout the Kingdom that his death was imminent and prayers were offered up for him in the various dioceses where he had preached missions as well as in convents and the numerous missionary societies and confraternities where he had conducted the spiritual exercises. The members of the Apostolic Missions and the Fathers of the Chinese College sent word they were united with him in prayer. Four days before he died he suffered a stroke, resulting in facial paralysis and loss of his power of speech, though he was still able to hear and showed signs of response when spoken to, especially by those whose voices were familiar.[26] On Tuesday evening, 31 July, it was clear that death was only a few hours away. The members of the community, with the exception of Villani, who was confined to bed, kept vigil throughout the night, filling his room and spilling out into the corridor. The prayers for the dying and the Litany of Loreto were repeated over and over again. He was still alive on Wednesday morning 1 August, but sinking rapidly. He was utterly peaceful and in no way agitated. Some time between eleven o'clock and midday, he drew his last breath, quietly and without struggle. Those who were watching hardly knew that he had passed away.

Word of his death spread rapidly. Within a few hours, crowds came to pay their respects and to venerate his remains, which were laid out in his episcopal robes on a catafalque in a temporary chapel on the ground floor near the entrance to the monastery. Next morning, Thursday 2 August, his obsequies were celebrated in the tiny church of St Michael, where he had so often preached and where, in his last years, he had spent so much time before the Blessed Sacrament. The church was filled with clerics and religious, with the result that the special preacher, Canon Fortunato Pinto from Salerno, delivered his panegyric to the people who were assembled in the square outside from a platform erected at the door of the church. At nightfall, the remains were returned to the temporary monastery chapel where, in the presence of the diocesan bishop and the civil authorities, they were formally identified and sealed in special coffins. Almost instinctively the correct procedures to facilitate the introduction of his Cause of canonisation were being adopted. With the formalities complete, the body was brought back to the church and interred in front of the High Altar at the epistle side. A simple slab announced: 'Here lies the body of the Most Illustrious and Most Reverend Monsignor Alphonsus Mary de Liguori, Bishop of St Agatha of the Goths and Founder of the Congregation of the Most Holy Redeemer.'[27]

The terms of his Will which he had drawn up before a Public Notary towards the end of 1775, and which he had kept up to date by adding codicil after codicil, as circumstances demanded over the ensuing years, were public knowledge. Hercules and his heirs were the main beneficiaries of his estate. Villani received his personal library and the rights to all his publications, as well as what remained of his episcopal pension. His two nephews were left copies of his spiritual books as well as paintings of the Good Shepherd and of Our Lady. Alessio and Brother Francis Anthony received considerable sums in cash in recompense for the services they had rendered him. Brother Francis Anthony later gave evidence at the process in Pagani that Alphonsus, before he died, saw to it that he received the bequest in cash so that he would be welcomed by the rector of whatever house he was assigned to, after Alphonsus' death.[28]

– *IV* –

Within a few months of the death of Alphonsus, the different processes were initiated which would lead, within a remarkably short period of time, to his elevation to the honours of the altar. In March 1788, Father Cardone was appointed Promotor of the Cause by Villani in Naples and De Paola in the Papal States; the two sections of the Congregation were united on this, at least. That same year the Ordinary Processes got under way in Pagani and St Agatha of the Goths, and were completed the following year. Seven years later when the necessary documentation and depositions were assembled, the cause of canonisation was formally introduced in Rome. The next stage was the opening of the Apostolic Processes which began in Pagani and Sant' Agatha, within a few months of each other. At the same time, Tannoia continued his own investigations as he prepared for the publication of his biography of Alphonsus which had been his life's work. Everything went smoothly with the progress of the Cause in Rome until the question of Alphonsus' conduct during the years of the *Regolamento* came up for examination. For many, this was the question most likely to prove an obstacle to the prospects of canonisation within a reasonable period of time. The Assistant Promotor of the Faith, Signore Gardellini, outlined the case against Alphonsus with great skill. He was ably assisted in his task by Father Leggio who maintained his stand against the course of action adopted by Alphonsus. Father Cardone found himself faced with a formidable task if the Cause were not to collapse or at least to be deferred indefinitely. The more he replied to the questions raised by Gardellini, the more difficulties arose; the influence of Leggio was palpable. 'God knows how much effort I have had to expend to overcome the arguments of Gardellini,' protested Cardone. Finally, he succeeded in convincing the Cardinals of the Commission specifically charged with examining the matter that, whatever the objective facts of the case might be, Alphonsus' conduct during the whole *Regolamento* debacle was not in any way an obstacle to the progress of the Cause of his canonisation.[29] To Cardone's great relief, Pope Pius VI, in a decree of April 1796, imposed silence on the whole question; it was not to be brought up again during the subsequent progress of the Cause. He was making amends for his attitude to Alphonsus during those difficult years when he failed to appreciate the complexity of the problem. Blasucci forbade Tannoia to make any reference to the division of the Congregation in the final volume of his biography; only in November 1796 did he permit the publication of the work, when it had been examined by Cardone to ensure that it did not depart in any way from the official line on the *Regolamento*.[30]

The progress of the Cause was then delayed by the French invasions of Rome in 1797 and 1809, which resulted, on both occasions, in the abduction of the Pope by French troops. Pius VI and his successor Pius VII were absent from Rome for years, during which time the Congregation of Rites for the canonisation of saints ceased to function. The process, however, passed a decisive stage in May 1807 when the decree declaring the heroism of Alphonsus' virtues was published. Towards the end of 1816 with peace more or less restored to Europe after the defeat of Napoleon, Alphonsus was beatified, just twenty-nine years after his death. In 1830 the decree 'Tuto' opened the way for his immediate canonisation. But the Redemptorist Congregation was unable to face the expense involved in the ceremony, and the superiors decided to wait until a number of candidates could be canonised together, thus enabling the financial outlay to be shared. So, nine years later, on 26 May 1839, Alphonsus was canonised with five others. Just fifty-two years had elapsed since his death, a remarkably short period of time for the canonisation process to reach a successful conclusion. Present in the basilica of St Peter's at the ceremony were his nephew Giuseppe and, in the words of the official gazette, 'other relatives of the *beatus*'. One can only surmise — and hope — that among these were his niece, Teresa, and his youngest nephew, Alfonsino, both of whom were certainly alive, though there is no explicit mention of their presence in any contemporary report. Present too were the superiors and members of the Redemptorist Congregation from the three sections into which it had been divided, Naples, the Papal States and the Transalpine Vicariate. In deference to protocol, the last of the Bourbons of Naples, Ferdinand II, no less odious than his grandfather Ferdinand, and his Queen, Maria Teresa of Austria, were in places of honour, enjoying whatever reflected glory the canonisation of the last great saint of Bourbon Naples brought to himself and his loathsome family. Significantly the General of the Jesuits ordered the decree of canonisation of Alphonsus to be proclaimed publicly in the church of the Gesù, a delicate tribute to a great admirer of the Society who had refused to accept the church for the ministry of his own Congregation when the Society was suppressed.[31]

The rapid spread of the religious Congregation he had founded brought the name of Alphonsus and his writings throughout the whole of Europe and into North America and Canada within a few years of his canonisation. His influence was dominant in the discussions leading to the definition of the doctrines of Our Lady's Immaculate Conception in 1858 and of Papal Infallibility in 1870.[32] His Moral Theology became accepted throughout the seminaries of the entire Catholic world, influencing the theological formation of saints like the Curé of Ars, with the result that the proposal to have him declared a Doctor of the Church met with considerable support among the bishops of the world. Those who were less than enthusiastic felt that St Francis de Sales had a prior claim, a point of view which Alphonsus himself would certainly have shared. However, in March 1871, in the immediate aftermath of the First Vatican Council, Pope Pius IX conferred on him this honour.[33] Eighty years later in 1950 Pope Pius XII named him as the patron of Confessors and Moral Theologians. There was nothing more the Church could do to honour the Saint of Bourbon Naples.

Epilogue

The Church canonises human beings. A false idea is prevalent that canonised sainthood somehow implies a human nature devoid of its imperfections and free of 'the heart-ache and the thousand natural shocks that flesh is heir to', an escape from being human instead of being totally human. Biographers of saints have much to answer for in this regard. True, there have been saints of undoubted innocence, of almost angelic purity. But neither their innocence nor their freedom from the urges of the flesh has brought them to the honours of the altar. The essential element remains the heroism of their struggle under grace to follow the gospel imperatives and to reproduce in their lives the virtues of the only model of sanctity, Jesus Christ. And the intensity of their struggle is determined by the obstacles they have to overcome.

The canonised saints of the Church have been of all ages, races and types. Among them have been kings and queens, soldiers and professors, rich and poor, aristocrats and homeless beggars. There have been saints whose human nature provided examples of much that is less than admirable in human beings; there have been angry, ambitious, scheming saints; there have been among them prostitutes and alcoholics. There have been canonised saints whom it would have been a pleasure to meet, others who might well have proved less than congenial companions. The variety of canonised sanctity, too, is equally broad, reflecting the sociological characteristics of time and place as well as the prevailing patterns of christian spirituality. To appreciate the different manifestations of christian holiness, from the anchorite of the desert to the factory worker or the alcoholic trade unionist of modern times, demands a sense of the presence of the Holy Spirit working at all times and in all places throughout the world. It demands too, an acceptance of the fact that the Church is authoritatively qualified to discern and proclaim the authenticity of His action in the lives of its members.

Alphonsus de Liguori was a man of his time and place, a Neapolitan of Bourbon Naples, highly intelligent, broadly educated, professionally a skilled lawyer. He was Neapolitan through and through, in his language, in his dealings with others. From the psychological point of view he presents an interesting case-history for a modern behavioural study of his scruples, his stubbornness, his anxiety complex, his sexual sensitivity. His spirituality with its devotional and ascetical practices was totally of his time and country.

The Church has canonised him first because she has recognised the authenticity of the action of the Holy Spirit in his life and the heroism of his struggle against the manifestations of the unredeemed human nature he inherited. While he may not be the most 'popular' of saints in the modern sense, there are innumerable souls who can identify with his struggles. In the lives of christian people, canonised saints play an important instructive role; they demonstrate how the gospel can be lived in practice. If the details of their lives are not to be imitated in every aspect, at least they inspire and stimulate, they encourage and reassure. The path to sanctity for Alphonsus was a painful one. He experienced sufferings of body, mind and soul; he knew disappointment, failure, misunderstanding, rejection and betrayal. When he breathed his last, the faint flame of life that flickered in his body was all that he had left to give back to God; he had been purified by the Spirit of everything else. The heroism of his perseverance in the path he had set himself was immediately evident. Father Corsano, a witness at the Ordinary Process at Nocera articulated perfectly the 'mystery' of his life:

> One must reflect on how the Lord wished to test the spiritual mettle of his servant through bitter sufferings. He was a man of vast learning, of brilliant talents, eminent for his writings on theological matters and the author of a considerable number of books. Furthermore, he was an expert in mystical theology since he was himself a contemplative and a mystic. He was a master of spiritual direction whose advice was sought in every aspect of human conduct, from the choice of a state of life to the appropriate moment for making one's decision. Everyone who consulted him received guidance which was at once perceptive and precise.
>
> And yet, while he had a hundred penetrating eyes for others, the Lord, who wished to increase the merits he had acquired, reduced him to blindness in his own regard. Every member of our Congregation, myself included, sought advice from him as regards the direction of souls. From every corner of the Kingdom other spiritual directors sought his advice, so much so that he was called the Master Guide, the Director of Directors.

But there is another purpose in canonisation besides the recognition of the personal struggle of the saints in their lives; the process is not an act of ecclesiastical narcissism. Alphonsus de Liguori belongs to that exclusive category of canonised saints whom the Church raises to the honours of the altar on account of the public role they have played in her life. Not merely have they lived their lives in faith, hope and charity as an example to others, but they have contributed to the manifestation of what the Church is in her eternal mystery. They have vindicated that church intellectually in their lectures and writings, they have defended it against the encroachments of the secular, they have clarified the norms of human conduct in its relation to God. This was the role Alphonsus de Liguori was raised up to play in the life of the Church in the eighteenth century. By canonising him fifty years after his death the Church recognised that fact and, at the same time, created the opportunity for him to continue his mission after his death. If, from some purely human points of view, he was an unlikely and perhaps inadequate choice for this task, then his life and work is just one more remarkable manifestation of the Lord's dealings with His people.

APPENDIX

Chronological list of Alphonsus' writings with page references to the text where relevant

1728	The Eternal Truths, 64–5, 190
1732	Hymns and Verses, 190
1734	Prayers to Our Lady for each day of the week, 190
1743	Novena in honour of St Teresa, 190, 348
	Short Way of Perfection
1743	Precis of Christian Doctrine
1745	Visits to the Blessed Sacrament, 33, 67, 190–91, 254, 379
1745	Reflections useful for Bishops 191–3, 342, 370, 377
1746	Letter concerning the Moral Implications of Cursing the Dead, 203–4
1748	Annotations to the *Medulla Theologiae Moralis* of H. Busenbaum S.J. In the course of the nine editions published during the saint's lifetime the title page changed to *Moral Theology of the Most Ill. and Rev. D. Alphonsus De Liguori, Bishop of S. Agatha of the Goths and Rector Major of the Congregation of the Most Holy Redeemer*, 67, 184, 204–5, 207–10, 220, 262–3, 274–8, 281–6, 332–443
1748	Reply to the Calumnies concerning Letter dealing with the Moral Implications of Cursing the Dead
1749	Dissertation in favour of the Moderate Use of the Probable Opinion, 266, 281, 426
1750	The Glories of Mary, 132, 263–4, 269–74, 398
1750	Consideration on Religious Vocation, 312
1751	Jesus hath loved us. Clock of the Passion
1751	Concerning the Refusal of Absolution to a Cleric 'habituato in vitio turpi', 275
1751	Rest for Scrupulous Souls, 74
1752	Lives of Father Sarnelli and Brother Vito Curzio, 131, 301
1754	On Conversing Continually and Familiarly with God, 291
1754	Rules for Correct Living

1755	Pratica del Confessore per ben esercitare il suo ministero (Praxis Confessarii), 50, 282–6, 349, 406
1755	Dissertation on the moderate use of the Probable Opinion, 281, 426
1755	Conformity with the Will of God
1756	Advice to newly approved Confessors
1756	Against the Errors of Modern Unbelievers called Materialists and Deists, 288
1756	Reply to an anonymous writer
1757	Rules for Seminaries, 338, 387
1757	A Short Treatise on the Necessity of Prayer, 291
1757	Examination of Candidates for Ordination
1757	Concerning the Cursing of the Dead, 203–6
1757	Advice to Priests for Assisting the Dying, 50–52
1757–59	Istruzione e pratica per un confessore (Compendium, Pratica Grande, Homo Apostolicus), 50, 284–6, 386
1758	Preparation for Death, 294, 477
1758	Nine Discourses for Times of Calamity
1758	Novena for Christmas, 294
1758	Novena for the Sacred Heart, 294
1758	Meditations in honour of St Joseph, 294
1758	Reply to a Letter concerning the Cursing of the Dead
1758	Preparation for Mass and Thanksgiving, 337, 513
1759	Dissertation concerning the Prohibition of Books, 359
1759	Prayer, the Great Means of Salvation, 291
1760	The Selva (Dignity and Duties of the Priest with two Rules of Life for secular priests), 336–8, 375
1760	The Exercises of the Missions, 246, 259
1760	The Mass and Office hurriedly said, 338
1760–61	The True Spouse of Jesus Christ, 266, 351–2
1761	Meditations for a Private Retreat of Eight Days
1761	Considerations on the Passion of Jesus Christ
1761	The Way of the Cross
1761	Letter to a fellow religious on the manner of Preaching with Apostolic Simplicity, 260–61
1761	Life and Death of Sr Teresa de Liguori, 28
1761	A Short Compendium of Christian Doctrine, 391
1762	Reply to a letter from Don Cipriano Aristasio
1762	Dissertation on the Moderate use of the Probable Opinion, 266, 281, 424
1762	The Truth of the Faith as evidenced by the Motives of Credibility, 288
1762	Method of Making Mental Prayer with Children during Mass
1764	For Confessors appointed to Rural Areas (Il Confessore Diretto), 268, 427
1764	Reply concerning the frequentation of Holy Communion against Don Cipriano Aristasio

1764	Examination of Candidates for Confession Faculties
1764	Questions to be asked of Priests who wish to engage in the Ministry of the Confessional
1764	Apologia in favour of the use of an equally Probable Opinion, 425
1764	Defence of Dissertation in favour of the moderate use of the Probable Opinion against Adelfo Dositeo, 424–6
1764	Rules for the Monastery of Our Lady Queen of Heaven at Airola
1765	On the moderate use of the Probable Opinion, 425
1765	Some Points Concerning the Matter of Frequent Communion
1765	An uncertain Law cannot induce a certain Obligation
1766	The Way of Salvation, 383, 428
1766	Life of Father Paul Cafaro, C.SS.R., 301
1767	The Truth of the Faith, 288
1767	Refutation of the Book *De l'Esprit*, 288
1767	Refutation of a work *On Preaching*
1768	Practice of the Love of Jesus Christ, 73, 428
1768	Arguments against Febronius, 429
1768	Instructions on the Ten Commandments for the Faithful, 427
1768	Five Points on which Preachers should instruct the Faithful, 427
1769	An Exposition and Defence of the Points of Faith discussed and defined at the Council of Trent, 288, 429
1769	On the Grace of Justification
1769	On the Acceptance due to the Definitions of a Council, 429
1769	Ceremonies of the Mass, 337
1769	Honoraria for Masses
1769	Apologia for his Moral Theology attacked as lax
1770	An Opinion, which is not convincing, in favour of an Obligation, does not impose an Obligation
1771	Sermons for all the Sundays of the year, 427
1771	Letter to a Bishop on the benefits of Missions
1771	Letter on the benefit of Spiritual Exercises made in Silence
1772	Triumph of the Church (History and Refutation of various Heresies), 141, 289, 429
1772	Sermons for the feast of St Joseph
1772	Sermons for the Clothing of a Religious
1773	Considerations on the Passion of Jesus Christ
1773	Considerations on some Spiritual Matters
1773	On the Truth of Divine Revelation, 289
1773	Is the use of a Probable Opinion lawful?
1773	Miraculous Discovery of the Blessed Sacrament in a parish in Naples
1773	Meditations on the Passion of Jesus Christ for each day of the week
1774	Explanation of the Psalms and Canticles, 34
1774	Explanation of the Moral System favoured by the author (Alphonsus Maria de Liguori), 427
1775	Advice to Priests appointed to assist those Condemned to Death, 50–52

1775	Victory of the Martyrs, 430
1775	The Sacrifice of Jesus Christ
1775	Exhortation to Religious in general
1775	Exhortation to a Nun to make progress in the Love of Jesus Christ
1775	Wonderful Manifestation of Divine Providence
1775	Reply to the Reforms of the Abbot Rolli
1775	Admonitions necessary for persons of every State of Life who wish to save their Souls
1775	Novena in preparation for the Feast of All Souls
1775	Divine Love and the means of acquiring it
1775	Consolation and Encouragement for a Soul in a state of Spiritual Desolation
1776	A Theological-Moral Dissertation concerning Eternal Life, 441–3
1776	Fidelity of Subjects to God renders them faithful to the Prince, 430–31
1777	Instruction to Preachers
1778	Exhortations addressed to the Nuns of the Most Holy Redeemer

NOTES

Abbreviations

A.G.H.R.	Redemptorist General Archives, Historical, Rome
Analecta	Analecta Congregationis SS. Redemptoris, Rome 1922–67
B.G.E.R.	Bibliographie Générale des Écrivains Rédemptoristes etc.
Falcoia, Lettere	T. Falcoia, Lettere à S. Alfonso Maria de Liguori, Ripa, etc.
Alfonso, Lettere	Lettere di S. Alfonso Maria de Liguori, I–III. Roma 1887–90
Spic Hist.	Spicilegium Historicum Congregationis SSmi. Redemptoris, Roma 1956 . . .
S.R.C. Informatio, etc.	Sacra Rituum Congregatione . . . Beatificationis et Canonizationis Ven. Servi Dei, Alphonsi Mariae de Ligorio . . . Informatio, Animadversiones, Responsio Super Virtutibus . . . Romae 1806
Tannoia	A.M. Tannoia, *Della Vita ed Istituto* . . . I–III Napoli 1798–1802
Telleria	R. Telleria, *San Alfonso Maria de Ligorio, Fundador* . . . Madrid 1950–51
Founding Texts	Founding Texts of the Redemptorists . . . ed. Hoegerl. Rome 1986

Chapter One, pp. 7–22.

1. As a young man Alphonsus wrote his name, *di Liguoro* or *Liguoro*. Later he changed to the form of *de Liguori* or *de' Liguori*. In his old age he was satisfied with *Liguori*. The branch of the family to which Alphonsus belonged was often referred to as the Liguori di Portanova from the *sedile* or *piazza* to which the family was attached.
2. T. Smollet, *Travels through France and Italy*, London 1949.
3. His life appeared in 1741: *Vita di Mons. Do. Emilio Giacomo Cavalieri, della Congregazione de' Pii Operai, Vescovo di Troia*, by D. Giovanni Rossi, a priest of the diocese of Troia.

4. The old Neapolitan ducat can conveniently be regarded as roughly equivalent to two American dollars though in those pre-inflation days its actual value was probably a lot more.
5. Tannoia is at his weakest in his account of Alphonsus' early years. It is here that recent research has yielded considerable insight into many aspects of those formative years.
6. Alphonsus was born on the outskirts of Naples at Marianella. The family then came to Naples about 1702 and lived in the parish of *Santa Maria dei Vergini* until about 1708. When Alphonsus began his law studies they moved nearer to the seat of the university at San Domenico Maggiore, parish of *Sant'Angelo à Segno*, (commonly called '*delle Anime del Purgatorio*') where they lived in the palazzo Cafaro in the Via Tribunali. Finally in 1717 they returned to the parish of *Santa Maria dei Vergini* to their palazzo at the Sopportico Lopez.
7. Gaetano Greco was born in Naples about 1680. None of his music appears to have been printed in his lifetime and only a few pieces are now known in MS. These are almost entirely for harpsichord and a selection of them from a MS in the British Museum was edited by J. S. Shedlock and published by Novello and Company.
8. The harpsichord was the favourite domestic keyboard instrument from Tudor times until the end of the 18th century. Naples in the 18th century was renowned for its harpsichord virtuosi. Domenico Scarlatti and Handel once competed, with the great music lover, Cardinal Ottoboni as adjudicator, to see which was the greater master of the instrument. They were judged equal. The usual 18th century Italian word for a harpsichord was *cembalo*, (which really means a dulcimer) or the more awkward *clavicembalo* (keyed-dulcimer). In the *Oxford Companion to Music*, P.A. Scholes 1955 tells us that the harpsichord is again being made and coming into use especially amongst connoisseurs who like to play — or less ambitiously, to hear played — old music, upon the instruments for which it was written. Alphonsus' harpsichord is still preserved in the Alphonsian museum attached to the Redemptorist house in Pagani.
9. Giambattista Vico, *Il Metodo degli Studi del Tempo Nostro*, ed. Antonio Corsano, Vallecchi Editore, Firenze 1937.
10. 'But I cannot forbear to mention three particular books, since they may have remotely contributed to form the historian of the Roman Empire: 1. From the provincial letters of Pascal, which almost every year I have perused with pleasure, I have learned to manage the weapon of grave and temperate irony, even on matters of Ecclesiastical solemnity; 2. The life of Julian, (the Apostate) by the Abbé de la Bleterie . . . ; 3. 'In Giannone's *Civil History of Naples* I observed with a critical eye the progress and abuse of Sacerdotal power and the Revolutions of Italy in the darker ages.' *The Autobiographies of Edward Gibbon*, ed. J. Murray London 1897. Excessive modesty cannot have been one of Gibbon's greatest defects.
11. The *sedile* were also called *piazze* or *seggi*. 'Wards' might be the appropriate English equivalent. The six *sedile* of Naples were: Capuana, Nido, Montagna, Porto, Portanova and Popolo.
12. P.L. Rispoli, *Vita del B. Alfonso Maria de Liguori*, Naples 1834.

Chapter Two, pp. 23–40.

1. S.R.C. Animadversiones R.P. Promotoris Fidei Super Virtutibus 5–6.
2. Evidence of Father Felix Verzella, Secretary and Confessor of Alphonsus during his episcopate, ed. A. Sampers. Spic. Hist. IX. 1961. 433.

3. S. Santagata, S.J., *La Vita di P. Giambattista Cacciottoli, Missionario della Campagnia di Gesu*, Naples 1751. 'La Signora D. Maria Anna di Liguoro, monaca nel chiostro di S. Girolamo prima di appressarsi alla communione per tal modo pativa di scrupoli che costretta era o a lasciare di communicarsi o a communicarsi con grande perturbamento.'
4. Venice, for example, had its *Incurabili* in which Francis Xavier and Ignatius Loyola laboured side by side.
5. Knowledge of Alphonsus' membership of the *Misericordiella* owes much to the researches of Father Orestes Gregorio, C.SS.R. *Contributi Bio-Bibliografici* 58–64. Alla *Misericordiella*.
6. The Promotor Fidei at the process of canonisation made some comments on Alphonsus' love for cards. In reply the Postulator of the Cause quoting St Thomas proved that to play games and recreate oneself was the virtue of Eutropelia!
7. Handel wrote his Agrippina during his visit to Italy; he spent over a year in Naples from June 1708.

    Dr Charles Burney went to the Teatro dei Fiorentini the very evening he arrived in Naples, Tuesday 16 October 1770: 'This theatre is as small as Mr Foote's (the new Haymarket in London), but higher as there are five rows of boxes in it.' Tour in Italy, 241.
8. Don Joseph's efforts to secure Alphonsus' *fidanzamento* (engagement) and subsequent marriage are well attested but at times with conflicting details. Tannoia, Landi, and Father Giuseppe Cardone among others give details of some of these efforts. But it is once again due to the researches of Father Gregorio, C.SS.R. that some clarification has been achieved. *Contributi Bio-Bibliografici* 48–58. The archives in Naples may have some surprises still in store for us in this matter, cf. Landi I, 28. A.G.H.R. XXV Summario & XXVII 17.
9. B.G.E.R. I. 117.
10. A.G.H.R. XXVI 60; XXVII 30.
11. A.G.H.R. XXVII 44.
12. A.G.H.R. SAM VI 10 35.
13. We have the explicit testimony of Alphonsus' brother Cajetan for this incident. A.G.H.R. XXVII 31.

    As regards his health, Alphonsus informed his father — what he must have known already — that he was not meant for marriage 'perche non di perfetta salute e putiva di petto'. Besides being slightly asthmatic at this time Alphonsus also suffered from chronic bronchitis all his life which was liable to develop into severe congestion of the lungs if he was not careful.
14. The Superior of the Vincentian house in Florence, Father Scaramelli, vouched for the authenticity of the incident with his own signature and the Seal of his Order. Since the families of the parties involved, so the account continues, were still alive the picture could not be kept in Florence nor the event made public there. The picture accordingly was sent to the Vincentian house in Naples and is still preserved in one of the monastery parlours. Every year the king of Naples, Charles III, sent his children to see the picture and to meditate on it.
15. *Visite al SS. Sacramento ed a Maria SS. per ciascun giorno del mese*. Opere Ascetiche di S. Alfonso M. de Liguori I, 369. Marietti Torino 1845.
16. Alphonsus de Liguori, Homo Apostolicus, Tractatus XIII. Punctum III. No. 24.
17. Archivo Vaticano Nunz. Nap. 449. 182: Ad primam tonsuram non promoveantur unigeniti; primogeniti; qui habent alium fratrem tonsura vel aliis Ordinibus insignitum.

18. Orestes Gregorio, Richerche intorno alla Causa Feudale Perduta nel 1723 da Alfonso de Liguori, estratto dall' *'Archivio Storico per le Province Napoletane'*, Vol. XXXIV (1953–1954).
19. Sorge published two small treatises on the legal aspects of the emperor's case against the Grand Duke of Tuscany in Naples in 1720 with which Alphonsus would certainly have been familiar. This material Sorge incorporated in his eleven-volume work *Iurisprudentia Forensis universi propemodum iuris materias . . . complectens*, which he published in Naples 1740–1744 and which he dedicated to King Charles III. The whole of volume 5 deals with *De Feudis*.
20. A.G.H.R. XXVII 33. Alphonsus described the case to his missionary colleagues in August 1758; one of them went to his room within half an hour and wrote down what Alphonsus had recounted. The saint's account makes quite clear the kernel of the whole case: 'il punto stava in dichiarare se un feudo era nuovo o antico. Il Padre nostro sosteneva che era vecchia e ci aveva fatto un lungo discorso. Quando uno de' guidici. . .disse che si fusso letto il Diploma della concessione, ove si trova espressa la clausola *in novum*. E pure questa scrittura era stata varie volte letta dal nostro Padre.' This account is confirmed in an account of the case based on information from Alphonsus' brother Don Cajetan. A.G.H.R. XXVI 31.
21. 'Alfonso e capo tuosto: con difficoltà si muove', cf. Antonio Altamura, *Dizionario dialettale Napoletano*, Naples 1956.
22. Most biographers place this incident later in the month, on the same day that Alphonsus seemed to hear the voice of God in the Incurabili telling him to leave the world. In this they follow Tannoia. Alphonsus himself does not mention the sword incident but he related his visit to the church during the novena of Our Lady's Assumption to his friend Don Salvatore Tramontano, and with all an old man's attention to detail recalled that the preacher had a German name. A.G.H.R. XXV 17c.

    G.A. Galante in *Guida Sacra della Citta di Napoli* 1872 states that the original sword was sold some time in the last century and the silver crown which now adorns the statue purchased with the proceeds.
23. A *Cuccagna* was originally applied to the village game of placing a ham or some similar eatable on top of a greasy pole; whoever climbed to the top claimed the ham. At the viceregal — and later the royal — court of Naples it was a more elaborate and more revolting affair. In one corner of the courtyard was placed an enticing array of every possible luxury, food, fruit, wine, etc. guarded by a pallisade. At the opposite corner a group of the poor of Naples was assembled and at a sign from the viceroy or president the mob swarmed towards the food. Whatever they were able to lay their hands on and keep they could take away with them. From the balconies the court and nobility looked on at the horse-play, enjoying the revolting scene of human beings trampling on each other and fighting like animals for food. Frequently many of the participants were seriously injured; at times deaths resulted. The *cuccagna* which celebrated the arrival of Charles of Bourbon in 1734 ended in disaster with the collapse of the scaffolding bearing the food; twenty-four of the participants were killed and over a hundred injured. Charles III and his court looked on in dismay from the balconies.
24. Years later Alphonsus speaking to a group of young Redemptorist scholastics said that one of the fundamental maxims of the Gospel teaching is 'what doth it profit a man if he gain the whole world and suffer the loss of his soul'. It was

this maxim which brought many saints to God, like St Ignatius Loyola, St Francis Xavier and many others. 'And to tell the truth it was this maxim which drew me also from the world. My father outlined for me the advantages that I could hope for in this world but I, reflecting that all is vanity and comes to an end quickly, resolved to leave the world and consecrate myself to God'. A.G.H.R. XXVII.

25. *Ippocondria* is not to be translated simply as hypochondria, a morbid state of depression usually associated with anxiety about health. In the meaning that it was used in the circumstances of Alphonsus' decision it contains undertones of 'spleen' and 'bitterness' with perhaps 'self-justification' and 'self-pity' included. See *Vocabolario degli Accademici della Crusca*, Florence, 1729–1738; 'E impazzito Alfonso de Liguori', A.G.H.R. XXVII 17.

Chapter Three, pp. 41–65.

1. Tannoia describes Don Joseph's acceptance of his son's vocation after hearing him preach in the basilica of the Holy Spirit: Vita. Lib. I c. XI 37. The year usually given is 1728. If that is correct it is clear that Alphonsus was not preaching the *Predica Grande*; it must have been some other minor exercise of the Mission. Unfortunately the registers of the Apostolic Missions for that particular year are missing. The registers for the following year 1729 show that during the annual general mission held in the basilica of the Holy Spirit, Alphonsus was not present on any evening but preached the morning sermon once, on 27 October. R. Telleria, Prima S. Alfonsi Palaestra Missionaria etc., Spic. Hist. VIII. 1960. 393.
2. The information about the three missionary congregations in the Naples diocese is based on Telleria's researches published in Spic. Hist. VIII, 1960, 393.
3. P.L. Rispoli, *Vita*.
4. I have kept distinct the meetings of Alphonsus and his companions as clerical students from those which he later on organised as a young priest — often with the same companions — and which are known as the *Cappelle Serotine*. S.R.C., *Summarium super dubio*, etc. 18–20.
5. G. Estius (1542–1613), born in Holland, spent most of his life in Douai. His commentaries on the Epistles of St Paul, published in 1614–1616, made him the foremost pauline authority of his era. Pope Benedict XIV called him Doctor fundatissimus. It was often said at the time: 'Maldonatus on the Gospels, Estius on the Epistles'.
6. Louis Vereeche, C.SS.R., *De Guillaume D'Ockham à Saint Alphonse de Liguori*, Rome 1986. James R. Pollock, S.J., *François Genet: The Man and His Methodology*.
7. *Breve Dissertazione sull'uso moderato dell'opinione Probabile*, Naples 1762, 90. *Risposta Apologetica* . . . 1762, cf B.G.E.R. I. 118.
8. *Avvertimenti a'Sacerdoti che assistono ai Condannati a morte*, Naples 1775, cf. B.G.E.R. I. 165.
9. O. Gregorio published an assessment of Alphonsus' first sermon in *Osservatore Romano*, 1 January 1960. The MS. is to be found in A.G.H.R. A.M. III. 249. An interesting internal detail is that Alphonsus referred during the sermon to *Blessed* (Beata) Margaret of Cortona; she was canonised in 1728 by Benedict XIII. The theme of this sermon found its way into at least three of the *Visits to the Blessed Sacrament*, nos. 7, 11 and 29. The theme of Christ the Good Shepherd was commonplace in popular devotional literature at the time and also in devotional art. There were even paintings of Our Lady under the title of *La*

Divina Pastora, the most acceptable of which was executed by the Neapolitan painter, P. Di Maio. It is also suggested that Alphonsus himself painted a picture of Our Lady under this title. D. Capone, *Il Volto di Sant'Alfonso*, Rome 1954, 116.
10. Council of Trent: sess. 23. Cap. XVI. Paolo Sarpi in his history of the Council commented with his usual maliciousness on the problem. Pallavicino went out of his way to reply in his *Istoria del Concilio di Trento*, Lib. XVIII Cap IX.
11. Archivio Vaticano: Nunz. Nap. Vol 449, f.176; Vol. 459, f.65. The account of the condition of the Naples clergy is taken from the thesis of Rev. Angelo Lanzoni, presented in the Pontifical University of the Lateran, *La riduzione del Clero nelle trattive fra la Santa Sede e la Corte di Napoli.*
12. Giovanni Giuseppe della Croce died at Naples in 1734. Alphonsus would have been aware of his reputation for holiness and extreme penance; he consulted him among many others concerning the establishing of his missionary society.
13. P. Hazard, *European Thought in the Eighteenth Century*, London 1954.
14. *Homo Apostolicus. Tract. Ult. Punctum IV*, 650 Marietti, Torino 1848.
15. Alfonso, Lettere I. 253.
16. Don Joseph gave him the rents of a house in the Toledo as his patrimony and this was increased by the incomes from the benefices which came to him from the Duke of Gravina Orsini and the Prince of Presicce Liguori, his kinsman. Finally, he was provided with a rich chaplaincy in the Cathedral.
17. Father Telleria discovered the original documents with the details of these legal transactions after long and patient search in the Notary section of the Neapolitan State Archives. Spic. Hist. V. 1957. 237–76. The document relating to Alphonsus' clerical patrimony, constituted legally 28 July 1724, is to be found in Spic. Hist. X. 1962. 334–6. The entries in the Neapolitan archiepiscopal archives confirming Alphonsus' admission to orders from Tonsure to Priesthood are also to be found there.
18. B. Croce, *Uomini e Cose della Vecchia Italia*, Bari 1956, II. 121. A. Santonicola, C.SS.R., *Sant'Alfonso e l'Azione Cattolica*. Pompei 1939.

Chapter Four, pp. 66–89.

1. A.G.H.R. XXVII 30.
2. O. Gregorio, 'Richerche intorno al libretto Alphonsiano della "Visita al SS.Sacramento"', Spic. Hist.IV.1956. 177–82. Unfortunately this research of Father Gregorio puts an end to the charming speculation that the publication of the book of 'Visits' was financed by Don Joseph, Alphonsus' father. There is a price to be paid for everything.
3. Alfonso, Lettere I. 234, 235, 239.
4. Alfonso, Lettere I. 3; Falcoia, Lettere 186, 220; O. Gregorio, *Mons. Tommaso Falcoia*, 1663–1743. 272.
5. P. L. Rispoli, *Vita*, 35.
6. D. Capone, 'Dissertazione e Note di S. Alfonso sulla Probabilità e la Coscienza'. Studia Moralia, I. 1963, 271.
7. The main source for this section of Alphonsus' life is the so-called 'Spiritual Note-Book' of the saint, mainly in his own handwriting and also referred to as 'Matters of Conscience'. The MSS. are preserved in A.G.H.R. under the indication SAM, VI, 9a, 9b, 10. The first competent study of this important source is the work of F. Ferrero, 'La Mentalidad Moral de San Alfonso en su Cuaderno Espiritual', Spic.Hist. XXI. 1973. 198–258.

NOTES

A transcription of Alphonsus's 'Libretto di Memorie' was made by Father Giuseppe Mautone (1765–1845), Procurator General and Postulator of the cause of canonisation. It is to be found in A.G.H.R. SAM IIIa, formerly MS. Mautone 9c. Father Mautone omitted certain phrases which he may have found embarrassing for one reason or another. A later transcript made by Father Domenico Mozzicarelli (1887–1972) has also to be checked carefully against the original.

8. On page 24 of his 'note-book' Alphonsus has two entries concerning the possibility that one Barb(ara)? and one Ter(esa)? had somehow incurred the penalty of excommunication. It is an intriguing possibility that this cryptic entry may have referred to his two sisters.
9. A.G.H.R. XXV 17c; XXVI 62; XXVII 15.
10. S. Alfonsi Mariae de Liguori, *Theologia Moralis*, ed. L. Gaudé, Romae, 1905, I. 6–10. It is not an exaggeration to say that what is contained in the 'note-book' is a rough draft of what is found in the *Moral Theology*. He wrote from his own experience. B.G.E.R. I. 76.
11. A.G.H.R. XXVII 44.
12. R. Telleria, 'Sacellum Scalense "S. Maria de Monte"', Spic. Hist. XI. 1963. 345–73. Considerable research has been done to ascertain the precise number and identity of the members of the group since there are conflicting accounts given by Alphonsus' contemporaries, Sportelli and Tannoia. There is also disagreement whether the sanctuary should be referred to as S. Maria di Monte or S. Maria dei Monti. Father D. Capone, the authority on the geography and traditions of Scala, uses both forms.
13. S. Majorano, *L'Imitazione per la Memoria del Salvatore*, 55.
14. S. Majorano, *L'Imitazione*, 55 quoting from Crotarosa'a autobiography.
15. About Crostarosa's understanding of religious life and missionary activity cf. Majorano, *L'Imitazione* 11 & 311; *Le Radici* 6–7.
16. Falcoia, Lettere 69–70.
17. S. Alfonso Maria *Homo Apostolicus* ed. Marietti, Torino 1848. Appendix I. Directio Animarum Spiritualium Nos. 19–23. 667–71.
18. Spic.Hist. XXVIII. 1975. 14–39.
19. Alfonso, Lettere I. 1–8.
20. Falcoia, Lettere 85.
21. Spic.Hist. XXIII. 1975. 26
22. Falcoia, Lettere 87.
    For the Rule of Crostarosa in its many redactions, cf. Founding Texts.

Chapter Five, pp. 90–110.

1. Perhaps in this we do less than justice to the Foundresses of Orders of Sisters. Women have shown less reluctance to assume the burden of establishing religious families; they are possessed of a finer sense of purpose in this than their male counterparts.
2. Andrea Sampers, *Corrispondenza Epistolare tra S. Alfonso e le Monache di Scala* . . . Spic. Hist. XXIII. 1975. 27–9.
3. A.G.H.R. SAM VI 10. 36 (Transcript. Mozzicarelli 17).
4. The original document concerning these revelations of Sister Maria Celeste is not extant. Years later, after 1749, she wrote an account from memory in her autobiography. Her scripture text united two texts of St Mark, 1.15 and 15.16.
5. Falcoia, Lettere 86 No. 24.

6. Analecta V. 1926, 44.
7. Falcoia, Lettere 87 No. 25.
8. Analecta III. 1924, 26 Depositiones Joannis Mazzini.
9. Falcoia, Lettere 89 No. 26.
10. Alphonsus de Liguori, *Riflessioni utili ai Vescovi* IX.
    In some biographies of Alphonsus it was stated that it was on returning from the fatigues of Nardo that Alphonsus and his companions went to Santa Maria dei Monti. But the visit to the hermitage above Scala took place nearly two years before. Once again we owe this correction of chronology to Father Telleria.
11. Arch. Vat. Concilio. Relat. dioec. Troiana a.1733.
12. Alfonso, Lettere II. 456–7.
13. With his own hands Pagano entered in Alphonsus' personal note-book on 29 March 1732 'chiamato per rivelazione per Padri spirituali senza poterlo mettere piu in dubio'. Transcript 26.
14. '*Matto, pazzo, ostinato, fanatico, ossesso, illuso, vanglorioso, per farsi nome nel mondo, borioso, superbo, pieno di se, svanito di mente, posto in testa di fare il fondatore, uscito di mente, si faceva diriggere da una monaca illusa.*'
15. S.R.C. Informatio Super dubio . . . 10 No.37.
    Responsio ad Animad. R.R.P.F. Super Virtut. . . . 27 No. 62.
    A.G.H.R. I. D. 34.
16. Analecta IV. 1925. 271 et seqq. Ripa wrote his account of the events connected with the founding of the new Institute many years after those events. His work was published in Naples in three volumes in 1832.
17. Falcoia, Lettere 102 and 107, nos. 34 and 37.
18. A.G.H.R. SAM VI 10 63, 64 (Mozzicarelli, 31).
19. Verdict of C. Sportelli in Spic. Hist. V. 1957. 235.
20. Spic. Hist. XXIII. 1975. It is quite clear from the correspondence that a number of letters both from Celeste and Alphonsus during this period have not survived. A similar fate must have befallen the 'conzaputa relatione' she had sent him.
21. Spic. Hist. XXIII 1975. 31–4.
22. Analecta V. 1926. 120–21.
23. Analecta V. 1926. 117.
24. Alfonso, Lettere 1. 16–19. This edition of St Alphonsus' letter, published in 1887, tentatively dated this letter March 1733, which is clearly incorrect. Father Capone is correct in recognising that it dates from September 1732, after Tosques' visit to Scala, and after Alphonsus had accepted Falcoia as his Director and before he left for Scala in November 1732.
25. Falcoia, Lettere 109–13, no. 38 'Con questo vi prego e v'impongo che rifiuti tutte le tante riflessioni che v'angustiano e vi molestiano'.
26. Tannoia Vol. I. L. II. C. I. 8. A.G.H.R. XXVII 10.
27. Spic. Hist. VIII. 1960. 437. Alfonso, Lettere I. 13.
28. A.G.H.R. SAM VI. 10. 66 (Transcript. Mozicarelli, 32).
29. R. Telleria, Documenta Vaticana de Apparitionibus Scalae. Spic. Hist. I. 1953. 67–82.
30. Tannoia places the Inauguration ceremony in the cathedral with a sung Mass of the Holy Spirit. More reliable sources place the ceremony in the hospice of the Sisters. I think the weight of contemporary evidence indicates this as the more likely, cf. *Le Radici*, 91. There are interminable arguments about details of the whole 1732 scenario in the life of Alphonsus. Who accompanied him to Scala? Did he go directly to Scala or via Castellamare? Was Falcoia waiting for

him in Scala or did they all go together from Castellamare to Scala? Was the inauguration in the cathedral with a large congregation or in the Hospice? etc. etc. Evidence given during the various Processes for canonisation offers conflicting accounts very often on these minor points. Even Tannoia contradicts himself, saying one thing at the Process of Beatification and then stating something quite different in his *Vita*. But these points, while interesting and at times of some significance, do not alter the main outline of the history of the events. Even Father Telleria in his later publications in the Spicilegium Historicum had to contradict facts which he stated some years before in his magisterial two-volume *San Alfonso Maria de Ligorio*. And so the present writer finds himself at times deciding on a particular fact or date knowing well that eminent researchers have settled for something different. But one has nearly always some eminent authority on one's side.

Chapter Six, pp. 111–135.

1. A.G.H.R. SAM VI 10, 66–7 (Trans. 32).
2. S.R.C. Animad. R.P.P.F. Super Virt. 14 No.27.
   Resp. ad Animad. . . . 49 Nos. 96, 53, 104.
3. Spic.Hist. X. 1962. 198–220. Letters of Tosques and Torni.
4. Tannoia dramatised Alphonsus' expulsion from the Apostolic Missions and casts Gizzio in the role of villain (Lib. II. Cap. III). The minutes of the society itself give a more sober account. Spic.Hist. VIII. 1960. 437–9.
5. There is a full account of the area of Tramonti and of this first missionary undertaking by Telleria in Spic.Hist. X. 1962. 179–217.
6. Falcoia, Lettere 121–22.
7. Tannoia Lib. II. Cap. IV.
8. Alfonso, Lettere I. 25.
9. *Le Radici* 352.
10. Falcoia, Lettere 142–5.
11. S.R.C. Anim. R.P.P.F. Super Virtutibus 18 No.15. 'Miror in tanto negotio disponendo, maturando, absolvendo animi constantiam, invictam intueor Ven. Alf. fortitudinem.'
12. Falcoia, Lettere 146.
13. This letter is to be found Alfonso, Lettere I. 20–32.
14. For the question of Alphonsus' accusations against Maria Celeste and the effect it had on the introduction of her Cause, and her letter of reply, called by some historians, as here, her *Apologia*, see Analecta VI. 1927. 48–60; Spic.Hist. XXIII.1957.21. *Le Radici* 138–163.
15. Analecta VI. 1927. 105–12.
16. G. Landi, Istoria I. 132.
17. Arch. Vat. Concilio. Relationes dioec. Caiacensis 1735.

Chapter Seven, pp. 136–168.

1. The *chinea* is described by Cornelia Knight in her autobiography published in London 1861. She witnessed it in 1780. It was finally abolished by Pius IX.
2. He was buried in the church of San Giovanni dei Fiorentini in Naples in the via Fiorentini. The church has since been demolished.
3. *Concessionis Tituli Doctoris* . . . Rome 1870. Animadversiones . . . 3 No.7.
4. Tosques was considered by the Bourbons in Naples to be an Austrian spy, one

more bizarre turn to the story of this amazing man. For the consequences for Alphonsus' father, see Spic.Hist V. 1957. 252.
5. Alfonso, Lettere I. 40.
6. Falcoia, Lettere 223; Analecta XI. 1932. 364.
7. Falcoia, Lettere 230 & 290.
8. Alfonso, Lettere I. 32–6.
9. Alfonso, Lettere I. 38–40.
10. The series of letters about novitiate training are to be found *passim* in Falcoia's correspondence with Alphonaus from September 1734 to the end of 1735.
11. G. Landi, *Istoria* I. 78.
12. A.G.H.R. XXVII 9a (c).
13. Alfonso, Lettere I. 62–65 Alphonsus is today venerated in Villa Liberi as the Patron of the city.
14. Epistolae C. Sportelli. ed. Henze 68–70; A.G.H.R. XXVII 39
15. A.G.H.R. I.D. 36 (4).
16. Alfonso, Lettere I. 79.
17. *Founding Texts* 321. Epistolae C. Sportelli, 50. The Vow formula mentioned that it 'can be dispensed only by the actual major superior or by the sovereign pontiff'. At the time there was apparently no major superior of the congregation.
18. A.G.H.R. XXVII 21. Alphonsus was preaching on Saturday 9 July 1757 when he made this remark.
19. *Le Radici* 225. Alphonsus' resolution about Falcoia 'dir sempre bene delle cose di Mgr. Falcoia e non lagnarsene' is to be found on page 282.
20. Falcoia, Lettere 393.
21. Spic.Hist. VIII. 1960. 443. Alphonsus' conferences must have been quite remarkable if the clergy remembered them after seven years. In these matters the duration of clerical memories can be quite brief.
22. De Meulemeester, *Origines* II. 229; *Le Radici* 286.
23. The account of the abuses the missioners were faced with can be found in Arch. Vat. Congreg. Council; Relat. Dioec. Neap. 1747 and in the folios of Sacra Visita 1741–1746, of Spinelli, in the archiepiscopal archives of Naples.
24. A.G.H.R. XXVII 10.
25. Epistolae C. Sportelli, 68–70; Falcoia, Lettere 433–9.
26. Technically from 21 July until the middle of August when the constellation Sirio, the Dog star, rises with the morning sun. *Solleone* is when the sun is in Leo.
27. *Le Radici* 289.
28. Epistolae C. Sportelli, 86; O. Gregorio, *Mons. T Falcoia*, 308. The whereabouts of the bishop's remains is unknown today.

Chapter Eight, pp. 169–199.

1. Founding Texts 326.
2. De Meulemeester, *Origines* II. 35, note 55.
3. *De Indole Juridica Votorum in Congregatione SS.R. ante annum 1749 emissorum* J. Pfab. Spic.Hist. IX. 1971. 280; Founding Texts 321.
4. Spic. Hist. XXV. 1977. 289–300.
5. Alfonso, Lettere I. 102.
6. Most of the details about the Pagani foundation can be found in G. Landi, *Istoria* I. 174.
7. One of the questions raised against Alphonsus at the process of canonisation by the *Promotor Fidei* was that he spent much of his lifetime engaged in court

quarrels — litigation in the royal and civil courts of justice. The 'Devil's Advocate' must have had an unusual sense of humour. In point of fact from the year 1740 Alphonsus was hardly ever free from some legal worry; there was hardly a year in which there was not some move against him or his congregation or one of his foundations. He sustained it all with remarkable patience, fighting every legal corner like the lawyer he was. But he was always the defendant, never the plaintiff. As I pointed out in an early chapter, court litigation was a way of life in 18th century Naples.

8. A.G.H.R. Historica XVIII C. Deliceto; Alfonso, Lettere I. 98 et seqq.
9. De Meulemeester, *Origines* II. 256.
10. For the importance of the Compendio of Bovino in the evolution the Rule of the C.SS.R. cf. Founding Texts 151.
11. F. Kuntz. Annales C.SS.R. . . . II. 363–6.
12. A.G.H.R. SAM 9c 67–73. De Meluemesater, *Origines* II. 261. There is an excellent theological analysis of this sermon in D. Capone, *Sant'Alfonso Missionario*, Naples, 1987, 75. There are a number of copies extant of various versions of the 18th century *Predicata della Chiamata*.
13. Epistolae C. Sportelli 121.
14. S. Alfonso Opere Ascetiche Vol. XV *La Vera Sposa di Gesù Cristo*, Rome 1935 passim.
15. Alfonso, Lettere I. 110.
16. De Meulemeester, *Origines* II. 273. Father Giuseppe Landi used similar language when describing his fellow countrymen of the Principato Citra near Persano. O. Gregorio, Un Cronista Settecentesco Eburino. *Rivista di Studi Salernitani* No.3. 1969.
17. Epistolae C. Sportelli 178–80.
18. Alfonso, Lettere I. 55 and 66.
    Alphonsus' letters to his father are published. It would be hard to imagine books more unsuitable for Don Giuseppe than those recommended to him by Alphonsus.
19. Alfonso, Lettere I. 112.
20. B.G.E.R. I. 56.
21. *Riflessioni utili a' Vescovi* . . . Marietti, Turin. Opere Ascetiche Vol. III. In many places at that time the local municipality, often referred to as *l'Univeraità*, arranged the mission, or if the priests of the locality did not want one, approached the bishop directly. In many cases they bore the cost of the mission from their own tax revenue or through grants from central government. This latter is what is meant when on occasions the King offers to support the work of the missions financially.
22. A.G.H.R. XXVII 30.
23. A.G.H.R. XXVII IV.
24. A.G.H.R. XXVII 21.

Chapter Nine, pp. 203–227.

1. B.G.E.R. I. 61–2; Alfonso, Lettere III. 1–2.
2. B.G.E.R. I. 68. There is some evidence according to de Meulemeester that the Dominican in question replied to Alphonsus' *Apologia* some years later.
3. Spic.Hist. XXIX. 1981. 72 et seqq. D. Capone, *S. Alfonso . . . lettore di Teologia*.
4. Alfonso, Lettere III. 459.
5. So many legends have grown up about St Alphonsus that it would require a special study to track them all down and refute them. After his death evidence was

given to Tannoia that 'once he left for Scala he never saw his parents' home again. When he went to Naples he stayed with Olivieri. When his father died he did not want to go home. At his mother's death he went but left after two days.' The emphasis here is inaccurate. Similar legends persist about other saints despite efforts to refute them — such for example, as that of St Aloysius Gonzaga refusing out of modesty to look his mother in the face. A.G.H.R. XXVI 67

6. St Teresa of Avila, *Libro de la Vida* ... Ch. 37.
7. *Adnotationes in Busenbaum* col. 250.
8. Tannoia T.I.L. II c.38.
9. For the evolution of the Redemptorist Rule, cf. Founding Texts. Sportelli, Epistolae, 178.
10. Alfonso, Lettere I. 118–122.
11. A.G.H.R. I c.33.
12. Alfonso, Lettere. I. 149. The principal examiners were Canons Simeoli and Blaschi.
13. Alfonso, Lettere I. 154–7.
14. The main source of the details concerning Villani's Roman visit are to be found in the letters he wrote back to Ciorani and which are preserved in the General Archives in Rome. A large number these are to be found in M. de Meulemeester, *Origines* II. 274–315.
15. Villani was the first one *canonically* entitled to do so. But Sportelli had jumped the gun when news of the likely change reached him. He signed himself 'del SS. Redentore' in a letter 15 January 1749. Sportelli Epistolae, 199.
16. Landi's account is published in de Meulemeester, *Origines* II. 316–23.

Chapter Ten, pp. 228-261.

1. Alfonso, Lettere II. 235, 27 June 1773.
2. Mannarini died 12 March 1775 at the age of 75. He was buried in the church of his Order at Lucera, thirteen miles from Foggia. His tombstone bears the simple inscription, *Congregationis SS. Sacramenti Fundator.*
3. Father Telleria found the Report of Cito in the Naples State Archives: Affari Ecclesiastici, Espedienti di Consiglio, V. 591.
4. Alfonso, Lettere I. 208, 25 December 1752. The Nuncio's Report to Rome is in Arch.Vat.Napoli, Vol. 237, ff.377–9.
5. Alfonso, Lettere I. 238.
6. Alfonso, Lettere I. 184.
7. Contributi Bio-Bibliografici, 241–3.
8. A.G.H.R. I.D. 35 No. 3 for Spinelli's reply. Proc. Ord. S. Agath. III. I.153 ter.
9. Alfonso, Lettere I. 252, 18 June 1754.
10. The truth about Alphonsus' conduct on the occasion of his mother's last illness and death is in startling contrast with the unfounded traditions in the matter which gained credence about him in the 19th century and which were adduced as the basis for quite indefensible practices in the area of filial pietas. Donna Anna chose for her burial place the Confraternity of the Immaculate Conception dei Nobili de Montecalvario in Naples, of which she was a life-long member. Taking into account the fact that Cajetan was also a priest, the distance between Naples and Beneventum, and the accepted custom in Naples of not delaying the burial, there is no ascetical conclusion to be drawn from the fact that Alphonsus did not return to Naples for his mother's burial.

11. B.G.E.R. I.110. F.de Mura, *Il Missionario Istruito*, Naples 1738. A historico-theological study of Alphonsus' missionary system is to be found in P.A. Mazzoni, *Le Missioni Populari nel Pensiero di Sant'Alfonso de Liguori*, Padua 1961, Pontificia Universitas Gregoriana.
12. Father Dominic Corsano, a Dominican, one of Alphonsus' confessors, declared at the process of beatification that Alphonsus said to him several times that he could not remember ever having *dismissed* a penitent without granting absolution. A long argument developed between the Promotor of the Faith and the *Ponens* of the Cause as a result of this evidence. The Devil's Advocate urged that it was unthinkable that Alphonsus should not have encountered in his whole missionary career, habitual sinners who lived in the voluntary proximate occasion of sin (to use the contemporary terminology) and whom it would have been impossible to absolve there and then. Much time was expended on this discussion at the Process, involving the theology of the *consuetudinarii and occasionarii*. There is no doubt that on a number of occasions Alphonsus *deferred* absolution, which, however, is different from *refusing* or *dismissing* a penitent without absolution. On his behalf it was claimed that he possessed a unique gift from God as a result of his personal holiness of life, which gave him such power over souls that by his patience and the force of his exhortations he was always able to dispose them for the fruitful reception of absolution, no matter what demands he was forced to make on them as regards abandoning the occasions of sin. It was also made clear that since the missioners remained in the area for several weeks, Alphonsus probably *deferred* absolution in certain cases to allow the penitent time to consider his situation and make the necessary decisions, in which case he or she would have returned to Alphonsus to receive absolution.

    S.R.C. Animadversiones R.P.P. Fidei Super Virtutibus, 15, No.31. Resp. ad Animad. R.P.P. Fidei 57, No.116 et seqq; Nova Positio Super Virtut. Animad. R.P.P. Fidei, 9–11, Nos. 20–26 Responsio . . . 56, No.107 et seqq. And cf. Rev.James Cleary, C.SS.R. Did S. Alphonsus Ever Refuse Absolution? *Irish Ecclesiastical Record*, LXII. 1943. 389.
13. *Il Confessore Diretto per le Confessione della Gente di Compagna* XII.25. One of the Fathers, giving evidence at the process of gathering information for Alphonsus' canonisation gave it as his opinion that Alphonsus' special gift from God was direction of souls and not only those souls who were most abandoned but also devout and spiritual souls who had need of being guided and directed in the way of the Lord. A.G.H.R. XXVI 65.
14. *La Presenza e l'opera dei Redentoristi del Mezzogiorno*, Napoli, 1987, 29.
15. 'There is greater need for instruction of the people than for preaching. The principles of religion are more impressed on them by means of instruction then by formal sermons.' O. Gregorio, *Sentimenti di Monsignore*. Spic.Hist. IX. 1961. 449. There was a very decided catechetical orientation in Alphonsus' mission system from the beginning, see Spic.Hist. IV. 1956. 261 et seqq.
16. Much has been written about this Neapolitan social custom and the moral problems it caused. An excellent study of the whole question is to be found in Jose Suescun, *La Moralidad de las relaciones prematrimoniales segun la doctrina de San Alfonso Mari de Ligorio y Su Tiempo*. Dissertatio ad Lauream. Pontificia Universitas Gregoriana, 1955.
17. A.G.H.R. XXVII 41.
18. Proc. Ord. S. Agath. III.1311. Evidence of Father Picone.
19. *Selva*. Pars III. Cap. VII par. VI.

20. The Crusca was an academy founded in Florence in 1583 which took the name Crusca, meaning chaff, with a sieve for its emblem, to symbolise its self-arrogated function of separating good linguistic usage from bad. It also published a dictionary, the *Vocabolario della Crusca*, referred to simple as *La Crusca*. Eventually the word *Crusca* became synonymous with pedantry and affectation, see Eric W. Cochrane, *Tradition and Enlightenment in the Tuscan Academies, 1690–1800*, Rome 1961, Edizione di Storia e Letteratura.
21. Proc. Ord. Nuc. I. 361 Spic.Hist. X. 1962. 39–40.
22. A.G.H.R. XXVII 21; S.R.C. Resp. ad Animad. R.P.P. Fidei Super Virt. 36–9 par. 73–81.
23. B.G.E.R. I. 116 No. 50.

Chapter Eleven, pp. 262–295.

1. The whole question of citations and references in the ascetical works of Alphonsus, which gave rise to considerable controversy in the last century in connection both with the granting of the title of Doctor of the Church and with the criticisms of German historians, is admirably treated by D. Capone, *Le Citazione nelle Opere Ascetiche di S. Alfonso*, in S. Alfonso M. di Liguori, *Opere Ascetiche*, ... Introduzione Generale, 293.
2. Alfonso, Lettere III. 437.

    The problems surrounding printing and publishing in Bourbon Naples is dealt with in S. Alfonso M. de Liguori, *Opere Ascetiche* are ... Introduzione Generale, Gregorio, Cacciatore, Capone, Rome 1960. cf. R. Bayon *Como Escribio Alfonso de Liguorio*, Madrid 194.
3. Alfonso, Lettere III. 272.

    S. Alfonso M. de Liguori, *Opere Ascetiche* ... Introduzione Generale, 13–14.
4. 'O you who would with Jesus go, must never with the S.J. go.'
5. G. Cacciatore, *La Letteratura degli 'exempla'*, Alfonso M. de Liguori, *Opere Ascetiche*, ... Introduzione Generale, 239.
6. C. Dillenschneider, *La Mariologie de S. Alphonse de Ligouri*, ... 2 vols. Fribourg 1931, 1934.
7. J. H. Newman, *A Letter addressed to the Rev. E. B. Pusey, D.D. on the occasion of his Eirenicon*.
8. *Le Glorie di Maria*, Pars I. Cap. V. Critical edition, Rome 1936, 160.
9. *Le Glorie di Maria* ... Appendix 7, 377; B.G.E.R. I. 87 No.27.
10. Alfonso, Lettere I. 191.
11. The firm of Remondini, which had been in existence for over a hundred years at this time, was among the most prestigious publishing houses in Europe. Founded by Giuseppi Antonio Remondini from Padua, succeeding generations of the family had added to the business and expanded into other aspects of the trade, such as paper making. They had branches in Rome, Bologna, Ferrara, as well as agents in the principal cities beyond the Alps. It was primarily his keen business sense which prompted Giuseppi Remondini, the head of the firm, to contact Alphonsus in the summer of 1755 with a proposal to bring out an edition of the *Moral Theology*.
12. It was only in the sixth edition of the *Moral Theology*, published by Remondini in 1767, that the name of Busenbaum disappeared completely from the title page. And then it was mainly due to the anti-Jesuit campaign being waged at the time. Alphonsus was afraid of bringing the anti-Jesuit fury down on himself and his Congregation. B.G.E.R. I. 66.

13. Alphonsus is now most commonly referred to as an 'Equiprobabilist' and the moral system he advocated as 'Equiprobabilism' which, in substance is similar to Probabilism but with modifying nuances in certain areas, see B.V. Johnstone, 'The Significance of the Moral Theology of St. Alphonsus . . .' *Studia Moralia*, Supplement, 1990, 80 n.9.
14. Alphonsus' treatises dealing with the speculative aspects of Probabilism have virtually identical titles — *'De Uso Moderato dell'Opinione Probabile'* — and are distinguishable mainly by date of composition and content.
15. *Theologia Moralis Sancti Alphonsi*, . . . ed. Gaudé, Vol. II.689. Lib. V. Tractatus Praeambulus. De Actibus Humanis in Genere.
16. (i) *Pratica del Confessore per ben esercitare il suo Ministero*, Naples 1755 in Italian. Referred to as the *Pratica piccola*. Translated into Latin and published in 1757.
    (ii) *Istruzione e pratica per un Confessore*, Naples 1757. 3 Vols in Italian. Referred to as *Pratica Grande* and *Il Compendio*. Published in Latin in 1759 as *Homo Apostolicus*.
17. Alfonso, Lettere III. 172.
18. One of the most amusing attacks on the Moral Theology of Alphonsus was made in England by the Rev. R.P. Blakeney, Minister of Christ Church, Claughton, Birkenhead, and published in London by the Protestant Alliance in 1846 under the title, *St. Alphonsus Liguori, or Extracts translated from the Moral Theology of the above Romish Saint, who was canonised in the year 1839, with remarks thereon*. Blakeney made the modest claim for his work that 'the exposure of Romish sentiments as expounded by the saint is one of the heaviest blows which the Church of Rome has received for a long time.' The work is based on a series of lectures which Blakeney delivered in the Assembly Rooms in Nottingham. The purpose of the lectures and the book was to prove, with particular reference to the moral teaching of Alphonsus, 'that Popery not only destroys the soul by its damnable idolatries but even the fairest temporal interests of mankind. Popery is a system of spiritual and corporal despotism. It is a prolific source of vice; it is a tremendous conspiracy against the welfare of the human family; the very masterpiece of the devil'. After an introductory chapter on the life of Alphonsus, the author continues to attack, first of all, Probabilism with which he is not too familiar, then the infallibility of the Pope as proved by Alphonsus, and a litany of 'errors' dawn from the *Moral Theology*. It was the misfortune of Alphonsus, with his personal refinement and even scrupulous attitude in matters concerning the sixth and ninth commandments, that his treatment of this subject and of the possible forms of human weakness should be singled out for special attack. At the end of almost 400 pages the author in a magnificent crescendo draws the attention of the British Parliament to the iniquities of Alphonsus and his moral writings: 'surely this is a subject which should at once be pressed upon the attention of the British Parliament, seeing that the liberties of the people are involved in it.'
19. The nuncio in Naples, Mons. Locatelli complained to Rome that the archbishop of Naples lacked both zeal and pastoral initiative. A. Vat. Napoli, vol. 415, 21 August 1762. In the same Fondo is an even more damaging indictment — though anonymous — of the Cardinal, who was placed in Naples, maliciously by Spinelli, 'ut comparatione deterrima sibi gloriam quaesivisset'. Vol. 596, 24 July 1762.
20. *Verita della Fede contro i Materialisti*, . . . etc. Naples 1767. Appendix I. *Confutazione del libro francese intitolato dello Spirito*.

21. *Verita della Fede*, Parte I. Cap. I, 3.
22. Alfonso, Lettere I. 414.
23. 'You are led to sin
    By the World, the Flesh and the Devil
    Pray, pray, if you
    Do not wish to be overcome.'

    This rhyme became even simpler in early Redemptorist preaching in English as 'If you pray, you will be saved; if you do not pray, you will be lost.' This aphorism of Alphonsus was not made up haphazardly nor in the enthusiastic amplification of a theme in a sermon; it is found again and again in his writings — *Vera Sposa di Gesù Cristo*, Cap. XX; *Selva*, III. c.12; *La Pratica di amar Gesù Cristo*, c. XVII.
24. Father Marin-Sola, O.P. wrote of this work: 'A juicio nuestro, este opusculo de San Liguori, titulado *De Magno Orationis Medio*, aunque pequeno en extension, no es de menor valor para las questiones de la predestinacion y de la gracia que los voluminosos in-folios de los grandes teologos de los siglos XVII y XVIII.' Ciencia Tomista, 1925, 14, 31; 1926, 53, 321–97. A full doctrinal study of this work of St. Alphonsus, its theological background, its eclecticism etc. is to be found in J. F. Hidalgo, *Doctrina Alfonsiana acerca de la accion de la Gracia Actual, Eficaz y Suficiente*, Marietti, 1954.
25. In his study of the doctrine of the Sacred Heart, Alphonsus used Père Gallifet, *Eccellenza e Preghi della divozione del Cuor di Gesù Cristo*, Venezia 1735. He also copied some prayers from it into his *Visits*. The actual copy which he used is still preserved in the Pagani Redemptorist Library.

Chapter Twelve, pp. 296–329.

1. A.G.H.R. XXVI 1b.
   The papal brief granting communication in the privileges of other Orders was dated 11 August 1757; the Royal Exequatur was granted six years later in 1763. *Documenta Authentica Facultatum et Gratiarum Spiritualium quas C.SS.R. S.Sedes concessit*. Ratisbon 1903.
2. Alfonso, Lettere I. 397.
3. So far, repeated searches in the Archives of the Propaganda Fide have failed to bring to light the correspondence concerning this official invitation and the subsequent negotiations. Many aspects of the whole affair remain far from clear and will not be clarified until these documents have been discovered. Maybe it is not without significance that none of the correspondence seems to have been preserved by Alphonsus in Pagani.
4. G. Landi, *Istoria* . . . II. 99; P. Blasucci, *Relazione delle Cose accadute nella Fondazione dell Casa di Girgenti*; etc. Spic.Hist. V. 1957. 70–110; Alfonso, Lettere II. 409; S. Giamusso, *I Redentoristi in Sicilia*, Palermo, 1960; Pietro Blasucci, *Alfonso de Liguori*, ed. Salvatore Giamusso, Palermo, 1987

   One morning in June 1760 while the negotiations for the establishment of a Redemptorist foundation in Sicily were in progress, Alphonsus was surprised to get a letter from the Bishop of Agrigento regretting that for the moment he was unable to send on the contributions which Alphonsus had requested. Since Alphonsus had not requested any money nor even dreamt of doing so — to use his own expression (Lettere I.438) — he realised at once that someone was using his name fraudulently to get money from the bishops of Sicily. A short

NOTES

while later Brother Francis Tartaglione, Alphonsus' agent in Naples, went to collect Alphonsus' mail at the clearing centre in the city and found a number of letters authorising Alphonsus to get certain sums of money from various agents in the city for the pious work he had in hand. It all amounted, according to Tannoia, to a considerable sum. By some fortunate coincidence Tartaglione arrived before the thief had time to collect his takings. Putting together certain points of evidence, Alphonsus was able to identify the culprit as a Neapolitan priest who was using his name for this purpose and who had already intercepted his correspondence with Remondini (Lettere III.141). Having explained the matter to the bishops, Alphonsus then inserted a notice in the official gazette, putting everybody on guard against anyone who would seek money in his name. He could not be persuaded, however, to denounce the cleric to the authorities, even in order, as they said, to deter others from similar action.

5. F. Kuntz, *Annales C.SS.R.* VI. 368. The bishop of the diocese was the remarkable Mons. Andrea Lucchesi, Prince of Campofranco. He was one of the most learned and cultured of the Italian hierarchy at the time and for those days, united an edifying pastoral zeal to his vast learning and culture. In his palace, he was, at this time, forming his famous collection of Latin, Greek and Arabic Codices as well as his collection of ancient Greek and Roman coins which he left as a legacy to the town of Agrigento as the Biblioteca Lucchesiana and entrusted to the care of the Redemptorists whom he had brought to the diocese.
6. A.G.H.R. XXVII 43; Proc. Ord. 5. Agath. III. fol.1111.
7. S.R.C. Resp. ad Animad. R.P.P. Fidei . . . 49 No. 96
8. *Homo Apostolicus*, Appendix I. Methodus vitae pro aliqua moniali quae exposceret dirigi per viam perfectionis.

    One of those instruments of penance, a frightening instrument with sharp metal points, is now preserved in the Museo Alfonsiano at Pagani where he died, and it is claimed that it belonged to him. It is called a *cardo*, which was of two types, one like a thistle head with spikes on the end of a cord, the other, like a spiked comb.
9. A.G.H.R. XXVI 14, 34. Father Landi was shrewd enough in his analysis of Alphonsus' character to point out his constant internal struggle against his passions, his evil inclinations and especially against his self-esteem. G. Landi, *Istoria*, I. 55–6; Alfonso, Lettere I. 301.
10. A.G.H.R. XXV 17c, 17e.
11. S.R.C. Animad. R.P.P. Fidei 14, No.28; Resp. ad Animad. R.P.P. Fidei 54, No.108.
12. Father Angelo Verdesca, A.G.H.R. XXVI 61. Verdesca later left the Congregation and died from poison taken in the chalice at Mass, 'more avvelenato nella sunzione del Calice'. Minervino, *Catalago dei Redentorist d'Italia*, Rome 1978.
13. Systematic excavations began at Herculaneum in 1738 under the direction of Alcubiere, the Spanish engineer in the service of Charles III. He later also took charge of the excavations at Pompei. In 1770, Dr Charles Burney visited the Royal Museum at Portici; 'I went this morning with a large party of artists to his Neapolitan majesty's Museum at Portici, having had an order procured by Mr Hamilton from the Marchese Tanucci for that purpose.' *Dr. Burney's Musical Tours in Europe*, ed. Percy A.Scholes, O.U.P. 1959, Vol.I 271.
14. Masone e Amarante, *S. Alfonso de Liguori e la Sua opera*. Naples 1987, 282–97.
15. Alfonso, Lettere II. 18, 24.
16. A.G.H.R. XXVI 62.

17. Alfonso, Lettere I. 256–65, 408.
18. Proc. Ord. S. Agath. III. 1323.
19. B.G.E.R. I. 73. *Avvisi spettanti alla vocazione religiosa; Considerazioni per coloro che sono chiamati allo stato religioso; Conforti ai novizi.* These works have appeared in various forms and under various titles in translations into different languages, *Choice of a State of Life, The True Redemptorist,* etc. When young Willle Doyle visited his brother Charles in the Jesuit novitiate in Tullamore, he was given a copy of Alphonsus' work on the Religious State; it changed 'the whole currents of my thoughts' and led him to join the Society of Jesus, see Alfred O'Rahilly, *Father Willie Doyle, S.J.* London 1925.

    The whole question of the theology of vocation to the priesthood and the religious life has been the subject of considerable investigation since the early years of this century and the teaching of St Alphonsus on the obligation of following a religious vocation has been subject to close scrutiny. cf. *Acta et Documenta Congressus Generalis de Statibus Perfectionis,* Rome 1952.
20. The parents of Constantino Santorelli and of the Buonapane brothers, Fabio and Vicenzo, among a host of others, appealed to the King against their sons entering the Redemptorist novitiate.
21. Alfonso, Lettere I. 298. Capuano was profesed in 1756 in Deliceto. He left the Congregation in 1781 because his conscience would not permit him to take an oath to accept the *Regolamento.*
22. *Avvisi spettanti alla vocazione religiosa,* Cap. 2.
23. A.G.H.R. XXVII 9a, 9c. This was one of those occasions when Alphonsus' irascible temperament got the better of him. The chronicler of the incident mentions that Father Spera felt the public humiliation very much and fell into bad health as a result, from which he never recovered. Bursars are usually made of sterner stuff — the truth is that Spera died of tubercolosis in 1762; Analecta XIX. 253.
24. Alfonso, Lettere II. 11–12 S.C.R. Resp. ad Animad. R.P.P. Fidei, 35, No. 71.
25. Alfonso, Lettere I. 569.
26. It is recorded that on occasions Alphonsus played the harpsichord in an effort to relieve him of his depressions.
27. Alfonso, Lettere I. 321.
28. Alfonso, Lettere I. 407. Father Ferrara was one of Alphonsus' official consultors for sixteen years. Ferrara may well have been the Father referred to in the Process of Canonisation as being more or less a thorn in Alphonsus' side — 'contrariavalo o nelle sue dottrine, o sentenze di Teologia morale, o per altri punti regolari appartenenti al buon governo della Congregazione'. S.R.C. Resp. ad Animad. R.P.P. Fidei 35, No.71.
29. Alfonso, Lettere I. 273; A.G.H.R. XXVII. 43.
30. Alfonso, Lettere I. 434.
31. Alfonso, Lettere I. 209.
32. The case of Father Apice figured largely in the exchanges between the Postulator of the Cause and the Promotor Fidei, see Resp. ad Animad. R.P.P. Fidei 42, No. 85. A life of Father Apice was published in Naples in 1816 by Father Saccardi.
33. Alfonso, Lettere I. 392-2. This is an abbreviated form of the letter. The original, since located in Argentina, is published in full in *Contributi Bio-Bibliografici,* 248–9.
34. In the administration of the Congregation during the last century, the Superior General, Father Mauron adopted a policy of *never* re-admitting to the

Congregation a member who had been dispensed, appealing, as he formally stated, to the principle laid down by Alphonsus-'vous savez en effet, que pour le bien commun, S. Alphonse a établi pour principe de ne jamais plus recevoir dans la Congrégation ceux qui ont eu le malheur d'en sortir une fois.' He applied this principle in the celebrated case of the unfortunate Father Vladimir Pecherin (1807–1885), and his successors continued this practice until well into this century. Mauron's interpretation of Alphonsus' practice was clearly incorrect and caused much suffering, verifying once again the wise dictum of St Jerome, *'multi labuntur errore propter ignorantiam historiae'*. Spic.Hist. XXI. 1973. 194–5; XXV. 1977. 319–20.

The great Francesco Sanseverino also wanted to go back but his request was not granted.
35. A.G.H.R. XXVII 7.
36. A.G.H.R. SAM III 285.
37. A.G.H.R. I. C 31.
38. One can find something similar in the letters of St Paul of the Cross. *S. Paolo della Croce*, Lettere. Rome 1924, Vol.2, 534.
39. Pagani Archives: S.A. 32.1961, 90–91.

Chapter Thirteen, pp. 330–354.

1. Charles was so scrupulous about not taking anything belonging to the Kingdom with him to Spain that he later returned a ring which he had himself found during the excavations at Pompei. Within a year of his return to Spain, his wife, Maria Amalia, died at the age of thirty-six, leaving him grief-stricken. He refused to marry again.
2. Brancone died in May 1758, to be succeeded by Julio de Andrea from whom Alphonsus expected great favours. Unfortunately, he was removed by Tanucci soon after the departure of Charles III for Spain. *Contributi Bio-Bibliografici*, 249.
3. Alfonso, Lettere I. 423.
4. Alfonso, Lettere I. 441.
5. *Selva*, Avvertimenti 6. *Opere Ascetiche* 1847, Vol. III. 6.
6. A.G.H.R. SAM III 373–9
7. Maria Abbondanza Rocchina, *Le Istruzioni di S. Alfonso ai Parroci nelle bibliotece Lucane. La Presenza e l'opera dei Redentoristi nel Mezzogiorno*, Naples 1987. These 'Rules of Life' were published as appendices to the *Selva*.
8. i. *Selva di materie predicabile ed istruttive per dare gli esercizi ai Preti, anche per uso di lezione privata, a proprio profitto*. Naples 1760; ii. *La Messa e L'Officio Strapazzati*. Naples 1760; iii. *Delle Ceremonie della Messa*. Naples 1769.

   Alphonsus published his first series of prayers of preparation for and thanksgiving after Mass in Naples in 1758; *Apparecchio e Ringraziamento per i Sacerdoti nel celebrare la Messa*. His second series of meditations and prayers were later published together in the various manuals of priestly devotion. A. Van Biervliet, *La Liturgie dans la Pieté Alphonsienne*, Esschen 1925.
9. Spic.Hist. IX. 1961. 115–28
10. A.G.H.R. XXVI 45.
11. Alfonso, Lettere I. 213.
12. Romeo de Maio, *Società e Vita Religiosa a Napoli nell'Età Moderna* (1656–1799) Edizioni Scientifiche Italiane, 1971.
13. Spic.Hist. V. 1957. 5.
14. *Riflessioni Utili à Vescovi*, par.6.

15. A.G.H.R. XXVII 27.
16. A.G.H.R. XXV 17.
17. Alfonso, Lettere I. 616.
18. Alfonso, Lettere I. 559.
19. A.G.H.R. XXVII 23.
20. Alfonso, Lettere I. 446.
21. Alfonso, Lettere I. 72. 422.
22. Alfonso, Lettere II. 181.
23. S. O'Riordan, 'The Influence of St. Teresa of Avila on St. Alphonsus Liguori', in *St. Teresa of Avila*, ed. Thomas and Gabriel, Dublin 1963.
24. Alfonso, Lettere I. 52.
25. *Praxis Confessarii*. Caput IX. Quomodo se gerere debeat Confessarius in dirigendis animabus spiritualibus.
26. A.G.H.R. XXVI 65.
27. A.G.H.R. XXV 17c.
28. *La Vera Sposa di Gesù Cristo*, Cap. I. 5–9.
29. *La Vera Sposa di Gesù Cristo*, Cap. XXIII. no. 8.
30. A.G.H.R. SAM III 339–41.

Chapter Fourteen, pp. 357–395.

1. Spic. Hist. IX. 1961; R. Telleria and A. Sampers, *Documenta circa electionem et consecrationem S. Alfonsi* . . . 269 A. Sampers, *Epistulae S. Alfonsi* . . .ineditae 1762–1775, 296.
2. Most of the Neapolitan hierarchy owed its appointment to the influence of Cardinal Spinelli and the Nuncio was disappointed at their lack of courage in the face of regalist encroachments. He placed the blame, nevertheless, firmly on the shoulders of Cardinal Sersale who was a great disappointment as archbishop of Naples. The Nuncio believed that one way to a better Church was the appointment of better bishops and for this he outlined two qualifications for any new candidate for a bishopric in the Kingdom, personal holiness and zeal for souls, and nobility of birth, the first for pastoral reasons, the second in order that he should be respected in Court circles.
3. A.G.H.R. SAM 111a 144. Alphonsus' name had been mentioned in connection with several bishoprics after his father's death. On several occasions his good friend Brancone had made proposals to him in the matter and eventually desisted only when Alphonsus said to him, ' Signore Marchese, if we are friends now, we will easily become enemies since I cannot possibly accept what you offer me.' Proc. Ord. S. Agatha 111.120v. There is historical proof that he was proposed for Palermo in 1747. It is said that one of the reasons that he abandoned Spinelli's missionary campaign and retired to Ciorani in 1741 was that Spinelli had suggested a bishopric to him. A.G.H.R. XXV.
4. B.G.E.R. I.103 No.41 1759, *Dissertatio de justa Prohibitione et abolitione liborum* . . .
5. Bruni's official title was 'adjutor in studiis'. His voice in the appointment to those Neapolitan bishoprics which were in the complete control of the Holy See aroused the ire of Tanucci who wrote to Cardinal Orsini in 1764, 'The character of the abbate Bruni, the dealer in papal bishoprics in this Kingdom, does little honour to the Pope, and a great injury to the King and this Kingdom, seeing that these bishoprics depend on an instrument so base and unworthy as he. This has caused great anxiety to my colleagues who have determined that

the Pope must be disabused.' But Bruni's character was, in fact, above all reproach, and what nettled the marquis was the type of bishop the sound judgment of Bruni proposed to the Pope. Spic.Hist. XI. 1961. 276.
6. A.G.H.R. XXVI 14.
7. Spic.Hist.IX. 1961. 280.
8. Alfonso, Lettere I. 470.
9. A.G.H.R. XXV.
10. Tannoia Lib. III. Chap. 1V. 16.
11. Alphonsus' fear of his episcopal responsibilities persisted with him until his retirement in 1775. A remarkable echo of his attitude is to be found in his account of Acacius in his *Storia delle Eresie*, Bk. 1. Chap. V. par.84. 'Speaking here of Acacius, it will serve as a warning to those whose ambition is the honour of becoming a bishop to reflect on the unhappy death of this unfortunate prelate . . . I tremble myself as I write this, seeing that I, too, am a bishop. Many who have been raised to this dignity have fallen away and have lost their souls and God. If they had remained just simple priests they would have more easily saved their souls. Prescinding altogether from the question whether those who ambitiously seek the episcopate are in a state of mortal sin, I cannot imagine how anyone who wishes to secure his eternal salvation could seek to become a bishop, thus placing himself, of his own volition, in all the dangers of eternal damnation to which bishops are exposed.' Whatever the quality of the history, these lines illustrate clearly Alphonsus' psychology in the matter of being raised to the episcopate.
12. Tannoia gives 14 June as the date of the episcopal ordination and mentions that Mons. Mastrilli, titular archbishop of Bethlehem and a Theatine, assisted. Lib. III. C.V. 22. The altar to St Aloysius Gonzaga is a masterpiece of Brother Andrea Pozzo and of baroque art. Dedicated in 1699, the centrepiece is in gleaming white marble, representing the apotheosis of the Saint. There are four columns of *verde antico*, interlaced with *bronzo dorato*. The urn of *lapis lazuli* contains the relics of the saint. At that time it was necessary to have a special Rescript granting permission to wear the skull-cap during the celebration of Mass, see Ephemerides Liturgicae, XXX. 1916. 36–41. A.G.H.R. XXVI. 14.
13. A.G.H.R. 1. C. 32 (a) & (b)
14. Verzella was to remain as secretary to Alphonsus for the greater part of his episcopate until he fell foul of the bishop's strict regulations about undue familiarity with convents of contemplative nuns. However, he was an important witness at the different Processes leading to Alphonsus' beatification. See *Notitiae Rdi. Felicis Verzella, Secretarii et Confessoris S. Alphonsis tempore episcopatus*; A. Sampers, Spic. Hist. IX. 1961. 373–438; Alfonso, Lettere II.205; III.409.
15. O. Gregorio, 'La diocesi di S. Agatha com'era ieri e com'e 'Oggi' Spic. Hist. IX. 1961.547; cf. *La Nostra Chiesa*, Bulletino Ufficiale della Diocesi di S. Agatha dei Goti. Oct.–Nov. 1960.
16. Proc. Ord. Nuc. II.796 From the many witnesses at the Ordinary Processes who claimed to have heard what was said as a result of listening at doors, it would appear that eavesdropping was widespread. Whatever we may think about the ethics, the practice has proved valuable to historians.
17. Alfonso, Lettere I.472.
18. A.G.H.R. XXVI 58 & 31. Verzella and Alessio Pollio provided a great deal of information about Alphonsus' years as a bishop. The 'senior seminarian' who ended as Mons. Giovanni Battista di Luccia, was responsible for preserving some of the poetic offerings from the seminary.

19. Spic. Hist. IX. 1961. 290–95, *Notitiae Statisticae Saec. XVIII super Diocesi di S. Agatha.*
20. Alfonso, Lettere III. 551; Spic. Hist. IX 1961, 420.
21. Alfonso, Lettere I. 475–6 Alphonsus took similar action against a prostitute from Naples who arrived in Santa Maria à Vico, Lettere II.497. When the Promotor Fidei brought up for discussion Alphonsus' action against the prostitutes of his diocese, the Ponens of the Cause pointed out that each bishop must act according to the circumstances of the diocese, the civil law of the area and the local customs. While the manner of dealing with the prostitutes at the time is totally repugnant to our way of thinking, it was still the law of Naples and did not appear strange to the local inhabitants. It was also part of the legislation of the Vth Lateran Council which Trent explicitly refused to alter. Sess. 24. De Reform. Matrim Cap.4.

    With regard to the similar case of Canon Petti, the Promotor Fidei did not object to Alphonsus' action in handing him over to the secular arm, but insisted that it should be clearly demonstrated that this was used as a last resort and that its purpose was to enforce otherwise ineffective spiritual punishments.
22. Alfonso, Lettere I. 501; II. 297. Spic. Hist. IX. 1961. 390.
23. Proc. Ord. Nuc. II.722
    Archiv. Stat. Napoli, Dispacci Ecclesiastici, 298. 44–45
    S.R.C. Animad. R.P.P. Fidei Super Virt. 20. No. 40 & 41. Respon. ad Animad. R.P.P. Fidei, 75, No. 147
    Proc. Apos. St. Agatha III. 1046 Evidence of Don Carlo Bruno of St. Agatha who was a witness of all he recounted.
    A.G.H.R. XXVI 37 & 40
24. Alfonso, Lettere I.483.
25. B.G.E.R. No.50. 116 Spic. Hist. IX. 1961. 407 No. 149
26. This incident evoked another objection from the Promotor Fidei at the Process, half-hearted indeed, since it was pointed out to him that Alphonsus was not in favour of venial sin, but that he was displeased that the mission should have begun with a sermon more suitable for those already converted to God and serving Him faithfully, than for the conversion of obstinate sinners, and the eradication of public immorality such as was indicated for Airola. Proc. Apos. St. Agatha, 1768. S.R.C. Animad. R.P.P. Fidei, Super Virt. 22. Responsio 85, No. 171–2.
27. Spic. Hist. IX. 1961. 407 No.50.
28. A.G.H.R. XXVI 37. Proc. Ord. S. Agatha II.839–939.
29. Proc. Ord. Nuc. II. 716, 768.
30. A.G.H.R. XXVI 65.
31. A.G.H.R. XXVI 44.52.
32. S.R.C. Resp. ad Animad. R.P.P. Fidei 80 No.161.
33. A.G.H.R. XXVI 56.
34. A.G.H.R. XXVI 52.
35. Benedict XIV. *Institutiones* 116. S.R.C. Animad. R.P.P. Fidei 221–2, No. 43. Resp. . . . 82–4, No. 165–8.
36. A.G.H.R. XXV and XXVI 67.
37. Proc. Ord. St. Agatha III. 1217 ter.
38. A.G.H.R. XXVI 65.
39. Proc. Apos. S. Agatha III.1051.
40. A.G.H.R. XVI 37. As regards the seminary Rule, cf. Spic. Hist. IX. 1961. 402.
41. A.G.H.R. XXVI 19.

42. Alfonso, Lettere III. 653–4.
43. A.G.H.R. XXVI 23. The Promotor Fidei objected to this telescoped way of speaking which was quite characteristic of Alphonsus right through his life. S.R.C. Animad. R.P.P. Fidei Super Virt. 26. No.53.
44. A.G.H.R. XXVI 15.
45. There are many references to Alphonsus' charity as a bishop. A.G.H.R. SAM 3a; XXVI 8 & 32; Proc. Ord. Nuc. II.I539.
46. A.G.H.R. XXV 17c.
47. Proc. Ord. St. Agatha II.613; A.G.H.R. XXVI 19. At the Process the Promotor Fidei had not sufficient words of praise for his pastoral solicitude for his flock and could offer no words of criticism. However, he suggested that if Alphonsus did not sin by defect he might have erred by excess. This was too much for the Advocate of the Cause who could only burst out in reply, 'Bone Deus!' — 'Good God!' in utter amazement. This is one of those rare occasions when a little colour comes into the whole Process which is so impersonal and objective.
48. Alfonso, Lettere III.620.
49. 'ob rationem temporum impraesentiarum decurrentium'.
50. There was considerable shadow-boxing on the part of the Promotor Fidei over the fact that Alphonsus did not summon a Synod. He argued at length on the matter, almost driving the Advocate of the Cause to distraction. It was certainly the least convincing argument to adduce against Alphonsus' canonisation. S.R.C. Animad. R.P.P. Fidei, 17, No.35. Resp.ad Animad. etc. 65 No.130.

Chapter Fifteen, pp. 396–422.

1. A.G.H.R. XXVII 6.
2. At the medical examination of Alphonsus' remains carried out from 1951– 1952, he was found to be without teeth, *edentulo*. Spic. Hist. IX.1961. 389–90.
3. Spic. Hist. IX. 1961. 389; Alfonso, Lettere 1.519.
4. Spic. Hist. IX. 1961. 395.
5. Alfonso, Lettere 1.555–8.
6. Alfonso, Lettere 1.569.
7. Unfortunately no copy of Alphonsus' letter of resignation to the Pope has been found.
8. A.G.H.R. XXVI.l9; Alfonso, Lettere I.569.
9. Alfonso, Lettere I.500.
10. Alfonso, Lettere I.621. Spic. Hist. IX.1961. 325–7. Despite the fact that Alphonsus drafted the letter in his own handwriting and then signed the final copy, drawn up by Verzella, the letter, apparently, was never dispatched to Rome. Perhaps a further scruple intervened.
11. Alfonso, Lettere II. 59–60. 205; A.G.H.R. XXVII 63.
12. A.G.H.R. XXVII 41; XXVI 5a.
13. Alfonso, Lettere 1. 477. For the meaning of *cicisbeo* and its significance see Chapter 18.
14. Alfonso, Lettere I.444–8.
15. Alfonso, Lettere I.478.
16. A.G.H.R. XXVI 67; Spic. Hist. IX. 1961. 434.
17. A.G.H.R. XXVII 67.
18. Proc. Ord. S. Agatha III.1445. The remark is not original; it is part and parcel of papal and episcopal folklore. A similar reply is attributed to the Medici Pope, Clement VII, with reference to Henry VIII's wish for a male heir.

19. Proc. Ord. S. Agatha III. 1483
20. Spic. Hist. IX. 1961. 340. The twin boys were baptised Giuseppe and Carlo Maria. Carlo Maria whom Hercules had legally constituted his heir, died as an infant in 1770. The funeral of the nephew of the bishop of St Agatha gave rise in Northern Italy at the time to a false report that the bishop of Sant Agatha had died.
21. *Documenta Miscellanea ad Regulam et Spiritum Congregationis Nostrae* . . . Romae 1904, 159–65.
22. Tannoia III. C. XXI. 102.
    Spic. Hist. I. 1953. 123. The anti-chapter sentiment in the Congregation was evident from the beginning. Epistolae Pauli Cafaro, Romae. 1934. 57: '*non tutti s'approveranno dal Capitolo Generale*'.
23. With the Chapter of 1764 we enter an area of extreme historical sensitivity, where the subsequent division between the houses of the Congregation in the Kingdom of Naples, and in the Papal States determine the attitudes to be adopted. Some held that Alphonsus did not approve of the Constitutions of 1764 while others asserted his full acceptance of them. The two contemporary historians of the Congregation, Tannoia in Naples, and Landi in the Papal States, adopted opposing positions. Landi, De Paola and Leggio regarded the Constitutions of 1764 as null and void. The division between the Congregation in Naples and in the Papal States crystallised around the so-called Tannoian Constitutions.

    Unfortunately there is no detailed account of the 1764 Chapter discussions; the original minutes have been conveniently 'lost'; cf. the excellent exposé of O. Gregorio, *Le Costituzioni Redentoriste del 1764*; Spic. Hist. I.1953. 119–44; and R. Telleria, *De Capitulo*, 1764, 145–68.
24. Alfonso, Lettere 1.577. This unpleasant letter of 1765 was omitted from those generally available to the members of the Congregation in English translations in the last century. Neither did it elicit comment from the Defensor Fidei during the process of canonisation. *Letters of St. Alphonsus Maria de Liguori*, Part 1. Vol.II, ed. E. Grimm, New York 1892.
25. Alfonso, Lettere I.522, 568; II. 8, 12, 21, 26, 149. As regards Melchionna, Alphonsus' judgment was vindicated. Melchionna persevered in the Congregation until his death in 1803 at the age of 70.
26. Alfonso, Lettere I. 612.
27. Alfonso, Lettere II. 19.
28. Alfonso, Lettere II. 25.
29. Alfonso, Lettere II. 39.
30. Alfonso, Lettere II. 6.
31. Alfonso, Lettere II. 177; Spic. Hist. IX. 1961. 362.
32. Alfonso, Lettere II. 53.
33. Alfonso, Lettere II. 48.
34. Alfonso, Lettere II. 55, 57, 58.
35. Proc. Ord. Nuc. III 1202 v.
36. A.G.H.R. XXV 17c.
37. The details of this illness were later described by Dr Ferrara. Obviously conscious of the fact that his medical expertise would go down to posterity, Ferrara made the most of his opportunity and describes the symptoms in great detail. At the process of canonisation Verzella and Alessio Pollio described the illness with considerably less medical élan. A.G.H.R. XXVI 55.
38. Alfonso, Lettere I. 87.
39. Alfonso, Lettere II. 122, 123, 126. At the process of Beatification the Vicar Forane of Santa Maria à Vico, Canon Liborio Carfora, declared that Alphonsus

took the Precious Blood by means of a silver tube, plated with gold on the inside. The Canon's evidence was just hearsay on his part as is abundantly proved by the evidence of Alessio Pollio and Brother Romito who contradicted it flatly, see Proc. Apos. S. Agathae, fol.763 tergo, 1097 tergo. The Promotor Fidei later objected to the fact that Alphonsus said Mass with the use of this fistula for the Precious Blood without seeking a Papal Indult, which in all likelihood would not have been granted at the time. He pointed out that Pope Benedict XIV at the end of his pontificate was unable to stand at Mass and hesitated to avail himself of the privilege of celebrating Mass while seated without considerable consultation with others on the point. It appeared to him an intolerable liberty on Alphonsus' part that he should have taken it upon himself to take the Precious Blood through a fistula without a papal indult. It was then clearly demonstrated to the complete satisfaction of the Promotor Fidei that Canon Carfora's evidence was inaccurate. Alphonsus did use a tube for drinking but he did not use it at Mass. It was then suggested to him that he should petition the Holy See for such a privilege but he absolutely refused to do so. Rather than seek a dispensation he went for several months without celebrating Mass. It was only when the Augustinian pointed out the alternative to him that he accepted the advice and then he always celebrated in private, never in public, and always assisted by another priest in cotta and stole.
40. Alfonso, Lettere II. 128, 131.
41. Alfonso, Lettere II. 122, 125, 129, 139.

Chapter Sixteen, pp. 423–440.

1. Alfonso, Lettere III.339: '*Ci fatico non solo io ma altri*'; B.G.E.R. I. 118 no. 52, 142 no. 76.
2. Alfonso, Lettere III. 182
   B.G.E.R. I. 119, *Breve dissertazione dell'uso moderato dell'opinione probabile*.
3. Alfonso, Lettere III. 229, 230.
4. L. Vereecke, *De Guillaume d'Ockham à St. Alphonse de Liguori*, Romae 1986, 559; B.G.E.R. I. 127, *Apologia dell'Illustrissimo e Rev. mo Mons. D. Alfonso de Liguori, Vescovo di Santagata de'Goti* . . .
5. B.G.E.R. I. 127–9; Alfonso, Lettere III. 238.
6. Telleria, II. 300–301.
7. Alfonso, Lettere III. 266.
8. Alfonso, Lettere III. 300.
9. Alfonso, Lettere II. 261, 281; III. 457.
10. B.G.E.R. I. 160, No. 96.
11. B.G.E.R. I. 122, No. 57.
12. Alfonso, Lettere III. 428; B.G.E.R. I. 131, No. 67; Alphonsus De Liguori, Opere Ascetiche (Editio Critica) X. *Via della Salute*.
13. B.G.E.R. I. 138, No. 73.
14. B.G.E.R. I. 140, No. 74.
15. Alfonso, Lettere III. 378.
16. Alfonso, Lettere III. 399.
17. Alfonso, Lettere III. 399–400.
18. R. Giglio, 'A Proposito di un Trattatello di Alfonso M. de Liguori poco noto . . ., *Alfonso M. de Liguori e La Società Civile del Suo Tempo*, Firenze 1990, 1.287. Giglio points out Alphonsus' usual stance in many contemporary debates. He accepts the situation as he found it; he refrains from entering into the debate concerning

NOTES

Church-State relations. He simply suggests a way of acting in certain circumstances which would be meritorious in the eyes of God.
19. Alfonso, Lettere II. 270.
20. Alfonso, Lettere II. 161–4.
21. Alfonso, Lettere II. 232–7.
22. Alfonso, Lettere II. 270.
23. Alfonso, Lettere III. 402–7.
24. Alfonso, Lettere II. 301, 372.
25. Alfonso, Lettere II. 270.
26. Alfonso, Lettere II. 305.
27. Tannoia, Lit. III. Cap. LV. p.282
28. Alfonso, Lettere II. 292.
29. Alfonso, Lettere II. 281.
30. S.R.C. Animad. R.P.P. Fidei 33. No. 65, Summarium Objectionale II. No. 8. Resp. ad Animad R.P.P. Fidei 123–6.

   Father Tannoia relates the incident without any great excitement in Lib. III. Cap. LV. 283. His source was one Agatha Viscardi, an employee of the Redemptoristines in St. Agatha. They had sent her to Arienzo where she claimed to have been present when Alphonsus stated that he had been assisting at the death of the Pope. She brought the news back to St Agatha and it was from the Nuns there and in particular from S. Maria Celestine of Divine Love, one of the first members of the St Agatha Community, that Tannoia got his information. In his *History of the Popes*, XXXVIII. 533, note 2, Pastor, quoting Pichler, makes passing reference to the 'entirely spiritual presence of St Alphonsus Liguori at the death bed of the pontiff'.
31. Alfonso, Lettere II. 306.
32. Alfonso, Lettere II. 306–10.
33. Spic. Hist. IX. 1961. 362.
34. Alfonso, Lettere II. 399, 340, 341; Spic. Hist. X. 1962. 20–35. A. Sampers, *Documenta Quaedam Romana circa S. Alfonsi Dimissionem Episcopatus anno 1775*.
35. Alfonso, Lettere II.343; Analecta XVII. 275

Chapter Seventeen, pp. 441–473.

1. 'I am better now than I have ever been for the past ten years', Alphonsus wrote in November 1776, Lettere II.396. By 1779, however, he was complaining that he was unable to walk, Lettere III.531. His room in Pagani was on the second floor. In Naples the ground floor or *pianterreno* is often referred to as the first floor with the result that Neapolitans referred to his room as being on the *third floor*. *Le Camarette di Sant'Alfonso nel Collegio di Pagani*; Spic. Hist. XVIII. 1970. 107.

   The Promotor of the Faith objected to the fact that on his retiring from his bishopric Alphonsus accepted such a considerable pension from the diocese and insisted on having a carriage and pair for himself at Pagani. 'Can this conduct be compatible with the practice of heroic poverty on his part?' S.R.C. Nova Positio. Animad. R.P.P.Fidei, Super Dubio, 8 par. 18, 19.
2. Proc. Ord. Nuc. II. 677 ter.
3. This story provides a good example of the folklore which gathers around saints. It is to be found in Proc. Ord. Nuc. II. 649 and was given in evidence by Father Nicola Contaldo. Father Orestes Gregorio recounts it in somewhat different form in *Monsignore si diverte*, 159.
4. Alfonso, Lettere II. 476–7.

5. B.G.E.R. I–168. No. 108.
6. Alfonso, Lettere III. 487.
7. 'sono aborriti i libri e specialmente le Morali dei Gesuiti', Alphonsus wrote to Remondini, Lettere III.514, cf. L. Gaudé, *Opera Moralia S.A.* T. I. XXII. Alphonsus wrote or dictated a series of letters to Remondini from December 1776 about the changes he wished introduced into the 8th edition, Lettere III. 490, 513 etc.
8. Maffei and Sarnelli continued to act together '*sotto acqua. La tempesta e grossa.*' Alfonso, Lettere II.153. For a while Alphonsus believed that the correct tactics were 'to lie low', II.150.
9. Alfonso, Lettere II. 313; 318–21; 331.
10. Alfonso, Lettere II. 362–3.
    Spic. Hist. XI. 1963. 5–6.
11. It is significant that the powers of the Rector Major were somewhat curtailed in the *Regolamento* of 1780. For the Villani proposals see Telleria, II.513, note 18.
12. Alfonso, Lettere II. 355.
13. Alfonso, Lettere II. 366.
14. Alfonso, Lettere II.372. While Sant'Angelo was geographically in the Kingdom of Naples, it was a papal enclave administratively.
15. Alfonso, Lettere II.372, 398. De Paola was to pay dearly for his special vocation in the Congregation.
16. Alfonso, Lettere II. 395, 398.
17. Tannoia Lib. IV Cap. V. 34
18. Alfonso, Lettere II. 414, 425, 428. III. 429; A.G.H.R. Historia XVIII A.12.
19. Alfonso, Lettere II. 448–9.
20. Alfonso, Lettere II. 502.
21. Tannoia IV. Cap.19. 94. Cf. the draft memorial Alphonsus drew up for Pius VI in Spic. Hist. XIV. 1966. 231.
22. Alfonso, Lettere II.505.
23. Alfonso, Lettere II.518-19.
24. Spic. Hist. XI. 1963. 38–9; A.G.H.R. IIB. 47; Telleria, II. 617, note 46.
25. The word *Regolamento* means a 'Rule' and could apply both to the Rule of Benedict XIV and the version approved by the Bourbon Court. In the history of the Congregation, however, it has been reserved exclusively for the document of March 1780.
26. Alfonso, Lettere II.539.
27. Tannoia Lib. IV. Cap. XX. 98. Another account puts the arrival of the Regolamento on 27 February.
28. D. Capone, *Mendacia Tannoiana* 8.
29. Alfonso, Lettere II.525-9.
30. Alfonso, Lettere II.534.539-42.
31. Alfonso, Lettere II.528. Alphonsus did not succeed in his efforts to restore his good name to Father Maione. The 'official' history has cast him in the role of an intriguing ambitious villain which he hardly deserved. Having being removed from office in the angry Assembly at Pagani in June 1780, he left the Congregation and died seven years later at the age of fifty-four. He deserved a kinder fate. Father Cimino showed greater resilience. He too was deposed in June 1780 and apparently expelled some time later. But he was personally acceptable to the Bourbons through whose influence he was appointed a bishop in 1798. He retired to Pagani where he was graciously received and died in the monastery as an oblate of the Congregation in 1818.

32. Alfonso, Lettere II.538.
33. The latest amd most convincing account of the origins of the *Regolamento* controversy is to be found in the unpublished *Mendacia Tannoiana* by Father D. Capone. In January 1780 a young Father in Naples, Cipriano Rastelli wrote *in confidence* to De Paola informing him that Alphonsus in concert with Maione was going to impose a new modified Rule on the Congregation. Only those who accepted would be allowed to remain in the Congregation. De Paola forwarded the letter with his own memorial to the Abbate Zuccari, Prosecretary of the Congregation of Bishops and Regulars. So much for confidentiality. Rastelli left the Congregation some months before Alphonsus died in August 1787, having caused considerable trouble. *Mendacia* 10.
34. Father Pavone describes Alphonsus' mental condition at this time in a memorial he presented to the Holy See in October 1780: '(Mons. Liguori) *non puo negarsi che sia sano di mente ma non puo negarsi pure che abbia perduto in gran parte il vigore della testa, motivo per cui alle volte detta qualche lettera con poca accuratezza*'. A.G.H.R. II A154.
35. Tannoia Lib.lV. Cap.21 107-8. No formal written minutes of this Assembly have been preserved, cf. Spic. Hist. XIV.'1966. 235. The best account of what took place is to be found in the memorial presented to the Congregation of Bishops and Regulars by Father Pavone in October 1780. A.G.H.R. II A15.
36. '*Accetiamo il nuovo Regolamento purche sia approvata dalla Santa Sede*', Memorial of Father Pavone, October 1780 to the Congregation of Bishops and Regulars. The same point is made by the Vicar, Father Cardone, in a memorial in December of the same year: 'La stessa Assemblea altro non disse se non l'accettava, ma colle necessarie reserve'. A.G.H.R. II A24.
37. D. Capone, *Mendacia* 23 says that the whole procedure was juridically absurd.
38. Tannoia, Lib. IV. Cap. XXVI. 129.
39. Kuntz. X. 138.
40. Alfonso, Lettere II.554.
41. A.G.H.R. II. A10.
42. A.G.H.R. II. A11.
43. The relationship between Tannoia and Leggio presents a problem for the historian. Dilgskron is of the opinion that Tannoia does less than justice to him in his life of Alphonsus. On the evidence of his correspondence with the Holy See, I am inclined to believe that, for whatever reason, Leggio sacrificed Alphonsus and his reputation in order to secure Papal support for the independence of the Redemptorists in the Papal States.
44. Alfonso, Lettere II.598.
45. Tannoia Lib. IV. Cap. XXIII. 115.
46. 'Help me, Mother Mary. Jesus, my Hope. I shall not be confounded for ever.'
47. Alfonso, Lettere II.557. The tragedy of the *Regolamento* was that Alphonsus and his advisers did not pursue their case directly and more energetically in Rome. As far as one can surmise they were not aware of the strength of feeling among the *Statisti* and they lost out to De Paola mainly through default.
48. Alfonso, Lettere II.584, 'non fanno piu conto di me'.
49. Alfonso, Lettere II.560-1.
50. Alfonso, Lettere II.563.
51. For the memorial of December 1780 see Alfonso, Lettere II.572-7. The first account of the whole situation was drawn up immediately after the Pagani Assembly but on the advice of Cardinal Banditi was not sent to Rome lest, for

some obscure reason, it should prove to be counter-productive. It was apparently sent to the nunciature in Naples instead where Servanti made use of it in *his* report to Rome in October 1780. Spic. Hist. XIV. 1966. 221-6.
52. Alfonso, Lettere II.601.
53. Alfonso, Lettere II.601. It is one of the anomalies in the complex history of those troubled years that Alphonsus was incorrect in his verdict that 'reunion is essential for the survival of the Congregation'. If reunion had taken place at that time the expansion of the Congregation due to De Paola's dynamism might never have occurred. In a paradoxical way it was the division of the Congregation that facilitated its remarkable expansion in the 19th century.
54. Alfonso, Lettere II.564.
55. Alfonso, Lettere II.598-9.
56. Kuntz X.281.
57. Alfonso, Lettere II.606-11; A.G.H.R. II A32.
58. A.G.H.R. II A34, 12. 'si e dovuto caminare all'oscuro perche non essendosi stata communicata ne la posizione ne il decreto della S. Congregazione ne il voto del preteso Procuratore Generale . . .'
59. A.G.H.R. II A32.
60. 'Stat in decisis per SSmum. sub die 22 Septembris 1780 et amplius non admittantur preces.' A.G.H.R. II A36.
61. A.G.H.R. II A36.
62. Tannoia Lib. IV. Cap.27 136-7 All the witnesses at the time were unanimous in describing his heroic resignation.
63. Kuntz. V.337.
64. Alfonso, Lettere II.619, 620, 627.
65. Clement Hofbauer entered the novitiate at Rome in October 1784. Sadly Alphonsus refrained from writing to him: 'I would write to him but the Lord does not wish me to interfere.' Tannoia Lib. IV. Cap. XXIX 148.
66. Alfonso, Lettere II.632. Alphonsus' letter to Pope Pius VI has not been found.
67. Analecta II. 1923. 29, 61, 103, 132.

Chapter Eighteen, pp. 474–487.

1. This comment of Tanucci was reported by Father Blasucci at the diocesan Process in Pagani.
2. Tannoia, Lib. III. Cap.XLVII. 246-7.
3. Alfonso, Lettere II. 531-3.
4. Evidence of Father Corsano at Proc. Ord. Nuc. 1.443. Giuseppe and his wife fell on evil days about ten years later with the coming of the French and the exile of the Bourbons. He lost his property and his considerable wealth and was, politically, *persona non grata*. His marriage, too, suffered. His wife with their only child, lived in Sorrento where she died in 1842, while he continued to live in Naples. In 1817, his sister, Teresa, the nun, took legal steps to protect her patrimony from suffering any loss as a consequence of her brother's financial dificulties. R. Telleria, *Super domibus Palatiatis Familiae S. Alfonsi*; Spic. Hist. XIII.1965. 98 et seqq.
5. Alfonso, Lettere II.567.
6. Alfonso, Lettere II.568.
7. Alphonsus used the colourful word, 'diruparvi' which means more than simply 'return to the world'.

8. Alfonso, Lettere II.594; Spic. Hist. XI.1963. 286. We do not know what pamphlet he sent her.
9. Alfonso, Lettere II.605, 'Le dame que frequentano le conversazioni ordinariamente perdono la grazia di Dio.'
10. Teresa had a dowry of 1,500 ducats plus 120 ducats per year by way of income. And an additional 500 ducats for the once-off expenses of her reception and profession. Spic. Hist. V.1957. 46 n.16.
11. Alfonso, Lettere II.655. S.R.C. Animad. R.P.P. Fidei . . . 35 No.69. Sister Brianna Caraffa, the superior of the Convent, reported to Alphonsus that Teresa was endangering her life through not eating sufficiently.
12. A.G.H.R. XXVII 27.
13. R. Telleria, *Alexius Pollio, S. Alfonsi Episcopi Servus*, Spic. Hist. X.1962. 256.
14. Proc. Apos. Nuc. Expositio Virtutum, 120 par.233. The evidence of Villani, Mazzini and Corsano at the Process in Nocera makes intensely interesting reading. It speaks volumes for their honesty and integrity that they did not hesitate to describe the more unpleasant aspects of Alphonsus' last years. Proc. Ord. Nuc. ff.270, 329, 465 ter; Proc. Ord. S. Agatha, fol.1873.
15. The Promotor Fidei contended that Alphonsus was not wholly *compos mentis* for a few years even before he resigned his bishopric. In his latter years, he was *Plene imbecillis*, he claimed. Some of the members of the Commission in the Sacred Congregation of Rites examining the Cause were of the opinion that Alphonsus' mental aberrations were transitory, not constituting a permanent condition. On the other hand there is a large volume of evidence to suggest that he was in full possession of his mental faculties. Villani, Mazzini, Corsano, Volpicelli, and the medical doctor, Desiderio, to name but a few of the witnesses, all testified to his mental alertness. They were equally insistent that at times he pretended to be stupid, ignorant, even childish in order to humble himself and control his natural vanity. *S.R.C. An quae obiiciuntur* . . . Summ. Resp. No.12.
16. A second spiritual note-book contains his scruples after 1775 and the directions given to him by his confessors and directors, see Regestum MSS. S. Alphonsi, ed. H. Arboleda Valencia, 377; No.359 in *Studia et Subsidia de Vita et Operibus S.A. de Liguori*. Romae 1990.
17. A.G.H.R. XXVII 44; Telleria, II. 743 n.18.
18. S.R.C. Summarium Objectionale 20, no.29. Respons. Ad Animad R.P.P. Fidei 133, no.281; Proc. Ord. Nuc. fol.881 ter.
19. Proc. Ord. Nuc. ff.321, 326.
20. Proc. Apos. Nuc. Expositio Virtutum, 118 par. 229; S.R.C. Summarium Objectionale 18, nos.19, 20: 'sfogo avanti del servo di Dio con gli atti impuri in se stesso'; cf.Proc. Ord. Nuc fol. 1227 et ter.
21. S.R.C. Animad R.P.P. Fidei, 38 par. 74; Resp. ad Animad R.P.P. Fidei 137 par.293-4; Summarium Objectionale 17 par.17.
22. A.G.H.R. XXVII 14.
23. S.R.C. Expositio Virtutum . . . ab anno 1775 ad annum 1787. Nova Positio super Virtutibus, Romae 1806; Animad. R.P.P. Fidei. An quae objiciuntur etc. no. 99. The Promotor of the Cause pointed out that not only were many of the ancient Fathers such as Gregory Nazianzen, Pachomius, Anthony similarly tempted sexually but also Catherine of Siena and Magdalen de Pazzi. A modern scientific medical examination of his skeleton has suggested that the sexual problems suffered by Alphonsus in his old age may have been due, at least in part, to the considerable deformity of the spinal column in the lumbar

region, which, in turn, affected the entire spinal nervous system, with particular reference to the lumbar nerve regions and the nerve-plexus controlling the genital organs. Prof. Dott. Gennaro Goglia, *Il corpo di Sant'Alfonso*. Spic. Hist. Vl. 1958. 76.

24. A.G.H.R. XXVII 12a.
25. A. Sampers, *Relationes medicorum Curantium circa S. Alfonsis valetudinem*. Spic. Hist. XII. 1964. 209 'non ha modo di liberarmi'.
26. D. Capone, *Il Volto di San Alfonso*, 78. Dr Desiderio refers to Alphonsus' loss of speech due to 'le convulsioni sopravenuteli pochi giorni prima di morire.' S.R.C. An. quae Objic . . . Respon. ad Animad. II.91
27. The inscription was in Latin: 'Hic jacet corpus Illustrissimi et Reverendissimi Domini Alphonsi Mariae de Ligorio (*sic*) Episcopi Sanctae Agathae Gothorum ac Fundatoris Congregationis Sanctissimi Redemptoris'.
28. Telleria, II.714. S. Alfonso, XIII 1942. 163-9 (*Monthly Review*, Pagani 1930–1950)
29. Alfonso, Lettere II.558-9; D. Capone, *Mendacia Tannoiana* 8.
30. D. Capone, *Mendacia Tannoiana*, 8; Kuntz XlV 52.
31. The non-appearance of the youngest of Hercules' sons, Alfonso Maria, usually referred to as Alfonsino, is intriguing. He had been baptised by Alphonsus and was destined for the Church. Before he was twelve, Alfonsino was promoted to an ecclesiastical benefice, which his uncle, Don Cajetan, relinquished in his favour. He accepted the benefice in legal form, symbolically 'kneeling in prayer before the altar and kissing it'. By 1783 young Alfonsino, aged sixteen, indicated that he had no intention of proceeding to accept clerical tonsure or continue on to priesthood. It was, as far as we can judge from the available indications, a keen disappointment for Cajetan, possibly also for Alphonsus, though there is no mention of the fact in any of his letters. Before he died the following year, 1784, Cajetan made his Will making the older brother Giuseppe his 'universal heir' and made no mention whatsoever of Alfonsino, who, up to that, had been his favourite nephew. What was the reason, if any, for his 'fall from grace'? Telleria. *Rev. D. Caietanus de Liguro, S. Alfonsi Frater eiusque Nepos Alfonsinus* . . . Spic. Hist. XIII 1965. 325 et seqq; G. Orlandi, *Centocinquanta anni fa Alfonso de Liguori veniva proclamato Santo*. Spic. Hist. XXXVIII 1990 237 et seqq.
32. R. Culhane, C.SS.R., 'St Alphonsus on the Immaculate Conception', *Irish Ecclesiastical Record*. Vol. LXXXII (1954) 391.
33. *Concessionis Tituli Doctoris . . . in honorem Sancti Alphonsi Mariae de Ligorio* etc. Romae. 1870.

BIBLIOGRAPHY

A recent publication *Studia et Subsidia de Vita et Operibus S. Alfonsi de Ligorio*, Rome 1990, (Bibliotheca Historica C.SS.R. Vol. XIII) has rendered a detailed list of manuscript sources concerning the life of Alphonsus superfluous. In this work H. Arboleda Valencia has published a register of all MSS concerning Alphonsus in the General Archives, *Regestum manuscriptorum S. Alfonsi in Archivo Generali Historica Redemptoristarum Romae* (A.G.H.R.). Otto Weiss has given a full account of the various works on the life of Alphonsus from Landi to Rey-Mermet, in *Alfons von Liguori und seine Biographen. Ein Heiliger swischen hagiographischer Verklarung und historischer Wirklicheit*. Giuseppe Orlandi has described the position concerning the Letters of Alphonsus in *La Corrispondenza di S. Alfonso M. de Liguori. Dall'Epistolario al Carteggio* while Fabricio Ferrero and Weiss have drawn up a bibliography of all recent studies connected with the saint. This monumental work of the highest scholarship will greatly facilitate all future students of the life of Alphonsus de Liguori.

The twenty-four or so handwritten volumes of the evidence given at the different stages of both the Ordinary and Apostolic Process leading to the Beatification and Canonisation of Alphonsus are in the A.G.H.R. and are indicated in the Notes when quoted. The printed volumes of the different Processes Rome, 1796–1815 are also referred to where appropriate.

Titles of works quoted occasionally in the text are given in the Notes to each Chapter and are not repeated here.

Acta Integra Capitulorum Generalium C.SS.R., Romae 1899.
'Alphonse de Liguori. Pasteur et Docteur', *Theologie Historique*, No. 77, Paris 1987.
Bayon, R., *Como Escribio Alfonso de Ligorio*, Madrid 1940.
Boland, S., *A Dictionary of the Redemptorists*, Romae 1987.
Bouvier, R. and Laffargue, A., *La Vie Napolitaine au XVIII Siècle*, Paris 1956.
Cacciatore, G. S., *Alfonso de Liguori e il Giansenismo*, Firenze 1942.

Capone, D., *Il Volto di Sant'Alfonso*, Roma 1954.
Capone, D., *Sant' Alfonso Missionario*, Napoli 1987.
Capone, D., *Mendacia Tannoiana* (MS).
Capone, D., *Le Prime Abitazione dei Redentoriste a Scala* (MS).
Capone, D., *Suor Celeste Crostarosa e Sant' Alfonso de Liguori*, Incontri-Spiritualita, Materdomini 1991.
Capone, D., *Introductio in Theologiam Moralem S. Alfonsi* (MS).
Capone, D., *De Theologa Morali Casuistica* (MS).
Capone, D. and Majorano, S., *Le Radici*, Materdomini 1985.
Catalago dei Redentoristi d'Italia 1732–1841, ed. F. Minervino, C.SS.R., Romae 1978 (Bibliotheca Historica C.SS.R. Vol. VIII).
Chadwick, O., *The Popes and European Revolution*, Oxford History of the Christian Church 1981.
Codex Regularum et Constitutionum C.SS.R., Romae 1896.
Concessionis Tituli Doctoris . . . in Honorem S. Alphonsi M. de Ligorio, Romae 1870 (Sacra Rituum Congregatio).
Contributi Bio-Bibliografici. Sant'Alfonso de Liguori: A. Gregorio, D. Capone, A. Freda, V. Toglia, Morcelliana 1940.
Cragg, G.R., *The Church and the Age of Reason (1648–1789)*, Pelican 1960.
Croce, B., *Uomini e Cose della Vecchia Italia*, Bari 1927.
De Carli, Ferruccio, *L.A. Muratori*, Firenze 1955.
De Liguori, Alphonsus M., *Theologia Moralis*. ed. L. Gaude, C.SS.R. I–IV, Romae 1905.
De Liguori, Alphonsus M., *Opere Ascetiche*, I–IV, Marietti Torino 1845.
De Liguori, Alphonsus M., *Opere Morali*, V–VII, Marietti Torino 1846.
De Liguori, Alphonsus M., *Opere Ascetiche* (Editio Critica) Roma 1933–.
De Liguori, Alphonsus M., *Lettere di S. Alfonso Maria de Liguori*, I–III. Roma 1887–90. See also Appendix.
De Maio, R., *Società e Vita Religiosa à Napoli nell'Età Moderna*, 1656–1799, Napoli 1971.
De Meulemeester, M., *Bibliographie Générales des Écrivains Rédemptoristes*, Louvain 1933.
De Meulemeester, M., 'La "Vita Divota" des Missions Napolitaines au XVIII S.', *Revue d'Ascétique et de Mystique*, 1949.
De Meulemeester, M., *Origines de la Congrégation du Très Saint-Rédempteur*, Louvain 1953–57.
De Mura, F., *Il Missionario Istruito*, Naples 1738.
Documenta Miscellanea ad Regulam et Spiritum . . . (C.SS.R.) Romae 1904.
Epistolae Ven. Pauli Cafaro, C.SS.R., Roma 1934.
Epistolae Ven. Servi Dei Caesaris Sportelli, C.SS.R., ed. C. Henze. Roma 1937.
Founding Texts of Redemptorists . . . ed. Hoegerl, C., Rome 1986.
Giamusso,S., *I Redentoristi in Sicilia*, Palermo 1960.
Giannantonio, P., *Alfonso M. de Liguori e la Società Civile nel Suo Tempo*, I.II. Firenze 1990.
Gregorio, O., *Monsignore Tommaso Falcoia, 1663–1743*, Roma 1955.
Gregorio, O., *Mons. T. Falcoia: Lettere à S. Alfonso de Liguori, Ripa, Sportelli, Crostarosa*, Roma 1963.

Gregorio, O., *Monsignore si Diverte*, Napoli 1987.
Hazard, P., *European Thought in the Eighteenth Century*, Pelican 1954.
Kuntz, Federico, 'Annales C.SS.R. I–III', MS, A.G.H.R.
Kuntz, Federico, 'Commentaria de Rebus C.SS.R., I–XX', MS, A.G.H.R.
Landi, Giuseppe, 'Istoria della C.SS.R', MS, A.G.H.R.
La Presenza e l'Opera dei Redentoristi nel Mezzogiorno, Napoli 1987.
Lettere dalla Sicilia a S. Alfonso, ed. Giamusso, S., Romae 1991 (Bibliotheca Historic C.SS.R. Vol. XIV).
Majorano, S., *L'Imitazione per la Memoria del Salvatore*, Romae 1978 (Bibliotheca Historica C.SS.R. Vol. VII).
Masone, E. and Amarante, A., *S. Alfonso de Liguori e la Sua Opera*, Napoli 1987.
Mazzoni, P.A., *Le Missioni Populari nel Pensiero di S. Alfonso M. de Liguori* (Dissertatio ad Lauream). Pontificia Universitas Gregoriana, Padua 1961.
Meiberg, A., 'Historiae Missionis Paroecialis Lineamenta', (MS thesis ad Lauream. Academia S. Alphonsi, Romae 1953).
Oppitz, J.W., 'Alphonsian History and Spirituality', (Ad Usum Privatum).
Pietas Alfonsiana Erga Matrem Gloriosam Mariam, Louvain 1951 (Relatio Actorum).
Pollock, J.R., 'Francois Genet: The Man and his Methodology', *Analecta Gregoriana* 1984.
Positio Super Virtutibus Januarii Mariae Sarnelli C.SS.R., Sacra Rituum Congregatio, Romae 1889.
Ripa, M., *Storia della Congregazione e del Collegio de Cinesi* . . . , I–III, Naples 1832.
Santonicola, A.M., *Sant'Alfonso e L'Azione Cattolica*, Pompei 1939.
Tannoia, A. M., *Della Vita ed Istituto del Ven. Servo di Dio Alfonso Maria Liguori*, I–III, Napoli 1798–1802.
Van Delft, M., *La Mission Paroissiale*, Lethielleux: Paris 1964.
Vereecke, L., *De Guillaume d'Ockham à St. Alphonse de Liguori*, Romae 1986 (Bibliotheca Historica C.SS.R. Vol. XII).
Vico, G., *Il Metodo degli Studi del Tempo Nostro*, Firenze 1937.

INDEX

Abelly, Louis, Vincentian, 48
Accadia, 184
Agrigento, 300
Airola, 368, 376, 378, 381, 391
Althann, Frederick, Cardinal and Austrian Viceroy, 19, 37
Amalfi, 244–5, 257, 472
Amarante, Biagio, C.SS.R., 211, 245, 257
Amatrice, 35–7
Anastasio, Casa (Scala), 131
Apice, Bernard, C.SS.R., 249, 299, 321, 346
Arienzo, 368, 371, 376, 390, 399, 419–21, 437
Arnaud, Antoine, *De la fréquente Communion*, 47
Arpaia, 377

Bagnoli, 368
Banditi, Francesco, Cardinal of Beneventum, 445, 447, 466
Bari, 1, 109, 210, 258
Benedict XIV, Pope, 56, 163, 178, 182, 205, 223, 232–3, 275, 278, 294, 332–3, 383, 400, 409–10, 414, 450–51, 456, 471
Beneventum, 207, 241–3, 257, 297, 399, 466
Bergamo, Mons., Bishop of Gaeta, 445, 466
Besozzi, Joachim, Cardinal, 220–21, 237
Bianchi della Giustizia (Confraternity), 49–52
Blasucci, Pietro Paulo, C.SS.R., 297, 299, 315, 323, 433, 444, 462, 473
Bonaccia, Dominico, 15
Borgia, Nicholas, Mons., Bishop of Cava and Aversa, 216, 241, 332, 360, 401, 405
Bottari, Giovanni, Mons., 268–9
Bovino, 176–7, 179, 205, 472
Brancone, Gaetano Maria, Secretary of State for Ecclesiastical Affairs, 136, 139, 165, 177, 199, 209, 230–31, 237, 305, 331
Bucciano, 376, 382, 389
Buonapane, Fabio, C.SS.R., 460
Busenbaum, Henry, S.J., 207, 220, 278, 332. cf. Chronological List of Alphonsus' Works, Appendix

Cafaro, Paul, C.SS.R., 2, 56, 73, 153, 164, 178, 211, 226, 301
Caiazzo, diocese of, 96, 132–5
Calabria, missions in, 2, 297–8
Capobianco, Albert, O.P., 268, 424
Caposele, cf. Materdomini
Cappelle Serotine, 62–5, 144
Caputo, Thomas, O.P., 357, 388, 419
Carafa, Francesco, Prince of Colubrano, 150
Carafa, Sister Brianna, 347, 420
Cardel, P., S.J., 333
Carmelite nuns, 94, 339, 348, 370
Cassano, 297
Castellamare, cf. Falcoia, Bishop of
Castelli, Giuseppe, Cardinal, 422, 437, 439
Castelluccio, 297
Cavalieri, Anna Caterina, Mother of Alphonsus, 10–13, 23, 242
Cavalieri, Emilio, Bishop of Troia, uncle of Alphonsus, 10, 39–40, 94
Celano, Gaetano, Neapolitan Lawyer, 415, 460
Charles III, King of Naples and Spain, 4, 136–68 passim, 193–6, 229–34, 265, 271, 330–32, 414, 451
Cimafonte, Pietro and Salvatore, architects, 320, 385, 390
Cimino, Fabrizio, C.SS.R., 361, 435, 444, 451–73 passim
Ciorani, 3, 33, 148–57, 169–72, 224–7, 444, 472–3
Cioranisti, 155, 449
Cito, Baldassare, 18, 20, 22, 70, 390, 415–16
Clement XIII, Pope, 294, 334, 357–66 passim, 401, 414, 418, 421
Clement XIV, Pope, 34, 422, 429, 435–7
Conza, 185, 472
Copertino, 94
Corrado, Bartolomeo, C.SS.R., 309, 457, 460
Croce, Benedetto, 63
Crostarosa, Julia, Ven. Maria Celeste, 77–85, 91–107, 120–27, 145, 167, 184, 242
Crostarosa, Ursula, 78–85
Curzio, Vito, the first brother in the new congregation, 112, 151, 155, 165, 212
Cutica, Vincenzo, C.M., 32, 39, 49, 97

[529]

INDEX

Danza, Flaminio, Mons. Bishop of St Agatha of the Goths, 357–8, 369–74, 382
de Alteriis, Michael, 46, 144, 147
de Filippo, Don Francis, pastor of Frasso, 377, 389, 439
de La Crusca, Academy, 255–61 passim, 376
de Leon, Ferdinando, the Avocato Fiscale, 444, 446–50
Deliceto, 2, 175–8, 231, 243, 431, 453
de Liguori, Alphonsus Maria
    family, birth, 9–15
    university studies, 15–20
    legal practice and law case, 20–37
    discernment of vocation, 23–40
    ordination, 41–54
    Chinese College, 59, 66–110
    Capelle Serotine, 62–5, 190, 264
    health and scruples, 46, 48, 54, 69–74, 243, 481, 483
    Scala and foundation of missionary society, 66–135
    relations with Bishop Falcoia, 99–168 passim
    elected Rector Major of new missionary society, 169–71
    efforts to secure royal approval, 193–9, 208–9
    Roman approval, 212, 214–23
    mission system, 246–55
    appointment as Bishop of St Agatha of the Goths, 357–66
    episcopal ordination, 364
    confirmation as Rector Major, 366–7
    his years as bishop, 369–440 passim
    ill-health as bishop, 399–403, 418–22
    move from St Agatha to Arienzo, 401
    efforts to resign his bishopric, 399–401, 422, 438–9
    retirement in Pagani, 441–85
    the *Regolamento* crisis, 450–73
    last illness and death, 479–84
    canonisation process, 485
    Doctor of Church, 487
    patron of confessors and moral theologians, 487
    writings, cf. Appendix, Chronological List of Alphonsus' Writings, 491
De Liguori, Alfonso Maria (Alfonsino), nephew of Alphonsus, son of Hercules, 409, 474, 486
De Liguori, Antonio, Benedictine, 11–12, 24
De Liguori, Cajetan (Gaetano), priest brother of Alphonsus, 11–12, 24, 54, 59, 242, 264, 362, 479
De Liguori, Don Giuseppe (Joseph Felix), father of Alphonsus 9–42 passim, 49, 52–4, 59, 108–9, 141, 180, 186–90, 197
De Liguori, Giuseppe (Peppo), nephew of Alphonsus, son of Hercules, 474–5, 484, 486
De Liguori, Hercules, youngest brother of Alphonsus, 12, 29, 74, 152, 187–90, 242, 264, 362–3, 365, 368, 398, 406–9, 416, 474–5
De Liguori, Maddalena and Barbara (Maria Luisa) twin sisters of Alphonsus, 11–12, 23–4, 189, 341, 416
De Liguori, Marianna, sister of Alphonsus, 24, 189, 416
De Liguori, Marianna, second wife of Don Hercules, 407–9
De Liguori, Maria Teresa, niece of Alphonsus, daughter of Hercules, 342, 408, 475–9
De Liguori, Rachele (Raquel), first wife of Don Hercules, 406
De Marco, Carlo, Secretary for Justice, 331, 365, 374, 404, 414, 449, 453
De Meo, Alexandro, C.SS.R., 238, 259, 263, 310, 423, 461, 473
De Muro, Philip, 246
De Nicolai, Giuseppe, Bishop of Conza, 184, 472
De Paola, Francesco, C.SS.R., 263, 309, 317, 431–73 passim, 485
De Robertis, Celestino, C.SS.R., 178, 197, 217, 237, 309, 346
De Sales, Francis, Saint, 1, 73, 307, 352
Dilgskron, Karl, C.SS.R., 3
Donato, Giovanni B., 100–102, 111–23, 297

Equiprobabilism cf. Probabilism

Falcoia, Thomas, Mons. Bishop of Castellamare, 68, 73, 77–89, 92–4, 99–169 passim, 253
Fatigati, Gennaro, Chinese College, 67, 395
Ferdinand IV, King of Naples, 4, 232, 305, 330–31, 342, 417
Ferrara, Geronimo, C.SS.R., 264, 320, 423
Fiorillo, Ludovico, O.P., 97–9, 110, 114, 134, 194
Firmo, 297
Foggia, 61, 80, 94–6, 127, 177, 180–84, 265

INDEX

Forchia, 376, 378
Frasso, 368, 370, 376–7, 389–90
Frosinone, 446–7, 461

Galliani, Celestino, Cappellano Maggiore, 196–9
Gallo, Salvatore, C.SS.R., 463–4
Garzillo, Francesco, C.SS.R., 186, 217
Genet, Francis, bishop and theologian, 48, 71, 280
Gentili, Antonio, Cardinal Prefect of the Congregation of the Council, 221
Gerard Majella, Saint, C.SS.R., 242, 483
Ghilini, Cardinal Tommaso Maria, 462–4
Giacchi, Bernard, Capuchin, 256–9,
Giannini, Augustin, Mons. Bishop of Lettere, 296, 305, 398
Giannone, Peter, Neapolitan author and regalist, 17
Gizzio, Peter, Canon, member of the Apostolic Missioners, 39–40, 43, 49, 97, 114–17
Gravina-Orsini, Duke, 35

Herculaneum, 308
Hofbauer, Clement M., 215, 471

Incurabili, Hospital, 25–40 passim

Janella, Dominic, temporary servant of Alphonsus, 363, 367
Jansenism, 266, 280, 291–5
Japan, mission to, 298
Jerome, Francis, S.J., Saint, 57, 246
Jorio, Giuseppe, missioner and theologian, 204, 210, 246, 275, 278, 281, 307, 375

Landi, Giuseppe, C.SS.R., 1, 208, 226, 257, 431
Lazzaroni, 62–5
Leggio, Isidore, C.SS.R., 431, 445, 457–70 passim, 475
Leon, Ferdinand, Procurator Fiscal of the Giunta degli Abusi, 44, 446, 447, 448
Locatelli, Giuseppe Maria, Papal Nuncio in Naples, 358
Lucchesi, Andrea, Mons. Bishop of Agrigento in Sicily, 300, 510
Lungro, 297

Maddaloni, Duke of, 368, 385, 399
Maffei, Antonio and Francescantonio, local lords of Deliceto, 229, 413, 415, 432
Maione, Angelo, C.SS.R., 373, 402, 435, 444, 448–73 passim
Mannarini, Vincenzo, 46, 75, 85, 93, 100–102, 107, 120, 143, 196–8, 229, 297
Manulio, Dominic, S.J., 50, 97, 129, 326
Maratea, 297
Margotta, Francesco, C.SS.R., 217, 318, 373
Maria Amalia, wife of Charles III, 67, 140, 194, 233–4, 331
Maria Carolina, wife of Ferdinand IV, 447
Marianella, birth place of Alphonsus, 11–13, 408–9
Materdomini (Caposele), 184–6, 452
Mazzini, Giovanni, C.SS.R., 34, 46, 73, 75, 85, 93, 109, 123, 144, 155, 227, 236–8, 361, 410–12, 419, 460, 480–82
Misericordiella, Confraternity of, 25–6
Montealegre, Marquis of, 194, 209
Montesarchio, 368
Mormanno, 297
Muratori, Ludovico, Antonio, 260, 267–75
Muscari, Giuseppe, C.SS.R., Abbot, 218–20, 223–7, 234–8

Nardo, 61, 94
Negrone, Mons. Andrea, Uditore of Pope Clement XIII, 358, 359, 361
Newman, John H. Cardinal, 273, 308

Oliviero, Angela, *Monaca di Casa*, 67, 194
Oliviero, Giovanni, 67, 191, 194, 217, 264

Pacifici, Emilio, 470
Pacifico, Angelo, pastor of S. Michele à Segno, 42
Pagani, foundation of, Chapters 1755 and 1764, Assembly 1780, 165, 173–5, 262, 410, 460, 476–87
Pagano, Thomas, Oratorian, 14–40 passim, 46, 48–50, 69–74, 76, 84, 93–100, 242, 280
Passionei, Dominico, Cardinal, 222, 268
Pastorano, 376, 389
Patuzzi, Giovanni, O.P., 265, 278, 281, 424–6
Pavone, Giuseppe, C.SS.R., 461
Pavone, Society of Missioners, 42
Pepe, Francesco, S.J., 195, 230, 269–72

INDEX

Pius VI, Pope, 232, 438–9, 463, 470, 486
Pius VII, Pope, 486
Pii Operai, missionary society, 42, 97, 114, 144, 166, 171, 204, 218–22, 253, 363, 375
Polignano à Mare, 61, 94
Pollio, Alexis, butler and Redemptorist brother, 367–441 passim, 480–85
Probabilism, 279–86
Puoti, Antonio, Mons. Archbishop of Amalfi, 241, 376, 397, 402–3, 405, 422
Puoti, Giuseppe Maria, 215, 394

Regolamento, 3, 195, 213, 232, 402, 413, 441–73
Remondini, publishers, 264–5, 276–8, 281, 285–95 passim, 424–31, 442
Ricci, Lorenzo, Superior General of the Jesuits, 333, 364
Ripa, Matteo, founder of the Chinese College, 66, 90, 98, 108
Romano, Canon Pietro, 81, 83, 101–2, 126, 151
Romito, Francis Anthony, Redemptorist brother, 367–485 passim
Rossi, Don Nicholas Matias, 466–7
Rossi, Saverio, C.SS.R., 56, 133–5, 144, 150, 151, 153, 165, 167, 226
Rubino, Nicholas, Vicar General of Saint Agatha, 367–440 passim

St Angelo à Cupolo, 241, 242, 301, 382, 415, 446, 456
Salerno, mission in, 245–6, 257, 472
Sambuca, Marquis, 448, 480
San Basile, 297
Sanseverino, Francesco, Novice, Pio Operaio, Archbishop of Palermo, 176, 220–23, 237, 275, 442
Sant' Agata dei Goti, 357–440 passim
San Felice à Cancello, 391
S. Maria à Vico, 368, 376, 380, 390, 420
Santoro, Antonio, Mons. Bishop of Scala, 104, 120, 127
Saracena, 297
Sarnelli, Angelo, Baron of Ciorani, 148, 164, 413
Sarnelli, Gennaro, C.SS.R., 66, 123, 128–30, 131, 159–64, 204, 292
Scala, 65–135 passim
Scalea, 297
Scarlatti, Alessandro, 13–14

Scifelli, foundation of, 433–6, 447
Sergio, Thomas, of the Pii Operai, 205, 220
Sersale, Antonio, Cardinal Archbishop of Naples, 240, 365, 418, 437, 444
Sicily, 299–301, 433, 446
Simeoli, Giuseppe, Canon of Naples, Censor, 268, 429, 437, 443
Society of Jesus, 216, 331, 375, 414, 416–17, 431, 435, 443
Spinelli, Giuseppe, Cardinal Archbishop of Naples, 41, 159–64, 179, 210, 215–17, 237, 239, 280, 292, 299, 357–9, 400, 450
Sportelli, Caesar, C.SS.R., 109, 123, 128, 144, 153–7, 164, 166, 277, 281

Tannoia, Antonio Maria, C.SS.R., 1–3, 208, 318, 410, 429, 431, 453–63
Tanucci, Bernardo, Marquis, Secretary of State for Justice, 20, 57, 139–40, 209, 241, 269, 289, 331, 373, 414, 422, 424, 444–5, 447, 453, 474
Tartaglione, Francesco, Redemptorist brother, 194, 217–23, 242, 264
Testa, Matteo, Capellano Maggiore, 209, 216, 449, 455, 472
Torni, Giulio, Director of the Apostolic Missions, Professor of Theology, 16, 43, 47, 61, 76, 97, 114, 116, 117, 216, 281
Tosques, Silvestro, 101–8, 115, 120–27, 141
Tramontano, Salvatore, priest friend of Alphonsus, 393, 419, 421
Tramonti, area of first missionary activity, 118
Troia, 10, 179–80

Vargas, Macciucca, Francesco, Marquis, 416, 444
Verzella, Felix, secretary of Alphonsus, 367–440 passim
Vico, Giovanni Battista, 16
Villa degli Schiavi (Liberi), 132–5, 146–51, 296
Villani, Andrea, C.SS.R., 73, 153, 195, 214, 217–27, 243, 309, 316, 363–7, 409–12, 417, 444–75 passim, 480–85
Vincentians, 26, 32, 147, 171, 190, 204

Zaccaria, Francesco Antonio, S.J., 277–8, 284, 332, 443